DATE DUE			

Mass Communication Review Yearbook

Mass Communication Review Yearbook

Volume 5

1985

Michael Gurevitch
Mark R. Levy
Editors

Steve M. Barkin
Edward L. Fink
James G. Webster
Contributing Editors

Published in cooperation with the
Center for Research in Public Communication,
University of Maryland

SAGE PUBLICATIONS
Beverly Hills London New Delhi

For information address:

SAGE Publications, Inc.
275 South Beverly Drive
Beverly Hills, California 90212

SAGE Publications India Pvt. Ltd.
M-32 Market
Greater Kailash I
New Delhi 110 048 India

SAGE Publications Ltd
28 Banner Street
London EC1Y 8QE
England

Printed in the United States of America

International Standard Book Number 0-8039-2499-2

International Standard Series Number 0196-8017

FIRST PRINTING

Contents

STRUCTURING REALITY

TELLING STORIES

PART III: MASS MEDIA AND THE INDIVIDUAL

About the Editors

MICHAEL GUREVITCH is a Professor in the College of Journalism and the Director of thc Center for Research in Public Communication at the University of Maryland. His current research interests include the relationship between media organizations and political institutions and media portrayals of public issues. He is coauthor (with Elihu Katz) of *The Secularization of Leisure* and (with Jay Blumler) of *The Challenge of Election Broadcasting*, as well as articles on political communication and uses and gratifications. He is also coeditor of *Mass Communication and Society* and *Culture, Society, and the Media*. He earned his Ph.D. from the Massachusetts Institute of Technology. Prior to joining the University of Maryland, he worked at the Open University and the University of Leeds, England, and the Hebrew University of Jerusalem.

MARK R. LEVY is an Associate Professor in the College of Journalism and a Research Associate of the Center for Research in Public Communication at the University of Maryland. His principal research interests are uses and gratifications theory; news comprehension; and the impact of new communication technologies, particularly home video cassette recorders, on audience behavior. His publications include *The Audience Experience with Television News* and (with Sven Windahl) "The Concept of Audience Activity." He is a coeditor of and contributor to *The Main Source: Learning from Television News*. Before earning his Ph.D. (in sociology) from Columbia University, he was a reporter with *The Record* in Hackensack, N.J.; a writer, editor, and associate producer with NBC News in New York; and an associate national affairs editor at *Newsweek*.

INTRODUCTION

Michael Gurevitch and Mark R. Levy

As the new editors of the *Mass Communication Review Yearbook*, we thought it appropriate to outline our approach to the editing of Volume 5 of the *MCRY* series and to convey our thoughts more generally about the scholarly enterprise chronicled in these volumes. Perhaps not surprisingly, the theme of our observations is continuity versus change. Despite the fact that virtually all newly installed editors face this dilemma, it in fact reflects our rationale for the structure of this book, captures the spirit of the articles that follow, and illuminates the condition of the field.

In planning this collection, we were immediately struck by the need for continuity and by the logic of that need. After all, the editors of the first four volumes in this series had bequeathed us a structure and format. And we suspected that based on previous volumes the readers and users of *MCRY* had formed expectations about the series. Beyond our desire to build on that identity, our academic socialization has taught us, correctly or not, that scientific progress is predicated on cumulation—the very process implied by the *MCRY* series. Finally, and far from least important, we were reluctant to tinker too much with a good thing—with past jobs well done.

Still, the urge for change was strong. No two groups of editors think precisely alike, hence the inevitability of change produced by the transfer of editorship. First, readers of *MCRY* should note that starting with this volume, *MCRY* has become a biennial—published every other year instead of annually. We trust that this will broaden and deepen the already rich pool of materials from which selections for this publication are made.

A second and more significant change is in the structure of the volume. As we see it, one of the major purposes of *MCRY* is to alert mass communication scholars to the shifting contours of the field. This task should be accomplished not merely through the volume's contents (which should remain primarily—but not exclusively—previously published works of exceptional quality and interest), but also by the way in which the book is organized.

Our awareness that the structure of this volume has intellectual implications led us to cast this collection in a form that differs somewhat from previous volumes of *MCRY*. Earlier volumes reflected attempts to represent the diversity of mass communication research. Thus all four preceding volumes first paid homage to perennial areas of research (effects, political communication, and the like) and then followed with topical sections ranging from violence in the media to information-processing, feminism, international communication, and new communication technologies.

While a concern with reflecting the diversity of mass communication research is a legitimate principle on which to base a yearbook, nevertheless it seemed to us to be deficient. It creates an impression, perhaps not completely warranted, that mass communication research consists solely of diverse areas, linked only by a vaguely shared interest in mass communication per se and not, as we believe it to be, a field with a short list of conceptual frameworks, widely understood to be legitimate if not universally accepted.

Another organizing principle, considered and rejected, was to focus the collection around the current debate in the field, which pits critical researchers (both Marxist and non-Marxist) against the traditionalists, who work largely in an empirical/behavioralist mode. That approach, we felt, would be counterproductive, partly because it perpetuates an unhealthy spirit of confrontation when dialogue is called for, partly because it shifts our attention from substantive issues to the wrangle itself, and partly because the debate has already had its share of exposure elsewhere. In addition, we felt it unlikely that the pool of published research from which we could draw would yield works that could be neatly classified into critical or traditional research. Indeed, even if our assumption proved false, the utility of this distinction—which alerted us in the past to sometimes unvoiced assumptions—is by now limited.

Instead we decided to structure this volume around the distinction between macro and micro studies. Macro investigations were defined as those addressing the nexus of media and society. Research dealing with issues pertaining to the relationship between the media and the individual were placed in the micro section. This macro-micro distinction was not always easy to apply, and sometimes the same selection clearly has both macro and micro aspects.

Still, we think the macro-micro distinction is useful, based as it is on the focus of the questions addressed. We have knowingly ignored the often considerable theoretical and methodological differences between studies assembled under the same heading in order to direct the reader's attention to the unit of analysis—society or the individual.

In lieu of an opening section labeled "Theoretical Perspectives," we decided to lead off with selections grouped under the heading "Identifying the Significant in Mass Communication Research." This, we hope, is not merely playing with words. First—and this is perhaps the most innovative aspect of this volume—we sought to establish a forum in which leading mass communication researchers would be given an opportunity to make a "personal statement" that would identify what they felt were the significant issues and offer an agenda for future research. Second, apart from their intrinsic value, these original contributions were designed to dispel, at least to some extent, the sense of *déjà vu* that often lingers over any collection, however strong, of previously published materials.

Following the general macro-micro distinction outlined above, we asked James Carey to write on issues of media and society, and Percy Tannenbaum to share his thoughts on the individual and the media. Moving somewhat beyond the macro-micro distinction, we commissioned Kurt and Gladys Lang to prepare a statement on mass communication research methods and Nicholas Garnham to write on new communication technologies and policies. Also included in Part I are four previously published articles that reflect on developments in the field. Like most observations made in hindsight, these articles offer both insights into the past and new directions for the future. Taken together, the eight selections in Part I add another important dimension to this yearbook: Not only does this volume "skim off the cream," offering a view of the state of the art in mass communication research, it also charts a course for the future based on both the accomplishments and the deficiencies of work already on the record.

Following Part I are two major groupings of articles, reflecting the macro-micro distinction: "Media and Society: Social Reality and Media Representations" (Part II) and "Mass Media and the Individual" (Part III). Finally, in a spirit of continuity with preceding volumes, we decided to retain the section on "Mass Communication Technology and Policy." Work in that area, it seemed to us, has breached the traditional boundaries of mass communication research and has established an identity of its own, not easily captured by the macro-micro distinction.

WHERE ARE WE GOING?

Having thus established the structure of this volume, its contents had to await the selection process. We solicited nominations from the 45 men and women who make up our international editorial board and found other articles through a call for papers addressed to the scholarly community at large. More than 200 studies were nominated; and with the help of our contributing editors, we made our selections.

Only when this work was completed could we stand back to look at "the big picture," attempting to discern the shape of the field as it emerged from the assembled materials. Indeed, the test of the validity of this collection lies, we believe, in the clarity with which it identifies the contours of the field and the answers it provides to the question, Where are we going?

The answers seem clear in some cases and rather ambiguous in others. Perhaps the most distinct pattern emerges in the macro section, the section on media and society. A preoccupation with the role of the media as constructors and definers of social reality seems to underlie most, if not all, of the articles in that section. There is a clear trend here—one that places the issue of the relationship between the media and social reality at the center of mass communication research. The history and development of this line of research deserves a closer look, perhaps along the lines taken in the article by Chaffee and Hochheimer on the evolution of political communication research in the United States. More likely, some of its origins can be traced to the impact over the last decade of the cultural studies tradition as developed in Europe, and especially in Britain, on American researchers. Other influences undoubtedly would include currents from American sociological traditions based in symbolic interactionism and phenomenology.

Although Carey, in his personal statement, still sees an entrenched resistance to cultural studies among American researchers, the evidence offered here suggests that by now the doors for cultural studies in the United States have been thrown wide open. Indeed we hope that Carey's plea, together with the stimulus provided by the work assembled in this volume, will encourage even more researchers to locate cultural studies squarely in the mainstream of American mass communication research. For such a development to occur, of course, attention still must be paid to finding a place in and establishing the relevance of cultural studies for schools of journalism and mass communication.

Another and somewhat different pattern emerges in the articles grouped under the heading "Reflections on Developments in the Field." These articles imply a readiness to take a critical look at the past. Here we find that even researchers who have invested considerable effort in developing certain lines of work are now prepared to reexamine their own intellectual commitments. As the introduction to Part I suggests, this can be taken as a sign of "disciplinary vigor," signifying the well-being of the field and perhaps also its growing maturity. We applaud and encourage work in that spirit.

By contrast, a more ambiguous picture emerges from the selections in Part III ("Mass Media and the Individual"). Most of the work in this section deals with the issue of media uses and effects. Perhaps because that research tradition has been with us for many years, it lacks a single dominant or innovative thrust that might have unified current work in the area. That is not to say, of course, that this line of work lacks significance, or that its potential contributions have been exhausted (although Carey argues to the contrary in his personal statement).

It is not likely that effects research will wither away in the foreseeable future—first, because many researchers have been trained in that tradition and remain committed to it, and second, because there will always be social and political actors who will support and demand such research. Nevertheless, even the outstanding work assembled in this volume strongly suggests that this general area of inquiry could benefit from a new sense of coherence and direction.

Judging from the selections in Part IV—"Mass Communication Technology and Policy"—a greater sense of coherence and direction is also called for in studies of the so-called communication revolution. Indeed, much of it appears to be motivated by a fascination with the "wonders"—real, potential, and imagined—of communications hardware, perhaps to the neglect of a host of other, more significant macro and effects issues. Similarly, there appears to be a lack of coherence in studies with a communications policy focus. Rather, what we have is a number of protracted debates, waged by cadres of antagonists arguing from irreconcilable positions over matters whose centrality to the general communication research agenda remains largely unexplicated.

On balance, however, the picture of the overall mass communication field that emerges from this volume is of a field still rich in diversity and still reflecting a plurality of scholarly interests. Another, somewhat less sanguine way to see it, however, is as a field in which various forces tug against each other, pulling in different directions. It is certainly too early to assess what the outcome of these pulls and pushes might be. Over this simmering intellectual stew loom the larger issues of the future of mass communication and of the future of the mass media as we know them in an era of rapidly changing technology.

At issue here is not the question of the intellectual superiority of one theoretical approach or another; nor the ascendancy, temporary or long-term, of any of the schools of thought that currently characterize the field. The future of the discipline hinges, rather, on our ability to identify that which will be significant, and to equip ourselves, theoretically and methodologically, with the most adequate tools with which to tackle those problems. Of course, the task of "identifying the significant" does not take place in a theoretical or social vacuum. It is informed by, indeed is rooted in, the social and theoretical perspectives that structure and frame our thinking about current as well as future issues. The current debate in the field is therefore as crucial for shaping the future of scholarship as it is for understanding its present condition.

A RESEARCH AGENDA

As noted above, one of our purposes in commissioning the four personal statements that open this volume was to elicit research guidelines or agendas for the different areas of work represented in this collection. We therefore consider it appropriate to conclude this introduction by offering our own agenda.

We do our work at the University of Maryland's Center for Research in Public Communication, the copublisher of this volume. As research associates of the center, we share in a general research philosophy and orientation. Our basic assumption is that the public (or mass) communication process ought to be viewed as an integrated whole in which the various actors and institutions are linked and interdependent; investigation of any part or aspect of this process ought to be located in its social, cultural, and political context. To assert this, of course, is neither original nor novel, but it does serve to draw attention to those issues and problems that span the different parts or levels of the public communication process and to bring to the fore those questions that highlight the holistic and integrated nature of the process.

Two additional principles characterize the center's research philosophy. The first emphasizes the special importance we attach to comparative, cross-cultural research. In a world in which global communication assumes ever-growing significance, no society remains a communication island unto itself. Issues ranging from the micro impact of mass communication through the structure of media organizations and the production of culture to the macro role of worldwide communication networks can best—some would say only—be explored through a comparative perspective.

The second principle that guides the center's work is an emphasis on policy-oriented research. We strive to be conscious of the implications of our research for questions of public policy, and, to reveal our value preference, we are guided by the goal of enhancing the contribution of mass communication research to the promotion of democratic institutions and practices.

Given these assumptions we now wish to single out a number of research areas that we believe constitute important sites for investigation. Our recommendations are grounded in the center's philosophy although not all center associates endorse these specifics, nor are they expected to do so. Indeed some researchers may even object to the very notion of a research agenda and consider pluralism or perhaps even anarchy the best guarantors of scholarly freedom and accomplishment. We share and uphold the spirit of such a position (also captured in Tannenbaum's essay in this volume—"To Each His/Her Own"), and regard the research ideas that follow not as an agenda in any constraining sense. Rather, we present it as our own statement of "the significant" in mass communication research and offer it for consideration by our colleagues *extra muros*.

The Media in the Nexus of Power Relations

The position of the media in the structure of power in society and their relationship to power-holding institutions is not, of course, an unexplored area. Much of the writing on this issue, however, tends to be speculative rather than empirically grounded. A notable exception is the issue of media ownership and control about which considerable data have now been gathered. The issues outlined below may be regarded as candidates for similar research attention.

Media-social elite integration. The main concern here is with the degree of social-cultural proximity and of political affinity that obtains between the media elite and other social elites. First, there is a need to examine the extent of structural differentiation (or integration) between these elites. Quite often this structural differentiation is blurred or eliminated through various formal (e.g., interlocking directorships) or informal bridges. There is also ample evidence to suggest that similarities in social and cultural background between members of various elites often, if not always, result in political and value affinities between them. There also may be an overlap of personnel, resulting, say, from the movement of media professionals into the political elite, and vice versa.

As the political persuasion process becomes more intense and specialized, boundary agencies are formed, in both political institutions and media organizations, staffed by individuals with experience in and familiarity with the "other" domain. In addition, there are varieties of informal contacts, fueled by mutual dependencies and affinities, that may generate greater responsiveness on both sides to each other's views and problems. Research into the variety of linkages between the media and political-social elites could shed light on the mechanisms that place the media in the nexus of power relations in society and that define their specific role within the social elite.

Source-professional communicator relations. Research on the relationship between the sources or originators of public communication messages and media professionals has been less than fully developed. Elsewhere Blumler and Gurevitch have stated the problem as follows:

> Much of what gets into news and current affairs reporting in the media originates in "news sources," yet little sustained work has been devoted to the orientation of media personnel to those organizations and individuals that comprise their major sources and that, simultaneously, also constitute the subjects of these news stories. The relationship of news professionals to their sources has been explained—as a function of the public relations activities of organizations and institutions keen to purvey their messages; as the products of institutional structures within which newswork is embedded; as the application of the tenets of media professional ideologies (e.g., "news values," "objectivity," "impartiality") and more generally as the outcome of a process of exchange, bargaining and mutual accommodation, tempered and constrained by the role definitions which prescribe and regulate the interaction between media professionals and their sources cum subjects of reporting. But again, little attempt has been made to consider whether these elements represent competing, alternative explanations of the relationship, or instead comprise a set of equally operative and mutually complementary and reinforcing factors, and if so, whether they invariably structure the resulting "stories" in the same manner or not. In addition, little attempt has been made systematically to explain the differential treatment that different information sources or institutions enjoy or suffer at the hands of newsworkers [Blumler and Gurevitch, 1982].

The view that news is controlled to a considerable extent by the sources of information on which newsworkers rely highlights the role of sources as one of the main influences that shape the news. The "interface" between sources of information and media professionals is thus an important point of convergence, where central influences on the production and content of the news interact. It is also, in the spirit of our "level-spanning" principle, an issue located at the conjunction of two "parts" or levels of the mass communication process.

Journalist's orientations toward social institutions. Another important dimension of the relationship between the media and the structure of power in society has to do with the orientations of media professionals, especially newsworkers, toward different social institutions and role incumbents whose activities and views they report. Ultimately, these orientations constitute an important influence on the framing of media portrayals of different areas of social life.

One example of this line of research can be found in a study by Blumler and Gurevitch of direct audio broadcasting from the Houses of Parliament in Britain

(Blumler and Gurevitch, 1982). The data gathered in the course of interviews with different groups of British broadcasters involved in the coverage of parliamentary activity suggested that those newsworkers regarded, and treated, the coverage of Parliament with varying degrees of "sacredness." This stemmed not from their professional orientation toward Parliament but rather from their extraprofessional values, those inherent in their roles as citizens who viewed Parliament as a symbol of British democracy.

Extrapolating from this framework, a case could be made that media portrayals of other social institutions are also influenced in a similar fashion. Thus those social institutions that embody, represent, or symbolize the consensual values of society might be treated as more "sacred" by the media, while those social groups or institutions that are regarded as being more remote from core values or that represent alternative, oppositional, or even "deviant" values will be treated by the media in a less sacred, more pragmatic fashion.

Sacred treatment implies a sympathetic media portrayal. Groups and institutions are portrayed as they would portray themselves—that is, in a manner that is governed by acceptance and respect for the values for which the institutions and groups stand. A pragmatic orientation, on the other hand, implies treatment determined primarily by professional news values, and consequently reflects the social values implicit in those news values. In Britain, Parliament is one institution likely to receive sacerdotal treatment. Another, perhaps more obvious example is the royal family. The trade unions in Britain, by contrast, are apparently less likely to be accorded such special treatment, as some research evidence suggests, and hence are more likely to complain of media bias. American examples of institutions given sacred treatment might be the presidency (although not necessarily the president); the Supreme Court; and perhaps some professions, such as medicine or even journalism itself.

By examining variations in the degree of sacerdotal coverage accorded different groups and institutions, it might be possible to construct a media view of the core consensual values of society. By comparing media representations of the value system of society with representations of that value system by other institutions (e.g., the educational system) or as measured through sample surveys of the general population, it might be possible to assess the degree to which media representations of social values are consonant with the values held by different parts of society. This could provide important insights into the role played by the media in cultivating a dominant ideology.

Orientations toward the media. The counterpart of the issue discussed above has to do with the orientations of different institutions, groups, and the public at large *toward* the media. Much has been said recently about the erosion of public trust in the media, and a number of incidents have been recorded in the United States of open conflict between the media and other social and political actors. Even an institution such as the White House which, following the argument above, could be expected to be treated in a sacred manner, continually signals its displeasure with the media. Indeed, recently the White House has launched its own news service, designed to overcome the filtering and packaging of its messages by so-called unsympathetic journalists. Media professionals have expressed puzzlement, annoyance, and outrage at these manifestations of mistrust, seeing in them a less than sacred respect for the position of the media as guardians of democracy and democratic values.

Research into public and institutional orientations toward the media, past and present, could illuminate a number of significant questions: (1) Are we indeed witnessing a meaningful change in the relationship between the media and society, or have the media always been the object of ambivalent attitudes? (2) If such a change can be documented, what are the causes of this change? (3) What might be the consequences, short- and long-run, for society and for the media, of changes in their historical relationship with society? and (4) What does this change signify, and what implications might it have for the analysis of the role of the media in the power structure of society?

Media Representations of Social Issues

The role of the media in framing public issues and shaping the terms of the discourse about these issues is by now recognized and acknowledged. Less often recognized is the notion that the media ought to be seen as a site on which various social groups, institutions, and ideologies struggle over the definition and construction of social reality. Alternatively, we could say that the media should be seen as the site on which a variety of more-or-less powerful and organized interests and perspectives contend in an effort to influence the public dialogue. Research into media treatment of *specific* public issues could shed light on that contest and illuminate the various mechanisms (e.g., language, professional practices and ideologies, the position of media organizations vis-à-vis other social actors) through which the debate is conducted. Work along these lines is exemplified by a number of studies conducted in Britain that focused on media portrayals of issues such as industrial relations, law and order, and the welfare system (Glasgow University Media Group, 1976, 1980; Golding and Middleton, 1982; Hall et al., 1978).

A number of assumptions underlay these studies. First, these studies assume that media presentations of specific issues are, by and large, uniform across all the media. Although some variation can always be found, these studies document the recurrence of a limited number of themes and images that can then be identified as the dominant ones. Second, the studies assume that these dominant images are consonant with the views held on these issues by the dominant groups in society, hence the ideological effect of the media.

These assumptions have received substantial support in the British studies mentioned above. Yet media professionals, anxious to defend themselves against accusations of bias or lack of impartiality, contend that the recurrence and the uniformity of the news "frames," if true, is dictated by the nature of the events or issues covered, rather than by any ideological preferences. Media researchers, on the other hand, have identified media practices, professional ideologies, and media organizational structures as the mechanisms that explain the thematic uniformity in the news. Using the British work as a benchmark, researchers in other countries may now wish to conduct comparative analyses of media presentations of the major public issues in their societies, with a view to explicating the factors and forces that best explain the shaping of the discourse of public issues in the news media.

It is not our argument that all such work should be guided by a search for a single, dominant message. Attempts to map the extent and limits of media functions as a "cultural forum" would be equally appropriate (Newcomb and Hirsch, this volume). Conceived of in these terms, research of this kind would facilitate theorizing about the role of the media as ideological agency; and, in keeping with our comparative thrust, encourage studies of how that role would vary across different social and media systems.

Encoding and Decoding

Another level-spanning set of issues has to do with the relationship between media messages and audiences. Two observations are especially pertinent here. First, it appears that after a decade or so in which research and theorizing about media effects has documented the cognitive contribution of the media, questions are now being raised about the efficacy of the media as contributors to audience members' knowledge and comprehension of their society and the world. Such doubts—one may perhaps talk of disillusionment—were caused primarily by findings that persistently highlight the very limited contribution of media exposure to information processing and increased knowledge.

Second, alongside the skepticism about the cognitive contributions of the media, there is an increasing awareness of the normative and ideological dimension of media messages. A view of the media as carriers and promoters of social norms goes back to the founding fathers of American mass communication research (Lasswell, Merton, and Lazarsfeld) who saw the media as agencies involved in the reproduction and transmission of cultural values and social norms. Thus while this insight has the patina of authority, it still had to contend for many years with the proposition, strongly endorsed by media professionals, that at least those formats of media content designed to convey information were, indeed, value free.

If, then, we discern, on the one hand, a failure of the media to increase effectively the levels of factual knowledge among audience members and, on the other hand, acknowledge the norm-providing function of media informational content, then important questions arise concerning the impact of news on its audiences. Researchers should therefore turn their attention to the impact of news as a constructor of interpretative frameworks for the audience. What is required then is a better understanding of the complexities of the encoding/decoding process.

Studies of the production of news have already provided important insights into the encoding process. Research into audience decoding of news (as well as of other media contents) is less well developed. The next important step, however, is to relate these two processes to each other. Studying either aspect of the overall process in isolation will yield only limited results. We should proceed to view the encoding/decoding process as an integrated whole, and study it as one of the keys for understanding the relationship between media messages, the meanings they carry, and audience perceptions of the social environment.

Communication Technology and Policy

The hardware of the new communication technologies and its potential effects has attracted considerable attention from communication scholars. But students of new technology and communication policy need to consider what, if anything, unites their disparate efforts. How, for example, are teletext systems and automated work stations related? What, save their newness and their reliance on computer technology, makes them the subject of a common research interest? Unless we seek ways to understand the new technology that draw on and extend past research traditions, we run the risk of becoming "chip-ologists"—practitioners of a scholarly discipline that blindly venerates processed sand.

Important questions about the new technology, however, can be framed in terms of the principles outlined above. One line of investigation, especially amenable to cross-national and level-spanning inquiry, might consider who benefits from the new technologies; in whose interest are the technologies designed, marketed, and used? Other research should probe the impact of new technologies on democratic processes. How, for example, is the growing diversity of information sources affecting citizen awareness of and participation in social and political life? To what extent are new modes of communication supplementing or replacing existing channels of talk between elites and publics, and within elites?

One final note about our research agenda and its relationship to this volume. Both the agenda and this collection grow out of our research interests and preferences. However, in choosing items for inclusion here we were also constrained by what was out there—the work of the scholarly community. It is not surprising, therefore, that some of the studies collected here do not fall under the specific items on our agenda. Still, we would contend that many do, and that, taken as a unit, the articles here exemplify the spirit and assumptions that also guide the work of the Maryland Center for Research in Public Communication.

ACKNOWLEDGMENTS

Now that we have provided a "biography" of this volume and have taken the liberty of outlining our own research agenda, we would like to thank those who have helped in this project. In particular, we want to thank our editorial board, whose tireless efforts as talent scouts provided much of the raw material presented herein. We especially want to thank Chuck Whitney and Ellen Wartella, our predecessors as editors of *MCRY*, who generously shared their experience with us. We also wish to acknowledge the contributions of Jim Carey, Percy Tannenbaum, Gladys and Kurt Lang, and Nicholas Garnham, who responded to our offer of a "soapbox" with personal statements marked by insight and excellence.

We are also grateful to Dean Reese Cleghorn of the College of Journalism, University of Maryland, for his continuing interest and support; and to Lisa Freeman-Miller, our editor at Sage Publications, who guided us through the review yearbook process with grace and good sense. Finally, but by no means least in our gratitude, we wish to thank Steve Barkin, Ed Fink, and Jim Webster, who truly earned their titles of contributing editors.

NOTE

1. The principal themes of this research agenda were developed in collaboration with Jay Blumler, associate director of the Maryland Center for Research in Public Communication.

REFERENCES

Blumler, Jay and Michael Gurevitch 1982. "Newsmen's orientations toward social institutions: the case of the broadcasting of Parliament." Centre for Television Research, University of Leeds. (mimeo)

Glasgow University Media Group 1976. Bad News. London: Routledge & Kegan Paul.

———1980. More Bad News. London: Routledge & Kegan Paul.

Golding, Peter and Sue Middleton 1982. Images of Welfare. London: Macmillan.

Hall, Stuart et al. 1978. Policing the Crisis. London: Macmillan.

PART I

IDENTIFYING THE SIGNIFICANT CHANGES IN MASS COMMUNICATION RESEARCH

INTRODUCTION

Mark R. Levy

Significant scientific research often begins with a good question—not any old itch (as Einstein put it) that's easily scratched, but a question so profound and initially so perplexing that it forces the scientist into that never-ending dialogue with life we call scholarship.

Asking good—let alone great—questions, however, is enormously difficult. There is no "Problematics 101" with easily applicable lessons. Rather, we must struggle with ourselves and our colleagues to define the intellectual agenda, to establish the significant questions for study.

The eight pieces in this section attempt just that: to mark the path, to identify those questions or issues—large as well as less large—that are worthy of serious and prolonged attention by the mass communication research community.

The first four selections are personal statements by leading mass communication researchers, commissioned by the editors of *MCRY 5*. In these pieces the authors share their thoughts on the various states of the discipline and suggest where we ought to go from here. In "Overcoming Resistance to Cultural Studies," Carey challenges mainstream communications research to come to grips once and for all with "the entire framework within which our studies proceed." Plunging deeply into the philosophical thicket, Carey examines both positivist and phenomenological opposition to cultural studies, and argues for an alternative approach informed by—but not a captive of—neo-Marxist and structuralist traditions. In the final analysis, Carey argues, the mass media must be considered a strategic field of research for general social science inquiry.

In "To Each His/Her Own," Tannenbaum calls, among other things, for increased scholarly attention to the nature of *vicarious* experience. "Deep truths about the nature of the human psyche," he contends, will be unearthed by communication scholars who take seriously the "lure" of mass entertainment.

And in opposition to current speculation and practice, says Tannenbaum, unintended or incidental effects of exposure to entertainment would be better understood with a set of mini-theories and micro-methodologies, fine tuned to temporally differing consequences of media use. Finally, Tannenbaum suggests greater research emphasis on the origins and development of communication "literacy," the principal mechanism by which vicarious experience is transferred.

Next, Kurt Lang and Gladys Lang review the basic strategies of "effects" research and answer the question implied in their title ("Method as Master or Mastery over Method") with a strong challenge to current practice. Research methods, say the Langs, have blinded scholars to side-effects, spill-over effects, and long-term effects; forced investigators to rely on obviously flawed self-reported measures; and led to overly individualistic modes of explanation. The solution, they suggest, is a greater willingness to experiment with multiple, often "soft," research methodologies, coupled with the application of an inverse inductive logic that seeks causes *from* fully documented effects.

In "Communication Technology and Policy," Garnham offers a *tour d'horizon* of the rapidly changing technology of communication and suggests that the convergence of computing and telecommunications poses urgent, new questions for both scholars and policymakers. A complex dialectic of centralization and decentralization is at work, says Garnham, with extraordinary implications for the public and private spheres. What's needed, Garnham contends, is research with a macro, interdisciplinary and cross-cultural focus that examines the political economy of the information society, the formulation of communications policy, and the societal impact of information consumption.

Following the four personal statements are four other articles, grouped under the subheading "Reflections on Developments in the Field." Each piece deals with a major area of communication research. In the section's most general selection, "The Beginnings of Political Communication Research: Origins of the 'Limited Effects' Model," Chaffee and Hochheimer trace the origins and early development of American political communication. They review the theoretical assumptions and empirical findings of the earliest political communications studies, contend that the work of Lazarsfeld and others created an unwarranted image of limited campaign effects, and show how that image was taken over more broadly by communication researchers. Only in the late 1960s and early 1970s, say Chaffee and Hochheimer, did researchers trained primarily as communications scholars begin to question the limited effects paradigm.

In "Space, Time, and Captive Communication History," Marvin argues that communication history has been held hostage by the ideology and customs of its intellectual "patron," the professional schools of journalism and mass communication. Peripheral to the mission of those institutions and neglected by mainstream historians, communication history has failed to produce work of substance. And, says Marvin, even so-called exemplars of communication history (such as Innis's much-vaunted cultural studies) hold little promise for rectifying the second-class citizenship of the communications historian.

As one of the earliest of the second-wave uses and gratifications researchers, McQuail offers a reexamination from within the tradition in the selection, "With the Benefit of Hindsight: Reflections on Uses and Gratifications Research." McQuail reviews briefly the intellectual history of the uses and gratifications approach, and asserts that the core concerns of the tradition (the choice, reception, and manner of audience response to the media) remain viable, but poorly studied. McQuail also rejects the gratifications paradigm's fundamentally behaviorist assumptions in favor of a "culturalist" model of the media experience, a model that he contends would allow a more adequate exploration of human culture.

In the final article, "The Implicit Assumptions of Television Research: An Analysis of the 1982 NIMH Report of Television and Behavior," Cook, Kendzierski, and Thomas use the 10-year follow-up to the Surgeon General's report on violence as a chance to take a broad-gauge look at television effects research. Most current research on television, they conclude, depends on individual rather than institutional levels of analysis; employs extremely simple models of the audience selection process; and overemphasizes the substantive importance of small but statistically significant effects. The authors also criticize television researchers for largely ignoring "sources of leverage" that might be used to improve television programming.

In summary, although the eight selections of Part I are disparate in substantive focus, they share at least two common perspectives. First, each of the authors essentially agrees with Whitehead's apothegm that "a science which hesitates to forget its founders is lost." The insights of all-purpose giants such as Marx, Weber, and Durkheim, the work of avatars such as Lazarsfeld, Innis, and Hovland, and even the contributions of contemporary leaders such as Hall, Gerbner, and Pool are evaluated with a skeptical eye. Our 10 authors, divided over metatheory and method, are nevertheless united by a critical (with a small "c") spirit.

Second, in rejecting—or at least rethinking—the founders, most of these selections also seek to promote a new and larger dialogue. That scholarly conversation, say our authors, should draw on both scientific and humanistic perspectives in order to understand mass communication as a cultural phenomenon.

Taken together, these two themes then are robust indicators of disciplinary vigor. It is most certainly a positive sign that the received traditions of our field are coming in for such scrutiny. Perhaps even more striking is that in criticizing research past, these authors are often self-critical—sometimes self-consciously so, sometimes not. That too is a strong indicator of disciplinary well-being. Finally, as a unit, these selections strongly suggest that something important is going on in mass communication research. As Clifford Geertz has observed, "Something is happening to the way we think about the way we think."

1

OVERCOMING RESISTANCE TO CULTURAL STUDIES

James W. Carey

The major issues that face students of mass communications, the macro issues, have been the same for the past 15 years. They concern the entire framework within which our studies proceed and, therefore, the nature, purpose, and pertinence of the knowledge we profess. In order to reorient this framework, I have been making an argument for a particular and distinctive point of view toward the mass media, for something I call, without originality, cultural studies. Much of that argument has been made by indirection, suggesting that the study of the mass media would be better served if we pretty much abandoned our commitments to certain forms of explanation that have dominated the enterprise over the last 50 years or so. We have had our equivalent of the quest for the Holy Grail: the search for a positive science of communications, one that elucidates the laws of human behavior and the universal and univocal functions of the mass media. It is time to give it up, to relinquish happily what John Dewey called a couple of generations back the "neurotic quest for certainty." To abandon the traditional framework would not only invigorate our studies, it would liberate us as well from a series of bad and crippling ideas, particularly from a model of social order implicit in this framework, a twisted version of utilitarianism, and form a rhetoric of motives that I have elsewhere called a power and anxiety model of communications.[1] I am suggesting that we unload, in a common phrase, the "effects tradition."

There is now, I believe, a large and compelling literature, one written from every point on the compass of knowledge, ethics, and beauty, attacking the behavioral and functional sciences on both epistemological and ethicopolitical grounds. Idealism and pragmatism have undermined the notions of objectivity and objective truth that ground the explanatory apparatus of such sciences. Marxism, existentialism, and a variety of continental philosophies have elucidated the baleful consequences of such sciences for politics and morals, for conduct and practice. However, it is not necessary to be either so contentious or so philosophical about the entire business. The argument can be made in the small rather than the large. Contrary to Bernard Berelson's dire prediction of 25 years ago, the field of mass communication has not withered away. In fact, it is a successful, growing, highly institutionalized academic enterprise. But, despite its academic success, as measured by courses, students, journals, and faculty, it is intellectually stagnant and increasingly uninteresting. It is also crippled by a widening gap between the ambitions of the students and the intellectual and ideological poses of the faculty. Part of the problem, although only part, is that the central tradition of effects research has been a failure on its own terms, and where it is not a failure, it is patently antidemocratic and at odds with the professed beliefs of its practitioners.[2] In political terms, it would be a greater failure if it were more of a success.

The effects tradition has not generated any agreement on the laws of behavior or the functions of communications of sufficient power and pertinence to signal to us that success has been achieved. The entire enterprise has degenerated into mere academicism: the solemn repetition of the indubitable. Our commitments are no longer advancing but impeding inquiry, reproducing results of such studied vagueness and predictability that we threaten to bore one another to death. The surest sign of this state of affairs is the long-term retreat into method at the expense of substance, as if doing it right guarantees getting it right. The sharpest criticism of the behavioral and functional sciences ushering forth from philosophical quarters are now dealt with by silence. Under these circumstances, we can continue to wait for our Newton to arise within the traditional framework, but that increasingly feels like waiting for Godot. Or, we can try to shift the framework and hold on to what is valuable in the tradition, even as we recast it in an alternative conceptual vocabulary.

Let me be clear on one point the speed readers always seem to miss. To abandon the effects tradition does not entail doing away with research methods—including the higher and more arcane forms of counting—that take up so much time in our seminars. Nor does it require turning up the academic temperature to 451 Fahrenheit and indulging in wholesale book burning. No one, except the congenitally out of touch, suggests we have to stop counting or that we can afford to stop reading the "classics" in the effects literature. However, this literature will have to be deconstructed and reinterpreted and the methods and techniques of the craft redeployed. I am trying to be ecumenical about this—not solely for reasons of decency, although that would be sufficient, but for a serious philosophical purpose. There will be no progress in this field that does not seriously articulate with, engage, and build upon the effects tradition we have inherited. A wholesale evacuation or diremption of the theories, methods, insights, and techniques so painfully wrought in the last half-century would be a sure invitation to failure. This is true if only because intelligence continually overflows the constrictions provided by paradigms and methods. But more to the point, the effects tradition attempted to deal with serious problems of American politics and culture, at least on the part of its major practitioners, and it is now part of that culture. Any attempt to avoid it will only consign one to irrelevancy.

However, to reorient the study of mass communication, we will have to change the self-image, self-consciousness, and self-reflection we have of the enterprise: our view of what we are up to, the history we share in common, how we are situated in the societies in which we work, and the claims we make for the knowledge we profess. This is both a little easier and much more painful a surrender than changing a reading list or substituting participant observation or close reading for factor analysis and linear regression equations. If we make the shift I have been recommending, we would, to borrow some observations from Richard Rorty (1984a), talk much less about paradigms and methods and much more about certain concrete achievements. There would be less talk about rigor and more about originality. We would draw more on the vocabulary of poetry and politics and less on the vocabulary of metaphysics and determinism. And we would have more of a sense of solidarity with both the society we study and our fellow students than we now have. Above all, we would see more clearly the reflexive relationship of scholarship to society and be rid of the curse of intellectual humanity: the alternating belief that we are either a neutral class of discoverers of the laws of society or a new priesthood endowed by credentials with the right to run the social machinery. We would, finally, see truth and knowledge not as some objective map of the social order, nature speaking through us, but, in the lovely phrase of William James, as that which is good by way of belief, that which will get us to where we want to go.

Cultural studies is a vehicle that can alter our self-image and carry forward the intellectual attitudes noted above. At the very least, this position entails recentering and thinking through the concept of culture relative to the mass media and disposing of the concepts of effect and function. Now I realize that only the excessively adventurous, consistently unhappy, or perpetually foolhardy are going to leave the cozy (if not very interesting) village of effects research for the uncharted but surprising savannah of cultural studies without a better map of the territory than I or anyone else has been able to provide. Filling that gap is a major task of the future. The best I can do at the moment is to encourage people to circle within an alternative conceptual vocabulary and an alternative body of literature that will assist in marking out this unclaimed territory. To make things familiar, if not exactly precise, this means connecting media studies to the debate over mass culture and popular culture, which was a modest but important moment in the general argument over the effects of the mass media in the 1950s. The debate itself will have to be reconstructed, of course. The basic lines of such reconstruction were set out in the early work of Raymond Williams and Richard Hoggart in England when they attempted to apply the anthropological or primitive society conception of culture to the life and peoples of industrial society: to the language, work, community life, and media of those living through what Williams called "the long revolution."

The connection of cultural studies to the work of Max Weber is more important yet, for Weber attempted to provide both a phenomenology of industrial societies—that is, a description of the subjective life or consciousness of industrial peoples, including the ends or purposes of their characteristic actions—and an analysis of the patterns of dominance and authority typical of such societies. Weber described this enterprise as "cultural science" during the interminable argument over *Naturwissenschaft* and *Kulturwissenschaft*. I much prefer cultural studies to cultural science because I abhor the honorific sense that has accumulated around the word "science." As Thomas Kuhn has recently remarked, the term "science" emerged at the end of the eighteenth century to name a set of still forming disciplines that were simply to be contrasted with medicine, law, engineering, philosophy, theology, and other areas of study (Kuhn, 1983). To this taxonomic sense was quickly added the honorific one: the distinction between science and nonscience was the same as the Platonic distinction between knowledge and opinion. This latter distinction, along with the correlative distinctions between the objective and the subjective, primary and secondary, is precisely the distinction cultural studies seeks, as a first order of business, to dissolve. More than that, I rather like the modest, even self-deprecating, connotation of the word "studies": It keeps us from confusing the fish story with the fish. It might even engender a genuinely humble attitude toward our subject and a sense of solidarity with our fellow citizens who are outside the formal study of the mass media while, like us, inside the phenomenon to be studied.

Cultural studies, on an American terrain, has been given its most powerful expression by John Dewey and in the tradition of symbolic interactionism, which developed out of American pragmatism generally. It was Dewey's student, Robert Park, who provided the most powerful analysis of mass culture (although he did not call it that) that was adapted to the circumstances of the country. Dewey, Park, and others in the Chicago School transplanted, without attempting to do so, Weberian sociology to American soil, although happily within the pragmatist attempt to dissolve the distinction between the natural and cultural sciences. Not so happily, although understandably, they also lost the sharper edges of Weberian sociology, particularly its emphasis on authority, conflict, and domination, and that will have to be restored to the tradition.

Names solve nothing, I realize, but they begin to suggest at the very least a series of concepts and notions within which media studies might fruitfully circle: experience, subjectivity, interaction, conflict, authority, domination, class, status, and power, to state but part of the catalogue. As I have earlier argued, it was precisely these connections and issues that formed scholars striking a minor but enduring theme of media studies during the ferment in the 1940s and 1950s: David Riesman, C. Wright Mills, Harold Innis and Kenneth Burke (Carey, 1983). Cultural studies, in an American context, is an attempt to reclaim and reconstruct this tradition.

I realize that, in an age of internationalism, I have set this argument out ethnocentrically. I do so to make a philosophical point and not a nationalist one. Since the advent of the printing press, at least, the arguments that comprise social analysis have been ethnocentrically formulated. To try to escape these formulations, to

try to import wholesale from somewhere else an analysis that does not develop roots on native grounds, is simply a pose, another way of being an observer. This is not to say that other voices from other valleys cannot make a major contribution. Weber has been mentioned; Marx cannot for long be avoided; and I have paid homage to Williams and Hoggart. On the contemporary scene one thinks of four foreign voices that have something of the right spirit to them: Habermas, Foucault, Giddens, and Bourdieu. But such voices must be embedded in, deeply connected with, the lines of discourse and the canons of evidence and argument that are only decipherable within the social, political, and intellectual traditions of given national, social formations.

The issues surrounding cultural studies have been very much complicated, as well as enormously enriched, by the increasing prominence in the United States of the work of the Center for the Study of Contemporary Culture at the University of Birmingham, and, in particular, that portion of the center's activity identified with Stuart Hall. Hall's work is theoretically, historically, and, often, empirically elegant and very much deserves the influence it has acquired. The center's research, while distinctively English in orientation and therefore in its limitations, draws heavily on certain traditions of continental theory and politics, particularly Marxism and structuralism, although interestingly enough not on critical theory of the Frankfurt School variety.

British cultural studies could be described just as easily and perhaps more accurately as ideological studies in that it assimilates, in a variety of complex ways, culture to ideology. More accurately, it makes ideology synecdochal of culture as a whole. Ideological studies, in Stuart Hall's lovely phrase, represent "the return of the repressed in media studies." Ideology, on this reading, was always the unacknowledged subtext of effects research. Differences of opinion described by psychological scales masked structural fault lines along which ran vital political divisions. The "consensus" achieved by the mass media was only achieved by reading the "deviants" out of the social formation: political difference reduced to normlessness. The positive sciences did not provide an analysis of ideology (or of culture) but rather were part of the actual social process by which ideological forms masked and sustained the social order.

This analysis, while radically undersketched, has had a rejuvenating effect on a variety of Marxist and neo-Marxist analyses of capitalist societies by North American scholars. Unfortunately, the ferment this rejuvenation has provided in the field is often described by the stale and unproductive contrast between administrative and critical research, a legacy left over from the years the Frankfurt school was in exile and, in truth, in hiding. But the difference between cultural studies and the positive sciences is not in any simple sense a mere difference between supporting or criticizing the status quo, although I suppose it is comforting for some to think so.

There are gross and important similarities between British and American cultural studies that derive from certain common origins and influences. Both trace their founding to the early 1950s and both have been influenced, to a greater or lesser degree, by the debate over mass culture and the work of Williams, Hoggart, and E. P. Thompson. Both have drawn extensively on symbolic interactionism, although in somewhat different ways. In the British case symbolic interactionism has been limited to providing an approach to the analysis of subcultures and the "problem of deviance," whereas it has provided a much more generalized model of social action in the American case. Similarly, both traditions have been influenced by Max Weber. The principal concept of Weber that has worked its way into British studies is that of legitimation, while the rest of Weber's analysis of class, status, and authority—important as that has been to American scholars—has largely been shorn away. Finally, British cultural studies has circled within a variety of meanings of ideology, meanings provided by the wider debate within Marxism, particularly by the encounter of Marxism and French structuralism. In fact, beginning from the work of Williams, Hoggart, and Thompson, British cultural studies have made a long detour through French structuralism and, like everything else these days, have been deeply divided over the encounter. Structuralism, in turn, has made little headway in the United States, where it must contend with the far more powerful formalisms provided by information theory and transformational linguistics.

These wide-ranging and often contradictory influences have been held in remarkable equipoise by Stuart Hall. He has shown an exceptional capacity to be open and generous in absorbing currents of thought while firmly fixed on centering cultural studies on ideological analysis within a neo-Marxist framework. However, despite the power and elegance of this analysis, I think it is likely to increase rather than reduce resistance to cultural studies in the United States. That resistance, however understandable, is, I believe, shortsighted.

The two dominant types of resistance to cultural studies take a positivist and a phenomenological form, although the labels—like all labels—are not quite adequate. As forms of resistance they overlap and have something important in common; however, they proceed from different origins and therefore end up in different dilemmas.

The positivist resistance to cultural studies, beyond the ever-present desire to maintain a distinction between hard science and soft scholarship, between knowledge and opinion, is grounded in a deep political instinct. The positive sciences, of which physics is the model and psychology the pretender, grew up in a distinct historical relation not only to capitalism but to parliamentary democracy. These sciences are the crowning achievement of Western civilization, far less ambiguous in many ways than either capitalism or democracy. Indeed, the positive sciences epistemologically grounded democracy, provided some guarantee that opinion could be transcended by truth, and, most of all, provided a model of uncoerced communication in terms of which to judge and modify political practice. In short, the positive sciences are historically linked to certain valuable practices that no one particularly wants to surrender. Therefore, cultural studies, in its attack on the self-understanding of the positive sciences, seems to buy into a moral and political vocabulary that is, if not antidemocratic, at least insufficiently sensitive to the ways in which valued political practices intertwine with certain intellectual habits. More than that, few can completely forget that the positive sciences shored up parliamentary democracy at a particularly perilous moment in its history—during the Depression and World War II. Positive science, anchored as it was in a notion of truth independent of politics, arrived at by open communication and in the doctrine of natural rights, was one means of withstanding the totalitarian temptation.

I think it is important to be sympathetic to this form of resistance to cultural studies, but in the end it is misplaced and counterproductive. Because the positive sciences shored up democracy at one bad moment, it is not necessary to conclude they can or will do it permanently. I have already suggested, in fact, that in the post-World War II phase, the positive sciences increasingly assumed an antidemocratic character that was implicit in the commitments of the behavioral and functional sciences. Notions of laws of behavior and functions of society pretty much obliterate the entire legacy of democracy; they substitute ideological and coercive practice for the process of consensus formation via uncoerced conversation.[3] The suggestion that positive science be substituted for uncoerced communication was first put forward, within our tradition, by Walter Lippmann in *Public Opinion*. John Dewey instantly responded to the book, describing it as the greatest indictment of democracy yet written. By the time of the Vietnam war, Dewey proved prophetic, for the behavioral sciences were central to that intellectual, moral, and political disaster.

Democracy may be damaged by the positive sciences but it does not need to be buttressed by them or defended and justified in terms of them. The valued practices and habits of the intellectual and political enlightenment can be better defended by what Richard Rorty (1984b) has called a "criterionless muddling through," by comparing those societies that exhibit qualities of tolerance, free inquiry, and a quest for undistorted communication with those that do not. We do not need to buttress this comparison by designating certain methods and theories as guarantors of the truth.

Of course, cultural studies consists of a thinly disguised moral and political vocabulary. But that is true of all intellectual vocabularies, including the vocabulary of the positive sciences. If students in this field have not learned it from Kenneth Burke perhaps they are no longer capable of learning, but conceptual vocabularies always contain a rhetoric of attitudes and a rhetoric of motives. There is no way of doing intellectual work without adopting a language that simultaneously defines, describes, evaluates, and acts toward the phenomena in question. Therefore, resistance to centering the question of ideology or of adopting cultural studies as a point of view toward the mass media is that it seems to commit oneself in advance to a moral evaluation of modern society—American in particular, the Western democracies in general, the mass media above all—that is wholly negative and condemnatory. It seems, therefore, to commit one to a revolutionary line of political action or, at the least, a major project of social reconstruction. The fear is real but it is a little silly, if only for the reason that there aren't any revolutionaries anywhere these days.

If the behavioral and functional sciences contain a moral and political vocabulary, then the problem is not to undertake the hapless task of sundering science from morals and politics but rather to recognize the inevitable interconnection of these forms of activity and to make them ever more explicit and defensible. The behavioral and cultural sciences should contain an analysis of ideology beyond the crude and reductive one they now have but they should also make explicit their own ideological implications and persuasions and defend them on their own ground, not by pretending that "science says" is an adequate defense. (A paradoxical fact of our times is that right-wing scholarship, as represented by neoconservatism, does not have much of an analysis of ideology; it just has an ideology. The Left has a dozen different analyses of ideology; it just does not have an ideology in the sense of a plan for political action.)

Cultural studies looks at ideology and theory as varying forms of expression within the same culture. They differ semantically, stylistically, and in terms of their conditions of expression and reception. They do not differ because one contains truth and one error, one knowledge and one opinion, one fact and one fancy, in some a priori way. The task is to see the characteristic kinds of difficulties our ideologies and our theories (and our culture) get us into and then to try to devise ways of getting out of those difficulties.[4] However, getting out will not be accomplished by getting rid of or devaluing ideology and culture in the name of science but by plunging the latter more deeply into the former. All forms of practice and expression, including science, are cultural forms and can only be understood in that light.

An instructive lesson here, although I am hardly in the business of extolling or applauding positivists and neoconservatives, was provided by Daniel Bell and Irving Kristol when they founded *The Public Interest*. The journal was established in 1965 at a moment when the orthodox (as opposed to the radical) Left was in control of American politics. Bell and Kristol felt the American society had been badly damaged by the social programs as well as the cultural and foreign policy initiatives of those in charge. *The Public Interest* was designed as a place for like-minded persons to work out a broad social program to change the direction of American life. They did not waste their time, I can assure you, on defending or explaining the theories and methods of the positive sciences. It was not for them to chase metaphysical bats around intellectual belfries. They simply gathered up a group of social scientists and left the church. They disappeared down the street. They didn't even leave a forwarding address or a note in the pew saying regards. They went off and built a different church on a different intellectual site, on a site that was not as easily shaken by an antipositivist critique. They systematically went about the task of using intelligence, irrespective of method and theory, to reground the social order, undertaking what Stuart Hall would call a hegemonic project but which we might more evenhandedly call a project of social reconstruction. They did not need an outmoded philosophy of science to ground their own image of democracy and intellectual work. Despite having written essays on the "end of ideology," they unabashedly admitted the interconnection between ideology and science and made a case, a remarkably successful case as it has turned out, for their own way of viewing the world and proceeding within it. The task for those who believe that current versions of cultural studies corrupt or compromise democratic practice is not a retreat into value-free objectivist science but to unearth, make explicit, and critique the moral and political commitments in their own contingent work.[5] In short, the answer is to move toward, not away from, a cultural studies viewpoint.

The phenomenological resistance to cultural studies is more difficult to characterize because it otherwise shares so much in common with cultural studies. Phenomenologists are quite willing to give up the entire positivist framework of the science of human communication or, at a minimum, to settle for a bargain in which the labor is divided between the sciences and humanities. They are willing to follow or work out a parallel path to cultural studies up to the point of using the mass media as a context within which to write a phenomenology of modern experience and consciousness: to describe the subjective life—the modern "structure of feeling" in Raymond Williams's arch but useful phrase—in relation to the media of communication, *one* of the paramount forms of experience in relation to which consciousness is formed. In practice, this means only going as far as the early work of Williams and Hoggart and particularly not into the intellectual, moral, and political quicksand one encounters when one starts romancing French structuralism. Phenomenologists, in the restricted sense I am using the term, are willing to commit themselves to a reconstruction of consciousness through methods as simple as *verstehen* or as complex as hermeneutics. While recognizing that modern consciousness is riddled by antinomy and contradictions formed in relation to and exacerbated by the mass media, and while standing in firm opposition to many forms of life in modern capitalist societies, phenomenologists resist moving power, conflict, domination, or any given set of sociostructural elements to the center of analysis.

Again, I am not at all unsympathetic to this resistance, but I think it is misplaced. It is clear, however, that ideological and cultural analysis can be simply another entry of the Platonic: The distinction between knowledge and opinion is simply replaced by a distinction between knowledge and ideology. The only gain here is the more explicit political reference of the word "ideology." But what, then, is one buying into by centering the ideological and political? When "ideology" becomes a term to describe an entire way of life or just another name for what is going on, then the rich phenomenological diversity of modern societies is reduced to a flattened analysis of conflict between classes and factions. Cultural—or ideological—studies replaces economics as the dismal science.[6]

Phenomenologists of all stripes are committed to the *varieties* of human experience as providing the deepest pleasure, the wasting resource, and the most complex explanatory problems in modern society. To strip away this diversity, even if it is described as relatively autonomous diversity, in order to reveal a deep and univocal structure of ideology and politics, is to steamroller subjective consciousness just as effectively as the behaviorists and functionalists did. One does not, on this reading, wish to trade the well-known evils of the Skinner box for the less well-known, but just as real, evils of the Althusserian box. Any movement, therefore, toward encompassing elements of social structure—class, power, authority—which explain away the diversity of consciousness is to head one down a road just as self-enclosing as the behaviorist terrain phenomenologists have been trying in one way or another to evacuate for most of this century. To put the matter differently, phenomenologists just cannot take seriously the claim they sense in ideological studies that, in Otto Neurath's (1935) familiar analogy, we cannot make a sailable boat out of the planks of the ship on which we are currently sailing but rather we must abandon ship altogether and start anew. Why abandon something of rich diversity in order to build something of self-enclosing monotony? It is precisely the phenomenological diversity of modern society and the extraordinary tensions of consciousness this produces, particularly in relation to the mass media, that is the most compelling problem, however critical or skeptical phenomenologists may be about the actual experience in modern Western societies.

I believe that both of these forms of resistance to cultural studies are of real significance and genuine importance—neither can be easily or summarily dismissed. I disagree with them, however. I have already said that I do not believe that social democracy needs to be propped up with the objectivist grounding of the positive sciences, that the latter are a weakness of the former. We can get along quite nicely by looking at intellectual work, including science, as a muddling through of the dilemmas that history, tradition, and contemporary life have placed before us. Neither do I think it is necessary to abandon the notion of ideology or to close our eyes to the forms of power, authority, and domination characteristic of the modern world in order to do justice to its phenomenological diversity. Conflicts and contradictions are as typical and often irremovable a part of our society as any other.[7] Ideology does, after all, play a larger role in modern life because coercion plays a much smaller role. Ideological state apparatuses have significantly displaced repressive state apparatuses, if that is what we wish to call them, and that is not necessarily a bad thing. No one has, as yet, doped out an adequate analysis of power, conflict, contradiction, and authority. That task remains. The problem was absolutely central to the rich, diverse, and melancholy work of Max Weber. In fact, part of the phenomenological resistance to cultural studies stems from the simple fact that notions of power and authority that were firmly attached in Weber to matters of action and subjectivity are now more often derived from Durkheim, the social integrationist, in whose work power and authority were invisible and unnoted. As a result, the analysis is constantly slipping into a functionalism, despite the most heroic attempts to prevent it from doing so. It is not absolutely given that the forms of inequality and domination typical of modern society are so odious that they can only be maintained by the silent and invisible agency of cultural reproduction, behind the backs, as it were, of its "subjects."[8]

In short, it is possible, I believe, to press forward with a form of cultural studies that does not perforce reduce culture to ideology, social conflict to class conflict, consent to compliance, action to reproduction, or communication to coercion.

More than that, despite the dangers and reservations acknowledged herein, cultural studies, in whatever form it survives, offers the real advantage of abandoning an outmoded philosophy of science (maybe even getting rid of the philosophy of science altogether) and centering the mass media as a *site* (not a subject or a discipline) on which to engage the general question of social theory: How is it, through all sorts of change and diversity, through all sorts of conflicts and contradictions, that the miracle of social life is pulled off, that societies manage to produce and reproduce themselves? Put in a slightly different way, how is it through communication, through the intergraded relations of symbols and social structure, that societies are created, maintained, and transformed?

NOTES

1. Utilitarianism has historically provided the basic model and explanation of social order in Western democracies and utility theory; therefore, it is the most influential form of social theory. Utilitarianism starts from the assumption that the desires that motivate human action are individual and subjective and are, therefore, either unknowable to the observer or purely exogenous. These subjective desires, these given and individual preferences, are expressed in human action as an attempt to maximize utility or the pleasure or happiness that the satisfaction of desire brings. Economic theory and capitalist economies are built upon this principle of the maximization of utility. The rest of the social sciences, generally unhappy because utility theory tends to skirt or assume away the problem of social order, desubjectivize utility, drive it outside of the head and into the objective world. But, the social sciences then relocate utility in our genes or in our environment or in our society. Social Darwinism and its latter day embodiment, sociobiology, are examples of the first strategy whereas behaviorism and sociological functionalism are examples of the second and third. It is these later positions, but particularly behaviorism and functionalism, that provide the underpinning for mass communication research. Indeed, communications research has been little touched by utility theory in either its economic or biological form except, and it is a big exception, that certain assumptions about language and communication (the theory of representation, the self-righting process in the free market of ideas) have undergirded economists' notions of the ways in which the quest for utility can also produce a progressive social order. The utilitarian conception of human conduct and society, then, is the implicit subtext of communication research, but it has been twisted out of its originally subjective framework and resituated in the objective world of environment and social structure. It is a form of utilitarianism nonetheless: the objective utilities of natural ecology, the utilities that promote the survival of the human population or the given social order. Now, it would be comforting to think that our small-scale empirical investigations are detached from these overarching solutions to the problem of social order but they are not. Our studies inevitably articulate "into" and "out of" these wider theories. They articulate out because they inevitably borrow language, concepts, and assumptions from the more encompassing intellectual environment; they articulate into the wider theories in that they provide evidence or they are used as evidence for and against the soundness of these social theories. Concepts such as attitude, effect, uses, and gratifications are borrowed from utility theory; evidence from effects studies are used to support one or another theory of mass society, usually the liberal, utilitarian, or pluralist theory. Indeed, the study of communication effects makes sense and has pertinence only insofar as it actively articulates with these larger positions. Unfortunately, there are no neutral positions on the questions that vex society.

2. Utility theory, as practiced by economists, produces the classic dilemma for democracy. If human agents are driven by subjective desire disconnected from the feelings of others, how do they manage to create and sustain the associated, cooperative form of social life we call democracy? Why

don't people always gouge one another to the limit, as they often do even in the best of times? No one has produced an adequate answer to that problem and it is usually dismissed with one or another metaphysical concept, such as the invisible hand of the market. The objective utility theorists give us an answer: Our genes, or our environment, or the norms of society, make us democrats, although I am here engaging in a bit of burlesque. Besides being a little too optimistic, objective utility theorists achieve an image of democracy at an enormous price: the surrender of any notion of a self-activating, autonomous, self-governing subject. The "new" subject is one controlled or constrained by the laws of biology, or nature, or society—laws to which he or she submits because he or she can hardly do otherwise. This is the image of humanity and the dilemma of democracy with which the entire tradition of mass communication research struggles. It is at the heart of our founding book, Lippman's *Public Opinion*. It is the reason why Paul Lazarsfeld's work was so important. *The People's Choice* turns out not to be the people's choice but the choice of an index of socioeconomic status. Such laws of behavior are antidemocratic either because they reveal a subject who is not fit for democracy or they can be used to control the subjects of a mere presumptive democracy. As so often happens in intellectual work, the answers we give become disconnected from the questions we were asking, or, better, they become actively suppressed.

3. If behind our subjective notions of what we are up to there lie in wait our genes, our conditioning history, or the functions of society exacting their due, then our subjective life, our intentions and purposes, are just so many illusions, mere epiphenomena. The only people who grasp the distinction between reality and appearance, who grasp the laws of conduct and society, are the ruling groups and those that do their bidding: scientific, technical elites who elucidate the laws of behavior and the functions of society so that people might be more effectively, albeit unconsciously, governed.

4. I have already suggested how it is that utility theory, the social sciences, and liberal ideology get us into a series of difficulties. How do we reconcile the individual desires unleased by capitalism with the demands of associated life, with the justice, equality, and mutual concern necessary for democracy? That dilemma is bad enough but as soon as we resolve it by the route open through the objective sciences (don't worry, justice is in our genes or in our institutions), we end up in a worse dilemma, a dilemma the Left has critiqued with precision. We have, then, a ruling class of social scientists—disinterested, of course—managing the social order on the basis of uncontaminated truth. We are entitled to be skeptical about such a priesthood. Once social scientists adopt the role of seers, we should entertain the notion that their position is not based on their knowledge but on their ability to monopolize positions of power and influence in the social structure. Again, it was Max Weber, who looked at intellectual credentials as a device of class closure, who was most trenchant on this point. The supply of valued things in a society, including valued occupations, is strictly limited. Work in industrial societies is hierarchically organized so that valued occupations can be identified and showered with income, amenities, and prestige. Preferred jobs are positional goods, as opposed to material goods, in the well-known distinction of the late British economist Fred Hirsch, and they are valued because they are in short supply. They are valued also because power attaches to them, the power to monopolize valued cultural resources—to monopolize objective knowledge, uncontaminated by ideology, knowledge only the social scientist can grasp. This is not a healthy climate for democracy. Forgive me if I don't announce how to get out of this fix, but we don't have a chance until we recognize the fix we are in.

5. Intellectual work, then, is contingent upon the entire framework of articulated social order—and the ideologies that articulate it—and does not usher forth from some Archimedean point in the universe—from some observer "out there," where, as Gertrude Stein said of Oakland, California, "there is no there there." If one objects to current versions of cultural studies, then the only answer is to analyze the articulations between theory, practice, and ideology present within the effects traditions: to give up, in short, the pose of the observer and to undertake, explicitly, the task of using intelligence to change, modify, or reconstruct the social order.

6. Economics became the "dismal science" for two interrelated reasons. First, utility theory reduced social life to the flywheel of acquisitiveness and accumulation. Economic man became the whole man, the only man. However, the repetitive dullness of acquisition was not the only dismal

prospect economics held out. Society became a "world without end, amen!" where the acquisitive itch could never be adequately scratched because of the Malthusian spectre. Every gain was balanced off by a rise in population, and the children that we love became merely the tyrants who turn the wheel of gain. Cultural studies can also turn into a dismal science if the phenomenological diversity of society is reduced to the single quest for power and domination. We are again laced to Axion's wheel. By evacuating diversity in the prerevolutionary era, we are left with only one motive with which to run the postrevolutionary society. But the pursuit of power will prove as exhausting and inexhaustible as the pursuit of wealth. The pursuit of power, and theories that rationalize it, nonetheless catches something of the predicament we are in. Power, and the prestige that goes with it, is as archetypal of a bureaucratic age as wealth was of the era of penny capitalism. There is no reason, however, except a positivist one, why a phenomenology of communications must avoid the phenomena of power and domination, lest all human relations and all symbols be reduced to the terms of power and politics alone. I support the phenomenological enterprise because I believe any healthy society will possess that part of its spirit that admits to the inevitable and desirable pluralizing of the varieties of experience. Just because you admit power to the household of consciousness and conduct, you do not have to let it occupy every room, although I admit that, like many an unwanted guest, you will have to struggle to prevent it from taking over the entire domicile.

7. We live in the lap of a vast series of contradictions. There is, for example, the contradiction of the employment market referred to earlier, a contradiction relevant to our experience in education. We observe in the swings of student interest among college majors a wholesale competition for positions in the occupational structure and, increasingly, attempts by parents to purchase with the tuition paid to prestige universities a place for their children in the occupational structure. This is an old story that federal aid and loan programs have more or less (largely less) democratized. That these occupational niches are thought to be entitlements, rewards for education virtue, disconnected from conduct or self-worth, presents one kind of contradiction. That such competition for jobs in an age in which automation widens the gulf between mechanical and immiserating work and the presumed glamour of the professions presents another kind of contradiction. Both of them exist in our classrooms every day, and we have no answer to them. If we remove those contradictions, we will have others, equally difficult and punishing, with which to replace them. This is not a call for resignation but just an admission that life goes on.

8. I suppose it would be nice if the social order worked by the silent reproduction of cultures and structures. It would spare us from all the misery that conflict and antagonism brings. Unfortunately, they do not work in this way. We live this reproduction in all its turmoil and ambiguity. In contrast to the Marxist tradition, Durkheim, the theorist of social integration, deliberately downplayed elements of power and conflict. Inspired by the complexity of anthropological studies of social reproduction, he invented notions of "collective representation" and "collective conscience" to explain how societies were held intact in the midst of conflict and strain. Although my chronology is off here, when he applied this analysis to modern societies he tried to show how capitalist societies depended for their very existence and stability on an inherited precapitalist society—the so-called precontractual elements of contract. *Gesellschaft* society, the society regulated by utility and contract, could not work without the integrative mechanisms of *Gemeinschaft* society: nonutilitarian values, beliefs, traditions, and the like. To the old slogan that money is to the West what kinship is to the rest, he added that kinship performs a continuing integrative function in advanced societies. In a sense, Durkheim inverts the relations of base and superstructure: The capitalist economy thrives on the root system of traditional society. This aspect of Durkheim has been of signal importance and usefulness. But just because culture provides the supportive background to contract, it is not necessary to argue that culture is unconscious, irrational, coercive, or automatic. To make this argument is to become either an objective utility theorist or a mechanical Marxist. This leap to culture as unconscious or part of the deep structure makes it difficult to distinguish Marxism from functionalism, except—and it is an important exception—that they make quite different evaluations of the social order that is being silently, automatically integrated.

REFERENCES

Carey, James W. (1983). "The origins of radical discourse on communications in the United States." Journal of Communication, 33:311-313.
Kuhn, Thomas (1983). "Rationality and theory choice." Journal of Philosophy, 80:567.
Lippmann, Walter (1922). Public Opinion. New York: Harcourt Brace.
Neurath, Otto (1935). "Pseudorationalismus der Falsifikation." Erkenntnis 5:353-365.
Rorty, Richard (1984a). "Science as solidarity." Paper presented to the symposium on the Rhetoric of the Human Sciences, University of Iowa, March.
———(1984b) "Solidarity or objectivity." Paper presented to the symposium on the Rhetoric of the Human Sciences, University of Iowa, March.

2

TO EACH HIS/HER OWN
A Personal Research Agenda for Micro Issues in Communication

Percy H. Tannenbaum

As a staunch believer in academic freedom, I take seriously the right of any investigator, most certainly members of university faculties, to select and pursue their own research topics. There are some qualifying conditions, of course: They must adhere to proper scholarly and scientific procedures and should be ready and willing to face the judgment of their professional peers as to the appropriateness and quality of the work, at least if they wish to be funded and have the product published. As such, I am naturally reluctant to foist on others of our ilk my personal values of what is and what is not proper and/or needed in the field of communication research. Particularly as one who prefers to focus my own research on problems as they arise—either as concrete events (e.g., my recent work on the broadcast of early election night projections) or as a passing idea that sounds right at the time (e.g., several periodic studies on animal communication over the years)—I would rather leave it to others to decide for themselves how they wish to spend their time and energy.

However, I must admit I do find most of current communication research rather dreary and uninteresting, both in topic and method, and I do confess to having an occasional urge to set things right. As Robert Hutchins was supposed to have said about doing physical exercise, I normally let such feelings lie dormant until they subside and disappear. But when somebody offers me the opportunity to mount a soapbox—in an annual review volume, yet—the temptation is just too great to pass up.

Of course, one brings a goodly amount of personal baggage (in my case, accumulated over the better part of a total career span) to such a venture. Thus it will come as no surprise that my suggestions for the future run much along the same lines as the themes that underlay much of my research in the past. I am, after all, much the same individual I was, with similar if not identical predispositions and prejudices—pet peeves and pet preferences—as previously. I have also had the good fortune, by and large, of being able to conduct research that followed my inclinations at the time, usually juggling several different types of studies at the same time (to relieve the tedious detail that accompanies most research). Even when I undertook a mild mid-career change of affiliation—joining a rather vaguely defined school of so-called public policy from a joint appointment in communication and psychology, both of which were becoming increasingly defined and narrowed—I remained the social psychologist I always was (old tigers with new spots, and all that) although I must admit I did go pretty far afield on some occasions (e.g., a recent study of the California medfly crisis as an example of the uneasy role of scientific expertise in public policy decision making).

FOCUS ON THE INDIVIDUAL

My background in psychology predisposed me to use the individual as the main unit for attention and analysis in communication behavior. In fact, in assessing group effects, we usually obtain measures on a number of individual subjects or respondents (or even individual message units in a content analysis) and then combine and transform into indices of association (correlations), relative frequency (e.g., for chi-square analysis) or central tendency (means, medians), with some allowance for variations among individuals. This focus on individual data and, more important, on the variation between them, was brought home all the more forcefully when I recently was asked to examine the cumulative (over several decades and dozens of studies) findings and their respective methods in five different research areas, all but one involving communication phenomena. Two related results stood out, both worth our earnest attention:

(1) Most—in these cases, all but a rare handful—findings in social research are really of *minority results*: Correlations that are judged to be statistically significant, and hence of theoretical importance, actually are rather small—most often between ±.12 and ±.36, rarely above ±.50—leaving the vast bulk of the variance unaddressed, let alone unexplained. Equally often, differences between groups in an experimental design are apparent in well below half the subjects changing as predicted, with the considerable majority of individuals either totally unaffected by the treatment or even showing a contrary influence. This is not to suggest that such findings should be summarily dismissed—clearly, even nonspurious results of statistically meaningful relationships need to be explored and, one hopes, explained. It is to suggest that we should not get carried away by them, as so often occurs. It is simply bad reasoning and bad theory to focus on such minority effects to the virtual exclusion of the majority findings, even when contradictory. When an obtained correlation accounts for less than 5% of the total variance, one has either left out one or more major factors in explaining the relationships or there are many such small influences involved. Either way, harping on the ones you have

chosen to isolate for theoretical explanatory purposes is inadquate at best and misleading at worst.

(2) The related finding is the high degree of *individual differences* in the behavior of different subjects within the same condition. This too is nothing new but it has been conveniently set aside in our zeal to seek general aggregate results. To be sure, this within-group variance is not completely overlooked—to the degree that it is high, the odds of finding a statistically significant relationship are lowered. But the time is probably long past due for us to not only accept these intrinsic interpersonal differences but to investigate them in their own right. Such findings—that people of the same population subgroup or people exposed to a common set of messages do not respond in kind—is as intriguing as between-group differences. Individuals apparently bring with them varying dispositions from the past and varying reactions to the present that limit or enhance how they respond to a common stimulus.

All this suggests (at least to the likes of me) that a fruitful line of inquiry would be to study such individual differences directly rather than consign them to a general "error" term. Certainly, there is no shortage of data. A good place to start to ferret out these differences and the reasons for them is in the form of secondary analysis of the findings of countless studies the past few decades of research have generated. What is lacking is a good theory of individual differences (one of the failings of psychology as a discipline) and an appropriate methodology for conducting such an assay, but that should be more interesting than conducting still another study of an already investigated phenomenon with the same intrinsically faulty methods.

THE NATURE OF VICARIOUS EXPERIENCE

My interest in communication began when I majored in psychology as an undergraduate and continued through my graduate training. Learning theory was in vogue at the time with attempts to account for how people acquired behaviors based on their experiences in immediate proximal environments of direct, personal experience shaping later behavior. However, I readily realized that this did not apply to much of my own learning, that which I acquired from others, often in remote places and times—my parents and others from the past, family and friends from the present, and, far from least, from being an avid reader of all sorts of publications, under the kindly guidance of a benevolent school system and a dedicated librarian. This clearly is indirect, vicarious experience—and it accounts for a good deal of people's knowledge, factual or fancied, of the world they live in and of the way they govern their own behavior in that world. In due time it dawned on me that such vicarious experience extended beyond the realm of information and learning for survival to that of emotion and of the pleasure and pain of that survival—in short, to the full range of human behavior.

To me, this fact of vicarious experience is still the very essence of communication as a field for scientific inquiry, and I accordingly commend it as a major item for one's research agenda. On intellectual grounds alone, it should be a rewarding area to which to direct one's talents and, if that doesn't grab you, it does abound with many fascinating applications, not the least of which is why people spend so much time with the mass media to begin with.

THE APPRECIATION OF ENTERTAINMENT

Why, indeed, do we devote so much of our leisure time in pursuit of media fare, often of an admittedly trivial, peripheral nature? Harkening back to the field's origins in journalism and rhetoric (at least as it has developed in the United States) and continuing through to the present, we seek to justify our forms of mass media institutions because they are central to providing needed information to a fact-hungry population. But are people, indeed, all that hungry for news? News programs (if they can still be called that at the level of local television) do command substantial enough audiences to warrant advertiser attention, but, given the choice between straight factual presentation and an adventure story or some situation comedy, the latter will win most of the time. This is no accident—much as our focus on factual learning from the media would suggest otherwise—and we avoid facing that fact at our own peril. For all these faults, the rating figures do not lie about the fact that so-called entertainment programs are the preferred fare on TV and in films and that many people read newspapers as much for the soft features as the hard news.

Serious scholars of communication cannot avoid this lure of entertainment if they wish to come to grips with the nature of the media and their role in contemporary society. There have been a few attempts to do so but these have been relatively meager compared to the vast set of questions on hand: Why are people motivated to seek amusement to the degree that they do? What, if anything, does it do for or to them? Is it a passing fancy, serving some momentary wants and needs, or are there longer-lasting goals involved? What are its consequences in the life of the individual audience member and, by extension, in the social groups to which they belong? For what it is worth, it is my earnest feeling that there are some deep truths about the nature of the human psyche to be unearthed here—anything that widespread, with some offerings (especially American ones) having almost universal appeal, must be inherently vital and fundamental. At the very least, it commands more serious attention from those who have chosen the mass media as their main field of scholarly investigation.

INCIDENTAL EFFECTS

Much has been said in recent years about the pervasive influences of the mass media, in general, and television, in particular, on the individuals and the society they inhabit. Theory in the field is not exactly specific—it is more as if anything used that much and spread that widely through the population must leave its marks along the way, whether creating false ideas, planting values (usually negative), or promoting the imitation of selected behavior patterns. These are difficult enough to demonstrate where the messages have deliberate aims toward producing certain effects. They are bound to be more difficult methodologically where possible effects are, at best, secondary, incidental by-products of the main purpose of the production.

The predominance of entertainment content in the media is a perfect case in point. Its main goals—to attract an audience, to amuse, to provide vicarious thrills—seem innocuous enough, even if it takes free liberties with the real world to do so. Could such selective action and varying emphases have more sinister influences, such as seriously distorting one's accepted views of reality, promoting more hostility and aggression, and the like? If anything, such concerns currently dominate American and European thinking about the media but, as noted above, the research demonstrations have not been terribly convincing.

The first step in improving this situation is to sharpen the theory. It is probably too broad and all-inclusive to be useful and to make more specific predictions. I would guess that partitioning off the kinds of effects would be a good start, followed by an attempt to explicate the mechanisms that may be involved in mediating between message exposure and immediate or more lasting consequences. We could then have a set of a mini-theories, different ones for different types of messages and possibly for different kinds of effects—probably a more faithful representation than a single overarching "general field theory" of communication effects. At the same time, it would be wise to incorporate the qualification introduced by intrinsic differences among the exposed individuals, as noted above.

The companion requirement is to develop a set of methodologies to match the theories—again, easier said than done, so much so that it may be a mere pipe dream. But can we go on as we are—knowingly using poor measures (our greatest failing, in my judgment), inadequate, even improper, samples, and cumbersome analytic procedures to tease out small (but not unimportant) effects when time-tuning is clearly called for, and so on? Something has to give here, and any general research agenda just cannot shirk the need for methodological improvement and innovation.

BUILDING BLOCKS OF COMMUNICATION "LITERACY"

Surely, one of the great achievements of the human species is its ability to communicate. I have tried to argue (above and at more length elsewhere) that such an ability is critical to individual and species survival in that it provides the essential mechanism for transferring remote vicarious experience, and that its elaboration in modality and form constitutes one of the critical features distinguishing humans from other species. Its biological, social scientific, and humanistic aspects continue to intrigue scholarly investigators, but we know all too little of its origins and the factors that govern its course of development.

Communication theorists and researchers clearly have a stake in this pursuit, and it is high time they tried to enter the search from their particular perspective (rather than serve as poor stand-ins for better-equipped researchers in the more established disciplines). Linguists and psychologists are finding out more about formal language development, some insights are to be gained from experimental studies in animal communication, and new work in computer simulation and artificial intelligence excites the imagination. Where do the mass communication researchers fit into all this?

It would seem to me that, for starters, they should look at their own turf—both the encoding and decoding processes of mass media messages. There are propositions to be gleaned from how the producers of such messages create their images. These are not haphazard or mere repetitions of professional norms. Rather, most often they are highly deliberate, with a lot of thought and effort into getting something communicated to a particular audience. The tricks of the trade come from long, sometimes arduous trial-and-error experience, and the degree to which they are successful (i.e., that a majority of the intended audience of a program comprehend and like what has been prepared for them) they represent implicit theories about how people learn and develop their media decoding capacity. These theories may not prove to be correct in the end but they merit a sincere hearing. One needs first to codify production practices into a set of formal propositions that can then be subjected to formal testing.

Observational and experimental studies with viewers make up the related strategy. Direct observation of children watching television turns out to be remarkably barren—they appear not to attend to the screen more than to concentrate on it; but if one makes the effort of viewing more instrumentally directed in some way, it is revealing what children can discern and comprehend. I have tried to con six- and seven-year-old inner-city children into believing that segments from a fiction drama came from a news show and vice versa but they wouldn't buy it. They clearly know one from the other, interpret them accordingly, and show a degree of sophistication in that interpretation—in effect, in taking fiction representations for what they are rather than as the truth—that might astound many of our colleagues in children's media behavior.

Adults are, of course, even more media-wise, although their viewing behavior and verbal expressions might lead you to believe otherwise. Their preferences may not be so obvious to them or to the observer but they are clearly willing to expend more time and energy (e.g., pedaling harder on a stationary bicycle to keep a fading image on the screen) for some programs—even repeats of favorite programs—than others, and do so with impressive consistency. Prosaic audience ratings data, gathered for different, commerical purposes, can be further mined for developing insights in media behavior. (For example, the outstanding sociological media fact for me is that while the audience for a series appears stable in size and composition from week to week, there is as much as 50% turnover in the actual individuals watching from one week to the next.) Especially if we examine such data in a panel study, and combine it with certain experimental interventions (e.g., deliberately omitting one or two episodes in a series, or even selected segments within an episode), we can probably determine optimal courses for developing TV savvy and chart the course for going from casual viewer to afficionado to media "maven."

A FORWARD LOOK

Any one of the above fields of inquiry, only sketched here quite sparsely, can provide the better part of a communication scholar's repertoire for an entire career. Taken together they provide a pretty fair definition for the program of a research institute or a full school of communication. Of course, it is only one person's preferred agenda and the reader would be wise to take it as such. Most will probably shrug it off and go on doing what they would have done anyway—which is just as well, as far as I am concerned, because without one's own motivation and curiosity the resulting research is often vapid. That is why I am not a fan of government or foundation undertakings that select a problem area and offer the temptation of financial support for proposals to deal with it, nor of agendas for research such as this one.

As for myself, I may from time to time continue to dabble in one or another of the above areas but I expect my future work will be quite different. Having made my bed, so to speak, in the public policy field, I intend to sleep in it for a while longer. The methodology there is quite different—essentially sorting out plausible options and evaluating them comparatively for legal, organizational, economic, and political feasibility, recognizing the need for trade-offs and being alert to potential unintended consequences—but rewarding intellectually. I do miss the excitement of conceiving and designing a neat laboratory study but I do relish dealing with real problems of the here and now, even if a good deal is of the quick-and-dirty type because some kind of answer is needed and cannot await the leisurely process of accruing academic research. But those entering this research area should be forewarned that it is no less demanding intellectually—quick-and-dirty does not mean sloppy—and the "proofs" demanded for supporting one's conclusions are no less rigorous. Relevant data are even harder to find, and pet ideological solutions are inadequate justifications in the political marketplace, where public decisions are finally made.

3

METHOD AS MASTER, OR MASTERY OVER METHOD

Kurt Lang and Gladys Engel Lang

Students of communication, like most social scientists, tend to locate themselves along a continuum that runs from empiricist to theorist. It is chiefly when it comes to diagnosing "what ails the field" that they tend to position themselves toward the extremes. At one end is the theoretical purist's position, which is predicated on the belief that there can be no breakthrough or worthwhile research without thorough reconceptualization. The argument is a seductive one. Theories have a grandeur that most empirical studies lack; the more abstract and speculative a theory, it sometimes appears, the higher its prestige, regardless of whether it can be tested. Yet for every theoretically pure position, there is an opposite but equally "pure" methodological stance. However few those methodologists who take the most extreme position, they would give top priority to the explication of exacting canons of research. For them the solution to problems facing the field resides in more data collected with better tools. They are accordingly disdainful of theoretical speculations untestable by the means at hand and thus see the main challenge in the development of research instruments. Progress is seen to depend on the quality of the tools and methods of research.

Like most social scientists, we do not consider ourselves theoretical or empirical purists. But, taking a step beyond this disclaimer, we elaborate in this essay on the interplay between theory and research, between concept and method, arguing that many of the "methodological" problems regarded by self-defined theorists as nothing but tactical or technical matters and of primary concern only to those committed to empirical research have, in fact, played and continue to play a crucial role in shaping our theories. Looking backward we are persuaded that solutions to methodological problems have had an inordinate influence on how we think theoretically about communication effects.

Perhaps our purists are nothing but strawmen, and our capsuled descriptions of their views may strike the reader as simpleminded parodies. Has anyone ever met either type of purist? Doesn't everyone agree that methodology and theory are inextricably intertwined? Doesn't every methods text—even of the cookbook variety—stress the need to state the research problem in the form of a hypothesis, with the hypothesis in its turn derived from some kind of high-level or low-level theory? Equally true, in discussions about the adequacy of measuring tools, isn't the emphasis as much on concept validity as on test/retest reliability and the elimination of observer bias? Yes, the relationship of methods to theory (and vice versa) is universally acknowledged. Nevertheless, simply to fasten on this acknowledgment is to miss the point: When it comes to actual practice, most of us still regard method as an auxiliary to theory. Thus we teach our students to begin with a theory and then find the appropriate methods, to make use of certain conventionally acceptable ways for resolving any methodological difficulty. Most important, we tend to follow our routines without considering how these formulae sometimes crystallize and constrain our thinking. Yet, in fact, we face a problem the physicists have long recognized: namely, the influence of the measuring tool on the direction of theoretical development.

Methods have affected the direction in which mass communication research has moved. Where once we used to question our judgment when our methods did not reveal what we intuitively knew to be there, many of us are now more likely to take a critical look at our methods. One senses a certain malaise. The critics themselves have come to recognize that even the best textbook solution, when carefully scrutinized, turns out to have serious limitations. If this is so, there no longer is any reason to be constrained by the way things have been done in the past.

EFFECTS

We begin by illustrating our general proposition on the effect of method on concept by reference to formulations about media effects, one of the central concerns of mass communication theory and research. Today's conventional wisdom stands in clear contrast to that of 20 years ago. Once again the media are considered effective. If nothing else, it is conceded that they tell people what to think about. In a similar vein, we are tempted to add, the methodology preferred by media researchers tells people what and how to think about the media. Surely, our methodological commitments help explain why during the two decades following World War II the media were judged largely ineffective, impotent, and, except for special situations, incapable of changing opinions, attitudes, or behavior. Thus it became a well-established proposition that apparently powerful media effects were more correctly attributable to other even more powerful nonmedia influences. Strange as it may seem today, until little more than a decade ago this was the prevailing view of mass media effects among social scientists.

Elsewhere, in examining the studies from which these conclusions were derived, we have argued that the methods favored during this "golden age" of communication research highlighted some aspects of the communication process and thereby cast a dark shadow over many others beyond the scope of these methods. To stray into these uncharted areas was considered all right for the journalist and the social critic, but the researcher who deviated from the conventional methods often had to pay a price. Some of the major academic journals were prone to reject their work. Many reviewers with an empirical orientation apparently felt that whatever was not substantiated in a particular way should be dismissed as pure speculation. So it came that during the 1950s and early 60s the notion that the media of mass communication had societywide or long-range effects was banished to the dark regions and consequently left unexplored, even though these should have been, as they once were, at the center of interest. For this period at least, many scholars were dissuaded from asking such basic questions as whether the media were promoting national unity or sowing the seeds of distrust and how they might be affecting the political system or contributing to the transformation of culture.

We have deliberately expressed our critique in this perhaps over-honed form in order to draw attention to the limits of the sample survey as the preferred form of measurement. The survey is a powerful instrument, but findings of "no effect" that helped make the search for media effects unfashionable had at least something to do with its logic. In the usual survey respondents are confronted with a series of standardized questions about what they know, like, think, favor, have done, or are about to do. They are also queried about their communication behavior. The latter then functions as the independent variable with inferences about communication effects usually derived from correlations between media exposure and questions that serve as the dependent variable. We do not deny that these procedures represent a logical and direct approach to the phenomenon. We recognize the ease with which one can incorporate them into any number of research designs, such as repeat surveys either of the same sample (panel) or of similarly constructed samples (time series) that provide before-and-after readings. These two versions are clearly preferable to a single survey limited to cross-sectional analysis, but the choice is heavily dependent on the resources available and the time pressure under which a study is conducted.

The more important procedural decision relates to the independent variable. Here the subject matter grants an investigator considerable latitude. Let us begin with a simple listing of the broad spectrum of potential effects that can be used as the measure of effects in such surveys. These include, first, certain effects on cognition. At this most elementary level, one could aim to explore the various ways in which mass communication directly creates awareness of events, personalities, roles, situations, issues, and even possibilities; or how mass communications can increase recognition of, and familiarity with, the symbols in the mass media content and the objects these symbols represent. All of these measures have been used. As a result, we have come to understand better than ever before that changes on one level do not automatically translate into corresponding changes on the next level. Awareness, recognition, and familiarity can develop without or together with effects on the actual content of people's beliefs and/or preferences. The strength of these persuasive effects has been a central issue.

A set of effects at still another level relates less to the specific content of memory, opinions, or beliefs than to the more general orientations that may underlie them. Mass communications can stir up interest, impart knowledge (or misinformation), develop sophistication, insight, and perhaps even skill and problem-solving ability of a general sort not directly related to the subject matter actually covered. One develops an outlook, a perspective, a mode of semantic processing. In addition, there may be reactions closer to the affective level, due partly at least to the inability to assimilate all content. Thus too much exposure to information or to unsuitably packaged information can produce confusion. Critics of the media have been particularly concerned that the quick succession of events, especially depictions of violence, may raise the level of tension and/or socialize children to antisocial behavior. Nor is this type of effect necessarily confined to younger age groups. Even adults, when alerted to danger, may become fearful; news of impending social problems may arouse widespread concern. Alternatively, mass communication can sometimes calm people, provide them with reassurance and instruction on how to cope with contingencies. To the extent that this "calming effect" inhibits people from acting on grievances or proves so narcotizing that they fail to develop a sense of civic responsibility, mass communication would indeed be functioning as the "opiate" of the people, as some have charged. How much and in what ways people orient their political, social, and personal behavior to what mass communication has made relevant remains one of the trickiest questions. It should nevertheless be apparent that the behavioral effects of mass communication encompass not only inducements to act and act in a certain way but also deterrents to action.

Regardless of which of these levels we should be focusing on, priority has been given to whatever holds promise of tangible payoff. The probability of payoff hinges on two things. The investigator must work with a reliable measure of effect. Usually questions or other indicators are aimed at only one or, at most, a few closely related effects. Because the measures have to be pretested, they have to be developed in advance. To change them once the survey is in the field is to put the study in jeopardy. The alternative strategy of open-ended questions focusing on specific content or types of content has been underutilized, although it has provided some interesting, although usually less than definite, results.

The probability of payoff also relates to relevance. Given the uncertainty about what to anticipate, the effects closest to the intended objective of the communicator and to the manifest content of the message have come in for the greatest amount of attention. One typically asks whether a certain message gets across or, in the case of entertainment, whether the program is enjoyed. What has this meant in practice? As an example let us look at the various studies, spanning some 20 years, on the impact of broadcasting election returns before polls have closed. Almost all have stated the issue in terms of the effect of early projections on vote decisions, on whether or not they have affected or could affect the outcome of an election. Little sustained effort has gone into assessing their effect on perceptions of politics and on beliefs in the legitimacy of the electoral process. It is almost as if one were to study the much criticized violent TV-fare only in order to ascertain how successful it was in pleasing and holding its target audience. Yet this is exactly the practice in market research, much criticized for its narrow vision. Why, then, should we be less critical of those who study any political communication in an election with the sole objective of measuring how many votes it may have changed?

Granted, many studies today define their objectives more broadly. A new generation of researchers may turn out to be more adventurous and inventive. Yet insofar as many of them still favor standardized procedures at the expense of ingenuity, they will in all likelihood continue to neglect a whole range of phenomena, often covert, that we include under the rubric of side-effects. Because of their covert nature and the subtle ways in which they work, these effects are easily overlooked. But people do respond even when manifestly rejecting the overt intent of a message, as an early experimental study by Cooper and Jahoda (1947) so convincingly demonstrated. The lack of overt shift toward what the communication advocates does not mean the absence of any response. It is probable, to say the least, that some elements of the communication whose overt message is rejected will nevertheless be assimilated. People do develop defensive strategies or they adapt in other ways. These "no effect" effects may be difficult to study but must be included within our purview.

Some studies have zeroed in on exactly this issue by explicitly differentiating between direct frontal attacks on opinions and attitudes and the peripheral infiltration into the cognitive field of influences not consciously dealt with. Most of this research is conducted in the context of persuasive communications, particularly as related to advertising, where the objectives of the communicator (or sponsor) remain paramount. Much of this work has been conducted in laboratory settings, where it is easier to control exposure and to detail the more subtle effects. While laboratory observations have helped us understand the complex nature of communication effects and the variability in individual responses to propagandistic messages, the behavior of the captive subject may not adequately replicate what is most salient in real life—a drawback that must be balanced against the failure of so many of the aggregate measures, obtained in surveys, to record effects of great consequence.

The dilemma is real and calls for nev and imaginative strategies to resolve it. Many analysts have approached the problem by way of multivariate analysis designed to tease out from the surrounding tissue of competing influences just what it is about a person or situation that accounts for differential responses. The research problem has, over the years, been progressively redefined: from ascertaining effects to an analysis of why some persons are influenced by a specific content in a specific way while others are not. Thus emphasis shifted to the conditions of susceptibility, with progress gauged by the number of intervening variables suggestive of such conditions that investigators were able to identify. Mass communication effect came increasingly to be seen as "mediated" and contingent on factors other than the media content itself. No longer were there any direct effects to contend with. In what came to be known as the "uses and gratification" approach, effect was seen as a function of what people do *with* the mass media rather than what these media do *to* them.

This catchy phrase does more than reiterate a simple but nevertheless essential truism: Communication effects cannot be understood without taking into account the orientation and frame of mind of the recipient. A strong preconception or a particular pattern of media use may function as an obstacle, or it may facilitate a particular response. But these and other variables with which the response is associated should not be allowed to deflect our attention from what is attributable to the media. It seems that a one-sided reliance on uses and gratifications as explanatory variables has dissuaded some researchers from even asking whether the mass media, whose ubiquitous presence they take as a given, makes any difference at all.

Surveys can be rich sources of information, but they also have certain weaknesses. One of these has to do with the uncertain validity of self-reports. Verification of attitudes, intentions, and other motivational states is often difficult and sometimes impossible. Of this the measures used in election studies provide a good example, notwithstanding the existence of voting registers that can be used to verify self-reports about having voted. Such checks nearly always turn up some study participants who falsely claim to have voted (usually for the winning ticket or candidate). Troublesome as these "fibs" may be, they are not frequent enough to discount the validity of most findings from well-conceived voting studies. But the acknowledgment that some people do not tell the truth highlights a fundamental problem: how to interpret the measure of change during an electoral campaign. What is the meaning of a stated intention to vote, obtained by an interview weeks before the election, by those who refused to admit being nonvoters? Did they deviate from this intention or did they never seriously intend to vote? It is the same with any other discrepancy between a stated preference, leaning, or intention to vote in a particular way when obtained in an interview situation without the subjective commitment implied by an actual vote. If a person claims in September to be favoring or leaning toward a party or candidate and/or intending to vote in a certain way, but then in November casts a ballot for the opposing candidate (or fails to vote), does this represent a change or a deviation from the intention or is it an artifact of the interview? To say the least, it is possible, even probable, that a disproportionate number of those who account for panel "turnover" never had any clear intention, that the expressed preference or leaning was nothing but an off-the-cuff response in order to cooperate with an interviewer. Yet, it is on such data that some interpretations of media effects hinge. Can we distinguish between a recorded "change" that appears to be a campaign effect attributable to mass media influence and a "silent vote," a deliberate noncommunication of actual voting intention that will be expressed only on election day by the secret marking of a ballot? Such questions concerning the validity of intentions stated in the interview situation remain despite the intricate, often ingenious, methods by which survey researchers screen out likely nonvoters and seek to simulate the act of casting a ballot.

Changes that are illusive rather than real add up to a strong argument for relying on indicators of actual behavior, but these, too, have their problems. Often there simply is no way for behavior to be documented or for readings to be taken at the right time so that surveys are forced to fall back on self-reports. Even then the link between behavioral changes and media exposure must still be established. To infer such a link without reference to the respondent's state of mind is risky. In other words, as communication researchers we cannot avoid dealing with how the presentations of objects, images, and information by the media are received, recognized, and interpreted by those exposed to them. To do this effectively requires valid measures of exposure together with authentic descriptions of the content to which people have been exposed.

EXPOSURE TO WHAT?

Most of us, when given a choice, would opt for a research design that incorporates controls over exposure. Unfortunately, such controls are generally beyond our capability. Outside the experimental laboratory, we have to depend on the occurrence of unique events as a way of pinpointing exposure—events that may include a moon landing, the shooting of a president, a few major speeches and televised debates as well as some entertainment spectaculars. Readings can be taken before other experiences and conversations have contaminated the impact directly attributable to exposure to the media coverage of the event. This may be a sound approach when dealing with short-term effects, but the longer the time span over which effects are sought, the more completely one is forced to rely on what respondents report about past exposure and/or communication habits.

Given any significant time lapse, some of the measures of exposure, when used as the independent variable, become highly suspect. Their validity depends on the accuracy of recall and that, as we can all attest, can often be faulty. In recounting their communication activity, people are prone to confuse their sources of information. Subjectivity is apt to become more rampant when gauging exposure over longer intervals. How does the average respondent, when asked "how much attention" was paid to an electoral campaign, judge what can be considered a "great deal" as opposed to "some" or "very little"? Or, questioned about which of several media they most "relied on," what does it mean to rely "most on television" as compared with print? As a rule, the interviewer neither tells the respondent what "a great deal" specifies or exactly what is the criterion of "reliance." Yet, problematic as measures obtained from these questions may be, we never seem able to do without them. It is from these self-reports on media use that the effects of mass media campaigns and the effects specifically attributable to television (as opposed to newspaper, radio, and other means of reaching the electorate) have been determined. Of course, longer and more searching series of questions would yield more reliable information, but they also increase costs and try the patience of the interviewee. Besides, they still generate self-reports.

Some research procedures are more interventionist, as when subjects are issued diaries with detailed instructions on record keeping. The substitution of technical devices directly attached to the set avoids the problem of faulty memory, but at some cost. Even when one-set families were the norm, the question of who was watching or listening and what, if anything, they could recall remained unresolved. Now, with the move to the multiset family and the dawning of the videorecorder age, the utility of technical devices has been further reduced. Still, as audience research has become big business, the search for technological solutions goes on. There are few alternatives because most people are not about to admit anthropologists (or other avid communication researchers) into their homes, where behavior can be directly observed.

However successful some procedures may have proved in counting people (or households) supposedly watching or listening at any given time, these have failed (actually, not even attempted) to describe the content to which the attentive user, unlike the inattentive one, would have been exposed or to describe the information or image solely available to the TV-viewer but not to anyone still exclusively oriented to print. As an analog to a methodological orthodoxy that demands that observations of exposure be distinct from observations of the response or effect, descriptions of content should be kept "objective" and not incorporate any elements of the audience response. This objectivity is normally to be achieved by dissecting the text into more rudimentary indicators, usually of a formal kind amenable to standardized description. The "meanings" extracted are derived from the analytic scheme imposed by the analyst.

On this issue—the analysis of content—as on others, there are two diametrically opposed schools of thought, one that stresses the "objective" description of content, preferably quantifiable, the other that approaches the problem of meaning from the perspective of semiotics. Descriptions in the form of content analysis can be flat. They are unlikely to catch the thick fabric of culturally acceptable layers of meaning that can be read into anything that serves as a text. Whereas the traditional content analyst deliberately aims to separate the text from its "reader," the semiotician refuses to recognize any content apart from the meaning the reader of the text sees in it. The code that is used to interpret the events, acts, or symbolic configurations that function as sign vehicles—to use old-fashioned positivist terminology—determines what it means. And as there is no universally valid code except, perhaps, on the most abstract level, attempts to construct one are doomed to fail. The few that have been proposed, such as the semantic differential, are only general schemas that abstract from the context in order to facilitate judgments along a few dimensions.

Content analysis, in the orthodox or pure sense, nevertheless has advantages. For one thing, it stipulates certain procedures for testing whether a text is consistent with an interpretation made within a particular code. On the basis of such tests, one can then develop inferences about the communicator, about the likely intent of the messages, and even about unintended nuances and latent meanings of which the communicator may not even have been aware. Similarly, the method enables the analyst to make judgments about the symbols and themes that audiences recognize, respond to, accept as valid, ignore, or interpret in a way at odds with their intended meaning. Comparing the symbols and themes in the content with the response implies a definition of effect in terms of congruence. One is almost driven to ask how well the implicit or explicit message gets across and what sequential pattern, amount of repetitiveness, complexity, or formal arrangement maximizes its acceptability. Thus the effectiveness of persuasive propaganda no less than the appeal of popular songs or soap operas is seen to reside in the resonance its dominant symbols and themes evoke within a target audience.

This is not the place to enumerate the technical difficulties encountered in using content analysis or to discuss the many ways in which objective description can be refined. The relevant question is whether one should preclude as an alternative the description of content in terms of what a sample of "readers" reads into it. In this alternative methodology, the objective communication content dissolves into a multiplicity of meanings, including some that the originator may never even have thought of. To be sure, these unexpected and unintended meanings, although somehow embedded in the message, exist only because that is how some people respond. But as long as the meanings read into the content are defined as real, they are for this group real in their consequences. They become part of the culturally enshrined symbolic environment. Methodologies that insist on a sharp separation of content, which is to be described objectively, and of meaning, which becomes an element in the response, are apt to consider certain divergences as misreadings and interpret them as communication failures. This has certainly been the practice in communication research that has focused on individual response to specific messages.

It strikes us that the treatment of cultural effects could benefit greatly if we paid more attention to how people constructed their view of the world by drawing on content with a presumably objective meaning. Some of the earlier mass communication studies took this approach, but the refinement of techniques has put them in some disrepute so that, until very recently, the area was very much left to the social critic. Yet it seems to us that some shift is required from textual to contextual analysis and, also, from the effect of exposure to specific content to exposure to a certain type of symbolic environment over longer periods of time.

UNITS OF ANALYSIS

In distinguishing between media effects on individuals and cultural effects of the media, we are introducing another methodological issue: the appropriate unit of analysis. Both the survey and the laboratory experiment, the two favored instruments of communication research, were uniquely suited for monitoring individual responses to communication. Given the power of these tools, it was probably inevitable that the unit of observation should also have become the unit of analysis. So it is that the theories building on the foundation of empirical communication research had a strong affinity with social psychology, with its atomistic orientation, rather than with collective behavior, which approaches its subject matter from an interactionist perspective.

To say that the bulk of studies in communication have been audience studies focusing on the effect of who says what to whom is not to downgrade their theoretical contribution. The genre has elucidated the potential barriers to getting a message across. Our conception of how one communicates effectively has become more complex as a result. These achievements have not, however, been matched by similar gains in our understanding of the sociological and cultural effects of mass communication. These effects have been shortchanged, if not altogether overlooked, given a research concentration on studies that take as their only measure of effect the responses of individuals.

Take the proposition that media effects in the direction of reinforcement predominate quantitatively over those in the direction of change. This is a strictly empirical generalization based on a variety of studies, mostly of the social psychological sort, in which the characteristics and circumstances of individuals were at the center of attention. It is during election campaigns that this preponderance has been repeatedly observed. In this setting the evidence in support of increasing partisanship and vote crystallization is fairly persuasive: As a campaign develops, those who care about the outcome look to the media to justify their prior leanings, however vague these may be. Far less persuasive is the more general inference drawn from these electoral and similar data: Mass communications in a pluralistic system generally function to uphold the status quo. A case can as readily be made for a different scenario: Heightening of the partisan dispositions on both sides produces polarization, so that what appears to be merely a reinforcement of dispositions already present in individuals may undermine consensus and become disruptive of the political system.

Another empirical generalization derives from studies of information campaigns. Rarely does a single campaign score more than modest gains, and what gains there are are usually concentrated among those with a prior interest in the subject so that the campaign provides those already well informed with even more information but fails to breach the ignorance of the vast majority. All media activity, one may conclude, just reinforces interests already in place without accomplishing much else. Yet any campaign may have two other important consequences. For one thing, it may raise, even if only modestly, the general level of information. Yet the upshot of this achievement may not be all to the good. If there are disproportionately large gains within one segment of the public, the campaign may only widen the information gap within the public, with serious consequences for the polity and institutions. Along this line, perhaps best known is the charge that *Sesame Street*, the children's TV program designed to close the gap between the reading readiness of poor and middle-class children, had only succeeded in enlarging it. Although it had helped those it was meant to help, it had helped the others even more. The dominant methodologies fail to address potential effects such as these.

Periodically, there is a concerted search for alternatives to the survey. Provocative and ingenious as some of the suggested substitutes have been, no equally powerful method has been offered to take its place. The problem, at least for the foreseeable future, is less one of replacement than of adaptation. The survey and other instruments for observing the responses of individuals have to be explicitly designed to provide data relevant to social and cultural effects. This requires ingenuity, most of which seems to have gone into the perfection of the measuring instruments. But why shy away from observations of a less systematic character, such as the various nonreactive and unobtrusive measures that we could find if only we would search for them? The hard data we routinely collect become more meaningful when analyzed in conjunction with observations from other perspectives.

TIME FRAMES

What is the proper time frame within which to observe effects? The answer seems to depend, in large part, on institutional demands. How long-term-minded can the researcher be, given the pressure for a quick and visible payoff to satisfy a sponsor, granting agent or promotion and tenure review committee? And while we may all be disinclined to wait for results in some distant future, the study of short-term effects suits the methodologist's disposition in other ways. Its model is the experiment in which one can control exposure in order to test for a specific effect before responses are subject to contamination from extraneous influences. Everyone is now aware of how tricky it is to generalize from effects observed in the laboratory to effects under natural conditions. But similar caveats hold when generalizing from any "immediately-after" effect, inside or outside the laboratory, to the role of mass communications as an agency of socialization. There has been some interest in the effect of television on children, particularly the younger ones, who by the time they go to school have consumed huge doses of television. But the socializing influence of the mass media is not confined to children. The process goes on continuously; it is never complete. Interest in the possible residues of childhood exposure has never been matched by an equal interest in the contribution of the media to the continuous socialization of adults.

First of all, many immediately-after effects do indeed erode, partly by way of normal forgetting and partly because they tend to be displaced by the stream of competing communications that continue to impinge on everyone. However, the same problems that confound generalization from the experiment can confound effects traceable to exposure to some specific content in a more natural situation. Immediately-after effects are apt to erode. Therefore, any inferences about more permanent and far-reaching effects—especially the role of mass communication as an agency of socialization—can be misleading.

As we extend the time frame, it becomes increasingly difficult to "control" exposure in ways that even remotely approximate the experiment. Our observations are no longer confined to the direct impact of exposure to some program, event, or other clearly defined set of messages. Long-term effects involve more than just the passage of time; they result from repeated exposure to similar content (the treatment of a prominent political actor), to certain types of content (realistic portrayals of violence), or to the content of a particular medium (the video coverage of an electoral campaign). If these ensuant communications reinforce the original message so that audiences progressively adapt, change their frames of reference, develop new modes of thought, and so on, then their effect becomes cumulative. Studies that concentrate on short-term effects are able to ignore these cumulative aspects; they are either treated as givens or analyzed as predisposing or contextual factors. This is something that a longitudinal study following individuals over time cannot afford. The effect of other concurrent influences must be separated from the effect of exposure. Insofar as this is achieved by introducing the appropriate statistical controls, the method tends to shift our focus away from the mass media and toward the individual. The correlates of effect often turn out to be the same as the correlates that govern exposure.

Nor have these methods taken adequate account of the possibility of spillover from those directly affected by mass communication. As a rule, this phenomenon has been placed under the rubric of interpersonal communication as it relates to opinion leadership. Thus face-to-face contact was made to appear as an alternative to mass media influence and not, as it should have been, as just one possible step in a chain reaction by which a climate of opinion develops. We are speaking of multiplier effects that, like the Keynesian budgetary deficits pumped into the economy, can change expectations; but in this case, the expectation relates not to material well-being but to what seems to be in or out of step with the time. The information gained from exposure counts for less than the image built up from what the media recognize. A view that appears in ascendancy, or dominates the media through powerful spokespersons, gains landslide proportions if the fear of being unpopular keeps those who see themselves in the minority from speaking out. The process operates on both the elite and the grass-roots level. Politicians intent on maintaining popularity become cautious; they do not wish to appear too "far out." There are similar dampening effects on the expression of supposedly unpopular opinions in casual exchanges among peers. This "spiral of silence" reinforces the climate of opinion from which it derives. The methods generally in use take little account of this process.

Ultimately these adaptations to the media image have reciprocal effects. These occur when the producers of content begin to collaborate with actors and institutions in order to stage events for the media, thereby influencing the world they appear to be merely mirroring. The dominant medium leaves its imprint on an entire historical period. Does this mean we should cede the analysis of contemporary developments to historians? Activities that are ongoing, unlike those that are past, can be studied as they are happening. One should take more advantage of such opportunities even if we only succeed in providing reliable data for future historians. Too often the emphasis on what can be reliably measured has deflected attention from the chance to study these cumulative, multiplicative, and reciprocal effects.

RESEARCH DESIGNS

Many points we have already made—whether in speaking of effects, measures of exposure, units of analysis, or time frames—could with equal justification have been considered in speaking of research design. Here, then, it should suffice to allude to some general strategies, strategies that reduce so far as possible the reliance on self-reports of media exposure and alleged changes in individual dispositions for which no method of validation exists. We want, in particular, to reiterate our belief that the most significant and interesting effects of mass communication occur over time, that they are cumulative and as much the result of spillover and institutional adaptation as attributable to any specific exposure or even combination of exposures, and that, therefore, we should be refocusing our attention on institutional, social, and cultural effects. The responses of individuals to mass communication obtained through surveys can be important data but only if supplemented and interpreted within an adequate framework.

The creative and venturesome researcher need not curse the crudeness of customary exposure variables. There are alternatives. One exists in the form of pairs of communities with different media situations, where a certain content is available in only one or where one, but not the other, has certain media facilities. A major occurrence in one community, if it remains local news, offers a natural opportunity for assessing the impact and consequences of a particular type of coverage. Likewise, one can compare communities in different time zones, with different ownership patterns, or operating under different traditions and/or regulations. In the past, when television was already a way of life in some areas but still a wonderment only heard or read about in others, there were golden opportunities for assessing the effects of new media. For the most part, these opportunities were missed. We have been willed only a few before-and-after studies of the effects of TV, and the ones we have are rather limited in their scope, virtually ignoring effects other than those observable on the individual level. The strategic moment passed all too quickly. Once a community came within the range of the TV signal, those who acquired television sets were already a self-selected group and those who did not were still subject to spillover.

Nevertheless, insofar as communication facilities are still unevenly distributed, one still finds, although only in a special and limited sense, "media-rich" and "media-poor" communities. Yet inquiries based on such a comparison cannot be productive unless the effects sought are clearly defined in relation to the specific nature of the contrast between communities. For instance, one might compare the impact of high-culture television in cities with a strong tradition of arts support and those lacking such. Does television fill a gap in the media-poor city? Does it lead to new cultural initiatives? One might likewise probe the effect of interference in the flow of content due to such barriers as language, national monopolies, geographical distances, and time zones. Here, too, a caveat applies. Studies of effect must be designed to take account of the full range of effects related to these differences.

One can also work backward—from effect to cause. In this kind of inverse inductive approach, one begins with a situation in which something we take to be at least in part a media effect has been fully documented. It can be a massive change of public opinion, as during Watergate, or a panic such as occurred during the famous "Invasion from Mars" broadcast or when the polio vaccine was first introduced; it can equally be a media-promoted change in style or the abandonment of time-honored practices as an accommodation to the media of mass communication. So intrinsically woven into the fabric of society are the media of mass communication that any collective behavior phenomenon or social movement can be used as the starting point for an intensive case study of mass communication effects.

The method is essentially diagnostic. It has problems, some of which can be overcome by a clear focus together with a precise statement of what is to be explained. Is it a specific event or reaction? The rise and decline of a cyclical phenomenon, or some kind of institutional change? Another problem is the difficulty one inevitably encounters in seeking to reconstruct significant communication patterns operant at several levels and to determine the content flow. One is forced to work from whatever records are available in order to ascertain what media content within the public domain served as the point of common orientation for various actors and to describe it in meaningful ways. Additional information on what was available to major participant groups and what had the greatest influence on each is imperative. So is a thorough evaluation of the specific historical context in which the media functioned.

The strategy incorporates the unique advantage of the case study approach. It allows the observation of a great many variables and influences that operate at different levels in relationship to one another. Insofar as the site or situation is well chosen, it may present opportunities not likely to be found in a sample based on random selection. While it is obviously desirable to identify the "critical" case in advance so one can conduct ongoing and on-site observations, this is not always possible. In that event, a case study encounters some of the same pitfalls as a survey. Still, a great deal can be learned from post-factum interviews with informants, while the many data bases in existence today (including routine polls) provide a far richer lode of source material than heretofore ever available. This means that the reconstruction need not depend solely, or even mainly, on retrospective data drawn from interviews but can rely on a great many different records and unobtrusive indicators.

Gaps in data are inevitable in post-factum research designs. These are the same kinds of gaps with which historians must always cope. Communication researchers interested in understanding media effects—of all kinds—sometimes have, like historians, to make the most of what they have. This requires that the case study be informed by an adequate theoretical perspective. The prime purpose of theory in this context is not the generation of hypotheses with high generalizability but the clarification—not necessarily the demonstration—of processes that influence outcomes. The media, as we all understand, do not operate in a vacuum, and any analysis needs to be cognizant of the specific historical setting in which they function. The traditions in some countries favor close cooperation between the media and the various establishments. Conversely, a potential public outburst may be contained by a lack of resources, absence of an associational infrastructure, or sheer repression. One cannot adequately deal with traditions and historical events without some recourse to a narrative and linguistic mode of analysis that takes account of the substantive content of the events under analysis.

A CLOSING NOTE

None of this will put to rest the debate about media effects. Mass communication, like other communication, does not affect people in the same predictable way that a physical force does. There are very considerable differences in the susceptibility of individuals to various kinds of influence. It is these differences that the conventional methodologies have elaborated. The road has been paved. It is the familiar and, therefore, the easy road to take, and many will follow it without much thought of where it leads. We must, however, realize that these methods, like all methods, have their limitations. The ones most widely used in the study of mass communication have been allowed to influence our definition of the problem of media effects far more than most of us want to admit. The fundamental question that should be on our agenda concerns what difference the presence of media makes. The query can be phrased more specifically to deal with television, with saturation, with pluralism, and so on. But, whatever the specific phrasing, as we go about our research we must not lose sight of the extent to which the media permeate the society. One cannot even conceive of politics, of education, of culture and leisure without them. Therefore, to study the complex nature of media effects demands flexibility and ingenuity. One simply cannot rely on conventional and textbook solutions in addressing issues that are of the greatest significance. We may want to master methodology but we cannot afford to let it be the master.

REFERENCE

Cooper, E. and M. Jahoda (1947) "The evasion of propaganda: how prejudiced people respond to anti-prejudice propaganda." Journal of Psychology 23: 15-25.

4

COMMUNICATION TECHNOLOGY AND POLICY

Nicholas Garnham

Current developments in communications technology are throwing up a range of policy problems of increasing importance and difficulty. The convergence of computing and telecommunications is dissolving the technological barriers that have separated the media from one another and underpinned policy toward them. Developments in satellite technology are decoupling cost and distance in transmission as part of a general trend, reinforced by fibre optics, for transmission costs to fall in relation to production costs and for the development of distribution capacity to outrun production capacity. Such developments are undermining national control of communications policy. At the same time the identification of the electronics sector by governments as the key to economic growth and international competitiveness is increasingly overlapping communications and industrial policy, often with deleterious effects on the former. Finally all these developments are part of a complex dialectic of centralization and decentralization with profound implications for the relationship between private and public spheres.

We have inherited a range of distinct technologies for the reproduction and distribution of information and entertainment: print, film, broadcasting, and telecommunications. These technological divisions not only determine our commonsense view of what the media are, they also in large part determine the division of scholastic labor, making it difficult for scholars to see the media system and policy toward it as a whole. Upon these divisions there have also arisen distinct institutional, economic, regulatory, and legal structures. The press operates in the market and policy toward it is largely determined by a notion of the "free press," which mitigates against—when not actually forbidding—state intervention. Film has exhibited a high level of U.S.-dominated international concentration, which has created in response a protective structure of state intervention and support for domestic film industries outside the United States. Broadcasting everywhere has been either a direct arm of the state or it has been franchised and tightly regulated as to both ownership and program content by the state. Telecommunications has been run as a common carrier under either a state monopoly or regulation.

We are becoming ever more able to convert these disparate forms of social communication into a common digital electronic or opto-electronic form for manipulation by computer and intermingled transmission as a single bit-stream on a shared digital pathway. This, in turn, is dissolving the conventional barriers between the media and throwing the basis of communications policy into confusion. Is videotex print publishing or broadcasting? Should cable be a common carrier like the switched telecommunications network or should it be regulated like broadcasting? Should the telephone company itself be allowed to control the provision of both text and TV services as well as voice and data over broadband networks? Will current technical developments favor—or should they be encouraged to favor—a plurality of competing delivery systems and associated information providers? Or, on the contrary, is the trend toward one unified digital pathway for all communication services, the so-called integrated services digital network (ISDN)? Are there social advantages to such a unification? If the path of technical plurality is followed, will this of itself also foster a plurality of information providers and information access or must such plurality be separately fostered by the regulation of cross-ownership and/or the imposition of common-carrier status on all physical distribution networks. If the ISDN route is followed how is such a massive and socially strategic monopoly to be controlled? By bringing all existing forms of regulation into question and by unleashing powerful new competitive forces, both nationally and internationally, into the communications arena to challenge the inherited regulatory structure, these developments are forcing us to reexamine the basic principles of communications policy.

When considering the debate on the impact of the new communication technologies and on the appropriate policy responses to them we find ourselves faced with two polarized views, one the mirror image of the other. The first, dominant view—that propagated by leading politicians and corporate publicists—vaunts them as "technologies of freedom," as bringers of the good tidings of the information society. According to this view, the technologies of broadband cable and satellite, of video-cassette and video-disc, of digital networks, will decentralize media power and create a world in which citizens, inhabitants of their "electronic cottages," will have access to an unprecedented cornucopia of information and entertainment at the touch of a key pad. On the other hand the pessimists—which, at least in the United States, constitute a beleaguered minority—see in these new technologies either the face of exploitative multinational capital (if they are Marxists) or the onward march of social rationalization (if they are Weberians).

Both positions possess partial truth. The general advance of the forces of production is liberating; many of the concrete technological developments are strongly determined by the dynamics of the capitalist world economy; there are powerful trends toward social rationalization within these developments. But they all share common faults. They fail to distinguish between the potential of a technological advance (in, for instance, microelectronics) and the actual concrete but always partial realization of that potential in applied technologies. They thus fail to take a nuanced view of the technology. They fail to distinguish between technologies used in production (such as computerized video editing), technologies used in consumer goods for the domestic consumption of communications goods and services (such as video-cassette recorders), and technologies of distribution, whether switched or unswitched (such as satellite and cable). They see the impact of this generalized technology as either all good or all bad. They thus simplify the policy choices by failing to see that technologies may be double-edged, having different effects on different social groups. Word-processing and home-working may be liberating for professionals and repressive for lower-level office workers; interactive cable may both increase consumer choice while at the same time enhancing corporate and state powers of manipulative control; the introduction of advanced, digital telecommunications may enhance economic productivity to the general benefit of all citizens, while at the same time causing a deterioration of service to those same citizens as domestic telephone subscribers. Finally both schools of thought too readily take the wish for the deed. They exaggerate the extent to which, under current conditions, the introduction of new technology can be planned and the social impact accurately predicted. The most powerful of economic actors—multinational corporations and governments—certainly have strategies, but, if only because they are in competition, their best laid plans may fail to come to fruition, as the strewn wreckage of plans to introduce video-disc, broadband cable, direct broadcasting satellite services, and domestic videotex bear witness.

These limits to the reach of human wisdom and perspicacity might lead one to endorse the values of piecemeal social engineering, as recommended by the philosopher Karl Popper in *The Open Society and Its Enemies*. Only such strictly delimited forms of social intervention were open, he argued, to the possibility of rigorous testing and falsifiability and thus offered an escape from the clash of incompatible, and irrational because irrefutable, social theories. But unfortunately the introduction of these new technologies illustrates the weakness of Popper's original thesis, for they are often systems that are either introduced with major and probably irreversible human consequences or they are not. Thus the piecemeal option is not available. Faced with this dilemma there are two policy responses. Either politicians say "leave it to the market" on the grounds that they will then bear no responsibility for the consequences, or they are drawn to dirigisme.

However, the most serious failing, if only because their view is dominant, lies with the optimists. They propagate a technological determinism that diverts attention from the real economic context that largely determines the outcomes of technological development and with which policy has to deal. Indeed one of the key characteristics of the current policy phase is the extent to which communications policies and the cultural policies that relate to them are determined by the priorities of economic and industrial policy. All OECD (Organization for Economic

Cooperation and Development) governments have identified their electronic and information sectors as the keys to international competitiveness and future economic growth. Certainly in Europe the introduction of broadband cable and direct broadcasting satellites is being pushed by governments at almost any cost to the ecology of the existing media systems, in order to create a home market base for high technology exports and the necessary infrastructure for the development of an information economy. There is certainly little enough evidence of any great public demand for these services. Even in the United States, where the government's role is less apparent, it seems clear that one of the major motives behind the decision to break up AT&T, whatever its effect on both national defense preparedness or the majority of telephone subscribers, was the desire to release AT&T to compete with the Japanese on the world telecommunication equipment and information technology markets. These pressures stemming from competition on the world market are part, as we shall see, of a general trend that is taking over control of communication and cultural policies from the nation state.

In the field of communication itself three economic trends can be identified behind the introduction of new communication technologies. The first is a search for new markets for domestic consumer goods, a search that is leading to a situation in which access to information and entertainment depends increasingly on ever higher levels of capital investment by individual consumers in their homes, which both raises their entry costs and locks them into patterns of domesticated, privatized consumption. The second is an increasingly intense fight, among advertisers and the providers of information and entertainment services as well as those marketing a growing range of financial and other retail services, for access to the domestic TV screen, in front of which people spend the bulk of their leisure time and on which they spend, at least in the United Kingdom, the largest proportion of their leisure expenditure. Third is the trend toward using advanced telecommunications techniques to increase productivity in the service sector and in office work.

These economic developments, and the technological developments they have spawned and by which they have been made possible, have unleashed powerful new economic forces in the communications sector that are now calling for that sector's deregulation. The deregulators are able to exploit the demonstrable confusion, contradictions, and illogicality that new technological developments have revealed in existing regulatory structures. As a result, policymakers are tempted, in the face of the real pressures and complexities involved, to take the easy way out and leave it to the market. The deregulators want the free press model to be applied universally across all media. They argue that developments in distribution technology undermine the case for broadcasting regulation by removing spectrum scarcity and the case for common-carrier regulation by destroying natural monopoly in the provision of the physical network. This argument fails for the following reasons. The case for broadcasting regulation rests not upon spectrum scarcity but upon the ability of a regulated system, under the special economic conditions of cultural production, distribution, and consumption, to deliver a wider range of choice to more people at lower cost than a free market system. The case for common-carrier regulation rests as much upon the natural monopoly inherent in the interconnectivity of a switched network as upon a natural monopoly in the provision of the physical network. Finally in its own field of print the free press model has, historically, demonstrated unequivocally its own inadequacy, producing not diversity and freedom of expression but powerful trends toward oligopolistic control and homogenization of an increasingly depoliticized content.

To date, the deregulation argument has been most extensively and forcefully deployed in the United States. The debate has taken place in the language of U.S. legal, regulatory, and political traditions. A notable recent example of this has been de Sola Pool's influential book *Technologies of Freedom*. For all its judicious and knowledgeable analysis of both technology and regulation, it exhibits an ethnocentric parochialism by resting its case on the First Amendment, which, although it has many virtues in a U.S. context, simply cannot be translated into the context of any other country let alone the international arena. Whatever the virtues of a deregulatory argument in the U.S. context (and it is important to stress that de Sola Pool himself does not adopt a simple deregulatory position as he recognizes resource scarcity and the fact that markets are themselves regulated and regulatory), it cannot easily be transfered to other political, economic, and cultural contexts, if only because of the sheer size and wealth of the U.S. domestic market and the power of the equipment- and program-producing industries built upon it. This would not matter if it was not the overt policy of the U.S. government and of U.S.-based multinationals to devote a great deal of energy, resources, and pressure to the export of deregulation, as recent U.S. actions within the ITU (International Telecommunications Union), UNESCO, and GATT (General Agreement on Tariffs and Trade) demonstrate, and if the U.S. example, half-digested and with the bad aspects left out, were not used as powerful propoganda in other countries' internal communications policy debates. The U.S. diplomatic and economic offensive in the communications field, both against other nations less powerful than itself and within and increasingly against international institutions, is particularly dangerous at a time when both economic and technological developments are undermining the ability of nation states to retain control over communications policy. This is not to decry the values of individual freedom, which, at least at the ideological level, motivate much of U.S. policy. But it is to stress that there are other policy traditions linked to alternative and equally valid political and cultural traditions and that from different viewpoints, from Europe for instance, the debate over deregulation looks very different.

Something of what is at stake in the argument between the deregulators and the regulators can be illustrated by the case of current debates over cable and satellite policy in Europe. We are here dealing with distribution technologies that are dependent for their success or failure on an existing structure of production and an existing level of disposable consumer income. Experience throughout Europe has shown that the development of distribution channels has outrun the capacity of the system of production to fill them at a cost that consumers will pay. Indeed the same phenomenon is observable in the United States, although the size and wealth of the U.S. domestic market makes the situation less acute. This is happening, moreover, at a time when, owing to the incidence of Baumol's disease, real costs of production are rising faster than real income because technology can only be used to enhance productivity to a very limited extent. Indeed the trend, as in the use of computerized video editing, is to increase production values rather than reduce costs. The only partial solution to this problem is to lower programming costs by maximizing returns to economies of scale in distribution on a world scale and to attract new sources of financial support. Thus pressure is building up all over Europe to relax quotas on domestically produced material on national TV and to increase advertising and sponsorship support with potentially serious harmful effects on the public service broadcasting tradition and upon the domestic program production industry.

This undermining of nationally based communication and programming policies is reinforced technologically by satellites' ability to decouple cost from distance in transmission and by the impossibility of excluding extensive cross-border signal spillover. Cable program providers in the United States, such as HBO (Home Box Office), can as easily supply European as U.S. cable networks and, as in the case of the U.S. film industry, their base in the dominant U.S. domestic market allows them to exploit bigger economies of scale than any European national operator and thus to offer service at very competitive prices. Similarly it is clearly the strategy of both Rupert Murdoch's Sky Channel and the U.S./Luxembourg Coronet consortium to fill the programming vacuum created by the development of cable and DBS with Europeanwide, advertiser-supported services.

The development of such services makes imperative the development of supranational policies and of bodies with powers to implement them. At present the United States and the countries of Western Europe have different programming policies designed to protect other media (for instance, limits on advertising or on the number of feature films that can be shown), to protect a domestic program production industry (for instance quotas on imported programming), to protect political life through rules on political broadcasting and election coverage, and to protect consumers through rules on advertising standards (including advertising to children and on advertising goods such as tobacco, alcohol, drugs). The danger at present is that the problem of harmonization will tend to lead to the acceptance of the lowest common denominator of such standards and, because there are no supranational structures competent to formulate communications policies with a democratic legitimacy that will make them stick, the needs of the multinational advertisers and program providers will dominate.

A major problem in Europe is that the free market model clashes not just with the public service tradition and with efforts to protect and foster national cultural production. It also conflicts with economic policy because there is not enough realizable economic demand under free market conditions to finance the infrastructural investment thought necessary. The result in the United Kingdom, for instance, has been pressure from potential TV program service providers to use

MATV (Master Antenna TV) and MDS (Multi-point Distribution System) systems rather than cable to provide the limited number of extra TV channels that might be viable. (There are possibly three of these—film, music, and sports channels—each, it should be noted, a monopoly in its own category.) They do not wish to invest in cable systems both because they are too expensive and because they cannot wait for them to achieve the penetration levels that would make programming viable. But for the government to accede to such a demand would be to go against its own policy for cable which was to finance the investment, in what was seen as essentially an economic infrastructural investment for information services, from the revenues of cable TV. Similarly, the U.K. government has had to abandon its plans for competition in direct satellite broadcasting despite its strong ideological commitment to competition, and instead encourage the formation of a single monopoly consortium of all interested parties, dominated by the existing networks. Even under these conditions the consortium is claiming that if programming is to be viable it must buy its satellite from a U.S. supplier rather than the United Kingdom, thus removing at a blow the original raison d'être of the whole project: to provide not more TV but a market for British satellite manufacturers.

For this reason France and the Federal Republic of Germany have chosen to use their national PTTs as the vehicle for system development on the grounds that only they can justify the huge, long-term investment required by integrating broadband cable development with the digitilization of the telephone network and by bundling the maximum number of services onto the network. Quite apart from the economic arguments, the technology of switched, interactive networks, with their need for universal interconnectivity and compatibility, makes central network control optimal. This is likely to be the case under both competitive market conditions as well as regulated conditions. If one entity is not to control all social information flows—an outcome both unacceptable politically and unworkable managerially—the above considerations would seem to point to the physical network, whatever its constituent technologies (cable, satellite, cellular radio, etc.), being operated under common-carrier regulations. This is in fact the policy adopted by de Sola Pool in his *Technologies of Freedom*. However, three problems immediately arise. First, as de Sola Pool himself points out, it may be necessary during the system's development period (especially under market conditions) if the necessary investment is to be attracted by acceptable amortization time-scales, for the system operator to benefit from the profits of service provision. (The alternative is a public subsidy via system investment to service providers.) In such a situation the problem is to decide at what point the system can operate viably as a common carrier and then to move to that position given the entrenched power the system operator will then possess. Second, even assuming common-carrier regulation, one cannot, as de Sola Pool does, then simply assume that the First Amendment can be allowed to handle content problems. For as de Sola Pool himself demonstrates, although he fails to draw the necessary policy conclusions: (1) The First Amendment can be and has been so widely interpreted by the Supreme

Court—across a spectrum from the public interest always overriding First Amendment rights to a position of extreme libertarianism that does not recognize any public interest as overriding those rights—as in effect to render it a shaky guide to future regulatory action. (2) The First Amendment tradition has signally failed to deal with the problem of corporate power in communication, making no distinction between the rights of individuals and those of corporations so far as freedom of expression is concerned. This issue is being made more not less acute by current technological developments that make available the computer's ability to monitor information consumption in great detail and with great accuracy. This in its turn makes possible the extensive commoditization of information. (3) The development of digital networks means that it may be both technically and economically optimal to place most of the signal-manipulating intelligence in the network along with the necessary network operating intelligence. In such a situation the network itself becomes a range of enhanced or value-added services and the distinction between content and carriage dissolves. It is for this reason that one of the crucial issues in current international negotiations within the ITU on the technical specifications for ISDN (Integrated Services Digital Network) is whether intelligence should be placed in the network or the terminals.

The deregulators, mainly the U.S. government and its multinational corporate allies, argue that intelligence in the network should be minimized and intelligence in the terminals be maximized on the logically correct grounds (from their point of view) that such a position optimizes competitive conditions. However, even though making terminals more expensive and minimizing economies of scale may favor the economic prospects of terminal manufacturers, it may also delay the spread of enhanced services to a mass public by raising the costs of access. Thus far from technology being determinant, decisions on technical standards will be determined by the balance of force between alternative views on regulation, market structure and the balance of social utility.

Finally, I want to raise some of the wider social issues associated with the development of the new communication technologies. First, the distribution technologies are being introduced in such a way as to reinforce the domesticated, privatized forms of cultural participation. The video cassette recorder, the video disc, cable, and satellite TV services are all designed to tie people ever more closely to their TV sets in domestic isolation. These technologies are all sold as being able to offer an ever-increasing range of choice with channels of programming directed at ever smaller and more narrowly targeted consumer groups. All this constantly reinforces our perception of ourselves as individual consumers rather than as citizen members of a wider social whole with generalized, common interests. Let me give one example of what I mean. Some advocates of the advantages of the new technology argue that the newspaper will cease to exist, being transformed into an electronic data base from which every information consumer can summon up, for printing out if necessary on their own printer, just that information that they require. But to destroy the newspaper is to destroy not just one vehicle for information among others but an important social organization. A newspaper is not just a primitive data base, as some advocates of the wired society seem to assume. It is a forum within which a distinct social group can talk to itself. It is not just a vehicle for individual expression but in itself an organizing force, as its close relationship to the development and the continued existence of political parties, at least in Europe, testifies. Moreover, to think that these new networks of electronic communication do not themselves also act as organizing forces would be a serious error. However, such networks will tend to organize people into sets of what Sartre called "serial relations"—that is to say, each of us will relate to one another via a center that defines us and then actually creates us in the image of the statistical artifacts of the marketing industry. The introduction of interactivity, far from liberating us, will make available at the center information on our patterns of consumption that will in its turn tie us ever more tightly and willingly into our targeted and isolated social groups. The same, of course, is true of the possibilities of working at home, or telecommuting, as it is called. The forms of sociality created by industrialization and urbanization, constituting the public sphere, upon which our very notions of democratic politics and civilized behavior are based, are threatened. Of course, it is true that switched networks offer us alternative possibilities of noncentralized, more participatory forms of social organization, but such forms will have to be actively worked for and policies constructed actually to block the far more powerful and deeply embedded social trends identified above. As in all questions of social policy, we are not dealing here with choices between good and bad but with the achievement of a balance between alternative goods—between individualism and sociality, between the necessary center and the periphery, between the private and the public. Technology determines no particular outcome to this constant historical process of defining the social good. It offers potentials and creates a network of contending forces. Only the properly political process of policy formation can resolve the dilemmas it presents.

What research agenda can we derive from this analysis? First, it is increasingly essential that research be organized on an interdisciplinary and cross-cultural basis. Analysis of the trends I have described and of appropriate policy responses to them requires the pooled expertise of economists, political scientists, lawyers, technologists, and social scientists. As these trends are now unavoidably transnational, any research project requires a comparative element, a sensitivity to the differing impact of these developments on different economic, legal, political, and cultural systems and to the ways in which these differing impacts feed back into relations between nation-states and cultures. More specifically, research needs to be directed at the following areas: (1) work of a theoretical nature on the political economy of information and on the structure, role, and development of the public sphere and its implications for social and political theory; (2) macroanalysis, at a national and international level, of the supply side of the information and cultural industries with particular attention to the impact of the shift to the telecommunications mode on the mode of cultural and informational production in general, on the structure of control and product mix of these industries; (3) detailed analysis of the communications policy formation process; (4) traditional media impact, effects, and content studies need to shift their attention to a macro-analysis of the consumption of information in all its forms and across all the social contexts in which that information consumption takes place, from the domestic to the public and work environments. What are the information needs and potentials for information usage of varying social groups? How do those needs and potentials interact with supply, encouraging some developments and blocking others? And what related roles can and should regulation and the market play in optimizing the satisfaction of those needs and with what varying effects on the distribution of social power?

REFERENCES

De Sola PooL, I. (1984) Technologies of Freedom. Cambridge, MA: Harvard University Press.

Popper, K. (1966) The Open Society and Its Enemies. Princeton, NJ: Princeton University Press.

5

THE BEGINNINGS OF POLITICAL COMMUNICATION RESEARCH IN THE UNITED STATES
Origins of the "Limited Effects" Model[1]

Steven H. Chaffee and John L. Hochheimer

INTRODUCTION

The intellectual history of U.S. political communication research is traced from its origins in the 1940 Erie County study by Paul F. Lazarsfeld and his colleagues at Columbia University, through the more psychological studies of voting centered for many years at the University of Michigan, to the contemporary era of studies by mass communication researchers. The Columbia studies created an image of the limited effects of the mass media on voting behavior, a paradigm taken over more broadly by communication scholars. Chaffee and Hochheimer argue that empirical support from the Columbia studies for the limited effects model was problematic, and was mainly a result of the studies' design and conduct, and the assumptions upon which they were based. The Michigan researches on voting during the late 1950s and 1960s largely relegated the mass media to a minor role. It was not until the late 1960s, when scholars trained in mass communication research began to engage in studies of political behavior, that the limited effects model began to be seriously questioned. ***E.M.R, F.B.***

The basic paradigm for research into the roles of mass communication in political processes has remained largely intact since the earliest major studies conducted in the United States (Lazarsfeld and others, 1944; Berelson and others, 1954). This paradigm projects an image of the "limited effects" of the mass media in the context of election campaigns, an expectation that has had profound influences on the conduct of research on mass communication in Europe as well as in the U.S., in the four ensuing decades. It has also had a considerable influence on public policy, particularly in defending new communication technologies (e.g., television) from governmental regulation or control in the United States. The argument that media need not be controlled because they have only minimal

[1]Portions of this chapter were presented in earlier papers delivered to the German Association for Journalism and Communication Research at Münster, Federal Republic of Germany, in 1982; and to the International Communication Association convention at Dallas, in 1983.

From Steven H. Chaffee and John L. Hochheimer, "The Beginnings of Political Communication Research in the United States: Origins of the 'Limited Effects' Model," pp. 263-283 in Everett M. Rogers and Francis Balle, eds., *The Media Revolution in America and Western Europe* (Norwood: Ablex, copyright 1982). Reprinted by permission.

political and social impact has been continually reasserted by the broadcasting industry. The now-venerable research on which this argument rests has rarely been subjected to fresh academic scrutiny.

Because the original studies were highly empirical, the analysis of media "effects" has long been regarded as the essence of empirical mass communication research, despite a growing body of work on media uses (e.g., Blumler and McQuail, 1969; Blumler and Katz, 1974), media institutions (e.g., Ettema and Whitney, 1982), working norms of the press (e.g., Tuchman; 1978, Schudson, 1978), and other non-effects themes. Because the early investigators brought a "marketing" orientation to the problem of politics, effects were sought that would take the form of "selling" one candidate or party in preference to another; only to the extent that a medium displayed a strong bias in favor of one side, and then only to the extent that this bias was reflected in the votes of that medium's audience, would more than "limited" effects be imputed to mass communication. Because, as Gitlin (1978) has pointed out, the field of marketing treats all topics of media manipulation homogeneously, it was assumed that what had been found (or not found) for politics would hold more or less equally for other topics, and vice versa (Katz and Lazarsfeld, 1955; Berelson and Steiner, 1964); thus the idea of "limited effects" was extended to the entire range of mass communication (Klapper, 1960).

While current scholars have been expanding the realm of communication research, rewriting much of "what we know" about the importance of mass media, it is essential as we approach a new era in communication technology to reexamine not only the earliest studies but also the assumptions that lay behind them. These basic assumptions, which remain with us to a great extent today, included the following:

1. That the act of voting is a consumer decision equivalent to the purchase of a product in the marketplace. From this assumption comes the definition of "political communication" as a message or campaign that effects a change in people's evaluations of candidates for office. In short, political communication is viewed as a marketing phenomenon, and research on this topic can be interpreted in terms of the study of a marketing problem.
2. That politics and communication can be assessed in contrast to an idealized system, in which all people should be concerned, cognizant, rational, and accepting of the political system, and in which the institutions of communication should be comprehensive, accurate, and scrupulously fair and politically balanced. This kind of assumption grew naturally from the use of "ideal types" in sociological theorizing of the 1930s and 1940s. Imagined ideal behaviors and systems were useful, in the absence of comparative

data, in that they provided a standard for interpretation of empirical observations in early studies.

3. That communication and politics are appropriately viewed from the top or power center rather than from the bottom or periphery of the system. The role of the media was conceived in terms of their effects, what they might do to people, rather than what people might be doing with the media (or without them). Politics was examined in terms of the needs of the political system, in particular the electoral component of that system, and from the perspective of political elites. These media-centric and elite-oriented approaches were quite congenial to the people conducting the studies and the funding sources that supported them.
4. That the processes involved in political communication are approximately equivalent across time and space. There was in the 1940s a growing appetite within social science for theoretical generalizations, broad conclusions about relationships between extensive variables, which were assumed to hold regardless of the empirical boundaries of a particular study. Gradually it was to be recognized that the field would have to settle for "theories of the middle range" (Merton, 1957), but at the beginning the method was to assert a proposition in as general a way as possible. The task of demonstrating the limits beyond which a statement would no longer hold was implicitly left to future research.

THE LAZARSFELD TRADITION

These intellectual assumptions and perspectives were brought into the communication research field most forcefully by the work of Paul F. Lazarsfeld of Columbia University. While they would not be accepted by many researchers today, the original studies based upon them are still treated as benchmarks against which contemporary research is to be compared. These early studies are the main object of our attention here.

In 1940 Lazarsfeld undertook his landmark study of the determinants of voting in the U.S. presidential election campaign (Lazarsfeld and others, 1944). Together with a follow-up study in the 1948 campaign (Berelson and others, 1954), these were the first major election studies to give concentrated attention to the role of the mass media—and also virtually the last for many years thereafter. The limited range of impact ascribed to the media in the Lazarsfeld studies so impressed itself on the minds of most social scientists that the general question of media "effects" on politics was not reopened until about ten years ago. Recently there has been a new flowering of research exploring the role of mass communication in political processes, breaking out of the mold established by Lazarsfeld in a number of ways. But, to a remarkable extent, most of the assumptions of the original studies continue to structure current research.

There have been, to be sure, studies of the media-election nexus that do not fit clearly into this analysis. Some refreshingly new research directions have been taken, and a number of *ad hoc* studies of particular elections across the years have been reported without reference to Lazarsfeld's original work. Journalists have also written a great deal about the role of mass media in politics, typically in ignorance of any empirical research on the topic. Still, the impact of the early studies on today's researchers remains pervasive. A fair measure is the recent *Handbook of Political Communication* (Nimmo and Sanders, 1981). A quick count of entries in the index to this comprehensive volume reveals that Lazarsfeld and Berelson both are cited in more than 40 locations; almost all of these references are to their 1940 and 1948 election studies. A recent analysis of citation networks in *Journalism Quarterly* (Tankard and others, 1982) suggests that those two monographs are the "classics of the field", along with Klapper's (1960) synthesis of the limited effects model.

A MARKETING ORIENTATION

The marketing orientation to research has been so intimately intertwined with much of communication research that it would seem inseparable to many scholars. The search for "effects" of the media stems from the concern of producers of goods to sell their products through the use of advertising, product and packaging design, pricing decisions, and so forth. The most effective marketing is that which realizes the largest increases in sales (i.e., positively influences the buying behavior of the largest segment of the target population). The "effect" of the media is then seen as the intervening factor that induces a more favorable perception of the product being marketed.

The focus of research, in this approach, is to differentiate factors characteristic of people, messages, and media to see where the most effective implementation of marketing techniques might be made. Lazarsfeld's training and basic research orientation made him a pioneering scholar in this burgeoning field.

Although he became known in the U.S. as a member of the sociology faculty at Columbia, Lazarsfeld's basic academic orientation was to the psychology of marketing. In a biographical note to a methodological article in *The National Marketing Review* (Lazarsfeld, 1935), he is described as "a member of the Department of Psychology of the University of Vienna who has been interested in applying psychological principles to the field of marketing research," having "conducted numerous marketing surveys in Europe" and more recently having "tested his principles in the laboratory of American marketing research."[2] His interest in voting as an example of a consumer decision is evident in his early article. His concern with media came a bit later, in the famous radio audience analyses that he conducted with Frank Stanton, later President of the Columbia Broadcasting System (Lazarsfeld and Stanton, 1942). The 1940 election study was planned as an assessment of the influence of the media on the vote, although when they came to writing up the report the evidence of media impact was considered weak enough that the purpose was broadened to that of discovering "how and why people decided to vote as they did" (Lazarsfeld and others, 1944, p. 1).

THE ERIE COUNTY STUDY

For their 1940 election survey, Lazarsfeld and his associates chose Erie County, Ohio, the center of which is the small city of Sandusky. Their panel design was described in *The People's Choice*, the slim (178 pages) monograph in which they reported their findings:

> Erie County, Ohio . . . was chosen because it was small enough to permit close supervision of the interviewers, because it was relatively free from sectional peculiarities, because it was not dominated by any large urban center although it did furnish an opportunity to compare rural political opinion with opinion in a small urban center, and because for forty years—in every presidential election in the twentieth century—it had deviated very little from national voting trends.
>
> In May, 1940, every fourth house in Erie County was visited by a member of the staff of from twelve to fifteen specially-trained local interviewers, chiefly women. In this way, approximately 3,000 persons were chosen to represent as closely as possible the population of the county as a whole.

---

[2]Merton (1968, pp. 504–505) ties Lazarsfeld directly to this line of the evolution of American marketing techniques: "As Lazarsfeld and others have pointed out, mass communications research developed very largely in response to market requirements. The severe competition for advertising among the several mass media and among agencies within each medium has provoked an economic demand for objective measures of size, composition, and responses of audiences." Merton continues: "And in their quest for the largest possible share of the advertising dollar, each mass medium and each agency becomes alerted to the possible deficiencies in the audience yardsticks employed by competitors, thus introducing a considerable pressure for evolving rigorous and objective measures not easily vulnerable to criticism."

> This group—the poll—resembled the county in age, sex, residence, education, telephone and car ownership, and nativity.
>
> From this poll, four groups of 600 persons each were selected by stratified sampling . . . Of each of these four groups of 600, three were reinterviewed only once each.
>
> (T)he 600 people of the panel were kept under continual observation from May until November, 1940. Whenever a person changed his vote intention in any way, from one interview to the next, detailed information was gathered on why he had changed. The respondents were also interviewed regularly on their exposure to campaign propaganda in all the media of communication—the press, radio, personal contacts, and others. (Lazarsfeld and others, 1944, pp. 3–5)

Thus, as Sheingold (1973) points out, the Columbia research had its analytical focus on decision-making, although the authors concluded that voting was primarily a group process. This led to a research agenda that looks at politics and voting as the sum of individual interactions with the media, "opinion-leaders", and so forth, rather than the social networks through which information and influence flow. Since self-report data are insufficient to study network structures, and since "network attributes are more important than individual attributes in determining the likelihood of new information reaching an individual" (Sheingold, 1973, pp. 714–715), the Columbia research design was largely inappropriate to understanding the dynamics of political behavior, communication flow, and information-seeking within the context of an electoral campaign.

In retrospect it is difficult to imagine what kind of evidence might have satisfied the expectations regarding media impact that led to the Erie County study. Lazarsfeld (1935, p. 35) distinguished between what he called "biological" and "biographical" determinants of an action, and "determinants of the first degree." The latter category might include the "circumstances" under which a decision is made, the person's "purpose", and "all the factors which carry this decision on until it has actually been executed." The task of a survey questionnaire is to ascertain "the *total* motivational set-up of the first degree," by which he meant the immediate motivating factors entering a person's thinking (Lazarsfeld, 1935, p. 36; emphasis his).

It is intuitively obvious that for most marketing decisions, many of these determinants are unlikely to be attributed by a consumer to the mass media. In approaching the vote as a type of consumer decision, Lazarsfeld asked voters in the post-election survey what sources had provided information that led them to arrive at their vote decisions, and which source had been most important to them. More than two-thirds mentioned newspapers or radio as a "helpful" source, while less than one-half mentioned any type of personal source (relatives, business contacts, friends, and neighbors). More than one-half said either radio or newspapers had been the single most important source, but less than one-fourth cited a personal source as important (Lazarsfeld and others, 1944, p. 127, 171). Despite this seemingly preponderant evidence of media impact, the authors concluded that "more than anything else people can move other people." The 1940 study came to be cited as the basis for the two-step flow model of personal influence mediating between voters and the world of public affairs (with the latter treated as one of many commodities to be marketed) (Katz and Lazarsfeld, 1955).

ELECTION CAMPAIGNS: A VERY SPECIAL TOPIC

Unlike most kinds of campaigns, an election campaign consists of competing messages for the opposing candidates; one candidate succeeds only if the other loses. In a marketing campaign, each of the competing brands might succeed to the extent that they capture a share of the market; in most product classes a number of alternative brands can succeed simultaneously. Much of everyday politics is conducted in a similar fashion. For example, oil companies successfully "market" the special interest of deregulation to the extent that they gain some relief from public controls as a result of their constant campaign on that theme. An election campaign is more finite in scope and time, and fits the marketing model much less well than does the ongoing clash and compromise of competing political interests. Generally in politics one would attempt to estimate the total impact of campaigning, but in a two-sided "zero-sum" election contest the result is represented by the net effect—i.e., all those effects favoring the winning candidate, minus those favoring the loser. This approach, which confuses an analysis of the campaign *process* with an analysis of the election *outcome*, constitutes a serious mismatching of research purpose to study design. The news media do not as a rule intend to serve the purposes of only one side in an election contest; rather they strive to illuminate decision-making processes by providing news and information about the candidates.

Although content analyses indicated that both radio and newspaper news coverage favored the Republican Party's cause in 1940, the newspapers (in Sandusky, Ohio, and its environs) were much more heavily slanted in this direction. Lazarsfeld suggested that this difference effectively offered "a medium for each party," although neither radio nor the newspapers were literally "for" the Democrats in Erie County. Changes in favor of the Republicans were almost twice as likely to be based mainly on a newspaper report (31 percent of changers) as on something heard on radio (17 percent). As they had loosely hypothesized, among those changing toward the Democrats the results were approximately the reverse: 30 percent based on radio reports, 20 percent on newspapers (Lazarsfeld and others, 1944, p. 132). These rather large contrasts are especially impressive when one considers that most news coverage, even in local newspapers of that time, was largely standardized wire service material selected according to professional norms of newsworthiness. It must have included a good deal of campaign-related material favorable to each side, regardless of the medium of transmission, and this would have tended to neutralize the net effect of a particular medium leaning toward one side or the other.

At the same time, very slight differences in the same directions were found regarding exposure to these two media, Democrats being slightly more exposed to radio than Republicans, and slightly less to newspapers.[3] The partisan differences in net effects, which were much larger than those in media exposure, were later to be treated as having been theoretically explained by selective exposure factors.

"Selective exposure" was thereafter destined to join the "two-step flow" as the major conceptual basis of the "limited effects" image of media impact (Klapper, 1960; Kraus and Davis, 1976). Neither had shown up as a major factor in the 1940 study, at least not in comparison with the evidence of direct effects—nor did they in any subsequent study. No multivariate comparisons were employed in the 1940 study, nor for many years thereafter (Chaffee and Miyo, 1982). No new measures or analyses appropriate to these questions were added in the 1948 Elmira study. The theoretical terms simply became "facts" independent of their empirical origins or lack thereof.

If a marketing orientation was not pursued very clearly in Lazarsfeld's data-analysis and interpretation, it certainly was in his study design. The vote was taken to be the ultimate criterion variable, as if it were the single most important political act a person can perform. This focus on voting has been followed by many researchers since the 1940s, so it must have some appeal to the democratic ear (Sears, 1969; Mendelsohn and O'Keefe, 1976). Certainly voting is an act of consequence in popular government, but so too are the contribution of time and money to a campaign, personal argumentation on behalf of a candidate, the display of campaign buttons and bumper stickers, etc. Indeed, all of these require more personal investment than does the simple act of casting a secret ballot at the end

---

[3]On an index where means for Republicans and Democrats differed by 5 scale positions, between-media differences within each party were not greater than 1.1 scale positions.

of a campaign. Far more consequential to the political process is organized political activity through groups representing various economic and social interests, as Lazarsfeld later pointed out (Lazarsfeld and Merton, 1948).

For all its importance in the selection of political leaders and the transfer through them of power from one societal interest or class to another, casting a vote is neither a very large event, nor a risky one, in the lives of most people. The political movements for union representation, women's suffrage, and equal political and economic rights for minorities have been important issues in this century's American political history, and involved millions of participants who devoted much more than votes to their causes. These movements involved the formation of large voluntary political organizations such as the Anti-Defamation League and the National Association for the Advancement of Colored People. The roles of mass media communication, both for informing members of such organizations and for disseminating messages to the general public, are crucial in large-scale organized political activity.[4] But in a field survey of individuals that is focused simply on voting, this role is almost totally obscured and politics is reduced to a single act of "the sale and purchase" of candidates when viewed from a marketing perspective.

CONTEMPORARY INFLUENCES ON LAZARSFELD

Much of the research interest in the vote was inherited by Lazarsfeld from the dominant research paradigms that immediately preceded his Erie County study. Perhaps the most important within the academic community was the work of Stuart Rice, a sociology professor at the University of Pennsylvania, who laid the basis for the behavioral movement in political science with his widely used volume *Qualitative Methods in Politics* (1928), and his reader *Methods in Social Science* (1931). Building on the growing interest in the 1920s in the concept of "attitudes", Rice was able to marshal a variety of ecological data to account for various kinds of election outcomes. These books were well known in the major social science graduate departments throughout the 1930s, and Lazarsfeld's reduction of community data to individual-level data through personal interviews was looked upon as a logical extension of the beginning that Rice had provided (Rossi, 1959).

A more immediate influence in concentrating attention on the vote as the main criterion were two books by Louis Bean, *Ballot Behavior*

---

[4]Interpersonal communication, and communication structured along internal lines of organization, are likewise essential for any successful political movement.

(1940), and *How to Predict Elections* (1948). Bean, whose methods constituted refinements and extensions of Rice's, was cited in *The People's Choice,* which contains only seven references to other work related to any aspect of the project. In *Voting*, the 1948 election study report, Bean is mentioned on the second page in a blanket reference along with Samuel Lubell and Louis Harris, well-known public opinion poll specialists.

But the person whose professional conception of research undoubtedly had the greatest influence on the design of the Erie County study was the pollster Elmo Roper. In the 1930s, Roper had built a successful and well-known marketing survey organization that had gradually refined sampling and interviewing techniques for public opinion polling. His firm contributed to the funding of the 1940 research "and he and his staff were most helpful in the planning and execution of the study" (Lazarsfeld and others, 1944, p. v).[5] Roper had built a public reputation by predicting election outcomes in advance, on the basis of sample surveys. It was most logical that a study he co-sponsored would adopt as its goal the explanation of the vote as a primary criterion variable.

From this perspective, the main effect of heavy attention to the news media and the content of the campaign was seen as that of rendering a voter more predictable. Lazarsfeld repeatedly emphasized that unstable voters, and those who voted contrary to their "predispositions", reported quite low levels of campaign exposure. The predispositions were measured indirectly, through demographic correlates: Democratic votes tended to be drawn from blue collar, low socioeconomic status (SES), Roman Catholic families, and those who considered themselves "labor", while the Republicans were supported by white collar, high SES, Protestant, business-oriented voters (Lazarsfeld and others, 1944). The presumed predispositions were not so much psychological as social. They heavily reflected the different class interests served by the Democratic Party of the New Deal and by its conservative Republican opposition, and were presumably translated into votes through communication about these differences. For many voters, this communication doubtless had occurred some years before the 1940 campaign. But each campaign produces new candidates and new circumstances and at least some people might have paid particular attention to the campaign to assure themselves that they were indeed voting in their own best interests.

The communication process by which demographic differences came to be viewed as class interests and in turn were translated into votes was never examined. Had it been, it is likely that mass communication would

---

[5]Other sponsors included the Rockefeller Foundation, Columbia University's Office of Radio Research, and *Life Magazine*. Their influence was not, however, nearly so evident in either conceptualization or execution of the study as was Roper's.

have been an important part of it, especially in connection with the Republican candidate, Wendell Willkie, who was little known to the public prior to his nomination (Barber, 1980) and who had no clear political definition during the campaign (Lazarsfeld and others, 1944, pp. 28–32). Then too, the year of 1940 brought constant news about the recovering economy, and of the war in Europe in which Roosevelt was progressively involving the United States. These factors, which weighed heavily in many voter decisions, were of course dependent upon the mass media for their transmission to people. But news usually cuts several ways, reinforcing, in this instance, both isolationists and interventionists in their views. While the total effect is often large, the net effect is usually quite small. Using multivariate regression analyses (which are common today, but were practically unheard of in 1940) we would probably characterize the role of the mass media in that campaign as an interaction with class-related and interest-related independent variables; as a predictor of the vote, media exposure habits would have little main effect but rather strong multiplicative effects.

Looking across the Lazarsfeld-Berelson election studies as a whole, it is reasonable to conclude that their purpose shifted from the original one of investigating the role of the mass media to that of explaining the direction of the vote (Rossi, 1959). This transition would be completed in the next phase of election research, the national surveys conducted by the Survey Research Center at the University of Michigan (Kraus and Davis, 1976). Before examining these studies, though, we should examine in detail some covert assumptions of the Lazarsfeld research tradition, assumptions that have been accepted with little question in the Michigan series and most smaller-scale studies in the same vein.

THEORETICAL GOALS AND ASSUMED HOMOGENEITIES

Lazarsfeld's group held as their general goal the development of theoretical generalizations about processes that enter into the development of vote decisions. If these scholars' initial ambitions in this regard were unreasonably high, they were soon tempered by the reality of handling field survey evidence (with all its uncertainties and imperfections). Their conclusions were always phrased in terms of general variables, in a fashion extending well beyond the empirical boundaries of their study. Typically these were bivariate theoretical relationships, such as, "The less interest people have, the more variable are their vote intentions" (Lazarsfeld and others, 1944; p. 68), or, "Interest in the campaign invariably increases as the campaign progresses" (p. 77). Bivariate relationships like these were derived from empirical analyses with one or two control variables at most, and then strung into longer sentences to produce more complex theoretical syntheses.

Berelson was particularly fond of cataloging these findings, which came to be called in the phrase of another influential colleague, Robert Merton (1957), "theories of the middle range." This seemingly modest term referred to a broad search for general "laws" of human behavior. The assumption that fundamental laws would be discovered in the highly specific context of a U.S. election campaign must have seemed ludicrous even in those early years of empirical social science.

An appendix of the Elmira study report presents a chart summarizing the evidenciary support across seven studies for more than 200 separate inferences. This approach of cataloging knowledge eventually led to the expansive volume *Human Behavior* (Berelson and Steiner, 1964), which covered a wide range of topics. Most of the generalizations they drew about mass communication have since been disproven in at least some circumstances. It would be difficult for most scholars today to accept such assertions as, "the mass media do not appear to produce substantial . . . reaction to violence" (p. 546), or, "the fuller . . . the interest . . . then . . . the more resistant [the audience] to uncongenial [communications]" (p. 542), in the face of continuing research of the past 15 years.

The error, and it was probably a necessary error in order to get their grand enterprise in motion in the first place, was that Lazarsfeld and Berelson made a number of assumptions about the homogeneity of the elements they were studying. These elements included the basic pieces of an empirical study: people, places, times, and such specifics as elections, vote decisions, media, and political parties. To some extent the concept of "history" as a threat to validity of an inference (Campbell and Stanley, 1966) covers this problem. In studying one election campaign, and then a second, it was hardly outrageous for the investigators to assume that a finding from the first that was replicated in the second would prove to be an enduring generalization, especially if it remained couched in the most general of terms. If history proved these conclusions to be bound to their time (the 1940s), it would be the responsibility of future generations of researchers to demonstrate this limitation by repeatedly testing the propositions produced by Lazarsfeld and Berelson. What happened, though, was quite different. Their findings were accepted by most academics as valid generalizations, and therefore as not standing in need of further testing. Only in recent years, as the number of active researchers in this area has noticeably expanded, have many of the original propositions been subjected to new tests. About as often as not, they have not survived these tests.

There are further difficulties inherent in the assumptions of a homogeneous population, on which the theoretical interpretations of Lazarsfeld and Berelson rested. Each member of their sample was treated as an equally weighted unit, which permitted application of random sampling and statistical models that were then coming into vogue. Lazarsfeld and others (1944, p. 3) asserted that they were studying "the *development* of votes and not their distribution" (emphasis theirs); but evidence of what was important was drawn mainly on the basis of the frequency with which certain behavior patterns occurred. The key analysis, which led to the conclusion that there had been little room for the media to have any impact beyond "reinforcement" of predispositions to vote in a particular direction, was based on a turnover table comparing May and October voting intentions (Lazarsfeld and others, 1944; p. 102–104). Anyone whose stated vote intention had not changed during this time was classified as either "reinforcement" (53 percent of all cases) or "no effect" (16 percent). By contrast, "conversion" from one side to the other was "by far, the least frequent result" (8 percent). It was this interpretation of marginals, coupled with the finding that those classified as "conversion" cases were low in attention to the campaign via the media, that led to the "law of minimal consequences" regarding media effects.

Had not the focus been exclusively on the vote, and specifically on within-campaign changes in voting intentions, and had not each case been weighted equally and relative frequencies been taken as the indicator of theoretical importance, a very different interpretation of the role of mass media could have been derived from the findings of the 1940 study—and of every election study since. Some people certainly weigh more heavily in the political process than others; Lazarsfeld noted the role of "opinion leader", people who influenced other people and who themselves relied heavily on the media for their political information. Much has since been made of the concept of opinion leader, often implying that they are somehow independent of and distinct from other people and the media. Media attention is much higher among those who are more likely to vote, who contribute their efforts to campaigns, and who are at the forefront of organized political groups and movements. Only on Election Day do all voters count equally; even then the non-voters are strongly defined by their lack of attention to the campaign. In the 1940s their lack of interest may have been tantamount to a lack of exposure, but this is not the case today. In the intensive campaigning via television and other media, even people with little political interest or partisan attachment are now reached by a heavy volume of campaign messages (Chaffee and Choe, 1980).

The decision to locate the 1940 and 1948 studies in small cities of the Northeastern U.S. was mainly dictated by economic and administrative imperatives. But in each instance a case was made for the appropriateness of the site selected as representative of the entire nation, almost as if theories of the middle range would emerge from communities of the middle range in terms of size, geographic, socioeconomic, and political characteristics. Erie County, Ohio, had "deviated very little from the national voting trends" (Lazarsfeld and others, 1944, p. 3), and Elmira, New York was close enough to a "normal" American community "to assure a realistic test of the generalizations" (Berelson and others, 1954 p. 10). The Columbia researchers did not assume that these local sites represented valid samples of a homogeneous national political community. But neither did they locate their studies in Harlem, New York; Cambridge, Massachusetts; or Atlanta, Georgia. These would have been more obviously atypical. They also would have provided more evidence of the competing factions, interests, and ethnic groups that exist in the very heterogeneous United States than did Erie County—which was in fact atypical by its very lack of political interest groups.[6] The Columbia researchers also consciously picked communities that were very stable politically. This choice reduced the likelihood of their finding much instability—the within-campaign change they considered a necessary condition for inferring media effects—at the level of the individual voter.

In selecting a single community the researchers also thereby selected its local news media. In the cases of Sandusky and Elmira, these media consisted mainly of pro-Republican newspapers in a stable Republican region, and a small number of (and thus little variety among) low-budget, local radio stations. The homogeneity of media provided in a single site greatly restricts the variance available for study, and consequently restricts as well the possible covariance one may detect between media content and exposure, and other variables. It was not until 1976 that a major election study would be conducted in two sites selected for their constrasting media resources (Patterson, 1980). By this time, with the coming of television and the demise of many local newspapers, there was not sufficient

---

[6]"Local union leadership had not been outstanding or progressive or particularly aggressive and local units were not active in their own state organizations. Labor was not an important influence in the county; the domination of business over labor was freely admitted by local labor leaders . . . labor did not form a political bloc as such, and no group or individual was able to deliver the labor vote. On the whole, the labor picture was apathetic rather than calm . . .

"There were no special interest groups in Erie County wielding important political influence. None of the ethnic groups—Negroes (sic), Germans, or others—formed an organized voting unit. The minority parties were not strong and there was no youth movement in the county (although there was a Young Republican Club). The votes of neither veteran nor fraternal groups could be delivered; and there were too few relief clients for them to be influential as a unit" (Lazarsfeld and others, 1944, pp. 12–13).

between-community variance to make a detectable difference in voter decision-making processes. We can only speculate on the possibility that the seeming imperturbability of voters in Elmira, New York in the volatile election year of 1948 might not have been very indicative of simultaneous events in media-rich New York City, the burgeoning suburbs of Los Angeles, or the Deep South of the "Dixiecrat" revolt against the liberal civil rights platform adopted by President Harry Truman's Democratic Party.

HISTORICAL SHIFTS

Lazarsfeld and Berelson can hardly be faulted for their limited samples of time frames. They happened to be working in the election years 1940 and 1948, and their implicit ahistorical assumption of the homogeneity of times was unavoidable. But subsequent scholars might have been more attentive to some major changes in the elements involved in voting behavior and theoretical statements about it, which occurred in the U.S. after 1948. The media system has, as noted, changed dramatically. Television has replaced radio as the most popular source of news, and cities where competing newspapers of rival political perspectives once thrived have come to be dominated by single (usually centrist) newspapers. Thus the arrays of media available to an individual vary considerably by time and place (Hochheimer, 1982). With a rising level of mass public education should come a concomitant increase in people's capacity to process complex political information. More than one-fifth of all adults—and undoubtedly a higher proportion among those who vote and otherwise participate in politics—receive one of the informative weekly news magazines, *Time* and *Newsweek*. If the "enlightened electorate" presumed by romantic democratic theorists ever existed, it ought to be more likely in the United States of the present day than it was in the 1940s. Berelson and others (1954, Ch. 14) in a somewhat pessimistic final chapter concluded that the voter they had been studying "falls far short" of standards of knowledge, principle, and rationality in reaching a decision. Whether that generalization would be as easily reached or accepted today is at least debatable, but it is certainly true that most people find electoral politics much less engaging an activity than do the researchers who study them. There is an inescapable "elitist bias" in academic evaluations of the intellectual performance of the typical member of society. Most evidence suggests voters have become better informed and more issue-oriented over the decades since the early voting studies (Nie and others 1976), although many would still fall short of an idealized standard.

Certainly American electoral politics has changed since the 1940s. Campaigns are conducted today not by political parties nearly so much as by professional campaign consultants, who specialize in direct mail solicitation, polling, advertising, and media relations. Whether for this reason or others, parties do not loom large in the public mind as they did when the original studies were undertaken. People in the U.S. today are less likely to say they belong to a party, and this measure is a less-strong predictor of the vote, than was the case 30 years ago (Nie and others, 1976). Votes seem to be determined by specific comparisons of candidates on issues, more than they are by party labels. In the studies of 1940 and 1948, the Columbia researchers emphasized how much voters distorted their perceptions of the candidates' positions so as to coincide with personal preferences and partisan allegiances. When the intellectual leadership in U.S. election research shifted to the University of Michigan in the 1950s, these assumptions, conclusions, and interpretations went with it, and party indentification became the core concept in predicting the vote.

THE MICHIGAN TRADITION: PSYCHOLOGICAL EXPLANATIONS

Party identification is a distinctly American way of "explaining" political processes, growing out of the unique political history of the United States. By the time social research began in this century the two-party system had become deeply ingrained in U.S. politics.

In today's era of relatively low allegiance to parties, it may be difficult to recall the deep-seated feelings that were once associated with the term "identification" when it was applied to partisan orientations. Freudian psychology, which stressed the importance of early emotional experiences and subconscious psycho-dynamic processes of adaptation to the outside world, had an enormous impact on American intellectuals of the 1920s and 1930s. The Freudian concept of "identification" was conceived as an affective bonding between the person and an ideal, or another person, or a group, a bonding that is considered essential to the development of a well-integrated personality (White, 1956, p. 200). Harold Lasswell (1930), who was highly intrigued by the possible application of principles of psychopathology to political processes, brought the most extreme version of this view into political science. In an elaborate speculation on the clashes between ego and id that he saw as involved in identification with a nation or a social class, he concluded that the large American middle class was particularly vulnerable to propaganda and suggested "devising expedients of mass management by means of significant symbols which induce the harmless discharge of collective insecurities" (Laswell, 1935, p. 233). There was thought to be, then, a strong need for identification with national symbols of power and with one's distinctive group, and these ties were acquired in an individual's early formative years within the family.

There is no evidence that this view of party identification as a primal force was ever adopted by the early election researchers. Lazarsfeld almost never used the term "identification"; his concept of "party preference" was measured by the self-reported frequency for candidates of each party. Only in the last major interview wave of the last Columbia election study (dated October 15, 1948) was a question asked about the person's psychological orientation toward political parties: "Regardless of how you may vote in the coming election, how have you usually thought of yourself—as a Republican, Democrat, Socialist, or what?" (Berelson and others, 1954, p. 361). This question represented a supplementary measure, near the end of the interview schedule; Lazarsfeld and Berelson were behaviorists.

Angus Campbell, who directed the major national election studies at the University of Michigan from 1948 until the late 1970s, was a psychologist. He viewed the determinants of the vote as psychological in nature, and party identification was pre-eminent among these. He impressed upon the Michigan studies his assumption that the explanation of voting behavior was to be found in the partisan attitudes of individuals (Campbell and others, 1960, pp. 64–75). Noting that Americans' party preferences "show great stability between elections", the Michigan group viewed this consistency as a product of an "individual's affective orientation to an important group-object in his environment," which they called party identification. The party was not viewed so much as representing a consistent class or interest thrust as it was simply a distinctive group in society "toward which the individual may develop an identification, positive or negative" (Campbell and others, 1960, pp. 120-122). This psychological attachment was not considered the same as regularity of voting for one party, although there was a strong empirical correlation between the two. This distinction allowed the central concept to jibe with the basic facts of the times: While the Michigan investigators were studying the 1952 and 1956 victories of the Republican President Eisenhower, they continued to find that most people reported that they considered themselves to be Democrats, not Republicans.

The origins of party identification were not so important in the Michigan studies as was the simple fact that this self-classification measure was a reliable predictor of the vote. When asked what their parents' party preferences had been, voters tended to describe them as consistent—both between mother and father, and between parent and child (Campbell and others, 1960, pp. 146–149). The validity of this retrospective measure was not tested, although it was of some concern. Campbell and others (1960) expressed some skepticism over the notion that party identification was typically learned at a very young age, or transmitted between generations within a family in association with strong emotional linkages to parent–child relations. Instead, they emphasized the many different kinds of political events and experiences that might account for both the acquisition and the later fluctuation of party identification.

IGNORING THE MASS MEDIA

That this fluctuation due to the flow of events might depend heavily on the kinds of political information brought to the person via the mass media did not enter the discussion of the Michigan scholars. From the 1948 study through that of 1972, use of mass media variables were generally limited in the Michigan questionnaires to one item per medium (radio, newspaper, magazine, and television) asking whether the respondent had heard or read any campaign program or story from that source. These experiences were treated as instances of political participation, somewhat weaker than such forms of campaigning as giving money, wearing buttons, or attending meetings, but nonetheless evidence of something greater than total apathy on the respondent's part. *The American Voter*, the highly influential monograph summarizing findings from the 1948, 1952, and 1956 national surveys, devoted only one paragraph specifically to the subject of mass media use during a campaign (Campbell and others, 1960, p. 92).

The message of this research for students of electoral behavior was clear: Party identification and other partisan attitude measures were strong predictors of the vote. The use of mass media was a type of "informal participation" which for a few people constituted "a principal means of relating to politics," but was generally not related to prediction of the vote and hence is of very little theoretical consequence. By relegating media-related activity to the status of a minor mode of political participation, the Michigan studies through the 1960s inadvertently insured perpetuation of the limited-effects model of mass communication. No new data relevant to the question of media effects would be gathered, so no new interpretations could be reached.

THE HYPODERMIC NEEDLE (MAGIC BULLET): A NON-TRADITION

It is often asserted that the limited-effects conclusions of Lazarsfeld and his associates were reached in reaction to an earlier image of the mass media that accorded them very powerful putative effects. The latter is often referred to as the "hypodermic needle model" in skeletal histories of the field (e.g., Schramm, 1971; Reeves and Wartella, 1982). The term "magic bullet" is also sometimes used to describe this supposed naive and long-discredited view. In a popular current introductory textbook, for example, De Fleur and Dennis (1981, p. 502) equate the "magic bullet theory" with both the "hypodermic needle theory" and "stimulus–response theory", defining them as the assumption "that all subjects will receive some critical feature of the message (the magic bullet) that will change them in the same way." This "legacy of fear" of massive media impact, they say, stimulated much of the mass communication research in this century. The studies by Lazarsfeld and others "opened a new era in thinking" by rejecting "the old hypothesis that the media have great power" (De Fleur and Dennis, 1981, pp. 294–297).

This widely accepted version of the field's history does not correspond to the published record as we have found it. Early studies of the impact of motion pictures on young people, sponsored by the Payne Fund in the late 1920s, were quite sophisticated in the complexity of their applied theory, although they were built upon a linear model of media effects (Rogers and Kincaid, 1981). The same film, it was found, affected children differently depending upon a child's age, sex, predispositions, perceptions, social environment, past experiences, and parental influence (Reeves and Wartella, 1982). None of the subsequent investigators of media effects in the 1930s and 1940s ever seems to have proposed a simple, direct effects model in which media content would be accepted and acted upon by large masses of people. The learning theory set forth by Carl Hovland in his experimental studies of propaganda film effects proposed a sequence of direct information inputs, followed by lesser impact at the levels of affect and conation (Hovland and others, 1949). Several of these experiments demonstrated large differences in effects due to intervening factors such as the person's mental ability. Hovland concluded that mass-scale direct effects should not be expected, although considerable impact is possible if a message is carefully designed for its audience.

Lasswell, in his darkest writings on the psychopathological side of politics (1930) and the need of atomized man in modern society for symbols of group identification (1935), considered that media messages that filled this kind of need for an individual would be gladly accepted as therapeutic. Somewhat parallel assumptions were being made in the planning of Nazi propaganda in Germany at the same time (Doob, 1950). This view was only speculation on Lasswell's part, however; his empirical research concentrated on analysis of media content, which reflected his deep interest in the manipulation of symbols.

In any event, Lasswell does not seem to have been on the minds of the early political campaign researchers. He is not cited in either of the Columbia election studies (Lazarsfeld and others, 1944; Berelson and others, 1954), and the only reference to him in *The American Voter* is in connection with individual differences or "personality" variables (Campbell and others, 1960, p. 499).

Although it is Lasswell who is most often cited as the author of a "hypodermic needle" model of direct effects (e.g., Schramm, 1971; Davis and Baran, 1981; Dominick, 1983), it is difficult to find the evidence in his own writing. At the most, this piece of imagery would have had a highly specific meaning in the context of Lasswell's essays of the 1930s. Writing in the depths of the Depression, he saw the threatening political movements sweeping Europe (such as Fascism and Communism) as almost inevitable outcomes of the isolation of the individual in an atomized society.[7] By bringing symbols of nationalism and group identity to such a person, he reasoned, political campaigns via the mass media could be effective because they would be welcomed by the person in the absence of any more satisfying social ties. A hypodermic needle is, of course, a method for injecting medication into an ailing body. Later research stressed the message strategy of "immunizing" a person against propaganda by "inoculation" with a belief defense (Lumsdaine and Janis, 1953; McGuire and Papageorgis, 1961; McGuire, 1964; Roberts and Maccoby, 1973). This extension of the medical metaphor may account for the extent to which the hypodermic needle model became embedded in the literature long after its supposed heyday.

The image of a "magic bullet" is also derived from a medical metaphor, and also seems to have been created as a straw man years after the supposed fact. In this case, the usage of the term represents almost precisely the *opposite* of its meaning in the popular literature on medicine. Far from an image of universal impact, a magic bullet is a specific medication, which hits only those few in the population who are diseased; it is "magic" because it passes through all the others without any effect on them.[8] The direct metaphor is that of a bullet that one could fire into a crowd, which would kill all one's enemies but leave friends and neutrals unharmed. Ironically, a literal magic bullet metaphor would accord rather well with the empirical image of political media effects we have distilled from the long research record since Lazarsfeld. As campaign messages diffuse through a population, they do indeed seem to pass through many people without noticeable impact on their thought or behavior, but it has been repeatedly demonstrated that a substantial minority who are seeking political orientation are affected when the content of the message coincides

---

[7]Elihu Katz, a leading student of Lazarsfeld's, summarized what was "in the air" if not explicitly to be found in the writings of the Columbia scholars, in this passage from a synthesizing article: "Until very recently, the image of society in the minds of most student of communication was of atomized individuals, connected with the mass media but not with one another" (Katz, 1960, p. 436).

[8]The Edward G. Robinson film, "Dr. Ehrlich's Magic Bullet," concerns the search for a cure for syphilis.

with their current needs (e.g., Chaffee, 1978; Weaver and others, 1981).

In sum, there does not seem to have been a general theory of massive media effects that was seriously proposed by empirical investigators of political behavior and mass communication.[9] With the development of new campaigning techniques and strategies, such a time may very well lie in the future (Rice and Paisley, 1981). It would seem, though, that the competitive arena of political campaigning (Chaffee, 1981) lends itself much less easily to this kind of eventuality than is the case with public health, environmental topics, and other activities on which audience predispositions are more likely to coincide with message intent.

THE CONTEMPORARY ERA

The publication of Joseph Klapper's *The Effects of Mass Communication* (1960) marked the watershed of the limited effects model. This highly influential volume weaves together the Lazarsfeld-Berelson middle-range theoretical propositions into one global generalization: The impact of mass media on public attitudes and behaviors, especially those in the political realm, should ordinarily be expected to be minimal. Not until after the 1972 election campaign, in which the media played an unmistakably central role, did additional measures related to mass communication get added to the questionnaires for the Michigan electoral research series (Miller and others, 1974). By this time a number of new currents of political communication research had begun to flow, in other academic settings.

---

[9]Many other writers, generally neither communication scholars nor social scientists, did write extensively about the great power of the mass media and why society should fear them. These popular writings are probably responsible for creating the hypodermic needle model that Lazarsfeld and his colleagues were later credited with destroying. Speculations about powerful media influences have been a major theme in both journalistic and novelistic literature throughout this century. Examples within academic circles include accounts of the role of the Hearst newspapers in crystallizing the Spanish–American War, analyses of Hitler's propaganda warfare, the panic created by Orson Welles's "War of the Worlds" broadcast, and the fear of Madison Avenue advertising effects as expressed in Vance Packard's book *The Hidden Persuaders*.

Scholars entering the field of mass communication research typically encounter these kinds of writings early on, before they begin to study empirical research. Consequently, the phenomenological introduction of the individual researcher to the field is usually one of progression from hypodermic-needle beliefs to a more measured comprehension of how mass communication processes actually work. It requires only a slight leap of inference to confuse this personal experience with the history that the ongoing research field itself has experienced, especially when the small literature on that history describes it in a way that matches one's personal experience. In preparing this chapter, the authors became acutely aware of this kind of confusion in their own earlier experience and thinking.

Throughout the 1960s evidence began to accumulate which suggested that the limited effects image was at best oversimplified and under many circumstances quite misleading. Its most thorough codification (Klapper, 1960) had stressed that there were a number of conditions that might produce strong, direct media effects. Klapper's qualified statements tended to get rounded off in summary treatments by other authors, however, and relatively few academics saw much promise in the study of the political impact of the mass media.

Politics, though, inexorably continued. Campaigns had to be mounted each election year, and it was difficult for researchers to ignore them. In 1958, a gubernatorial candidate in California tried a political gimmick of then-rising popularity, an election eve "telethon." Schramm and Carter (1959) conducted a survey of the potential audience for this program, and found that few of those who listened or called in were not already his supporters. This expensive campaign event failed for lack of an audience, due to selective exposure (and the candidate lost the election to boot). The limited effects model seemed to fit.

Two years later, however, Carter (1962) found a campaign situation that did not provide much opportunity for the audience to select itself according to partisan predispositions: the series of televised debates between John F. Kennedy and Richard Nixon in the fall of 1960. In a then-rare test of the prevailing wisdom, he tested panels of pro-Kennedy and pro-Nixon voters on their knowledge of factual items that each candidate had presented during the course of the first debate. Among those individuals who had watched the entire debate, there was no difference in recall based on which candidate the voter favored. Nixon partisans recalled what Kennedy had said as well as what Nixon had said, as did Kennedy supporters. Katz and Feldman (1962), in their comprehensive review of all studies of the 1960 debates, called this finding "most intriguing."

The more general conclusion from the 1960 debates studies, though, was that they had mainly served as "image-building" events, giving the young Kennedy a chance to demonstrate that he was more "experienced" and had qualities of "leadership", according to various panel studies. The net impact of the debates on the vote was slight, although enough to help Kennedy win a very narrow victory. Even if recall were not selective, and if the two-candidate format limited the opportunity for selective exposure, party identification was still a regnant concept and the debates were treated as a unique exception to the rule of limited effects (Pool, 1963). In retrospect, though, Carter's (1962) finding was not an anomaly, but the beginning of a new wave in mass communication research.

By the early 1960s a number of former journalists were emerging from newly-established doctoral programs in mass communication research in the U.S. A marketing orientation is not particularly comfortable for scholars who view the media through the eyes of reporters, nor is the belief that the media are of little consequence in politics. These news-oriented researchers tend to conceive of the role of the news media as primarily one of informing—rather than directly persuading—people, and consequently have focused increasing attention on the cognitive effects of political communication. For example, McCombs and Shaw (1972) initiated study of the "agenda-setting" power of the media. The "uses and gratifications" served by the media's public affairs content were first investigated by Blumler and McQuail (1969) in Great Britain, and have since been enthusiastically pursued in the United States (e.g., McLeod and Becker, 1974; Mendelsohn and O'Keefe, 1976). The importance of the news media in informing young people of pre-voting age about politics has been demonstrated in several studies (e.g., Chaffee and others, 1970; Hawkins and others, 1979). But even as they diverge from the Lazarsfeld tradition in their selection of dependent variables and conception of the media's role, these recent departures retain many characteristics of the early studies: election campaign settings, large-sample field surveys, predominantly individual-level data-analysis, and the search for enduring generalizations. The debt of contemporary researchers to Lazarsfeld and his colleagues is clear, and it is recognized. The Erie County study remains one of the most-cited sources in political and mass communications research even in the 1980s (Paisley, 1984).

We have dwelt at length on the earliest studies of mass media in U.S. election campaigns, and emphasized the extent to which they have influenced later research. This brief effort at historical scholarship has impressed upon us several conclusions of a historical nature, involving both the history of our field and the extent to which interpretations of research findings should be considered relative to their historical times and places.

HISTORY OF THE FIELD

The "received history" of mass communication research as brought to us in brief prefatory chapters and paragraphs written since 1960 does not correspond to the actual work in the decades of the original studies, if we are to judge from the published record of that time. The earliest studies stressed that media impacts are contingent on personal orientations and accordingly differ from one person to another. No empirical study has, to our knowledge, ever purported to demonstrate a universal, massive pattern of media impact. The "hypodermic needle" and "magic bullet" images represent misinterpretations of metaphors drawn from medicine, and appear to have been "straw men" created some years later as a naive conception against which the limited-effects model could be contrasted. The conclusion that media effects are limited was based on assumptions derived from the field of marketing, and is in the process of being discarded as assumptions more appropriate to the communication functions of public affairs media are applied to research.

The assumption that communication and political influence are unidirectional linear processes has also come under considerable criticism of late. Dervin (1980b) argues that the source-to-receiver image of communication flow may be backwards; in the area of communication and development, Hornik (1980) used the term "feedforward" to refer to the idea that the initiative for a communication program may often lie with the person who is eventually to receive the information. Rogers and Kincaid (1981) point out that the linear perspective captures only one-half of the "convergence" process that comprises communication. Sheingold (1973) contends that the most useful contribution sociology can make to voting research will come from the analysis of the communication networks through which political information flows. From a viewpoint of intellectual history, the early studies—which were designed in ways that precluded the empirical examination of concepts of these more sociological kinds—probably served to retard the development of social theories of political communication even though the studies were often conducted by sociologists.

THE RELATIVITY OF RESEARCH DATA

Empirical research findings need to be interpreted in the context of the historical time and place in which the data were gathered. Estimates of the percentage of individuals who behave in a particular way, or of the strength (or even the direction) of bivariate relationships, should be constructed only very tentatively on the basis of a single study. Whereas the groundbreaking researchers could reasonably give their research monographs generic titles like *Voting* and *The American Voter*, we have found that certain of their generalizations do not hold up in the face of historical change. Today it is becoming common to find time-specific and locale-specific labels attached to the titles of research reports that deal with general variables: "in the Carter–Reagan Campaign", "during the 1984 U.S. Election", and the like. This reflects a new found awareness that quantitative results may differ widely from time to time and place to place, as the conditions of media and politics vary.

It is still quite possible that certain findings will prove to be generalizable. The strong correlation between public affairs knowledge and newspaper reading, for example, seems to hold up consistently in various settings. We would not fault the pioneers of our field for putting forth their intitial results as generalizations, because they assumed that it was understood that these propositions were always open to subsequent test. But now that more than four decades of studies have accumulated, an empirical reassessment of those propositions is long overdue. We have not attempted to reconstruct a set of empirical propostitions in any systematic way in this chapter, We believe that a re-analysis of the underlying assumptions should be the first step in such an undertaking. We expect that some generalizations are indeed attainable, but that many findings will prove to be specific to the conditions of a particular study. Careful comparison of these differing conditions can produce new hypotheses for testing, hypotheses that would help to explain why such very different relationships between similar variables are to be found under different circumstances.

RELATIVITY OF RESEARCH PERSPECTIVES

An additional point we wish to stress is that the "effects" orientation of political-marketing research assumes a fundamentally linear model of communication from source-to-receiver, and a system-down model of politics. These are not the only conceptual possibilities, nor even the preferable ones, as Rogers and Balle suggest in the introductory chapter of this volume.

The source-to-receiver view is unidirectional, seeing the person whose decisions and other behaviors are at stake as the intended target of messages. In a campaign context, messages are studied for their effects upon voter perceptions and behaviors, and how they may influence the outcome of the election. The system-down perspective posits the behavior of the "ideal" or "proper" citizen, and leads to studies of the extent to which the voter approaches the model of behavior established by the scholar. This approach may result from top-down definitions of politics (Lemisch, 1969). The paradigm of politics as voting behavior, a normative and stable process, has remained virtually unchallenged throughout the history of political communication research, even as the focus may have shifted toward cognitive and professional communication criteria. The behaviors of political actors continue to be interpreted almost entirely within the confines of electoral campaigns, as if "politics" consists simply of attempts to attain public office, an activity that is concentrated in the short period prior to each election. There is as yet in the study of political communication no analog to the "convergence" model of communication outlined elsewhere in this volume by Rogers, although some empirical beginnings have begun to appear (e.g., Eulau and Siegel, 1981).

The assumption of homogeneity as to people, places, media, and political cultures that is permitted by the early narrow view of political communication reduces us to a "stipulated static paradigm for research" (Meyer and others, 1980, p. 264). It is ironic that in the United States, probably the most heterogeneous country in the western world, statistical parameters to describe "typical" political processes and "the American voter" have been the object of so much of our research. In a country where voting by 60 percent of the eligible citizens has come to be considered a "heavy" turnout in national elections, more attention might well be given to other, perhaps more profound forms of political communication and action.

A reversal of the conceptions of communication and politics would be an essential step in this direction. Brenda Dervin (1980a, 1980b; Dervin and others, 1982) and Rita Atwood (Atwood and Dervin, 1981), among others, have recently been arguing that the source-message-channel-receiver (S-M-C-R) picture of communication processes puts matters backwards. In line with the psychology of "becoming" (Rogers, 1979), they see people as active creators of their own information, defined as the sense one makes of the world while moving through time and space. The media, from this person-oriented perspective, can be seen as the lenses through which the world is viewed and which structure the ways in which the person makes his or her particular sense of it (Hochheimer, 1982). Similarly, a person-centered perspective would view political socialization in terms of the needs and capacities of the person developing from childhood into adolescence, and thence on into adulthood. For example, Wackman and Wartella (1977) have studied children's reactions to television advertising from such a developmental perspective. Most research on political socialization, however, has assumed that the standard of comparison is a stipulated political system, toward which the young person is expected to become socialized. More person-oriented research, reversing both the S-M-C-R and system-down models, is likely to enrich our understanding of political communication in the future.

The political dynamics of elections vary over time. Sheingold (1973) suggests that the dynamics of the decision-making process lying behind voting also varies with differences in historical situations. The electorate itself changes over time, too. Women, blacks, and people without property were, in various times and places, excluded from voting. Party alignments have shifted dramatically due to changing economic and social conditions. For example, the Democratic "Solid South" that was formed in the wave of post-Civil War Reconstruction has become an increasingly Republican New South in the past 20 years of civil rights struggles, influx of new industry, rising affluence, and, perhaps, media influences.

The media, too, change over time, both as cause and as effect of political, social, and economic change. The content, form, and uses of a medium interact with a changing environment to remain in flux (Williams, 1974). Thus, the search for the political role of the mass media constrains the analysis of communication and of politics. Both are processes; both evolve. We need not remain constrained by the assumptions upon which Lazarsfeld, his colleagues, and their scientific descendants constructed their research. We can learn from the past as we look to the future.

Our broadest recommendation, then, is that the study of historical change should be reintroduced into the analysis of political communication. Politics, in the words of Lord Acton, "is the one science that is depositied by the stream of history." Mass media serve both as a central component in the political process, and as an enduring record of its history. The search for ahistorical theory has unnecessarily impoverished our understanding of that process and of that record.

REFERENCES

Rita Atwood and Brenda Dervin (1981), "Challenges to Social-Cultural Predictors of Information-Seeking: A Test of Race vs. Situation Movement State," Paper presented at the International Communication Association, Minneapolis, MN.

James David Barber (1980), *The Pulse of Politics*, New York: Norton.

Louis H. Bean (1940), *Ballot Behavior*, Washington, DC: American Council on Public Affairs.

Louis H. Bean (1948), *How to Predict Elections*, New York: Knopf.

Bernard Berelson, Paul F. Lazarsfeld, and William McPhee (1954), *Voting*, Chicago, IL: University of Chicago Press.

Bernard Berelson and Gary Steiner (1964), *Human Behavior: An Inventory of Scientific Findings*, New York: Harcourt, Brace and World.

Jay G. Blumler and Elihu Katz (1974), *The Uses of Mass Communication*, Beverly Hills, CA: Sage.

Jay G. Blumler and Denis McQuail (1969), *Television in Politics: Its Uses and Influences*, Chicago, IL: University of Chicago Press.

Angus Campbell, Philip E. Converse, Warren E. Miller, and Donald E. Stokes (1960), *The American Voter*, New York: Wiley.

Donald T. Campbell and Julian C. Stanley (1966), *Experimental and Quasi-Experimental Designs for Research*, Chicago, IL: Rand-McNally.

Richard F. Carter (1962), "Some Effects of the Debates," in Sidney Kraus (ed.), *The Great Debates*, Bloomington, IN: Indiana University Press.

Steven H. Chaffee (1978), "Presidential Debates: Are They Helpful to Voters?", *Communication Monographs, 45*, 330–346.

Steven H. Chaffee (1981), "Mass Media in Political Campaigns: An Expanding Role," in Ronald E. Rice and William J. Paisley (eds.), *Public Communication Campaigns*, Beverly Hills, CA, Sage.

Steven H. Chaffee and Sun Yuel Choe (1980), "Time of Decision and Media Use in the Ford-Carter Campaign," *Public Opinion Quarterly, 44*, 52–69.

Steven H. Chaffee, L. Scott Ward, and Leonard P. Tipton (1970), "Mass Communication and Political Socialization," *Journalism Quarterly, 47*, 647–659.

Steven H. Chaffee and Yuko Miyo (1982), " Selective Exposure and the Reinforcement Hypothesis in the 1980 Presidential Campaign: An Intergenerational Panel Study." Paper presented to the Association for Education in Journalism, Athens, OH.

Dennis K. Davis and Stanley J. Baran (1981), *Mass Communication and Everyday Life*, Belment, CA: Wadsworth.

Melvin L. DeFleur and Everette E. Dennis (1981), *Understanding Mass Communication*, Boston, MA: Houghton Mifflin.

Brenda Dervin (1980a), "Information as a User Construct: The Relevance of Perceived Information Needs to Synthesis and Interpretation," Paper presented at the Research and Educational Practice Unit, National Institute for Education, Washington, DC.

Brenda Dervin (1980b), "Communication Gaps and Inequities: Moving Toward a Reconceptualization," in Melvin Voigt and Brenda Dervin (eds.), *Progress in Communication Sciences, Volume 2*, Norwood, NJ: Ablex.

Brenda Dervin, Thomas L. Jacobson, and Michael S. Nilan (1982), "Measuring Qualitative and Relativistic Aspects of Information Seeking: A Test of a Quantitative-Qualitative Methodology," Paper presented at the International Communication Association, Boston, MA.

Joseph R. Dominick (1983), *The Dynamics of Mass Communication*, Reading, MA: Addison-Wesley.

Leonard W. Doob (1950), "Goebbels' Principles of Propaganda," *Public Opinion Quarterly, 14*, 419–42.

Heinz Eulau and Jonathan W. Siegel (1981), "Social Network Analysis and Political Behavior: A Feasibility Study", *Western Political Quarterly, 34*, 489–499.

James S. Ettema and D. Charles Whitney (eds.) (1982), *Individuals in Mass Media Organizations: Creativity and Constraint*, Beverly Hills, CA: Sage.

Todd Gitlin (1978), "Media Sociology: The Dominant Paradigm," *Theory and Society, 6*, 205–253.

Robert Hawkins, Suzanne Pingree, Kim Smith and Warren Bechtolt (1979), "Adolescent Responses to Issues and Images," in Sidney Kraus (ed.), *The Great Debates*, Bloomington, IN: University of Indiana Press.

John L. Hochheimer (1982), "Probing the Foundations of Political Communication in Campaigns: The Dispersion Process of Media." Paper presented to the International Communication Association, Boston, MA.

Robert Hornik (1980), "Communication as Complement in Development," *Journal of Communication, 30*, 10–24.

Carl I. Hovland, Arthur A. Lumsdaine, and Fred D. Sheffield (1949), *Experiments on Mass Communication*, Princeton, NJ: Princeton University Press.

Elihu Katz (1960), "Communication Research and the Image of Society: Convergence of Two Traditions," *American Journal of Sociology, 65*, 435–440.

Elihu Katz and Jacob J. Feldman (1962), "The Debates in the Light of Research: A Survey of Surveys," in Sidney Kraus (ed.), *The Great Debates*, Bloomington, IN: Indiana University Press.

Elihu Katz and Paul F. Lazarsfeld (1955), *Personal Influence*, New York: Free Press.

Joseph T. Klapper (1960), *The Effects of Mass Communication*, New York: Free Press.

Sidney Kraus and Dennis Davis (1976), *The Effects of Mass Communication on Political Behavior*, University Park, PA: Pennsylvania State University Press.

Harold D. Lasswell (1930), *Psychopathology and Politics*, Chicago, IL: University of Chicago Press.

Harold D. Lasswell (1935), *World Politics and Personal Insecurity*, New York: McGraw-Hill.

Paul F. Lazarsfeld (1935), "The Act of Asking Why in Marketing Research," *National Marketing Review, 1,* 26–38.

Paul F. Lazarsfeld, Bernard Berelson, and Hazel Gaudet (1944), *The People's Choice*, New York: Duell, Sloan and Pearce.

Paul F. Lazarsfeld and Frank Stanton (1942), *Radio Research, 1941*, New York: Duell, Sloan and Pearce.

Paul F. Lazarsfeld and Robert K. Merton (1948), "Mass Communication, Popular Taste, and Organized Social Action," in Lyman Bryson (ed.), *Communication of Ideas*, New York: Harper and Brothers.

Jessee Lemisch (1969), "The American Revolution Seen from the Bottom Up," in Barton Bernstein (ed.), *Towards a New Past: Dissenting Essays in American History*, New York: Vintage Books.

Arthur A. Lumsdaine and Irving L. Janis (1953), "Resistance to 'Counter-Propaganda' Produced by One-Sided and Two-Sided 'Propaganda' Presentations," *Public Opinion Quarterly 17,* 311–318.

Maxwell E. McCombs and Donald L. Shaw (1972), "The Agenda-Setting Function of the Press," *Public Opinion Quarterly, 36,* 176–187.

William J. McGuire (1964), "Inducing Resistance to Persuasion: Some Contemporary Approaches," in Leonard Berkowitz (ed.), *Advance in Experimental Social Psychology, Volume 1,* New York: Academic Press.

William J. McGuire and Demetrios Papageorgis (1961), "The Relative Efficacy of Various Types of Prior Belief-Defense in Producing Immunity Against Persuasion," *Journal of Abnormal and Social Psychology, 62,* 327–337.

Jack M. McLeod and Lee B. Becker (1974), "Testing the Validity of Gratification Measures Through Political Effects Analysis," in Jay G. Blumler and Elihu Katz (eds.), *The Uses of Mass Communications*, Beverly Hills, CA: Sage.

Harold Mendelsohn and Garrett J. O'Keefe (1976), *The People Choose a President*, New York: Praeger.

Robert K. Merton (1957), *Social Theory and Social Structure*, New York: Free Press.

Robert K. Merton (1968), *Social Theory and Social Structure*, New York: Free Press.

Timothy P. Meyer, Paul J. Traudt, and James A. Anderson (1980), "Nontraditional Mass Communication Research Methods: An Overview of Observational Case Studies of Media Use in Natural Settings," in Dan Nimmo (ed.), *Communication Yearbook, 4,* New Brunswick, NJ: Transaction Books.

Warren E. Miller, Arthur Miller, and F. Gerald Kline (1974), *The CPS 1974 American National Election Study*, Ann Arbor, MI: University of Michigan, Center for Political Studies.

Norman H. Nie, Sidney Verba, and John R. Petrocik (1976), *The Changing American Voter*, Cambridge, MA: Harvard University Press.

Dan D. Nimmo and Keith R. Sanders (1981), *Handbook of Political Communication*, Beverly Hills, CA: Sage.

William Paisley (1984), "Communication in the Communication Sciences," in Brenda Dervin and Melvin J. Voigt (eds.), *Progress in Communication Sciences, Volume 5*. Norwood, NJ: Ablex.

Thomas E. Patterson (1980), *The Mass Media Election*, New York: Praeger.

Ithiel de Sola Pool (1963), "The Effect of Communication on Voting Behavior," in Wilbur Schramm (ed.), *The Science of Human Communication*, New York: Basic Books.

Byron Reeves and Ellen Wartella (1982), "For Some Children Under Some Conditions: A History of Research on Children and Media." Paper presented at the International Communication Association, Boston, MA.

Stuart A. Rice (1928), *Quantitative Methods in Politics*, New York: Knopf.

Stuart A. Rice (1931), *Methods in Social Science: A Case Book*, Chicago, IL: University of Chicago Press.

Ronald E. Rice and William J. Paisley (1981), *Public Communication Campaigns*, Beverly Hills, CA: Sage.

Donald F. Roberts and Nathan Maccoby (1973), "Information-Processing and Persuasion: Counterarguing Behavior," in Peter Clarke (ed.), *New Models for Mass Communications Research*, Beverly Hills, CA: Sage.

Carl R. Rogers (1979), "The Foundation of the Person-Centered Approach," *Education, 100*, 98–107.

Everett M. Rogers and D. Lawrence Kincaid (1981), *Communication Networks: Toward a New Paradigm for Research*, New York: Free Press.

Peter H. Rossi (1959), "Four Landmarks in Voting Research," in Eugene Burdick and Arthur J. Brodbeck (eds.), *American Voting Behavior*, Glencoe, IL: Free Press.

Wilbur Schramm (1971), "The Nature of Communication Between Humans," in Wilbur Schramm and Donald Roberts (eds.), *The Process and Effects of Mass Communication*, Urbana, IL: University of Illinois Press.

Wilbur Schramm and Richard F. Carter (1959), "Effectiveness of a Political Telethon," *Public Opinion Quarterly, 23*, 121–126.

Michael Schudson (1978), *Discovering the News: A Social Life History of American Newspapers*, New York: Basic.

David O. Sears (1969), "Political Behavior", in Gardner Lindzey and Elliot Aronson (eds.), *The Handbook of Social Psychology, Volume 5: Applied Social Psychology*, Reading, MA: Addison-Wesley.

Carl A. Sheingold (1973), "Social Networks and Voting: The Resurrection of a Research Agenda," *American Sociological Review, 38, 712, 720.*

James W. Tankard, Tsan-Kuo Chang, and Kuo-Jen Tsang (1982), "Citation Networks as Indicators of Journalism Research Activity." Paper presented at the Association for Education in Journalism, Athens, OH.

Gaye Tuchman (1978), *Making News: A Study in the Construction of Reality*, New York: Free Press.

Daniel B. Wackman and Ellen Wartella (1977), "A Review of Cognitive Development Theory and Research and the Implication for Research on Children's Response to Television," *Communication Research, 4*, 203–224.

David H. Weaver, Doris A. Graber, Maxwell E. McCombs, and Chaim H. Eyal (1981), *Media Agenda-Setting in a Presidential Election*, New York: Praeger.

Robert W. White (1956), *The Abnormal Personality*, New York: Ronald Press.

Raymond Williams (1974), *Television: Technology and Cultural Form*, New York: Schocken Press.

6

SPACE, TIME, AND CAPTIVE COMMUNICATIONS HISTORY

Carolyn Marvin

In the now conventional discussion of the disappointing quality of communications history within the field (Carey 1974; Stevens and Garcia 1979; McKerns 1977), the most obvious thing perhaps has not quite been said: For most of its existence the study of communications history in the United States has been a captive of its patron, the professional media training program. While research on problems that are central to communications history has flourished outside the field in recent years (Clanchy 1979; Darnton 1979; Eisenstein 1979; Havelock 1982; Stock 1983), investigation within it has remained detached from the shaping minds and influences of historiography in the last half-century. Communications scholars have contributed little to the work and thinking of mainstream historians, nor have they been influenced in any very perceptible way by the rather spectacular and fruitful developments that have vivified recent historical discourse (Stone 1980; Higham and Conklin 1979; Le Roy Ladurie 1979; Braudel 1969; Rabb and Rotberg 1982). The fact that there has been little discussion of this point is a troubling sign, I think, of the degree to which the relationship between communications history and its patron is still a stifling one, though lately it is a symbiosis showing distinct signs of strain.

This situation is not unique in historical studies associated with professional training. In 1959 Bernard Bailyn, the distinguished historian of the American Revolution, warned historians of American education, a group constituted within similar professional curricular boundaries, of the hazards of isolation from the active center of historical research, writing, and teaching (Bailyn 1960). He faulted especially the restrictive definition of education as a subject for research to formal instruction alone, as though an understanding of other educational forms and prac-

From Carolyn Marvin, "Space, Time, and Captive Communications History," in Mary S. Mander, ed., *Communications in Transition: Issues and Debates in Current Research* (New York: Praeger, 1984), pp. 20-38. Copyright 1983 by Mary S. Mander. Reprinted by permission.

tices were not essential to an intellectually serious history of education, and as though the history of formal instruction could properly be understood apart from them. Bailyn advised educational historians not to confuse the justification of current professional norms and notions with the pursuit of historical understanding. All past instruction had not prophetically aimed, as conventional historiography had it, at the profession of teaching and the institution of schooling as educational practitioners had come to believe in it in the twentieth century. The impulse among educational historians to discover in history the "intimate relationship between their hitherto despised profession and the destiny of man" was motivated by understandable but not scholarly concerns (Bailyn 1960, p. 8).

The parallels with communications history are painful and exact. Communications history within the field has been, on the whole, an isolated endeavor. Its clients certainly have not been historians of all persuasions, or even an educated public, but mainly journalism teachers and their students. The subject matter of communications history also has been organized around a professional notion of what counts. Its research focus generally has been limited to the history of professional mass media. Even within that narrow compass, this meant for years an exclusive concern with the history of printed media. The history of spoken discourse, of telephony, telegraphy, museums, libraries, parades, festivals, correspondence, of literacy, of graffiti, of fashion and etiquette, of sound and visual recording, dance, maps, gossip and taboo, of the sonic landscape, of prayer, of the organization of knowledge, of dictionaries, spelling, and a thousand other components of communications have not merely been ignored or slighted within the field. They have barely been recognized.

Finally, the questions addressed by captive communications history have emerged primarily from modern professional constructions of the proper role of the elite urban press projected on past time.[1] From the fixed-point frame of reference in which captive communications historians have worked, the modern urban press is an end-point of evolution, if not exactly a professional perfection of autonomous news media institutions and products, increasingly professional news staffs, and whiggishly maturing audiences. The rosy reconstruction of journalism history as a morality play in which bad journalists and big government struggle against good journalists and emerging professional standards portrays the past as a quainter, somewhat less accomplished version of our own present, as "the present writ small," to borrow Bailyn's description of educational historiography (1960, p. 9).

There are certainly journalism historians who do not accept this traditional framework for press history, and who believe that the concerns of communications history should be broader. Such discussions alarm some guardians of the applied professional curriculum. They fear that an expansion of communications history or any other nonapplied area of the curriculum will reduce the time students have for cultivating professional skills. Others are concerned that such changes could endanger the academic legitimacy of the applied curriculum, the traditional raison d'être for most communications programs, and the final protector of the journalism historians themselves, who have no protectors elsewhere. This practical tension between the applied and academic curriculum within communications programs has furnished the terms of what debate there has been among the captive historians and their patrons.

THE UNEXAMINED LIFE OF THE AMERICAN NEWSPAPER

In my view this issue, though serious, is not the most crucial one for communications history. I believe the structural distortions of a profession-driven concept of communications history are much deeper. To take one pertinent example, I believe that even the meaning of the historical term "newspaper" has a falsely secure ontological and analytical status; that we know much too little about the adequacy of the evolutionary model of the past taken for granted in journalism history; that the shape of newspaper history never has been examined independently of powerful professional notions of what ought to be and to have been; that what is regarded as the "solid basis of fact" (Carey 1974, quoting Theodore Peterson, p. 3) needing only amendment by inspirited investigators may be neither solid nor fact.[2]

Consider how the authors of The Press and America, a standard reference work, and the bedrock text for most college courses in journalism history, set the conceptual boundaries of their entire historical narrative with a definition of their subject that has remained unchanged through four editions (Emery and Emery 1954, 1962, 1972, and 1978). (For statistics on journalism history text use, see Endres 1978, p. 2.) Inexplicably adapted from a 1928 German text (Groth 1928, pp. 21ff) and offered without theoretical justification or elaboration, this definition sees the "true" newspaper as a commodity published by mechanical means at least weekly, available to all at a single price, concerned with news of interest to a "general public," pitched to an "ordinary" literary skill, timely within the possibilities of available technology, and economically stable "as contrasted to the fly-by-night publications of more primitive times" (Emery and Emery 1978, pp. 4-5; see Dickinson 1929, pp. 9-11 for a contemporary review of Groth).

This list will be perfectly intelligible to journalists, since it reflects a commonsense professional mythology about what newspapers ought to be. Its categories are meant to be roomy enough to surround a large amount of history, including periods when the newspaper was not yet "complete." They suggest that the historical event, newspaper, is a special conceptual, commercial, and moral achievement with fixed characteristics marked by their absence or presence and level of mature development. In this setting the task of newspaper history can only be to explain how past historical actors learned by a series of successively fewer errors and bad guesses to solve the (correctly conceived and real) problems of our present. To make past actors responsible for historical goals that describe modern aspirations is a peculiar and unsupportable charge on the interpretation of the past.

There are other difficulties. To what audience does the term "general public" refer for historical periods in which literacy (what skills at what level of difficulty?) was not yet an "ordinary" achievement in the United States? Does the specification of a criterion of literacy suggest that real newspapers can be apprehended only privately? If so, why? Why is an economically "stable" newspaper more truly a newspaper than one that is not? (What does this criterion suggest about the current classification of The Times of London?) Why wasn't the "party press," the unabashedly partisan early republican press format, that of a "true" newspaper and ours the primitive, or by turn, decadent version?

Such unexamined notions go to the heart of traditional newspaper history. Consider, for example, efforts to establish an origin point for the newspaper in the "newes letter," traditionally regarded as one of the earliest newspaper formats in spite of the model its name suggests (as though it were a misguided effort that could have striven to be the New York Times if its producers had understood things properly).[3] The newes letter was comprised of items from private letters, from other newes letters, and from "correspondents" who might be traveling friends of the newes letter proprietor. It was distributed, at first irregularly, to the same taverns and coffeehouses that served as distribution points for letters from abroad and as places to converse about them. Newes letters frequently invited return correspondence and occasionally provided blank pages for readers to add their own news for forwarding to friends. The newes letter was less often the focus of its early proprietors' livelihoods than a sideline or extension of more significant communications roles that did provide such focus. Newes letter proprietors might be local postmasters within whose responsibilities all letters, including newes letters, fell, or job printers working also as booksellers, innkeepers, and general store keepers, occupations that constituted the central nervous system of local communication.

The newes letter was not an immature or fumbling prototype of objective journalism striving for the anonymous perspective familiar to modern audiences, but an elaboration of customary habits of letter writing and public discourse in communities of mutually acquainted persons. The newes letter practiced the conventions of the personal letter, the private professional mercantile newsletter, and the tavern conversation, all personal communication forms with established public dimensions. While all these forms contributed to the social invention of the modern newspaper, none was a quaint or deficient version of it.

We know relatively little about the homogeneity or distribution of early news forms from one town or community to the next, or about differences in their appearance and function in localities with different histories and cultural mixes, different geographic, economic, and social circumstances. We know less about the social economy of personal letters, conversations in coffeehouses and taverns, the postal service, the pulpit, or networks of personal friendship and gossip. Taken together, the practices of these oral and written forms in public and private settings constituted ecologies of discourse that should be a principal object of the study of the history of communications.

INSTITUTIONAL AND ARTIFACTUAL MODELS

Our ignorance reflects the prevailing model of the historical newspaper, a taxonomic illusion that treats evidence and event as coterminous. The newspaper has been confidently charted through history as a communications event fully contained in a product, a concrete object with natural outlines set neatly in relief against the past and following self-generated internal rules of development. Instead of placing the newspaper within larger systems of social signification and practice, systems partly reflected in the newspaper but also surrounding and containing it, historians have located the newspaper either in the relatively impoverished context of editorial practices organized around and through the professional newsroom or against the thinnest of background narratives of American political history.

The narrow logic of this institutional model was inherited both from the newspaper profession and from the self-consciously scientific "new" historians of the late nineteenth and early twentieth centuries. In emulation of the much admired examples of nineteenth-century biology and philology, the new historians constructed ambitious institutional histories conceptualized in abstraction from social life at large, and purportedly demonstrating the forward evolutionary movement of human affairs.

The chronologies, periodizations, and organizing concepts they devised framed their subjects for years to come (Handlin 1979, pp. 43-110; Hofstadter 1968, pp. xi-xvii, 3-43).

Journalism historiography faithfully adhered to the reigning historical model of institutions cast in splendid and improving isolation. The stand-alone evolutionary model pried the newspaper of journalism history loose from the rest of the social life and helped preserve it from challenges to its interpretive validity. That model has not worked very much better for the modern newspaper, for it is not only the origin of the "true" newspaper that is in doubt. For example, the captive historians have failed to explore, because their artifactual categories could not suggest them, the historical connections between certain important features of the newspaper-as-wire-service-outlet and network broadcasting.

With the emergence of a national wire service monopoly and a monopoly national telegraph network, local newspapers were often transformed into, or created precisely for the purpose of becoming, outlets on a national electrical communications grid for identical and exclusive "programming" transmitted from a central point. Concentration of news sources and conventions of editorial selection and presentation now strongly associated with broadcasting were familiar to audiences long before the invention of wireless technology and provided economic and cultural templates for its development. Perhaps because communications historians have not asked, conventional historical wisdom continues to see a nineteenth-century newspaper where it has not existed for 100 years. The habit of packaging communications practices and phenomena in the deceptively solid forms and products of technology conceals strategic cultural details and functions that are not isomorphic with any single technological application.

This is not a question of providing a richer or more adequate context, conceived as a kind of pastel wash around the imagined edges of events, but the question of an historically legitimate model of communications. Michael Schudson (1978) has recently challenged the captive mold by casting the penny press of the 1830s in the role of inventor of "objectivity" instead of merely a stage in its evolution, a characterization that augments the traditional reputation of the penny press as inventor of the local feature story. Schudson does not, however, explore why objectivity and local news were new to urban journalism. Were earlier entrepreneurs less imaginative (a notion that sometimes passes for explanation in captive history), or had the rhythm and pattern of life in earlier communities provided other, better networks for collecting, sorting, and distributing familiar and surprising knowledge? Did modern news devices mend deficiencies in older, quainter forms that might have disappeared earlier but for more talented entrepreneurs in the heroic mold, or were structures of social communication reorganized around new relationships in community life and new models for understanding and expressing them?

The "problem of journalism history" (Carey 1974) may be something like the discovery in anthropological and development circles that labels like "peasant" and "tribe" had been too generally applied to widely diverse groups and dissimilar practices.[4] Once investigators began to consider these labels in light of evidence that could be fully appreciated only after they had begun to loosen their intellectual grip, a host of notions that seemed incontrovertibly true and plausible also began to unravel in their wake. The variety of cultural phenomena masked by those labels belied much of the ideological overlay that had connected and supported them. The question for communications history is whether the term "newspaper," and others like "print culture" and "literacy," are applied too generally to dissimilar phenomena, or to misdivide other phenomena that are better grouped together along new classificatory axes.

It must be said that journalism historians have come by the contemplation of their own navels honestly. They, too, are victims of history. In a public description of his plans for one of the first full-scale journalism schools at Columbia University in 1904, Joseph Pulitzer vowed that through all phases of the ambitious historical training he envisioned for journalists "would run the idea of progress, especially the progress of justice, of civilization, of humanity, of public opinion, and of the democratic idea and ideal" (Pulitzer 1904). Pulitzer's perspective was the Progressive one of his period, shaped in the Midwest, shared not only by politicians and reformers but reflected also in the work of academic historians like Turner, Becker, Robinson, Beard, and Parrington.

These scholars and their disciples provided models and organizing questions to which journalism historians of the 1920s and 1930s, a breed that flourished especially in the land-grant schools of the Midwest, turned for their vision of American history. The coincidence of terms in the title of one of the first serious products of the new historical consciousness in journalism, Willard G. Bleyer's Main Currents in the History of American Journalism (1927), and Vernon Parrington's influential Progressive History, Main Currents in American Thought (1927), suggests the attentiveness of early journalism historians to the intellectual ferment of their time. But the Progressive view that took root in the first professional schools of journalism in accord both with the foremost model of American history at the time of their birth and the expectations of a profession in pursuit of intellectual legitimacy never really moved again.

Why? The answer to this question is speculative, but probably not mysterious. It can be sought in the intellectual isolation of journalism historians in their graduate training, in their departments, and in the universities where they work. In most graduate communications programs, core courses provide training in theory and basic research technique, and specialized seminars allow students to pursue special topics or to explore relationships between marginal and mainstream areas. In most graduate programs, communications history is still a special area with a small range of courses. Aspiring communications historians are slighted not only in basic history but often do not get adequate training in their chosen specialty. An awareness of debates and discoveries in history at large, or of the narrower range of work bearing directly on communications history, is built <u>out</u> of the structure of most graduate training in communications history.

The meagerness of this intellectual diet is sometimes justified by pointing to the limited teaching opportunities for historians in professionally based communications programs. It is strengthened by the conviction of other communications faculty that communications history of the usual kind is adequate for students, that it requires and deserves no more than commonsense training. Nor have journalism historians found sympathetic support from colleagues elsewhere in the university, who are often suspicious of the legitimacy of all professional faculty. Journalism historians frequently enjoy little of the camaraderie and support from other academicians, particularly in history, which provides the informal intellectual give and take that disciplines, encourages, and legitimates much academic work.

The mutually constructed nonintercourse between many communications programs and outside academic departments finds communications historians twice exiled. While scholars with history Ph.D.s are regarded as too academically specialized and insufficiently socialized to professional curricular goals to be hired in most communications programs, an advanced communications degree with a history specialization is also inadequate qualification for an appointment in history. Historians with primary training in communications are not prominent in professional scholarly associations of historians, and prominent historians are not active in associations for communications scholars. While these may be problems for communications historians to work out gradually in the course of disciplinary and curriculum evolution, they help explain, I think, why communications historians in the field have blazed few new trails through their own subject.

Permission to take the substantial intellectual risks that are necessary to build a field of knowledge requires an intellectual support system, either in curriculum structure and teaching opportunities in the field, or in a network of sympathetic scholars beyond it. It must include even the freedom to repudiate one's own intellectual heritage. Lacking the confidence of a discipline that takes its own risks, poorly placed to displease its patron, captive communications history has never dared enter the main arena of academic history to insist on the power of its subject to mark a path to the center of historical thought. Claiming only a small and derivative historical territory for its own, journalism historians never imagined a history of communication that might be more than a decorative bauble on the Progressive framework, or might expand and deepen Progressive hypotheses and rebuild them with the special materials available to journalism and communications historians. The failure of captive communications history must be measured by this inability to offer a genuinely fuller understanding of the past, but must also be seen in terms of the limiting conditions faced by many of its scholars.

PRESSURES FOR CHANGE

Ironically, the materials of communications history are just those that might have involved its researchers in the issues that have so engaged mainstream historians during the dramatic twentieth-century shift to social history. Until recently this shift of emphasis has taken place without reference to the work of communications historians, who nevertheless have a critical investment in the relationship of popular to elite history, the history of literacy, the history of large demographic shifts, the history of technology, women's history seen as the expanding area of public discourse permitted them, and the broadly conceived history of the imaginative and practical routine of daily life. This does not mean that mainstream history can or should dictate the program of so-called special areas like communications history.[5] It has always been necessary for historians working at the margins to prove the validity of their claims to center stage.

Although the inadequacies of Progressive journalism history are widely conceded, this dissatisfaction results only partly from internal scholarly discussion. Pressure for change is also a response to changes in the academic fortunes of journalism education and the rising worldly success of what has confusingly been labeled empirical communications studies.[6] During the fiscally prosperous 1960s and 1970s, teachers of professional journalism and social scientists of communication waged a kind of cold war over their shared curriculum. The ascendant star of social scientific approaches to a variety of topics and problems, including the press itself, gave social scientists growing leverage over communications budgets, curricula, and terminology. "Journalism" programs increasingly became "communications" programs.[7] Especially in an age fascinated by television, journalism historians seemed to have little to offer.

To the extent that their legitimacy depended on the tolerance of their professional colleagues, the shift of academic prestige away from vocational journalism training toward experimental and survey research sometimes deprived journalism historians, possessors of modest status outside the field, of status inside many communications programs as well. While the Association for Education in Journalism (organized as a wholly academic group in 1949 in a departure from the more customary partnership of professional journalists and journalism educators) has included organizations of journalism historians since 1951, the International Communications Association, organized in 1950 to further social scientific research in communications, still has no communications history group of any kind.[8]

The appearance of _Journalism History_ in 1974 was a visible sign of the increasing exclusion of journalism historians from traditional forums of communications research. From its first issue _Journalism History_ made itself a center for debate about what a reinvigorated journalism history might be, launching that discussion with an article by James W. Carey, a respected and influential spokesperson for what is usually called the American cultural school of communications studies, which Carey recommended as a research perspective to students of communications history.[9] The cultural school has claimed for its intellectual turf the study of thoughts, feelings, and sensibilities in specific social milieux. It seeks to go beyond descriptive "facts" and institutional analyses of communicative expression to a determination of deeper social meanings, an empirically and theoretically elusive goal in much of the school's work. Although its followers have been articulate about the difficulty of investigating such meaning with the usual assumptions and techniques of communications research, they have not developed rigorous alternative strategies and methodologies that _are_ suited to such problems (Christians and Carey 1981).[10] Whether meanings that satisfy cultural investigators have some claim to validity or are simply possible glosses of significance subject only to the aesthetic preferences of interested observers is not an issue the cultural school has successfully resolved.

The declared allegiances of the cultural school are to Durkheim, Park, Dewey, Thomas, Mead, Wirth, Cooley, and others generally regarded as founding members or early formative influences on the Chicago school of sociology. The cultural school's own subject list for sociological inquiry rests heavily on the historical presumption that an existing organic social unity, variously defined, was destroyed in the movement from community to society. The major temporal markers of that transformation also have varied with the problem under consideration, but most advocates of cultural studies would probably agree that whatever starting point for social disintegration is chosen, things have only gotten worse, and that the technologization of communication is largely responsible for rendering human experience demeaningly vicarious and artificial.

This is a sweeping historical hypothesis, in support of which there has emerged no cultural school of communications history research, properly and self-consciously speaking, no distinctive corpus of cultural research models, data, or strategies. The cultural school's definition of social life as communication has produced a few scholars to carry the debate, in Fernand Braudel's words, "right into the heart of history" (1969, p. 73).[11] Because the cultural school has generated no substantial historical body of knowledge of its own, its champions have had to look elsewhere for evidence to support a typically nostalgic construction of history, sometimes without adequate guidelines for judging the quality of historical work cited in behalf of that perspective.

The American cultural school's resistance to the intellectual evangelism of contemporary social science has also not been entirely consistent. While members of the school have questioned the capacity of reductionist models to handle and explain complex social meaning, they have also appealed to models of inquiry in anthropology, ethnography, and sociolinguistics — that is, to social sciences whose practitioners have labored to develop highly rigorous models and methodologies that are capable of approaching some aspects of human meaning and experience in an explanatorily rich and empirically reliable way (for example, Hymes 1967).

GRAND THEORY IN MEDIA HISTORY

There is an historian whose work exemplifies for some enthusiasts of cultural studies a theory of history that treats communications as the nerve center of social possibility and change. Harold Adams Innis conceived Western history as a succession of competitive struggles of centuries' duration among communications technologies serving competing elites and cultural values. His thesis has seldom been examined in light of its historical adequacy. Innis's most extended presentation of his communications theory of history, Empire and Communications (1950), is a somewhat breathless account of what almost seems to be a list of every important fact in communications history from 4000 B.C. to 1950. In fact, this historical narrative is perilously sketchy. A second book, The Bias of Communication (Innis 1951), offers only a slightly expanded analysis. Innis does not present his chronology of historical events as unique or possessed of multiple levels of explanation and structure, but as the epiphenomenal expression of great technological transformations in media that constitute the bone structure of historical epochs.

Innis set himself the problem of accounting for the rise and fall of "empire" in the history of such transformations. He hypothesized that empires rise out of partnerships between durable media and portable media, and that the outcome of adversarial encounters between civilizations depends on the comparative efficiency with which media controlled by contending powers facilitate the administration and control of territory on the one hand and the succession and continuity of authority on the other. Innis did not elaborate this hypothesis in sufficient historical detail to explain the mechanics of its claim, much less to make them convincing. He never proved whether the real history behind history is the history of media, as he asserts, or whether media only carry the struggles of history on their backs, and explanations of fundamental change lie elsewhere.

For Innis, assertions of media presence count as declarations of historical efficacy in the absence of detailed evidence for concrete media effect in particular historical circumstances. When Innis does note specific historical claims, the result is sometimes jarring. His account of the French Revolution in this sentence, "The policy of France, which favoured exports of paper and suppression of publication and which increased printing in Holland and England, created a disequilibrium, which ended in the Revolution" (1950, p. 159), is not credible and not atypical. Minus an argument from detailed evidence, Innis stretches the fabric of history across a spare two-dimensional frame of "time" and "space" coordinates said to be manifest in communication — the process, according to Dewey, in which society exists. The hopeful and immodest ambition of this attempt to sort vast and complex collections of human experience into typologies devoid of any obstinate paradoxes of particularity owes something to a reductive structuralism that has characterized not a little recent social science theory.

Innis's fundamental historical dynamic does not begin at this abstract level. It begins in the plausible argument that political and cultural control over space requires the capacity to move information easily from the center of power to its periphery and back, from which it follows that the portability of the medium is a critical factor. In a parallel way, he argues, successful control over the imaginative time of tradition requires media like stone that endure. Less plausible is the next level of the argument, in which the physical characteristics of media generate typical habits of thought and disposition for entire cultures. If media last, according to this claim, then the cultures to which they belong respect tradition and permanence. If media move information rapidly across space, then the cultures to which they belong value life that is fast paced and present-oriented.

Innis uses the term "bias" to specify media orientation. Time-biased media render the passage of time unimportant in the transmission of messages. However far back in time a message is launched, it remains unimpeded and undistorted. People separated by generations can have the same message in their hands. Time-biased messages fade over space. Spoken language, clay, parchment, and stone are time-binding media, according to Innis (1950, pp. 7-8, and passim; 1951, pp. 3-4, 33-34, and passim). They are typically durable and difficult to transport. They are said to foster hierarchy, decentralization, provinciality, religious tradition, and permanence. Space-biased media render the expanse of space unimportant in the transmission of messages. From no matter how geographically distant a point a message is launched, it remains unimpeded and undistorted. Space-biased media are light and fragile and permit those separated by vast reaches to have the same message in their hands. Space-biased media are ephemeral, and the messages they carry fade over time. Paper, celluloid, and electronic signals are space-binding media. They are said to give rise to centralization, bureaucracy, secularism, imperialism, and force.

The elliptical narrative in which this scheme is presented leaps from technological "fact" to social "effect." Though Innis's theory of media determinism radically challenges conventional historical explanations of political change, it seems to have no consequences at all for conventional periodizations, nor for conventional labeling and sequences in political history. The "facts" on which it is built are culled from a variety of secondary sources without discussion of the interpretive contingencies on which such facts depend. Innis treats categories like technological innovation, bureaucracy, decentralization, religion, and secularism as if they described razor-sharp, clean-boundaried, precise, and unproblematic phenomena, just as he finds it expedient to characterize Greek or British or French culture along one or two dimensions. Students of culture may be justifiably suspicious of this reductive tendency in the historical description of complex civilizations.

Innis also takes the operation of time and space biases as ideally effective. He assumes an always successful connection between centers of power and peripheries of spatial and temporal geography, an identity between the possibility of control and its reliable exercise that was rarely borne out in the premodern historical record with which he is particularly concerned, and probably operates more erratically in the present than is generally assumed. The representation of shifts in media efficiency as transformations of enabling conditions requires a supporting history of transportation effectiveness, an element largely missing in the Innisian account.

Absent a history of transportation, media and the values they embody compete for dominance by a process Innis also never analyzes or elaborates empirically. Just as some media are always present and by implication effective for Innis, so some media are always dominant in a way that has determinative cultural consequences. Theoretically, dominance is the result both of leaps in efficiency, or effective competition among media, and monopolies of knowledge, or failed competition. Monopolies of knowledge have the same evils as economic monopolies in stifling adaptiveness and diversity. They occur when obstacles of cost or skill give effective control of particular media to exclusive groups. Monopolies of knowledge introduce social instability and "invite" challenge from competing media and bodies of knowledge. Social stability, of which empire is the most dramatic historical example, occurs when a single authority controls both space-binding and time-binding media.

In Innis's narrative, "dominant" sometimes means politically dominant in the sense of being administered or controlled by reigning political authority. At other times it means socially dominant (in the sense of being the channel through which most people communicate most of the time), or economically dominant (though Innis, whose work was mostly in economic history, never offers figures comparing media for this purpose), or morally dominant (in the sense of dictating prevailing values). At different points it has all these meanings, but they are assumed rather than demonstrated, and this makes them tautological as well.

Innis writes as if "space-binding" and "time-binding" were mutually exclusive, independent, and constant physical properties of media operating _on_ culture. In the details of his historical account, however, the effective properties of old and new media constantly shift in relation to one another, as if there were after all an ecology of mutually adjusted communications functions. Innis specifies no general principle for circumstances in which the physical characteristics of media fully shape the social expression organized by their means, or, alternatively, in which they do not. In the resulting confusion, cultural characteristics exactly opposite from those predicted by a "technological" definition of media are occasionally attributed to media in particular historical situations.

Innis portrays the ancient Babylonian empire, for example, as an uneasy alliance between a temple-based priesthood in the south organized around sacred writing on clay tablets, and a centralized, militarily ambitious northern monarchy organized around stone media and architecture (1950, pp. 26-54). The heaviest and most enduring of all ancient media is thus held responsible for classic space-binding cultural traits of military expansion and secular political interest, where, according to the theory of media bias, there should be an overlapping and unconquerable constellation of time-binding influences on social organization.

Either spatial and temporal biases are potentially equally present in all media and are variously elicited in circumstances that can be specified, or they reside separately and unvaryingly in media with distinctive physical characteristics. They cannot logically do both. Having argued that the success of Hitler's aural and therefore temporal radio appeal was a theoretically consistent reaction to the distortion of Western civilization by the spatiality of the printed word, for example, Innis cannot then claim that radio overcame the impulse of printing toward decentralized nationalism, and successfully commanded vast new territories, without contradicting himself (1951, pp. 80-81). A world constructed in the spatial, centralized image of print cannot also be a decentralized community battling the paradoxically expansionist tendencies of an ephemeral aural medium like radio.

Besides making such a posteriori adjustments without explanation, Innis frequently introduces external factors to explain media effects without acknowledging the extratheoretical character of this extramedia explanation. He makes much, for example, of the strength of the Greek oral tradition, which he credits with resisting the absorptive threat of a written alphabet and with being the "reason" the Greeks were able to break the advancing wave of Persian empire (1951, pp. 53, 58-59, 66, 75, 84). Since all ancient cultures had an oral tradition of some kind, what made that tradition strong in one culture instead of another was not the oral tradition itself and must be explained in other terms. If external influences determine the effectiveness of media and even, as in the case of Babylonia, shape that effect in violation of some inherent "bias," then it is not media that make a historical difference, but other political, economic, and religious factors that operate through them.

These are not the only logical puzzles in Innis's theory. Except to construct the history of media competition in a deterministic and narratively dramatic way, it is not clear why any medium should be capable of only a single bias at a time, or how it is that "space" and "time" are mutually exclusive categories of analysis. Media do not exist as communications phenomena or events except in socially invented practices for transmission, storage, and retrieval. Innis seems to have regarded storage and retrieval not as variable social practices but as consistent extensions of assumed transmission properties of media, and to have classified all media accordingly.

The actual history of memory innovations drastically diminishes the suggestiveness of Innis's scheme for sorting media by the presumed consequences of bias. While Innis has argued, apparent contradictions aside, that print is as pure a case of spatial bias as history offers, Elizabeth Eisenstein (1979) has argued that the most important consequence of the printing press was to make writing permanent. While manuscripts were fragile and unevenly dispersed across geographical space, and survived best when they were inspected least, typographical fixity saw the printed word through all disasters that had previously diverted human energy from cultural preservation. Eisenstein, as is now well known, argues that several cultural renaissances that preceded the quattrocento Renaissance failed to take hold for lack of effective preservative techniques. After Eisenstein, it is difficult to argue convincingly that print is ephemeral. In Innis's terminology, print binds space *and* time with equal success.

If the capacity to move information over long distances and to store a lot of it are significant measures of media effectiveness, the two watershed developments in communications history after language and writing are printing, which greatly increased the capacity for transmitting and storing written messages, and computing, which is telegraphy with a memory, radio with a memory, and television with a memory. What printing did for writing, computing does for all electronic media.

These definitions of effectiveness are seriously inadequate, however, most of all because they leave the crucial problem of meaning unaddressed. The very anthropologists, ethnographers, and sociolinguists to whose example the enthusiasts of cultural studies have so strongly appealed argue that the pattern and richness of meaning can be established finally only in its particularities (Hymes 1967). Few cultural enthusiasts would be likely to insist that culture is so inconsequential a system of human meaning that messages moved over time and space will arrive undistorted in circumstances of utterly different cultural dimension and significance. That very notion, however, is the thrust of a theory of technological determinism. Innis failed to realize that meaning is not in the technological object, but only in the particular practices to which society puts it. Every technological object is already the expression of meanings and choices in a larger social order. Innis's error was the same as that of the journalism historians who assumed that media are objects with natural outlines, rather than a range of possibilities responding to changes in cultural time and space.

CONCLUSION

It is not surprising that communications history, increasingly studied by scholars outside the tradition of journalism history, shows signs of becoming an adopted child of social history. This shift is a significant and positive departure from its traditional and not notably successful emulation of Progressive institutional history in departments of journalism and communications, and from its acquiescence in that setting to the practical priorities and intellectual categories of professional journalists. Communications history cannot win its fight for intellectual dignity as a captive of professional ideology. Wherever communications history is subordinated to an applied curriculum, it will be distrusted both by professionals who see it as having an irremediable outsiders' perspective on what insiders know and by mainstream historians who see it as the impossible object of irreconcilable intellectual commitments. Whether it can do better under the auspices of social history than it has done as a grudgingly tolerated helpmeet of political history is a more uncertain question. Even the most critical and painstaking attempt to reconstruct the evidence of the past can only use categories that make sense in whatever the present may be. In that sense, all history is Whig history and is in need of constant rediscovery and reinterpretation.

The work of Harold Innis has sometimes been offered to communications historians as an alternative to the generally conceded inadequacies of conventional journalism history. This chapter argues that Innis's schematic media determinism is theoretically and empirically inadequate to the serious account of communications history its students seek. The formulation and investigation of fruitful historical problems in communications or any other area does require, though it cannot be dictated by, disciplined engagement in the central debates within mainstream history, something that also cannot be achieved so long as communications history remains within the warm circle of professional media concerns.

NOTES

1. For evidence of an assumed equivalence between the so-called elite press and newspapers deemed worthy of historical inquiry, see Merrill 1969, Chapters 1-4; and Nevins 1959.

2. Frank Luther Mott once explained that he always worked "with someone looking over my shoulder, as it were — with the sense of writing in a kind of collaboration with someone else, as my wife, a colleague, a close friend . . . . When I write on a journalistic topic, that collaborator is most often another ink-stained wretch" (see Casey 1965, p. 81).

3. Typical examples of reading the present back into the past, and judging the past by modern professional standards, are found in Gordon 1977, pp. 8-13, and Mott 1962, p. 15. A fairer picture of American journalism, comparative rather than evolutionary in presentation, is Marzio 1973 and Lee 1937.

4. I am indebted to Pamela Sankar for discussion on this point.

5. The perils of mainstream appropriation of emerging historical areas are clearly illustrated in the text of an address by Allan Nevins, then president of the American Historical Association, to the Committee on History at the 1959 Association for Education in Journalism Convention in Eugene, Oregon (1959). Nevins surveyed journalism historiography and concluded that: it had been insufficiently critical in identifying good and bad journalism (by standards unspecified, but evidently assumed); that journalism historians had done a poor job of discovering novel evidence to assist in the construction of a fuller political history, as though the only "real" history were political history; and that historians should confine their energies to newspapers worthy of having their history preserved, a criterion that, from Nevins's perspective, excluded most American dailies.

6. For example, Daniel J. Czitrom (1982) titles a chapter on the recent movement of social scientific perspectives into the field of communications, "The Rise of Empirical Media Study: Communications Research as a Behavioral Science, 1930-1960," (pp. 122-46). This is a misnomer. Journalism and communications history were always intended to be empirical, that is, to make and test propositional statements on the basis of evidence. Czitrom and others perhaps improperly confuse the term "statistical" with "empirical."

7. As early as 1944, however, Ralph D. Casey (1944, p. 56), then director of the University of Minnesota School of Journalism, was advising his colleagues at the National Council on Professional Education for Journalism that "the forward-looking teachers acknowledge that today's school of journalism is properly a _school of communications_." As an exercise in social prognostication, this article is chiefly interesting for its inability to identify what would be the chief new demands on journalism schools in the postwar era.

8. The evolution of these groups is recounted in Summary of Roundtables 1951; Official Minutes 1952; Conversation with Emery 1980.

9. Following Carey's (1974) article in its inaugural issue, _Journalism History_ devoted the entirety of another issue to further discussion and replies to Carey. "A Symposium: History in the Journalism Curriculum" was the topic of Vol. 3 (1981). Though _Journalism History_ has also devoted issues to Native American Indian journalism (1979) and to women's history and journalism (1975), these efforts do not so much challenge basic constructions and assumptions of traditional journalism history as attempt to disguise a seriously flawed theoretical structure by giving it a fashionable vocabulary.

10. Christians and Carey advance four standards for qualitative research, including naturalistic observation, contextualization, maximized comparisons, and sensitized concepts. Nowhere, however, do they wrestle with the translation of these rhetorical notions into concrete research procedures. Much, for example, is made of taking "social wholes" into account in interpretation (p. 355), but no effort is made to specify what a social whole is, so that an aspiring researcher can decide if he or she has gotten hold of one. Similarly, the discussion of maximized comparisons never considers whether or under what circumstances particular comparisons are inappropriate and invalid. In its claim to present strategies and standards for "qualitative" research, this article, the only one I am aware of that represents the culturalist contribution to such discussion in communications, is not merely disappointing but theoretically and methodologically inadequate.

11. Classic culturalist preambles include Carey 1975 and Park 1923.

REFERENCES

"American Indians and the Media: Neglect and Stereotype." 1979. *Journalism History* 6 (2).

Bailyn, Bernard. 1960. *Education in the Forming of American Society*. Chapel Hill: University of North Carolina.

Bleyer, Willard Grosvenor. 1927. *Main Currents in the History of American Journalism*. New York: Houghton-Mifflin.

Braudel, Fernand. 1969. *On History*. Trans. Sarah Matthews. Chicago: University of Chicago Press.

Carey, James W. 1974. "The Problem of Journalism History." *Journalism History* 1 (1):3-27.

———. 1975a. "Communication and Culture." *Communication Research* 2:173-91.

———. 1975b. "A Cultural Approach to Communications." *Communication* 2 (1):1-22.

Casey, Ralph D. 1965. "The Scholarship of Frank Luther Mott." *Journalism Quarterly* 42 (1):81.

Christians, Clifford and James W. Carey. 1981. "The Logic and Aims of Qualitative Research." In *Research Methods in Mass Communication*, ed. Guido H. Stempel III and Bruce H. Westley, pp. 342-62. Englewood Cliffs, N.J.: Prentice-Hall.

Clanchy, Michael T. 1979. *From Memory to Written Record: England, 1066-1307*. Cambridge, Mass.: Harvard University Press.

"A Conversation with Edwin Emery." 1980. *Journalism History* 7 (1):20-21.

Czitrom, Daniel J. 1982. *Mass Media and the American Mind: From Morse to McLuhan*. Chapel Hill: University of North Carolina Press.

Darnton, Michael. 1979. *The Business of Enlightenment: A Publishing History of the ENCYCLOPEDIE, 1775-1800*. Cambridge, Mass.: Harvard University Press.

Dickinson, Burrus. 1929. "A German Text on Journalism." *Journalism Quarterly* 6 (2):9-11.

Eisenstein, Elizabeth. 1979. *The Printing Press as an Agent of Change*. 2 Vols. London: Cambridge University Press.

Emery, Edwin and Michael Emery. 1978. *The Press and America; An Interpretative History of the Mass Media*. Englewood Cliffs, N.J.: Prentice-Hall.

Endres, Fred. 1978. "Philosophies, Practices, and Problems in Teaching Journalism History." *Journalism History* 5 (1):2.

Gordon, George N. 1977. *The Communications Revolution: A History of Mass Media in the United States*. New York: Hastings House.

Groth, Otto. 1928. *Ein System der Zeritungskunda*. Vol. 1, pp. 21ff. Mannheim: J. Bernsheimer.

Handlin, Oscar. 1979. *Truth in History*. Cambridge, Mass.: Harvard University Press.

Havelock, E. 1982. *The Literate Revolution in Greece and Its Cultural Consequences*. Princeton, N.J.: Princeton University Press.

Higham, John and Paul K. Conklin, eds. 1979. *New Directions in American Intellectual History*. Baltimore: Johns Hopkins University Press.

Hofstadter, Richard. 1968. *The Progressive Historians: Turner, Beard, and Parrington*. Chicago: University of Chicago Press.

Hymes, Dell. 1967. "The Anthropology of Communication." In *Human Communication Theory*, ed. Frank E. X. Dance. New York: Holt, Rinehart and Winston.

Innis, Harold A. 1950. *Empire and Communications*. New York: Oxford University Press.

———. 1951. *The Bias of Communication*. Toronto: University of Toronto Press.

"Journalism History and Women's Experience: A Problem in Conceptual Change." 1964. *Journalism History* 8 (1).

Lee, Alfred McClung. 1937. *The Daily Newspaper in America*. New York: Macmillan.

Le Roy Ladurie, Emmanuel. 1979. *The Territory of the Historian*. Trans. Ben and Sian Reynolds. Paris: Gallimard.

Marzio, Peter C. 1973. *The Men and Machines of American Journalism: A Pictorial Essay from the Henry R. Luce Hall of News Reporting*. Washington, D.C.: National Museum of History and Technology, Smithsonian Institution.

McKerns, Joseph P. 1977. "The Limits of Progressive Journalism History." *Journalism History* 4 (3):88-92.

Merrill, John C. 1969. *The Elite Press: Great Newspapers of the World*. New York: Pittman.

Mott, Frank Luther. 1962. *American Journalism*. New York: Macmillan.

Nevins, Allan. 1959. "American Journalism and Its Historical Treatment." *Journalism Quarterly* 36 (3):411-22, 519.

"Official Minutes of the 1952 Convention." 1952. *Journalism Quarterly* 29 (3):502.

Park, Robert Ezra. 1923. "The Natural History of the Newspaper." *American Journal of Sociology* 29 (10):80-98.

Parrington, Vernon. 1927. *Main Currents in American Thought*. New York: Harcourt, Brace and World.

Pulitzer, Joseph. 1904. "The College of Journalism." *North American Review* 578 (570):641-79.

Rabb, Theodore K. and Robert I. Rotberg, eds. 1982. *The New History, NJ: The 1980s and Beyond*. Princeton, N.J.: Princeton University Press.

Schudson, Michael. 1978. *A Social History of American Newspapers*. New York: Basic Books.

Stevens, John D. and Hazel Dicken Garcia. 1979. *Communications History*. Beverly Hills, CA: Sage Publications.

Stock, Brian. 1938. *The Implications of Literacy: Written Language and Models of Interpretation in the Eleventh and Twelfth Centuries*. Princeton, N.J.: Princeton University Press.

Stone, Lawrence. 1980. *The Past and the Present*. Boston: Routledge and Kegan Paul.

"Summary of Roundtables at Urbana Convention." 1951. *Journalism Quarterly* 28 (3):547.

"A Symposium: History in the Journalism Curriculum." 1981. *Journalism History* 8 (3-4).

7

WITH THE BENEFIT OF HINDSIGHT
Reflections on Uses and Gratifications Research

Denis McQuail

□—*Uses and gratifications research has had a history of over forty years, and shows continued signs of lively activity, despite a good deal of criticism and some disappointment amongst its own practitioners. This article, written from a position within, or close to, the tradition, expresses some regret at the failure to deal adequately with questions of "culture gaps" and "knowledge gaps." It suggests that the failure lies partly in the dominance of one behavioristic paradigm and suggests an alternative "culturalist" model of the media experience which might help re-orient research to important, but neglected, matters.*

HISTORICAL PERSPECTIVE

THIS TRADITION of research has been the object of a good deal of denigration as well as advocacy. It started life in the early 1940s as a fairly simple and straightforward attempt to learn more about the basis of appeal of popular radio progams and about the connection between the attraction to certain kinds of media content and other features of personality and social circumstances. Happily without the name with which it is now irrevocably saddled, it was one of several lines of advance in the new branch of social science concerned with mass communication. Its origins and underpinnings included: a simple wish to know more about the audience; an awareness of the importance of individual differences in accounting for the audience experience; a still fresh wonderment at the power of popular media to hold and involve their audiences; and an attachment to the case study as an appropriate tool and an aid to psychological modes of explanation.

There was enough work accomplished by the time that Klapper (1960) put together his review of research to allow an overview which still bears reading. There had also been some development of theory and method, as the exploratory case study gave way to the more systematic collection of numerical data and to the testing of hypotheses by statistical methods. The early research was quite diverse, although as it developed, there was some bias towards television and towards the child audience. This may simply reflect the circumstances of the time, when television was becoming

Mr. McQuail is Professor of Mass Communication, University of Amsterdam, Netherlands.

From Denis McQuail, "With the Benefit of Hindsight: Reflections on Uses and Gratifications Research," *Critical Studies in Mass Communication*, Vol. 1, No. 2 (June 1984), pp. 177-193.

established on both sides of the Atlantic and was being perceived as the new threat or promise in the socializing of young children. An additional factor, however, is probably a view of television as a continuous and undifferentiated use of time by children which was more amenable to analysis according to broad categories of type of content than was either book or film. Both film-going and reading had also largely ceded their "social problem" character to the new medium and were looked at almost benignly. By the time television came to be investigated in any large scale way during the 1950s and early 1960s (e.g., Himmelweit et al., 1958; Schramm et al., 1961), the method of "uses and gratifications" research was sufficiently developed for it to be used as an instrument for investigating this large, undifferentiated, allocation of time by children. The appeal of the approach was its potential for differentiating within an otherwise seemingly featureless field of media behavior and providing variables of attention to television, beyond that of sheer amount, which could be related to possible causes of "addiction" or to the consequences of over-indulgence.

It is interesting to recall how broadly defined and diverse this field of research was at least until the early 1960s. It covered: inquiries into the allocation of time to different media; relations between media use and other uses of time; relations between media use and indicators of social adjustment and relationships; perceptions of the functions of different media or content types; and reasons for attending to media. It would be hard to distinguish much that is now placed within the "tradition" from other kinds of media research. The common strand was, nevertheless, a concern with the "function" of media, in its several senses, but especially the question of the kind and the strength of motive for media use and the links between such motives and the rest of experience.

1960 as a Turning Point

The decade of the 1960s has been treated as a watershed in respect of more than one feature of mass communication research and, however exaggerated this picture or distorted by hindsight, there are some reasons for so regarding it. Firstly, it was a time when communication research appeared to "take off" once more, certainly in Europe, as the social sciences became better established and discovered post-war energy and direction. Even in the United States, there seemed to occur a new beginning after the golden age of communication research whose passing was mourned by Berelson (1959). Secondly, there was a coming to terms with the accumulating evidence about media effect or the lack of it. Thirdly, there was the fact of television as a new medium of seemingly immense appeal, if not effect. Fourthly, although later in the decade of the 1960s, there was a growing tendency in the social sciences to react against "positivist" methods and concepts and against functionalism in its several variants. The favored modes of thinking were more "social-critical," interpretative, anti-scientistic, ethnographic, phenomenologistic. The particular turning point for uses and gratifications research seemed to follow the (rather obscure) publication of an important article by Elihu Katz in 1959, which provided a manifesto of a kind and a number of key slogans and terms. Thus:

> ". . . less attention [should be paid] to what media do to people and more to what people do with the media. Such an approach assumes that even the most potent of mass media content cannot ordinarily influence an individual who has no 'use' for it in the social and

psychological context in which he lives. The 'uses' approach assumes that people's values, their interests, their associations, their social roles, are pre-potent and that people selectively 'fashion' what they see and hear to these interests." (Katz, 1959, p. 2)

While the thoughts expressed in this vein, belonging more generally to the "rediscovery of people," were very important for the blossoming of more research on media use (especially in connection with the re-assessment of media effects), the development was running counter to the stream of critical theory and research of the later 1960s.

Revival and Redefinition of the "Uses" Tradition

While early conceptions of the process of media effect had a place for a notion of audience response as a type of independent effect (Klapper had considered media gratifications almost exclusively in this light), researchers now turned to the possibility of using a motive or a satisfaction as an intervening variable in its own right. This was guided in part by the early use of indicators of interest as a relevant way of categorizing an audience (Lazarsfeld et al., 1944), and by the accumulation of evidence that audience choice and reaction were always selective in systematic ways. Thus, one of the innovations in the search for better concepts and methods of inquiry in relation to media effect was to take more account of the kind and strength of motivation of the relevant public. The guiding thought was that effects would be more likely to occur where a corresponding or relevant motive existed on the part of the receiver (e.g., Blumler and McQuail, 1968). In turn, this had a place in the development of theory and research concerning the active or "obstinate" audience (Bauer, 1964) and of interactive, in place of one-way, models of media influence. The rise of television has increased the demand for research into audiences that would go beyond head-counting and reach some more qualitative accounting of the audience and help relate program provision to various audience demands by ways other than pure market forces (Emmett, 1968/69). More "qualitative" audience research could be seen as a "half-way house" between the collection of "ratings" and the ultimate delivery of evidence about the longer-term social effects of the new medium, allowing some provisional evaluation of what might be going on.

The advance and then retreat of positivism and functionalism concerned uses and gratifications research especially during the late 1960s and early 1970s for a number of reasons. Firstly, most of the research involved was inescapably cast in the functionalist mold. The theory and research described by Klapper (1960) already presupposed a distinct functionalist framework in which media use is likely to be interpreted as a means of adjustment to, or reaction in, a system of connected personal relations or a wider social context. Moreover, the concepts and methods typical of the research were essentially individualist, psychologistic and had a strong leaning towards the "variable analysis" which had been an early target for more holistically-minded sociologists (e.g., Blumer, 1956) and historically-minded media theorists (e.g., Smythe, 1954). What came to be viewed, by the early 1970s, as typical of the tradition was a) functionalist in conception; b) individualist in method of data collection; and c) lending itself to multivariate statistical analysis. It embodied the methodological advances of the period with the demonic characteristics which became, increasingly, an object of disdain by the "critically" minded; that is, positivism, scientism, determinism, value-neutrality, and conservatism. There is more to be said of this, but first attention should be given to one additional strand in the complex of problems in which this research tradition has landed itself.

USES AND GRATIFICATIONS AND THE STUDY OF POPULAR CULTURE

Somewhat ironically, the main point of Katz' 1959 article was to suggest that the "uses" approach could help build a bridge to the humanistic tradition of popular culture. One source of the approach had been the New School of Social Research at Columbia University, with a measure of influence from the original Frankfurt School and having a mixture of sociopolitical, psychological and cultural concerns. There were thus historical and circumstantial as well as methodological grounds for Katz' suggestion. However, the various strands mentioned had tended to separate, and elsewhere they had barely come together. In Britain, for instance, the analysis of (mainly written) cultural forms had largely been carried out by academics applying somewhat elitist values mixed with social and political concerns. The influence of Q. D. and F. R. Leavis from the 1930s onward led to a greater (though still somewhat disdainful) attention to the popular arts, which eventually did bloom into a new school of socio-cultural analysis, with Raymond Williams, Richard Hoggart and Stuart Hall as prominent representatives and pioneers. Even so, the separation between the "culturalist" examining "texts" and the social scientist looking at audiences tended to persist. Again, there is another potentially long story and it is sufficient for now to say that Katz' call for a rapprochement based on the typical methods of "uses" research and of the analysis of texts and cultural forms, within a broadly humanistic program did seem to have some potential. It seemed, in particular, to offer an exit from the sterile debate between critics of mass culture and its defenders (cf. Rosenberg & White, 1957) and allow in evidence some representation of the voice of the "consumer." The new research approach would be a way of giving people a voice in cultural matters much as surveys had done in relation to political and social issues. It might even offer a way of testing the proposition of some sociologists and critics of mass culture that mass media served to perpetuate capitalist society. An early version of this view is to be found in the work of a pioneer in "uses" research: "Psychologically the effect (of escapist fiction) is distraction from somewhat habitual anxieties. Sociologically, the effect is to reduce the violence of assault on the existing social structure by cooling the discontent of underprivileged groups. The reading of anything at all which takes the reader's mind from his [sic] troubles has this cooling effect" (Waples et al., 1940, p. 123). In a similar vein, Irving Howe later described mass culture as filling the leisure hours of industrial workers, providing "relief from work monotony without making the return to work too unbearable" (Howe, 1957, p. 497).

It can be said at this point that Katz' call for a bridge-building was never really taken up, if it was ever heard and taken seriously. Certainly it did not lead to any notable bridge-building and was pushed aside by the greater attraction, to social scientists, of seemingly powerful data analysis techniques and, to humanists, of new literary-critical theory and method. Literary-cultural concerns were led even further away from positivism and functionalism, which came to be associated with manipulation and conservatism. Thus, the ground which had seemed so fertile for the development of humanistic "uses" research proved rather sour. The two main strands of relevant work were even further apart. The reasons are well analysed from the "cultural" side by Carey and Kreiling (1974), but ten years after their analysis and suggestion for an accommodation, there seems little progress to report.

What Went On?

The substance of the post-1960s renascence of uses and gratifications research, which still continues, can only be summarily characterized by a few key references. The account given here cannot pretend to be either full or unbiased, given the participation of the present writer in some of the work. However, an essential aspect of the tradition is its diversity and lack of coordination or of a common program. The wide currency and convenience of the shorthand label "uses and gratifications," the targeting of fairly coherent critiques by single authors, the use of the term "functionalist" as a blanket description, have all tended to exaggerate the degree to which the approach shares an identity and common philosophical and scientific basis. What we now see as evidence is a series of projects, which can be classified under a few broad headings. Firstly, there have been many studies of children and media, especially: Schramm (1961); Riley and Riley (1951); Maccoby (1954); Himmelweit and Oppenheim (1958); Furu (1971); Noble (1975); Greenberg (1974); various, mainly European, researches collected by Brown (1976); ongoing work in Sweden (e.g., Hedinsson, 1981; and Johnsson-Smaragdi, 1983). Secondly, there has been a good deal of attention to political communication and media gratifications. This is well-reviewed by McLeod and Becker (1981) and may be thought to begin with the work of Blumler and McQuail (1968). Thirdly, there have been numerous studies of particular forms and the basis of their appeal, including: McQuail et al. (1972); Mendelsohn (1964); Levy (1978); Tannenbaum (1980); and many others. Fourthly, there have been studies of media and wider social integration, the most significant being that of Katz et al. (1973). Fifthly, there have been studies of information-seeking and of the more cognitive aspects of media use: Atkin (1972); Kline et al. (1974); and Kippax and Murray (1980). Finally, we can distinguish a set of contributions to the development of theory and the formation of models. Some of these are to be found in Blumler and Katz (1974), and more recent examples include Blumler (1979) and Windahl (1981).

Criticism

The diversity mentioned earlier refers to theory, methods, aims and the kinds of media content studied. No common model, set of procedures or purposes informs the tradition, despite the attempts of Katz, Blumler and Gurevitch (1974) to give some shape to the assumptions that have guided "uses" research and to assess the state of the art. Ten years after that rendering of account there is probably no greater unity and there is some reason to look back on the direction taken by the revived tradition. Criticism of the approach has been lucidly and not infrequently expressed, notably by Chaney (1972), Elliott (1974), Carey and Kreiling (1974) and Swanson (1977). There have been three main lines of attack or sources of dislike: one relating to its theoretical underpinnings and associated method; another to its social and political implications; a third to its model of man and its way of handling cultural phenomena. The main theoretical charge is that it is essentially lacking in theory and such theory that it has is inadequate and confused. The common element of many studies seems to be a certain way of devising lists of verbal statements about media or media content which are labelled, variously, as "use," "gratification," "motivation," "satisfaction," "need," etc., implying distinctions and a conceptual status which cannot be validated. If there is a theory, according to critics, it is pure tautology moving from measured satisfaction back to an imputed need or forwards from a need to a use and gratification, with no independent way of measuring need, or even any coherent theory of needs, and certainly no way of determining the direction of influence between measured "need" and media use. The lack of theory is said to lead to a misuse of empirical method, to the extent that verbal statements or aggregate statistics derived from responses to verbal statements are reified to become new constructs supposed to stand for the gratifications offered by media content. At times these new constructs are seen merely as reflections of social class or other background variables and when used instead of the latter, they are likely to by mystifying and distorting.

The social and political objections advanced from a perspective of critical theory rest mainly on the view that the incurable functionalism of the method ties the researcher to a conservative model of a social system in which all adjustment is for the best and which ends up portraying all kinds of media content as helping individuals to adjust. The method, as typically practiced, can only increase the chances of manipulation, since it adduces psychological and social reasons why people like what they get which can easily be turned to support the view that people get what they like, thus blunting any possible critical edge in the application of new knowledge which comes from the research.

The "cultural" objection has several grounds but, most centrally, exception is taken to the utilitarianism and behaviorism of the whole underlying model, in which cultural "behavior" is treated as both determined and instrumental and rarely as "consummatory" or an end in itself. The version of the meaning of cultural consumption as derived from statements or recognitions of statements by individuals is regarded as a poor substitute for an overall view in which the ritual nature of culture is recognized along with its great diversity of meanings. There is also a wider reluctance to accept a value-free and mathematical treatment of matters which should be seen as evaluative and qualitative and not amendable to sociological categorization. From a cultural point of view there seems to be no recognition, or use, of any kind of aesthetic theory.

While there has been no systematic demolition job on the results of uses and gratifications research, as distinct from its theory (except, selectively, by Elliott, 1974), there has been disappointment over the yield of findings which might add up to an explanation of media choice or which clearly show the part played by media in the process of effects. There is, seemingly, very little predictive power in any current index of motivation, in respect of effects. In his early review of the field, Klapper (1960) had already pointed to inconsistencies and low explanatory power in the first batch of studies. For the most part, the evidence we have still comprises certain consistent patterns linking one "gratification" with another and some gratifications with either social background variables or media use, or both. Perhaps this line of criticism is not taken very far because of its rather general application to mass communication research.

THE CENTRAL POINT OF THE TRADITION

The point of summarizing criticism is not to offer a new defense and assessment, but to consider the possibilities for future work, taking account of objections which deserve to be taken seriously. Before doing so, it is worth re-asserting the importance of the broad questions with which this tradition has always been concerned. It derives from a conviction that what is central for mass communication is not message-making or sending and not even the messages themselves, but the choice, reception and manner of response of the audience. In turn, an attention to the audience requires a sensitivity to the full range of meanings of that experience and thus to its diversity and fragility. It also means accepting that making, sending, choosing and responding to media messages involves a set of understandings which are, up to a point, shared by "makers" and "receivers" and which are usually both complex and unspoken. Thus diversity, ambiguity and even some mystery are to be expected on the "side" of production and content as well as on the "side" of reception. This is to underline the impossibility of artificially separating the question of audience experience from the sources of that experience in content itself. Nor can it be separated from aspects of the context in which the experience takes place—where, with whom, under what circumstances, through which channel. It may appear from these remarks that a true study of the media experience has to be about everything—society, culture, human behavior—and, for this reason, it is unlikely to be theoretically satisfying to everyone. Underlying the controversies of this kind of research is a pull in several directions: towards society as "first cause;" towards cultural content as the true determinant of response; or towards explanations to be found in individual behavior and personality.

It is worth being reminded of some of the relative success of the research tradition as it has been practiced, partly to redress the balance, partly to account for the appeal of the line of work. One apparent success has been to express, in differentiated verbal formulas, which are widely recognizable and available for consistent use, key elements of the image or dominant associations of specific media cultural products and kinds of media experience. The verbal expressions show some stability across cultures and over time and yet the methods used are sensitive enough to record differences in the perception of similar kinds of material. Information of this kind is often open to interpretation in terms of differences of plot, style or format and it does seem that cultural analysis and audience analysis can be mutually enriching. The research has also identified and given names and definitions to a set of "functions" of media-cultural experience which help to make sense of the innumerable details of audience reaction. These possibilities lend themselves, further, to making comparisons between media and between different audience groups which would otherwise be impossible.

We have, thus, the basic terms for discourse about media content and experience which have been discovered, drawn together and ordered by empirical procedures, rather than invented or put forward as concepts. This means that some form of three-way exchange is possible between the makers of culture, the audience and social scientists. This may be more a potential than an actuality, but the existence of something like a common terminology has been demonstrated (Himmelweit et al., 1980) and it is a necessary precondition for talking sensibly about the audience experience. Without this accomplishment, it would be difficult to approach the central issue of whether content "produces particular values and patterns of behavior amongst its devotees or do its devotees become devotees because of the values and behavioral tendencies they already possess" (Klapper, 1960, p. 190).

While the achievement in respect of explanation and interrelation of different kinds of evidence about people and their media use has been modest, it is not wholly lacking. There are too many, albeit scattered, indications of clarifying or meaningful associations between expectations from, and ideas about, media and other relevant indications of choice to doubt that approaches to media, as expressed in the terms developed by this tradition (and there is really no alternative source except introspection and invention) are not independently influential. In other words, on some occasions at least, prior experience, behavior, tendencies and values shape attention and response, and it would be untenable to claim otherwise and unreasonable to claim total agnosticism. Uses and gratifications research has added to the concepts and instruments of research a valid status. Thus, *something* can usually be identified as standing for a differentiated view of content and experience of its reception which is not simply the idiosyncratic outlook of one individual, nor simply a secondary expression of a personality trait, or a surrogate for a location in an organization or a society, or merely a description of the item of content itself. It is, or can be, independent in the statistical sense of being open to use as a separate variable with some explanatory power of its own. It is also independent, in the semantic sense, in being conceptually different from these other similar or related things which have been named. The problem, of course, lies not with this claim itself (although it is not uncontested), but with what to do if one accepts it, since it is almost impossible to find an acceptable name for this *thing*. There are too many names for it and the choice of any one presupposes a theoretical schema which can take the researcher into deep waters. Uses and gratifications researchers have found something by empirical investigation, they know some of its properties and uses, but they do not really know what it is. If this *is* the case, it gives some support to criticism of the approach as the poorer for its lack of theoretical foundation.

A Readjustment of View

There are several ways of coming to terms with the problems encountered in the progress of this research tradition, if one accepts the continued value of the enterprise, and it would be out of keeping with the spirit of this tradition to present any single blueprint for survival and prosperity. There are those who would not accept that serious problems have been encountered, beyond what is the normal result of academic competition, fundamental theoretical divergences and the inevitably slow growth of scientific knowledge. To the present writer, however, it seems that there are grounds for disappointment in the history of the tradition to date and that the research in the main direction being currently taken is not very likely to deliver all of its early promise. This refers especially to the understanding of cultural experience and to the explanation of variations which might be of relevance for social-cultural policy. Thus, one of the original aims of the research was to shed light on both "cultural-gaps" and "knowledge-gaps" in society and suggest ways of reducing them. This may no longer seem a very urgent goal in an era of media abundance, media deregulation and cultural relativism, but the facts of communication inequality are barely changed and the theoretical interest of the associated questions remains high. By contrast, although the fruits may still lie just beyond our grasp, the work that continues to be done does seem to have a potential for clarifying the process of media effect.

The tradition of uses and gratifications research has thus seemed to reveal an inescapable bias: despite its diversity it tends towards what can most conveniently be called a "dominant paradigm," however overworked and tendentious that phrase has become. This paradigm or model is no secret and is to be read from the "state of the art" assessment by Katz et al. (1974). It involves: a view of media consumption as a logical and sequential process of need-satisfaction and tension-reduction, relating the social-psychological environment to media use; a set of assumptions about the audience (notably its activity, rationality, resistance to influence, capacity for reporting about itself); and a recommendation to value-relativism on the part of the investigator. This basic paradigm has organized much work and continues to lend itself to further elaboration and application in research (Palmgreen, in press). It is in fact more flexible than it sounds and can provide a powerful framework for looking at media in a wider social and cultural context. Yet it is also, not inconsistently, imperialistic, perhaps too powerful and tending to develop Moloch-like characteristics in the sacrifices which it demands from its devotees. These sacrifices are mostly in the form of a narrowing of vision and a submission to the ever-growing machine of data-collection and elaborate statistical analysis of numbers formed from much less substantial qualities.

While admitting an element of exaggeration in this picture, it does not seem very useful now to worry about the main component parts of the paradigm, although each merits critical attention, but better to consider whether there is really any alternative. In passing, it may be remarked that the components of the framework most in need of critical attention have to do with the "activity" assumption and the concept of "use," "gratification," "function," etc. There are many questions about the meaning of "activity," about the degree of activity that has to be present to sustain the program of empirical work, about how much of whatever kind of activity really exists in given audience situations. The dispute about the nature of the central concept has already been discussed, without resolution, but it does appear that the main choice lies between three (not mutually exclusive) possibilities: a concept of need related to the current circumstances of the audience member; a description or "image" of the key features of media content or the media experience; a satisfaction or gratification obtained or expected. Each of these has a different conceptual status, whichever word is chosen, and each has some place in the work typical of the research tradition. The suggestion which follows, although it involves a radical departure from the dominant model, would not, if adopted, render all work until now and all current debate redundant. It would, however, introduce some new concepts and change the balance of discussion. It would also move the model- (or road) building to a new site.

AN ALTERNATIVE BY-WAY

If there is a broad highway in the development of uses and gratifications research, it can be characterized by an elaboration of models, by its statistical methods and its theory for relating social and cultural experience "forward" to media use and its later consequences and back again to experience. I worked on some sections of the road and travelled some way along it, by adapting a "uses" approach to the study of political campaign effects and by trying to establish connections between social background and media use (McQuail et al., 1972). The suggestion which follows is for a return to the bridge-building between the social sciences and the humanities, urged by Katz, but never really achieved. Broadly, it may be described as involving a "cultural-empirical" approach, using some of the concepts and advances of "main-road" work, but with some new concepts added and all within a new framework or model. A good many of the new elements are untried and the proposal has, consequently, a very tentative character.

The uses and gratifications "main road" approach has tended towards utilitarianism and determinism, treating "consumption" of media content of all kinds as having a place or purpose in larger schemes of individual need-gratification. A cultural approach would be much more likely to consider "consumption" of culture as an end in itself (the "consummatory" view urged by Carey and Kreiling, 1974) and, in any case, requiring an understanding in its own right and not only as a stage in some behavioral process of adjustment. Attention should thus be concentrated on the making of choices and on the meaningful encounter with cultural products. Towards this end, a distinction will have to be made between the more "cultural" kinds of content and the more informational kinds—between affectual/imaginative and cognitive spheres. This kind of distinction is often made for practical reasons, but most uses and gratifications theory adopts fundamentally the same model for all kinds of imputed need and media use, partly because different kinds of content can serve the same function, partly because the underlying process is held to be the same.

The first model suggested is intended to deal with the "non-cognitive" area, with audience use of fiction, amusement, drama or spectacle, which appeals to the imagination or seeks to provide various kinds of pleasure at the time of use, and has no consciously intended application afterwards in the rest of life. It seems advisable to take some account of the built-in purpose of media content, as well as the purpose formed by the audience member, although this practice has seemed to fall victim to an exclusive policy of "taking the audience point of view." Moreover, if cultural experience is to be considered according to its functionality or utility in a more or less behavioral model, it is reasonable to suppose that some kinds of media fare will be less amenable to this kind of treatment than some others. Indeed, it may be necessary to treat some media experiences not only neutrally in this respect, but as if according to a *counter-behavioral* stance. This is an important feature of the alternative conceptual framework sketched below.

The key proposition (it is no more) on which the following rests is that cultural experience (what happens at the time of attention to media) be treated as a generalized process of involvement, arousal or "capture." To the observer there is little to see except varying degrees of rapt attention and to the participant, the most salient aspect of the experience is an awareness of "being lost" in something, "involved," "carried away," "caught up," "taken out of oneself," or simply "excited" or "thrilled." There are conventional variations of expression for this according to the kind of content—whether comedy, tragedy, adventure, romance, etc.—but there seems to be an underlying similarity of what is meant by these kinds of expression and what is experienced in terms of mental and physiological reaction. The precise nature of this generalized sensation lies outside the scope of this essay and probably of the social sciences, but if it is so pronounced and familiar a phenomenon as presupposed here, we should not be denied the chance to include it in a conception of media use. Although our primary interest is in the giving of meaning to this fundamental general experience, we do need some concept of what it is. The evidence of its existence is mostly of a commonsense kind, but there is research and theory to support the contention. It seems that a measureable factor of general "arousal" in relation to television, at least, does exist and correlates with motivation to continue attending to media (Tannenbaum and Zillman, 1975; Tannenbaum, 1980). There is no reason why this should not also be true of other media. It also seems from studies of audience evaluations of media content that there is a general factor of liking, which is closely connected with the attribution of a quality of being "absorbing," involving or exciting (Himmelweit et al., 1980). The rather scarce work that has been done in this area does at least seem to justify the proposition advanced above.

To go beyond the fact of this sense experience and relate it with its typical content, we can propose that the essence of this general sensation is to *free* the spectator/reader/listener mentally from the immediate constraints and/or dullness of daily life and enable him or her to *enter into* new experiences (vicariously) which would not otherwise be available (except by use of the imagination). The media-cultural experience is thus potentially a powerful aid to, or substitute for, the imagination, enabling a person to enjoy a variety of emotional experiences and mental states—involving joy, anger, sexual excitement, sadness, curiosity, etc. We can identify with people and share the illusion of living in interesting situations or observe it all, with inside knowledge, from a privileged position and one of physical and emotional security. Many of these processes have been described or presumed by writers about culture since the time of Aristotle, although rather little has found its way into the models of uses and gratifications research. There is no need or space here to enlarge on this tradition, except to emphasize the most vital point that whenever we are "caught up" or "captured" in a drama, story or spectacle, we are, by definition, also cut off, not only from the constraints of the moment and a less interesting reality, but also from our own past and future. Consequently, there is likely to be a positive *dissociation* from social circumstances and future consequences. This is often part of the conscious purpose and pleasure of "exposure" to cultural experience—we do want to be somewhere or someone else, with no thought for the future. Insofar as this is true, it does undermine a major premise of the mainstream uses and gratifications model, which holds that media use is often a direct reflection of pre-media experience and in some underlying way is structured as to its amount and kind by the rest of experience. The implication of what has just been written is that, if there is a relation, it may well be of a contradictory or quite unpredictable kind. In the view advanced here, the essence of audience "activity" is a process of self-liberation, however temporary, from everday self and surroundings. Consequently, there is no obvious way to make causal connections between media experience and behavior.

There are some important practical consequences of all this for a revision of the dominant model of the process of mass media use. First of all, as noted above, we should treat affective/imaginative content separately from cognitive content, since the arousal-involvement factor is either less relevant or of a different kind. In Himmelweit's (1980) study of audience judgement, the most "highly rated" of the television programs assessed was "The News" and "absorbing" was one of the terms applied to it "very much," but it was only one of five "stylistic attributes" applied, rather than a single main criterion, as it was for other popular fictional programs. Secondly, the generalized "arousal" factor should not be included in the lists of gratifications or satisfactions and should be treated on another level, as a prior condition of attention or for what it is, as a general factor, which finds several more specific forms of expression, according to the individual or the content concerned.

Further elaboration is needed in order to cope with these "second order" concepts. In a "culturalist" model it is appropriate to use the concept of culture itself and it can be used in two senses. Firstly, "culture" in the collective sense as the body of objects and practices which pertains to, or is available to, a given group or public, or subset of society. It is in this sense, for instance, that the term "taste culture" (Lewis, 1980) has been used—to indicate a more or less structured set of preferences. A member of the media public can only choose from, or have ideas about, what is available physically or is accessible and familiar by reason of a collective situation and provision. Cultural differentiation is an important element in the model of media use because it is a directing or constraining factor in choice. It may have much to do with class and social position, but more generally it has to do with closeness and familiarity, more so probably than with individual competence, skill, or any "need" for culture.

The second relevant sense of culture is that of individual "taste." Again an old term, disregarded in the "dominant paradigm," perhaps because of its vagueness and its connotation (and denotation) of a subjective state of mind and of the making of value judgements. But it is probably no more imprecise than other functionalist terms and subjective choice and assessment is central to the old as well as the proposed new model. Cultural taste provides the key to selection amongst what is offered by the (collective) culture and is essentially arbitrary and unaccountable. If it were accountable it would explain the differences of preference for genres, themes and authors. It is evidently not entirely random, but the regularities that do appear, such as gender differences in choice as between, for example, "adventure" and "romance" are really an aspect of collective cultural distribution which makes the former less accessible to girls from an early age and steers them towards "romance." While "taste" relates to choice of content and habits of use, it is usual and perhaps only possible to describe it in terms of content. Media content (and most cultural production) is constructed according to a knowledge of tastes and likely preferences, and has some built-in appeal to a sector of the potential public.

There is one further element in the scheme of things which provides a bridge to the dominant behavioral model described above, helping to characterize and differentiate the vicarious experience and emotion offered by culture more finely and objectively than does the concept of taste. This element is *content.* Thus, affective media content can be differentiated according to the specific experience offered and gained. In practice, such gratifications, assuming the experience to be wanted, are hard to identify except by general types of content—much as in taste specification of basic themes, plots and genres. A given genre or type of content normally promises and gives a set of experiences of a predictable kind, which might have to do with curiosity about human situations, or laughter, or sex, or tension and release, or mystery, or wonder and so on. These (and others) are the satisfactions which people claim to expect or receive from the media and which are to be found both in descriptions of cultural (media) content and in lists and typologies of media gratifications. There is a necessary place in a culturalist model for the reflection on (and anticipation of) emotions, thoughts and sensations evoked by the cultural experience. There remains, nevertheless, a difficulty, familiar to uses and gratifications researchers, of distinguishing between the general and the particular, and between expectation and satisfaction.

TWO MODELS

Little more need be said before setting out the main terms and their sequence of a model of cultural (affective) experience (Figure 1). One may point out that "general expectation of involvement," "taste" and "satisfaction" can easily be associated with different things and thus be used as orientations towards, or descriptions of, several different things: a theme; a genre or type; a medium or channel; an actual media experience (specific film, television viewing, reading a particular book); an author or performer; a particular work. The situation in this respect is not very different from the case of conventional uses and gratifications research, where "gratifications," etc., are used to differentiate media and types of content. In both the cultural and the "uses" model, we can also use the same terms to characterize people. This should not lead to confusion, since quite different statements are involved. For example, it is quite different to say that someone has a taste for thrillers than to

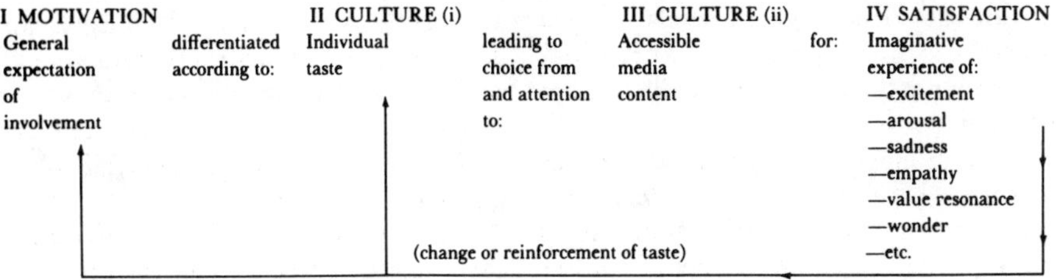

FIGURE 1
A CULTURAL MODEL

say that someone's "need for escape" is met by thrillers. In general, the lexicon of terms in a developed cultural model would depend on and say more about the specific content than about people and circumstances. Finally, the model, as drawn in Figure 1, is also sequential, since the general inclination to seek cultural experience precedes actual involvement, as does the pattern of taste. Actual media experience does lead to some awareness and reflection on what has happened, with some consequences for future cultural choice, and other more immediate consequences depending on the specific content and the degree of satisfaction obtained.

It is neither possible, nor really necessary, to give a full account of what an equivalent cognitive model (Figure 2) would look like, because of limitations of space and time and because such a model would not deviate too sharply from relevant components in the dominant paradigm. However, there are important differences of conceptualization from the cultural model. Firstly, the arousal/involvement factor would be replaced by a general factor of interest/curiosity. In turn, this would divide according to a set of interests, which are equivalent to cultural tastes and, in a similar way, a mixture of the arbitrary and the socially or culturally given in a particular environment. Thus some people are interested in football for reasons which are mysterious to some others, yet there are regularities in the aggregate distribution of interest in football, which show it to go with some other characteristics. As with "culture," information is variably available or accessible according to social position. Finally, there are specific gains or satisfactions which can be accounted for, much as in the uses and gratifications tradition, as uses and benefits, such as: helping in decisions and choices; opinion formation; providing subjects for conversation, etc. On the whole, one would expect more certainty of relationship between prior experience, information choices and satisfactions obtained. The key difference from the previous model (and at the same time, the factor which links this model to the dominant paradigm) is the absence of that *disconnection* between ordinary life and the moment or cultural experience. The motivating factor is one of connection and extension rather than disconnection.

CONCLUSION

It is early to assess the prospects for such an approach, or its implications for

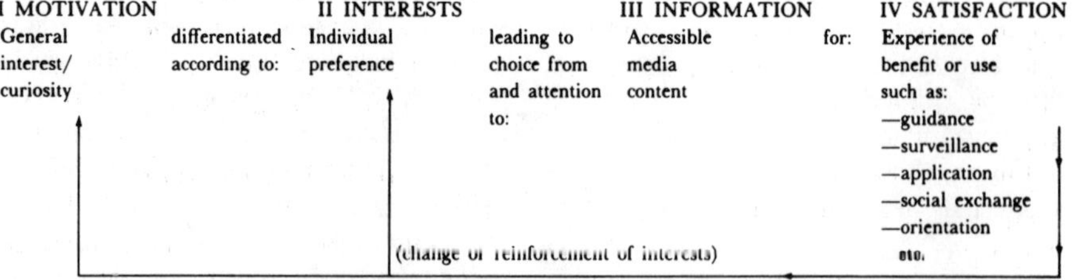

FIGURE 2
A COGNITIVE MODEL

the research tradition as a whole. It needs itself to be tried out empirically, either in the collection of new data, or in reworking existing data, since there could be a considerable overlap between the kind of work generated by such a cultural model and what has been done already. At some points it clearly challenges the established tradition, at others it might be supportive or supplementary. The most fundamental challenge is to the notion of a direct causal connection between background circumstances, cultural choice and the "effects" of cultural experience. In effect, this model resurrects the notion of "escape" as a dominant motive for media use and emphasizes discontinuities, although the "escape" may well be subjectively perceived in a positive light—thus as escape into a better world (of the imagination). An example of the potential complexities of this model, which might baffle practitioners of causal analysis is offered by Zillman's (1980) suggestion that, contrary to the thesis of the school of "cultivation analysis" (e.g., Gerbner et al., 1976), it is not "scary" television which leads to a scary world view, but the experience of actual worry and anxiety which leads people to watch "scary" television precisely because it fictionally heightens fear and tension and then releases it. It is the second part of this process which, according to Zillman, might be sought out for its positive benefits. This is a simple enough proposition, but the chance of testing it by content analysis and surveys is virtually zero.

On the positive side, the framework suggested here may, by reviving the notion of "taste" and the value judgements which go with that concept, add to the refinement and accuracy of description of content and improve our understanding of individual differences. It can also help to increase sensitivity to essentially "cultural" attributes. The notion of "taste" (and, on the cognitive side, "interests") may also help to clarify the nature of the central concept of the tradition (use, gratification, motive, etc.) which has proved virtually impossible to pin down. On the one hand, it offers one other possible meaning, perhaps only compounding the problem by so doing. On the other hand, the separation of a generalized "drive" or "set," as motivational factor, from its specific manifestations in taste, choice and satisfaction may open the way to a more consistent treatment (or multiple treatment) of the second order concept.

In the end, one has to make a rather important choice as to whether one really wants to know most about *culture* (its origin, production, meaning and use), or about *people* in audiences (their identity, attributes, reasons for being there), or about individual *behavior* (kind, frequency, causes, consequences, interconnections), or about *society* and the working of the media within it. It is unlikely that any one paradigm or model can serve all four purposes and the one sketched here has most relevance for the first. The main thrust of the uses and gratifications tradition has been towards the construction of a major highway which serves to link all four purposes in one investigative enterprise. Real highways do facilitate very long, fast, journeys by large vehicles (research teams), but they also change the landscape they traverse, have restricted views and stimulate travel for its own sake or that of the vehicle. By comparison, the byway mapped out for reaching one rather limited goal of knowledge might be slow and winding, but should enable one to see more on the way and keep one generally in closer contact with nature. □

REFERENCES

Atkin, C. K. (1972). Anticipated communication and mass-mediated information seeking. *Public Opinion Quarterly, 36,* 188–199.

Bauer, R. A. (1964). The obstinate audience. *American Psychologist, 19,* 319–328.

Berelson, B. (1959). The state of communication research. *Public Opinion Quarterly, 23,* 1–6.

Blumer, H. (1956). Sociological analysis and the "variable". *American Sociological Review, 21,* 683–690.

Blumler, J. G. (1979). The role of theory in uses and gratifications studies. *Communication Research, 6,* 9–36.

Blumler, J. G., & Katz, E. (Eds.). (1974). *The uses of mass communications.* London and Beverly Hills: Sage.

Blumler, J. G., & McQuail, D. (1968). *Television in politics.* London: Faber.

Brown, J. R. (Ed.). (1976). *Children and television.* London: Collier Macmillan.

Carey, J. W., & Kreiling, A. L. (1974). Popular culture and uses and gratifications. In J. G. Blumler & E. Katz. (Eds.), *The uses of mass communication* (pp. 225–248). London and Beverly Hills: Sage.

Chaney, D. (1972). *Processes of mass communication.* London: Macmillan.

Elliott, P. (1974). Uses and gratifications research: A critique and a sociological alternative. In J. G. Blumler & E. Katz. (Eds.), *The uses of mass communication* (pp. 249–268). London and Beverly Hills: Sage.

Emmett, B. (1968/69). A new role for research in broadcasting. *Public Opinion Quarterly, 32,* 654–665.

Furu, T. (1971). *The functions of television for children and adolescents.* Tokyo: Sophia University.

Gerbner, G., & Gross, L. (1976). Living with television: The violence profile. *Journal of Communication, 26,* 2, 173–199.

Greenberg, B. G. (1976). Gratifications of television viewing and their correlates for British children. In J. G. Blumler & E. Katz. (Eds.). *The uses of mass communication* (pp. 71–92). London and Beverly Hills: Sage.

Hedinsson, E. (1981). *Television, family and society.* Stockholm: Almquist & Wiksel.

Himmelweit, H. T., Oppenheim, A. N., & Vince, P. (1958). *Television and the child.* London: Oxford University Press.

Himmelweit, H. T., Swift, B., & Jaeger, M. E. (1980). The audience as critic: A conceptual analysis of television entertainment. In P. H. Tannenbaum. (Ed.), *The entertainment functions of television.* (pp. 67–97). Hillsdale, NJ: LEA.

Howe, I. (1957). Notes on mass culture. In M. Rosenberg & D. M. White. (Eds.), *Mass culture: The popular arts in America* (pp. 496–503). New York: Free Press.

Johnsson-Smaragdi, U. (1983). *TV use and social interaction in adolescence.* Stockholm: Almquist & Wiksel.

Katz, E. (1959). Mass communication research and the study of culture. *Studies in Public Communication, 2,* 1–6.

Katz, E., Blumler, J. G., & Gurevitch, M. (1974). Utilization of mass communication by the individual. In J. G. Blumler & E. Katz. (Eds.), *The uses of mass communications* (pp. 19–32). London and Beverly Hills: Sage.

Katz, E., Gurevitch, M., & Haas, H. (1973). On the use of mass media for important things. *American Sociological Review, 38,* 164–181.

Klapper, J. T. (1960). *The effects of mass communication.* Glencoe: Free Press.

Kippax, S., & Murray, J. P. (1980). Using the mass media: Need gratification and perceived utility. *Communication Research, 7,* 335–360.

Kline, G., Miller, P. V., & Morrison, A. J. (1974). Adolescents and family planning information. In J. G. Blumler & E. Katz. (Eds.), *The uses of mass communications* (pp. 113–136) London and Beverly Hills: Sage.

Lazarsfeld, P. F., Berelson, B., & Gaudet, H. (1944). *The people's choice.* New York: Duell, Sloan & Pearce.

Levy, M. R. (1978). The audience experience with television news. *Journalism Monographs, 55.*

Lewis, G. H. (1980). Taste cultures and their composition. In E. Katz & T. Szescko. (Eds.), *Mass media and social change* (pp. 201–207). Beverly Hills and London: Sage.

McLeod, J., & Becker, L. B. (1981). The uses and gratifications approach. In D. Nimmo & R. R. Saunders. (Ed.), *Handbook of political communication* (pp. 67–100). Beverly Hills and London: Sage.

McQuail, D., Blumler, J. G., & Brown, J. R. (1972). The television audience: A revised perspective. In D. McQuail. (Ed.), *Sociology of mass communications* (pp. 135–165). Harmondsworth: Penguin.

Maccoby, E. (1954). Why do children watch television? *Public Opinion Quarterly, 18,* 239–244.

Mendelsohn, H. (1964). Listening to radio. In L. A. Dexter & D. M. White. (Eds.), *People, society and mass communications* (pp. 239–269). Glencoe: Free Press.

Noble, G. (1975). *Children in front of the small screen.* London: Constable.

Palmgreen, P. (in press). The uses and gratifications approach: A theoretical perspective. In R. N. Bostrom. (Ed.), *Communication Yearbook 8.*

Rosenberg, B., & White, D. M. (Eds.). (1957). *Mass culture.* Glencoe: Free Press.

Riley, M. W., & Riley, J. W. (1951). A sociological approach to communications research. *Public Opinion Quarterly, 15,* 444–460.

Schramm, W., Lyle, J., & Parker, E. B. (1961). *Television in the lives of our children.* Stanford: Stanford University Press.

Smythe, D. W. (1954). Some observations on communication theory. *Audiovisual Communciation Review, 12,* 24–37.

Swanson, D. L. (1977). The uses and misuses of uses and gratifications. *Human Communication Research, 3,* 214–221.

Tannenbaum, P. H., & Zillman, D. (1975). Emotional arousal in the facilitation of aggression through communication. In L. Berkowitz (Ed.). *Advances in experimental social psychology* (Vol. 8, pp. 149–192). New York: Academic Press.

Tannenbaum, P. H. (1980). *The entertainment functions of television.* Hillsdale, NJ: LEA.

Waples, D., Berelson, B., & Bradshaw, F. R. (1940). *What reading does to people.* Chicago: University of Chicago Press.

Windahl, S. (1981). Uses and gratifications at the crossroads. In G. C. Wilhoit & H. de Bock (Eds.), *Mass communication review yearbook* (pp. 174–185). Beverly Hills: Sage.

Zillman, D. (1980). The anatomy of suspense. In P. H. Tannenbaum (Ed.), *The entertainment functions of television* (pp. 133–163). Hillsdale, NJ: LEA.

8

THE IMPLICIT ASSUMPTIONS OF TELEVISION RESEARCH
An Analysis of the 1982 NIMH Report on *Television and Behavior*

Thomas D. Cook, Deborah A. Kendzierski, and Stephen V. Thomas

IN 1969, Senator John Pastore called on the surgeon-general to organize a research effort designed to discover whether television violence increases aggressiveness in children. The surgeon-general appointed a Scientific Advisory Committee that commissioned research on the topic and in 1972 issued a report concluding that television violence does indeed cause aggression, at least in some children. In 1979, some researchers suggested to the surgeon-general that it would be useful to

---

Abstract The authors analyze some of the assumptions underlying most current research on television. They emphasize the dependence on (1) an individual rather than an institutional level of analysis; (2) a model of research utilization that pays little explicit attention to where sources of leverage lie for changes in programming; (3) extremely simple models of the selection processes associated with different levels of television viewing; and (4) uncritical appraisals of the consequences of effects that many would call small or modest. These issues are illustrated by a general discussion of the NIMH report on *Television and Behavior* and specific discussion of "mainstreaming" and the effects of television violence.

In 1972, POQ's editors invited Leo Bogart to prepare an extended review article of the Surgeon-General's Study of Television and Social Behavior (POQ 36:491–521). When the 10-year follow-up study was released by NIMH in 1982, the editors asked Thomas D. Cook, a distinguished psychologist noted for his research on television, to perform the same function.

Thomas D. Cook is Professor of Psychology and Urban Affairs, Deborah A. Kendzierski is a Postdoctoral Fellow in Social Psychology, and Stephen R. Thomas is completing his Ph.D. in Mathematics, all at Northwestern University. An earlier version of this paper was prepared for the Committee on Research and Law Enforcement and the Administration of Justice of the National Research Council of the National Academy of Sciences, whose financial help is gratefully acknowledged. Thanks are due to George Comstock, Ronald Milavsky, and Rowell Huesmann for providing the authors with unpublished materials, and to Fay L. Cook, Leonard Eron, George Gerbner, Ronald Kessler, Ronald Milavsky, Horst Stipp, and David Pearl for comments on a prior draft. Special thanks are also due to Eric Rein Muchnik, whose Bar Mitzvah commentary on Esau and Jacob made it all possible.

From Thomas D. Cook, Deborah A. Kendzierski, and Stephen V. Thomas, "The Implicit Assumptions of Television Research: An Analysis of the 1982 NIMH Report on *Television and Behavior*," *Public Opinion Quarterly*, Vol. 47, No. 2 (Summer 1983), pp. 161-201.

assess the newer literature. According to the foreword to *Television and Behavior: Ten Years of Scientific Progress and Implications for the Eighties* (NIMH, 1982) he agreed that this would "provide opportunity to be more definitive regarding television's causal influences on violent and aggressive behaviors of viewers as well as to address an increasing number of questions about the medium's impact on viewers' functioning." And so a new research effort began under the direction of David Pearl at the National Institute of Mental Health (NIMH).

Its aims were to review the most recent literature on television entertainment—"the kinds of programs watched by most of the audience, most of the time," and "to elucidate research findings and their implications for public health and future research." The foreword also notes that the report, while "relevant to public policy . . . makes no recommendations and does not issue specific prescriptions." Yet the foreword also adds, "We would anticipate . . . that persons bearing responsibility for policy and for television industry practices would be interested in the findings for use in decision making. Also the report should be of substantial help to parents and others who seek to know of both the positive and adverse effects of the medium and of the ways in which they can influence them." Thus, readers are encouraged to believe that the report has action implications, but it is left up to them to decide what they are.

The report was released in 1982 in two volumes about five months apart. The first volume is a summary, and the second contains the 24 literature reviews on which the first volume is based. Two related themes continually occur throughout the NIMH report: that current entertainment programming has largely negative effects, and that researchers have identified alternative types of programming that have more prosocial effects. We want to examine the principal negative claims in the report: that television violence causes aggression, and that a distorted world presented on television causes heavy viewers to see the real world as more hostile and scary than it really is. We also want to explore what is known about prosocial effects that might be brought about, especially concerning children's programming and the use of television for promoting public health.

For each of these issues, we try to assess the degree of scientific support for the report's major findings, and we also examine the conditions under which the findings might be used to modify programming. This last emphasis clashes with the report's stated aim of presenting the "facts" and letting readers draw their own implications. However, the report does make the claim that current programming has mostly negative effects that could be reversed with different programming. This claim has fairly obvious action implications, the report's disclaimer notwithstanding. We probe these implications, and deal especially with how the report's major claim is related to the sources of leverage that currently exist for making programming changes. But before exploring these issues, we want to analyze the scope of the NIMH report in order to force out some of its implicit assumptions.

The Scope of the Report

The report's scope can best be understood by comparing its coverage of televison research with the coverage implied by Himmelweit's (1980) comprehensive model of the field, which is presented in Figure 1. Himmelweit postulates a set of elements that determine both how television affects viewers and society and how viewers and society affect television. These are: the norms of a country; the institutions that impinge on its broadcast industry (e.g., in the U.S. these would include the FCC, Congress, and various advocacy groups); the structure of the broadcast industry itself (e.g., networks, local stations, production companies); the technological state of the art (e.g., the availability of multichannel cable); the industry's outputs (largely the advertisements and news and entertainment shows that are produced); viewer perceptions of these outputs; the attitudes and values of the viewing audience; and the stable social and psychological attributes of specific groups within the audience (e.g., race, age, level of education, etc.).

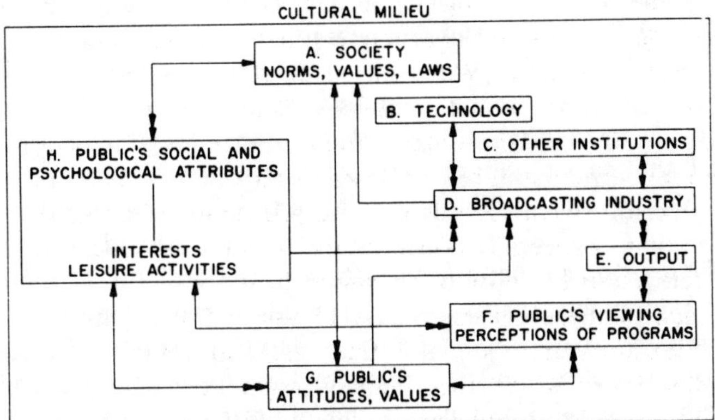

Direction of strong influences. Direction of some influences.

SOURCE: Himmelweit (1980).

Figure 1. Himmelweit's Model of Television and Its Influences

With the help of Himmelweit's model we can trace the priorities in previous television research. Most of it explored how the industry's output influenced viewer perceptions and how these perceptions affected attitudes and behavior. The causal agent was usually television considered globally, and any differentiation of content was largely to explore dramatic violence as a presumed cause. Children were studied most often, usually as individuals. Institutions rarely came under study. Thus, only a part of Himmelweit's model was explored; and in her judgment, it is a part that has less influence on the socialization of children than general cultural norms or the social beliefs of the particular groups to which children belong.

The NIMH report re-creates one of the past priorities, since nearly all of Volume 2 concerns children—how television relates to their information processing, imagination, affective development, academic achievement, and critical viewing skills; how it relates to aggression, sex-role development, the acquisition of consumer habits, and learning about sex. But another past priority is not re-created, since only about 10 percent of Volume 1 and 20 percent of Volume 2 deal explicitly with violence, though the topic arises as a minor theme in many other places. Instead, the report places relatively more stress on prosocial programming, thereby contributing to an enlargement of the scope of television research along with Comstock et al. (1978) and Withey and Abeles (1980).

But contrast this enlarged scope with the elements from Himmelweit's model that are left largely or totally unexplored. Where in the report are the extended discussions of the structure and functions of the broadcast industry so that one can understand better the types of programs that are broadcast? The report does contain two (of 24) chapters on the industry and its place in society. But this strikes us as an underemphasis when exploring programming content that is presumably influenced by a complex set of economic, political, sociological, managerial, and historical forces. To be sure, the industry is difficult to study. For example, the networks resent outsiders from academe, who are thought to have too little appreciation of the pressures on broadcasters and who often seem to hold alien conceptions of television's function. Nonetheless, research on the industry is vital for anyone who wants to understand how programming decisions are made or who wants to identify research questions with leverage either for theoretical understanding or for programming changes.

A second part of Himmelweit's model not explicitly covered in the NIMH report concerns the institutions that interface with television. Television is financed by companies that want to advertise, and a powerful industry has developed to commission, produce, and market these advertisements. We know relatively little about how advertisers and the advertising industry influence television and are influenced by it. Another institution affecting television content is the Federal Communications Commission (FCC), which determines the issuance and renewal of station licenses. We know relatively little about how the FCC actually operates, what the forces are sustaining it, and under what conditions it will move against stations because of their programming. Other institutions influencing the content of television include Congress, the courts, advocacy groups, and public opinion in general. Such institutions are rarely mentioned in the NIMH report.

Even if we consider only television programming, the NIMH report still has a restricted scope. In particular, little consideration is given to public affairs programming or to the medium's role in stimulating consumption, each of which may have important social-structural implications. What if, for instance, news coverage on television (a) makes a media-genic style necessary for political candidates to be selected and elected; (b) weakens political parties and local machines because skillful candidates can go more directly to voters; (c) plays a major role in the setting of political agendas; (d) influences voter turnout; or (e) modifies public opinion through the repeated presentation of dramatic footage about political events (e.g., as in the Vietnam War)? The NIMH report is not as comprehensive as its title, *Television and Behavior*, suggests. It would be more accurately described as a report on "The Psychological Consequences of Television Entertainment at the Individual Level, with Special Reference to Children."

Why does the report have these emphases? We can only speculate. They probably reflect the momentum of received research traditions, which had to play a major role in the report once the decision was made to review past research rather than fund new studies. Also, the emphases may reflect the NIMH sponsorship, with the institute's inevitable preference for psychological variables. The composition of the Advisory Committee, whose members helped choose the topics and reviewers, may also have played a role. Of its seven members, we would classify five as having an exclusive orientation toward the psychological, and the other two as exhibiting the same paradigmatic bias in much (but not all) of their work. The committee had no economists or sociologists of the media, no one trained in political science, administrative studies, or policy sciences, and no one from the networks or other parts of the broadcast industry.

But to be fair, we should note the difficulty of studying television in the way that Himmelweit's model suggests. Such research would have to be associated with reciprocal causal influences, multiple institutions, and different levels of analysis. Anyone who appreciates the difficulties of studying even one-way causal influences from television to children will blanch at exploring all of Himmelweit's model, however comprehensive it may be in capturing the reality of television for those who want to explain it or for those who want to change it. We should also note that, within the report, both Chaffee and McLeod et al. lament the dearth of studies at the family level. This means that some authors did recognize the need to move beyond individuals to higher-order aggregates. However, these are only two sets of authors and they limit their analysis to the family, leaving out of consideration political, economic, and other social institutions. Thus, they do not seriously challenge our view that the NIMH report is less broad in scope than its title, *Television and Behavior*, suggests.

Prosocial Programming for Children

Throughout the NIMH report runs the message that television could portray themes other than adventure, violence, and titillation; that it could instead portray cooperation, altrusim, and self-control; that it could promote healthier lifestyles; and that it could even model proven strategies for coping with life's common problems. A fundamental change in television's functions is implied in this advocacy. We move from the primacy of delivering potential customers to advertisers at the lowest cost per thousand to the primacy of using television to entertain while also promoting physical and emotional health and embodying the more interpersonally binding American values. Make no mistake: A fundamental challenge implicit in the NIMH report is to the exclusively commercial rationale for entertainment television in the U.S. today. To examine the prosocial focus in the report, we now turn to the first of our two substantive domains: prosocial programming for children.

The major chapter on this topic is by Rushton, who succinctly summarizes research from experiments in both laboratory and field settings that supports the proposition that television can teach children and adolescents behaviors widely recognized as altruistic, friendly, indicative of self-control, and effective in coping with fear. Prosocial issues are also discussed in other chapters: Dorr suggests that television can teach empathy and the ability to recognize emotions; Singer claims that television content can stimulate the imagination, but that cartoons do not; and Rubinstein and Sprafkin report an original study which they interpret as showing that a prosocial television diet can induce prosocial behavior in persons aged 8 to 18 who are institutionalized because of poor social functioning.

Dorr and Singer admit that there is not much evidence for their hypotheses, while the research of Rubinstein and Sprafkin is preliminary and difficult to interpret. However, Rushton's case is based on many studies that converge impressively in their results. The television stimulus in these studies consists of (a) films that were created especially for research; (b) specific shows from the "Mister Rogers" or "Sesame Street" series; or (c) special viewing diets created by restricting the child's exposure to prosocial programs taken from tape libraries. The reader might well wonder what effects such shows would have in home settings where it may be easier for attention to wander, where antisocial models and events are interspersed with the prosocial, and where competing activities are available in the form of other channels, video recordings, or play. From the network perspective, the most important attribute of programs is their ability to attract and hold an audience, despite competition for the child's attention.

While holding the audience is the end of commercial broadcasting, for most researchers it is merely the means. This disjunction of perspective is very salient in Rushton's chapter, for it contains no mention of how attractive a prosocial diet would be to children of different ages. The only authors to consider the issue are Rubinstein and Sprafkin, who conclude from their own study that attention did not differ between adolescents exposed to a typical television diet and adolescents exposed to a prosocial one. While an important first step, this still does not speak to the prior question of whether children will spontaneously *select* prosocial programs, especially when there are alternatives that include action-packed shows and a variety of non-television activities. Individual networks probably fear that, if they introduced more prosocial programming, they would be at a competitive disadvantage. Their need for large audiences dictates research not just on the effects of prosocial content, but also on the ability of such programming to first capture, and then hold large audiences. Without such research, the networks have every reason to fear prosocial television in the sense we are using the term.

This can be seen by examining "Mister Rogers," "Sesame Street," and the "Electric Company." They are widely acclaimed as prosocial programs; yet it is noteworthy that none of the networks has tried to create such programming. On network television, children's programs continue to be almost nonexistent on weekdays and to feature cartoons on Saturdays. Indeed, one of the few live shows—"Captain Kangaroo"—was recently pushed back to a timeslot when we would all like our children to be asleep and, not surprisingly, the ratings soon killed the show. Nowhere in the NIMH report is there an extensive analysis of the economics of the media and of the paucity of incentives for the networks to improve children's programming.

We probably understand at a very coarse level the reasons for the networks' lack of interest. Children are captivated by cartoons, which cost relatively little to produce; in determining purchasing decisions children play a role, but it is not usually the major one; the child market is shrinking because of demographic trends; and children's abilities and interests change markedly from one narrow age band to another, limiting the potential audience for most shows. In this last respect, action-packed cartoons are somewhat of an exception, since they hold children of 4, 8, and 12 in a way that no program can that is aimed at the specific needs of a particular age group. For all these reasons, we have to conlude that it is no accident that the productions of the Children's Television Workshop have not been extensively imitated by the networks.

In theory, the difficulty of having prosocial material broadcast can be circumvented through regulation, subsidies to the networks, or the eventual control by the federal government of a children's channel in the narrowcast era. Each of these has distinct drawbacks, is highly controversial, and, in the short run at least, is only a remote practical possibility. The omnipresent reality is: Even if prosocial programming were effective with children and adolescents when it was watched, why should the networks broadcast it? Certainly, they do not seem worried by the head-to-head competition with prosocial programs on public television on Saturday mornings. We presume that the networks have examined the ratings and are not moved to modify their current practices. They have probably also examined the ratings of the current children's channel on cable television and are aware of the relatively small audiences, the financial losses being incurred, the steady drift in the programming toward action-packed cartoons, and the escalating talk about the possibility of advertising in the near future. With these advertisers will come pressure to increase audience size so that the channel may come to look more and more like network television. To achieve large audiences will require a departure from the fundamental tenet of prosocial television for children: That each age group has specific needs and skills that require different types of programming, much as different types of textbooks are needed at each grade in schools. The problem with such wisdom from developmental psychology is that to implement it would realize small audiences and so be poor business.

A final note is worth making about what is absent from the report's discussion of prosocial programming. The cited evidence comes almost entirely from short-term experiments which show what exposure to prosocial content *might* achieve if it were watched. No longitudinal studies are reported which probe the effects of differences in spontaneous exposure to prosocial content, both during children's viewing hours and at other times, when indeed most viewing by children actually takes place. The absence of such longitudinal studies may be due to researchers' doubts about whether there has been enough prosocial content to make an analysis meaningful, or it may reflect the researchers' personal conviction that the results are self-evident. However, all the inferential traps that beset longitudinal studies of violence—traps that we will soon discuss—pertain to studies of prosocial effects, and it would not be realistic to expect either clear answers or large effects. Nonetheless, effects may be larger than with violent programming, especially if one assumes that the child's everyday world more often models and rewards prosocial than antisocial behavior.

The Uses of Television for Health Promotion

In his foreword to *Television and Behavior*, Herbert Pardes, the Director of NIMH, wrote that the work "intends primarily to elucidate research findings and their implications for public health and future research." Thus, the hope is expressed that the report will spell out the implications of research for public health policy or practice.

The section of Volume 2 on public health contains introductory comments by Hamburg and Pierce outlining future research needs, which in their estimation largely revolve around the use of television as a major adjunct to other means of developing and enhancing healthful behavior. Next is an essay by Gerbner, Morgan, and Signorielli detailing the results of content analyses of the ways in which mental health, doctors, nutrition, safety, smoking, and alcohol are portrayed on television. Solomon then presents an essay on health campaigns in which he uses successful and less successful campaigns to illustrate the principles on which he thinks a successful campaign depends. Finally, Rubinstein and Sprafkin lament the dearth of knowledge about the roles that television plays with institutionalized patients, and they then present the results of a preliminary study on prosocial television for institutionalized children and adolescents.

Within the limits imposed by the sampling frame of only one week's dramatic content, Gerbner and his colleagues demonstrate some areas in which the reality of television distorts the reality beyond television. Among their claims are that portrayals of the mentally ill correspond more with stereotypes than with professional knowledge; that doctors are represented as omniscient and omnipotent; that children's shows and advertisements are a nutritionist's nightmare; that adult characters spend more time snacking than eating meals; that major characters are almost universally slim and attractive; that smoking is rare, while alcohol abounds and is often used to "solve" personal crises. The argument is that television distorts reality, has harmful effects, and fails to attain the prosocial ends it could (apparently) attain so easily.

The chapter on television portrayals of health does not deal with leverage. How can those who want the content of television changed to reflect healthier practices bring this about when (a) the broadcast industry has little internal incentive to produce or air such materials; (b) external pressures to portray healthier behavior are limited by the First Amendment, a docile FCC, a Congress many of whose members are unwilling to take on the networks, and a low level of organized citizen interest to reform television; (c) companies in the multibillion-dollar food industry want a competitive edge through advertising; and (d) the networks already monitor advertisers' claims about health products and probably feel they are sufficiently responsible about health matters? Indeed, the networks could probably point to the apparent low frequency of portrayals of smoking and claim how responsible they are. Interestingly enough, we do not know why so little smoking is shown, and if there has been any decline, we do not know why it has occurred. Studying the smoking issue with writers, producers, and others might give insight into industry practices and suggest leverage points for how alcohol might also be treated. After all, the networks have little to fear from the relevant industry, for hard liquor cannot now be advertised on television, though beer, wine, and other products of liquor-producing conglomerates can be.

The essay by Solomon puts forth, in the author's own terms "only one idea. It is time to stop asking . . . 'Do the mass media work in health?' and start asking 'How can we best make them work?' " He answers his own question: through adequate problem analysis (using basic knowledge of the health problem under attack), by careful media selection and use (based on knowledge in communication research and practice), by appropriate message design (derived from theories of attitude and behavior change), and by evaluation aimed at improving the campaign. But we must not be complacent about any of these answers. At any one time medical research is open to multiple interpretations. Note, for example, the recent changes in belief about the role that different types of cholesterol play in cardiac involvement. Communication research is also far from definitive on all issues. Do we know, for example, whether a media campaign will be effective by itself or whether it needs a face-to-face complement? The Stanford Heart Health Project, with which Solomon has been connected, is ambivalent on this count, for some data suggest the need for face-to-face services while other data suggest that the media will be just as effective without these services. As to behavior change, Bandura's social learning theory provides the currently preferred strategy in the three health promotion campaigns being funded by the National Heart, Lung, and Blood Institute and in the University of Pennsylvania project in Lycoming County, Pennsylvania. But this theory is more a framework of concepts to be considered in developing change campaigns than a blueprint for specific actions. It raises consciousness, but hardly details action plans.

More important than Solomon's suggestions are the issues he hardly raises, particularly about how community health promotion campaigns gain and hold their audiences. Solomon is most concerned with the question: "Given that we reach target audience members, how can we change them?" Thus, he considers the program "Feeling Good" a success despite the fact it went off the air because of poor ratings, even by the standards of PBS. The hope was that "Feeling Good" would re-create the success of "Sesame Street." It did not, and for important reasons that should give pause to anyone who wants to use television to promote practices deemed more healthy. Children of 4 are relatively more homogeneous than adults in their interests and background knowledge. They bring comparable cognitive structures to viewing and can mostly be motivated to view by a fast pace, kindly muppets, and cartoons. They probably also want to learn about letters and numbers, know little about these matters before age 4, and when they display their knowledge are sometimes rewarded by significant others. Contrast this with adults. They come from many different generations and have had very different levels of education and experience with health systems. Moreover, adults are (presumably) more motivated to watch television for entertainment than for health education, and few external rewards exist for gaining more health knowledge. If all, or even part, of this analysis is correct, public education about health matters is not likely to get over the first hurdle that commercial networks absolutely have to clear: the gaining and holding of a large audience.

The recent experimental health promotion campaigns do not rely on television alone. They are multimedia approaches, using television, radio, newsprint, and posters. Moreover, they have large community components involving physicians, nurses, and other public health workers as well as key local decision makers and local community organizations. Also, health screening is used to detect individuals at serious risk. Such an eclectic approach seems reasonable for gaining awareness, transmitting information, modeling recommended practices, and reinforcing compliance with these practices. However, it also reduces television's major advantage for public policy—its potential ability to reach large audiences at a low per person cost. In the large-scale demonstrations that Solomon analyzes, issues of cost-effectiveness loom large, not only in the sense of whether such campaigns should be preferred over sickness-oriented medicine, but also in the sense of whether television should be preferred over radio, print, etc. for those functions for which television is relevant.

If a decision were made that television is cost-effective in adding to a campaign, funds for televised health promotion would still have to be obtained. The broadcast industry is not likely to take upon itself the task of producing and airing such shows, because small audiences will be expected. Their interest would probably be limited to some talk show appearances, public service announcements, and regular paid advertisements. Some local stations may be persuaded to run low-cost specials, but it is not clear how many would do this or which time slots they would assign. We already have one cable channel that deals exclusively with health matters and that will soon reach most of the nation, and we may later have others. But who will support these channels financially, as advertises or subscribers? Some of the potential advertisers of a health channel have, after all, no desire to be associated with wellness. Sickness is their trade. Also, what will the profile of subscribers be like? Will it be biased toward the more or less affluent, the younger or older, the healthier or sicker? Will the need for finance mean that much of the programming is locally produced? If so, what will be its ability to capture and hold large audiences in light of the competition from other channels producing more expensive and more professional fare full of action and adventure?

Let us imagine that some production is funded from federal, state or local sources that also purchase air time for shows or advertisements that promote healthy practices. This should help improve the quality of programming over locally produced, low-budget shows. But how comfortable will public agencies feel with so much exposure and vulnerability to dissenting public voices about which behaviors are healthy and about how tax monies should be spent? Health promotion campaigns in which television plays a major role will be expensive and probably funded either out of the public purse or out of cable company set-asides for progamming that originates locally. The current broadcast industry has few incentives to be active in promoting public health. The NIMH report does not deal with this issue or with where the money might come from for future programming in the health promotion area.

The foregoing remarks suggest the need for a hard-headed analysis of television's role in health campaigns. Should it be used to advertise the telephone numbers of local prevention services, to raise awareness through appearances on talk shows and the local news, to broadcast well-advertised health specials, or to broadcast regular series on health? In most of these contexts, it seems to us more appropriate to talk about "Television and Its (Minor?) Role in Health Campaigns" rather than to talk, as Solomon does, about "Health Campaigns on Television."

Effects of Television's Distorted World

THE CULTIVATION HYPOTHESIS

Content analyses have shown that television presents a social reality which differs from the world in which we live. For instance, violence occurs on television atypically often, men outnumber women three to one, and minorities, blue-collar workers, young children, and the elderly are underrepresented (Gerbner et al., 1980). Gerbner and his colleagues have suggested that this television world reflects power relationships in U.S. society, with men and whites being dominant, and women, children, and blacks tending to be seen as victims. Gerbner and his associates have also maintained that exposure to this distorted world makes heavy viewers more sexist, anomic, fearful of crime, and negative in their stereotypes of the elderly. They further claim that this process of cultivating perceptions homogenizes society, reducing the degree of diversity that would pertain if there were no heavy viewing of television. The claims of Gerbner and his colleagues are frequently discussed in the NIMH report.

Several chapter authors note that, when multiple controls are simultaneously employed to control for third variable "causes" (cf. Hughes, 1980; Hirsch, 1980), some of the relationships published by Gerbner decrease to a level not different from zero. This has been demonstrated, for example, with the fear of walking alone at night, with other indicators of being a crime victim, and with the perceived fairness of bringing a child into the world. However, other relationships remain above zero even after multiple controls have been simultaneously employed. Thus, Tyler (1980) found that mass media presentations of crimes still influenced estimates of the general crime rate; Neville (1980) found that television exposure still influenced interpersonal mistrust; and Gerbner et al. (1980) discovered that viewing was still related to anomie among respondents with some college education.

A puzzle is presented by the finding that, after multiple controls have been instituted, viewing remains significantly related to some dependent variables but not others. Within the NIMH report, Comstock sought to solve the puzzle by postulating that heavy viewing cultivates pessimism about the world in general but does not increase one's personal fear of being a crime victim. Hawkins and Pingree concluded that television viewing increases interpersonal mistrust and estimates of the prevalence of crime but does not affect either personal fear of being victimized or alienation, defined as judgments about how the unjust world affects oneself. The preferred hypothesis seems to be that television affects general beliefs about how the world is but not particular fears of how it will affect oneself. The theoretical mechanism underlying this hypothesis is presumably that beliefs about how the world affects oneself depend more on actual life experiences and social networks than on television, whereas perceptions of how the world is in general depend more on vicarious experiences that extend one's knowledge beyond the necessarily restricted external world with which one has direct contact. This reconciliation of apparently conflicting findings begins the important task of specifying the conditions under which individuals base their opinions more on vicarious than on real experience. Also, it provides a contingency context for limiting Gerbner's general cultivation hypothesis, replacing the question "how does heavy viewing affect X" with "under which conditions does heavy viewing affect X."

However, we should not forget that, while the correlations between television exposure and general beliefs about the world remain above zero even after multiple simultaneous controls have been instituted, they are still extremely modest—mostly in the .10 to .20 range. Moreover, they can be interpreted as causal only if the assumption is accepted that the control variables fully model the true selection process whereby heavy and light viewers come to hold different worldviews for reasons having nothing to do with television. Not everyone will agree that the control variables typically used in research on Gerbner's hypothesis fully model the relevant selection differences. Some psychologists might postulate that withdrawn people watch television more often and see the world as more fearful for reasons that relate more to their earlier direct experiences in the world than to the television fare they have seen. Scholars favoring such a selection model would worry about the extent to which the typical control variables—age, gender, income and the like—function as sufficiently good proxies to remove statistically all the effects of withdrawal. Such scholars might well contend that adding a valid measure of psychological withdrawal to the analysis might make the modest partial correlations between television and general beliefs shrink even further, perhaps to zero. If it did, there would be no point trying to reconcile why multiple controls shrink some relationships to zero. Thus, the task Comstock and Hawkins and Pingree set themselves depends on assuming that past research has used credible selection models—an assumption not everyone would be willing to accept.

MAINSTREAMING

Gerbner has acknowledged the shrinkage of correlations that results when multiple controls are used simultaneously, and his response has been to modify his general hypothesis about the effects of heavy viewing. He now maintains that such viewing should distort perceptions of reality only with individuals belonging to social groups whose view of the world is discrepant from the mainstream presented on television. Heavy viewing can obviously not have the same effect on social groups that already subscribe to the mainstream. Gerbner's revised hypothesis specifies a statistical interaction between level of viewing and whether the respondent does or does not belong to a group that already believes in the television mainstream. A corollary is that there will be more variability in perceptions of the world among light viewers from a variety of different social groups than among heavy viewers from the same groups. It is in this last sense that Gerbner now claims that heavy television viewing is homogenizing society.

Numerous instances of mainstreaming are cited in the NIMH report, all of which depend on three inferences. First, content analysis is used to infer the nature of the television mainstream; second, surveys are used to infer the social groups which, in the aggregate, believe in the television mainstream; and third, a graph (or some equivalent) is presented which shows that heavy viewers from groups with perceptions generally discrepant from the television mainstream nonetheless perceive the world much like heavy and light viewers from groups with the same worldview as television. Thus, Gerbner and his colleagues (1980) report that (a) the television world is scary; (b) persons with less education tend to be more anomic and mistrustful than persons with more education; and (c) heavy viewers with high education rate the fearfulness of the world more like heavy viewers with little education than like lighter viewers with more education. They also note that (a) alcohol is frequently consumed on television; (b) surveys suggest that people in better health are more likely to drink than people in poorer health; and (c) the drinking habits of heavy viewers in poor health are more like those of heavy viewers in good health than like those of light viewers in poor health. Research since the NIMH report provides more evidence. Morgan (1982) (a) used content analyses to argue that the behavior of boys and girls is presented stereotypically on television; (b) he used surveys to infer that girls' beliefs about gender-appropriate behavior are less stereotyped than boys'; and (c) finally, he showed that girls who view heavily have more stereotyped beliefs than girls who view less heavily and that their beliefs are close to those of boys whatever the boys' viewing level. Gerbner et al. (1982) argued that television presents political views that are middle-of-the-road, and they went on to show that, in terms of anti-comunism and support for restrictions to free speech, liberals and conservatives who view heavily are more alike than liberals and conservatives who view less often. Within the NIMH report, Gerbner, Morgan, and Signorielli show (a) that television frequently portrays snacking and the eating of fattening foods; (b) that people from high-income groups are more concerned about their weight than people from lower-income groups; and (c) that heavy viewers with high income are less concerned about their weight than their lighter viewing counterparts and are just as unconcerned as low-income persons in general.

The number and variety of demonstrations of mainstreaming are impressive and clearly merit closer methodological scrutiny. To begin this process, we will use the last example above since it permits us to make concrete a number of general points. The first concerns the characterization of the television mainstream. While this may be clear in many instances, it may not be in others. For instance, Gerbner and his colleagues maintain that the television mainstream is characterized by snacking and a lack of concern with the health implications of food. Yet they also contend that the majority of television characters are slim—indeed, slimmer than most Americans. Are we to conclude from the presentations of eating on television that there is little concern with health; or are we to conclude from the slimness of heroes and heroines that eating well is a feature of the lifestyle of persons worth emulating? Standards need to be established and defended for inferring what the television mainstream is. It will not always be obvious.

Second, in analyses of mainstreaming it is typical to trichotomize viewing for each of the different groups examined. This would seem to unconfound viewing and group membership. But it need not, for within any viewing category the social groups can still differ in average viewing. To make this clear, imagine our example of eating in three income groups. Among those viewing television more than four hours per day, the lowest income group may have viewed five hours on the average, the middle income group five and one-half hours, while the highest income group may have viewed eight hours. If this were the case, one would have to consider whether the data in the NIMH report are due to a simple effect of viewing in the highest viewing category or to the crucial statistical interaction of viewing and group membership on which an inference of mainstreaming depends. Tests of mainstreaming should treat viewing as a continuous variable, taking care not to truncate prematurely when creating the heaviest viewing category. The current practice of creating this category by truncating at four or five hours of viewing per day may lead to a range within the category that is so wide that it masks group differences in viewing. Better would be truncation at more hours per day or perhaps a transformation of the untruncated viewing variable to make it more normally distributed.

A third problem concerns the correlates of viewing levels and group membership. In our example, there are probably many ways in which high-income people who view heavily differ from their counterparts who view less, some of which will be related to a lack of concern with weight. To give only one possibility, those who spend more time viewing might be less active socially and may therefore have less need to be concerned about their weight and general appearance. Third variable controls always need to be dealt with in analyses of mainstreaming. Controlling for these variables is particularly complicated because group variables correlated with television viewing and a concern with weight are potentially *both* confounds *and* stratification variables whose interaction with viewing constitutes a test of the mainstreaming hypothesis. Thus, if the frequency of social activities were correlated with a concern with weight, why should one test the mainstream hypothesis by stratifying on income rather than on the frequency of social activities? Should one not stratify on each variable, as well as on any other group variable that is related to a concern with weight? If one chooses to stratify only by income, as in the NIMH report, one should have a rationale for selecting this variable over others; but none is specified in the report. Research on mainstreaming has not yet developed explicit criteria for selecting one possible stratification variable over another and has ignored the possibility that most group correlates of the dependent variable can logically function both as tests of mainstreaming and as possibly spurious third variable causes.

A fourth problem concerns how to control for third variables once one has decided what the stratification and control variables will be. The few cases in the mainstreaming literature that have used multivariate controls have employed linear regression, whose appropriateness needs defending. This is because one way of formulating the mainstreaming hypothesis is that the regression of viewing on concern with weight should take one form for low-income persons and a different form for high-income persons. As a result, the overall regression of income on concern with weight may not always be linear. When multiple controls are used, the analysis should always be preceded by tests of the linearity assumption. If the tests indicate nonlinear regression, and linear adjustments are nonetheless made, spurious conclusions will probably result. They can also result if the assumption of linearity holds. This is because the control variables constitute a multivariate selection model that may be incomplete or inadequately operationalized. There is no way to escape the great difficulties inherent in choosing selection models in television research, particularly where the research is cross-sectional, as has been the case with studies of mainstreaming to date.

A fifth methodological problem concerns the falsifiability of mainstreaming. Hirsch (1981) has pointed to the relationship between mainstreaming and resonance, the latter being a process that Gerbner has hypothesized will cause group differences to increase among heavy viewers. This is the opposite to what mainstreaming brings about. Until there is an exact theoretical analysis of the conditions under which mainstreaming and resonance occur, it will not be possible to falsify either construct. For instance, had our example not shown a convergence of belief among heavy viewers from income groups with different aggregate levels of concern about weight, it would have been possible to argue that mainstreaming had occurred but that its effects had been masked by the countervailing effects of resonance.

The literature on mainstreaming is so new that all of the implicit assumptions of tests of the hypothesis have not yet been forced out and critically examined. However, enough preliminary data exist to convey a sense of excitement, albeit an excitement tempered by the need to probe unresolved methodological issues. What makes the mainstreaming hypothesis more credible than earlier, more global assertions about the effects of heavy viewing is that television's effects are now made contingent on the interaction of viewing and group membership. This means less widespread and thus more modest effects. For example, television is now thought to undermine a concern with eating and weight, not among all high viewers, but only among those who enjoy high incomes. The affected subgroups will sometimes be relatively small when expressed both as a percentage of all persons and as a percentage of all persons in the particular social group that does not agree with the television mainstream. Indeed, heavy viewers with high incomes probably represent a relatively small percentage of all high-income persons, and certainly a lower percentage of their group than viewers of lower-income groups. But such modest percentages need not always be the case. For instance, in Morgan's (1982) analysis of sex-role stereotyping, we suspect that the heavy-viewing girls represent no smaller a percentage of all girls than the heavy-viewing boys do of all boys. Nonetheless, Gerbner's new hypothesis about mainstreaming is more modest in its presumed scope of effects than was the earlier and less differentiated hypothesis about cultivation.

A final point needs to be made in trying to understand the scope of the mainstreaming hypothesis. If some heavy viewers are indeed moved toward television's distorted mainstream, this is not a mainstream in which "anything goes." Television does not move heavy viewers toward radical values or beliefs. Both the politics and the economics of the industry dictate that television keep to the middle ground, that it avoid confrontation with regulators and organized interest groups, and that it attract sponsors by presenting programming acceptable to a large heterogeneous audience. Fringe ideas and characters rarely appear on television, and when they do the context makes clear their social unacceptability. However, within these boundaries numerous leanings can be expressed, and researchers are only now begining to characterize them empirically. For example, Gerbner and his colleagues (1982) maintain that the television mainstream tilts toward the political right on issues of segregation, communism, and civil and personal rights, and that it tilts toward economic populism when federal spending is at issue. Subtle analyses are needed of any network leanings within the restricted range of the acceptable where the television mainstream operates. But none are detailed in the NIMH report, nor is this presented as an area for future research.

Television Violence

The NIMH report is more definite than the surgeon-general's in concluding that television violence causes aggression. Indeed, this conclusion is repeated in many chapters in both volumes. Although an "official" conclusion is clear, a chapter by Milavsky et al. (1982) offers a dissenting opinion based upon the authors' own research. In his overview to the chapters on violence, Rubinstein notes that the dissenting opinion of Milavsky et al. is based on a single study that is discrepant with most past findings and is likely to be debated. The last is certain, for the study is of the type called for in the surgeon-general's report. It is longitudinal, television exposure and aggression are carefully measured, and the data analysis is state of the art. Thus, readers of the NIMH report may be in a quandary: the report unambiguously and frequently concludes that television violence causes aggression; yet an apparently exemplary new study within the report fails to support this same conclusion. Let us now examine the evidence for each of these conclusions.

THE CONVENTIONAL SOCIAL SCIENCE WISDOM

The NIMH report contains a literature review of the violence issue by Huesmann that accurately reflects the opinion of many other scholars (e.g., Comstock, in press; Parke et al., 1977). Only a minor part of Huesmann's chapter deals with whether television violence increases aggression, for like most others he believes that the issue is closed. His belief rests on the consistency of past findings from laboratory and field experiments, cross-sectional surveys, and panel studies. To accept such consistency as a basis for believing that television causes aggression, one must logically accept (a) that the different methods do not share biases operating in the same direction; and (b) that the past studies using unbiased methods have been accurately reviewed. Huesmann does not examine these issues, to which we now turn.

It is obvious why laboratory experiments might exaggerate any link between television violence and aggression for normal children in everyday settings. Experiments have to produce aggression to discriminate between the outcomes of different treatments. Yet aggression is a relatively rare event. So, experiments are designed (a) to minimize internal inhibitions against aggression, (b) to minimize external cues sanctioning aggression, and (c) to maximize the clarity and intensity of short-term experimental treatments that have been deliberately chosen because they are likely to foster aggression. Although appropriate for discriminating between treatments, this strategy is not obviously relevant to regular television programming in the home, where internal cues against aggression may operate more powerfully, situational cues sanction aggression, and television aggressors are punished, usually by characters with prosocial qualities that are themselves presumably worthy of emulation. Also, the violent scenes on television are interspersed with many different types of activity, and viewers are free to watch intermittently or with low levels of involvement.

Positive bias is also likely in cross-sectional surveys where the amount of exposure to violence is correlated with aggression scores, holding constant background variables that are thought to correlate with viewing and agression. The adequacy of this approach depends on how completely selection differences between heavier and lighter viewers are modeled and how well the constructs in the model are measured. Usually, the selection models are primitive, involving demographic variables such as age, race, sex, etc., which are presumably proxies for the true (and unknown) psychological and social factors that cause differences in exposure to violence. Campbell and Boruch (1975) have argued that "underadjustment" is likely to occur in this situation so that, while some of the true selection difference will be removed, not all of it will. The synchronous correlation between viewing and aggression is positive, although usually small—in the .15 to .25 range. If Campbell and Boruch are correct, some of the background differences between heavier and lighter viewers will not have been removed, and estimates of the relationship between television and aggression will be somewhat inflated. Not everyone agrees with Campbell and Boruch. Cronbach et al. (1977) believe that overadjustment will sometimes occur, and that the adjustment can even be perfect, though we would never know when it was. Our point is *not* that underadjustment bias has occurred in all past cross-sectional studies of television and aggression; it is only that a plausible case can be made that the bias might have operated.

Huesmann mentions six reports of field experiments involving random assignment in nonlaboratory settings. Four were said to have yielded evidence of a positive relation between violence viewing and aggression, the exceptions being Feshbach and Singer (1971) and Wells (1973). However, the study by Loye et al. (1977) is also an exception since the data show that the group assigned to a television diet of high violence was no more likely to commit hurtful behaviors than the controls. Moreover, the experiment of Stein and Friedrich (1972) showed weak effects confined to a subgroup of initially more aggressive children and, according to Parke et al. (1977), this result failed to replicate (Sawin, 1973). Thus, four of the six studies are problematic. Of the two others, the work of Leyens et al. is also included as one of three experiments reported in Parke et al. (1977), which therefore emerges as the crucial report claiming to find effects of television violence. However, these field experiments deal with institutionalized children; regular television viewing was forbidden, possibly creating frustration; and in two studies the boys assigned to view aggressive films were initially more aggressive. In our view, the field experiments on television violence produce little consistent evidence of effects, despite claims to the contrary; and the instances where an effect is claimed involve populations that seem to be initially more aggressive.

It is widely agreed that the best method for studying television effects involves longitudinal panel studies. Unfortunately, the state of the analytic art has recently changed. The formerly advocated analysis based on cross-lagged pannel correlations is misleading when test-retest correlations differ between variables. Then, the less reliable measure will spuriously appear to be causal (Cook and Campbell, 1979; Rogosa, 1980). Television viewing is nearly always less stable than aggressiveness, as in the study by Lefkowitz et al. in the surgeon-general's report and in the original data that Huesmann includes in his chapter in the NIMH report. It may also be the case with Singer and Singer (1980), who used cross-lagged panel analysis. Thus, a bias may also have operated in past panel studies to produce a spurious relationship between television and aggression.

Like most summaries of television violence and its effects, the NIMH report is somewhat uncritical in its claim that the question has been answered and in its implication that the effect is widespread. The reliance on evidence from multiple methods is admirable—in the abstract. But the viability of such a strategy depends on the absence of biases operating in the same direction across all of the methods. In our opinion, such biases *may* have operated, although we have no direct evidence that they did or that they operated to produce totally spurious effects rather than merely inflating true ones. Yet no analyst in the NIMH report tackled these issues, which are certainly not handled in meta-analyses of the violence literature (Hearold, 1979). Until they are tackled and put to rest, doubts about the consequences of television violence will not be stilled, certainly not because of a committee decree or the frequently voiced consensus of a scholarly community. And until they are tackled, we will have to rely disproportionately on panel studies which involve state-of-the-art design, measurement, and data analysis. We examine two such studies below, beginning with Milavsky et al. (1982). To examine their work we rely, not on the summary in the NIMH report, but on their published book.

MILAVSKY, KESSLER, STIPP, AND RUBENS

Approximately 2,400 elementary students between 7 and 12 years of age were surveyed over a three-year period beginning in 1970, together with 800 boys between 12 and 16. The survey was repeated six times for the elementary sample, and five for the older sample. The interval between adjacent waves varied, ranging from 3 to 12 months for the elementary sample and 5 to 19 months for the older sample. Television exposure was measured with a program checklist. Students indicated how many episodes of each program they watched, and an estimate of total exposure over the preceding four weeks was obtained. A violence exposure measure was also derived by weighting programs according to adults' perceptions of the amount of violence in them. To measure aggression, younger children rated which of their classroom peers tried to hurt others by pushing or shoving, by hitting or punching, by saying mean things, or by lying to get others in trouble. The four items were summed so that each child received a score based on the percentage of classmates nominating him or her as aggressive. A self-report aggression measure was used with the teenage boys. Separate indices were formed of personal aggression (four items), aggression against a teacher (two items), and property aggression (one item on stealing and another on property damage). These items were assessed by noting how many times youngsters reported engaging in such an act during the last four weeks. A delinquency index of six items was also constructed. Teenagers indicated the last time they were badly beaten up, arrested, participated in a gang fight, stole a car, hurt someone to get his money, or purposely hurt someone with a knife. Responses were coded 0 or 1 depending on whether the event had occurred within the last three months and were then summed to create a delinquency scale.

The basic causal model can be expressed in equation form as:

$$A(t) = a + b^*A(t-1) + b^*TV(t-1) + u(t).$$

Stated verbally, aggression at one time is made a function of aggression and television viewing *at a prior time*. The earlier aggression variable, $A(t-1)$, functions to remove the simplest form of selection difference associated with the fact that some children are more aggressive than others at the time $(t-1)$ measurement takes place. The television variable tests whether viewing violence at an earier time adds to the predictability of later aggression once earlier aggression levels have been statistically controlled. Since aggression and television viewing were measured six times within the elementary sample, the model was used to evaluate each of the 15 possible wave pairs. Thus, when Waves I and VI are being contrasted, the model tests to what extent television viewing for four weeks in 1970 adds to the predictability of aggression in 1973. A major assumption of the model is that the prior aggression and television variables are measured without error. Since this assumption is manifestly false, Milavsky et al. estimated LISREL models for each wave pair in addition to the basic regression model.

Milavsky et al. concluded: (a) that the findings for boys and girls were quite similar; (b) that the lagged television variable was associated with many small positive coefficients, of which no more were statistically reliable than may be due to chance; and (c) that when socioeconomic status was included in the model as an additional control variable, the predominance of positive coefficients disappeared for elementary boys and the size of the coefficients decreased for elementary girls and teenage boys.

It is worthwhile displaying the major results from the LISREL analyses of children in the elementary sample with valid data. These are not much different from the basic regression results in the NIMH report. Table 1 shows that the estimates for the lagged television variable are small and rarely reliable. However, for both boys and girls the estimates are predominantly positive, suggesting that viewing television violence may have a small effect on aggression. The tendency is clearer for boys than girls. However, there is clearer evidence of the same effect with a large subset of girls. In the final column of Table 1 we also present basic model results for all the girls who attended schools classified as middle class and white. These constitute 70 percent of the total sample of girls, and are of special

Table 1. Results of LISREL Analyses by Milavsky et al. for Elementary Boys and Girls

Wave Pair	*Duration*	*N (Boys/ Girls)*	*A (t-l) Beta (Boys/Girls)*	*TV (t-l) Beta (Boys/Girls)*	*TV (t-l) Beta*[a] *(Middle-Class Girls)*
I–II	5 mos.	364/391	.724/.749	–.046/–.090	–.004
I–III	9 mos.	356/384	.714/.691	–.018/–.024	.013
I–IV	1 yr.	349/369	.668/.682	.038/.008	.051
I–V	2 yrs.	211/236	.624/.496	.096/.078	.032
I–VI	3 yrs.	112/113	.571/.651	.160/–.024	.137
II–III	4 mos.	413/426	.876/.801	.046/.087*	.058
II–IV	7 mos.	409/408	.792/.676	.124*/.132*	.092*
II–V	1 yr./7 mos.	240/245	.694/.638	.014/–.006	.015
II–VI	2 yrs./7 mos.	121/123	.699/.601	.070/.213*	.144
III–IV	3 mos.	497/491	.885/.825	.078*/.068*	.041
III–V	1 yr./3 mos.	291/292	.753/.657	.015/–.043	.022
III–VI	2 yrs./3 mos.	147/133	.663/.610	.133*/.141	.200*
IV–V	1 yr.	301/296	.759/.513	–.043/.074	.088
IV–VI	2 yrs.	161/134	.721/.723	.059/–.022	.082
V–VI	1 yr	188/153	.750/.650	.075/.109	.109

* $p < .05$, all aggression coefficients are significant.

[a] Coefficients in this column are from OLS, not LISREL, analyses.

substantive importance because of the claim that controls for SES make the positive lagged coefficients shrink to zero. Yet for these middle-class girls the coefficients do not shrink to zero, despite the probable restriction in SES variance in the analysis.

A second point needs to be made about the results. Table 1 shows that the lagged coefficients representing the "effect" of television appear to increase with time, suggesting a larger effect the longer the delay between watching television and aggression being measured. The table is somewhat confusing because of instability in the estimates that we would presume to be greater the longer the delay interval. This is because attrition was greater with longer delays. The effect we are discussing can be seen more clearly in Figure 2, where the delay variable is expressed in six categories of equal width—a delay of 0–5, 6–11, 12–17, 18–23, 24–29, and 30–36 months—and where each data point represents the mean of all lagged coefficients falling within the time category. Figure 2 shows clearly that the coefficients tend to increase with time. The major exception is with the 18–23 month category, where the Wave V data are overrepresented. In nearly all our analyses, Wave V provided unusual data for reasons of which we are not sure.

Table 2 presents some of the results from the NIMH report on teenage boys. The analysis involved taking the data from adjacent waves and testing how viewing at the first wave was related to

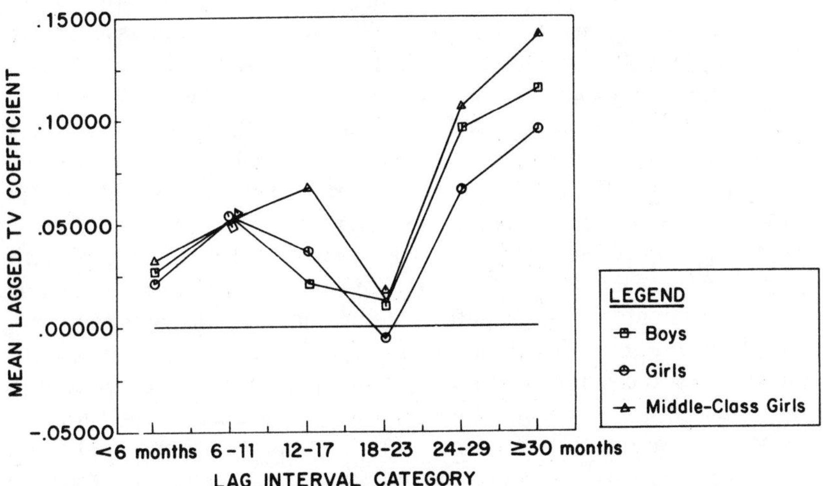

Figure 2. Relationship Between Lagged Television Coefficients and Delay Between Measurement Waves (Elementary Sample)

Table 2. Results of the LISREL Analyses for Teenage Boys

Pair	*Duration*	*A (t-1) Beta*	*TV (t-1) Beta*	*Mean TV (t-1) Beta*[a]
Personal aggression (N = 285)				
I–II	5 mos.	.530	−.023	.000
II–III	7 mos.	.443	.058	.034
III–IV	1 yr./7 mos.	.454	.094*	.058
Teacher aggression (N = 272)				
I–II	5 mos.	.546	.044	.090
II–III	7 mos.	.420	.036	.004
III–IV	1 yr./7 mos.	.236	.074	.030
Property aggression (N = 291)				
I–II	5 mos.	.418	−.059	.024
II–III	7 mos.	.320	.144*	.124
III–IV	1 yr./7 mos.	.408	−.025	−.044

Delinquency aggression (N = 172)[b]

Predicted probability of initiating delinquent behavior among teens with earlier television scores of . . .					*t-Ratio of b*
(5th percentile)	*(10th)*	*(50th)*	*(90th)*	*(95th)*	
.212	.229	.304	.436	.508	2.01*

* $p < .05$, all aggression coefficients are significant.

[a] Unweighted average over *all* wave pairs of identical duration. No statistical tests were conducted.

[b] This result is from a logit, not LISREL, analysis.

aggression at a later wave, holding constant *all* prior aggression waves, *all* previous television measures, and the relationship between the television measure whose causal influence is being assessed and the immediately preceding measure of aggression. Table 2 reports the lagged coefficients for the first three adjacent wave pairs, where the sample size is largest and the delay interval increases. Although there are two wave pairs separated by five months (I–II and IV–V) we report only the former, since it has not been subjected to as many controls removing the effects of prior television viewing. For the measure of personal aggression, which most closely corresponds with the measure used with elementary boys and girls, the results indicate that two of three lagged coefficients are positive and that their magnitude increases with the length of delay. For the measure of teacher aggression, the lagged coefficients are again positive but there is no evidence of greater magnitudes with longer delays. For the measure of stealing and damaging property, the results are inconsistent. Since these analyses use only part of the data, we in addition present the unweighted averaged lagged coefficients across all tests with the same lag period. The same patterns result for personal aggression (non-negative coefficients that increase with delay), for teacher aggression (positive coefficients that are not related to delay), and for reported stealing and damaging property (inconsistent results).

It is difficult to interpret the results presented for the delinquency scale. Since acts of delinquency are rare and distributions are extremely skewed, Milavsky et al. conducted logit analyses for all wave pairs. However, they acknowledge that only three of the six items were asked at Wave I and that responses were disproportionately prone to error at that time. Hence, we assign little weight to the Wave I results. Milavsky et al. also acknowledge that the responses at Waves III and V could not be edited as they were at Waves II and IV. Also, disproportionately few adolescents seem to have reported new acts of aggression between Waves IV and V, entailing a particularly skewed distribution and correspondingly insensitive analysis of Wave V data. Assuming linear increases, our reanalysis of their Table 10.6 shows that, per month, about 33 new acts were reported between Waves I and II (probably because of the new delinquency items added at Wave II), and about 8 new acts were reported between Waves II and III as well as between Waves III and IV, whereas only 3 were reported per month between Waves IV and V. Since the basic analysis was of the percentage of adolescents *who committed any kind of delinquent act for the first time in the prior three months*, it seems that for analyses of Wave V there were only about 9 adolescents distributed across all the different levels of viewing television violence. For these reasons, we also assign little weight to the results using Wave V.The three wave comparisons that remain—between Waves II, III, and IV—all show positive relationships between the amount of viewing and subsequent delinquency, with only one being statistically reliable; but it covers the longest time period of 25 months and is shown at the bottom of Table 2. Milavsky et al. concluded from the equal number of positive and negative coefficients that viewing television violence was not related to subsequent delinquency. But this conclusion is based on all waves of data, and so it fails to use what is known about the lack of correspondence between Wave I and other measures, about wave differences in the quality of measurement, and about the particularly skewed margins at Wave V, where the results could change dramatically if a few cases were reclassified. We remain agnostic, therefore, about the relationship between television violence and subsequent delinquency.

Milavsky et al. noticed the plurality of positive over negative lagged coefficients in Table 1, and they probed whether they could make this relationship disappear. They found that when an indicator of family socioeconomic status was entered into their basic model, the plurality disappeared for boys. They also found that when indicators of gender and school socioeconomic status were included in an analysis of boys and girls combined, the positive coefficients disappeared and no evidence remained of larger coefficients with longer delay intervals. However, the authors analyzed many third variables, and no a priori rationale was offered for singling out SES. Moreover, in the most crucial analysis, SES had to be used as a school-level variable although aggression was measured at the individual level. Also, Table 1 showed that lagged television coefficients are consistently positive and increase with time for girls in middle-class schools. Thus, the stratification by SES has not made *all* lagged relationships between television and aggression disappear, although there is presumably still considerable variability in home SES within higher SES schools. Finally, we have to note that analyses comparable to those of the girls were not presented for boys using the school-level measure, and that the individual-level analyses of the boys' data are not convincing because more than half of the cases are missing, irrespective of whether household income or *mother's* employment status (blue collar, white collar nonprofessional, or professional!) is used as the control variable. In our opinion, the need exists to explore complex interactions involving gender, SES and television viewing, but we are not sure that the measures of SES available to Milavsky et al. are adequate to perform this task.

Delayed effects of television would be expected by anyone who assumes that viewing violence has its impact through the slow buildup of influences attributable to cumulative viewing. Milavsky et al. realized that their model might underestimate cumulative effects, and they addressed the issue directly. Their first step was to estimate a regression model in which aggression was the dependent variable and controls were instituted for *all* the previous levels of aggression and the most recent television score. Thus, when aggression at Wave IV was the dependent variable, aggression at Waves I, II, and III were the controls together with television viewing at Wave III. The next step was to estimate a "cumulative" model that included the same variables plus all prior television measures—i.e., those at Waves I and II. The final step was to test whether the multiple R-square was higher for the cumulative than for the comparison model. Since it was not, Milavsky et al. concluded that cumulative viewing does not increase aggression.

However, they tested whether previous measures of viewing violence increased the prediction of aggression *over and above the prediction attributable to viewing violence in the period immediately prior to the measure of aggression*. In our previous example, this would be equivalent to testing whether television viewing at Waves I and II adds to the prediction of aggression at Wave IV over and above the prediction already provided by television viewing at Wave III. This is not equivalent to testing whether the effect of *all* previous viewing is zero, which we interpret to be a more relevant definition of "cumulative viewing." Further, their cumulative model controls for all prior aggression measures and not just the initial one. This means that, if the earliest television measures affected subsequent aggression, these influences would be removed as part of the control for aggression. Thus, in a four-wave model where A = aggression and TV = viewing television violence, a control for all aggression prior to Wave IV would remove the effects of the causal path $TV_2 \rightarrow A_3 \rightarrow A_4$. Alternative cumulative models need to be postulated and tested that include: (1) all direct paths from prior TV measures to the dependent variable—i.e., from $TV_1 \rightarrow A_4$, $TV_2 \rightarrow A_4$, and $TV_3 \rightarrow A_4$; (2) all indirect paths from early TV to later aggression via intermediate aggression—i.e., from $TV_2 \rightarrow A_3 \rightarrow A_4$; (3) all indirect paths from earlier aggression to intermediate TV to later aggression—i.e., from $A_2 \rightarrow TV_3 \rightarrow A_4$; and (4) all paths from early to later TV measures—i.e., from $TV_1 \rightarrow TV_2 \rightarrow TV_3 \rightarrow A_4$. It will be difficult to test models that incorporate all the ways that television violence might affect aggression, and the analyst might be better served bracketing unknowable "true" effects rather than trying to estimate a single point that represents the cumulative effect of television. For the present, however, the crucial point is that the cumulative model of Milavsky et al. fails to include all the paths through which television violence might affect aggression and so may provide an underestimate of the "true" effect.

Another problem in the work of Milavsky et al. is the considerable departure from normality of the aggression dependent variables. The consequences of the skewed distributions should be considered in light of the sample sizes that are inevitably smaller with longer lags and more specific subgroups. Thus, for elementary boys the largest sample size is 497 when contrasting Waves III and IV, and the beta for the lagged TV variable is .078 ($p < .05$). In contrast, the sample size is only 112 when Waves I and VI are compared, and the beta, while higher (.160), is not reliably different from zero. Because of the grossly nonnormal distributions and small sample sizes for the longer lags that are of greatest relevance for a cumulative model, it is difficult to place confidence in the tests of statistical significance reported by Milavsky et al. and regularly used by them as a screening mechanism for deciding whether "effects" have occurred. Instead, we prefer to look to magnitude estimates and stable patterns of replication.

Anticipating the critique that their basic regression analysis was not sensitive enough to detect true effects at conventional levels of statistical significance, Milavsky et al. conducted a sensitivity analysis. They took five of the variables with the largest synchronous correlations with aggression and substituted these for the television variable in the basic lagged regression analysis for two-wave data. Since three of the five substitute measures resulted in consistent and reliable lagged associations with aggression, the authors concluded that their method was sensitive and that their failure to detect reliable effects of television violence was not due to the model's insensitivity with the data on hand. Unfortunately, the sensitivity analysis cannot carry the inferential burden attributed to it. First, the authors selected, a posteriori, variables with the highest cross-sectional correlation with aggression. Yet there are important theoretical and practical reasons for examining the lagged relationship of television violence to aggression. Second, Milavsky et al. tested whether *any* effects can be detected. This is less meaningful than testing whether effects of a predetermined magnitude can be detected.

Milavsky et al. foresaw every problem we have brought up and their foresight far outstrips conventional practice. However, we believe that their analysis nonetheless (a) failed to probe strong models of television's cumulative impact; (b) failed to probe the possibility of interactions between television viewing, gender, and SES levels; (c) did not fully probe the implications of consistently positive small coefficients and larger estimates with longer lags; and (d) relied excessively on tests of statistical significance that have questionable power because of badly skewed distributions and only moderate sample sizes for analyses involving longer time lags.

We are not inclined to claim that the study by Milavsky et al. "proves" any conclusion. Fortunately, a second panel study is available that tested a similar (but not identical) causal model. The work is by Huesmann et al. (1982), a version of which was published in the NIMH report. However, that version used an inadequate analysis based on cross-lagged panel correlations. The work we now review involved a better analysis.

HUESMANN, LAGERSPETZ, AND ERON

Each year for three years, Huesmann et al. surveyed elementary school children in grades 1–5, 758 from the U.S. and 220 from Finland. Program checklists were used to measure television viewing. Students indicated their favorite shows and rated their viewing frequency. These responses were summed and weighted according to the program's violence rating, as determined by two judges. A peer-rating measure of aggression was used, for which children were told to consider only behaviors in the current school year. Also, a four-item index was constructed of the child's self-rated similarity to characters who were described as engaging in specific aggressive behaviors. This was intended as a measure of identification with aggressive characters. The basic regression model was like Milavsky et al. in that the dependent variable was aggression in 1978, and aggression in 1976 was statistically controlled. However, the viewing measure was of one type of *cumulative* exposure to television violence (i.e., the sum of violence exposure for 1976 and 1977) rather than the single viewing term mostly preferred by Milavsky et al. Also Huesmann et al. added grade level to their model.

The results were similar to Milavsky et al. in direction, magnitude, and the low frequency of statistical significance. Thus, for American girls the standardized regression coefficient for the lagged television variable was .135 ($N = 221, p < .05$), while for U.S. boys it was .079 ($N = 191$), for Finnish girls it was .012 ($N = 85$), and for Finnish boys it was .110 ($N = 80$). However, Huesmann et al. chose to interpret the findings as evidence of an effect, whereas Milavsky et al. chose to interpret coefficients of comparable magnitude as evidence of no effect.

Huesmann et al. tested a second model with boys in which later aggression was studied with prior aggression being entered before a term formed from the product of viewing and the extent to which boys thought they were like aggressive television characters. The authors found that the interaction coefficients were reliably different from zero in both countries, and concluded that the link between television violence and subsequent aggression may be mediated through children identifying with violent fictional characters and not applying enough reality discount to what they watched. However, this conclusion depends on the interaction term not being correlated with the main effect of television. Since Huesmann et al. specifically concluded that a main effect was present, they also estimated a model in which prior television viewing was included. This reduced the interaction coefficient to a level that was no longer statistically reliable. Thus, the hypothesis that causal impact is mediated through identification with aggressive fictional characters remains promising but not proven for boys and untested for girls.

WHAT DO WE KNOW ABOUT TELEVISION VIOLENCE?

Our analysis of the past evidence for a causal link between television violence and aggression suggests that there is less consistency in the results than claimed and that consistent biases *may* have operated to inflate past estimates. Our reanalysis of the newer panel studies by Milavsky et al. and Huesmann et al. suggests that: (a) no effects of television violence emerge that are so large as to hit one between the eyes; (b) early measures of viewing television violence add to the predictability of later aggression over and above the predictability afforded by earlier measures of aggression; (c) these lagged effects are consistently positive, but not large, but (d) they are rarely statistically significant, although no reliable lagged negative effects have been reported.

The evidence indicates that a small association can regularly be found between viewing violence on television and later aggression when individual differences in aggression are controlled at one time. But is the association *causal*? If we were forced to render a judgment, it would be: Probably yes. Milavsky et al. conducted scores of subanalyses controlling for third variables that might be related to television viewing and later aggression over and above any relationship through earlier aggression. It seems that, of these, only SES analysis made the pattern of small positive coefficients disappear, and for reasons given earlier we are not impressed by the analyses of SES. Also, Leonard Eron has reported to us that entering an individual-level SES variable into the causal model of Huesmann et al. failed to make their lagged coefficients shrink to zero. Thus, the lagged relationships seem to have withstood all tests except one; and that failure is open to debate. Even so, this is not the same as withstanding tests based on third variables that theory indicates are spurious causes; and third variables can always be discovered of which no theoretician has yet conceived. Consequently, proof of causation is never possible, and judgments on this issue always have to be made. In our judgment, the lagged effects are probably causal.

This judgment is also influenced by the past literature. In particular, the randomized experiments in laboratory settings very strongly suggest that violence on the screen *can* cause aggression in normal populations, even though they do not speak directly to whether televised violence causes aggression in other settings. Further, the slowly growing file of case studies of imitative violence (summarized by Comstock, in press) indicate that events which are rare in real life have sometimes been committed soon after they were televised as part of a dramatic fictional show or a news account. This suggests that television violence *can* cause violence in nonlaboratory settings on the part of presumably abnormal people. Thus, there is strong evidence of causation in the wrong setting (the laboratory) with the right population (normal children), and in the right setting (outside of the laboratory) with the wrong population (abnormal adults). Such auxiliary evidence does not provide proof that the lagged associations obtained by Milavsky et al. and Huesmann et al. with the right population in the right setting represent causal connections; but it does provide circumstantial evidence of such connections.

WHAT DO THE SMALL LAGGED ASSOCIATIONS "MEAN"?

By conventional statistical criteria, these lagged associations account for trivial proportions of the explained variance in aggression even after corrections for unreliability. Also, most of the aggression measures are indistinctly related to behaviors that are obviously antisocial. Some tap into "boisterousness," others into "incivility," and very few tap directly into behaviors that we know lead to physical violence in the home or to problems with the law. Until intrepid (or foolhardy) econometricians undertake television research, we will not have grounded statements of the form "For each million hours of viewing television entertainment we have X murders, Y assaults, and Z cases of child abuse."

Unfortunately, there is no credible research on the extent to which the aggression measures typically used in television research predict to overt aggression and criminal behavior. Nonetheless, we are prepared to surmise that the relationship between viewing television violence and committing violent acts of the type universally abhorred in the U.S. will be even smaller than the already modest relationship between television violence and acts of boisterousness and incivility. It seems to us highly unlikely that television plays more than a minor role in directly producing violence and violent crime in the U.S. Certainly, its role is likely to be minimal when compared to many other social forces. Yet unlike these other causes of violence, television can be controlled technically, largely by limiting what is transmitted.

Although the effects of television may be small *on the average*, we do not yet know how the quality of interpersonal relations is changed when the general level of incivility among a large number of children is raised, whether by .5 percent, 1 percent or 2 percent. Also, the estimates of Milavsky et al. and Huessmann et al. represent an average, and a small number of the children who make up the average may suffer much larger consequences. Further, studies of television violence begin with children who have been watching television for several years, and they end well before the children have stopped watching violence. If effects increase in magnitude with more years of viewing or with longer delays between viewing and measuring effects, then the panel studies we examined in detail may have underestimated cumulative effects that can only be sensitively estimated from very large studies covering the two decades from infancy to late adolescence. All these limitations suggest that we have little basis for assessing the implications of the small lagged relationships between television and aggression observed over three years; and we cannot interpret them either as indicators of the need to reform entertainment programming or as indicators of the need to drop the violence issue as a dead end.

The NIMH report is too complacent, we believe, in its reasons for believing that television violence causes aggression and in its failure to describe the size of obtained effects. It is also inadvertently misleading in failing to discuss the implications that follow if the effects are considered "small" and if their relationships to physical violence or criminal behavior are unclear. Many readers understand "aggression" in terms of physical violence with intent to harm or as criminal behavior, and not as the "incivility" that the majority of past measures of aggression mostly tap into. Still, in interrelating the issues of prosocial and antisocial programming, the NIMH report does change in an important way the debate on television violence. We are now asked to measure the effects of such violence not only in terms of the aggression it might cause, but also in terms of the opportunities for positive growth that television violence precludes. For anyone who accepts this new frame for reference, the "small" direct effects of television violence inevitably understate the total direct and indirect costs of this type of programming.

Where Is the Leverage for Programming Changes?

It is difficult to predict how the NIMH report will be used. The theory of research utilization undergirding it seems to be the traditional theory of most basic researchers. It can be characterized as: Publish what we know to be the facts, and let them generate their own uses. The hope is that journalists, legislators, or judges will read the report and use its findings in ways that directly lead to programming changes, perhaps through regulation or creating public pressure on the networks. Another hope may be that individual parents will use the report to regulate their children's viewing; and another may be that future books on the media will cite the findings and influence how writers, producers, network executives, activists, and parents come to think about television.

The same theory of research utilization seems to be widespread among academic researchers of television. Most of them seem to care little about how their research is used. Their goal is a theoretical understanding of television and its roles in society. Other researchers care more about usage but are frustrated by the knowledge that academic research has rarely led to programming changes. The most salient exception to this generalization is offered by the surgeon-general's report of 1972, which led to the short-lived family viewing hour and may have contributed to what the CBS Office of Social

Research (1981) believes has been a small decrease in television portrayals of violence over the last 10 years. But the uses of the surgeon-general's report were not as dramatic or as longlasting as hoped, and may have been as much due to the short-lived pressure and publicity generated soon after the time of publication by Senator Pastore and the academic research establishment as to the quality of the evidence about the dangers of television violence.

It is not realistic to expect that the NIMH report will be used by the FCC to justify regulatory changes (Krattenmaker and Powe, 1978; Bollinger, 1982). This is partly because of the difficulty of establishing clear and present dangers from television. It is also partly because the FCC has been docile in the past and is financially dependent on a Congress whose members do not like to oppose the networks. Further, the courts have traditionally upheld the current dominant interpretations of the First Amendment that make government intervention into program decisions extremely difficult. The courts are also enjoined to seek the least harmful means of dealing with any negative effects of television. These are more likely to involve educating parents to control the selector knob better than decisions to modify program content, which would reek of censorship. The censorship issue is most salient with portrayals of real-life violence on the news. If television violence is harmful and should be regulated, surely this should apply to the news as well as entertainment programming, if the two can ever be clearly differentiated. For all these reasons, it is highly unlikely that the FCC will seek to regulate television content any more than it already does.

It is also difficult to affect change through influencing public and political opinion in ways that force the networks into "voluntary" change. Few Americans are so dissatisfied with the content of current television that they are willing to pressure legislators, to boycott certain advertised products, or to create events critical of programming that get extensive press coverage. Organized lobby groups are now trying to reduce the violence and sex on television or are attempting to reform children's advertising. But none of these poorly funded groups seem to us to be effective in significantly modifying the nature of television programming and advertising. They are indeed bothersome to the networks and may even be effective within the limits imposed by their size. Moreover, we do not know how television would be if they were not there as watchdogs. Nonetheless, their national impact does not seem large, and it is our impression that the networks treat them more like annoying gnats than strategically targeted missiles. Yet under different conditions the public interest groups could be more effective nationally, and we are not willing to assume that public pressure can never push the networks into "voluntary" change.

A third political source of leverage is through the broadcast industry's own attempts at self-improvement. The National Association of Broadcasters has standards which producers try to follow and which can be changed; the networks' own research staff studies the popularity of programs and the factors in them that make for popularity, and their findings can help change programs; the research staff also uses behavioral science consultants to comment on story plans in order to force out their potential for harm, and this process is attended by staff from departments concerned with standards. Finally, writers and producers have their own artistic standards, some of which can also change.

Little academic research speaks to the information needs of these groups within the broadcast industry, since the research deals with effects and not with ways to gain and hold audiences. There are some exceptions. For instance, Belson (1978) substituted the question of which types of violent programming cause aggression for the more traditional question of whether violence causes aggression, hoping to discover those forms of exciting violence that hold audiences but do not have harmful consequences. With a similar intent, Himmelweit et al. (1980) examined the nonviolent characteristics of programs that hold audiences, while in the NIMH report Comstock used laboratory experiments to detail the factors in violent programming that lead to less aggression. While useful in intention, these particular strategies have resulted in a limited payoff for industry self-improvement. To give only one example, Belson claimed that sports, cartoons, and slapstick comedy do not increase aggression, while realistic dramas and Westerns do. To ask writers and producers to eliminate or reduce realistic drama would be like asking them to refrain from exercising their craft on all interesting topics dealing with everyday life. More cogent would be research questions about the types of realistic violence that do and do not influence aggression.

In the more applied social sciences it is customary to ask, Where are the sources of leverage for change? and to follow this with the question, How can research best speak to the sources that have been identified? This approach involves different assumptions from those undergirding the model of use in the NIMH report and most academic research, where one begins with the assertion: This is what we know, and follows it with the question, How can this knowledge be used? In our opinion, the academic model has not yet produced much usage because it is not sensitive to where change can be effected. The knowledge is relevant to regulatory change, but such change is hardly possible given the stance of the FCC and the courts. It is also relevant to groups that want to reform television, but these groups are not now powerful or particularly effective. And while some kinds of knowledge might be used by the broadcast industry for self-improvement, the research community in universities is not producing information of this type. It is concentrating on effects of television and is ignoring the industry's desire to identify only the subset of programming changes that manifestly does not compromise audience size. Although academic research on television is somewhat successful in cataloging effects and beginning to understand why they come about, it is largely unsuccessful in using research to improve the entertainment content of television. One reason for this is that much television research is undertaken without first identifying where leverage for programming change exists and then tailoring the research to the pressure points identified.

Where, then, does leverage lie? Unfortunately, we are not as sure of an answer as we are of the importance of the question and of the need to explore it. In our opinion, the best place to start such an exploration is to go to Himmelweit's model and examine the broadcast industry (the networks, production companies, local stations, and advertising agencies) from a multidisciplinary perspective. This would stress the internal economics of the industry, its politics, sociology, and management, and it would also probe how the industry is linked to the institutions with which it interfaces (the FCC, Congress, high technology companies, university-based researchers, law firms representing the networks, activist groups, and various other public opinions). In such research the nature of schedules, shows, and advertisements would be dependent as well as independent variables; the predominant unit of analysis would be institutions rather than individuals; the methods would be historical and qualitative as well as quantitative; the causal models would involve reciprocal as well as unidirectional causal influences; and a special emphasis would be placed on the leverage points already identified so as to explore the conditions under which regulation, public opinion, and internal standards can help bring about changes in programming.

Such research would do more than fill out some of the glaring blanks in Himmelweit's model. It might also lead to information about specific sources of leverage of which we are not now aware and to which research could speak. We cannot be certain that research on the institutions related to television will eventually provide a theory of leverage for programming change. But we are confident that such research cannot influence programming less than the future research plans outlined in the NIMH report. Basically, these call for more of the same, but with a somewhat greater emphasis on new technology, on how adults as well as children are affected by television, on prosocial rather than antisocial effects, and on causal explanatory models instead of simple bivariate causal relationships. Since the NIMH priorities for the future overlap heavily with the research emphases of current television research, we feel all the more obliged to suggest the need for an alien perspective on the report's assumptions that may help alleviate the current impotence of television research (a) through study at the institutional rather than the individual level, and (b) through an explicit search for knowledge of leverage points that may affect programming changes. We have few illusions about how easy such research will be, particularly because the broadcast industry is private, is suspicious of the implicit elitist values of most researchers, and has few incentives to be cooperative with researchers. Nonetheless, much can be done with persistence, the creative use of public documents, and with access to individuals who have firsthand knowledge of the industry because they are or have been in it.

Conclusion

We are convinced, in general, that the NIMH report presents a reasonable summary of current knowledge about television, its effects and its potential. Our reservations touch upon a lack of realism in dealing with how the potential for prosocial effects can be realized; a lack of concern with the generally modest, if not small, negative effects of television; and an exaggerated sense of the confidence we should place in many past findings. The report convincingly takes us beyond the "no effects" era of Klapper (1960), when television was held mostly to reinforce already established beliefs and behaviors; but it does not convincingly take us as far as the authors of the report want to go in portraying television as a source of negative effects of immediate and pressing concern and as a force that could easily be harnessed for more prosocial ends. Evidence of negative effects is apparent, as is evidence of the potential for prosocial accomplishments. What is missing in the NIMH report, as in nearly all television research, are mechanisms for going from the evidence produced by television researchers to changes in television practice. We would be happy indeed if this article helped create a debate about whether such mechanisms are important, what they might be, and how they might be researched. Personally, we are apprehensive about the good to be gained from more television research of the dominant type conducted in the past and advocated for the future in the NIMH report. Such research produces descriptive findings, and helps begin the process of causal understanding. But since this type of television research places university-based scholars in a relationship of antagonism or irrelevance to those responsible for television practice, it needs supplementing with approaches that have a greater likelihood of directly and indirectly shaping the content of entertainment programs.

References

Belson, W. A.
1978 Television Violence and the Adolescent Boy. London: Saxon House.

Bollinger, L. C.
1982 "The First Amendment and the regulation of television violence." Paper prepared for Workshop on Television and Violent Behavior, Committee on Research on Law Enforcement and the Administration of Justice, National Research Council, Washington, D.C.

Campbell, D. T., and R. F. Boruch
1975 "Making the case for randomized assignment to treatments by considering the alternatives: six ways in which quasi-experimental evaluations tend to underestimate effects." In C. A. Bennett and A. A. Lumsdaine (eds.), Evaluation and Experience: Some Critical Issues in Assessing Social Programs. New York: Academic Press.

CBS Office of Social Research
1981 "Network prime-time violence tabulations for 1980–81 season." Unpublished manuscript, CBS, New York.

Comstock, G. A.
In press "Media influences on aggression." In A. Goldstein (ed.), Prevention and Control of Aggression: Principles, Practices and Research. New York: Pergamon Press.

Comstock, G. A., S. Chaffee, N. Katzman, M. McCombs, and D. Roberts
1978 Television and Social Behavior. New York: Columbia University Press.

Cook, T. D., and D. T. Campbell
1979 Quasi-Experimentation: Design and Analysis Issues for Field Settings. Boston: Houghton Mifflin.

Cronbach, L. J., D. R. Rogosa, R. E. Floden, and G. G. Price
1977 "Analysis of covariance in nonrandomized experiments: parameters affecting bias." Occasional Papers, Stanford University, Stanford Evaluation Consortium.

Feshbach, S., and R. D. Singer
1971 Television and Aggression: An Experimental Field Study. San Francisco: Jossey-Bass.

Gerbner, G., L. Gross, M. Morgan, and N. Signorielli
1980 "The 'mainstreaming' of America: violence profile no. 11." Journal of Communication 30:10–29.
1982 "Charting the mainstream: television's contributions to political orientations." Journal of Communication 32:100–27

Hearold, S. L.
1979 "Meta-analysis of the effects of television on social behavior." Unpublished doctoral dissertation, University of Colorado.

Himmelweit, H. T.
1980 "Social influence and television." In S. B. Withey and R. P. Abeles (eds.),

Television and Social Behavior: Beyond Violence and Children. Hillsdale, NJ: Erlbaum.

Himmelweit, H. T., B. Swift, and M. E. Jaeger
1980 "The audience as critic: an approach to the study of entertainment." In P. Tannenbaum (ed.), Entertainment Functions of Television. Hillsdale, NJ: Erlbaum.

Hirsch, P.
1980 "The 'scary world' of the nonviewer and other anomalies: a reanalysis of Gerbner et al.'s findings of cultivation analysis, Part I." Communication Research 7:403–56.
1981 "On not learning from one's own mistakes: a reanalysis of Gerbner et al.'s findings on cultivation analysis, Part II." Communication Research 8:3–37.

Huesmann, L. R., K. Lagerspetz, and L. D. Eron
1982 "Intervening variables in the television violence-aggression relation: a binational study." Unpublished manuscript, University of Illinois at Chicago Circle.

Hughes, M.
1980 "The fruits of cultivation analysis: a re-examination of the effects of television watching on fear of victimization, alienation, and the approval of violence." Public Opinion Quarterly 44:287–302.

Klapper, J. T.
1960 The Effects of Mass Communication. New York: Free Press.

Krattenmaker, T. G., and L. A. Powe, Jr.
1978 "Televised violence: First Amendment principles and social science theory." Virginia Law Review 64:1123–1297

Leyens, J. P., R. D. Parke, L. Camino, and L. Berkowitz
1975 "Effects of movie violence on aggression in a field setting as a function of group dominance and cohesion." Journal of Personality and Social Psychology 32:346–60.

Loye, D., R. Gorney, and G. Steele
1977 "Effects of television: an experimental field study." Journal of Communication 27:206–16.

Milavsky, J. R., R. C. Kessler, H. Stipp, and W. S. Rubens
1982 Television and Aggression: The Results of a Panel Study. New York: Academic Press.

Morgan, M.
1982 "Television and adolescents' sex role stereotypes: a longitudinal study." Journal of Personality and Social Psychology 43:947–55.

National Institute of Mental Health
1982 Television and Behavior: Ten Years of Scientific Progress and Implications for the Eighties (D. Pearl, L. Bonthilet, and J. Lazar, eds.). Rockville, Md.: NIMH.

Neville, T.
1980 "Television viewing and the expression of interpersonal mistrust." Unpublished doctoral dissertation, Princeton University.

Parke, R. D., L. Berkowitz, J. P. Leyens, S. West, and R. J. Sebastian
1977 "Some effects of violent and nonviolent movies on the behavior of juvenile delinquents." In L. Berkowitz (ed.), Advances in Experimental Social Psychology (Vol. 10). New York: Academic Press.

Rogosa, D.
1980 "A critique of cross-lagged correlation." Psychological Bulletin 88:245–58.

Sawin, D. B.
1973 "Aggressive behavior among children in small polygroup settings with violent television." Unpublished doctoral dissertation, University of Minnesota.

Singer, J. L., and D. G. Singer
1980 Television, Imagination and Aggression: A Study of Preschoolers' Play. Hillsdale, NJ: Erlbaum.

Stein, A. H., and L. K. Friedrich
1972 "Television content and young children's behavior." In J. P. Murray, E. A. Rubenstein, and G. A. Comstock (eds.), Television and Social Behavior (Vol. 2): Television and Social Learning. Washington, D.C.: Government Printing Office.

Tyler, T.
1980 "Impact of directly and indirectly experienced events: The origin of crime-related judgments and behaviors." Journal of Personality and Social Psychology 39:13–28.

Wells, W. D.
1973 "Television aggression: replication of an experimental field study." Unpublished manuscript, University of Chicago.

Withey, S. B., and R. P. Abeles (eds.)
1980 Television and Social Behavior: Beyond Violence and Children. Hillsdale, NJ: Erlbaum.

PART II

MEDIA AND SOCIETY
Social Reality and Media Representations

INTRODUCTION

Steve M. Barkin

The 11 articles in this section are presented under two headings: "Structuring Reality" and "Telling Stories." Despite differences in emphasis and approach, all the selections share two fundamental assumptions: that mass communication is a social process involving the construction of meaning, and that questions of media content and performance are connected to the larger issues of social organization and cultural context.

In the first group of articles, Adoni, Cohen, and Mane examine perceptions of social conflicts as they appear on television news and as they occur in society. Subjects in their study were able to differentiate between media portrayals and social reality according to the perceived complexity, intensity, and solvability of the conflicts. Differences in perception were a function of individuals' direct experience and dependence upon the media as sources of specific information.

Hallin and Mancini compare Italian and American news broadcasts to illustrate the relationship between journalistic form and political structure. Broadcast news in the United States is characterized as thematic and interpretive; in Italy, as fragmented, referential, and less consciously symbolic. These differences, the authors suggest, stem from varying definitions of the public sphere and the role of journalists in the two countries.

Dayan, Katz, and Kerns present an anthropological view of television "pragmatics," the nature of audience involvement with a text. They point out that the televised trips of Pope John Paul II, conveyed as participatory celebrations, offer spectators an opportunity to undergo a pilgrimage of their own, a symbolic adventure outside oneself.

Morley also examines the audience's role in the construction of meaning. Focusing on the decoding of media messages—specifically those of the British current affairs program *Nationwide*—he suggests that differences in audience readings are considerable, and relate to a society's underlying distinctions of class and subculture.

Hackett's essay presents a series of challenges to the theoretical underpinnings of conventional research on news bias. His argument is for a broader conceptualization of both the nature of language and the journalist's role as agents in the framing of events.

Newcomb and Hirsch discuss a model for understanding the texts and processes of television that incorporates the notion of active audiences constructing a multiplicity of meanings. The television text is viewed as an open-ended, socially diverse forum, raising questions and allowing disparate and even oppositional responses from its audience. The authors contend that media messages are open to a wide range of interpretations and that audiences make meaning by selecting that which touches experience and personal history.

Budd, Craig, and Steinman open the unit on "Telling Stories." They offer a thematic analysis of one episode of television's *Fantasy Island* in which the myths of entertainment are directly linked to the myths of commercials. As the fictional program raises problems and possibilities for its audience to consider, the targeted commercials propose solutions in the form of consumer products. The result according to the authors is a dramatized form of dream fulfillment.

Bell examines themes in Australian news reports of drug-related issues. In stories about drugs, a structured set of interacting agents play out a limited number of scenarios. The author finds that those who use and abuse drugs are portrayed as passive victims, whereas "experts pronounce, authorities judge, helpers warn, scientists debate, bureaucrats plan." Defining drug use as a social problem, Bell argues, is a textual assertion of the remedial power of the state.

Eason's analysis of the "new journalism" places storytelling in its broadest context—as an epistemological act, a way of organizing experience. Two modes of new journalism, designated ethnographic realism and cultural phenomenology, are distinguished. The two approaches reflect alternative ways of responding to cultural change and creating meaning.

Radway's study demonstrates the nature of text-reader interaction among a small group of romance readers. As an interpretive community, romance readers contextualize stories within the social circumstances of their own lives. The author notes that the uses of reading itself will vary between communities and will influence the meanings drawn from any text.

Nord presents a historical case study of newspaper coverage of labor-management disputes in the late nineteenth century. The Chicago *Times, Tribune*, and *Daily News* had clear political differences but, more important, shared professional values that, Nord suggests, structured the presentation of events.

ON CONTEXTUALIZING THE TEXT

The central role of stories and storytelling in mass communication is either an explicit theme or an underlying premise in all these selections; media texts are treated throughout as important social and cultural documents. The notion of story has been for some time at the heart of dramaturgical approaches to communication. Because the construction of meaning is, to begin with, a process of creating and manipulating symbols, the nature of stories in a particular society may be expected to cast light not only on the processes of its communicators, but on the values of the society itself.

By now this is a familiar rationale for the textual analysis of media products: The text taken as a cultural artifact, the message as the object of a structural investigation, whether its concerns be literary, linguistic, or semiological. Collectively, the articles in this section raise another point, however: The text, isolated from the processes used to create it and, especially, from the audiences who actively interpret it, provides at best only part of the picture.

Curiously, perspectives on mass media and society grounded in the social construction of reality have tended to be message centered. The irony is that messages themselves may not sufficiently account for the *social* aspects of communication. Every symbolic universe, Berger and Luckmann observe, is a human product "whose existence has its base in the lives of concrete individuals," with no "empirical status apart from these lives." If meanings are in fact "intersubjective," both audiences and communicators are participants in its construction.

Many of these authors would insist that meanings are indeed multiple. Newcomb and Hirsch find in television a home for cultural diversity; Adoni, Cohen, and Mane demonstrate the variability of audience perceptions; Dayan, Katz, and Kerns locate "pilgrimages" not on the screen but in the lives of spectators; Morley and Radway suggest that reading and viewing can be processes of retextualization, of the social reconstruction of reality.

Radway's study is particularly useful in revealing the congruence of disciplinary concerns. As communication scholars turn to modes of decoding and to cultural anthropology, literary critics question whether metaphors, themes, and even the act of reading mean the same things to different people. The concept of "interpretive communities" bridges mass communication research and literary analysis, and promises to enrich both fields.

These chapters also may represent the current state of unhappiness with conventional forms of content analysis. Hackett makes the case most explicitly: Adding up descriptive signifiers has proved too frequently to be a surface exercise that underestimates the role of language in constituting reality. A catalogue of verbs, modifiers, and sentence constructions may not be enough to capture a mediated reality. Worse, it may actually obscure the broader process of framing ideas and events.

Some penetrating questions remain. If the media in effect present a first draft of reality, which audiences then edit, revise, and reformulate, how are we to define—or redefine—media's ideological and pedagogical roles? Is there a mechanism linking social structure, cultural context, and the processing of language? Such questions cannot be addressed by treating messages and audiences as discrete, separate, or static—as essentially unrelated to one another.

Those whose work is included here are concerned with a cultural analysis of mass communication as a network of symbolic environments rather than narrowly focused media studies. That these selections can neither be labeled message centered nor audience based is a telling comment on the authors' perspective: that the construction of meaning is a socially defined, thoroughly interactive process. In making a case for contextualizing the text, these authors provide a compelling argument for contextualizing mass communication research itself in the study of culture.

9

SOCIAL REALITY AND TELEVISION NEWS
Perceptual Dimensions of Social Conflicts in Selected Life Areas

Hanna Adoni, Akiba A. Cohen, and Sherrill Mane

Perceptions of social conflicts in television news and in "reality" are organized according to their complexity, intensity and solvability, and also according to their different life areas.

This study investigates simultaneously the perception of social, political and economic conflicts as they occur in society, and as they are portrayed by television news. We chose conflicts as the subject of the investigation because of three considerations: first, the ubiquity of conflicts in society and their importance in the processes of social change;[1] second, the dominance of conflicts as a subject of news content;[2] and third, the claim of the Critical Approach to mass culture as represented by the Frankfurt School of scholars and their followers[3] that media depictions of society, which emphasize consensus and minimize the importance of social conflicts, are fundamental to the role of the mass media in ensuring the existence of the social and political status quo.

Manuscript accepted for publication, August 1983.

The research reported here was sponsored by the Israel National Council for Research and Development. We would like to thank William J. McGuire of Yale University for his helpful comments on the conceptual part of the project. Thanks are also due to Gideon Drori, Hillel Nossek and Debbie Steinberg for serving as able, industrious and insightful graduate research assistants throughout the project. We wish to acknowledge our colleagues Elihu Katz and Yitzhak Roeh at The Communications Institute of The Hebrew University as well as Louis Guttman and Samuel Shye at the Israel Institute for Applied Social Research for their comments, suggestions and encouragement. And finally, Yaakov Schul for his assistance with some of the statistical analyses.

[1]Albert F. Eldridge, *Images of Conflict* (New York: St. Martin's Press, 1979); Anthony Oberschall, *Social Conflict and Social Movements* (Englewood Cliffs: Prentice Hall, 1973).

[2]Herbert J. Gans, *Deciding What's News* (New York: Pantheon Books, 1979); Johan Galtung and Marie Holmboe Ruge, "The Structure of Foreign News," *Journal of Peace Research* 2:64–91 (1965).

[3]T. W. Adorno, "Television and the Patterns of Mass Culture," in *Mass Culture: The Popular Arts in America,* eds. Bernard Rosenberg and David Manning White (New York: The Free Press, 1957); Leo Lowenthal, "The Triumph of Mass Idols," in *Literature, Popular Culture and Society,* ed. Leo Lowenthal (Palo Alto: Pacific Books, 1961); Stuart Hall, "Culture, the Mass Media and the Ideological Effect," in *Mass Communication and Society,* eds. James Curran, Michael Gurevitch and Janet Woolacott (London: Edward Arnold, 1977).

We chose to study television news because of common findings that it serves as an important source of political information and civic awareness.[4] Other studies which investigated the role of television in the process of the construction of reality focused on entertainment (fictional) contents.[5] Notwithstanding the assumption that television fictional contents are involved in the process of the construction of social reality, the lack of attention by researchers to *news* contents, purported by some to be a reflection of "reality," warrants this added research direction.

The main hypotheses of this study, to be elaborated below, are based on the media-dependency hypothesis[6] which suggests that the degree of media contribution to the perception of social reality is a function of direct experience with various social phenomena and the dependence on the media as sources of information about them. Direct experience and the degree of remoteness of different life areas from the individual in the perception of social reality are also central in various phenomenological theories on the social construction of reality.[7] These theories suggest that the individual's subjective reality is organized in terms of "zones of relevance" which differ in their degree of remoteness from the "here and now" of his or her existence. According to these theories various social processes such as socialization, acquisition of language and learning of social roles transmit basic everyday knowledge enabling the individual to function in society. These theories, however, do not discuss the role of the mass media in these

---

[4]Steven H. Chaffee, Marilyn M. Beeck, Jean Duvall and Donna Wilson, "Mass Communication in Political Socialization," in *Handbook of Political Socialization,* ed. Stanley A. Renshon (New York: The Free Press, 1973); Margaret Conway, A. Jay Stevens and Robert G. Smith, "The Relation Between Media Use and Children's Civic Awareness," *Journalism Quarterly* 52:531–538 (Autumn 1975).

[5]George Gerbner and Larry Gross, "Living With Television: The Violence Profile," *Journal of Communication* 26:172–199 (Spring 1976); George Gerbner, Larry Gross, Michael F. Eleey, Marilyn Jackson-Beeck, Suzanne Jeffries-Fox and Nancy Signorielli, "TV Violence Profile No. 8: The Highlights," *Journal of Communication* 27:171–180 (Spring 1977); George Gerbner, Larry Gross, Marilyn Jackson-Beeck, Suzanne Jeffries-Fox and Nancy Signorielli, "Cultural Indicators: Violence Profile No. 9," *Journal of Communication* 28:176–207 (Summer 1978); George Gerbner, Larry Gross, Michael Morgan and Nancy Signorielli, "The 'Mainstreaming' of America: Violence Profile No. 11," *Journal of Communication* 30:10–29 (Summer 1980); George Gerbner, Larry Gross, Nancy Signorielli, Michael Morgan and Marilyn Jackson-Beeck, "The Demonstration of Power: Violence Profile No. 10," *Journal of Communication* 29:177–196 (Summer 1979); George Gerbner and Nancy Signorielli, "Women and Minorities in Television Drama 1969–1978," (The Annenberg School of Communication, University of Pennsylvania, 1979); Robert P. Hawkins and Suzanne Pingree, "Using Television to Construct Social Reality," *Journal of Broadcasting* 25:347–364 (Fall 1981).

[6]Sandra Ball-Rokeach and Melvin L. DeFleur, "A Dependency Theory of Mass Media Effects," *Communication Research* 3:3–21 (January 1976).

[7]Peter Berger and Thomas Luckmann, *The Social Construction of Reality* (Garden City: Doubleday, 1966); Alfred Schutz, *The Phenomenology of the Social World* (Evanston: Northwestern University Press, 1967).

processes, except for minor references. Thus media dependency theory provides this missing element in attempting to understand peoples' perception of reality.

Television and Social Conflict

The literature is rife with definitions of social conflicts. The present study adopted Kriesberg's definition of social conflict as "a relationship between two or more parties who believe they have incompatible goals."[8] In our opinion, this general formulation is appropriate in studying the perceptions of conflicts which differ from each other in terms of issues in contention, the means used to pursue goals and the alternative solutions to the conflict situations.

Any symbolic representation of reality is based on selection and editing of material derived from reality, and thus depicts only a certain part of reality and portrays it from a specific point of view. Accordingly, in formulating hypotheses concerning the contribution of television news to the perception of social conflicts, we assumed that television news is affected by these inherent processes. The following is an attempt to suggest, on the basis of sociological and media literature, three main dimensions of social conflicts which may be considered as the central foci of such "bias." These dimensions are complexity, intensity and difficulty of resolution of social conflicts.[9]

Complexity. The focus on the complexity dimension stems from the argument that television news coverage tends to simplify social conflicts. While the sociological literature maintains that any conflict in society has several stages, television news focuses only on its manifest stages, and minimizes the presentation of its underlying causes, the opponents' motivations, and in general, the analysis of social conflicts as gradually unfolding social processes.[10] According to Murdock,[11] this type of simplification is the result of the "event orientation" which determines that processes leading to an event do not themselves make the news. In the absence of explanations of

---

[8]Louis Kriesberg, *The Sociology of Social Conflicts* (Englewood Cliffs: Prentice-Hall, 1973).

[9]Another attempt to define dimensions of social conflicts appears in the work of Ross Stagner, *The Dimensions of Human Conflict* (Detroit: Wayne State University Press, 1967) which has some overlap with the present conceptualization but also differs in several respects.

[10]Glasgow University Media Group, *Bad News* (London: Routledge and Kegan Paul, 1976); Paul Hartmann and Charles Husband, "The Mass Media and Racial Conflict," in *Sociology of Mass Communications,* ed. Dennis McQuail (Harmondsworth: Penguin, 1972); Gaye Tuchman, *Making News* (New York: The Free Press, 1978).

[11]Graham Murdock, "Political Deviance: The Press Presentation of a Militant Mass Demonstration," in *The Manufacture of News,* eds. Stanley Cohen and Jock Young (London: Constable, 1973).

the underlying causes of social conflicts, television news presents events as being "caused" by the immediately preceding acts of groups or individuals thereby creating the impression that dissent is confined to small and marginal groups in society. A further simplification is the typical depiction by television news of social conflicts as struggles between two well-delineated opponents[12] while in many conflict relationships there are actually more than two parties, including mediators, who are pursuing incompatible goals.

Intensity. The notion of the intensity dimension is derived from the claim that television news tends to present only the more intense moments of social conflicts.[13] Tuchman[14] illustrates this point with the example of news coverage of riots. While during riots there are periods of lull, "news reports usually ignore this, collapsing the course of riots into continuous intensive activity." Hall[15] observed that the characteristic form of coverage of social conflicts is "actuality without context" and that this is obtained by the concentration of the news media on "vivid sound and image." Furthermore, the presentation of intensive activity usually centers around groups who are not identified with the economic and political powerholders of society. For example, the Glasgow University Media Group[16] found that in the television news coverage of industrial strikes in Britain, management representatives are generally interviewed in their offices—a quiet setting connoting reason, authority and responsibility, whereas strikers are shown in "action" at mass meetings and pickets—settings implying that they are the major sources of the discord.

Solvability. The third and final dimension of social conflicts, that of the difficulty of solvability of social conflicts (referred to henceforth as "solvability"), is derived from the suggestion that television news tends to present social conflicts as "incidents soon to be resolved rather than permanent conflicts of interests."[17] According to the sociological analyses of social conflicts, the difficulty of resolution depends on the nature of the incompatible goals pursued by the opponents and on the estimated costs of the possible outcomes to the parties involved and/or to uninvolved people or groups.[18] For example, social conflicts over basic values and resources such as power, status, civil rights or religion are more difficult to resolve than conflict over issues such as economic benefits. Murdock[19] contends that as a

---

[12]Edward J. Epstein, *News From Nowhere* (New York: Vintage Books, 1973).

[13]Stuart Hall, "A World At One With Itself," in *The Manufacture of News, op. cit.*

[14]Tuchman, *op. cit.*

[15]Hall, "A World At One With Itself," *op. cit.*

[16]Glasgow University Media Group, *op. cit.*

[17]Gans, *op. cit.*

[18]Oberschall, *op. cit.*

[19]Murdock, *op. cit.*

result of the "event orientation" the social conflicts covered by television news appear to be short termed and easily solved. The underlying message of this type of presentation is that society is essentially characterized by consensus, and that the consequence is the reinforcing of the status quo. Connel, Curti and Hall also claim that as a result of the ethical and professional importance of objectivity, neutrality and balance, the presentation of television news gives the solutions to the conflicts the appearance of being in the general interest rather than exposing the advantages which the ruling classes gain from them.[20]

In sum, according to the literature on media and culture, presentations of social conflicts in television news tend to diverge from the complexity, intensity and solvability of social conflicts as they occur in society. Furthermore, television news tends to create a fairly uniform and stereotyped picture of social conflicts, while the sociological analysis points out the diversity and variety of these social phenomena.

Media Dependency Theory

Most of the studies cited above concentrated on the study of media contents and production constraints and assumed that the simplified and distorted picture of reality which is presented in television news indeed gets through to the audience and shapes their opinions and world view. We wish to suggest that this is an oversimplified view of media effects on the perception of social reality. Media dependency theory seems to provide a more useful theoretical framework for an empirical investigation of the contribution of the media to the process of the social construction of reality in general, and to the perceptions of social conflicts in particular.

According to this hypothesis, people depend on the media for information about social phenomena which are remote from everyday life experiences to a greater extent than they are dependent on the media in learning about social phenomena which they experience directly. However, very few empirical studies provide evidence to support this theory.

Rarick, Townsend and Boyd,[21] for example, found that perceptions of real policemen were diversified ranging from positive to negative, whereas perceptions of policemen on television were homogenized and favorable. In addition, in a British study, Hartmann and Husband[22] found that people living in areas with little contact between racial groups perceived race relations in

---

[20] Ian Connell, Lidia Curti and Stuart Hall, "The Unity of Current Affairs TV," *Working Papers in Cultural Studies, No. 9* (Center for Contemporary Cultural Studies, University of Birmingham, 1976).

[21] David L. Rarick, James E. Townsend and Douglas A. Boyd, "Adolescent Perceptions of Police: Actual and as Depicted in TV Drama," *Journalism Quarterly* 50:438–446 (Autumn 1973).

[22] Hartmann and Husband, *op. cit.*

line with the news media coverage to a greater extent than those from high contact areas. They also found that those living in high contact areas defined the racial situation using a greater variety of terms than those living in low contact areas. Also, Doob and MacDonald[23] found that fear of victimization is related to television viewing only for adults living in high crime areas but not for those living in low crime areas.

Personal Experience and Social Conflict

In the present study we hypothesized that the differential perception of the complexity, intensity and solvability of social conflicts between the "real" world and television news will depend upon the individual's personal experiences with social conflicts. Thus, more personal experience and less dependency on television news will result in the greatest differentiation between the two realms of reality. In order to test this hypothesis we examined three kinds of social conflicts differing in terms of their presumed remoteness from the life experience of adolescents: conflicts concerning school integration, labor relations and political terrorism. We assumed that adolescents have the most personal experience with the first type of conflict which generally occurs in their own schools and neighborhoods. Conflicts concerning labor relations are more remote from the adolescents' life experience as most of them do not work for a living or at most are employed part-time during school vacations. However, they could acquire some experience via their parents and by themselves being consumers of various services such as transportation and education. The third type of conflict is that of political terrorism with which most people do not have direct experience and depend almost entirely on the mass media for information about this.[24]

On the surface, it may appear that the conceptualization of the present study contradicts the concept of "resonance" suggested by Gerbner et al.[25] This is not the case, however; the two might even be complementary. Gerbner and his colleagues argue that in cases of high congruence between what people see on television and their "everyday reality or even perceived reality," the television content will be accepted as a faithful depiction of reality and the cultivation effect will be amplified. This may be the case with

---

[23]Anthony W. Doob and Glenn E. MacDonald, "Television Viewing and Fear of Victimization: Is the Relationship Causal?" *Journal of Personality and Social Psychology* 37:170–179 (February 1979).

[24]The study by Galtung and Ruge, *op. cit.,* presents several criteria according to which journalists select foreign news items for use in their newspaper. One of these criteria relates to the distance or proximity of the item being considered to the country where it will be reported. The authors demonstrate that this criterion is indeed used by journalists. However, Galtung and Ruge do not deal at all with the perception of the distance or proximity of the news item from the point of view of the reader.

[25]Gerbner, Gross, Morgan and Signorielli, *op. cit.*

fictional contents (on which Gerbner and his colleagues base their findings), given the assumption that people do not initially expect substantial congruence or identity between fictional contents and reality, and generally speaking, do not make a comparison between a specific event and its symbolic representation on television. However, when dealing with *news,* the subject of the present research, we assume that the viewer in fact becomes aware of even the slightest degree of incongruence between reality and television because he or she does initially expect television to "reflect" reality. This perceptual process is reinforced when people actually participate in specifically reported, or in similar events, and can compare "what happened there" to what they saw on television. In other words, what is critical in this context is the interaction between the viewers' experiences and their predispositions as to what the relationship between reality and the television genre is, or ought to be.

Even Gerbner and his associates, in their recent work,[26] interpret their findings taking into account the notion of direct experience. They found that the tendency for "heavy" viewers to have negative perceptions of elderly people is stronger for adults under 30 than for those over 30. Their explanation was that younger adults are more remote from old age and are consequently more influenced by television depictions of older people. Thus, all these findings seem to be congruent with the notion that the contents of perceptions of social reality, based on direct experience, are qualitatively different from the contents of perceptions based on other sources, as suggested by both the media-dependency hypothesis and the phenomenological theories.

Research Hypotheses

In the present study we tested three specific hypotheses. First, there will be a distinction between the perception of social reality and its portrayal in television news for all the dimensions and life areas. We expected that the conflicts in the realm of social reality will be perceived as more complex, less intense and more difficult to solve than their portrayal in television news.

The second hypothesis concerns the magnitude of differentiation between the two realms of reality across the three life areas, which are ordered according to the degree of their remoteness from the individual's life experiences. Accordingly, we expected that the differentiation between the two realms of reality will be greatest for the conflicts concerning school integration and minimal for the political conflicts.

The final hypothesis states that the structure of the perceptions of social

[26] Gerbner, Gross, Morgan and Signorielli, *op. cit.*

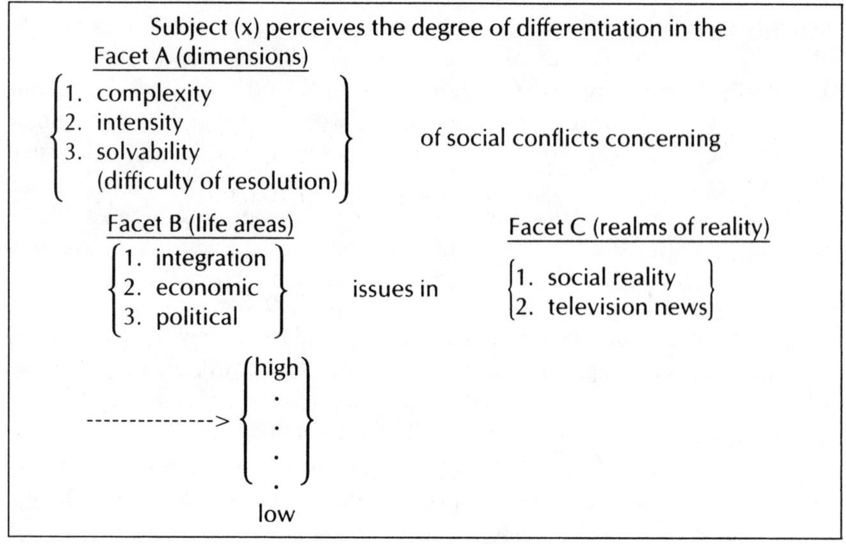

Figure I Mapping Sentence

conflicts in social reality and television news will both be organized according to the three conflict dimensions (complexity, intensity and solvability) and the three life areas (integration, economics and politics). The structure will be tested by means of correlations among the various perceptual elements. Accordingly, the correlational structure among the elements of the perception of "real" conflicts will be more diversified (lower correlations among them), while the structure of the perceptions of media portrayals of conflict will be more homogeneous and uniform (higher correlations among them).

A summary of the theoretical arguments is presented in the following "mapping sentence" which is used to define both the content of the variables and the common range of their response categories.[27] In the present mapping sentence there are three facets: the dimensions of social conflicts, the social subsystems or life areas, and the realms of reality.

The elements of Facet A (the dimensions) are unordered. The elements of Facet B (the life areas) are arranged according to their assumed distance from everyday life experience of adolescents, with conflicts concerning integration being closest to the respondents and conflicts in the political life area being most remote from them. As for Facet C (the realms of reality), the elements are ordered in terms of their degree of mediation, namely the conflicts as they occur in social reality are unmediated whereas the conflicts as they appear in television news are mediated via the news organizations.

[27] Shlomit Levy, "Uses of the Mapping Sentence for Coordinating Theory and Research: A Cross Cultural Example," *Quality and Quantity* 10:117–125 (June 1976).

Method

The Sample

The sample consisted of 425 12th grade students in several high schools in Israel. The sample was representative of the entire high school population of the country in terms of gender and socio-economic status.

Procedure

The research was carried out in December 1979. Two graduate students were responsible for the administration in each classroom with an average of 15 students per room. The objective of the study was explained to the respondents as follows: "We come from the Hebrew University and we are interested in studying what young people in Israel think about social conflicts. To be sure that you understand what we mean by 'social conflicts' we are going to show you three news reports that were shown on the evening news some time ago."

At this point three 2-minute news items were shown, one concerning each of the social life areas: for the political life area the item dealt with an airplane hijacking in Europe committed for political blackmail; for the labor relations (economic) life area the item reported on a strike at a food factory; and for the social integration life area the item dealt with an attempt to prevent the integration of children from socially heterogeneous neighborhoods in one school. For each subgroup of the sample the items were shown in one of the six possible orders of presentation.

The news items were actually produced with the aid of Israel Television newsmen based on "scripts" prepared by the researchers. The "scripts" were based on the findings of Levin[28] which indicate that television news depictions of social conflicts on each of these subjects are highly uniform and that the same basic dramatic elements occur in all of them. The level of complexity and intensity were designed to be "moderate" in all of the items.[29] However, as solvability could be viewed as a dichotomous variable,

---

[28]Esther Levin, "Dramatic Elements in TV News Portrayal of Conflicts in Three Life Areas," (The Communications Institute, Hebrew University of Jerusalem, 1979).

[29]Levin's (1979) study was based on an analysis of numerous news items which could be ranged from high to low in terms of their intensity and complexity. For example, a news item on a hijacked airplane showing an actual attempt to rescue the hostages and/or victims of such an occurrence was considered as highly intense; a similar news item only showing the airport and a long shot of the hijacked airplane would be considered as low intensity. Items considered as "moderate" in intensity would typically show the hijacked airplane and the negotiations going on. As for complexity, a news item would be considered to be highly complex if it referred to many parties to the conflict and/or numerous issues involved. An item was considered to be low in complexity if only two parties were mentioned or only one issue (the minimum for any conflict). A "moderate" degree of complexity typically involved few (3–4) parties and 2–3 issues.

two versions were produced for each item—one with and one without a solution. The items were produced using film footage purchased from the Visnews agency and from segments shot by the research team. The items were judged by a group of television journalists and researchers as well as by a group of high school students in a pilot study to be highly authentic and of broadcast quality.

Our rationale for the use of the news items was to provide the respondents with a common reference regarding the nature of social conflicts, thus the news items would serve as a "triggering mechanism" to evoke their perceptual responses. We should stress, however, that the reason for showing the news items was *not* to test the effect of the specific items nor the manipulation of the solvability variable. Nevertheless, the two different versions *were* used in order to avoid biasing the respondents in any particular direction. As a precaution, the responses to the different versions were examined and no significant differences were found. This allowed us to combine the data of all the respondents for the data analyses. Moreover, given the hypotheses of the study, we could also argue that by presenting the respondents with *television* news items as examples of social conflicts, a bias could result in which the respondents would be less inclined to differentiate between television news and social reality. Hence, such a procedure would mean stacking the cards against us. This point should be kept in mind when examining the results of the study.

The Questionnaire

Three questions were developed for each of the dimensions of perception, with parallel questions for both realms of social reality. Each question had four response categories ranging from low to high. For all of the questions a high score indicated high complexity, high intensity and high difficulty of solvability. By way of illustration, we present the questions on the school integration conflict. Slight wording differences make them applicable for the other conflicts as well.

The three questions on the complexity dimension were: "How many parties are generally involved in conflicts concerning school integration?," "How many different opinions are generally involved in conflicts about school integration?" and "How many facts does one need to know in order to understand conflicts regarding school integration?" The comparable questions in the realm of television news were: "How many parties are usually presented on TV news in connection with conflicts on school integration?," "In TV news, how many differing opinions are presented concerning conflicts on school integration?" and "How many facts does one need to know in order to understand conflicts on school integration as presented by TV news?"

The questions on intensity were: "To what extent do the parties involved in conflicts on school integration use extreme means?," "To what extent do people involved in conflicts on school integration become emotional?" and "To what extent do people involved in school integration conflicts act in an aggressive manner?" For the realm of television news the proper modifications were made.

Finally, the questions on the solvability dimension were: "What proportion of conflicts on school integration are solved?," "To what extent are the parties involved in conflicts on school integration usually willing to give up their demands in order to reach a solution?" and "If a solution in a conflict on school integration is reached, how long does it generally last?" Here, too, the necessary modifications were made to make these questions applicable to the realm of television news.

Thus, for each realm of reality there were 27 questions, nine for each of the three dimensions in each of the three life areas. The first set of 27 questions for all the respondents were those concerning the realm of social reality followed by the 27 questions on the realm of television news. We decided upon this order of presentation of the questions in order to stack the cards against the hypothesis of the study by allowing the respondents, if they so wished, to respond to the questions on the "real" world using the presented television stimuli as reference points.[30]

At the end of the questionnaire there were several demographic questions. The entire session lasted about 35–45 minutes.

---

[30]We specifically checked to what extent this bias may have occurred by adding a control group consisting of 109 12th grade students. This group did not view the news stimuli and only answered the questions pertaining to the realm of social reality. We found no significant differences regarding the perception of social conflicts in society between the respondents in the control groups and the respondents who saw the news items. This finding is crucial indeed as it provides retroactive justification for our not having separated the data collection into two sessions, one for the questions about the "real" world and the other for the presentation of the news items and the questions concerning the world of television news. Since doing this study, we also conducted a more expanded replication with several modifications. We presented the same questions concerning social conflicts in television news, the "real" world and with the addition of the world of television fiction to a sample of 417 11th grade students. The 91 questions were presented in one session. However, the questionnaire was produced in six versions, one for each possible order of the three "worlds." Moreover, the questionnaire was administered without showing the respondents any stimuli. The entire session lasted 40–50 minutes with only several of the respondents showing any signs of fatigue. We subsequently performed a test between the responses provided by the respondents in the six subgroups based on the different versions of the questionnaire, using one-way ANOVAs. Of the 91 tests run, only three were significant with no consistent pattern of differences between the subgroups. One-way ANOVAs were also done for the 27 indices and we found that none were significant. We consider these results to be quite important evidence, indicating that the presentation of the questions concerning the different worlds of reality in the same session did not affect the findings. Moreover, and perhaps even more important, the actual analyses of the data contrasting television news and the "real world" were almost identical to those in the present study, thereby providing even more stable and reliable results.

Table I
T-tests for Differences Between Perceived Magnitudes of Dimensions of Social Conflicts in Social Reality and Television News (N = 425)

	Means for Social Reality[1]	Means for TV News[1]	t
Integration Complexity	8.17	6.03	13.87*
Integration Intensity	7.76	7.77	n.s.
Integration Difficulty of Solvability	8.07	7.41	3.91*
Economic Complexity	7.35	6.28	5.52*
Economic Intensity	8.42	7.75	5.41*
Economic Difficulty of Solvability	8.23	7.40	6.28*
Political Complexity	8.07	7.35	4.19*
Political Intensity	10.27	9.71	3.89*
Political Difficulty of Solvability	8.83	8.32	2.88*

[1]The minimum possible score for each dimension is 3 and the maximum possible score is 12.

*$p < .01$ (one-tailed)

Note: For each t-test the number of cases is slightly reduced from 425 due to listwise deletion of data.

Results

We tested the first hypothesis by comparing the differences between the responses to the questions concerning the two realms of reality summed separately for the three dimensions in the three life areas. Table I presents the means and the results of the t-tests for related measures performed between the two realms of reality.

Of the nine t-tests, eight were significant. As expected, for all the life areas, the complexity and the difficulty of solvability of social conflicts were perceived as greater in the realm of social reality as compared with television news. Contrary to the hypothesis, however, conflicts were perceived as more intense in social reality compared with television news for two life areas (economics and politics) and no difference was found for the integration conflicts.

The second hypothesis was tested by computing a weighted mean score for the "severity" of social conflicts in each of the three life areas. For this, we combined the responses on the three dimensions, in each realm of reality and computed differences between the "severity" scores in the two realms of reality. In the case of the conflicts concerning school integration, which we considered to be the least remote from life experience, the difference between the means was 2.80. For the economic conflicts, which we presumed to occupy a medium level of remoteness from life experience, the difference was 2.58, and for the political conflicts, which we presumed were most remote in terms of life experience, the difference was 1.79. In all cases the differences were highly significant using related t-tests. This demonstrated that the largest perceptual difference between social reality and television news was in the case of conflicts which were least remote from the individual's life experience, and the smallest gap was in the case of conflicts most remote from one's experience. A simultaneous test of significance between the three pairs of comparisons was done using an ANOVA with repeated measures. The overall main-effect for the three conflicts was highly significant. The contrasts performed indicated, however, that the difference between the school integration conflict and each of the other two conflicts was significant, but the difference between the political and economic conflicts was in the predicted direction, but not significant. These findings generally support the hypothesis derived from media dependency theory.

We tested the third and final hypothesis by means of Smallest Space Analysis (SSA) which is employed in direct correspondence with the mapping sentence.[31] The SSA algorithm presents each variable by a point in the Euclidean space. The distance between any two points in the space decreases as the correlation between the variables increases. The SSA map which we present describes the structure of, and the degree of differentiation between, the perception of social conflicts as they occur in society and as they are presented in television news. The SSA map in Figure II is based on a matrix of Pearson correlations. Data reduction was done for each dimension by combining the responses of its relevant questions. We justified this by the relatively high positive correlations within each subset of responses. Thus the map presents 18 points, nine for each of the two realms of reality.

The two-dimensional SSA map clearly demonstrates the division of the space according to Facet A (the dimensions) which divide the map into three triangular areas, accordingly labelled. The map also organizes the data according to Facet C (the realms of reality). This is depicted by linking all the data points belonging to the "real" world, thus forming an approximation of a circle with the data points of the world of television news lying within its perimeter.[32]

When considering the structure of the perception of social conflicts, the tendency toward differentiation is ever further reinforced. As noted, the area within the circle of Figure II is the domain of television news. The relatively closer proximity of these variables suggests a more stereotyped and homoge-

---

[31]Samuel Shye, ed., *Theory Construction and Data Analysis in the Behavioral Sciences* (San Francisco: Jossey-Bass, 1973).

[32]We should note that linking the data points was done on the basis of the *a priori* hypothesis concerning the structure. Thus, according to the SSA procedure, slight deviations are acceptable (in the present case the integration conflict in the world of reality) as long as the coefficient of alienation is below .15 (in the present case it was .13 which is considered quite satisfactory).

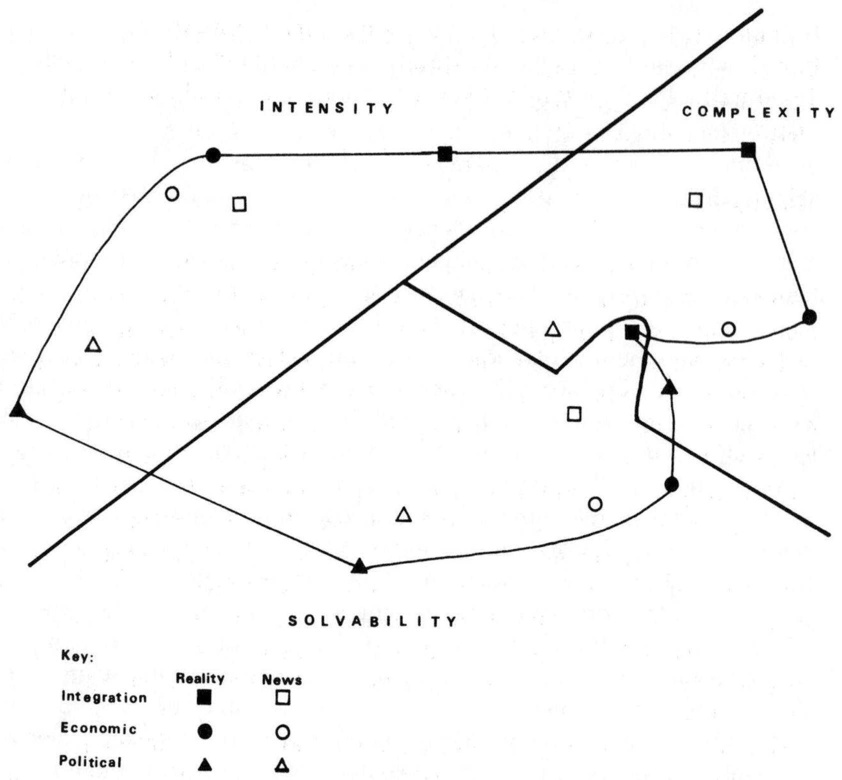

Figure II Structure of Perceptions of Social Conflicts in Social Reality and Television News (SSA Map)

neous view of social conflicts in television news as compared with the greater spread of the variables in the "real" world. This notion is indeed supported by two additional SSA maps (which were created but not presented here for the sake of brevity). One is of the perception of social conflicts in the realm of social reality and the other is for the perception in the world of television news. These separate maps show that in each of the realms of reality the differentiation by dimensions of perception is highly visible. And yet, the subdivision according to Facet B (the life areas) is well differentiated in the realm of social reality but is totally blurred in the realm of television news.

In examining Figure II one can get a glimpse of this interpretation. The data points for the integration conflict (represented by the squares) are located in the upper right half of the map; the data points for the political conflict (the triangles) are generally located in the lower left of the map; while the data points of the economic conflict (the circles) generally lie in the center of the map in between the data points of the other two life areas. As noted above, this order of the elements of the life area facet was clearly visible in the map of the world of reality but was not present in the map of the world of television news. Since Figure II presents the data of both worlds, the picture there is only partially discernable. In any event, as noted earlier (see Footnote 29), the data from the replication yielded almost identical results to the SSA map in the present study.

Discussion

The major finding of this study is that young people are able to differentiate between social reality and television reality. Despite the sought-after objectivity of news which purports to describe reality "as it is," people *are* able to make this important distinction.[33] As we expected, we indeed found that social conflicts in reality were considered to be more complex and more difficult to solve than in television news. Contrary to our expectation, however, was the fact that social conflicts in reality were perceived as more intense than in television news. This, despite the claim that television news emphasizes movement, action and violence. This is probably due to the tendency of the respondents to differentiate between the dimensions, on the one hand, but also to view social conflicts in their totality, as if to consider their total "severity." Thus, when social conflicts in the "real" world are perceived as more complex and as more difficult to solve, they are also considered as more intense, according to the presumed internal logic of "the more, the more."

Gerbner and his colleagues, in their discussion of the "cultivation hypothesis," emphasize that viewers implicitly learn and accept television assumptions about social reality, but do not necessarily attribute them to television. The present study focuses on an additional aspect of the perception of reality which is not emphasized in Gerbner's research, namely the ability to differentiate between different "realities." Our findings suggest that young people are able to consciously differentiate between what they learn from television and what they learn from their direct experience. Moreover, in Gerbner's studies, the amount of television exposure is the main independent variable which determines the degree of acceptance of television reality as social reality. In our research, however, the amount of exposure to television news was found to be unrelated to the ability to differentiate between the different "realities."

Of the entire sample used, a large majority of the adolescents habitually

---

[33]One might possibly argue that merely by asking the respondents two separate sets of questions concerning television news and reality could make the distinction more conscious in their minds. This is no different, however, for any situation when any questionnaire is used to ask questions on different topics. Moreover, as indicated above, the order of the questions did not affect the responses, hence this phenomenon could at most reinforce the differentiation but not create it in the first place.

watch television news at least several times during the week, if not nightly, while there was absolutely no case of a "non-viewer" in the sample. This fact corroborates other findings that Israeli adolescents, as well as the general population, are heavy news viewers, in addition to being heavy news readers.[34] More directly pertinent are the results of a direct test which we performed on the data in which we separately analyzed the responses of the nightly viewers of television news versus the relatively less frequent viewers. We found no differences in the ability to make the distinctions between the two realms of reality when controlling for exposure to television news. We suggest that the contribution of the degree of exposure to television news to the perceptions of social reality should hopefully be examined in a population which is more heterogeneous in its news viewing patterns.

We believe that our findings support a more refined approach to the study of interaction between social reality and its symbolic representations. Television may indeed contribute to the perception of social reality, but the extent and the scope of its contribution is determined by the amount of direct experience with social phenomena in different life areas, as suggested both by the media dependency theory and the phenomenological theories.

Our conclusions also suggest that the claims made by the critical theorists regarding powerful ideological effects of the media concerning the perception of social reality might possibly be exaggerated. The fact that people are able to differentiate between social reality and television news may serve as a barrier against an overwhelming effect of television on the construction of subjective reality. The relationship between the degree of differentiation and the degree of acceptance of the underlying cultural assumptions of television contents has not been conclusively established.[35] This issue could be seen as a further elaboration of our study, but was not tested directly.

In spite of what we suggest in this paper, we must also stress that the importance of the evidence concerning television's contribution to the perception of social reality in life areas which are remote from the individual's direct experience should not be miminized. According to the findings we have just reported, the perceptions of political life seem to be most vulnerable to the influence of television. In terms of the critical approach to mass communication, this may spell danger for the central social institutions which are responsible for distribution and organization of political ideology in society.

---

[34]Hanna Adoni, "Formation of young people's political opinions: a comparison of the mass media and primary groups as sources of information during the 1977 elections in Israel," *Fernsehen und Bildung* 13½ (1979); and Itzhak Roeh, Elihu Katz, Akiba A. Cohen and Barbie Zelizer, *Almost Midnight: Reforming the Late Night News* (Beverly Hills: Sage, 1980).

[35]Robert P. Hawkins and Suzanne Pingree, "Some Processes in the Cultivation Effect," *Communication Research* 7:193–226 (April 1980).

10

SPEAKING OF THE PRESIDENT

Political Structure and Representational Form in U.S. and Italian Television News

Daniel C. Hallin and Paolo Mancini

The metaphor of the mirror has always attracted observers of the media,[1] just as it once attracted theorists of language.[2] It has been used in many ways, both simple and sophisticated. Media people themselves often describe the news as a more or less literal reflection of "the course of events," a conception particularly useful for warding off political criticism.[3] Others have likened the news image to the images of a fun-house mirror, distorted by such factors as the organizational structure of the media, but still essentially reflective. And many have described the media as mirrors not so much of "reality" as of culture, or politics, or social structure, reflecting in their standards of judgment the cultural or social framework or the political balance of forces of their society.[4]

The metaphor is true enough in certain ways. But just as language is not really separate from the "world" it "pictures,"[5] the media do not stand apart from the social processes reflected in the content of the news. Just as language is embedded in the "forms of life" in which we use it, constituted by and helping to constitute those forms, the media are an integral part of political and social life. Their function, as we understand it in modern liberal societies, is primarily to provide a running, day-to-day *representation* of the life of the community. But *how* they do this, the form of representation they employ, varies greatly, shaped by the structure of those very political and social processes that they attempt in one way or another to "reflect" and by their own role in those processes. And there is every reason to believe that these forms of representation, in their turn, profoundly affect the conduct of politics and the character of social interaction.

University of California, San Diego; Istituto di Studi Sociali, Università di Perugia.

From Daniel C. Hallin and Paolo Mancini, "Speaking of the President: Political Structure and Representational Form in U.S. and Italian Television News," ***Theory and Society,*** **Vol. 13, No. 6 (November 1984), pp. 829-850. Copyright 1984 by Elsevier Science Publishers B. V. Reprinted by permission.**

This article compares the presentation of news in two liberal democracies. It is a study of television coverage in the United States and Italy during President Reagan's trip to Europe in June, 1982. There are many reasons one might expect television news to differ between these two countries. The two political systems are of course very different. The American system is presidential, the Italian parliamentary. The United States has two political parties, loose in ideology and organization; Italy has many parties with much tighter organization and clear ideological orientations. The United States is a world power with military and political interests around the globe; Italy is not.

The media themselves, moreover, are very differently organized in the two countries. American television networks are owned by private corporations and operated for profit. The main nation-wide broadcasting company in Italy, Radiotelevisione Italiana or RAI, is state-owned, directed by a board elected by parliament. RAI does broadcast advertisements, but most of its income is provided by subscription fees paid by television viewers; in 1980 66 percent of RAI's revenues from broadcasting and related activities came from subscription fees, which were payed in that year by 73 percent of Italy's households, 28 percent from advertising.[6] Of the three channels operated by RAI, two, the ones we will be concerned with here (TG1 and TG2), have partisan and ideological attachments. One is pro-Catholic, employing managers and journalists close to the Christian Democratic party; the other is secular, and close to the parties of the non-communist left. The third is essentially a cultural channel, focusing on regional matters. After thirty years of uncontested monopoly for the state-owned company, recent legislation now allows the existence of private and commercial networks. But these networks are still barred by law from broadcasting news simultaneously over the entire nation; they do not, therefore, compete with RAI's national news broadcasts. Local news is of little importance in Italy, either on public or private television. The news broadcasts of TG1 and TG2, which are 30 and 45 minutes in length, respectively, without commercial interruptions, are watched by over half of the Italian population each night, TG1 by 15 million Italians and TG2 by 5 million.

We will show how these differences affect not only the *content* of television news, in the sense of the kinds of political actors and activities that are covered, but also the *form of representation*, the conventions of narrative employed. We will argue that it is in these differing forms of representation that the differing conceptions of politics in the two societies are most profoundly embodied. And we will try to spell out tentatively some of the political consequences that seem likely to flow from them. As Michael Schudson has written:

> The power of the media lies not only (and not even primarily) in its power to declare things to be true, but in its power to provide the forms in which the declarations appear. News in a newspaper or on television has a relationship to the real world not only in content but in form; that is, in the way the world is incorporated into unquestioned and unnoticed conventions of narration, and then transfigured, no longer a subject for discussion but a premise for any conversation at all.[7]

The news in the United States and Italy reflects the differences between the two political systems, emphasizing different institutions and actors. But that is not all. The "pictures" of political life provided by the media of the two societies, first of all, present to their respective audiences differing conceptions of what politics is about: even as mirrors of political life the media are active constructors of meaning. The media of the two countries, moreover, not only mirror the forms of political life of their respective societies, but *embody* them. Because they are embedded in such different political contexts, the media themselves play very different roles: reporting the news in Italy is not the same kind of activity as reporting the news in the United States. Political structure thus comes to be embodied in certain ways of speaking about politics, conventions of communication that in their turn profoundly affect the possibilities for political discourse in the society.

This study is based on an analysis of ten Italian and fifteen American news broadcasts – all the major network evening news coverage from the week of June 7–11, 1982. This is, of course, a limited amount of material; we intend this analysis as an illustration of a certain approach to the study of news, not as a comprehensive survey of either Italian or American television coverage.[8] Any cross-national comparison of news faces the problem that news will vary not only because of different conventions of reporting – which we are interested in here – but also because the domestic political context is different, and the international context of different relevance. But the week we have chosen is a relatively good one for comparison. It was dominated by three international events of great importance to both countries: President Reagan's trip to Europe, which included a stop in Rome to meet with Italian President Pertini and with the Pope, the Israeli invasion of Lebanon, which had just begun, and the war in the Falkland Islands, which was approaching its final stages. (Italy, incidently, has a special interest in Argentina, which has many citizens of Italian descent, including Leopoldo Galtieri, who was President during the Falklands War.) Domestically both countries were involved in elections of roughly comparable importance. In the United States primary elections were held in many states on June 8. In Italy, on June 6, elections were held for some city and county councils. The Italian elections were of slight significance in themselves, but were regarded as an important indicator of the strength of the various parties; a large part of the news on

June 7 was devoted to the results and the reactions of the various parties to them.

Content: News as Mirror, Mirror as Frame

The news does, of course, mirror in its content the political structure of the society. Figure 1 summarizes the major subjects and political actors covered by American and Italian television during Reagan's trip to Europe. Two differences are particularly important.

American television, in the first place, gave far more coverage to foreign politics during this week of war than Italian television: foreign politics occupied 60 percent of the coverage in the U.S., 30 percent in Italy. This is not, certainly, a typical figure for foreign coverage on American television. It is a good illustration of the often-observed fact that the American media

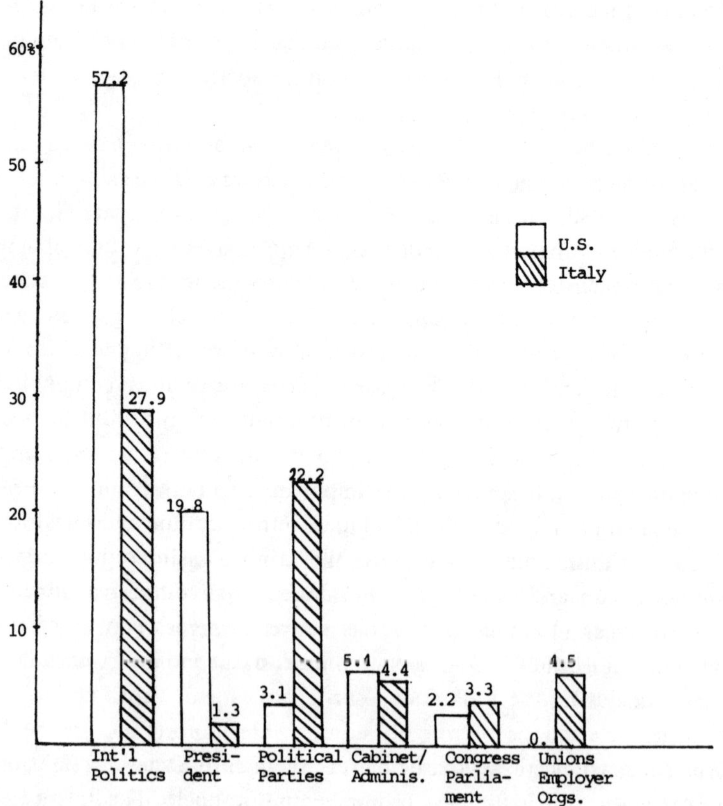

Fig. 1. Percent of total television time devoted to selected subjects and actors in U.S. and Italian news broadcasts.

cover foreign politics when U.S. interests are at stake. Foreign politics is defined for purposes of this analysis as the internal politics of foreign countries and relations among them, and does not include relations of Italy or the United States with other countries. Reagan's trip is therefore considered a domestic rather than a foreign story for American news. But it nevertheless provided the occasion for an unusual number of stories about European politics. And of course the United States was deeply involved in the diplomacy that surrounded both the Falklands war and the war in Lebanon, with the consequence again that coverage of these areas was exceptionally high. Nevertheless, estimates of the *average* level of foreign coverage in American TV news range from about 30–37 percent, still larger than the figure for Italian news during this period of international tension.[9]

The second difference has to do with the political actors who appear in the news. The prime actor in American coverage is the President; in Italian, the political party. Nearly 20 percent of American coverage concerned President Reagan; Italian television devoted less than 2 percent of its time to President Pertini, and an additional 4 percent to the government of Prime Minister Spadolini. Twenty-two percent of Italian news, on the other hand, was devoted to the parties, compared with about 3 percent of American news.

These differences are neither surprising nor difficult to explain (nor, incidentally, are they peculiar to this time period, when the American President was abroad, though this certainly heightens the President's visibility on the American news[10]). The President of the Republic is in fact a minor figure in Italian politics, and even the Prime Minister and his cabinet are transient creatures of shifting coalitions: Italy has had 44 governments in the 38 years since World War II. What is constant and powerful in Italian politics is the party. In the United States by contrast the party rarely acts as a unit except – and then to a limited extent – in support of a presidential campaign. As for the difference in foreign coverage, it is an excellent illustration of the version of the mirror theory that holds that news reflects culture and social structure. American and Italian news reflect world politics differently; they do not show the same picture of the world. But their differences of emphasis "mirror" real differences in the role the two countries play in international affairs. The United States has much more extensive international involvements than Italy.

But though they are in a sense obvious, these differences in news content are not trivial – not without significance for the political culture of the two societies. Even in mirroring society the media frame it:[11] they reflect back to society not just events, not unmediated reality, but a particular *conception* of politics embodied in that society's political life. This becomes clear if we look at the differences of emphasis in domestic coverage in a slightly different way. The attention in American news is devoted primarily to institutional and administrative spheres: it deals with the executive branch of government, with those actors, the President and other administration officials, who stand at the head of governing institutions. The emphasis in Italy, on the other hand, is on the *political* sphere. Italian news devotes the greatest part of its attention not to official governing institutions but to the process of political and ideological debate and the actors who participate in that process. If we compare coverage of the institutions of government, on the one hand (including the presidency, the cabinet, the courts, public administration, local government, and the police), and those of political debate on the other (Congress/Parliament, the parties, and finally, unions and employers' organizations – which received 4.5 percent of Italian coverage, none in the U.S.), U.S. coverage includes 27 percent devoted to the institutional sphere and 5 percent to the political. For Italy the figures are 16 percent institutional and 31 percent political. (Nearly half of Italian coverage of governing institutions deals with the police and lower courts, and their battle with the Red Brigades.)

So politics appears in American news as government, in Italian as debate and party activity. Politics also tends to appear in American news – because of the focus on international politics – as an affair of the nation as a unit; in Italy as a matter of conflict among social and political groups within the nation. The particular emphases reported here are of course affected by the context: they would have been somewhat different if we had chosen a different period of time, a time for example when President Reagan had been fighting with Congress over the budget rather than traveling abroad. But given the context of this week, in many ways closely comparable for the two societies, U.S. and Italian journalists made very different sets of choices. The Italians focused heavily on the local elections held on June 6; American journalists chose largely to ignore the June 8 primaries, and to focus instead on foreign politics and the President's trip to Europe. These choices reflect the political priorities of United States and Italy; at the same time they are an important part of the process by which those priorities are maintained as an ideological framework.

Forms of Representation

"In comparison to newspaper news," Paul Weaver has written, "television news is far more coherently organized and tightly unified, and this is true of the individual . . . story as well as of the . . . news aggregate. . . . [T]he TV news program tends to present a single unified interpretation of the day's events *as a whole*. . . ."[12] The reason for this difference, Weaver argues, is that television news is organized in time rather than space. The television audience must therefore be carried along by the narrative. It is not free, like the newspaper audience, to browse at will from story to story, and cannot be allowed to stray; its attention must be maintained continuously. A definite theme or story line is thus essential.

And indeed, television news in the United States is characterized by its thematic, unified presentation. But the imperative lies in the institution and its social role, not in the technology per se. Italian television shows none of the thematic unity that characterizes its American counterpart. Here are the anchors' introductions to two news broadcasts, one Italian and one American:

> RAI TG1, June 7, Valentini: "Lebanon, the Falklands – from our headlines you already know about the disquieting development of the situation in the Middle East and about the growth of military activity in the archipelago contested by England and Argentina. These, surely, have been the subjects most discussed during the Roman talks that Reagan, after the visit to the Pope, has had at the Quirinale with President Pertini and at Palazzo Chigi with Prime Minister Spadolini. The presence of Reagan in Rome constitutes, with the two serious international events going on just now, one of the outstanding events of this day, together with the results, that so far we know only partially, of the elections for the city councils of about eighty municipalities, which indicate, up to now, a likely victory of the Socialist Party and of the other secular parties. But let's see what is going on in Lebanon."
>
> ABC *World News Tonight*, June 7, Frank Reynolds: "Good evening. If this had been almost any other day it would, indeed, be big news that the President of the United States is at Windsor Castle, seat of the British monarchy, especially since Mr. Reagan came here right after a visit to the seat of the Papacy and a meeting with Pope John Paul. They talked, the President and the Pope, of peace; and we'll have a full report later. But this has really been another day of war, so we begin the broadcast, tonight, with the latest on the latest war, the one in the Middle East. Up the road in London, at our foreign desk, here is Peter Jennings."

The Italian broadcast begins with a list of headlines; the day's events are interpreted by the journalist only in the sense that certain ones are listed as especially important. The American broadcast begins with a frame: it opens with a set of contrasting images – war on the one hand, peace, authority, tradition, religion, on the other – which places all the day's events within a sort of cosmology, giving them both coherence as part of a single story and meaning as part of a moral order.

To a large extent, the unity of American news broadcasts during this week was achieved by organizing them around the central figure of the President. NBC's June 7 report is an excellent example. Tom Brokaw, one of NBC's two "anchors" (the terminology is significant: they are not just announcers), was traveling with the President in Europe. Anchoring the international portion of the broadcast from No. 10 Downing St., he wrapped up each international segment of the broadcast, and the broadcast as a whole, by bringing it into relation to the President's trip: "and tomorrow, when President Reagan will come here to No. 10 Downing Street, that war [in the Falklands] will be the major subject of attention." The broadcast was thus provided both with a central actor, the President, and a central setting, No. 10 Downing Street. On subsequent days, international events continued to be tied together by an emphasis on their relation to the President's trip. This is an unusually high level of unity even for an American news broadcast; the journalists made a special effort to integrate the news during this week, due probably both to the unusual complexity of international news and to the availability, in the President's trip, of a compelling organizational device. But the *tendency* to unify is typical of American news. Av Westin, once Executive Producer of ABC *World News Tonight*, writes:

> Stories . . . should be combined into a logical progression that threads its way through the day's news. The audience ought to be guided through the news so that it doesn't have to make sharp twists and turns to follow and understand what is going on. My preference is to divide the lineup into segments. In each segment, a narrative of sorts is fashioned, weaving together stories that relate to one another.[13]

An Italian news broadcast, in contrast, has little internal logic, and never has a central theme, setting or actor.

At the level of the individual news report, the same contrast of representational form can be seen once again. The American report is both "storylike" and interpretive; it is constructed to convey a certain understanding of events. The Italian report could be called "referential." It does not offer meaning within itself, but refers the viewer elsewhere: it provides a review, a list, of the interpretations offered by political actors outside of journalism. Here again are two examples:

> RAI TG1, June 7, 1982 (following a report giving election returns): "What do the political forces say about the results we have heard so far, even though they are only partial? One finds, of course, great satisfaction on the socialist and secular side with the good returns for these parties. As for the Christian Democrats, they underline the satisfying results they got in an administrative election in which, generally, the DC never achieves as good a position as in a political or general election. . . . But now we have to wait and see what will be the effect of these results on the general political situation because, although it is true that this has been a minor race, it comes just before an important discussion among the parties of the majority.
>
> Meanwhile, a comment from Craxi, Secretary of the PSI [Socialist] . . .
>
> From the point of view of the PSDI [Social Democratic], this election confirms that . . .
>
> From the Republicans, there is a statement of Del Pennino that . . .

The judgement of Zanone, Secretary of the PLI [Liberal] is that . . .

From the Communist side, Cossuta observes that . . .

Finally there is a statement of Almirante of MSI [Fascist]. Almirante says that . . .

These are the comments that have been delivered so far.

NBC, June 11, 1982, Roger Mudd: In an effort to act responsibly and pass a budget, any budget, House Democrats and Republicans joined forces today and passed, 219 to 206, the Republican version of the budget. Lisa Meyers reports.

Lisa Meyers: . . . More than 18 billion would be cut from domestic spending, most of it programs for the poor. . . . Majority leader Jim Wright likened it to the practice of medieval bleeders.

Wright: And if the patient does not respond to the first bleeding and indeed gets worse, just bleed him some more.

Meyers: Until the very end, it was questionable whether the house could muster the courage to pass anything.

Representative: I suggest to you the country won't go to hell without a budget.

Meyers: But leaders of both parties argued otherwise. . . .

Minority leader Robert Michels: If the bipartisan substitute goes down we all go down. . . .

Meyers: Wright pleaded for every member to vote for something.

Wright: To do otherwise, to vote against both, would be a craven cop-out and a retreat from responsibility.

Meyers: This budget must still be reconciled with the one which passed the Senate. . . . Then the House will have to wrestle with a compromise budget, a prospect which excites no one.

The Italian report, like most of RAI's political reporting, is divided into a three-part structure: announcement of event, interpretations of the parties, and (though this part may often be omitted) interpretation of the journalist. The order of presentation varies, but most reports on domestic politics contain these three elements. The journalist's interpretation (in this case, marked by the phrase "We must wait to see") is always easily recognizable, and in fact is frequently marked off by a phrase that identifies it as interpretation: "How can we interpret this?" "What does it mean?" or simply, "In other words."[14]

The NBC report, on the other hand, has no such divided structure, nor are the journalists' interpretations separated either from the reporting of the event or from the reporting of the views of party representatives. The structure of the report is a *narrative* structure, though of course a simple one: it sets the scene and describes the stakes, builds to a moment of crisis ("until the very end, it was questionable whether the House could muster the courage. . . ."), achieves a resolution, and closes by setting the stage for the next "episode." And embedded in the narrative there is a political interpretation: Congress moved so slowly on the budget that in the end any budget was better than none; it is to be hoped that there won't be any squabbling that will delay final passage any further. It is the journalist, as narrator, who controls the interpretation of reality. The statements of the political actors do not stand independently, as they do in the Italian report, but are woven by the journalist into her story.

The difference in the role of interpretation and framing is the most important difference in representational form between U.S. and Italian news, but it is by no means the only one. We will summarize here three other important differences. For reasons we will explore in the following section, all of the representational conventions discussed here are closely interrelated.

Use of Visual Images. The conventions of Italian TV news are essentially, to return to Weaver's distinction between print and television journalism, print conventions. Not only does Italian television not employ the conventions of unified, thematic presentation that mark American TV news, it also makes little use of the visual characteristics of the TV medium. A good deal of the Italian news report is simply read by the announcer, without any accompanying visual images. And film is used primarily as background to the verbal narrative. It is generally unedited, often of poor visual quality, and often only loosely related to the meaning of the report. The film that accompanied RAI's reports on Reagan's visit with the Pope was filled most of the time with unidentified people milling about on the periphery of the event; reports from Moscow and Washington were narrated over street scenes. Film in Italian television is referential rather than rhetorical; it *shows* the scene but most of the time has nothing to *say* about the event. In American television it is different. Film, and increasingly other visual images ("graphics"), are central to the semantic structure of the story. They are primarily symbolic: American television uses film not so much to show Windsor Castle or Beirut or the President and the Pope, as to *represent* tradition, war, diplomacy.[15]

The Role of the "Common Man." Television news in the United States devotes a good deal of attention to the private citizen. This tendency was somewhat less marked than usual during the week of our study because of the focus on international politics; it is especially in stories on domestic economics and public policy that American journalists are so fond of investigating the impact of events on "common" men and women. Nevertheless, nearly a third, approximately 48 of 150 people who appeared on U.S. television news during this week were "non-official" – civilians in Lebanon, families of British soldiers in the Falklands, arms control protesters and other civilians in Germany, and so on.[16] Italian television, on the other hand, is almost exclusively concerned with the institutionalized public sphere. Rarely does anyone appear on Italian television news who does not represent an organized participant in the political process.

Relation to Audience. Television journalists in the United States rarely speak in the first person; they used it only a handful of times during the week of our study. Italian newscasters use first person routinely. U.S. and Italian newscasters, moreover, mean different things when they do use first person. To an American newscaster, "we" means the news organization: "Up the road in London, at our foreign desk. . . ." When an Italian newscaster says "we," on the other hand, he means himself and the audience: "Let's see what is going on in Lebanon." (This usage, incidently, is sincere: the Italian announcer has in fact not yet seen the report from Lebanon, and will therefore be just as much informed by it as the audience.) The television journalist in the United States, in other words, will not normally "cross the screen" to put himself "on the side" of the audience in relation to events (CBS commentator Bill Moyers is an exception here); while the Italian announcer routinely moves back and forth across that invisible boundary.

Political Structure and Representational Form

The most obvious explanation for this pattern of differences is that American TV news is commercial and Italian is not. American television sells the attention of a mass public to advertisers; its most fundamental task as a business is to generate and maintain that attention. The news divisions of American networks are by no means their major money-makers, and to some degree they are exempted from the commercial imperatives that dominate other forms of programming. But the exemption is limited: although it has lower ratings than any other major form of programming, news can by highly profitable, and its profits depend directly on audience size. *CBS Evening News*, for instance, had profits of $28 million in 1980.[17] In the late seventies and early eighties, when CBS faced increasing competition from ABC, a slide in the network's ratings from 27 percent of the audience to 24 percent lowered the price of a 30-second advertising spot on the *Evening News* by as much as $10,000.[18] With about eight minutes of commercials in a 30-minute broadcast, this would add up to a revenue loss of roughly $160,000 a night. In order to keep its hold on the audience, American TV news adopts a set of conventions that serve to involve the viewer emotionally. The form it employs is essentially cinematic, combining visual imagery with narrative structure.[19]

For Italian television, by contrast, "ratings" are not a pressing concern. RAI has a relatively stable base of revenue in the subscription fees that provide nearly two thirds of its income from broadcasting. As for the 28 percent of that income that is dependent on advertising, this too has until very recently been quite stable. Before 1983, when competition from commercial television intensified, the demand for RAI's legally limited amount of advertising time exceeded the supply by a considerable margin. The national news broadcasts are still protected from commercial competition. Budgetary allocations, finally, are made to RAI's three channels from a common revenue pool, and are not directly related to audience size. The economic structure that ties the budget of an American news program closely to the size of its audience is thus not present in Italian television. Italian TV news, of course, faces organizational constraints of its own, which in part account for its particular conventions of reporting. Italian news is political rather than commercial, and political in a certain way. While the primary constituency for American television is the advertiser (and therefore the consuming public), the constituency for Italian television is the political party system (and the public as political observers or participants). Italian TV news is essentially a utility maintained by the parties to inform the public about their views and activities. Hence the characteristic disjointed, non-narrative structure of the Italian news report: announcement of event, statements of the parties, journalist's interpretation.

But the distinction between a commercial and a political news organization is not by itself an adequate explanation for the differences between the American and Italian systems. In fact, the contrast between U.S. and Italian TV news in some ways *reverses* the contrast most commonly drawn between the commercial journalism of America and the political journalism of Europe. The rise of commercial mass media that began in the United States with the penny press of the 1830s was associated with a shift away from the active political role the newspaper had played in the late eighteenth and early nineteenth centuries.[20] As the commercial press developed, newspapers became both more entertainment-oriented and more committed to the ideal of a professional, politically neutral "objective" journalism. Many European countries, fearing quite reasonably that commercialization would destroy the newspaper as an active participant in political debate, subsidize the party press.[21] But when one compares American and Italian TV news (as we shall see in a moment, the print media in Italy are another matter altogether), it is the American news that is the more active, that puts forth political interpretations and, as we shall see, that often plays a critical role vis-à-vis political authority, while Italian news is much more neutral, passing on in dry "objective" style the official statements of established parties.

Why should this be? The answer seems to lie in the differing structure of the public sphere in the two societies. We use the term "public sphere" in the Habermasian sense, but its application to modern liberal societies requires a word of explanation. For Habermas, the public sphere was the area of political life, established with the rise of bourgeois society, in which private individuals, those outside the formal institutions of government, took part in the discussion of public affairs.[22] The participatory, decentralized public sphere described by Habermas has been superseded by a process of political communication dominated by large-scale institutions: political parties, unions, and other organized associations of the private sector, and the mass media. The element of continuity is that there remains in modern liberal society an arena of political communication outside the formal control of the state. It is this arena we refer to here as the public sphere.

The public sphere is structured very differently in the United States and Italy: it is, in a sense, empty in the United States, while in Italy it is filled to overflowing, and solidly, even rigidly institutionalized. And this profoundly affects the role that journalism plays in the two societies. Political interpretation is provided in Italy by the institutions that have traditionally dominated the modern public sphere – political parties, unions and industrial associations, and parts of the print media, many of which are oriented toward political commentary rather than news coverage in the American sense. There is no need, therefore, for the television journalist to play an active interpretive role – and no reason for the parties, having control over the state broadcasting company, to allow journalism to usurp their function as arbiters of political meaning.[23]

In the United States, on the other hand, the institutions of the public sphere are weak. Newspapers have for the most part abandoned their earlier role as vehicles for the expression of political opinion.[24] The parties are entrepreneurial parties in the sense of Schumpeter and Downs – loose coalitions organized for the purpose not of expressing unified ideologies but of competing for political office.[25] And unions and other private organizations function for the most part as "interest groups," pressing particular demands, often behind the scenes, rather than attempting to mobilize public opinion around general ideological perspectives. There is thus a kind of vacuum in the American political system, an absence of the institutions which in liberal democracies have traditionally performed the function of interpreting political events. That vacuum is filled primarily by two institutions (which exist in a close, though not always comfortable relation to one another): the presidency[26], and journalism. Journalism is thus the primary institution of the American public sphere: it is the major institution outside of the State itself which performs the function of providing political interpretation and critique.

No wonder, then, that journalism in the United States has developed into an institution that is both more active and more autonomous than Italian journalism.[27] It is, in fact, somewhat artificial to say that journalism exists at all as a single, recognizable institution in Italy. Italy has two journalisms, and neither of them has the autonomy of function, organization, and ideology that American journalism has. Many of the print media in Italy are oriented toward providing political commentary, a function that they share with the other institutions of political debate. And if print journalism in Italy shares the functions of the political parties, television journalism serves them. The Italian television journalist is, both in training and in terms of actual power relations, a party functionary. The journalist is trained in the party apparatus, and can be transferred by the party if his or her work displeases its leadership. American journalism, by contrast, has developed into a separate political institution, with a set of functions and an ideology that are more or less its own. American journalists are not only free of direct political control, their political loyalty is primarily to journalism itself rather than to any distinct political tendencies. They see themselves, and are socialized, as members of an autonomous profession of journalism.

It is important to note, as Schudson has pointed out, that the idea of a profession of journalism developed in the United States primarily during the Progressive era, a period, that is, when party organizations were losing both influence and respect, and "good government" was contrasted with bad – that is, partisan – politics, when, in short, the traditional institutions of the public sphere were on the decline.[28] And it was simultaneous with the rise of the professional ideal that American journalism began not only to tell stories, something it had done since the rise of the penny papers, but to understand its function in terms of providing expert commentary on political affairs. A second significant increase in the interpretive activity of American journalism occurred during the late 1960s and early '70s, again, a period when political parties were losing influence, and this time also a period when the presidency, which has shared with journalism the function of political interpretation, was losing credibility as well.[29]

So the unified, thematic character of the American news report results not only from the imperatives of commercialism, but also from the central role journalism plays in the American political system. In the absence of other institutions, it falls upon journalism to play the active role of giving meaning and structure to the events of public life. Together these two characteristics of

American journalism account for its particular conventions of representation, as contrasted with Italian news: the greater tendency to frame and interpret, the use of narrative structures, the more extensive use of visual images and their integration into the semantic structure of the story. The journalist plays a more active social role in the United States than in Italy in two senses, both as a link in the chain of economic communication, as an entertainer and salesman, and as a provider of political meaning. And American journalism is an active creator of "publicity" in two corresponding senses: it generates the public attention, the mass audience, which makes possible the communication of commercial images, and it opens up an arena for the public discussion of political affairs. And because journalism as an institution plays a more active social role in the United States, the journalist plays a more active role in the presentation of news, working over the raw material of political information and giving it form both as entertainment and as comment on the meaning of events.

The greater centrality of journalism as an institution in the United States also explains what at first might seem a paradox in the contrasting relations of American and Italian journalists to their audiences. In a sense, American TV news seems populist in its style, compared with Italian. As we have seen, American television covers the "common man" much more; Italian television focuses almost exclusively on political officials. Italian news also tends to be presented at a relatively sophisticated level of discourse, making routine use of political jargon accessible only to those familiar with political affairs. At the same time, however, we have seen that Italian journalists are in a sense more familiar with their audiences than American, establishing relationships with them both by "crossing the screen" through a use of the first person that includes the audience, and through the use of performatives[30] that disclose directly to the audience the journalist's role in the presentation of the report. American journalists, by contrast, always stand apart from the audience.

How are we to make sense of these seemingly contradictory patterns? The answer lies in the fact that American journalists are "public" figures in a sense that Italian journalists are not. Because of the special role they play as interpreters of reality, American journalists must present a persona of authority that will legitimate the power they obviously possess. This they do in a number of ways – the identity of American journalism, because it plays multiple roles, is complex – two of which are particularly important here. First, they present themselves as *professionals*, who because of their training in certain methods and rules of conduct, are competent to make judgments that no one outside the profession is competent to make. Second, they present themselves as, and in a certain sense, are in fact, *representative* of the public. Journalism in the United States is (as many newspapers call themselves) a sort of "tribune of the people": in the absence of other institutions that could represent the interests of the public against those of the State, journalism fills that role. It is a role that on the one hand endows journalists with authority, setting them apart from the public at large and requiring them to act in a manner that confirms their public status,[31] and on the other hand – particularly given an individualist political culture which places a high value on the wisdom of the "common man" – requires them frequently to adopt a populist stance, to act as advocates for the interests and perspectives of the ordinary citizen.

Because they have so little power, in contrast, the Italian newscasters have neither much need for authority, nor much opportunity to take upon themselves the role of representing anyone. The parties and other institutions of the public sphere perform the role of representing the citizen vis-à-vis state power, as well as the role of interpretation. The journalists are merely public servants whose task it is to transmit information to those concerned with politics. They speak to the public as people who have specific information to pass on, but no authority either to represent them or to interpret for them the meaning of that information. It should be added that the commercial nature of American television news also pushes the journalist in a populist direction, requiring a presentation accessible to the widest possible audience. The Italian journalist is not so constrained, and speaks to an audience assumed to be familiar with political language and issues.

What Does It Mean?

The implications of these two forms of journalism are too numerous and too complex for us to give a full account of them here. We will close, however, by noting tentatively several that seem to us particularly important.

Because of the differing forms of representation of the two media systems, first of all, certain types of political action and certain types of actors "come across" much better in each system, and this has important implications for the nature of both political authority and political debate. A narrative requires a hero: the conventions of American TV news therefore place a premium on individual political leadership.[32] Both in the underlying message they convey about the nature of politics and in the conditions they create for effective communication, these conventions would seem to favor the centralized political authority of the Presidency. Their implications for Presidential power may, however, be complex. The image of the President in American news coverage results as much from the needs of journalism as from the real nature of Presidential power: there is no guarantee that the President can live up to the role in which he is cast. The imperative of creating an image of heroic leadership may be more a liability than an asset to American Presidents in a period of economic decline and political confusion.

As for political debate, the narrative conventions of American journalism make it very difficult for abstract political ideas to be dealt with, and focus attention instead, as has often been observed, on contest: the clash of presidential contenders, the test of wills between the President and Congressional leaders.[33] For Italian news, on the other hand, it is precisely the process of ideological debate that dominates the news, and the actions of political leaders appear as secondary to that debate. Italian TV news therefore seems likely to reinforce the prevailing pattern of Italian politics: a strong and stable party system; weak and unstable central government.

There is, at the same time, another wrinkle to the differing relations of U.S. and Italian TV news to political authority. Italian news rests content with the reporting of official statements, both from government and from the parties, and rarely provides any information or perspective beyond the bounds of official discourse. American journalism, on the other hand, is more active than Italian not only in the presentation of news, through framing, interpretation, and the creation of narrative, but also in the gathering of information. The American journalist not only interprets a story but much of the time investigates it: he or she takes a camera to the scene in search of visual images, interviews the people affected by a policy or a conflict, seeks out "sources" within a political bureaucracy that can give more information than was contained in the official statement. The news thus spills out beyond the bounds of official discourse.

This last characteristic of American journalism, combined with the observation that the search for heroes may, in the end, make it more rather than less difficult for a President to maintain his authority, has prompted many observers to describe the American media as a force generally destructive of political authority.[34] And indeed, compared with Italian TV news, American TV much more often plays a critical role. This was evident in the week of Reagan's trip to Europe: despite the intense focus on Presidential diplomacy, the news that week was by no means consistently favorable in its portrayal of the President. It was, in fact, a major theme of the news that week that the President's trip was largely a "media event," calculated to enhance Mr. Reagan's image both at home and abroad.

But the relation of American journalism to political authority is in fact intensely ambivalent and very unstable. We noted above two ways the American media legitimate the enormous power they possess as, in a sense, substitutes for the traditional institutions of political debate: by presenting themselves as professionals, standing above political ideology, and by presenting themselves as representatives of the "common man." There is also another way they legitimate their power: by identifying themselves with the authority of the State. When the journalist turns to official sources for legitimation,[35] the unified form of American news story takes on a new meaning: the journalist will now take the "frame" provided by government officials, and organize a story in which the official interpretation appears as the only interpretation possible. American journalism is thus at times a much more active critic of political authority, and at times a much more active instrument of it, than Italian journalism, which tends to maintain a constant, respectful distance.[36] The public sphere in the United States is thus more volatile than that of Italy. For all the shifting of governments in Italy, the public sphere remains more or less static. The news year after year reflects the same spectrum of ideological positions. In the United States, on the other hand, the public sphere can expand and contract within fairly large bounds, depending on the relation between the media and the state: it can, in periods when the media identify closely with the State, virtually collapse into the latter, so that the official interpretation of events dominates political discussion almost entirely, or it can expand to the point that political authorities spend most of their time trying to seize control over the elusive process through which political events are given meaning and public opinion formed.

There is, finally, much about the form of television journalism in both societies that is destructive of the ideal of a politically active public. American TV news is politically exclusive in two senses. It is exclusive, first of all, in the sense that it presents the interpretation of political events as belonging to a sphere that includes the journalists themselves and other political elites, but does not include the audience. This message is implicit in the treatment of the television screen as an impenetrable barrier. In Italy, political thinking is assumed to take place on both sides of the screen, which represents only a line between those who have current information and those who don't yet have it. In the United States politics takes place only behind the screen, and members of the public can become a part of it only to the extent that they are represented there by the journalists.

And television journalism in the United States is exclusive in the second sense that it offers only a single interpretation of events, an interpretation, moreover, that is presented as though it were embedded in the events themselves and therefore not subject to question.[37] While Italian news offers a series of alternative interpretations (including the journalist's), clearly marked out as interpretations, the interpretation in an American news report is built into the narrative itself, both in its verbal and visual components. This is true even in the case of the very typical story for American television that balances a statement from one political actor with an opposing statement from another. In such a case, there is generally a higher-order interpretation that the journalist employs to frame the other two; the ultimate message, in fact, will often be the fecklessness of political debate. This characteristic of the news report results at least in part from the awkward political position that American journalism occupies. It is an institution endowed with enormous and very visible power as the central "producer" of political meaning, but that at the same time has little solid basis of legitimacy. The institution deals with this problem in part by concealing its power (from itself as well as the public – it is largely an unconscious process) through adherance to the professional norms of objectivity. The practices of "objective journalism" in effect require that the meaning of the story be made to appear as though it emerged from the facts themselves, without the journalist's intervention.[38]

In certain ways, Italian news is clearly more open than American: it treats the audience as participant in the political process; it also presents a range of alternative interpretations of any event, clearly marked as interpretations. In another way, however, Italian news is more closed: political discussion remains strictly within the bounds of discourse defined by the party system. The news provides little independent interpretation or information. It also speaks, as we have seen, in a language accessible only to those with a relatively high level of political sophistication: the addressee of Italian news is the party activist. And because of the lack of framing, events appear in Italian news in an extremely fragmented form,[39] with the consequence, once again, that it is accessible only to those viewers with sufficient political sophistication to place it within a context of their own. American television, in contrast, through the simplicity and apparent unity of its narrative form, strives to make the news accessible to the entire public, albeit in a way that assigns to the public a passive role in the construction of meaning.

NOTES

1. Data for this article are drawn from research funded by a grant from RAI – Radiotelevisione Italiana, Verifica Programmi Trasmessi. We would like to thank Herbert Kitschelt and Michael Schudson for their comments on drafts of this article, and Helene Keyssar for guidance through the literature on cinema. The comments of the anonymous reviewers were also quite helpful.
2. We are thinking primarily of the early Wittgenstein, *Tractatus Logico-Philosophicus*, (Atlantic Highlands, NJ: Humanities Press, 1974).
3. Edward Jay Epstein, *News From Nowhere*, (New York: Vintage, 1974), 13–15.
4. Gaye Tuchman discusses this version of the mirror theory in *Making News*, (New York: Free Press, 1978), 182–183.

5. Ludwig Wittgenstein, *Philosophical Investigations*, (New York: Macmillan, 1958).
6. *Relazione e Bilancio 1980*, (Roma: RAI-Radio-Televisione Italiana, 1981).
7. Michael Schudson, "The Politics of Narrative Form: The Emergence of News Conventions in Print and Television," *Deadalus*, 111: 4 (Fall, 1982), 98.
8. Remarkably little has been written comparing the media of different countries. One review of the literature – not terribly out of date because not terribly much has been done since it was written, can be found in Jay G. Blumler and Michael Gurevitch, "Towards a Comparative Framework for Political Communication Research," in Steven H. Chaffee, ed., *Political Communication: Issues and Strategies for Research*, (Beverly Hills: Sage Publications, 1975).
9. Note that Reagan's trip was considered a domestic story for U.S. news, but a foreign story for Italian news, except when Reagan was in Italy. Figures for international coverage on U.S. TV are from James F. Larson, "International Affairs Coverage on U.S. Evening Network News," in William C. Adams, ed., *Television Coverage of International Affairs*, (Norwood, NJ: Ablex, 1982), Table 2.2, and Robert Frank, *Message Dimensions of Television News*, (Lexington, Mass.: Lexington Books, 1973). The average level of foreign coverage in Italy is about 20 percent, according to *Le notize dei telegiornali*, RAI Verfica Programmi Trasmessi n. 41, Roma, 1982.
10. On the centrality of the President in U.S. news see Herbert Gans, *Deciding What's News*, (New York: Pantheon, 1979, 9.
11. On the concept of "frame" see Tuchman, *Making News*, ch. 1 and Todd Gitlin, *The Whole World is Watching: Mass Media in the Making and Unmaking of the New Left*, (Berkeley: University of California Press, 1980). "Media frames," Gitlin writes (p. 7), "are persistant patterns of cognition, interpretation, and presentation, of selection, emphasis and exclusion, by which symbol-handlers routinely organize discourse, whether verbal or visual."
12. Paul Weaver, "Newspaper News and Television News," in Douglass Cater and Richard Adler, eds., *Television as a Social Force*, (New York: Praeger, 1975), 84–85. Martin Esslin makes a related argument: "in essence a dramatic medium, television from the beginning has been compelled by the special requirements of its nature – its own inner logic – to put its emphasis on material with a dramatic, emotional, personalized content." *The Age of Television*, (San Francisco: W. H. Freeman, 1982), 61.
13. Av Westin, *Newswatch: How TV Decides the News*, (New York: Simon and Schuster, 1982), 66.
14. Paolo Mancini, "Prescriptive Doing in Television News Reporting," paper presented at the International Sociological Association, Mexico City, 1982.
15. On the symbolic functions of television images see William Gibson, "Network News: Elements of a Theory," *Social Text*, Fall, 1980.
16. The figure is approximate because some people are hard to classify – lower-level civil servants, for example.
17. Lawrence W. Lichty, "Video versus Print," *The Wilson Quarterly*, 6: 5 (Special Issue, 1982), 57.
18. Sally Bedell, "The Upstart and the Big Boys Head for a Showdown," *TV Guide*, 30 (Feb. 6, 1982), 5–8.
19. See Sharon Sperry, "Television News as Narrative," in Richard P. Adler, *Understanding Television: Essays on Television as a Social and Cultural Force*, (New York: Praeger, 1981). The parallels between U.S. television news and cinema – or to be precise, western narrative cinema – are too complex to be developed fully here. They include a linear narrative form into which all elements, both visual and verbal are integrated [see Noel Burch, *To the Distant Observer*, (Berkeley: University of California Press, 1979)], and that is "illusionistic," which purports, that is, to allow us to view reality "just as it is," and a related claim to provide the audience with an intimate relation to its "characters," without, however, requiring the viewer to step out of the purely private role of viewing what unfolds [See Stanley Cavell, *The World Viewed*, (New York: Viking Press, 1971); Helene Keyssar, *Frogs with Wings: The Films of Robert Altman*, forthcoming].
20. Michael Schudson, *Discovering the News*, (New York: Basic Books, 1978); Dan Schiller, *Objectivity and the News*, (Philadelphia: University of Pennsylvania Press, 1981).
21. Anthony Smith, ed. *Newspapers and Democracy*, (Cambridge, Mass.: MIT Press, 1980).
22. Jürgen Habermas, *Strukterwandel der Öffentlichkeit*, (Berlin: Luchterhand, 1962); Jürgen Habermas, "The Public Sphere: An Encyclopedia Article (1964)," *New German Critique*, 1: 3 (Fall, 1974). Habermas's book is not available in English. We will cite the French edition, *L'Espace Publique*, (Paris: Payot, 1978). See also Daniel Hallin, "The American News Media: A Critical Theory Perspective," in John Forester (ed.), *Critical Theory and Public Life*, forthcoming.
23. See Giovanni Bechelloni (a cura di), *Il mestiere di giornalista*, (Napoli: Liguori, 1982).
24. The newspaper – in case this is confusing – continues to be central to the American public sphere, but the form of its activity changes from that of expressing explicit political opinion to that of providing authoritative information and interpretation. Most of what we say here

about the political role of American TV news (and a good deal of what we say about forms of representation), applies to newspapers as well as television.

25. Joseph A. Shumpeter, *Capitalism, Socialism and Democracy*, (New York: Harper and Row, 1950); Anthony Downs, *An Economic Theory of Democracy*, (New York: Harper and Row, 1957).
26. On the U.S. President as arbiter of political meaning see Richard E. Neustadt, *Presidential Power; The Politics of Leadership with Reflections on Johnson and Nixon*, (New York: Wiley, 1976), 167–173.
27. Cf. Jeffrey C. Alexander, "The Mass News Media in Systemic, Historical and Comparative Perspective," in Elihu Katz and Tamas Szecsko, eds., *Mass Media and Social Change*, (Beverly Hills: Sage Publications, 1981). As Alexander argues, the active role the American news media play as providers of normative interpretation is closely related to the fact that they are "differentiated" from the institutions of political debate. Beyond that point of agreement, however, our analysis diverges from Alexander's. We would argue, first of all, that the weakness of the institutions of political debate in the United States, which Alexander treats as an unfortunate coincidence, is in fact a necessary historical condition for the development of autonomous media on the American model, and that the media in turn reinforce that weakness both through the underlying messages they convey about the nature of politics and through the conditions they establish for successful political representation. The tendency for a "differentiated" media to "sell out" or collapse into the state is not merely accidental, either: it results, as we argue below, in part from the lack of a basis of political legitimacy that an autonomous media suffers from. Finally, "differentiation" seems to us a misleading term. The separation of the news media from institutions of political debate is simultaneous with their partial fusion with the economic institutions of the "culture industry," and the political institutions of State administration.
28. Schudson, "The Politics of Narrative Form."
29. Paul H. Weaver, "The New Journalism and the Old – Thoughts after Watergate," *The Public Interest*, 35 (Spring, 1974); Anthony Smith, *Goodbye Gutenberg*, (New York: Oxford University Press, 1980).
30. A "performative" is an utterance the purpose of which is to perform some social action, in this case to establish the bounds of the authority the speaker claims in making the statement that follows. See J. L. Austin, *How to Do Things With Words*, (New York: Oxford University Press, 1962).
31. In this sense there is an interesting parallel between the American journalist's relation to the "public" – that is, to the private citizens who make up its audience – and the pre-bourgeois relation of the noble to "common man." "Le statut de seigneur . . . est en soi neutre au regard des catégories 'public' et 'privé;' mais celui qui est le dépositaire représente ce statut publiquement: il se désigne et se présente comme l'incarnation d'une authorité . . . [L]e rapport des laïcs au clergé illustre la manière dont 'l'entourage' fait partie de la sphère publique répresentative tout en étant exclu – l'entourage est privé au sense où tout *private soldier* est exclu de la dignité de représentant et des honneurs militaire bien qu'il 'en fasse partie.'" Habermas, *L'Espace Publique*, 19, 20.
32. See Sperry, "Television News as Narrative," and Paul Weaver, "Is Television News Biased," *The Public Interest*, 26 (Winter, 1972).
33. See, for example, Thomas E. Patterson and Robert D. McClure, *The Unseeing Eye*, (New York: Putnam, 1976).
34. E.g. Michael J. Robinson, "American Political Legitimacy in an Age of Electronic Journalism," in Douglass Cater and Richard Adler, (eds.), *Television as a Social Force*, (New York: Praeger, 1975); Stanley Rothman, "The Mass Media in Post-Industrial Society," in Seymour Martin Lipset (ed.), *The Third Century*, (Chicago: University of Chicago Press, 1979); Samuel Huntington, *American Politics: The Promise of Disharmony*, (Cambridge: Harvard University Press, 1981), 203–205; Austin Ranney, *Channels of Power*, (New York: Basic Books, 1983).
35. See, for instance, Leon V. Sigal, *Reporters and Officials*, (Lexington, Mass.: D.C. Heath, 1973).
36. There are occasions – particularly when the parties are united in identifying a threat to the existing political order – when the Italian newscaster also acts as a representative of the official perspective. This is true, most notably, in coverage of terrorist activities.
37. This argument needs to be qualified a bit. In *form*, an American television report is organized as though it had a unified message. But that formal unity is often an illusion: it is often possible to identify conflicting or at least disjointed frames, coexisting within the same news story. During the week of our study, for example, many reports were divided in their framing of Reagan's trip, accepting its symbolism at one moment at face value, yet presenting it in the next moment as image-making. One CBS report thus began with film of the ceremony that accompanied the President's visit to London, coupled with the statement that "President Reagan today became a part of British history," and ended with a discussion of the image the President hoped to convey on American television by associating himself with the

symbolism of British monarchy. These conflicting frames were not integrated into any coherent larger framework; at the same time, however, they were not acknowledged as different interpretations, and the story proceeded from one to the other as though no shift in point of view had taken place.

38. Gaye Tuchman, "Objectivity as a Strategic Ritual: An Examination of Newsmen's Notions of Objectivity," *American Journal of Sociology*, 77 (January, 1972).
39. Franco Rositi, *Informazione e complessità sociale*, (Bari: De Donato, 1978). Italian political life can be seen as both static and fragmented: the same ideological conflicts persist year in and year out. And Italian TV news reflects both these characteristics, the first in the lack of unifying frames, the second in its tendency to remain rigidly within the established bounds of debate. American TV news is certainly fragmented in its own way, particularly if one looks at it over time. But each story and broadcast is presented in such a way that it *seems* to the audience to have some unity of meaning (see note 37 above). The media of both societies can thus be seen as "reflecting" different forms of a common malaise, an inability to achieve a working consensus on basic social perspectives through political debate. In Italy this leads to a fragmentation of perspectives, in the U.S. to the imposition of an illusory unity.

11

ARMCHAIR PILGRIMAGES
The Trips of John Paul II and Their Television Public: An Anthropological View

Daniel Dayan, Elihu Katz, and Paul Kerns

This paper deals with what happens when images or practices specific to a societal subsystem--the church--are exported into the realm of the media, into the realm of "common sense culture." It proposes an analysis of some of television's major religious events: the trips of Pope John Paul II. These trips are viewed, within his perspective as "pilgrimages." They are viewed on the other hand, within our own perspective--that of media students--as televisual ceremonies or "media-events."

What we wish to explore here is the nature of a celebratory experience, an ambiguous one, since it offers itself simultaneously as a liturgy and as a show. We are obviously involved in "pragmatics," questioning the nature of spectatorial involvement with a given television text. We are also addressing an anthropological issue, trying to identify a very unorthodox ritual experience, asking whether or not it fits within any of the existing maps of ritual territory. To avoid an early dismissal of our object of study, or what amounts to the same, a rigid distinction between the event before television and the event on television, the first being acceptable as ritual while the second would be dismissed as irrelevant to anthropology, we have relied on Victor Turner's theory of ritual, a theory whose broad scope and high level of abstraction permitted us to consider seriously the ritual monsters born of religious experience and communications technology.

Pope John Paul II's trips are usually described as pilgrimages. They are part of a long string of television shows in which he performs, a solitary figure clad in ample robes, on a background of rapidly shifting skies, landscapes or crowds; a catholic satellite of sorts, emitting his fatherly "beep" at regular intervals, in different languages, all around the globe.

Papal trips and ritual performances are undoubtedly television shows of almost unprecedented magnitude. (Easter mass, in Rome[1] is attended by 350,000 people and broadcast to 32 countries.) But are they pilgrimages? If they are, whose pilgrimages are they? The Pope's? The attending audiences'? The television spectators'? This last question is less absurd than it seems at first sight, and deserves to be rephrased: can you be a pilgrim while in your living room?

Answering positively implies, as Walter Benjamin's French disciple, Jean Baudrillard,[2] would put it, that television's spectacle of a ceremony is not simply a representation but a <u>simulation</u> of it, one which maintains the power of the ceremony, its symbolic efficacy. In fact, if one accepts that symbols have any power at all, why should one deny the same power to symbols of symbols? How less symbolic are the latter? Television, one might say, only offers the <u>image</u> of a ceremony. But what is the <u>referential</u> ceremony itself if not a metaphor, an image or an echo of some mythical belief or truth? Television is a mass-medium. So is the Catholic Church. Both deal with images and images of images, echoes of echoes. The difference is that the Catholic Church relies on a theatrical model of publicness, confronts ritual performance with audience reaction in a shared, congregative space, while television proposes a cinematographic model of publicness, a spatial and possibly temporal separation between the realms of performance and reaction. John Paul II fully uses television's power to reach world-wide audiences. But interestingly he avoids

This paper is inspired by the work of Walter Benjamin. We are also indebted to Peter Brown's studies of religious practices in late antiquity for the way in which his treatment of the themes of "adventus" and "translation" permit us to apply Benjaminian concerns to the subject of popular piety. We will develop this connection in a further paper. See, in particular, Peter Brown, *The Cult of the Saints: Its Rise and Function in Latin Christianity,* Chicago: University of Chicago Press, 1981. The "media events" project to which this paper belongs has benefited from the John and Mary Markle Foundation.
From Daniel Dayan, Elihu Katz, and Paul Kerns, "Armchair Pilgrimages: The Trips of John Paul II and Their Television Public: An Anthropological View," *On Film*, No. 13 (Fall 1984), pp. 25-34.

converting the Vatican into a full-time studio. By visiting country after country, by spending most of his time on "pilgrimage," he makes sure that the new medium does not obliterate the former; that televisual Catholicism does not erase the internal diversity of the Catholic Church, its roots in national or regional tradition. John Paul II tries to maintain some amount of ceremonial "aura";[3] he tries to establish, as if in answer to Daniel Boorstin,[4] that the ceremonies he performs are not "pseudo-events," that they are directed to those primary audiences who physically attend them, and only secondarily reach television spectators.

We wish to suggest here that such is not the case; that the spectators of the Pope's televised pilgrimages are anything but secondary, that, in many ways, these pilgrimages are primarily theirs. The process which Walter Benjamin showed at work in his analysis of the "work of art in the age of mechanical reproduction" is now taking place in a number of other domains.[5] The semiotic practices involved in political or religious discourses are subjected to a thorough re-textualization aimed at guaranteeing their reproduction, or, more exactly, their electronic transmission. This "re-textualization" is an aesthetic and a rhetorical mutation. The original event is no longer the "true" event, but some form of a "prop." As to the realm of copies, of images, it progressively absorbs the weight of social reality. Under these conditions, what happens to religious practices? And, to be specific, where lies the reality of a televised pilgrimage?

I. THE SYNTAX OF PILGRIMAGES. A TURNERIAN VIEW

While in principle a "pilgrim" may be a person who travels for secular <u>or</u> religious reasons, the notion has acquired an increasingly religious dimension. Historically, one can distinguish different types of pilgrimage. One consists in following in the steps of Jesus. The Easter ceremony organized in Rome turns the Coliseum into a <u>via dolorosa</u> where John Paul II is seen walking to and meditating on each successive stage of the passion. The other consists in traveling to shrines, shrines whose prominence as pilgrimage centers can result from various historical reasons, but towards which modern pilgrims tend to adopt similar behavior. Analyzing this behavior, Victor Turner stresses the emphasis which is placed on "devotion and personal piety." The shrine is seen as an "instrument of rechristianization deployed against the advancing secularization of society." One can remark already that shrines are thus functionally equivalent to television papal broadcasts.

In their **Image And Pilgrimage In Christian Culture,**[6] Victor and Edith Turner apply to pilgrimages the model of <u>rites-de-passage</u> which Victor Turner borrowed from the Belgian folklorist Van Gennep and developed into his own theory of "liminality." A <u>rite-de-passage</u> always includes a moment of separation from the rest of society for those undergoing the rite, and, at the end of it, a moment corresponding to their reaggregation in the community where they now hold a new status. The period which starts with separation and ends with reaggregation is a period during which the participants in the ritual are "betwixt" and "between" assigned social roles. They are, so to speak, on a threshold, neither in nor out, in a social limbo of sorts, in a state which Turner called "liminal."

Victor Turner defines liminal states as metatextual commentaries on society's daily practices. The usual, quotidian paradigms (society's <u>structure</u>) are subjected

The Pope is a Catholic satellite of sorts, emitting his fatherly "beep" at regular intervals.

to a fundamental reevaluation or revision. For a while (for the duration of the liminal period), they are suspended, set aside. Social life is then taken over by another set of rules, by a set of anti-rules. This alternative structuration is what Turner calls "<u>anti-structure.</u>"

Structure implies role repartition and social hierarchy. During the liminal period, the suspension of both allows for new possibilities of contact between participants in the ritual where relationships are no longer restrained by normative role attributions. As a group they experience their oneness, enter into the realm of <u>communitas.</u> Answering this unusual mode of relation between people, new connections between ideas become possible. Individuals experiencing a liminal period go through a process of examining radical possibilities. Liminality is a creative period. It opens up possibilities for an eventual transformation of forms or norms. Extending the realm of the liminal to include artistic or literary forms,[7] Victor Turner stresses that liminality is not only a period of transition but one of invention. Turner goes further

and suggests that societies that undergo a dramatic change usually do so because of ideas discovered or potentialities experienced during liminal moments.

All this creativity of the liminal period constitutes, in contrast to the indicative mode of culture (the way things are, in everyday life), a subjunctive mode of culture, one which covers the domains of what could be and of what ought to be. The realm of the subjunctive is an ambiguous one since it encompasses what is desirable and what is possible; since it encompasses communitas as a moral fiction and as chimaeras of carnival. Both, however, are potentially creative; both transform liminality into a social laboratory of sorts: a cognitive laboratory in one case, an experiential laboratory in the other.

Being inherent in the ritual logic and thus universal, the process of liminality is far from foreign to the practices of the Catholic Church. However, the Catholic Church seems to have conceived of liminality primarily in terms of specialized religious orders. The liminal state is not defined chronologically as a stage, a moment, an interval. It relates to the spatial metaphor from which Turner coined his word. It is a borderline, a margin, a zone on the threshold of society, a "specialized state involving the entire life of the deeply devoted." Monastics and contemplatives do not need to be pilgrims. Their entire life is spent in liminality, in a no man's land of sorts between this world and the next. However, for the common man, for the ordinary believer, another type of liminality is available: the "infrequent adventure of pilgrimage," an adventure where you encounter subjunctiveness not inside youself, as in the case of the mystic, but outside the limits of your daily world. Pilgrimages become active quests, "exteriorized mysticism," extrovert pursuits. Pilgrimages have a clear temporal structure, but, since they do not allow for a transformation in the pilgrim's status, they cannot really be assimilated to rites-de-passage. Their liminality is imperfect, approximative. They are almost liminal, or, to use Turner's term: liminoid.

A pilgrimage starts by an act of separation.[8] The pilgrim interrupts the regularity of his normal duties, dissociates himself from his familiar surroundings, severs for a while affective or institutional ties. His decision to undertake a (long) journey to the shrine allows him access to another (deeper) level of existence. Placed in a situation of vacancy, of unboundedness--if not freedom—the pilgrim enters the liminal stage of his trip. He is now liberated from profane social structure. He has lost his status and a large part of his identity. He has become partially anonymous: a pilgrim. It is a time of examination, a time of looking back at life, a time of reevaluation. The pilgrim's world has lost its weight. Its constitutive elements are allowed to enter new and unexpected combinations, to reorganize themselves in his mind. But the point of the pilgrimage is not to perform a liberation. It creates a void which must be specifically filled, a state of heightened receptivity to a given set of messages. As Philip Elliott stresses, "subordination to authority is even present in the transition phase of the rites of passage, that most cohesive moment which has provided the basis for Turner's argument that there is another model of society to be set alongside the structural one...The liminal phase (concerns) individuals who submit together to the general authority of ritual elders."[9]

Thus the pilgrimage ends and culminates with the experience of the shrine. This experience is stricly controlled. It is shaped by a ceremonial pedagogy. The pilgrim is here to be powerfully exposed to architectural, pictorial, musical, ritual manifestations of the "Christian structures of thought and feeling." Sensorially displayed in various symbolic forms, these structures are defined by Turner as "root paradigms." Impressing themselves vividly on the pilgrim, they now fill the void, occupy the emptiness created by the journey's liminality. Time is ripe for reaggregation. Loading liminality with "anti-structural" but nevertheless orthodox messages, shrines "reorient" the symbolic world of the pilgrim. Pilgrimages start as invitations to freedom but end up in submission, reach their apex when the symbols displayed during the collective mass succeed in evoking a commonness of feeling among the heterogeneous assembly of pilgrims. This likeness of experience changes their assembly into a communitas, injects a new power into the root paradigms, acts as their confirmation. Strengthened in their faith, the pilgrims are ready to be sent back to their daily life. They are now living messages, or more precisely, they can--as can all witnesses--be used as media.

II. SACREDNESS IS IN THE JET

John Paul II's trips are referred to as "pilgrimages." Paradoxically it is only when the Pope does not leave Rome and symbolically walks in the steps of Jesus in the arena of the Coliseum that his action best fits a definition of pilgrimage. When the Pope travels, he is received with all the pageantry called for by state occasions. But is he a pilgrim?

Obviously he does not change status when he undertakes his numerous journeys. If anything, his status is enhanced, his stature magnified. He is a head of state, a king of sorts, and his genial mixing with the crowds in no way abolishes the structural role which makes him stand aside and above those who come to greet him and get a glimpse of the pontifex maximus.

However the papal journeys have highlights and culminate in his visits to shrines. During such visits the Pope's status fades away, gives precedence to his role as a believer, as a man whose prayer meets popular religiosity on its very grounds, as a man who shares the collective fervor for the Marian figures of Lourdes, Guadalupe, or Yasna-Gora. But in such intensely emotional moments, he is at least as much concerned with the presence of the believers as he is with the focus of their beliefs. The Pope is visiting a shrine. First of all he is paying homage to the crowds on the site of the shrine, telling them that he shares their faith, that he does not despise or frown upon their style of worship. By adopting this style the Pope expresses respect for a given religious tradition. The act of worship he performs at the shrine is certainly intense and sincere. It differs from that of a pilgrim in that it is not an end in and by itself. It is a means for a gesture which turns the believers themselves into shrines.

As for the believers, their presence on the holy ground of the shrine has multiple motives. Have they, on their own, undertaken the personal adventure of pilgrimage, stepped out of their usual identities, entered that uneasy phase of inner dialogue which prepares them for their encounter with the holy remains or symbols? Do they even expect such an encounter to take place? Didn't they come instead with their relatives, neighbors and friends in search of an equally uplifting but quite different experience: that of witnessing the Pope's encounter with the same symbols, his own experience, his own faith?

The shrine becomes a pretext (one that can almost be disposed of or replaced), the occasion of a date, of a double fascination, of an intersubjective exchange between the Pope and the crowd. Each looks unto the other to recognize his--or their--own faith. Shrines lose their privileged status, their power of locally fixating sacredness, of making it present on a given spot. Shrines lose their "aura." Visiting them is a necessary part of the event. Not its definition. Shrines are no longer exclusive, powerful, undisputed magnets. Sacredness emanates from the august visitor as much as it emanates from the visited space. Papal visits have a "performative"[10] value: that of converting their halts into as many shrines. Airport landing grounds are kissed in prosternation and this gesture confers a sanctified dimension on the whole land of the visited country. Urban zones or rural spots which stand in collective memory for human greatness or suffering are changed into instant altars, improvized bridges towards transcendence. Poland's Auschwitz is attracted within a Christian discourse of sacrifice and redemption and the suffering of its inmates translated into "martyrdom." John Paul II's jet travels are not a pilgrim's progress towards sacredness. Sacredness is already in the jet.

Papal trips are advertized as pilgrimages. But are they *acted* as such? If so, who is the pilgrim? And where the shrine? Let us suggest the connection between papal journeys and another aspect of Catholic ritual; a ceremony long obsolete, since it moves back to late antiquity and the Catholic Middle-Ages; yet one which seems curiously modern: the *adventus*.[11]

The arrival of the emperor or hero into a community in late Roman history was governed by specific ceremonies that established the importance of the event. Usually the ceremony of *adventus* began at the outskirts of the city. It was there that the people gathered initially to greet the arrival. The entire city was expected to turn out. For a particular group not to be present meant rejection. This initial visit allowed the people of the city to see who this person was, both by sight, and by the *panegyrics* that would be given at the *adventus*. The role of the panegyrist was essential in giving meaning to the event.[12] Panegyrists of the fourth century did not attempt to create literature or historiography. In contrast to the Pindaric paradigm of celebratory poetry, they used familiar metaphors or descriptions to allow their audience to understand the meanings[13] assigned to the event. The panegyrist was supposed to perceive the importance of the event and then to transcribe it by way of speech to the people, offering the reason why the ordinary activities of city-life had been suspended. Following the initial greeting outside the city, guest and community were prepared to engage in the official reasons for the visit.

To summarize, the *adventus* ceremony seems uncannily familiar. One recognizes in it the scenography of state visits, of countless television events with their repertory of three major roles: that of the guest hero; that of the welcoming crowd (nowadays reduced to synecdochic proportions); that of the media panegyrists whose task it is to make (correct) sense of the event and to tell the invisible mass of home-based spectators why the live broadcast

John Paul II's jet travels are not a pilgrim's progress towards sacredness. Sacredness is already in the jet.

they receive on their TV sets calls for the suspension of all other activities.

The model of the *adventus* is slightly too broad to be really relevant to the case at hand. Any politically oriented "media event"[14] is in some way an *adventus*, no matter how profane. However, *adventus* ceremonies may have a truly religious dimension, one which was introduced in the Middle Ages to celebrate the installation of religious relics. These ceremonies--"translations"--invert the dynamics of pilgrimage. While pilgrimages are movements taking people to relics, translations take relics (or fragments of relics) to people in order to ensure in each community "some presence of the sacred."[15] Relics are "divided, then divided again," and scattered throughout the Catholic world. What becomes ritualized is no longer the active journey, the quest for the sacred, but its reception. This "reception"--the very term has a flavor of communications theory--takes the form of an *adventus*.

While they have many features in common with pilgrimages, papal journeys seem much closer to the dramaturgy of translations. The pope, as an almost relic (he is heir to St. Peter's throne), as an emanation of the sacred, comes to people and blesses their communities. But he does so in two ways. He comes to be greeted by the huge crowds that gather in adventus in his honor. He also comes to the "invisible mass,"[16] to the diasporic myriad of television spectators who greet him from the recesses of their darkened living rooms. In the adventus he is the guest of an assembly symbolically representative of the whole of society; he faces a social microcosm where now, as well as in medieval times, the stress is on unanimity within diversity. In the living rooms, his presence fits neatly within an aesthetics of television brilliantly characterized by Michael Arlen as evolving around the theme of hospitality; as modelled on the circumstances of home-based viewing and thus structured as an infinite modulation of the ritual of "ice-breaking"; as a constant repetition of the motive of the encounter as a never-ending stream of people introducing other people and as a litany of "hosts and guests": hosts of the talkshows; of the game shows; news anchors; permanent figures of serials; guest speakers, guest players, guest experts, guest stars. The adventus pours into the living room where it is modulated into a family occasion. The family occasion blends in, is absorbed by, the adventus. Being focused on the same guest erases boundaries between the two occasions, between their respective audiences, achieves a quasi-fictional identification between television spectators and the crowds who hail the pope.[17] Does this mean that these two audiences undergo the same experience?

III. TELEVISION PILGRIMS?

One should distinguish the event as performance, as the acting out of a given dramatury, from the event as a provoked experience. One should distinguish here what Barthes called the "writing" of the event,[18] its praxis, the models internalized by its actors, from its "pragmatics," the effects which the event as a text produces on its spectators. Television spectators go through a specific adventure. They have a specific role and a specific script. This script has to be inferred from the very existence of a television genre, a genre which in previous studies, we chose to call "media-events."[19] Our media-events have many features in common with some of the phenomena analyzed among others by Kurt and Gladys Lang, Philip Elliott, Steven Lukes, Edward Shils, David Chaney, Daniel Boorstin, Pierre Nora.[20] They are markedly different from Pierre Nora's monster events in that the genre we are addressing does not encompass print media. Ritualized as it might be, the discursive model of l'affaire falls outside of our preoccupation with events which must have a ceremonial, participatory dimension, a dimension which we think can only be realized through those media which allow "live" broadcasts (radio, television). Our events might be reminiscent of Daniel Boorstin's "pseudo-events," a notion which comes very close to Benjaminian grounds by evoking images without originals, events that are not only publicized but produced by the media. But Boorstin's perceptive description of pseudo-events falls short of pointing at the potential emergence of a new semiotic regime. He only sees in them a transgression of the real vs. image paradigm and morally condemns them for turning social reality into a semiotic chaos. Boorstin's "pseudo-events" are doubly irrelevant to our genre. In a narrow and almost juridical sense, our events are not "pseudo-events," because they are media-sponsored but originate outside the media.[21] In a larger sense, it is Boorstin's concept which we find at fault since juridical litigation about what is media-originated and what is not may easily turn into casuistics. Political institutions are mass-media. So is the church. All produce events. Their events are not "truer" than purely televisual ones. They may only be more "felicitous," an Austinian concept which takes us away from the somewhat irrelevant paradigm of true (referent) vs. false (image) and suggests another paradigm, that of expressive events, of symbolic manipulations which one is situationally entitled—or not—to perform, and which, as a consequence, capture—or fail to capture—public imagination. The logic of Boorstin's position is essentially one of distrust for simulacra of all kinds. It leaves no room for symbolic occasions. We refuse to fall on one or the other side of the "pseudo" line. Our events are not imaginary train crashes. They are truly ceremonial occasions.

The recurrence of such events on television constitutes them into a genre characterized by a few frequent—almost constant—textual patterns, patterns which can be found in the Pope's journeys but also in such events as the moonlanding, the funeral of J. F. Kennedy, of Lord Mountbatten, of Anwar Sadat, or the latter's visit to Jerusalem, to take only a few examples. Semantically, these events are focused on "great men" or "heroes" engaged in symbolic action. In the case of dead heroes, this symbolic action is maintained by simply being turned into a "passion." Death is mobilized and put to work as "sacrifice."

The celebrated action (or passion) has two main dimensions. It is "extraordinary," "unheard of," "historical," "a turning point," "beyond imagination." In short, it is perceived as an irruption in daily life of the realm of the possible. Simultaneously it is an action that is "heroic," "admirable," "commendable." A realization of Kant's categoric imperative, it is universal, is offered as a model, exemplifies what all behaviors should be. It is not only an action but a lesson ushering into existence what usually belongs to moral fictions, to worlds that ought to be. Our events present themselves as doubly subjunctive. They exemplify new possibilities; they embody a desirable state of things.

Television is a mass-medium. So is the Catholic Church.

Syntactically our events are characterized by an unusual utilization of television formats. Their broadcast provokes a cancellation of all other programs and, often, a suspension of ordinary life. Television uses here what has been described as its most powerful weapon: the power of interrupting its own structural flow.[22] Simultaneously television relinquishes some of its mastery over its discursive product. The event is broadcast "live," theoretically open to potential accidents (even though the multiplicity of cameras on different locations usually leaves open the options of multiple "editing routes" and that of camouflaging any unforeseen incident). It treats the event as a happening which it relates in a style which is frequently that of classical cinema, with its rhetoric of shot/reverse shot displaying the points of view of heroes or crowd members. But this "fictional" treatment is in fact what television strives for and only intermittently achieves. The very fact of attempting it, no matter how discontinuously, stands in contrast to the aesthetics of the news where images are treated like illustrations, and statements are either paraphrased or reduced to quotation-size. In the news-speakers' discourse both images and statements are submitted to and encased within a syntagmatic continuity.[29] The syntagmatic coherence of the news as a text derives from the event itself (another characteristic of fiction) and the commentator's speech acquires a connotative, interstitial status. Television portrays its own role as that of a "phatic" channel and the journalistic training of its personnel loses much of its relevance.

Journalists function like priests, or, more precisely, like panegyrists. They are not meant to read through the event (to assess it, to evaluate it), but to read on it what the event has to say about itself. Since the event calls for our emotions, its commentators are allowed to express their own and the norm of objective neutrality is dismissed in favor of a counternorm which may reach the level of

The Pope comes to the invisible mass, to the diasporic myriad of television spectators who greet him from the recesses of their darkened living rooms.

sportscasting hysteria. If daily television news can be considered part of society's structure, what we find here might be characterized as the anti-structure of television rhetorics.

Pragmatically the event is submitted to conditions of reception which contradict a converging ensemble of descriptions or theories stressing the theme of television as "wall-paper in motion." Again "media-events" come out as anti-structural. They are watched deliberately and in groups constituted for the occasion. They are experienced in highly social situations of party-giving and dressing-up, and serve as a prelude to an intense telephonic activity. Media-events provoke a strengthening of social ties—immediate or distant—an upsurge of communal feeling. The spectatorial experience is that of a renewed communitas.

Subjunctiveness, anti-structure, communitas. Media-events include in one way or the other each of the ingredients whose sum defines Turner's liminality, a liminality which one could already guess from their interruptive status. Thus the genre as a whole is liminal and the experience it provokes, that of communitas. One is tempted, however, to describe this experience in greater detail, to ask questions about its temporal structure, about the nature of its flow. In fictional cinema we have tried to show that the spectators are somehow "constituted," "processed," "performed" by the filmic text.[24] What are the symbolic processes which impress themselves upon me and orchestrate my attitudes, feelings or emotions as a spectator of televised events? This question attributes an active role to a text, but seems paradoxical only if one confines media discourses in a "constative" role and ignores their "performative" nature. What we wish to describe here has nothing to do with the consequences of the text, with its ulterior effects. It does not concern the aftermath of the televised event, but its very experience.

The televised event always starts in advance of the actual ceremony. While the event is an interruption in the flow of life, it is an anticipated interruption. During the days which precede the event, a progressive build-up is organized by networks or channels, leading to a steady multiplication of event-related items. This process has an almost hypnotic value. It refocuses social life on one of its elements, enlarges that element out of proportion, and, after establishing its overwhelming importance, it seals it off, organizes around it a sanitary cordon of sorts, prevents it from mixing with any other event or social concern. This process which we have described in detail[25] continues when the event reaches its ceremonial phase. The event must be kept pure. Failing to protect it is perceived by the media personnel as a broken taboo. Thus the unease expressed in **Four Dark Days** by CBS commentator on Kennedy's funeral, when the events force him to comment about another death, that of Lee Harvey Oswald, when a ludicrous repetition of murders poisons with a flavor of "farce" the lofty climate of the ongoing tragedy. The event is sacred. Anything else is profane. Television provides the separation between one and the other, or, to use Turner's term, it provides the "limen." By its intense —intensive—anticipation of the event, and by isolating the event from all the rumours of daily life, television performs for its spectators an initial rite of separation; it performs on their behalf the pilgrim's commitment. They have been forcefully diverted from other social concerns, placed in a situation of expectation and vacancy. They are empty vessels. The pilgrimage is well on its way.

As a ceremonial occasion, the event itself consists of a symbolic reordering of social life. The paradigms which rule a society's perception of its historical existence are powerfully, "exercitively"[26] altered, replaced or suspended. Israelis might live in peace with their Arab neighbors. Poles might openly live up to the standards of their Catholic faith. Earth might stop being the subjective center of the universe ... This reordering is symbolic, not only because it alters ways of thinking or conventions, but also because it offers no guarantee of lasting beyond the ceremonial occasion. In fact the ceremony offers itself as a metaphor for its own potential consequences. Seeing the Pope perform huge masses in Warsaw somehow means that Polish Catholicism is already free. Seeing Sadat land in Jerusalem tells you in a way that peace in the Middle-East has already come about. Seeing Nixon's aides face the probing of the Senate Judiciary Committee already places them in a position of culprits. In an interesting semiotic ambiguity, the metaphor of a process gives itself to be read as its index, and may indeed become this index by the mere virtue, by the "performative" power of the metaphor; by what Levi-Strauss called "symbolic efficacy."[27]

The symbolic reordering of social life is made posible by invocation or manipulation of sacred

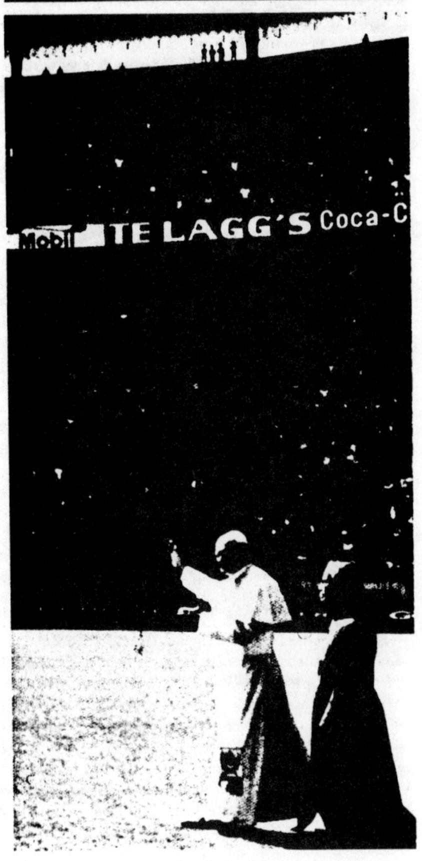

symbols, of "root paradigms." The event presents itself as a pedagogy during which the fundamental signifiers of a society's continuity are called upon, ritually displayed either for their own sake or for legitimizing the event's further purposes. Sadat in Jerusalem pays homage to the memorial of the holocaust. Taking account of the diversity of his--at least double--audience, his speech combines allusions to Mohammed's visit to Medina Jews and references to the (superficially) shared theme of the sacrifice of Abraham.[28]

The event is finally received in a state of communitas. We have already mentioned that the spectators are usually assembled in viewing parties, but we wish to insist here on television-performed communitas, to evoke once again television's textual treatment of the ceremonial grounds, with its reliance on fictional techniques of shot/reverse-shot. This treatment provokes the identification of television spectators with the attending crowds, simulates in them an oceanic feeling, an euphoric loss of the limits of the self, a new, imaginary, communal corporality.

"Media-events" thus appear to be not only a liminal form, but one which, though structurally different, is experientially similar to that of pilgrimages. Curious pilgrimages indeed, since they are motionless pilgrimages, pilgrimages without striving and without aura, pilgrimages in an armchair. The elusive quality of the shrine with its protective architecture, with its aesthetics of reticence, is replaced by an emphasis on obviousness, exhibition, display. Placed under the sign of Daedalus, the earth-flavored progress towards the unknown has been replaced by aerial, Icarean overviews. Paradoxically television pilgrimages tend to adopt a point-of-view which used to be described as that of God. And yet, the mystery remains. In the age of electronic simulations the experience which comes closest to pilgrimage is not that of the traveling Pope nor that of the traveling crowds that meet him. It might be that of their television witnesses.

This paper was presented at the Conference on Sociology of Religions "Il fattore religione nelle societa complesse," University of Padua, March 1983.

We wish to thank for their suggestions Pierre Motyl, Shaul Feldman and Prof. Don Handelman (Hebrew University, Jerusalem), Dr. William Gibson (UCLA) for his helpful comments on the rhetorics of network news, and Professors Gustavo Guizzardi and Enzo Pace (Universita degli Studi, Padova).

NOTES

1. April 1984.

2. Jean Baudrillard, "La précession des simulacres," **Traverses**, No. 10, (Paris: Minuit, February 1978).

3. Walter Benjamin, "The Work of Art in the Age of Mechanical Reproduction," **Illuminations** (New York: Shocken, 1969).

4. Daniel Boorstin, **The Image. A Guide to Pseudo-Events in America** (New York: Harper & Row, 1964).

5. Benjamin.

6. Victor and Edith Turner, **Image And Pilgrimage in Christian Culture** (New York: Columbia University Press, 1978).

7. Victor Turner, "Process, System and Symbol: A New Anthropological Synthesis," **Daedalus**, 1977.

8. Turner, **Image and Pilgrimage.**

9. Philip Elliott, "Press Performance as a Political Ritual," Centre for Mass Communications Research, University of Leicester, February, 1978.

10. J.L. Austin, **How To Do Things With Words** (Cambridge: Harvard University Press, 1962).

11. Paul Kerns, "Papal Visit to the U.S. as Pilgrimage," Annenberg School of Communications, August 1982. See, also: Peter Brown, **The Cult Of The Saints** (Chicago: University of Chicago Press, 1981); A. Dupront, "Pelerinages et lieux sacres," **Mélanges F. Braudel** (Toulouse: Privat, 1973); Patrick Geary, **Furta Sacra** (Princeton: Princeton University Press, 1978); A. Kendall, **Medieval Pilgrims** (New York: G. Putnam, 1970).

12. Aristotle distinguished three types of speech: political or advisory; juridical; and speeches for the entertainment of the audience. Panegyrics was considered in the latter category.

13. Using as a model a famous sociological distinction, one could distinguish the "ascribed" meaning of events from their "achieved" meaning. The "ascribed" meaning is performatively imposed on the event, here and now, by the panegyrists and their successors. The "achieved" meaning is retrospectively "construed" by hermeneutics, for example by historians. However, one can still wonder--as does Barthes--whether historical reading is not a performative in disguise and, therefore, a retrospective ascription.

14. In the celebratory sense we give to this phase, and which the third section of this paper will make explicit.

15. Kerns.

16. A new meaning of Elias Canetti's phrase.

17. See, on the function of shot/reverse shot in the pragmatics of fiction film; Dayan, "The Tutor Code of Classical Cinema," **Film Quarterly**, (Berkeley: University of California Press, Fall 1975).

18. R. Barthes, "L'écriture de l'évènement," **Communications**, No. 13, (Paris: Le Seuil, 1968).

19. E. Katz, D. Dayan, and P. Motyl, "In Defense of Media-Events," **Communications In The XXIst Century** (New York: Wiley and Sons, 1981).

20. Kurt and Gladys Lang, **Television And Politics** (Chicago: Quadrangle Books, 1968); Philip Elliott, "Press Performance..."; Steven Lukes, "Political Ritual and Social Integration," **Sociology**, Vol. 9, no.2, May 1975; E. Shils and M. Young, "The Meaning of Coronation," **Sociological Review**, Vol. 1, no.1, 1953; David Chaney, "A Symbolic Mirror of Ourselves. Civic Ritual in Mass Society." **Media, Culture And Society**, no.5, 1983; Daniel Boorstin, **The Image**; Pierre Nora, "L'evenement monstre," **Communications** No. 18, (Paris: Seuil, 1972).

21. Katz, Dayan, Motyl, "In Defense of Media-Events."

22. See Robert Vianello, "Notes Towards A Theory of Television Enunciation," UCLA, 1983.

23. Discourse is used here both in the usual sense, and in the more specific Benvenistian sense.

24. D. Dayan, "Le spectateur performé," **Hors-Cadre** No. 2, (Paris: Presses Universitaires de Vincennes, Winter 1984).

25. D. Dayan, E. Katz, "Rituels publics à usage privé: métamorphose télévisée d'un mariage royal," **Les Annales: Economie, Société, Civilisation** (Paris: Arman Colin, January 1982).

26. J.L. Austin.

27. C. Levis-Strauss, **Structural Anthropology** I (New York: Basic Books).

28. Tamar Liebes, "Sadat's Speech in the Knesset," Hebrew University, 1980.

12

CULTURAL TRANSFORMATIONS
The Politics of Resistance

David Morley

Mattelart has pointed to the fact that forms of popular resistance to, and subversion of, dominant cultures have rarely been studied. The point here, he argues, is that while the 'receiver' of communications is often considered as a passive consumer of information or leisure commodities, it is nonetheless true that the audience does not necessarily read the messages sent to it within the cultural code of the transmitters. The way in which the subaltern groups and classes in a society reinterpret and make sense of these messages is therefore a crucial problem for any theory of communications as a mode of cultural domination. At the macro level of international cultural relations, he argues, the consequences of a message being interpreted in a different way from what its senders intended may be quite radical. He asks:

> In how many countries do the Aryan heroes of the television series, Mission Impossible, fighting against the rebels, undergo a process of identification which is the exact opposite of that intended by the imperialist code, and how often are they viewed as the 'bad guys' in the story? (Mattelart & Siegelaub 1979, p. 27)

Mattelart warns that any notions of ideological domination must be employed with great care and recommends that the idea that imperialism invades different sectors of society in a uniform way be abandoned in favour of an analysis of the particular milieux which favour or resist penetration.

In the domestic context, the argument alerts us to the relation between the dominant ideological forms of the media, and the subcultures and codes inhabited by different classes and class fractions within British society. Cohen and Robbins (1978) argue that the specific popularity of Kung-fu movies within working-class youth culture is to be understood precisely in these terms. It is an instance of an ideological form securing some recognition and purchase within a particular section of the media audience to the extent that it 'fits' with the subcultural forms in which this class-fraction understands and articulates its own particular experience:

> The fascination of the content of Kung-fu movies for working class kids goes side by side with their unconscious recognition of its narrative style or 'grammar', as one which is identical with their own. They can read it effortlessly. (p. 98)

This is not simply a question of 'objective correspondence' between situations protrayed in a given movie and 'the more subterranean realities of living in a "hard" working-class area' which would allow a simple process of identification at the level of content. These authors maintain that the crucial factor in play is:

> ...the linkage of two forms of 'collective representation' which have radically different historical origins and institutional supports. If the linkage is possible at all, it is because there is an objective correspondence between some oral traditions in working-class culture and some genres produced by the mass media. It is a correspondence of form, rather than content, and where it doesn't exist, the impact of the mass media on working-class consciousness is entirely negligible. Finally, both in the history of the class, and in the life history of those growing up into it, the narrative forms of oral culture pre-date those of the mass media and constitute a kind of permanent infra-structure, which condition and limit the effectivity of the latter. (p. 99)

This is to argue that the structures of imperialism and of class domination, when introduced into the study of communications, pose the problem of audience responses to and interpretations of the mass media as a critical area of research.

Communications: a broken circuit?

We are faced with a situation in which there is a potential disjunction between the codes of those sending and those receiving messages through the circuit of mass communications (cf. Hall 1973, pp. 18-19; Eco 1972, p. 121). The problem of (non-)complementarity of codes at the production and reception ends of the chain of communications is indissolubly linked with the problem of cultural domination and resistance. In a research project on Nationwide (a popular current affairs magazine programme on BBC television), we attempted to pose this as a specific problem about the degree of complementarity between the codes of the programme and the interpretative codes of various sociocultural groups. (Brunsdon & Morley 1978; Morley 1980). We were concerned to explore the extent to which decodings take place within the limits of the preferred (or dominant) manner in which the message has been initially encoded. However, there is a complementary aspect to this problem, namely the extent to which these interpretations, or decodings, also reflect, and are inflected by, the codes and discourses which different sections of the audience inhabit, and the ways in which these decodings are determined by the socially governed distribution of cultural codes between and across different sections of the audience – that is, the range of decoding strategies and competencies in the audience.

To raise this as a problem for research is already to argue that the meaning produced by the encounter of text and subject cannot be 'read off' straight from textual characteristics. The text cannot be considered in isolation from its historical conditions of production and consumption. And an analysis of media ideology cannot rest with an analysis of production and text alone.

> The 'meaning' of a film is not something to be discovered purely in the text itself...but is constituted in the interaction between the text and its users. The early claim of semiotics to be in some way able to account for a text's functioning through an immanent analysis was essentially misfounded in its failure to perceive that any textual system could only have meaning in relation to codes not purely textual, and that the recognition, distribution, and activation of these would vary socially and historically. (Hill 1979, p. 122)

Thus the meaning of the text must be interpreted in terms of which set of discourses it encounters in any particular set of circumstances, and how this encounter may restructure both the meaning of the text and the discourses which it meets. The meaning of the text will be constructed differently according to the discourses (knowledges, prejudices, resistances etc.) brought to bear by the reader, and the crucial factor in the encounter of audience/subject and text will be the range of discourses at the disposal of the audience. The crucial point here is that individuals in different positions in the social formation defined according to structures of class, race or sex, for example, will tend to inhabit or have at their disposal different codes and subcultures. Thus social position sets parameters to the range of potential readings by structuring access to different codes.

Whether or not a programme succeeds in transmitting the preferred or dominant meaning will depend on whether it encounters readers who inhabit codes and ideologies derived from other institutional areas (e.g. churches or schools) which correspond to and work in parallel with those of the programme or whether it encounters readers who inhabit codes drawn from other areas or institutions (e.g. trade unions or 'deviant' subcultures) which conflict to a greater or lesser extent with those of the programme.

This is to say that if a notion such as that of a 'preferred reading' is to have any value it is not as a means to abstractly 'fix' one interpretation over and above others, but rather to account:

> For how, under certain conditions, a text will tend to be read in particular ways because of the way meaning is placed through the articulation of particular aesthetic, social and historical codes. (Hill 1979, p. 123)

It follows, then, that:

> The task of ideological analysis is [that] of accounting for how meanings are generated for and through particular audiences...accounting for the processes of signification through which particular meanings are produced in specific contexts. (p. 123)

The message: encoding and decoding

In outline, the premises on which we base our approach are as follows:

- a The production of a meaningful message in television discourse is always problematic 'work'. The same event can be encoded in more than one way.
- b The message in social communication is always complex in structure and form. It always contains more than one potential 'reading'. Messages propose and prefer certain readings over others, but they cannot be entirely closed around one reading: they remain polysemic.
- c The activity of 'getting meaning' from the message is also problematic practice, however transparent and natural it may seem. Messages encoded in one way can also be read in a different way.

Thus, the communicative form and structure of the encoded message can be analysed in terms of its preferred reading: the mechanisms which prefer one, dominant reading over the other readings; the means which the encoder uses to try to win the assent of the audience to his particular reading of the message. Special attention can be given here to the control exercised over meaning, and to 'points of identification' within the message which transmit the preferred reading to the audience.

It is precisely the aim of the presenter to achieve identification with the audience through mechanisms which gain the audience's complicity and 'suggest' preferred readings. If and when these identificatory mechanisms are attenuated or broken, will the message be decoded in a different framework of meaning from that in which it was encoded? Broadcasters undoubtedly make the attempt to establish a relationship of complicity with the audience (Brunsdon & Morley 1978) but there is no justification for assuming that the attempt will always be successful.

The structure of the audience: decodings in cultural context

We might profitably think of the media audience not so much as an undifferentiated mass of individuals but as a complex structure of socially organized individuals in a number of overlapping subgroups and subcultures, each with its own history and cultural traditions. This is not to see cultural competence as automatically determined or generated by social position but to pose the problem of the relation between, on the one hand, social categories and social structure and, on the other, codes, subcultures and ideologies. In this perspective the primary relationships for analysis are those between linguistic and cultural codes and patterns of class (cf. Bernstein 1971; Rosen 1972), race (cf. Labov 1969) and sex (cf. Lakoff 1976; Spender 1980). We are therefore proposing a model of the audience, not as an atomized mass of individuals, but as composed of a number of subcultural formations or groupings whose members will share a cultural orientation towards decoding messages in particular ways. Individual members' readings will be framed by shared cultural formations and practices. Such shared 'orientations' will in turn be determined by factors derived from the objective position of the individual reader in the social structure. These objective factors must be seen as setting parameters to individual experience although not determining consciousness in a mechanistic way: people understand their situation and react to it by way of subcultures and meaning systems (Critcher 1975).

Bernstein's work on sociolinguistic codes and his hypothesis of a correlation between particular social (class) categories and codes is of obvious relevance to any theory of the media audience, in terms of how different sections of that audience may relate to different kinds of messages – perhaps through the employment of different codes of interpretation. However, Bernstein's scheme is highly simplified: it contains only two classes (working and middle) and two codes (restricted and elaborated), and no attempt is made to differentiate within these classes, nor within their 'corresponding' codes. Rosen attacks Bernstein for his mechanistic analysis of the working class as an undifferentiated whole, defined simply by economic positions, and argues that Bernstein ignores factors at the level of ideological and political practice which 'distinguish the language of Liverpool dockers from that of...Coventry car workers' (Rosen 1972, p. 9). Rosen is here attempting to extend the terms of the analysis by insisting on the operation of non-economic factors. He rejects the argument that linguistic codes are determined by 'common occupational function' and presents a case for differentiating within and across class categories in terms of 'history, traditions, job experience, ethnic origins, residential patterns, level of organisation' (p. 6).

Bernstein's oversimplistic formulation of the relation between classes and cultural codes, and his neglect of cultural differentiation within classes, is to some extent paralleled in Parkin's attempt to produce a typology of 'meaning systems' in relation to class structure. Parkin's treatment of class structures as the ground of different meaning systems (1971, ch. 3) is a fruitful if crude point of departure which provided some basic categories for Hall's (1973) hypotheses about typical decoding positions. The key question at issue is that of the nature of the fit between, say, class, socioeconomic or educational position and interpretative codes.

Following, but adapting Parkin, we have suggested three hypothetical-typical positions which the decoder may occupy in relation to the encoded message. He or she may take the meaning fully within the interpretative framework which the message itself proposes and 'prefers': if so, decoding proceeds within, or is aligned with, the dominant or 'hegemonic' code. Second, decoders may take the meaning broadly as encoded; but by relating the message to some concrete, located or situational context which reflects their position and interests, they may modify or partially inflect the meaning. Following Parkin, we would call this a 'negotiated' position. Third, the decoder may recognize how the message has been contextually encoded, but bring to bear an alternative frame of interpretation, which sets aside the encoding framework and superimposes on the message an interpretation which works in a directly oppositional way – an oppositional, or 'counter-hegemonic' decoding.

Parkin elaborated these positions as three possible and typical positions of different classes in relation to a class-based hegemonic ideology. We have transposed them in order to describe possible alternative ways of decoding ideologically constructed messages. Of course, Parkin's conceptual framework is limited in that it provides only a statement of the three logical possibilities: that a given section of the audience may either share, partly share, or not share the dominant code in which the message has been transmitted (Morley 1974). If the three basic decoding positions have any sociological validity it will necessarily be at the very broad level of what one might call class competencies in the reading of ideological messages. Even at this level, further distinctions may have to be made: for example between a version of the negotiated position which reflects a deferential stance towards the use of the hegemonic code, or one which reflects a subordinate stance, as defined by Parkin, where messages cast at a general or abstract level are subject to negotiation when referred to a more limited or sectional interest.

Much of the important work in this respect consists in differentiating Parkin's catch-all category of 'negotiated code' into a set of empirically grounded subvariants of this basic category, which are illustrated in the sociological work on different forms of sectional and corporate consciousness (cf. Parkin 1971; Mann 1973; Nichols & Armstrong 1976). The crucial development from this perspective has been the attempt to translate Parkin's three ideal types (which are themselves a considerable advance on any model which sees the audience as an unstructured aggregate of individuals) into a more sensitive model of actual decoding positions within the media audience.

There remains, however, one critical problem in the attempt to integrate the sociological work of authors such as Parkin into a theory of communications. This is the tendency to directly convert social categories (e.g. class) into meanings (e.g. ideological positions) without attending to the specific factors which govern this conversion. It is simply inadequate to present demographic and sociological factors such as age, sex, race or class position as objective correlates or determinants of differential decoding positions without any attempt to specify *how* they intervene in the process of communication. The relative autonomy of signifying practices means that sociological factors cannot be 'read in' directly as affecting the communication process. These factors can only have effect through the (possibly contradictory) action of the discourses in which they are articulated.

Audiences and ideologies: methodological and empirical questions

I will now attempt to illustrate some of these theoretical arguments by drawing on material from the Nationwide research project (see Brunsdon & Morley 1978 and Morley 1980 for a full account of this project). The research was designed to provide an analysis of the programme discourse and then to ascertain which sections of the programme's audience decoded in line with the preferred /dominant codes, and which sections operated negotiated/oppositional decodings.

Two videotaped Nationwide programmes were shown to 29 groups drawn from different social and cultural backgrounds, and from different levels of the educational system. Our procedure was to gain entry to a situation where the group already had some existence as a social entity – at least for the duration of a course. The videotape showings and the subsequent interviews were arranged to slot into the context of their established institutional settings as far as possible.

The groups usually consisted of between five and ten people. After the viewing session the discussion was taperecorded (usually about 40 mins duration) and this was later transcribed in full to provide the basic data for the analysis. The project used the 'focused interview' method originally developed by Merton and Kendal (1946). Thus the interviews began with non-directive prompting designed to establish the 'working vocabulary' (Mills 1939) and frame of reference of the groups, and the order of priority in which *they* raised issues, before moving on to a more structured set of questions based on our programme analysis.

We were particularly concerned to identify the nature of the groups' 'lexico-referential systems' (Mills 1939) and to examine how these systems related to those employed by the broadcasters. Our questions were designed to reveal whether audiences used the same words in the same ways as the broadcasters, in discussing different topics in the programme; whether the groups ranked issues and topics in the same order of priority as that given in the programme discourse; and whether there were aspects of topics not discussed by the broadcasters that were specifically mentioned by these groups. The decision to work with group rather than individual interviews followed from our desire to explore the extent to which individual 'readings' are shaped by the sociocultural groupings within which they are situated.

We attempted to work as far as possible with the raw data of actual speech instead of trying to convert responses into immediately categorizable forms. Although this choice raised problems which we cannot claim in any sense to have solved, it did allow us to bring into focus the question of the relation between the forms of speech employed by broadcasters and those employed by respondents.

We took as axiomatic Voloshinov's (1973) concept of the multi-accentuality of linguistic forms, the impossibility of establishing simple one-to-one correspondences between particular linguistic features and ideological structures.[1] Our main concern was the broader level of conceptual frameworks and perspectives, in so far as these (usually at the level of implication or assumption) could be detected from the actual linguistic usage of the respondents. Our main guide to this was an application of Gerbner's method of 'proposition analysis' (Gerbner 1964), which allows one to identify the patterns of argument and assumption, and the cognitive premises, underlying particular responses. This is done by reconstructing declarative statements in terms of the simple propositions which support or underpin them, thus attempting to explicate the assumptions which must be held in order for it to make sense to give particular answers to questions raised in the interviews.

While this is evidently a controversial area, where responses may be interpreted differently, we would argue that it must remain the primary level of analysis. This is because only when the baseline assumptions embedded in a particular discourse have been explicated, when we have some sense of its overall pattern, can we move on to an analysis of how particular forms or signifiers function within the context of that discourse. Thus, while there remains in this approach a problem about the sensitivity of the linguistic tools which the analysis employs, this focus on the underlying patterns of assumption is a necessary preliminary before more precise methods of formal linguistic analysis can be productively employed.[2]

Classes, codes, decodings

The problematic proposed here does not attempt to derive decodings directly from social class position or 'reduce' them to it. It is always a question of how social position, as it is articulated through particular discourses, produces specific kinds of readings or decodings. These readings can then be seen to be patterned by the way in which the structure of access to different discourses is determined by social position. The question is which cultural repertoires and codes are available to which groups, and how do they utilize these symbolic resources in their attempt to make sense of messages coming from the media?

Although the project as a whole investigated decodings made by groups across a range of class positions, I shall, in order to focus the comparisons more sharply, deal here only with the differences between the decodings made by three kinds of groups, all sharing a roughly similar working-class position or background. These groups were, first, young apprentice engineers and metallurgists, second, groups of trade union officials and of shop stewards, and third, young black students at a college of further education.

Of these groups it was the apprentices who most closely inhabited the dominant code of the programme. Their decodings were mostly closely in line with the dominant/preferred meanings of Nationwide. This seemed to be accounted for by the extent to which the lads' use of a form of populist discourse ('damn all politicians – they're all as bad as each other...it's all down to the individual in the end, isn't it?') was quite compatible with that of the programme. Although the dominant tone of these groups' responses to Nationwide was one of cynicism, a resistance to anyone 'putting one over' on them, most of the main items in the programme were, in fact, decoded by these groups within the dominant framework or preferred reading established by the programme. They tended to accept the perspectives offered by and through the programme's presenter. The situation here seems to be the converse of that outlined by Parkin: here we have working-class groups who cynically claim to be distanced from the programme at a general level but who accept and reproduce its ideological formulations of specific issues. The 'commonsense' interpretations which the programme's presenters offer seem 'pretty obviously OK' to these groups too, and Nationwide's questions are justified as 'natural' or 'obvious' – and therefore unproblematic: 'They just said the obvious comment didn't they?'

The groups involved in the activities and discourse of trade unionism produced differently inflected versions of negotiated and oppositional decodings, depending on their social position and positioning in educational and political discourses. There is a profound difference between the groups who are non-union, or are simply members of trade unions, and those with an active involvement in and commitment to trade unionism — the latter producing much more negotiated or oppositional readings of Nationwide. So the structure of decoding is not a simple function of class position, but rather the result of differential involvement and positioning in discourse formations.

Further, there are the significant differences between the articulate, fully oppositional readings produced by the shop stewards as compared with the negotiated/oppositional readings produced by the trade union officials. This, we would suggest, is to be accounted for by the greater distancing of the stewards from the pressures of incorporation which full-time officials experience, which thus allows them to inhabit a more 'left-wing' interpretation of trade unionism.

The trade union officials on the whole inhabit a dominant/populist inflected version of negotiated code and espouse a right-wing Labour perspective. They are regular Nationwide watchers and approve both the programme's mode of address and ideological stance — 'I find that quite interesting...there's something in that programme for everyone to have a look at...'; 'It seems to be a programme acceptable to the vast majority of people.' They accept the individualistic theme of the programme and accept the programme's construction of an undifferentiated national community which is currently suffering economic hardship: to this extent they can be said to identify with the national 'we' which the programme discourse constructs. However, this is at an abstract and general level: at a more concrete, local level — that of directly economic 'trade union' issues — they take a more critical stance, and specific items within this category are then decoded in a more oppositional way (the classic structure of the negotiated code).

It is the shop stewards who spontaneously produce by far the most articulate, fully oppositional reading of the programme. They reject the programme's attempt to tell us what 'our grouse' is and its attempt to construct a national 'we' — 'They want "*we*"...they want the average viewer to all think "we"...' And they identify this Nationwide form of presentation as part of a general pattern: 'I mean, take Nationwide, add the *Sun*...the *Mirror* and the *Daily Express* to it...' This is a pattern in which: 'Union leaders are always being told "You're ruining the country!"'

Finally, the black students made hardly any connection with the discourse of Nationwide. The concerns and the cultural framework of Nationwide are simply not the concerns of their world. They do not so much produce an oppositional reading as refuse to 'read' it at all. These groups are so totally alienated from the discourse of Nationwide that their response is in the first instance 'a critique of silence'. In a sense they fail, or refuse, to engage with the discourse of the programme enough to deconstruct or redefine it. They are clear that it's not a programme for them, it's for 'older people, middle-class people'; it doesn't deal with their specific interests – 'Why didn't they never interview Bob Marley?' – and it fails to live up to their standards of 'good TV' defined in terms of enjoyment and entertainment (in which terms Today and ITV in general are preferred to Nationwide and BBC).

To this group Nationwide is 'so boring' it's not interesting at all': they 'don't see how anyone could watch it'. There is a disjunction between the discourse of their own culture and that, not simply of Nationwide in particular, but of the whole field of 'serious TV' ('BBC is definitely boring') and of party politics ('God that's rubbish'). Moreover, these groups reject the descriptions of their life offered by the programme. They can find no point of identification within the programme's discourse about the problems of families in Britain today – a discourse into which, the programme presenters have claimed, 'most people in Britain' should fit. Their particular experience of family structures among the black, working-class, inner city community is simply not accounted for. The programme's picture of family life is as inappropriate to them as that offered in a 'Peter and Jane' reading scheme:

> It didn't show one-parent families...the average family in a council estate – all these people seemed to have cars, their own home...property...Don't they ever think of the average family?

Now this is precisely what Nationwide would claim to think of: the point here is that the representation of 'the family' within the discourse of Nationwide has no purchase on the representation of that field within the discourse and experience of these groups – and is consequnetly rejected.

However these are statements at the level of gross differences of orientation between the groups, and they should not blind us to the differences, divisions and overlaps which occur within and among these groups. For example, although the apprentice groups were generally in sympathy with the programme and identified with the perspectives on events offered by its presenters, they did at times find it hard to relate to the programme's style of presentation or 'mode of address' (Neale 1977). At this point they frequently invoked Nationwide's ITV competitor as being 'more of a laugh' or 'better entertainment' and were, to this extent, alienated from the discourse of the BBC programme.

Moreover, if we are to characterize the apprentice group as decoding in a dominant mode, we must recognize that this is only one version, or inflection, of 'dominant code': within the study there were groups from quite different social positions (bank managers, schoolboys, teacher training students) whose decodings shared some of the dominant characteristics of those made by the apprentice groups, but which diverged from theirs at other points. Thus the category of dominant code would need to be differentiated, in terms of the material in this study, to account for different versions (radical and traditional Conservative, deferential, Leavisite) of the dominant code.

Equally, we must distinguish between different forms and formulations of negotiated and oppositional readings, between the 'critique of silence' offered initially by the black students, the critical reading (from an educational point of view) articulately expressed by some of the higher-education groups (though this itself varied, with topic-critical readings being made by these groups on moral and social issues, but dominant code readings being made by the same groups on economic and trade union issues), and the various forms of 'politicized' negotiated and oppositional readings made by the trade union groups.

These are simply instances of a more general phenomenon of differentiation within and across the basic categories derived from Parkin's scheme which we would need to take account of in developing an adequate model of the media audience. We need to understand the process through which the multiplicity of discourses in play in any social formation intersect with the process of decoding media material. The effect of these discourses is precisely to lend variety to decodings. Thus, in each of the major categories of decoding (dominant, negotiated, oppositional) we can discern a number of varieties and inflections of what, for purposes of gross comparison only, is termed the same 'code'.

Conclusions

This quick sketch of a large quantity of material at least allows us to see clearly the fundamental point that social position in no way directly, or unproblematically, correlates with decoding. The apprentice groups, the trade union and shop stewards groups and the black college students can all be said to share a common class position, but their decodings of a television programme are inflected in different directions by the discourses and institutions in which they are situated. In one case the framework derives from a tradition of mainstream working-class populism, in another from trade unions and Labour party politics, in another, from black youth subcultures. In each case the discourses in play inflect and organize the groups' responses to and decodings of the media material shown.

Any superficial resemblance between this study of television audience and the 'uses and gratifications' perspective in media research is misleading. In the latter, the focus would be entirely on what individuals 'do with' messages.[3] But the different responses and interpretations reported here are not to be understood simply in terms of individual psychologies. They are founded on cultural differences embedded within the structure of society; cultural clusters which guide and limit the individual's interpretation of messages. To understand the potential meanings of a given message we need a cultural map of the audience to whom that message is addressed – a map showing the various cultural repertoires and symbolic resources available to differently placed subgroups within that audience. Such a map will help to show how the social meanings of a message are produced through the interaction of the codes embedded in the text with the codes inhabited by the different sections of the audience.

Notes

1 For some useful recent work in this area, which attempts to establish patterns of relation between formal linguistic features and ideological frameworks, see Kress & Trew 1978 and Fowler *et al.* (1979).

2 For a critical look at the use of the concept of 'codes' within cultural analysis, see Corner 1980.

3 Carey & Kreiling 1974 give an account of the relation between 'cultural studies' and the 'uses and gratifications' approach. The present work owes its main categories and concepts to the cultural studies tradition.

13

DECLINE OF A PARADIGM? Bias and Objectivity in News Media Studies

Robert A. Hackett

☐—*This essay outlines emerging empirical, methodological, and epistemological challenges to several key assumptions associated with conventional research on news bias. These assumptions are: (1) the news can and ought to be objective, balanced and a reflection of social reality; (2) the political attitudes of journalists or editorial decision-makers are a major determinant of news bias; (3) bias in news content can be detected with existing reading methods; (4) the most important form of bias is partisanship. It is concluded that the concepts of structured orientation and ideological effectivity are more fruitful than that of partisan bias, and that the concepts of bias and objectivity ought themselves to be objects of research rather than evaluative standards.*

BIAS, or its commonly accepted opposite, objectivity, are the concepts which most citizens link with the political or ideological role of the news media. The concepts are enshrined in administrative guidelines for broadcasters, and they are sometimes adopted by disgruntled politicians. Spiro Agnew's 1969 denunciation of the networks' "nattering nabobs of negativism" is perhaps the best-known attack by an American politician on the news media for alleged ideological bias—in this case, for being too sympathetic to radical protest. Interest groups which monitor the media frequently adopt similar terms of reference. For instance, a study by the International Association of Machinists (1981) concluded that U.S. network news was overwhelmingly procorporate rather than prolabor. And of course journalists themselves use the concepts of bias and objectivity to assess their own work. Objectivity has been described as "the emblem" and "keystone" of American

Mr. Hackett is Assistant Professor of Communication, Simon Fraser University. *The author wishes to thank Stuart Hall, Lawrence Grossberg, Leslie Pal, Rick Gruneau, Edwin Black, Graham Knight and Liora Salter for their comments on an earlier draft of this manuscript. This research was supported by a grant from the I.W. Killam Scholarship Fund, University of Alberta.*

From Robert A. Hackett, "Decline of a Paradigm? Bias and Objectivity in News Media Studies," *Critical Studies in Mass Communication*, Vol. 1, No. 3 (September 1984), pp. 229-259.

journalism (Schudson, 1978, p. 9; Doll & Bradley, 1974, p. 256).

Not surprisingly then, academics have also adopted bias and objectivity as organizing concepts in many studies of journalism. Students of news production, from Breed (1955) to Sigelman (1973), often took for granted the distinction between the biased editorial "policy" which may be enforced by newspaper publishers, and the ideal of journalistic objectivity—skeptical though they might have been of its realization in practice. Numerous content analyses have sought to evaluate the objectivity of news coverage of election campaigns, issues, policies, institutions, movements, or politicians. Much of this research was inspired by Agnew's charges of "liberal" bias in network news (Adams, 1978, p. 20).

However, the utility of bias and objectivity as conceptual tools in the analysis of the media's ideological functioning is increasingly being called into question. For instance, Hall, Connell and Curti (1976, p. 91) have argued that bias is a "wholly inadequate conception" which "does not exhaust in any way the relation of TV to the political."

The challenges to the bias/objectivity couplet are broad-ranging, and hinge on questions of evidence, methodology, *and* epistemology. It is the aim of this article to outline some of the main thrusts of these critiques.[1] The next section proposes some key assumptions of conventional bias research, which are then critically examined. Finally, in light of these critiques, some tentative suggestions are offered for future directions in the analysis of the news media as a political and ideological institution.

BIAS AND OBJECTIVITY

What is conventionally understood by the concepts of bias and objectivity in the media? A schematic presentation here cannot do justice to the historically evolving issues and nuances evoked by those terms. (For historical discussions of news objectivity, see Schudson, 1978; and Roshco, 1975.) Suffice it to note that most definitions in common language regard news bias as the intrusion of subjective "opinion" by the reporter or news organization, into what is purportedly a "factual" account. Thus MacLean (1981, p. 56) suggests that "When a story does not distinguish clearly between its author's interpretations and the facts being reported, it is a biased or slanted report."

It has sometimes been noted that the concept of news bias has two moments which are not entirely consistent. One is a lack of "balance" between competing viewpoints; the other is a tendentious, partisan "distortion" of "reality." The ambiguity is suggested by the Doll and Bradley (1974, p. 256) survey of journalism textbooks for synonyms and antonyms of reportorial bias. On the one hand, the moment of imbalance is suggested by the synonyms "preferential," "one-sided," and "partial," and by the antonyms "equal," "equally-forceful," "neutral," and "fair." On the other hand, the moment of distortion is suggested by the terms "warped," "distorted," "indirect," and "stereotyped," versus "straightforward," "factual," "factually accurate," and "truthful." In journalistic practice, the goals of balance and accuracy (non-distortion) may not always be compatible. To take a simple example, in the 1972 U.S. election campaign, George McGovern made many more public appearances than did the incumbent Richard Nixon. To have "balanced" the television exposure of the two candidates would have "distorted" the strategies and progress of the campaign.

Related to the distortion/imbalance distinction, there is a tension between impartially reporting contradictory truth-claims by high-status sources, on the one hand, and independently determining the validity of such truth-claims, on the other. The media's uncritical amplification of Senator Joe McCarthy's unfounded accusations made journalists acutely aware of this tension, and now the concept of objectivity is sometimes taken to include interpretive and analytical reporting (Roshco, 1975, pp. 48–57).

Such ambiguities in journalistic norms are reflected in the differing operational definitions and measures used in bias research. Both the "imbalance" and the "distortion" concepts have been adopted. Leaving aside questions of epistemology, the "distortion" approach is *technically* feasible if alternative accounts or appropriate benchmarks are available. Possible benchmarks include the full transcripts of a politician's speech; the perception of participants or interviewed sources in a reported news event (Lang & Lang, 1953; Lawrence & Grey, 1969); and government statistics on crime (Davis, 1952) or workforce distribution and work stoppages (Glasgow University Media Group, 1976). The "distortion" criterion may be considered especially appropriate when there do not exist contending viewpoints of equal legitimacy, thus rendering the criterion of balance inapplicable. Such would be the case, for example, in studies of news about international relations, an area where journalists are not expected to balance their presentation between pro- and anti-American (especially Communist) viewpoints. Only when foreign policy (e.g., the Vietnam war after 1968) generates sufficient division within legitimate political circles must the media take balance into account. More normally, foreign affairs coverage would be considered biased only if it *distorts* reality in a politically motivated direction. Thus Chomsky and Herman (1979), whose work can be regarded as a less traditional bias study, argue that U.S. news coverage of Third World repression, and America's role in such repression, is distorted by the media's subordination to the interests and outlook of U.S. political and economic elites. Methodologically, they compare, not coverage of two competing parties or viewpoints, but rather mainstream media accounts with alternative evidence (from government documents, international human rights and relief agencies, the foreign press, and—some might say paradoxically—evidence scattered within the American media themselves).

Balance or equality of coverage is the more usual standard adopted in bias studies, no doubt because appropriate benchmarks are not always available, and because it is legally enshrined. The U.S. Communications Act, and the Federal Communications Commission's fairness doctrine, oblige broadcasters to provide "reasonable opportunity for the discussion of conflicting views on issues of public importance" in news programming, to "permit answers to personal attacks occurring in the course of discussing controversial issues," and to provide equal time for all political candidates, if any one candidate is given time outside of news programming (Brundage, 1972, pp. 531–532, 537). However, even researchers who agree that bias equals dyadic imbalance differ in their methods. True, many of them measure the air-time or news-space accorded each side, and make judgements of direction (favorable, negative, neutral or mixed) of statements or news items about each party. But beyond such basic procedures, variations exist. For example, McQuail suggests several possible manifestations of bias: explicit argument and compilation of evidence favoring one view; a tendentious use of facts and comments, without any explicit statement of preference; the use of language which colors an otherwise factual report and conveys an implicit but clear value judgement; and the omission of points favoring one side, in an otherwise straight news report (McQuail, 1977, p. 107).

Hofstetter and Buss (1978, p. 518) reject three potential definitions of bias: outright lying, distortion by emphasizing certain facts but not others, and the aggrandizement of certain values or mores. The authors suggest that while common in popular polemics, these concepts may not be very useful in scientific investigation. Occupational norms and sanctions render deliberate lying and distortion infrequent, while values do not provide objective benchmarks for the identification of bias. Instead, they propose that bias be treated as "selectivity," which "may or may not lead to the unbalanced, inequitable or unfair treatment of individuals or issues." Hofstetter (1976, pp. 33–34) further distinguishes between political bias resulting from the partisan preferences or ideological convictions of news persons, and structural biases which are due to the character of the medium or the imperatives of commercial news programming. Patterns of reporting which are similar within each medium but different between media are held to constitute *prima facie* evidence of structural bias. Within-medium variation suggests the possibility of political bias. As the authors concede, the researcher using this approach cannot identify *which* reporter or news organization is presenting biased coverage "without many additional assumptions and evidence" (Hofstetter & Buss, 1978, p. 522). Nor can this approach deal with biases which pervade the entire media.

Some authors have developed more specific catalogues of techniques by which journalistic "opinion" may surreptitiously be merged with "fact" in the presentation of news stories. (See, e.g., Cirino, 1971, pp. 134–179; MacLean, 1981, pp. 30–46; Efron, 1971, pp. 102–121.)

By contrast, Doll and Bradley (1974, pp. 258, 262) abandon the attempt to define bias. Instead, they treat it negatively, as the absence of objectivity, which they operationalize as equal time and positional emphasis to the major candidates and parties, the use of neutral or objective language, the use of evidence to support reported conclusions and to provide a balanced account, and the avoidance of gratuitous statements.

Notwithstanding such variations in conceptualization and methodology, bias studies tend collectively to accept the following assumptions:

1. The media can and ought accurately to reflect the real world, in a fair and balanced way. The concept of bias implies the possibility of a zero-degree unbiased or objective account of events. (Sometimes this assumption is explicitly made, e.g., "The detection of bias is crucial to the maintenance of democratic institutions and the people's right to *unbiased* [italics added] political information." See Hofstetter and Buss, 1978, p. 528.) The ideal of objectivity suggests that facts can be separated from opinion or value judgements, and that journalists can stand apart from the real-world events whose truth or meaning they transfer to the news audience by means of neutral language and competent reporting techniques. Accord-

ingly, news media would offer a faithful compression of the day's most newsworthy events—those most relevant and interesting to the audience. Unbiased media would accord quantitatively and qualitatively balanced coverage to the contending, legitimate political perspectives.

2. The most important potential obstacles to the presentation of such a balanced and accurate account of the world are the political prejudices or social attitudes of communicators, who allow their values or selective perceptions to bias their reporting.
3. When such biases appear in news content, they can readily be detected through existing methods of reading or decoding.
4. The most important form of political or ideological bias in the media is witting or unwitting favoritism towards one major candidate, party, political position or interest group over another.

The following sections consider critical challengers to each of these respective assumptions.

CAN NEWS REFLECT REALITY?

In the preceding section, I noted a tension between "balance" and "nondistortion" as practical criteria of objectivity. They are also incompatible at an epistemological level. A relativist, Mannheimian epistemology underlies the notion that bias is avoided by balancing between competing, incompatible worldviews, each with its own (limited and partial) validity. By contrast, the goal of avoiding distortion implies a positivistic, nonrelativist affirmation of the ultimate knowability of "the straight facts," whose visibility is temporarily obscured by the biased journalist.

Beyond their incompatibility, both notions of bias have been subjected to a telling epistemological critique. Skirrow (1979, pp. 28–29) argues that to attack TV news on the grounds of imbalance, is unwittingly to reinforce the very idea on which the news implicitly depends—that a plurality of viewpoints approximates truth. Skirrow argues, for instance, that it is ludicrous to suggest, as did one BBC program, that "there could be a neutral stand on exploitation and racism." The program in question "balanced" the film *Last Grave at Dimbaza,* depicting some of the poverty and oppression of South African blacks, with a South African government production "which showed black people driving around in cars in the apparently affluent and happy township of Soweto."

It is not that journalists consciously work from a well-developed, abstract theory of knowledge. Epstein (1974, pp. 44–77) shows that networks' attempts to balance the news are partly a response to government fairness rules and to the concerns of affiliate stations. Tuchman (1971/72) argues that the journalist's presentation of conflicting truth-claims is one of several "strategic rituals" of objectivity, by which news workers protect themselves from such occupational hazards as missed deadlines, libel suits, and superiors' reprimands. Such concerns are eminently practical and political, not philosophical. Nevertheless, although journalists often report conflicting statements from sources without trying to assess their validity, it can be held that there is at least an implicit truth-claim in such a juxtaposition. Sometimes it is explicit. Epstein has described the dominant "'dialectical' model for reporting controversial issues" as follows:

> The correspondent, after reporting the news happening, juxtaposes a contrasting viewpoint and concludes his synthesis by suggesting that *the truth* [italics added] lies somewhere in between. (Epstein, 1974, p. 67)

Such an approach can be epistemologically justified only by a position of social agnosticism and relativism, which regards the validity of different ideas as limited by the partial perspective of the group which produces them. The familiar paradox of relativism raises itself: what, then, justifies the truth-claims of news organizations themselves? Moreover, far from being in some absolute sense neutral, news balance generally leads the media to reproduce the definitions of social reality which have achieved dominance in the electoral political arena.

The alternative conception, that journalistic objectivity results in an undistorted view of the facts, is subject to many of the same criticisms that have been directed against positivism in general. This position implies that the journalist and the news media are detached observers, separable from the social reality on which they report; that truth or knowledge depends upon the observer's/journalist's neutrality in relation to the object of study; that the news medium, when "properly used," is neutral and value-free, and thus can guarantee the truthfulness of "the message." That is, the news can potentially transmit an unbiased, transparent, neutral translation of some external reality. Through the news, objects and events in the real world can be known to us as they "really are" (Skirrow, 1979, pp. 25, 30).

Several arguments have been advanced against this position. First, the news media *unavoidably* structure their representation of social and political events in ways which are not pregiven in the events themselves. Thus, researchers of news production overwhelmingly reject the "mirror" metaphor which is sometimes put forth by media spokespersons. Altheide (1976) argues that due to the organizational features of news work, local TV news inevitably decontextualizes events and recontextualizes them artificially in accordance with "the news perspective." As internal factors which shape the news, Tuchman (1978) identifies the news gathering net (the location of correspondents, camera crews, etc.), bureaucratic interactions within news organizations, and the rhythms of news work, with their associated "typifications" of newsworthy events and processes. Drawing upon organization theory, Epstein argues that the most critical demands which structure the scope and form of American network news are the budgetary limitations imposed by the assumption that improving the news show will not proportionately increase ratings or advertising revenue; the need to maintain the network's base audience for the prime-time schedule which follows the supper-hour newscasts; the need of affiliate stations for news of national scope, which results in the "nationalizing" of local happenings; and the federal government's fairness regulations.

Other critics argue that, quite apart from *journalism's* mediation of the social world, *language* itself cannot function so as to transmit directly the supposedly inherent meaning or truth of events. In part, this is because labelling implies evaluation and context. In David Morley's words, neutral value-free language "in which the pure facts of the world could be recorded without prejudice" is impossible, because "evaluations are already implicit in the concepts, the language in terms of which one observes and records" (Morley, 1976, pp. 246–247). And as Hall and colleagues note regarding the media's use of such labels as "mugging":

> They not only place and identify those events; they assign events to a context. Thereafter the use of the label is likely to mobilise *this whole referential context,* [italics in original] with all its associated meanings and connotations. (Hall, Critcher, Jefferson, Clarke, & Roberts, 1978, p. 19)

Hall (1982) also argues that such connotations are not fixed and pregiven, as in a dictionary, but rather are a product of political struggle over signification.

Studies which demonstrate the unavoidable editorial and linguistic mediation of events, nevertheless, leave open the possibility that the media stand separate from the events which they observe and report. This latter assumption is challenged by the argument that the social and political world is not a pregiven, "hard" reality for the media to reflect; it has to be socially constructed. Moreover, far from constituting a detached observer, the media help actively to construct that world.

Altheide and Snow (1979, pp. 10, 12, 15, 146) go so far as to argue that modern American society is dominated by a "media logic," by which they mean "the process through which media present and transmit information," a process whose elements include the various media and their formats. In previous centuries, media reflected the form of the dominant institutions. But in the modern era, media themselves "are the dominant force to which other institutions conform," including "the entire political process" which is now "inextricably tied to the logic of media work and has been transformed by it into an extension of media production."

One need not accept such sweeping media determinism to acknowledge the interventions of journalism in society and politics. One example is the widespread production of what Boorstin (1980, p. 11) labelled "pseudo-events," which are preplanned or incited, and which have the primary purpose of being reported or reproduced. News conferences and most political speeches are examples of pseudo-events which are arranged for media propagation, and which would not occur in its absence.

Apart from the deliberate production of pseudo-events, news media may influence the very social or political trends which their reports supposedly reflect. Thus television has been credited with undermining party identification and altering the qualities of successful presidential candidates. A complex example derives from the work of Hall and his colleagues. They have investigated interaction between (a) reports of "mugging" in the British press; (b) increased sensitivity to this apparently new crime by police, judiciary, and public; (c) the upsurge of "mugging" incidents in police crime statistics; and (d) the emergence of a "moral panic" over the issue in British society. Simply to contrast types of crimes reported in the press, with government crime statistics (as did Davis' 1952 study of crime news in Colorado newspapers), would be to overlook this dialectic. Moreover, it would risk according bureaucratically-generated statistics an epistemological primacy which must be justified rather than assumed.

Molotch and Lester (1974, p. 105) radically problematize the very concept of "event," and thereby explicitly question the notion on which the concept of "bias" depends: that "the media stand as reporter-reflector-indicators of an objective reality 'out there,' consisting of knowably 'important' events of the world." Rather, what counts as an "event" is socially determined: events are what we are accustomed to pay attention to. An event, in their definition, is an occurrence (any cognized happening) which is used creatively for time-demarcating purposes. Occurrences become events according to their usefulness to an individual (or organization) trying to order experience. Different people or institutions may have different, even conflicting, "event needs," and hence will attempt to order or define reality in different ways. In such a case, an "issue" has arisen. However, with the exception of accidents or scandals (which are leaked by nonofficial informers), most press stories are "routine events" which are promoted by political and bureaucratic power-holders: the "event needs" of the news promoters (political or bureaucratic sources) and the news assemblers (journalists) are complementary. Similarly, Fishman (1980, chaps. 2, 3) argues that "bureaucratic phase structures," by which institutions transform complex happenings into procedurally defined "cases," provide the criteria of relevance and the mechanisms of time-demarcation which define "events" for the media. As an example, the journalist covers "crime" as a set of discrete bureaucratically-organized cases, each beginning with the arrest (or the reported perpetration of a crime) and ending with the sentencing. Conversely, the institutional organization of event detection results in the creation of "non-events" which cannot be seen under the institutional scheme of interpretation, but can be seen under a different one. Thus, the media help actively to *constitute* reality, even if it is only by amplifying and conferring legitimacy upon the structuring of social processes achieved by political/bureaucratic institutions. Therefore, one cannot make a radical distinction between the world of social processes and events, and the news media which are supposed to *reflect* them. As Hall has put it, reality cannot be viewed as simply a given set of facts, but rather as:

> the result of a particular way of constructing reality. The media defined, not merely reproduced, "reality." Definitions of reality were sustained and produced through all those linguistic practices (in the broad sense) by means of which selective definitions of "the real" were represented. It implies the active work of selecting and presenting, of structuring and shaping: not merely the transmitting of an already-existing meaning, but the more active labour of *making things mean*. (Hall, 1982, p. 64)

So language (and the media) must be regarded as a structuring agent, rather than a neutral transmission belt which can refer directly to a world of non-discursive objects. As Hall (1982, pp. 70–71) notes, two rather different epistemological positions can be derived from this argument:

> A Kantian or neo-Kantian position would say that, therefore, nothing exists except that which exists in and for language or discourse. Another reading is that, although the world does exist outside language, we can only make sense of it through its appropriation in discourse.

The first (Kantian) position represents the more radical rejection of the notion that media bias distorts an external reality. Thus Fiske and Hartley (1978, p. 161) argue that:

> Reality is never experienced by social man in the raw. Whether the reality in question is the brute force of nature, or men's relations with other men, it is always experienced through the mediating structures of language. And this mediation is not a distortion or even a reflection of the real, it is rather the active social process through which the real is *made*.

For Bennett (1982, p. 295), Hall's position that the media help to define social reality is not radical enough, since it "keeps alive the concept of media as mirror at the same time as it contests it." He wants to eliminate fundamentally the distinction between the realm of social reality, and the realm of representations, a point which applies not only to the media but also to language. Signification is "a process which actively constructs cognitive worlds rather than simply passively reflecting a pre-existing reality."

Bennett (pp. 307–308) further claims that it is impossible directly to counterpose "the truth" against "allegedly distorting systems of signification." No such system can permit the real to speak through it without modification. Instead, analysis should shift from "the investigation of the relationship between sign and 'reality' to that of the relationship between signs, the play of signification upon signification within a structured field of ideological relationships."

Such a position will be more familiar to many social scientists in the form of Althusser and Balibar's (1965/1970) concept of "theoretical problematic," and Kuhn's analysis of the role of "paradigms" in the development of science. Kuhn argues that science has never proceeded by a direct comparison of statements with empirical fact; rather, scientific work during periods of "normal science" proceeds within a dominant paradigm—an ensemble which includes symbolic generalizations, "metaphysical" aspects such as the belief in broad models, scientific values, and "exemplars" (i.e., concrete problem-solutions that students learn as part of their socialization into a scientific discipline). For Kuhn (1970, p. 77), the falsification of theories by direct comparison with nature is merely a "methodological stereotype." While Kuhn hedges on the question, he *can* be taken as saying that theories are incommensurable, and determine their own criteria of validity.

Similarly, Althusser has been interpreted as arguing that the adequacy of a problematic is indicated by its *internal* coherence, its systematicity. Thus, in Sumner's (1979, p. 181) view, science for Althusser is "that field of significance which most systematically connects itself, or . . . that body of concepts which explains itself the best." This kind of position raises the specter of idealism and theoreticism, and is vulnerable to the criticism that:

> Systematicity provides no guarantees . . . that the theory is an accurate and explanatory "cognitive appropriation of the real." Scientific theory may be systematic; however, its condition of existence is not systematicity but rather that it explains the nature, mediation and movement of practical appearances and thus acts as the theoretical expression of concrete social relations.

In my view, the first (Kantian) position to which Hall alluded above, tends towards a linguistic determinism which overestimates the self-determination of signification, and overprivileges the semiotic at the expense of other aspects of social practice. It does not seem necessary to accept this position in order to reject the claim that media reports must either passively reflect or actively distort reality. There may indeed be no world of self-evident pristine "hard facts," standing outside of socially-constructed meaning and language, for journalistic (or scientific) discourse to operate upon. And it must be granted that if journalism actively participates in the struggle over the signification of events, then we cannot simply accuse the news of "distorting" their "real" meaning. Nevertheless, as Sumner maintains, there *are* "concrete social relations." And for some purposes, journalism can be assessed on the basis of its adequacy as a "theoretical expression of concrete social relations."

FROM BIAS TO IDEOLOGY

A fourth assumption of the bias paradigm is the definition of bias as favoritism towards one major party, candidate or interest group over another. Many studies have asked whether the media are fair in covering competition between Democrats and Republicans, liberals and conservatives, supporters and opponents of Administration policy. (See, e.g., Doll & Bradley, 1974; Efron, 1971; Hofstetter, 1976; Lowry, 1971; Meadow, 1973; Pride & Richards, 1974; Pride & Wamsley, 1972; Robinson, 1983; Russo, 1971/72; Stevenson et al., 1973.)

Should we conclude from the apparently general absence of partisan bias, that the news media are ideologically inert? No. Such an electorally oriented notion of bias and fairness is a very limited one. For example, research based on it takes for granted a State-supervised structure of legitimated access to the realm of public political debate. Thus in the FCC's words, fairness rules are not intended "to make time available to Communists or to the Communist viewpoints" (cited in Epstein, 1974, p. 64). It may well be, as Robinson (1978, pp. 202, 206) suggests, that previous bias studies have focused too narrowly on election campaigns, precisely where broadcasters have learned to tread carefully; political bias may be more evident in coverage of interest groups. A few studies suggest this may be the case; Efron (1979) found bias against nuclear power, while the International Association of Machinists (1981) found a preponderance of corporate over labor viewpoints. But even Robinson's proposal runs the risk of confinement within an implicitly pluralist view of society, a view which makes it possible to ignore both the class structure of power within which such electoral and interest competition occurs, and the relationship between ideology and that structure of power.

While the question of media *balance* continues to inspire research and debate, critical media scholars are increasingly drawing on the broader conception(s) of *ideology*. As discussed below, the view that news operates as ideology, fundamentally broadens and even contradicts the view that news messages are biased in accordance with the motivations of communicators. Indeed, Hall (1982) has argued that the very emergence of a new "critical paradigm" in media studies hinged on the rediscovery of ideology. The space left vacant by the absent concept of ideology was partly (mis)filled by the notion of "propaganda," conceived as messages intended to deceive and/or persuade. (Some implications of this were discussed in the preceding section on the methodology of analyzing bias.)

The political polarization and radicalization of the 1960s helped to rekindle interest in ideology by problematizing the assumption of consensus which had dominated orthodox American social science. In the work of Talcott Parsons, for example, society was assumed spontaneously to cohere around a central value system. How wide and deep was this consensus, how it was maintained in a class-stratified society, and in whose interests it operated, were questions rarely raised. But cracks began to appear in the monolith. In the sociological study of deviance, for example, the "power to define the rules of the game," and hence the power to define deviance, came to be recognized as a problem, ultimately leading to the query: In whose interests are the rules defined? Similarly, in political science, "power" was being reconceptualized, from something observable in the making of decisions, to the ability to keep potentially threatening issues out of the political arena ("nondecisions"), to the capacity to influence the very wants and perceived self-interests of those who are relatively powerless (Hall, 1982, pp. 60–65). Such developments inexorably led to theorizing about ideology, and its role in the mass media as an institution which could purvey ideas, influence wants, and help to define social reality. Seen in this light, the long-acknowledged "reinforcement" effect of the mass media could be reinterpreted as part of a legitimizing or hegemonic process.

Considerable ink (and blood) has been spilled over the issue of what constitutes ideology, and how one identifies it. Even *within* the Marxist tradition, which above all others introduced the concept into modern social thought, "ideology" has been variously defined. In the remainder of this section, only a few of the more pertinent conceptions can be outlined, and some of their possible applications in media studies considered, in order to show how they transcend or subsume the concept of "bias."

Although useful work has been done on the specific occupational ideology of journalists, the following three conceptions concern ideology as a "global" societal phenomenon:

1. A system of ideas, values and propositions which is characteristic of a particular social class, and/or which expresses the political and economic interests of that class. Insofar as these ideas are conceived to be "distortions" of real social relations, or alternatively, as contradictory to "real" class interests, the term "false consciousness" can be applied to them.
2. The necessary, everyday appearances of capitalism. For example, it *appears* that wages are the full price of labor, and that the sale and purchase of commodities is an equal exchange between individuals. Insofar as these appearances correspond to a practical reality of capitalist relations of production, they cannot simply be dismissed as "false consciousness." Nevertheless, by "naturalizing" capitalist social relations, ideology serves, as Hall (1977, pp. 322–325, 337–338) puts it, to "mark, conceal or repress" the "antagonistic foundations of the system"—namely, "class domination, the class-exploitative nature of the system, the source of this fundamental expropriation in the sphere of production, the determinacy in this mode of production of the economic. . . ."
3. The creation or interpellation of human subjects, the provision of subjective identities, of the type necessary to capitalist production relations (Althusser, 1969/1971, pp. 127–186).

The above conceptions share an insistence that ideology is rooted in social conditions of existence, primarily class relations. However, the second and third conceptions move away from a concept of a superstructure hanging over an economic base, towards a view of ideology as a constitutive element in the relations of production, and in their reproduction.

Ideology as Framing

Research based on the first conception (ideology as "pictures of the world" serving class or State power) is the *least* removed from traditional bias inquiries. The manifestations of ideology are perceived in terms not entirely unfamiliar to bias researchers. Thus Chomsky and

Herman (1979, pp. 3–79) see the evidence of the free press' subordination to American imperialism in the following: the omission of embarassing topics; selective emphases of fact; the generally uncritical treatment and high degree of access accorded to pro-American sources of information; the lack of context given to alleged Communist excesses; the favorable depiction of American actions and client states; the loaded use of labels such as "terrorism" and "police action"; and even outright lies. These types of evidence (though not the theory!) can be found in some of the more conventional bias studies.

Nevertheless, the search for class-biased "pictures of the world" in media content, is a broader and more advanced enterprise than the search for favoritism towards one party, candidate, or group. Thus in its analysis of British television coverage of industrial relations, the Glasgow University Media Group (1976, p. 267) asserts that:

> Our analysis goes beyond saying merely that the television news "favour" certain individuals and institutions by giving them more time and status. Such criticisms are crude. The nature of our analysis is deeper than this: in the end it relates to the picture of society in general and industrial society in particular, that television news constructs. This at its most damaging includes . . . the laying of blame for society's industrial and economic problems at the door of the workforce.

A similar conception underlies the notion of news "frames" or "frameworks." Gitlin (1980, p. 7) defines media frames as "persistent patterns of cognition, interpretation, and presentation, of selection, emphasis, and exclusion, by which symbol-handlers routinely organize discourse, whether verbal or visual." Thus David Morley (1976, p. 246) who studied British media coverage of industrial conflict, argues that more important than journalistic balance is "the basic conceptual and ideological framework through which events are presented and as a result of which they come to be given one dominant/primary meaning rather than another." Morley documents coverage of the 1973 gas strike, in which:

> programmes were often balanced in the sense that they had a gas board spokesman claiming that the strike, through lowering gas pressures, was causing danger to the public, and a union representative claiming that safety precautions were being observed and that therefore the public were not endangered. But analysis must also deal with the problems of how and why the strike comes to be presented primarily in *these* terms—in this case in terms of the possible dangers it might cause to the public. (Morley, 1976, p. 246)

To take an American example: television coverage of the conflict in El Salvador might have featured Reagan administration spokespersons claiming that the rebels were receiving substantial Soviet or Cuban aid. These spokespersons might have been counterbalanced by other politicians questioning the veracity of the administration's claims. But the analyst must also question why the conflict is signified as a potential extension of Communist influence (and perhaps also, why U.S. "national security" is so defined that this represents a potential "threat"). Many other perspectives are possible—for example, that the Salvadoran people are so oppressed by the U.S.-backed regime that they are entitled to receive whatever aid they can, from any quarter. If the conflict were instead framed as one between rich and poor, such aid might be at best a secondary issue.

Such framing is not necessarily a conscious process on the part of journalists;

it may well be the result of the unconscious absorption of assumptions about the social world in which the news must be embedded in order to be intelligible to its intended audience. Thus the Glasgow University Media Group (1980, p. 402) argues that the news, and the dominant social ideologies, are integrally related. The latter are "the connecting link between the so-called 'facts' of the news and the background assumptions which enable us, the audience, to understand those 'facts'." Similarly, Hall (1982, p. 72) argues that particular accounts may be ideological, "not because of the manifest bias or distortions of their surface contents, but because they were generated out of, or were transformations based on, a limited ideological matrix"—a set of rules and concepts for making sense of the world which is systematically limited by its social and historical context. This set or matrix constitutes a "deep structure" which is activated by journalists quite apart from their conscious awareness, let alone their intentions deliberately to deceive or manipulate.

It may well be that the very forms by which television news conveys its impartiality and neutrality serve to disguise (or render invisible) such underlying ideological assumptions. Thus, the appearance of "balance" between competing politicians, the presentation of "both sides of the story," may serve to deflect the viewer's attention from the question of why the issue is being cast in *these* terms, or why it is an "issue" at all, and why *these* individuals (usually officials of bureaucratic institutions, or high-level elected politicians) are accorded the right to define the issue. Therefore, it may be counterproductive to insist merely that journalists adhere to the *forms* of impartiality, since this may simply help to make the news even more effective in disguising its *underlying* ideological framework.

Ideology as Naturalization

The argument can be taken a step further: not only do the rules of impartiality *disguise* the ideological messages in TV news; they are an essential *part of* television's ideological functioning. This can be seen if we move to the second conception of ideology offered above, the "naturalization" of social relations. In this case, the relations of political power exercised through the parliamentary State. Hall, Connell, and Curti (1976) focus on the relationship between broadcasting and the State as it is manifested in the format of British current affairs television programming. They argue, essentially, that broadcasting supports the political system as a whole, but this support does *not* take the form of violating the norms of balance and impartiality so as to give an advantage to one electoral party over another. Rather, the ideological function is twofold. In its treatment of "current affairs," TV largely accepts and reinforces the definitions of issues which have prevailed in the political domain. The leading spokespersons of the established parties are accorded privileged access to the media, where they have the opportunity to amplify those definitions. This process makes viewpoints which lie outside the consensus (as articulated by the established parties) seem irrational or illegitimate—if those viewpoints receive any attention at all. The media both establish a "Parliamentary and Electoral framework of relevance" in their handling of political issues (at the expense of alternative issue agendas and political prescriptions), and legitimize Parliamentary government itself. The work of current affairs television is critical "in raising the

Parliamentary form of the State to the universal level—in generalising it for the whole social formation, signifying it as natural, as taken-for-granted, beyond the power of history and time to modify or dismantle" (Hall et al., 1976, p. 91).

But this ideological work by television is accomplished *through* the rules of impartiality and balance, and not by the occasional lapse or departure from them—"bias" in the conventional sense. Rather,

> the "skewing" of the access system towards the authoritative spokesmen of Parliamentary and Party politics is no well-kept secret. It is, in the minds of the broadcasters, precisely what a balanced coverage of politics *is about*. . . . In this sense, the media, in Current Affair television, do not represent in a biased way (ideologically) the structure of political power and its dominant mode of operation: the media *accurately* reflect and represent the prevailing structure and a mode of power. It is in politics and the State, not in the media, that power is *skewed*. (Hall et al., 1976, p. 92)

Bennett (1982, p. 306) describes the media's ideological function in this respect as "a 'double-dupe' system, an ideological form which effects a contraction of the sphere of public debate whilst simultaneously engendering the illusion that that sphere is entirely free and open."

There are several links missing from the above argument. First, the "skewing of access" in favor of spokespersons for the dominant parties is of little interest unless one accepts the premise that the capitalist State (and its structuring of political representation and debate) is not truly democratic or popular. Second, the argument largely evacuates the exercise of class power from the media to the State. Thus it cannot account for situations (e.g., Chile under Allende) where a bourgeois press agitates against a leftist government. Third, the authors do not discuss the specific mechanisms by which the routine editorial criteria of objectivity are enforced, and hence a structured orientation towards the State and the dominant parties maintained. Moreover, the question must be raised: What factors (apart from State power) ensure that those routine criteria retain their effectivity and their credibility amongst broadcasters and their audiences?

Notwithstanding such caveats, the argument summarized above usefully points to the ideological role of broadcasters' "impartiality." In his analysis of TV coverage of the "Social Contract" (the British Labour government's policy of "voluntary" wage restraint during the 1970s), Ian Connell (1980a, p. 140) applies and extends the argument. A precondition of television's effectiveness in establishing the dominant political perspectives as "common sense," "moderate public opinion" or "the consensus," is the separation and fragmentation of TV coverage from the actual events covered. In other words, part of television's ideological work consists precisely in presenting itself as *non*ideological, and in aligning itself with a similarly, apparently nonideological class-transcendent public and national interest. It is as if television states that "we" (the nation, the public, consumers, TV journalists) are nonideological; "we" represent good, sound common sense. The problem is with "them" out there (that irresponsible group of workers on strike, that particularly unfair or inefficient employer) who are ideologically motivated, or who have allowed their narrow interests to override the public welfare. It is *not* that television achieves its ideological effect by monolithically favoring, for example, management over union viewpoints.

The ideological separation which television makes between its own accounts of events, and those events themselves, is paralleled by the way TV news seeks to position or situate the viewing audience: viewers are addressed as passive onlookers for whom the media personnel speak, by contrast with (and separated from) the protagonists who make speeches or initiate news events. This ideological operation, this positioning, is effective for two reasons. First, it is subtly embedded in the codes of visual presentation on TV news. For example, with rare exceptions, only journalists are accorded the privilege of addressing the camera directly; interviewees and speech-makers are filmed at an angle. Second, television's separation reproduces an already established political ideology—the notion that the "nation as a whole" can be divided into those who are "done by" (consumers, commuters, taxpayers, the public, the silent majority, and so forth) and those who "do" (politicians, the unions, militants, etc.). The verbal depiction of actors on TV news further divides this latter group into a hierarchy of activists, differentiated according to legitimacy and/or representativeness. Gibson (1980, pp. 100–101) makes a similar point: television divides interviewees into discursive "adults" who are permitted to present their case at length, and those who are reduced to the status of sloganizing "children."

Ideology as Interpellation

The role of TV's apparent impartiality and neutrality is even more central in some theories of television which draw upon the third conception of ideology mentioned above—its interpellation of subjects. For illustration, I shall focus here on analyses of realism and its relationship to the positioning of the television audience.

As part of the same process of making knowledge possible, discourse serves to position human beings, subjects, in certain ways. The discourse of television news (or discourses, for as Barthes (1964/1967) suggests, television may be a complex system combining aural, visual and other levels) is targeted towards particular subject position(s). The viewer is invited, as it were, to accept a certain position in order to read or decode the message. As Coward and Ellis (1977, p. 50) argue with regard to the novel, "The whole process is directed towards the place of a reader: in order that it should be intelligible, the reader has to adopt a certain position with regard to the text."

Now, TV news is preeminently a *realist* discourse. Realist narrative is the dominant way of using language in bourgeois society. It is a mode in which

> Language is treated as though it stands in for, is identical with, the real world. The business of realist writing is, according to its philosophy, to be the equivalent of a reality, to imitate it. . . . (Coward & Ellis, 1977, p. 47)

Realism thus seeks to establish an identity (or at least an equivalence) between signifiers (loosely speaking, words or other symbols), signifieds (concepts), and their extralinguistic "real world" referents. But such an identity is an illusion, if only because even within a single language, a signifier does not univocally point towards a single signified which in turn clearly delineates a single referent. As Hartley (1982, p. 22) puts it, "signs do not have a fixed internal 'meaning,' but only meaning-potentials, which are actualized in use." Moreover, different languages may generate different sets of signifieds, which "slice up" reality in different ways. The best-known example is the multiple concepts which the Inuit have in place of our speech community's single concept of snow. Concepts, or signifieds, are a product of language, not "natural, given entities corresponding to distinct parts of the world out there" (Hartley, p. 16).

Yet realism functions to conceal the productivity of language. Like the capitalist market, realism stresses the product and represses its production. It matters not that "realism is produced by a certain use of language, by a complex production; all that matters is the illusion, the story, the content" (Coward & Ellis, 1977, pp. 46–47). Realist narrative does not appear to be the voice of an author; rather, "its source appears to be a true reality which speaks" (p. 49).

In an article in *Screen,* Colin MacCabe (cited in Woollacott, 1982, p. 106) identified the "classic realist text" as one in which there is a "hierarchy among the discourses which compose the text and this hierarchy is defined in terms of an empirical notion of truth." Within the realist novel, one discourse, the narrator's, is presented as the voice of truth; other discourses (e.g., particular characters) are subordinated to it, marginalized, rendered as partial perspectives. In MacCabe's view, the essential features of the "classic realist text" included:

> firstly, its inability to deal with the real as contradictory and secondly its positioning of the subject in a relationship of "dominant specularity." The dominant discourse in a classic realist text effects a closure of the subordinated discourses and the reader is placed in a position "from which everything becomes obvious." This is achieved through the effacement of the text's signifying practice, through the concealment of its construction. (Woollacott, 1982, p. 106)

So too with TV news. The newscaster's or reporter's voice is that of truth. Only he or she is accorded the privilege of introducing or concluding news items, of direct address to camera, of sustained voice-over narrative. All nonjournalistic interviewees and actors occupy lower rungs on the ladder of access.

As suggested by survey data consistently showing television to be the public's most trusted news medium, TV news is a particularly potent form of realism, because it can combine its narrative with a visual level of discourse. The verbal narrative seeks constantly to effect "closures" of meaning, to tie up the loose ends of interpretation, to present a picture of our society as one with institutionalized forms of conflict but without fundamental contradictions. The visual discourse seeks to convey a sense of immediacy, a sense that "you-are-there" watching the narrated events unfold before your very eyes. The film stands as the guarantor of the narrative's validity. Consequently, the evidence of editorial mediation must be rendered as unobtrusive as possible in TV news presentation. A widely used text on the production of TV news, for example, warns apprentice journalists to avoid editorial techniques in which "the viewer becomes aware of the editing process," which "distracts his attention from the content" (Green, 1969, p. 131)—as if the codes of editorial construction were not also part of the "content." Walter Cronkite's famous sign-off phrase, "And that's the way it is," exemplifies TV news' claim to reproduce the real.

While there has been some debate over whether realism in general is necessarily bourgeois (Woollacott, 1982, p. 107), TV realism can be seen as supportive of capitalist social relations in several general ways. In part, it helps to disguise the ideological framing of events. Moreover, the (illusory) reflection of the real world in TV's verbal and visual sign-systems may be a precondition for TV's ability to naturalize dominant social relations. But beyond that, TV realism is important for the ways it seeks to position or situate members of the audience. We have seen that according to Connell, the listener/viewer is situated as a passive observer, a mere consumer of the news, a member of the public who is "done to" by active and manipulative politicians, union leaders, militants, etc. The "consumer angle" of news reporting is evident, for example, in the overwhelming focus of strike coverage on the disruptive impact on services; at the thematic level in TV news, our concerns as workers (rather than consumers) are rarely addressed. Realism aids this positioning of the viewer as passive consumer, by denying his or her productivity even at the level of producing meaning. Such a positioning can be seen as complementary to advertising, in the mass marketing of commodities. From an analysis of the expository form of *CBS Evening News,* Bill Nichols (1981, p. 175) argues that "the structure of the program works to quiet, not arouse, the emotions, to win assent for the proposition that what happens 'out there' need not perturb." A comparison of the commercials with the news portion of the CBS newscast suggests that:

> If we were asked to look but remain passive before [during the news items], here [during the advertisement] we are asked to look and become active. We're asked to do something, to change, indeed to improve something. But what we're asked to improve is not the world but our own private situations or selves. And this improvement does not demand spiritual striving or political struggle, it simply requires the purchase of commodities.
>
> A displacement of values occurs. The news which refers to what should be our real conditions of existence becomes something almost imaginary, something highly mediated and punctuated by closure. The commercial message, which is indeed an imaginary message, becomes posited as the real, as an integral part of our lives, the part we can control and change. (Maaret Koskinen, quoted in Nichols, 1981, pp. 175–176)

If the commercials evoke dissatisfaction in order to incite us to individualized consumption, with the news events, "That's the way it is." In canalizing our attention away from the possibilities of political action, and towards privatized consumption, news and the commercials are complementary opposites: they both position viewers as depoliticized consumers.

Skirrow (1979, p. 35) takes the analysis of positioning in a somewhat different but complementary direction. She argues that by claiming and seeming to present facts impartially for the viewer to judge, TV news gives the viewer "a sense of being above and outside the actions displayed, and of having a god-like relation to them." Such a position is compatible with capitalism's need for subjects who feel themselves to be autonomous, free, self-determining, and who hence will voluntarily submit themselves to relations of exploitation, which appear as relations of exchange between equal and free individuals.

Analyses of this type must presently be considered tentative, speculative and exploratory. But they clearly do suggest the possibility that TV news' forms of impartiality and objectivity constitute an essential *part of* television's ideological work, rather than the primary criteria *against which* we should identify "biased" journalism.

FINAL REFLECTIONS

So long as the State enforces existing definitions of balance and fairness in broadcasting, so long as objectivity remains part of journalists' occupational self-definition, and so long as media organizations themselves find it in their own political and economic interests to pursue "due impartiality" (to the point of conducting their own in-house content analyses to monitor news balance) (Lower, 1970), bias research will continue to be conducted. Yet its theoretical underpinnings seem to be trembling. No longer can we simply assume the possibility of unbiased communication, of objective and detached reporting on an allegedly external social and political world. No longer can objectivity be taken as the opposite of ideology in the media, if indeed the forms and rhetoric of objectivity help to reproduce dominant political frameworks, or position the media audience as passive observers and consumers. No longer can we rely on inadequate and speculative methods for reading ideology "in" news content.

Must we then reinvent the wheel in order to analyze the news media as a political and ideological institution? Ought we to discard the very concepts of bias and objectivity? To accept these concepts unreflectingly as the criteria for evaluating news coverage, would be in effect to patrol the media on behalf of the State and the dominant political parties. Surely this is not a satisfying role for critical students of mass communications!

On the other hand, bias and objectivity are so embedded in popular and political debate that to ignore them would court isolation. Nor are these concepts entirely without normative and empirical merit. We would presumably prefer orthodox objectivity to the deliberate propagandizing of nineteenth-century journalism. And where the partisan prejudices or self-interests of news producers *do* influence content, we would want to know about it. Most important, the concept of bias, however inadequately, does raise for popular debate the question of journalism's ideological effectivity within a class-stratified society.

Rather than dismiss the concept out of hand, I propose that research could fruitfully proceed in two directions. First, make bias and objectivity, as rhetorical devices and practical norms, themselves the object of investigation, rather than the standards by which we evaluate *other* objects (e.g., news content). The following lines of inquiry seem promising:

1. As Bruck (1981, p. 17) proposes, we could "investigate the politics of the bias rhetoric, look at who raises the bias issue, when and why, and check the discourses and interests carrying it"—and, one might add, the impact on news production. There have been some interesting starts. Gitlin (1980, pp. 269–282) discusses the role of intervention by media executives and politicians under conditions of political crisis, when the normal routines of journalism provide an opening for opposition to the hegemonic ideology. Dreier (1982) undertakes a similar study of the "ideological mobilization among business leaders" to limit perceived antibusiness bias in the US media during the 1970s.
2. In order to demystify and denaturalize it, we could follow Schudson's (1978) lead, and analyze the historical, philosophical and political/economic roots of journalistic objectivity. We could also examine the practical and social consequences of objectivity. What do journalists mean by objectivity? How do they implement it in practice? Is it a norm sufficiently strong to override pressure from media owners and executives who want to set "policy"? Does increasing recruitment from schools of journalism encourage the entrenchment of

objectivity as a pan-occupational norm? Tuchman's (1971/72) discussion of "strategic rituals" attempts with some success to specify what objectivity means in journalistic practice. But as Bruck notes (p. 18), her adherence to ethnomethodology renders her indifferent to the question of the broader social significance of her findings. In particular, what are the consequences of objectivity for journalism's structuring and dissemination of information, issues and images?

The second broad direction for media research involves displacing the concept of "bias" with that of "structured orientation." By abandoning the notion of unbiased communication, we can avoid being sidetracked by the search for standards of balance and nondistortion. Instead, we would analyze the various types of systematic orientations and relationships which unavoidably structure news accounts. These factors may indeed include partisan favoritism or political prejudices. But they also include criteria of newsworthiness, the technological characteristics of each news medium, the logistics of news production, budgetary constraints, legal inhibitions, the availability of information from sources, the need to tell stories intelligibly and entertainingly to an intended audience, the need to package news in a way which is compatible with the commercial imperative of selling audiences to advertisers, and the forms of appearance of social and political events. All these factors and others shape the media's functioning as an ideological institution.

I have suggested that at least three conceptions of ideology may be fruitful in media studies: the "frames" or set of social assumptions promoted in the news; the "naturalization" of social relations; and the interpellation of the audience. The strategy I am proposing would relate the various structured orientations or imperatives of news production to their consequences for one or more levels of ideology.

To be sure, there are problems with some of the existing research on media and ideology. First, insofar as researchers turn their findings on news frames into an accusation of departure from objectivity, they have failed sufficiently to transcend the bias paradigm. They ignore the limited, electorally-defined nature of the media's own claims to impartiality. Since journalists never *claimed* to be neutral between police and criminals, elected governments and militant unions, or parliamentary parties and radical protesters, why go to considerable length to demonstrate this type of "bias"? The Glasgow University Media Group (1980), for example, accumulated massive evidence to show that British television journalism adopted and amplified the contentious wage-push theory of inflation, which underpinned the Labour government's policy of wage restraint. From this, the authors argued that far from being objective and impartial, the news reproduced the social assumptions of the powerful. Connell (1980b) criticizes this inference, countering that it is precisely *through* the broadcasters' adherence to *due* impartiality (which takes into account the "weight" of opinion) that the wage-push theory dominated coverage.

A second problem with some "ideological bias" research is its failure to substantiate its claim that media representations *distort* social reality. Sometimes the media analyst simply counterposes news coverage of a social phenomenon such as deviance, with his or her own favorite sociological theory, which may not enjoy universal acceptance even within the discipline (Anderson & Sharrock, 1979, pp. 371–372). In comparing the news with other records or explanations, media students ought more carefully to recall the socially constructed nature of all ways of making sense of a situation, before judging the news to "distort."

A related temptation is to criticize the news as if it were inadequate sociology, or mere propaganda. A precondition of this type of critique is to ignore the specificity of news as, for example, a form of narrative oriented to providing "acquaintance-with" daily events rather than "knowledge-about" social processes.

Finally, theorists of ideological bias frequently fail to specify the mechanisms which link media frames with their social conditions of production. The analyst may simply posit "structural correspondences between features of the social setting and features of media output" (Anderson & Sharrock, 1979, p. 373). This syndrome may include a tendency too readily to assign responsibility for propagating a particular news frame to "the dominant class," which is assumed to control the means of cultural production. Such class reductionism surely provides explanations no more adequate than the political/attitudinal model to which it is similar. The strategy of linking structured orientations with ideological consequences is intended to avoid such reductionism.

Clearly the move from "bias" to "ideology" in media studies is no guarantee against naivety or triviality. Yet it seems essential if we are to grasp adequately the political roles of journalism.

To the extent that ideological orientations can be inferred from the study of news content alone, we clearly must move beyond the dyadic methodology of bias research, which compares the amount of news space or the evaluative direction of statements about "each side." Various aspects of observable content have ideological relevance, including the types of topics which are selected or excluded; the kinds of people or institutions accorded varying degrees of access; the vocabulary in use (e.g., the labelling of social phenomena); the explanatory and evaluative themes employed, and the links between them; and nonverbal stylistic elements.

However, neither this type of diversified content analysis, nor the structuralist search for underlying codes, really mend the Achilles' heel of existing reading methods. That is, their speculative nature, their lack of integration with a theory specifying the forms of appearance that a particular ideological formation will assume in media texts. Sumner (1979, pp. 238–245) has proposed an "historical materialist" method for reading ideology in the news (or other cultural forms). In his method, one must analyze not only media texts, but also the inner logic of the ideology and its linkages with social relations, its historical conditions and forms of appearance, and the internal determinants and social context of the news media. This is clearly an enormous task. Yet it is arguable that by comparison with exclusively content-based research, case studies of news frames (or "preferred readings") *interacting with* their social context have already contributed more to our understanding of the media as an ideological force. Previously mentioned in this essay are studies of audience decoding of a current affairs program, the interaction between mass media and the New Left of the 1960s, and the emergence of a "moral panic" over "mugging" in Britain (Morley, 1980; Gitlin, 1980; Hall et al. 1978).

Finally, the challenge to the bias paradigm has implications for radical media politics. Connell (1980b) argues that the conventional notions of objectivity and balance cannot be the basis for the demands which the left makes on the mainstream media. (Nor, by extension, can they underpin "alternative media" practice.) Needed, he says, are entirely new editorial criteria. Questions must be raised. Is this possible without being seen to produce mere "propaganda?" How important are audience expectations of objectivity as a constraint on potential alternative media practice? What would be the political consequences if mainstream journalists themselves came to regard objectivity as ideological or illusory? Is it not sometimes politically useful to mobilize on the basis of demands for "balance" and "objectivity," just as the liberal rhetoric of human rights or equal opportunity may sometimes be turned in radical directions? Such questions can only be addressed through collective debate and practice. □

NOTE

[1]This paper, focusing as it does on the substantive grounds on which the "bias" paradigm is being challenged, cannot deal at length with the social, political and intellectual factors and movements which underlie such challenges. Briefly, we may say that such forces include the anti-individualist, anti-psychologistic, and anti-behavioralist epistemological assault mounted by French structuralism, and imported into English-language media studies via British Marxism and feminism. Structuralism is briefly discussed in this article, as is the revival of theorizing about ideology, yet another such intellectual force.

REFERENCES

Adams, W. C. (1978). Network news research in perspective: A bibliographic essay. In W. Adams & F. Schreibman (Eds.), *Television network news: Issues in content research* (pp. 11–46). Washington: George Washington University.

Altheide, D. L. (1976). *Creating reality*. Beverly Hills: Sage.

Altheide, D. L., & Snow, R. P. (1979). *Media logic*. Beverly Hills: Sage.

Althusser, L. (1971). *Lenin and philosophy and other essays*. (B. Brewster, Trans.). New York: Monthly Review Press. (Original work published 1969)

Althusser, L., & Balibar, E. (1970). *Reading capital*. (B. Brewster, Trans.). London: New Left Books. (Original work published 1965)

Anderson, D. C., & Sharrock, W. W. (1979). Biasing the news: Technical issues in 'media studies.' *Sociology, 13,* 367–385.

Barthes, R. (1967). *Elements of semiology*. (A. Lavers & C. Smith, Trans.). New York: Hill and Wang. (Original work published 1964)

Belkaoui, J. (1979). A critical assessment of media studies. *Alternate Routes, 3,* 94–127.

Bennett, T. (1982). Media, 'reality,' signification. In T. Bennett, J. Curran, M. Gurevitch, & J. Woollacott (Eds.), *Culture, society and the media* (pp. 287–308). London: Methuen.

Black, E. R. (1982). *Politics and the news: The political functions of the mass media*. Toronto: Butterworths.

Boorstin, D. J. (1980). *The image: A guide to pseudo-events in America*. New York: Atheneum.

Breed, W. (1955). Social control in the newsroom. *Social Forces, 33,* 326–335.

Bruck, P. A. (1981). The social production of texts: On the relation production/product in the news media. In *Working papers in communications*. Montreal: Graduate Program in Communications, McGill University.

Brundage, G. S. (1972). Rationale for the application of the Fairness Doctrine in broadcast news. *Journalism Quarterly, 49,* 531–537.

Burgelin, O. (1972). Structural analysis and mass communication. In D. McQuail (Ed.), *Sociology of mass communications* (pp. 313-328). Harmondsworth, England: Penquin.

Chomsky, N., & Herman, E. S. (1979). *The political economy of human rights: Vol 1. The Washington connection and Third World fascism.* Montreal: Black Rose Books.

Cirino, R. (1971). *Don't blame the people.* Los Angeles: Diversity Press.

Clark, D. (1980). The state of cultural theory: A review of past and present fashions. *Alternate Routes, 4,* 105–156.

Connell, I. (1980a). Television news and the Social Contract. In S. Hall, D. Hobson, A. Lowe, & P. Willis (Eds.), *Culture, media, language* (pp. 139–156). London: Hutchinson.

Connell, I. (1980b, August). [Review of *More bad news*]. *Marxism Today,* 30–32.

Coward, R., & Ellis, J. (1977). *Language and materialism.* London: Routledge and Kegan Paul.

Davis, F. J. (1952). Crime news in Colorado newspapers. *American Journal of Sociology, 46,* 325–330.

de Camargo, M. (1972). Ideological analysis of the message: A bibliography. *Working Papers in Cultural Studies, 3,* 123–141.

Doll, H. D., & Bradley, B. E. (1974). A study of the objectivity of television news reporting of the 1972 presidential campaign. *Central States Speech Journal, 25,* 254–263.

Dreier, P. (1982). Capitalists vs. the media: An analysis of an ideological mobilization among business leaders. *Media, Culture and Society, 4,* 111–132.

Drew, D. G. (1975). Reporters' attitudes, expected meetings with source and journalistic objectivity. *Journalism Quarterly, 52,* 219–224, 271.

Efron, E. (1971). *The news twisters.* Los Angeles: Nash Publishing.

Efron, E. (1979). The media and the omniscient class. In C. E. Aronoff (Ed.), *Business and the media* (pp. 3–32). Santa Monica, CA: Goodyear.

Epstein, E. J. (1974). *News from nowhere.* New York: Vintage Books/Random House.

Evarts, D., & Stempel, G. H. (1974). Coverage of the 1972 campaign by TV, news magazines and major newspapers. *Journalism Quarterly, 51,* 645–648, 676.

Fishman, M. (1980). *Manufacturing the news.* Austin: University of Texas Press.

Fiske, J., & Hartley, J. (1978). *Reading television.* London: Methuen.

Gibson, W. (1980). Towards a theory of network television news. *Social Text, 3,* 88–111.

Gitlin, T. (1980). *The whole world is watching.* Berkeley: University of California Press.

Glasgow University Media Group. (1976). *Bad news.* London: Routledge and Kegan Paul.

Glasgow University Media Group. (1980). *More bad news.* London: Routledge and Kegan Paul.

Green, M. (1969). *Television news: Anatomy and process.* Belmont, CA: Wadsworth.

Griffith, T. (1974). A few frank words about bias. *Atlantic Monthly, 233,* 47–49.

Hall, S. (1975). Introduction to *Paper voices: The popular press and social change,* by A.C.H. Smith, E. Immirzi, & T. Blackwell. London: Chatto and Windus.

Hall, S. (1977). Culture, the media and the "ideological" effect. In J. Curran, M. Gurevitch, & J. Woollacott (Eds.), *Mass communication and society* (pp. 315–348). London: Edward Arnold.

Hall, S. (1982). The rediscovery of 'ideology': Return of the repressed in media studies. In M. Gurevitch, T. Bennett, J. Curran, & J. Wollacott (Eds.), *Culture, society and the media* (pp. 56–90). London: Methuen.

Hall, S., Connell, I., & Curti, L. (1976). The 'unity' of current affairs television. *Working Papers in Cultural Studies, 9,* 51–93.

Hall, S., Critcher, C., Jefferson, T., Clarke, J., & Roberts, B. (1978). *Policing the crisis: Mugging, the state, and law and order.* London: Macmillan.

Hartley, J. (1982). *Understanding news.* London: Methuen.

Hofstetter, C. R. (1976). *Bias in the news: Network television coverage of the 1972 election campaign.* Columbus: Ohio State University Press.

Hofstetter, C. R., & Buss, T. F. (1978). Bias in television news coverage of political events: A methodological analysis. *Journal of Broadcasting, 22,* 517–530.

Holsti, O. R. (1968). Content analysis. In G. Lindzey & E. Aronson (Eds.), *The handbook of social psychology* (Vol. 2, 2nd ed., pp. 596–692). Reading, MA: Addison-Wesley.

International Association of Machinists. (1981). IAM project report. *Television: Voice of corporate America.* Reprinted from *The Machinist.*

Kerrick, J. S., Anderson, T. E., & Swales, L. B. (1964). Balance and the writer's attitude in news stories and editorials. *Journalism Quarterly, 41,* 207–215.

Kristol, I. (1975, May 19). Business and the 'new class'. *The Wall Street Journal,* p. 8.

Kuhn, T., (1970). *The structure of scientific revolutions* (2nd ed.). Chicago: University of Chicago Press.

Lang, K., & Lang, G. E. (1953). The unique perspective of television and its effect: A pilot study. *American Sociological Review, 18,* 3–12.

Larrain, J. (1979). *The concept of ideology.* London: Hutchinson.

Lawrence, G. C., & Grey, D. L. (1969). Subjective inaccuracies in local news reporting. *Journalism Quarterly, 46,* 753–757.

Lichter, S. R., & Rothman, S. (1981). Media and business elites. *Public Opinion, 4*(5), 42–46, 59–60.

Lower, E. (1970). Fairness, balance, and equal time. *Television Quarterly, 9,* 46–53.

Lowry, D. T. (1971). Agnew and the network TV news: A before/after content analysis. *Journalism Quarterly, 48,* 205–210.

MacLean, E. (1981). *Between the lines.* Montreal: Black Rose Books.

McQuail, D. (1977). *The analysis of newspaper content.* Study for the Royal Commission on the press. London: Her Majesty's Stationery Office.

Meadow, R. G. (1973). Cross-media comparison of coverage of the 1972 presidential campaign. *Journalism Quarterly, 50,* 482–488.

Molotch, H., & Lester, M. (1974). News as purposive behaviour: On the strategic use of routine events accidents, and scandals. *American Sociological Review, 39,* 101–112.

Morley, D. (1976). Industrial conflict and the mass media. *Sociological Review, 24,* 245–268.

Morley D. (1980). *The 'Nationwide' audience: Structure and decoding.* London: British Film Institute.

Nichols, B. (1981). *Ideology and the image.* Bloomington: Indiana University Press.

Pride, R. A., & Richards, B. (1974). Denigration of authority? Television news coverage of the student movement. *Journal of Politics, 36,* 637–660.

Pride, R. A., & Wamsley, G. L. (1972). Symbol analysis of network coverage of Laos incursion. *Journalism Quarterly, 49,* 635–640, 647.

Robinson, M. J. (1978). Future television news research: Beyond Edward Jay Epstein. In W. Adams & F. Schreibman (Eds.), *Television network news: Issues in content research* (pp. 197–212). Washington: George Washington University.

Robinson, M. J. (1983). Just how liberal is the news? 1980 revisited. *Public Opinion, 6*(1), 55–60.

Roshco, B. (1975). *Newsmaking.* Chicago: University of Chicago Press.

Russo, F. D. (1971/72). A study of bias in TV coverage of the Vietnam war: 1969 and 1970. *Public Opinion Quarterly, 35,* 539–543.

Schudson, M. (1978). *Discovering the news.* New York: Basic Books.

Sigelman, L. (1973). Reporting the news: An organizational analysis. *American Journal of Sociology, 48,* 132–151.

Skirrow, G. (1979). Education and television: Theory and practice. In C. Gardner (Ed.), *Media, politics and culture: A socialist view* (pp. 25–39). London: Macmillan.

Stempel, G. H. (1969). The prestige press meets the third-party challenge. *Journalism Quarterly, 46,* 699–706.

Stevenson, R. L., Eisinger, R. A., Feinberg, B. M., & Kotok, A. B. (1973). Untwisting *The news twisters:* A replication of Efron's study. *Journalism Quarterly, 40,* 211–219.

Sumner, C. (1979). *Reading ideology.* London: Academic Press.

Tuchman, G. (1971/72). Objectivity as strategic ritual: An examination of newsmen's notions of objectivity. *American Journal of Sociology, 77,* 660–679.

Tuchman, G. (1978). *Making news.* New York: The Free Press/Macmillan.

Weaver, P. H. (1972). Is television news biased? *The Public Interest, 26,* 57–74.

Woollacott, J. (1982). Messages and meanings. In M. Gurevitch, T. Bennett, J. Curran, & J. Wollacott (Eds.), *Culture, society and the media* (pp. 91–111). London: Methuen.

14

TELEVISION AS A CULTURAL FORUM
Implications for Research

Horace M. Newcomb and Paul M. Hirsch

A CULTURAL BASIS for the analysis and criticism of television is, for us, the bridge between a concern for television as a communications medium, central to contemporary society, and television as aesthetic object, the expressive medium that, through its story telling functions, unites and examines a culture. The shortcomings of each of these approaches taken alone should be obvious.

The first is based primarily on a concern for understanding specific messages that may have specific effects and grounds its analysis in "communication" narrowly defined. Complexities of image, style, resonance, narrativity, history, metaphor, and so on are reduced in favor of that content that can be more precisely—some say more objectively—described. The content categories are not allowed to emerge from the text, as is the case in naturalistic observation and in textual analysis. Rather they are predefined in order to be measured more easily. The incidence of certain content categories may be cited as significant, or their "effects" more clearly correlated with some behavior. This concern for measuring is, of course, the result of conceiving television in one way rather than another, as "communication" rather than as "art."

The narrowest versions of this form of analysis need not concern us here. It is to the best versions that we must look, to those that do admit to a range of aesthetic expression and something of a variety of reception. Even when we examine these closely, however, we see that they often assume a monolithic "meaning" in television content.

AUTHORS' NOTE: We would like to express our appreciation to the John and Mary R. Markle Foundation for support in the preparation of this chapter and our ongoing study of the role of television as a cultural forum in American society. This chapter was originally published in *Quarterly Review of Film Studies,* 1983, Vol. 8(2). © Redgrave Publishing Company, South Salem, NY.

From Horace M. Newcomb and Paul M. Hirsch, "Television as a Cultural Forum: Implications for Research," pp. 58-73 in Willard D. Rowland, Jr. and Bruce Watkins, eds., *Interpreting Television: Current Research Perspectives* (Beverly Hills, CA: Sage Publications, 1984). Originally published in *Quarterly Review of Film Studies*, 1983 Vol. 8(2). Copyright by Redgrave Publishing Company, South Salem, NY.

The concern is for "dominant" messages embedded in the pleasant disguise of fictional entertainment, and the concern of the researcher is often that the control of these messages is, more than anything else, a complex sort of political control. The critique that emerges, then, is consciously or unconsciously a critique of the society that is transmitting and maintaining the dominant ideology with the assistance, again conscious or unconscious, of those who control communications technologies and businesses. (Ironically, this perspective does not depend on political perspective or persuasion. It is held by groups on the "right" who see American values being subverted, as well as by those on the "left" who see American values being imposed.)

Such a position assumes that the audience shares or "gets" the same messages and their meanings as the researcher finds. At times, like the literary critic, the researcher assumes this on the basis of superior insight, technique, or sensibility. In a more "scientific" manner the researcher may seek to establish a correlation between the discovered messages and the understanding of the audience. Rarely, however, does the message analyst allow for the possibility that the audience, while sharing this one meaning, may create many others that have not been examined, asked about, or controlled for.

The television "critic" on the other hand, often basing his work on the analysis of literature or film, succeeds in calling attention to the distinctive qualities of the medium, to the special nature of television fiction. But this approach all too often ignores important questions of production and reception. Intent on correcting what it takes to be a skewed interest in such matters, it often avoids the "business" of television and its "technology." These critics, much like their counterparts in the social sciences, usually assume that viewers should understand programs in the way the critic does, or that the audience is incapable of properly evaluating the entertaining work and should accept the critic's superior judgment.

The differences between the two views of what television is and does rest, in part, on the now familiar distinction between transportation and ritual views of communication processes. The social scientific, or communication theory, model outlined above (and we do not claim that it is an exhaustive description) rests most thoroughly on the transportation view. As articulated by James Carey, this model holds that communication is a "process of transmitting messages at a distance for the purpose of control. The archetypal case of communication then is persuasion, attitude change, behavior modification, socialization through the transmission of information, influence, or conditioning" (Carey, 1975a).

The more "literary" or "aesthetically based" approach leans toward, but hardly comes to terms with, ritual models of communication. As put by Carey, the ritual view sees communication "not directed toward the extension of messages in space but the maintenance of society in time; not the act of imparting information but the representation of shared beliefs" (Carey, 1975a).

Carey also cuts through the middle of these definitions with a more succinct one of his own: "Communication is a symbolic process whereby reality is produced, maintained, repaired, and transformed" (Carey, 1975b). It is in the attempt to amplify this basic observation that we present a cultural basis for the analysis of television. We hardly suggest that such an approach is entirely new, or that others are unaware of or do not share many of our assumptions. On the contrary, we find a growing awareness in many disciplines of the nature of symbolic thought, communication, and action, and we see attempts to understand television emerging rapidly from this body of shared concerns.[1]

TELEVISION AS LIMINAL REALM

Our own model of television is grounded in an examination of the cultural role of entertainment and parallels this with a close analysis of television program content in all its various textual levels and forms. We focus on the collective, cultural view of the social construction and negotiation of reality, on the creation of what Carey refers to as "public thought" (Carey, 1975a). It is not difficult to see television as central to this process of public thinking. As Hirsch (1982) has pointed out, it is now our national medium, replacing those media—film, radio, picture magazines, newspapers—that once served a similar function. Those who create for such media are, in the words of anthropologist Marshall Sahlins, "hucksters of the symbol" (Sahlins, 1976). They are cultural bricoleurs, seeking and creating new meaning in the combination of cultural elements with embedded significance. They respond to real events, changes in social structure and organization, and to shifts in attitude and value. They also respond to technological shift, the coming of cable or the use of videotape recorders. We think it is clear that the television producer should be added to Sahlins's list of "hucksters." They work in precisely the manner he describes, as do television writers and, to a lesser extent, directors and actors. So too do programmers and network executives who must make decisions about the programs they purchase, develop, and air. At each step of this complicated process they function as cultural interpreters.

Similar notions have often been outlined by scholars of popular culture focusing on the formal characteristics of popular entertainment (see Cawelti, 1976; Thorburn, 1982). To those insights cultural theory adds the possibility of matching formal analysis with cultural and social practice. The best theoretical explanation for this link is suggested to us in the continuing work of anthropologist Victor Turner. This work focuses on cultural ritual and reminds us that ritual must be seen as process rather than as product, a notion not often applied to the study of television, yet crucial to an adequate understanding of the medium.

Specifically, we make use of one aspect of Turner's analysis, his view of the liminal stage of the ritual process. This is the "in-between" stage, when one is neither totally in nor out of society. It is a stage of license, when rules may be broken or bent, when roles may be reversed, when categories may be overturned. Its essence, suggests Turner,

> is to be found in its release from normal constraints, making possible the deconstruction of the "uninteresting" constructions of common sense, the "meaningfulness of ordinary life," . . . into cultural units which may then be reconstructed in novel ways, some of them bizarre to the point of monstrosity. . . . Liminality is the domain of the "interesting" or of "uncommon sense" (Turner, 1977: 68).

Turner does not limit this observation to traditional societies engaged in the *practice* of ritual. He also applies his views to postindustrial, complex societies. In doing so he finds the liminal domain in the arts—all of them.[2] "The dismemberment of ritual has . . . provided the opportunity of theatre in the high culture and carnival at the folk level. A multiplicity of desacralized performative genres has assumed, prismatically, the task of plural cultural reflexivity" (Turner, 1977). In short, contemporary cultures examine themselves through their arts, much as traditional societies do via the experience of ritual. Ritual and the arts offer a metalanguage, a way of understanding who and what we are, how values and attitudes are adjusted, how meaning shifts.

In contributing to this process, particularly in American society, where its role is central, television fulfills what Fiske and Hartley (1978) refer to as the "bardic function" of contemporary societies. In its role as central cultural medium it presents a multiplicity of meanings rather than a monolithic dominant point of view. It often focuses on our most prevalent concerns, our deepest dilemmas. Our most traditional views, those that are repressive and reactionary, as well as those that are subversive and emancipatory, are upheld, examined, maintained, and transformed. The emphasis is on process rather than product, on discussion rather than indoctrination, on contradiction and confusion rather than coherence. It is with this view that we turn to an analysis of the texts of television that demonstrates and supports the conception of television as a cultural forum.

THE COMPLEXITY OF IDEOLOGICAL COMMENTARY IN TELEVISION

This new perspective requires that we revise some of our notions regarding television analysis, criticism, and research. The function of the creator as bricoleur, taken from Sahlins, is again indicated and clarified. The focus on "uncommon sense," on the freedom afforded by the idea of television as a liminal realm helps us to understand the reliance on and interest in forms, plots, and character types that are not at all familiar in our lived experience. The skewed demography of the world of television is not quite so bizarre and repressive once we admit that it is the realm in which we allow our monsters to come out and play, our dreams to be firmed into pictures, our fantasies transformed into plot structures. Cowboys, detectives, bionic men, and great green Hulks; fatherly physicians, glamorous female detectives, and tightly knit families living out the pain of the Great Depression; all these become part of the dramatic logic of public thought.

Shows such as *Fantasy Island* and *Love Boat,* difficult to account for within traditional critical systems except as examples of trivia and romance, are easily understood. Islands and boats are among the most fitting liminal metaphors, as Homer, Bacon, Shakespeare, and Melville, among others, have recognized. So, too, are the worlds of the western and the detective story. With this view we can see the "bizarre" world of situation comedy as a means of deconstructing the world of "common sense" in which all, or most, of us live and work. It also enables us to explain such strange phenomena as game shows and late night talk fests. In short, almost any version of the television text functions as a forum in which important cultural topics may be considered. We illustrate this not with a contemporary program where problems almost always appear on the surface of the show, but with an episode of *Father Knows Best* from the early 1960s. We begin by noting that *Father Knows Best* is often cited as an innocuous series, constructed around unstinting paeans to American middle-class virtues and blissfully ignorant of social conflict. In short, precisely the sort of television program that reproduces dominant ideology by lulling its audience into a dream world where the status quo is the only status.

In this episode Betty Anderson, the older daughter in the family, breaks a great many rules by deciding that she will be an engineer. Over great protest she is given an internship with a surveying crew as part of a high school "career education" program. But the head of the surveying crew, a young college student, drives her away with taunts and insensitivity. She walks off the job on the first day. Later in the week the young man comes to the Anderson home where Jim Anderson chides him with fatherly anger. The young man apologizes and Betty, overhearing him from the other room, runs upstairs, changes clothes, and comes down. The show ends with their flirtation under way.

Traditional ideological criticism, conducted from the communications or the textual analysis perspective, would remark on the way in which social conflict is ultimately subordinated in this dramatic structure to the personal, the emotional. Commentary would focus on the way in which the questioning of the role structure is shifted away from the world of work to the domestic arena. The emphasis would be on the conclusion of the episode in which Betty's real problem of identity and sex role, and society's problem of sex role discrimination, is bound by a more traditional conflict and thereby defused, contained, and redirected. Such a reading is possible, indeed accurate.

We would point out, however, that our emotional sympathy is with Betty throughout this episode. Nowhere does the text instruct the viewer that her concerns are unnatural, no matter how unnaturally they may be framed by other members of the cast. Every argument that can be made for a strong feminist perspective is condensed into the brief, half-hour presentation. The concept of the cultural forum, then, offers a different interpretation. We suggest that in popular culture generally, in television specifically, the raising of questions is as important as the answering of them. That is, it is equally important that an audience be introduced to the problems surrounding sex role discrimination as it is to conclude the episode in a traditional manner. Indeed, it would be startling to think that mainstream texts in mass society would overtly challenge dominant ideas. But this hardly prevents the oppositional ideas from appearing. Put another way, we argue that television does not present firm ideological conclusions—despite its *formal* conclusions—so much as it *comments on* ideological problems. The conflicts we see in television drama, embedded in familiar and nonthreatening frames, are conflicts ongoing in American social experience and cultural history. In a few cases we might see strong perspectives that argue for the absolute correctness of one point of view or another. But for the most part the rhetoric of television drama is a rhetoric of discussion. Shows such as *All in the Family,* or *The Defenders,* or *Gunsmoke,* which raise the forum/discussion to an intense and obvious level, often make best use of the medium and become highly successful. We see statements *about* the issues and it should be clear that ideological positions can be balanced within the forum by others from a different perspective.

We recognize, of course, that this variety works for the most part within the limits of American monopoly capitalism and within the range of American pluralism. It is an effective pluralistic forum only insofar as American political pluralism is or can be.[3] We also note, however, that one of the primary functions of the popular culture forum, the television forum, is to monitor the limits and the effectiveness of this pluralism, perhaps the only "public" forum in which this role is performed. As content shifts and attracts the attention of groups and individuals, criticism and reform can be initiated. We will have more to say on this topic shortly.

Our intention here is hardly to argue for the richness of *Father Knows Best* as a television text or as social commentary. Indeed, in our view, any emphasis on individual episodes, series, or even genres, misses the central point of the forum concept. While each of these units can and does present its audiences with incredibly mixed ideas, it is television as a whole system that presents a mass audience with the range and variety of ideas and ideologies inherent in American culture. In order to fully understand the role of television in that culture, we must examine a variety of analytical foci and, finally, see them as parts of a greater whole.

We can, for instance, concentrate on a single episode of television content, as we have done in our example. In our view most television shows offer something of this range of complexity. Not everyone of them treats social problems of such immediacy, but submerged in any episode are assumptions about who and what we are. Conflicting viewpoints of social issues are, in fact, the elements that structure most television programs.

At the series level this complexity is heightened. In spite of notions to the contrary, most television shows do change over time. Cavell (1982) has recently suggested that this serial nature of television is perhaps its defining characteristic. By contrast we see that feature only as a primary aspect of the rhetoric of television, one that shifts meaning and shades ideology as series develop. Even a series such as *The Brady Bunch* dealt with ever more complex issues merely because the children, on whom the show focused, grew older. In other cases, shows such as *The Waltons* shifted in content and meaning because they represented shifts in historical time. As that series moved out of the period of the Great Depression, through World War II, and into the postwar period, its tone and emphasis shifted too. In some cases, of course, this sort of change is structured into the show from the beginning, even when the appearance is that of static, undeveloping nature. In *All in the Family* the possibility of change and Archie's resistance to it form the central dramatic problem and offer the central opportunity for dramatic richness, a richness that has developed over many years until the character we now see bears little resemblance to the one we met in the beginning. This is also true of *MASH,* although there the structured conflicts have more to do with framing than with character development. In *MASH* we are caught in an antiwar rhetoric that cannot end a war. A truly radical alternative, a desertion or an insurrection, would end the series. But it would also end the "discussion" of this issue. We remain trapped, like American culture in its historical reality, with a dream and rhetoric of peace and a bitter experience that denies those aims.

The model of the forum extends beyond the use of the series with attention to genre. One tendency of genre studies has been to focus on similarities within forms, to indicate the ways in which all westerns, situation comedies, detective shows, and so on are alike. Clearly, however, it is in the economic interests of producers to build on audience familiarity with generic patterns and instill novelty into those generically based presentations. Truly innovative forms that use the generic base as a foundation are likely to be among the more successful shows. This also means that the shows, despite generic similarity, will carry individual rhetorical slants. As a result, while shows like *MASH, The Mary Tyler Moore Show,* and *All in the Family* may all treat similar issues, those issues will have different meanings because of the variations in character, tone, history, style, and so on, this despite a general "liberal" tone. Other shows, minus that tone, will clash in varying degrees. The notion that they are all, in some sense, "situation comedies" does not adequately explain the treatment of ideas within them.

This hardly diminishes the strength of generic variation as yet another version of difference within the forum. The rhetoric of the soap opera *pattern* is different from that of the situation comedy and that from the detective show. Thus, when similar topics are treated within different generic frames another level of "discussion" is at work.

It is for this reason that we find it important to examine strips of television programming, "flow" as Williams (1975) refers to it. Within these flow strips we may find opposing ideas abutting one another. We may find opposing treatments of the same ideas. And we will certainly find a viewing behavior that is more akin to actual experience than that found when concentrating on the individual show, the series, or the genre. The forum model, then, has led us into a new exploration of the definition of the television text. We are now examining the "viewing strip" as a potential text and are discovering that in the range of options offered by any given evening's televiewing, the forum is indeed a more accurate model of what goes on *within* television than any other that we know of. By taping entire weeks of television content, and tracing various potential strips in the body of that week, we can construct a huge range of potential "texts" that may have been seen by individual viewers.

Each level of text—the strip as text, the television week, the television day—is compounded yet again by the history of the medium. Our hypothesis is that we might track the history of America's social discussions of the past three decades by examining the multiple rhetorics of television during that period. Given the problematic state of television archiving, a careful study of that hypothesis presents an enormous difficulty. It is, nevertheless, an exciting prospect.

INTERPRETIVE VARIANCE

Clearly, our emphasis is on the treatment of issues, on rhetoric. We recognize the validity of analytical structures that emphasize television's skewed demographic patterns, its particular social aberrations, or other "unrealistic distortions" of the world of experience. But we also recognize that in order to make sense of those structures and patterns researchers return again and again to the "meaning" of that television world, to the processes and problems of interpretation. In our view this practice is hardly limited to those of us who study television. It is also open to audiences who view it each evening and to professionals who create for the medium.

The goal of every producer is to create the difference that makes a difference, to maintain an audience with sufficient reference to the known and recognized, but to move ahead into something that distinguishes his show for the program buyer, the scheduler, and most importantly, for the mass audience. As recent work by Newcomb and Alley (1983) shows, the goal of many producers, the most successful and powerful ones, is also to include personal ideas in their work, to use it as all artists use their medium, as a means of personal expression. Given these goals it is possible to examine the work of individual producers as other units of analysis and to compare the work of different producers as expressions within the forum. We need only think of the work of Quinn Martin and Jack Webb, or to contrast their work with that of Norman Lear or Gary Marshall, to recognize the individuality at work within television making. Choices by producers to work in certain generic forms, to express certain political, moral, and ethical attitudes, to explore certain sociocultural topics, all affect the nature of the ultimate "flow text" of television seen by viewers and assure a range of variation within that text.

The existence of this variation is borne out by varying responses among those who view television. A degree of this variance occurs among professional television critics who like and dislike shows for different reasons. But because television critics, certainly in American journalistic situations, are more alike than different in many ways, a more important indicator of the range of responses is that found among "ordinary" viewers, or the disagreements implied by audience acceptance and enthusiasm for program material soundly disavowed by professional critics. Work by Himmleweit (1980) in England and Neuman (1980) in America indicates that individual viewers do function as "critics," do make important distinctions and are able, under certain circumstances to articulate the bases for their judgments. While this work is just beginning, it is still possible to suggest from anecdotal evidence that people agree and disagree with television for a variety of reasons. They find in television texts representations of and challenges to their own ideas, and must somehow come to terms with what is there.

If disagreements cut too deeply into the value structure of the individual, if television threatens the sense of cultural security, the individual may take steps to engage the medium at the level of personal action. Most often this occurs in the form of letters to the network or to local stations, and again, the pattern is not new to television. It has occured with every other mass medium in modern industrial society.

Nor is it merely the formation of groups or the expression of personal points of view that indicates the working of a forum. It is the *range* of response, the directly contradictory readings of the medium, that cue us to its multiple meanings. Groups may object to the same programs, for example, for entirely opposing reasons. In *Charlie's Angels* feminists may find yet another example of sexist repression, while fundamentalist religious groups may find examples of moral decay expressed in the sexual freedom, the personal appearance, or the "unfeminine" behavior of the protagonists. Other viewers doubtless find the expression of meaningful liberation of women. At this level the point is hardly that one group is "right" and another "wrong," much less that one is "right" while the other is "left." Individuals and groups are, for many reasons, involved in making their own meanings from the television text.

This variation in interpretive strategies can be related to suggestions made by Stuart Hall (1980) in his influential essay, "Encoding and Decoding in the Television Discourse." There he suggests three basic modes of interpretation corresponding to the interpreter's political stance within the social structure. The interpretation may be "dominant," accepting the prevailing ideological structure. It may be "oppositional," rejecting the basic aspects of the structure. Or it may be "negotiated," creating a sort of personal synthesis. As later work by some of Hall's colleagues (Morley and Brunsdon, 1978; Morley, 1980) suggests, however, it quickly becomes necessary to expand the range of possible interpretations. Following these suggestions to a radical extreme it might be possible to argue that every individual interpretation of television content could, in some way, be "different." Clearly, however, communication is dependent on a greater degree of shared meanings, and expressions of popular entertainment are perhaps even more dependent on the shared level than many other forms of discourse. Our concern then is for the ways in which interpretation is negotiated in society. Special interest groups that focus, at times, on television provide us with readily available resources for the study of interpretive practices.

We see these groups as representative of metaphoric "fault lines" in American society. Television is the terrain in which the faults are expressed and worked out. In studying the groups, their rhetoric, the issues on which they focus, their tactics, their forms of organization, we hope to demonstrate that the idea of the "forum" is more than a metaphor in its own right. In forming special interest groups, or in using such groups to speak about television, citizens actually enter the forum. Television shoves them toward action, toward expression of ideas and values. At this level the model of "television as a cultural forum" enables us to examine "the sociology of interpretation."

Here much attention needs to be given to the historical aspects of this form of activity. How has the definition of issues changed over time? How has that change correlated with change in the television texts? These are important questions that, while difficult to study, are crucial to a full understanding of the role of television in culture. It is primarily through this sort of study that we will be able to define much more precisely the limits of the forum, for groups form monitoring devices that alert us to shortcomings not only in the world of television representation, but to the world of political experience as well. We know, for example, that because of heightened concern on the part of special interest groups, and responses from the creative and institutional communities of television industries, the "fictional" population of black citizens now roughly equals that of the real population. Regardless of whether such a match is "good" or "necessary," regardless of the depiction of blacks on television, this indicates that the forum extends beyond the screen. The issue of violence, another deserving close study, is more mixed, varying from year to year. The influence of groups, of individuals, of studies, of the terrible consequences of murder and assassination, however, cannot be denied. Television does not exist in a realm of its own, cut off from the influence of citizens. Our aim is to discover, as precisely as possible, the ways in which the varied worlds interact.

Throughout this kind of analysis, then, it is necessary to cite a range of varied responses to the texts of television. Using the viewing "strip" as the appropriate text of television, and recognizing that it is filled with varied topics and approaches to those topics, we begin to think of the television viewer as a bricoleur who matches the creator in the making of meanings. Bringing values and attitudes, a universe of personal experiences and concerns, to the texts, the viewer selects, examines, acknowledges, and makes texts of his or her own.[4] If we conceive of special interest groups as representatives of *patterns* of cultural attitude and response we have a potent source of study.

On the production end of this process, in addition to the work of individual producers, we must examine the role of network executives who must purchase and program television content. They, too, are cultural interpreters, intent on "reading" the culture through its relation to the "market." Executives who head and staff the internal censor agencies of each network, the offices of Broadcast Standards or Standards and Practices, are in a similar position. Perhaps as much as any individual or group they present us with a source of rich material for analysis. They are actively engaged in gauging cultural values. Their own research, the assumptions and the findings, needs to be reanalyzed for cultural implications, as does the work of the programmers. In determining who is doing what, with whom, at what times, they are interpreting social behavior in America and assigning it meaning. They are using television as a cultural litmus that can be applied in defining such problematic concepts as "childhood," "family," "maturity," and "appropriate." With the Standards and Practices offices they interpret *and* define the permissable and the "normal." But their interpretations of behavior open to us as many questions as answers, and an appropriate overview, a new model of television is necessary in order to best understand their work and ours.

THE CULTURAL FORUM MODEL

This new model of "television as a cultural forum" fits the experience of television more accurately than others we have seen applied. Our assumption is that it opens a range of new questions and calls for reanalysis of older findings from both the textual-critical approach and the mass communications research perspective. Ultimately, the new model is a simple one. It recognizes the range of interpretation of television content that is now admitted even by those analysts most concerned with television's presentation and maintenance of dominant ideological messages and meanings. But it differs from those perspectives because it does not see this as surprising or unusual. For the most part, that is what central story telling systems do in all societies. We are far more concerned with the ways in which television contributes to change than with mapping the obvious ways in which it maintains dominant viewpoints. Most research on television, most textual analysis, has assumed that it is thin, repetitive, similar, nearly identical in textual formation, easily defined, described, and explained. The variety of response on the part of audiences has been received, as a result of this view, as extraordinary, an astonishing "discovery."

We begin with the observation, based on careful textual analysis, that television is dense, rich, and complex rather than impoverished. Any selection, any cut, any set of questions that is extracted from that text must somehow account for that density, must account for what is *not* studied or measured, for the opposing meanings, for the answering images and symbols. Audiences appear to make meaning by selecting that which touches experience and personal history. The range of responses then should be taken as commonplace rather than as unexpected. But research and critical analysis cannot afford so personal a view. Rather, they must somehow define and describe the inventory that makes possible the multiple meanings extracted by audiences, creators, and network decision makers.

Our model is based on the assumption and observation that only so rich a text could attract a mass audience in a complex culture. The forum offers a perspective that is as complex, as contradictory and confused, as much in process as American culture is in experience. Its texture matches that of our daily experiences. If we can understand it better, then perhaps we will better understand the world we live in, the actions that we must take in order to live there.

NOTES

1. See Silverstone (1981) on structural narrative analysis, Fiske and Hartley (1978) on the semiotic and cultural bases for the analysis of television, Thorburn (forthcoming) on the aesthetics of television, Himmleweit et al. (1980) and Neuman (1980) on the role of the audience as critic, Gitlin (1979) and Kellner (1979) on hegemony and new applications of critical theory, Lull (1979, 1980) and Meyer et al. (1980) on audience ethnography and symbolic interactionism, and, most important, the ongoing work of the Centre for Contemporary Cultural Studies at Birmingham University, England, as recently published in Hall (1980) on the interaction of culture and textual analysis from a thoughtful political perspective.

2. In various works Turner uses both the terms "liminal" and "liminoid" to refer to works of imagination and entertainment in contemporary culture. The latter term is used to clearly mark the distinction between events that have distinct behavioral consequences and those that do not. As Turner suggests, the consequences of entertainment in contemporary culture are hardly as profound as those of the liminal stage of ritual in traditional culture. We are aware of this basic distinction, but use the former term in order to avoid a fuller explanation of the neologism. See Turner (1974, 1979).

3. We are indebted to Professor Mary Douglas for encouraging this observation. At the presentation of these ideas at the New York Institute for the Humanities seminar in The Mass Production of Mythology, she checked our enthusiasm for a pluralistic model of television by stating accurately and succinctly, "there are pluralisms and pluralisms." This comment led us to consider more thoroughly the means by which the forum and responses to it function as a tool with which to monitor the quality of pluralism in American social life, including its entertainments. The observation added a much needed component to our planned historical analysis.

4. We are indebted to Louis Black and Eric Michaels of the Radio-TV-Film department of the University of Texas-Austin for calling this aspect of televiewing to Newcomb's attention. It creates a much desired balance to Sahlins's view of the creator as bricoleur and indicates yet another manner in which the forum model enhances our ability to account for more aspects of the television experience. See especially Michaels (1982).

REFERENCES

Carey, James (1975a) "A cultural approach to communications." *Communication* 2 (1).

Carey, James (1975b) "Culture and communications." *Communication Research* 2 (1).

Cavell, Stanley (1982) "The fact of television." *Daedalus* 111 (4).

Cawelti, John (1976) Adventure, Mystery, and Romance. Chicago: University of Chicago Press.

Fiske, John and John Hartley (1978) Reading Television. London: Methuen.

Gitlin, Todd (1979) "Prime time ideology: the hegemonic process in television entertainment." Social Problems 26 (3).

Hall, Stuart (1980) "Encoding and decoding in the television discourse," in Culture, Media, Language. London: Hutchinson.

Himmleweit, Hilda et al. (1980) "The audience as critic: an approach to the study of entertainment" in P. Tannenbaum (ed.) The Entertainment Functions of Television. Hillsdale, NJ: Lawrence Erlbaum.

Hirsch, Paul (1982) "The role of popular culture and television in contemporary society," in H. M. Newcomb (ed.) Television: The Critical View. New York: Oxford University Press.

Kellner, Douglas (1979) "TV, ideology, and emancipatory popular culture." Socialist Review 45 (May-June).

Lull, James T. (1979) "Family communication patterns and the social uses of television." Communication Research 7 (3).

______ (1980) "The social uses of television." Human Communication Research 7 (3).

Meyer, Tim, Paul Traudt, and James Anderson (1980) "Non-traditional mass communication research methods: observational case studies of media use in natural settings," in D. Nimmo (ed.) Communication Yearbook 4. New Brunswick, NJ: Transaction Books.

Michaels, Eric (1982) "TV tribes." Ph.D. dissertation, University of Texas at Austin.

Morley, David (1980) "Subjects, readers, texts," in S. Hall. Culture, Media, Language. London: Hutchinson.

Morley, David and Charlotte Brunsdon (1978) Everyday Television: "Nationwide". London: British Film Institute.

Newcomb, Horace (1982) Television: The Critical View. New York: Oxford University Press.

______ and Robert Alley (1983) The Television Producer as Artist in American Commercial Television. New York: Oxford University Press.

Neuman, W. Russell (1980) "Television and American culture: the mass medium and the pluralist audience." (unpublished)

Sahlins, Marshall (1976) Culture and Practical Reason. Chicago: University of Chicago Press.

Silverstone, Roger (1981) The Message of Television: Myth and Narrative in Contemporary Culture. London: Heinemann Educational Books.

Thorburn, David (forthcoming) The Story Machine. New York: Oxford University Press.

Thorburn, David (1982) "Television melodrama," in H. M. Newcomb. Television: The Critical View. New York: Oxford University Press.

Turner, Victor (1974) "Liminal to liminoid, in play, flow, and ritual: an essay in comparative symbology." Rice University Studies 60 (3).

Turner, Victor (1977) "Process, system and symbol: a new anthropological synthesis." *Daedalus* 106 (2).

Turner, Victor (1979) "Afterword," in B. Babcock (ed.) The Reversible World. Ithaca, NY: Cornell University Press.

Williams, Raymond (1975) Television, Technology, and Cultural Form. New York: Schocken.

15

"FANTASY ISLAND" Marketplace of Desire

Mike Budd, Steve Craig, and Clay Steinman

"For the show's characters. . .there is the therapy of fantasy; for its audience, especially those women whose genuine problems, fears, wishes, and needs are treated but neither satisfied nor confronted, there is only the fantasy of therapy."

At any moment between the hours of 10 and 11 p.m. on January 17, 1981, an estimated 33 million Americans were tuned to an episode of the ABC television series "Fantasy Island." And it seems likely that many of them are regular viewers of the show. Yet, despite the significance of television programs such as "Fantasy Island" to the U.S. economy and life within it, they have not been studied with appropriate seriousness and depth. The examination of TV in the U.S. has chiefly consisted of statistically aided content analysis, in which events are tabulated over a relatively large number of cases and conclusions are then deduced. But standard content analysis, as a rule, in measuring surface content, leaves crucial issues untouched.

Like most American television entertainment, "Fantasy Island" consists of stories presented in "invisible" (3, p. 24) classical Hollywood style. This realist form so dominates commercial television that, for most audiences, it is either the only conceivable visual narrative structure or, in practice, does not seem to be a structure at all. The form borrows from the classical cinema techniques of editing, camera work, sound, and performance that are designed to make themselves invisible while making visible imaginary yet coherent story spaces with psychologically

Mike Budd, Steve Craig, and Clay Steinman are Associate Professors in the Department of Communication, Florida Atlantic University.

From Mike Budd, Steve Craig, and Clay Steinman, "'Fantasy Island': Marketplace of Desire," *Journal of Communication*, Vol. 33, No. 1 (Winter 1983), pp. 67-77.

motivated characters (4, pp. 57–59). How these forms are seen is as much a product of the system as of the style itself. Our impression is that many otherwise critical, aware, and socially concerned Americans consider shows such as "Fantasy Island" harmless and escapist (with the possible exception that some seem to recognize the objectification of women as harmful). But this reaction, like any other to the material, is itself a product of social forces and cultural forms.

Realist technique greatly enhances the masking of cultural values present in entertainment programming. As Roland Barthes has pointed out, myth becomes invisible (as myth) to the extent that it "consists in overturning culture into nature or, at least, the social, the cultural, the ideological, the historical into the 'natural' " (2, p. 165). From this perspective, viewers absorbed by "Fantasy Island" are not only watching "stories" but also are unconsciously and unevenly working through myths that reinforce dominant cultural values, with all their contradictions. Further, as Barthes argues, those who control the mass media manipulate this process in a general way for their own purposes. In the final analysis, entertainment exists on commercial television only to support an audience for advertising; as form follows function, therefore, the myths of entertainment programming must inexorably be linked to the myths of commercials. Both stories and ads, for example, frequently exploit the myth that female perfection does exist and that it consists of sexual allure and skills in the kitchen.

This article provides a symptomatic analysis of "Fantasy Island" designed to help illuminate what American television generally keeps from conscious view.

We chose to study "Fantasy Island" because of its high ratings and because it seemed to us to exemplify the promises and denials that mark culture industry entertainment products. We chose the January 17 episode—with no advance knowledge of its specific qualities—because its date of broadcast was convenient for our work. Examination of other episodes of "Fantasy Island" and other programs indicates that our study of this episode yields widely applicable conclusions, although, of course, different shows have different specific characteristics. For instance, while "Fantasy Island" and "M*A*S*H" are hardly identical, our research indicates that they have more in common in design, functioning as glad-handing sales agents for the commodity culture, than is generally acknowledged. Evidence for the claims we make about the design of "Fantasy Island" in the January 17 broadcast is available, although we only mention that episode's specifics when it seems helpful. At the same time, we make claims about that episode only if we have been able to find no counter-examples in other prime-time broadcasts of the show.

According to ABC's figures, roughly 43 percent of those who watched "Fantasy Island" that January 17 were adult women and 30 percent were adult men. About 15 percent were teenagers and another 12 percent were children age 12 and under. While the viewing motives of each of these audiences (and no doubt groups within them) might be investigated, here we concentrate on adult women because, as a vehicle for advertising, ABC has made women between 18 and 49 the primary target audience for its series shows (5). "Fantasy Island" also needs male viewers to keep its ratings up, both by their own presence and by their willingness to join women on Saturday nights in front of the set, so the show's travel, adventure, and emotional motifs seem designed to approximate for its audience the experience of "going out." (In this respect—and others—it is like "Love Boat," which is produced by the same company and precedes "Fantasy Island" in the Saturday night schedule.) Its mixture of excitement and romance may indeed provide just what many couples are looking for toward the end of a weekend evening. We will argue, however, that "Fantasy Island" and cultural forms like it carry with them and produce much more than the entertainment that viewers might seek.

The stories that comprise each episode of "Fantasy Island" involve fantasies: quite conscious wishes, evidently familiar enough to viewers that they need only be named for a story about them to be plausible. These fantasies, in turn, may touch those hardly conscious desires which Freud referred to as "phantasies" (7, p. 47). There are usually two fantasies per show (each with at least one guest star) and each typically revolves around a wish to solve a personal problem. Regularly present are Mr. Roarke (Ricardo Montalbán), the proprietor of Fantasy Island, and Tattoo (Hervé Villechaize), Roarke's assistant and foil.[1] They introduce and interact with the characters portrayed by the guest stars, which helps give the stories a week-to-week consistency. As a marketed product, the show thus enjoys the advantages of both an anthology (flexibility in plots and characters) and a series (format continuity and viewer loyalty). This format no doubt stems in part from the belief of production and network executives that "viewers will not watch a series regularly unless they see a familiar face" (10, p. 27). The editing of the show uses the series regulars as what Frank Capra calls "reactive characters," whose reactions at certain key moments cue the audience as to how to respond to events in the stories. Whatever its effects, this editing structure—a part of practically all narrative television in America and virtually all commercial narrative films—is designed to heighten viewers' sense of involvement and ward off potential confusion.

In the episode we studied, a high school art teacher named Kermit Dobbs (Donny Most, in "The Artist and the Lady") wishes a fling as a talented painter, and Elizabeth Blake (Eve Plumb, in "Elizabeth's

[1] Beginning in the fall of 1981, the regular cast also included Wendy Schaal as Julie, Roarke's goddaughter, who complements and occasionally substitutes for Tattoo as Roarke's assistant.

Baby"), anticipating a childbirth she knows will kill her, wants to see into her child's future. On every show, the fantasies are socially acceptable and politically conservative: no one asks to experience hermaphroditism or to be a drug dealer or to live in an environment free from racism or carcinogenic wastes. Often the episodes close on the beginning or reinforcement of a nuclear family in which father knows best. All this takes place within a Disney World–TV ad–country club–"gentleman's retreat" environment whose greenery and smiles, sparkling waters and soft talk may obscure its Old Testament patriarchal regime. In every episode we have seen, the dreamer pays and submits to the Law of Roarke in exchange for Roarke organizing the fantasy's temporary realization.

The intercutting of the two story lines may serve (perhaps unintentionally) to reinforce reciprocally the themes that can be found in each. Principal among these are those themes involving the construction of a happy familial relationship sealed more by the promise of long-term affection than by the pleasure of short-term sex. Despite the increasing sexual explicitness of prime-time television, old-fashioned love and romance continue as dominant myths, probably because they most reliably deliver the "demographics of the supermarket" (1, p. 73) desired by many television advertisers: women in the 18–54 age range. This does not mean that the makers of "Fantasy Island" particularly care to promote family romance or that most of their viewers necessarily desire it above other forms, but that, in order to attract viewers, those responsible for the show have an interest in making sure its stories are comforting and comfortable to watch for the target audience.

In the two "fantasies" of the episode we studied, sexual pleasure outside of long-term commitment is associated with pain and unhappiness.

Offending characters are ritually punished: Kermit is unjustly chased and beaten for the lascivious conduct of an artist for whom he is mistaken; Maybelle (Jenny Sherman), a married woman who tries to seduce Kermit, is perpetually frustrated in her efforts and spurned by other characters. At one point in the show, Elizabeth sees her future daughter, Lisa (Alison Arngrim), turn to prostitution because she feels unloved by her family. While the program leeringly lingers over scenes of Lisa as a prostitute, script and direction both seem designed to assure viewers that Lisa's life of selling sex is degrading and frightening. Meanwhile, parental and romantic love (both supportive of the nuclear family) are portrayed as the proper path to fulfillment and contentment.

As this representation of Lisa's prostitution indicates, "Fantasy Island" contains sharp contradictions between the sexual values reproduced in the plots (e.g., casual sex leads to unhappiness) and the voyeuristic design of the women as displayed. In the title sequence, ingenues packaged as island "natives" run from Roarke's house to greet the visitors to the island—both those in the arriving airplane and those viewing at home. The female characters throughout each episode are remarkably similar in appearance, dress, and makeup, representing what the modern commodity culture defines as "beautiful" (6, 9). The contradiction between voyeuristic spectacle and puritanical plot line is perhaps most clearly visible in one short filler sequence seemingly unrelated to the two stories.

In this sequence, Roarke and Tattoo visit Santa Claus, who is evidently taking a post-seasonal vacation on Fantasy Island. An exuberant Santa proudly opens his toy sack to show Tattoo the "gift" Roarke has given him—a blonde, about the age of the Lisa character, clad only in a bathing suit. When Santa expresses concern that the woman might catch cold at the North Pole, Roarke tells Santa to dig deeper into his bag. Santa discovers a full-length fur coat. "What is a present if it isn't gift wrapped, eh, Mr. Claus?" asks Roarke. Thanking Roarke, Santa pushes his smiling woman-as-sex-object back into his sack, tosses it over his shoulder, and departs with gleeful "ho-ho-hos."

Evidently, it is acceptable on "Fantasy Island" for Santa (and viewers) to fantasize about possession of a "dream girl." Roarke and Tattoo react with smiles as Santa takes possession of his gift, the epitome of commodified womanhood. Yet, in a different sequence a few minutes later, Lisa's face shows signs of horror as her pimp auctions her off in a not-dissimilar arrangement. While the Santa sequence is presented with tongue in cheek, it is apparently not intended to be ironically connected to the other story. The show straddles a similar contradiction when the "masterpiece" Kermit paints turns out to be a billboard-sized nude, ogled by the visitors to "Fantasy Island" and perhaps many viewers at home. Yet Kermit finds his happiness not in sexual exploitation but in romantic satisfaction with Deborah (Michelle Pfeiffer), who says she loves Kermit for what the painting reveals to her about his "mind and heart."

The romantic side of this contradiction seems to be stressed in the commercials broadcast during "Fantasy Island," which typically naturalize patriarchal values in the shopping center of the nuclear family. Commercials are placed in six groups or "pods," as the networks refer to them, at approximately 2, 15, 28, 40, 50, and 58 minutes into the hour.

Figure 1: Six key program/commercial "flows" in "Fantasy Island"

Flow 1

Program: Mother's concern for child's happiness.
Commercial: Life cereal makes children happy.

Flow 2

Program: Mother perceives a problem (narrative disequilibrium).
Commercial: Itching solved by Caldecort salve.

Flow 3

Program: Mother tries to help family member (child).
Commercial: Man helps family member (sister) with A-1 sauce.
Commercial: Wife helps family member (husband) with Sucrets.

Flow 4

Program: Woman revealed as perfect wife-to-be for man—combines passion and wholesomeness.
Commercial: Perfect wife/mother combines beauty and working skill with desserts by Duncan Hines.

Flow 5

Program: Mother reunites family, generations (narrative closure).
Commercial: Cream of Wheat reunites old friends, generations.
Commercial: A.T.& T. reunites old friends, generations.

Flow 6

Program: Characters link present with future through traditional institutions.
Commercial: Parkay margarine links present with past through traditional institutions (country store).
Commercial: Mighty Dog links present with past through traditional institutions (Old West).

The program/commercial flow of contemporary television has its origins in preceding culture industry forms. Hollywood had earlier adapted its narrative style to highlight and sell the stars who appeared within its products. In television, following radio, the narrative form was altered to provide pre-commercial build-ups or suspenseful "hooks" to hold audiences for the program through the breaks. But the narrative also functions to sell something outside—or next to, intercut with—itself as well. American television's use of commercial inserts, rather than clusters at each program's end, becomes particularly pertinent here.

Raymond Williams has examined the overall relations between television segments as flow—a sequence of programs and commercials, spanning several hours, which are planned by networks and seen but not thought of by viewers as a unit (11, pp. 90–93). Flow describes a unity, a sequential wholeness, that overrides both the spurious published lists of programs and the habitual, naturalized perception of television as composed of separate parts. Many in the industry who think of programs as interruptions of commercials may be as accurately characterizing the flow as are viewers who usually think of commercials as interruptions of programs.

In Figure 1, we focus exclusively on the flow created by the relation between the program segment immediately preceding the pod and the first (and sometimes second) commercial, abstracting the program material to its narrative function and the commercials to their dramatized situations. All the transitions move from "Elizabeth's Baby" to a commercial except the fourth, which moves from "The Artist and the Lady." If programs do function to create audiences for commercials, then transitions into a group of commercials will be more important than those moving back out to the program.

This way of looking at "Fantasy Island" makes it possible to see how sexual, familial, and other desires invoked by the program can be covered by an ad within minutes.

As this episode of "Fantasy Island" demonstrates, commercials respond fairly directly to the problems, desires, and fantasies articulated in the program's narrative by promising gratification through products. The program part of flow 2, for example (see Figure 1), ends with Elizabeth discovering that her husband Steven (Don Reid) will, at some point after Lisa's birth (and Elizabeth's death), move, remarry, and have two more children. This leads to Lisa at age 12 feeling unloved (and leads later to her prostitution), Elizabeth crying about her daughter's future, and Roarke first telling her she cannot interfere and then embracing and consoling her.

In the commercial that immediately follows, a woman is shown scratching her wrist feverishly. Her face cannot be seen but quite visible is a man in a three-piece suit (his is brown while Roarke's is white). Prominent in the frame are the words that are keyed onto the screen as the man says them, while in the background the scratching continues: "The more you scratch, the more you risk infection." And then: "Short of a prescription, nothing is more effective in helping to keep you from scratching your itch to infection than new Caldecort." What in part constitutes the flow—and makes it so important to understand—is the way in which buying Caldecort is proposed as a solution only a moment or so after a fictional problem has been detailed. And in both program and commercial, the authoritative voice dispensing advice involving women is a well-dressed, middle-aged white man. Ads thus become an inseparable part of the repetitive flow of lack, enticement, and pseudo-satisfaction. No conspiracy or conscious hidden manipulation by the network is necessary. The flow is possible because of the iconography of television, its mise-en-scène, its découpage, its converging patterns of narration in programs and commercials.

There are a number of ways to account for this convergence. Commercials and programs have similar purposes—programs sell themselves; commercials sell products. Like the episodes of "Fantasy Island," the commercials seek their fortunes by promising satisfaction of audience desires and by avoiding the risk of threatening confrontation. The makers of "Fantasy Island" and of its commercials would seem to know roughly the same things about the same audience—at least as they imagine it. And yet, as far as we can tell, producers, writers, and directors in network television are far less knowledgeable about their shows' audiences than one might think, given the millions of dollars at stake. In August of 1981, one of us told the directors of episodes of "Fantasy Island" and "Three's Company" that the bulk of commercials on their shows were aimed at women. They expressed mild surprise, apparently because both shows are known for the ways they display and make jokes about women's bodies. Other program-makers consulted in Hollywood that month said that they had, at most, a vague idea of their shows' demographics. Everyone contacted said that, when taping or filming, they had no idea what commercials would be broadcast with a given show.

While some industrial constraints on program-commercial relations do exist at the network level, where contradictory material may be excluded prior to airing,[2] more important may be the constraints involved in the makers' rather uniform sense of what is appropriate for audiences, as well as those constraints governing the hiring decisions of network and production company executives. "I make what I like and feel I have a general sense of what people like," Don Weis, director of

[2] Early in 1981, a spokesperson for ABC told us that two guidelines were followed in placing prime-time commercials: do not place ads for competitors next to one another, and protect advertisers against inadvertent connections with program material (an airline with a show involving a plane crash, for example).

many television shows and films, told one of us on a "Fantasy Island" outdoor set in August of 1981. But he would not have been there if the values exhibited in his work were at odds with those of the show's backers and presumed target audience. The flow, then, can and does exist in the absence of any routine, conscious effort to structure certain types of commercials at certain narrative points.

On this episode of "Fantasy Island," as the narrative moves from problem to solution, from disequilibrium to equilibrium, from search to discovery, the product is there at every step, showing the way, providing therapy for what ails the characters in the commercials and, less obviously, in the program as well. In this way, the specific program-commercial interrelation changes from complementarity to harmony over the hour, not because the commercials have changed but rather because the pattern of juxtaposition has been altered. Every commercial moves from problem to solution in one easy step. The program, however, moves through three narrative stages: defining the problem, making the solution visible, and closing unsettled accounts. As a result, in flows 1–3, the product does what the program's character herself cannot—helps another family member; in flows 5 and 6, the advertised product and "Fantasy Island" character both serve to unify families or generations through "traditional" activity. In between, in flow 4, Duncan Hines helps Deborah's commercial counterpart change into what patriarchal culture tends to define as a perfect, loving wife, just after Deborah, for the first time, has been represented as being suitable for Kermit.

It is the phantasies of adult women—the show's primary target audience—which are primarily at stake here.

Dependence—on consumer products, on culture industry forms, on the "feminine" images on which they trade—is what is being sold to the female audience members. "Elizabeth's Baby" attempts to take up two concerns that may now be salient for adult women in the audience: the anxieties of child-rearing and the fearful future of the nuclear family. Both of these problems—as they are conventionally posed to women in magazines, soap operas, and popular novels—appear to be present in displaced form in the story of Elizabeth and her daughter. "The Artist and the Lady," with its aggressive objectification of women, would seem initially to be aimed more at masculine fantasy, but it provides a position for many women viewers as well. At flow 4, the only one that does not begin with Elizabeth's story, Deborah and Elizabeth become functionally similar at the climactic point of the narrative. Elizabeth's is the story of the restoration of a nuclear family threatened not by changes in the economy or sexual mores but by nature (her death), and it is only at this moment that she can, through helping Lisa to escape from prostitution, become what she "is"—a mother. Deborah's is the story of the formation of a nuclear family, and it is only at this moment that she becomes what she "is"—a wife, in contrast to the meretricious Maybelle. At the same time, Elizabeth's action results in Steven's leading of the successful rescue of Lisa, which seems designed to signify his reassertion of his position as father, in Lisa's resumption of her position as daughter, and in Lisa's eventual assumption of her position as wife and mother (shown in a photograph from the future near the episode's end). Also, at the same time, Deborah's assumption of the role of wife leads to Kermit's assumption of the husband's position.

Around flow 4, parallels between story/story and story/commercial intensify. As the two narratives intersect at this critical moment across the problematic of the nuclear family, one can displace the other. As a wife-in-the-making, Deborah's lead-in for the wife in the dessert commercial fuses variations on the stereotypes of mother and whore. The result is two fantasies of feminine perfection under patriarchy, at the point in the flow when the narrative moves to align itself with the problem-solution form of the commercials. After the commercial break, the show literalizes the mother/whore combination, as Elizabeth dresses as a prostitute to effect her rescue of Lisa. In both commercial and show, all that is supposed to matter is eventually resolved. For the show's characters, who within the hour are shown to have come better to understand themselves through the experience Fantasy Island provided them, there is the therapy of fantasy. For its audience, especially those women whose genuine problems, fears, wishes, and needs are treated but neither satisfied nor confronted, there is only the fantasy of therapy.

By the end of virtually every episode of "Fantasy Island," the visiting characters are ready to return to the situations they earlier wished to escape, the fulfillment of their fantastic desires most of all having helped their own self-understanding, their efforts to cope, smiling. (Rarely, for example, has a character said that he or she could not face going back.) As the show is constructed according to a search-discovery model with a therapeutic gloss, to the extent that viewers are taken with its thrust, the closure of the show might reassure them about the sensible order of social relations. For, like the visiting characters (who may function as figures for those who have visited with ABC for an hour), viewers at the episode's end have faced no serious challenge to their everyday life or outlook and have had a more or less pleasant experience in the process—at least on the surface.

What brings tens of millions of Americans to "Fantasy Island" each week seems to be a combination of something like voyeuristic visual pleasure and the satisfaction of identification with the narrative process that classical cinema has traditionally exploited (8). Using devices such as reactive characters, seeking to ensure a sense of simple certainty for audiences at every point, moving through the story in formulaic ways that allow viewers a feeling of mastery over experience, works such as "Fantasy Island"—no matter how outlandish, how inane—offer an imitation of what it might be like to feel actively at home in the world. Desire for these pleasures may be rooted in the "unsatisfied wishes" which Freud saw as the "driving power behind phantasies" (7, p. 47). "Fantasy Island" cannot address them, since its form is based on that very control desire seeks to overturn. Its manufactured fantasies are an attempt to "take up," to contain and control, unsatisfied wishes, rooted in fundamental desires yet shaped by years of dependence and frustration. Because of this, such fantasies reveal, symptomatically, the inadequacy of their representation of those wishes, the contradiction between phantasy as desire and fantasy as product.

Through fantasy as product, the commercials offer solutions of a kind, in a way that parallels the two stories in our episode: consume, follow conventional ways of living, respond to your perceived limitations by being more of what you are. Seemingly responsive to many viewers' contradictory interests in objectifying sexual spectacle and in idealized romance, trading on many viewers' fears and anxieties about both sex and family, helping to sell viewers products by most subtly connecting them to genuine fears and needs, this episode of "Fantasy Island" generates myths that relate to the problems of everyday contemporary life in ways that are irrational. For millions of viewers, objects of alienation become objects of desire and, as such, may lose those markings that might otherwise reveal their source and trajectory, their function, for those who trade in the commodity culture's unadvertised products: anxiety, displeasure, poison, and pain. And yet they retain their explosive potential: to stir wants that could be met only in a realm in which phantasy's promise engendered a taste of plenitude and phantasy's experience the fulfillment of a dream.

REFERENCES

1. Barnouw, Erik. *The Sponsor: Notes on a Modern Potentate.* New York: Oxford University Press, 1978.
2. Barthes, Roland. *Mythologies.* Edited and translated by Annette Lavers. New York: Hill and Wang, 1972.
3. Bazin, André. *What is Cinema?*, Volume 1. Edited and translated by Hugh Gray. Berkeley, Cal.: University of California Press, 1967.
4. Bordwell, David and Kristin Thompson. *Film Art: An Introduction.* Reading, Mass.: Addison-Wesley, 1979.
5. "CBS Breaks ABC's Hold on Women." *Variety,* February 11, 1981, p. 89.
6. Fischer, Lucy. "The Image of Woman as Image: The Optical Politics of Dames." *Film Quarterly* 30(1), Fall 1976, pp. 2–11.
7. Freud, Sigmund. "The Relation of the Poet to Day-Dreaming." In Benjamin Nelson (Ed.) *On Creativity and the Unconscious: Papers on the Psychology of Art, Literature, Love, Religion.* New York: Harper Colophon, 1958, pp. 44–54.
8. Mulvey, Laura. "Visual Pleasure and Narrative Cinema." *Screen* 16(3), Autumn 1975, pp. 6–18.
9. Rabinowitz, Paula. "Commodity Fetishism: Women in 'Gold Diggers of 1933.' " *Film Reader* 5, 1982, pp. 141–149.
10. Whitney, Dwight. "It Took a Second-Choice Actor, a Little-Known Dwarf and a Discredited Script to Make a Runaway Hit Out of Fantasy Island." *TV Guide,* March 1, 1980, pp. 26–30.
11. Williams, Raymond. *Television: Technology and Cultural Form.* New York: Schocken, 1974.

16

DRUGS AS NEWS
Defining the Social

Philip Bell

Since the early 1970s sociologists of the media have emphasized the ways by which news values and professional mediations constitute 'interpretive frameworks' of a highly consensual, conservative kind. Although most recent analysis has focussed on the semiotics of media discourses, the 'consensual paradigm' persists.

In 1974 Young argued that mass media share with other organs of popular social knowledge a set of assumptions about normality which is 'functional for the maintenance of diligent, consistent work and the realization of long-term productive goals.' The consensus image of society rests on (at least) three premises:

(1) People are seen to share common definitions of reality — agree as to what is normal and deviant behaviour; what activities are praiseworthy and what condemnable.

(2) This consensus is seen to be functional to an organic system which they see as society. Behaviour violating the consensus is dysfunctional.

(3) The major content of this model is geared to a neo-Keynesian image of the economy, a nuclear family image of sexuality, and a mundane concept of religious experience (p.233).

Thus the mythical hedonistic spontaneity of drug use is emphasized in media images of non-productive self-indulgence while the ingestion of alcohol and tobacco, being widely accepted as consistent with formal work values, must be understood, however contradictorily, as not dysfunctional or, alternatively, as constituting a problem within the consensus, not an attack on its central values.

The central tenet of the 'Consensual Paradigm', as Young later characterized it, is that

> *media operatives use a particular paradigm of reality in order to understand events in the real world. This paradigm, or 'inferential structure', is consensual in, its basis. That is, it bifurcates the world into a majority of normal people who are possessed of free will, and a deviant minority...acting outside rationality* (1981: 393).

The persistence of the paradigm can be seen in texts such as Hartley's *Understanding News.* He states that ' ...the notion of "the consensus" is a basic organizing principle in news production' (1982: 82), and argues that the media continually explain away political dissent as anti-social deviance. He cites Hall et al's 'concentric circles' model of the paradigm, and emphasizes the functional consequences of news ideology for the maintenance of what the media define as 'civilized society' (1982: 85).

In this paper I wish to argue that this paradigm is simplistic, even in the case of reports of drug-related issues in the press and on TV,

From Philip Bell, "Drugs as News: Defining the Social," *Australian Journal of Cultural Studies*, Vol. 1, No. 2.

the very area where it might be expected to apply. I will first discuss the general findings of a content analysis of one year's press reports on drug-related issues, briefly describe a semantic analysis of news headlines, and then reconsider the Consensual Paradigm in the light of a Foucault-inspired analysis of drug news discourses.

First, the content analysis (see Bell, 1982: 19-97):

All items which concerned drug-related matters that appeared in the New South Wales press between October 1, 1980 and September 30, 1981 were collected for analysis. A drug-related item was one which used the word 'drug(s)', 'addict(s)' or the name of a drug or drug class in its headline(s) or in its first sentence of text. All the major daily and Sunday papers published in New South Wales in the period were included in the study.

Additionally, samples of three other types of newspaper were included for comparision: seventeen Sydney surburban newspapers, seventeen from the North Coast (Health) region of New South Wales and the same number from the rest of the country area of the State.

Each item was classified in terms of the type of drug(s) on which it was principally focussed (Drug-Type) and according to the 'type of story' or its principal thematic concern. (Clearly this requires a judgement by the coder concerning the main focus of the item relative to many subsidiary or secondary themes.)

During the twelve month period under review, 1274 news items concerned drugs or drug-related issues. Forty percent of these included the word 'drug' or the name of a drug or drug class, at least once in their headlines (including sub-heads).

Table 1 indicates the percentage of drug-related items which were principally concerned with particular drugs or drug-classes.

Order	Drug Type	%
1.	Compendium	27.2%
2.	Alcohol	16.2%
3.	Cannabis	15.9%
4.	Narcotics	15.1%
5.	Prescription	11.1%
6.	Tobacco	8.9%
7.	Over-the-Counter	2.9%
8.	Illicit (other)	2.0%
9.	Other substances	0.8%
	n = 1274	

Percentages of items on different types of drugs all newspapers combined.
Table 1

Themes and Problems — Relative Emphases

Table 2 shows the major thematic emphases of items (ignoring drug-type) for all newspapers combined. The wide range of content classifications which were heavily represented in news items suggests that newspapers did not exclusively concentrate on discrete incidents and events (such as crimes) but that they reported very heavily both policy and research aspects of drug-related issues.

Order	Major Thematic Emphasis	%
1.	Research 19.1%	
2.	Individual Drug Offences	16.7%
3.	Education — Prevention	16.6%
4.	Drug Syndicates	12.3%
5.	Government Policy	10.0%
6.	Health	9.5%
7.	Agencies	5.2%
8.	Drug Seizures	3.1%
9.	Industry	2.4%
10.	Media	2.4%
11.	Drugs — Sport	1.3%
12.	Drugs — Driving	1.2%
13.	History	0.2%
	n = 1274	

Percentages of items classified by major thematic emphasis, all newspapers combined.
Table 2

I will not consider the detailed findings of this analysis, but wish to concentrate on their general implications for the model of media and society outlined in my introduction. But two additional findings should be noted: (1) The groups most frequently nominated in relation to 'drugs' are children (including 'youth'), women, and the elderly. (2) There are many references to 'foreign' racketeers and to foreign countries, which connote threat and/or sinister conspiracy to corrupt 'Australia', Australians and other nominated potential victims.

Drug syndicates, drug seizures and individual drug offences (including driving) accounted for exactly 33.3% of all items. Thus a general dichotomy might be asserted between reports on deviant/illegal behaviours on one hand and on social-administrative functions on the other, the latter being about twice as common as the former.

The results suggest that news reports confirm the view that drug *consumption* is the principal social issue. This might serve much the same ideological ends as explicitly blaming the victim, for it displaces complex social problems on to the consumers of drugs who are then seen as being in need of legally-sanctioned 'correction', or of medical or psychological help. This assumes the appropriateness of massive social welfare intervention at the level of those (villains) who facilitate or cause drug consumption. Hence the symptoms of a drug-using society are ritualistically portrayed as the disease itself, and the social welfare and legal apparatuses are visible as the mechanisms for controlling or alleviating these symptoms. Just as individual criminal behaviour is reported without any social or historical context, so too with drug-related behaviour. Any possible relation to complex social conditions or processes (such as poverty, or unemployment, for instance) is largely avoided. 'Drugs' and related issues, although constantly the focus of professional and administrative attention, seem strangely divorced from real political-economic determinations.

I also conducted a semantic analysis of newspaper headlines, based rather loosely on the work of Kevelson (1977) and Kress and Hodge (1979). This confirmed and extended the conclusions drawn from the more conventional content analysis. I focussed on the specifications of agents and processes in active- and passive-voice headlines (and text). Briefly, four classes of 'actant' were distinguished, interacting in a set of structured mini-narratives. The four were Heroes, Helpers, Villains and Victims.

Heroes either win battles, save victims or fight on another's behalf. They are reported as achieving these goals in the active voice. The prevalent headline metaphor of war-like conflict is given its natural personification in the wide range of heroic actors that 'fight', 'save', 'win', and 'raid' on society's behalf:

POLICE PHONE-TAP BLITZ ON DRUG RING *(Sun,* 19.1.81).
MP CALLS FOR WAR ON NARCOTICS TRAFFICKERS *(Australian,* 23.12.80).
DRUG FIGHT LEADER TO ADDRESS MEETING *(Gunnedah Independent,* 20.10.80).
POLICE ACTION SAVES DRUGGED GIRL *(Murwillumbah Daily News,* 7.10.80).
SUPER-FORCE SET TO CRUSH DRUG CHIEFS *(Daily Telegraph,* 1.7.81).
POLICE HIT TWEED DOPE PLANTATIONS *(Murwillumbah Daily News,* 6.3.81).

In the above content analysis many of the items under these rhetorical headline condensations would have been classified in terms of thematic emphasis or problem definitions which give little indication of their semantics. For example, the item 'War on drugs may feel cuts' (*Daily Mirror*, 24.8.81) is an 'Education-Prevention' item, a classification which ignores (as content analysis inevitably must), the fact that the headline relies on highly predictable metaphors.

Hence, it is possible that, *semantically*, many items of an apparently neutral or descriptive-informational kind may incorporate stereotypic 'frameworks of interpretation'. It remains a moot point, then, whether the overt 'content' of an item or the semantic-grammatical structures which link it to other interpretive frameworks are the more salient. Either way, one class of 'heroes' which is represented in items of various thematic emphases consists of experts — spokespersons for governmental agencies, scientific-medical experts and representatives of 'knowledge and surveillance' aspects of drugs as an assumed social problem. These spokespersons and experts are grammatically active and are incorporated into similar (although less metaphorically potent) frameworks of interpretation to other heroes involved in the 'fight against drugs'. But even representatives of bureaucracy may be represented as knights in shining armour who fight by means of knowledge and words: DRUG FIGHT LEADER TO ADDRESS MEETING *(Gunnedah Independent*, 28.10.81). Similarly, governments themselves can be construed as antagonists in the battle, with their spokesperson seen as the embodiment of a will to win the battle with 'drug chiefs':

> *The Federal Government is to join forces with NSW Victoria and Queensland to topple the overlords of crime and drug trafficking (Daily Telegraph,* 1.7.81).

Medical, paramedical, academic and other experts constitute an arm of this fight in that they provide intelligence, suggest strategy, and make public the battle plans by which the administration of society seeks to control drugs as a social, legal or medical problem.

So the category 'heroes' includes both 'helpers' ('police, doctors and social workers', above) in their capacity of concerned caring professionals, as well as those who moniter, research, and/or inform the public about 'drugs' (more precisely , the dangers thereof). Notice that items which feature helpers do not usually nominate precise villains (nor, indeed, acts of villainy) but speak instead of vague nominalizations such as 'glue-sniffing among (not by) *children.'* Thus agents of social control are of two kinds — those who fight villains and villainy (heroes) and whose who help victims (and alleviate suffering). Schematically, therefore, the relationships between the principal classes of actors are:

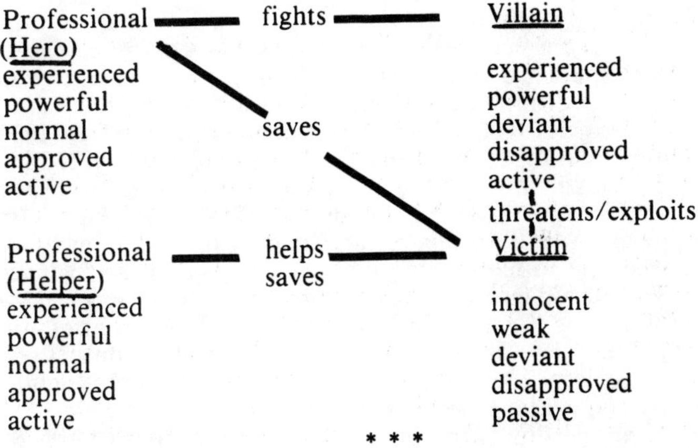

* * *

In drug items a structured set of interacting agents can be identified which play out a limited set of stories, repetitively making sense of drugs in terms of how the professional agents of social knowledge and control (helpers and heroes) fight for, help, and save, a society which is itself represented by analogy with the passive and ignorant (potential) victims of the intrinsic power of drugs or of the villainy of powerful exploiters.

The Consensual Paradigm reconsidered

I began by outlining the 'interpretive frameworks' by which news is conceptualized in the deviance-consensus model. I have suggested that the representation of drug-related issues is more complex than that model would predict. This is because 'drugs' assume newsworthiness in a heterogeneous range of story genres: scientific, medical, criminal or human interest, for example. On either a narrowly empirical analysis or in terms of a more conceptually complex semantic analysis, the interpretive frameworks into which drug issues are integrated frequently concern the administering, social-welfare, interventionist arm of the State. They are not restricted to individual deviance in isolation. This is not really surprising, for as Gandy argues, health (and much social-welfare) news is highly 'subsidized': it is usually a result of the cheap sources of routine information channelled from the bureaucracy, academic researchers or drug companies which are 'rewarded' by public relations exposure when a source is taken up:

> *The government, both elected officials and career bureaucrats, are the principal sources of information in the(se) routine channels* (1980: 104).

Of course, the police and courts also furnish much of the information on which drug stories are routinely built and dependence on all such sources is magnified by the inability of reporters to evaluate critically the literature received.

It is, therefore, important to note that the most commonly reported classes of items are those most directly dependent on routine (even self-serving) sources of information. 'Drug stories' are one shop-window for the display of the bureaucracy's and research institutions' own activities. The 'heroes' and 'helpers' in drug-related items are not merely individual actors in a morality play which is functional to the conservative ideological requirements of Capitalist society: or, at least, not in the way that the 'Consensual Paradigm' underlying much 1970's media research might suggest. Young (1981) who has recently criticized this paradigm, argues that the deviance-consensus model identified in various media contexts — for example, social welfare (Golding and Middleton, 1982) — need not imply a monolithic 'left-functionalist' theory of the relation between media and society. The Consensual Paradigm has simply become, Young asserts, a new orthodoxy.

The Marxist version of this paradigm argues that conflict between classes is concealed, for instance, by the assumption that 'we' — ordinary consumers, 'the nation' or 'the economy' — have one consensual interest — classless and natural. The key characteristics of Consensual Paradigm theory are:

> *a rational, voluntaristic notion of human action, a notion of society being held together by a mystification directly functional to the ruling class, and the coercive nature of reality hidden beneath the surface of consensual appearances* (Young, 1981:394).

In the case of particular issues, such as drug-use or strikes, the media may use folk-devils to 'present a negative image of ourselves and to lecture the population on the rewards of conformity' (1981:403). Further, strikes and crimes are 'explained' individualistically, not in terms of the structures of capitalist society.

It is possible to interpret the detailed findings of my study as supporting the Consensual Paradigm. Criminal deviance and psychological abnormality loom large in the representation of drugs as social problems, while the restriction of interest to issues of individual consumption confirms the displacement of structural problems by individual deviance. However, the complementary representations of scientific-welfare and bureaucratic agencies and pronouncements must also be explained. Drug news is not merely 'bad news', supportive of an illusory consensus. It does not simply construct an imaginary social unity, quivering yet reassured in the face of deviance and potential social disorder.

Young rejects the view that the apparent consensus assumed by the media is monolithic and conservative. He characterises the Consensual Paradigm interpretation of news as follows:

> *The media select anomalies of social actors and justice and render them into news stories, which in their denouement, plump for a suitable aetiology (which does not threaten social order) and appropriate nemesis (which balances social accounts). Moreover, the specific deviant groups selected are in fact either innocuous or else comparatively low in any rational list of anti-social activities* (1981:400).

Young sees this model as simplistic for two reasons. First, media institutions are relatively autonomous of the State, and second, particular media must accommodate to the real, if contradictory, locations of working class audiences and readers. Thus he argues for a potential dysfunctionality at the heart of capitalism which the mythologies of news can never make coherent, being based on the sphere of circulation, the world of appearances.

Even 'good news' such as the bureaucracy disseminates, which might serve an explicitly social control function, may be contradicted by the need for news to accommodate to its potential readers (what Young terms its 'audience function'). Thus

> *[The] relative autonomy, stemming from both audience demand and the struggle for a free and principled media leads to media — particularly at specific times and places — which in their focus on anomaly and injustice are far from presenting 'a world at one with itself'* (p.416).

Because of the conflict between the press's 'control' and 'audience functions',

> *justice is not always seen to be done: a sense of anomaly, outrage, and injustices sells news, not the soothing principles suggested in Paradigm Theory...*(p.412).

Yet Young admits that, despite such bad news (for the State), the continued faith which subjects have in the institutions of the State requires explanation.

So, rather than contradicting the Consensual Paradigm, Young seems merely to qualify it, to make it more subtle by emphasizing that audiences work on, and in part produce, the forms of message they receive. But he avoids asking how the media might help to maintain faith in the agents of the State, preferring to assert that not all audiences merely gobble up the inevitable products of consensual ideology.

Rather than focussing on the individual deviant, analysis might foreground the ways by which the State itself is represented. Like Young, I wish to avoid the negative conceptualization of ideology as 'illusion', 'mystification' or merely as a form of 'imaginary coherence'. I want to look not at what drug stories conceal, distort or mystify, but at what they reveal, assume, and generally display.

My argument centres on the ways by which the modern State is represented through the discourses of news. If there is a consensual assumption at the basis of various news genres, it consists in the ways the various agencies and administrative functions of the State are represented in relation to the individual, not merely in the rituals of deviance-defining bad news. It is surprising that few studies of drug-related issues in the media have sought to understand the overwhelming presence of scientific, bureaucratic-administrative, and medical discourses which inform such items. Almost invariably the individual-in-the-news has been the focus of research. Ironically, the researchers seem then to have attributed this same narrow preoccupation to the media themselves. Yet what is clearly on display in press reports of drug-related issues is what Foucault terms 'the administration of bodies and the calculated management of life' (1981: 140), not simply individual violations of assumed consensual norms.

I will detour briefly through Foucault's work on the histories of sexuality and of discipline and punishment during the period characterised by what he sees as the increasing 'governmentalization of the state' (1979:26).

Foucault traces the history of sexuality by means of a 'strategical model, rather than a model based on law' (1981:102). That is, he argues that social power is not maintained simply by virtue of formal legal codifications administered 'from above', but through the 'multiple and mobile field of force relations wherein far-reaching but never completely stable effects of domination are produced' (1981:102):

> *In concrete terms, starting in the seventeenth century, [ ] power over life evolved in two basic forms; these forms were not antithetical, however; they constituted rather two poles of development linked together by a whole intermediary cluster of relations. One of these poles — the first to be formed, it seems — centred on the body as a machine: its disciplining, the optimization of*

its capabilities, the extortion of its forces, the parallel increase of its usefulness and its docility, its integration into systems of efficient and economic controls, all this was ensured by the procedures of power that characterized the disciplines: an anatomo-politics of the human body. The second, somewhat later, focussed on the species body, the body imbued with the mechanics of life and serving as the basis of the biological processes: propagation, birth and mortality, the level of health, life expectancy and longevity, with all the conditions that can cause these to vary. Their supervision was effected through an entire series of interventions and regulatory controls: a bio-politics of the population. The disciplines of the body and the regulations of the population constituted the two poles around which the organization of power over life was deployed. The setting up, in the course of the classical age, of this great bipolar technology — anatomic and biological, individualizing and specifying, directed toward the performances of the body, with attention to the processes of life — characterized a power whose highest function was perhaps no longer to kill, but to invest life through and through' (1981:139).

The consumption of behaviour- and mood-altering substances clearly activates similar disciplines and regulatory controls in so far as they are represented in the contemporary media: bodies and pleasure are medically and normatively described; children and women are at issue as potential victims because they are the central foci of either protective-pedagogical or pleasure-power relationships. Perverse pleasure is self-indulgence and therefore is exposed to the glare of psychiatric, legal and other normative examination. Foucault, analysing the history of sexuality, points out that the confession replaced the 'judgement of God', and has itself been medicalized and psychologized from the 19th Century. We are enjoined to speak about sex continually; sexuality is dangerous, but central to the meaning of life — both at the species and individual level; it is secretive, unknown but knowable; confession can reveal the truth to the powerful (e.g. medical) 'master'; sex is critical in the distinction between normal and pathological. The hedonistic/individualistic focus of media discourses about drug use clearly echoes many of these preoccupations. Drug use is now at the erotic-confessional stage as a topic of media concern. The media construct drug use as a medical, scientific, administrative, social, and, therefore, personal problem: the private and the public bodies, their contested boundaries, their normal functioning and their 'administered efficiencies' are at issue:

The judges of normality are present everywhere. We are in the society of the teacher-judge, the doctor-judge, the educator-judge, the socialworker-judge; it is on them that the universal reign of the normative is based (quoted in Sheridan, 1980:162).

The popular media circulate and render 'natural' the assumption that 'crime is a departure from the norm, a sickness to be understood if not cured...[and]...provide[s] a justification for the examination of the entire population' (Sheridan, 1980: 162):

If the development of the great instruments of the State, as institutions of power, ensured the maintenance of production relations, the rudiments of anatomo- and bio-politics, created in the eighteenth century as techniques of power present at every level of the social body and utilized by very diverse institutions (the family and the army, schools and the police, individual medicine and the administration of collective bodies), operated in the sphere of economic processes, their development, and the forces working to sustain them (Foucault, 1981: 141).

Following Foucault, Kress defines a 'discourse' as a 'mode of talking', which

. . . in relation to certain areas of social life which are of significance to a social institution . . . will produce a set of statements about an area which will define, delimit and circumscribe what it is possible and impossible to say with respect to it and how it is to be talked about (1983: 2).

The discourses which are woven together in various reports on drugs in the press and on television consistently derive from the scientific, bureaucratic and normative institutions. The 'factual', balanced discourse of news itself hierarchically organizes these into complex texts about drugs as a social problem of a particular kind.

In the example below ('Drugs Spread in Schools') these discourses are patent: the pedagogical, medical, scientific, legal, bureaucratic and behavioural discourses are subsumed under the 'factual-revelatory' structure of the text. Following the factual generalization of the first sentence, the text alternates between reports of the testimonies of various social agencies or their spokespersons and factual claims located in the investigative-revelatory mode of the (bylined) journalist-expert.

The caring (maternal?) discourse is then juxtaposed with the descriptions of psychologically deviant behaviour in youth. Thus the item moves through various evidences of the 'social problem' to locate the social in the behavioural. Control of behaviour under the ultimate sanction of death is the point of intersection of the various discourses. The 'ways of talking' about drugs here are transparent and unexceptional — experts, evidence, youth and death are the predictable semantic foci. But this very typical item is but one textual realization of possible ways of speaking the relationship between the State and its subjects, one possible way of constructing a subject of the discursive practices mobilized.

Sydney Sun-Herald — 5th October, 1980.

NOW 'BIGGEST HEALTH PROBLEM' DRUGS SPREAD IN SCHOOLS

By Tony Blackie

The abuse of barbiturates, pain killers and tranquillisers is now the major health problem in NSW schools.

The Australian Federal Police Drug Unit says that eight years ago it was difficult to find a school with a drug problem, but now it is hard to find a school without one.

Health Department statistics show that problems with these drugs are not confined to one area of the city or to one social group

The drugs account for almost twice as many deaths as heroin each year.

Barbiturates are supposed to be obtained only by prescription but are readily available on the streets — as *The Sun Herald* found last week when a reporter was offered a variety of the drugs after making contact with users in Bankstown and Manly.

'FRIGHTENING'

The Australian Medical Association has called on its members to try to find alternatives for barbiturates when prescribing medication.

The AMA Federal Council says that barbiturate abuse is now the major drug problem in Australia.

Barbiturates are depressants which induce a floating feeling. Among users they are called 'goof-balls' and 'downs', because of drowsy effects.

Tolerance to barbiturates develops quickly, requiring larger doses or the use of alcohol to produce the same effects.

The drugs can also produce a hypnotic effect, sending the user into a half-sleep state.

According to Mrs Beverly Sheridan, coordinator of the Drug Crisis Centre at Yagoona, an education programme should be started in Sydney's schools with children as young as 10.

'The problem is becoming much worse,' she said. 'If you wait until they are 16 it's too late — they have already been experimenting.

'Once that happens they feel that the drugs make them feel good, and people preaching the consequences of drug abuse will mean nothing to them.'

While we were talking, a 15-year-old boy staggered out of one of the Crisis Centre's rooms.

He had been taking a mixture of alcohol and barbiturates the night before and was still in a drug-dazed state.

He was unable to walk properly, bumping into furniture and

unable to talk coherently.

A heroin addict sitting opposite said: 'That's the most worrying thing of all. It's frightening, these kids getting into chemicals and mixing them with alcohol.

'It's a quick death, and it's worse than heroin addiction because that stuff is legal and they can kill themselves within the law.'

SURGERY THEFTS

A mixture of barbiturates and alcohol can kill without warning because the alcohol speeds up the effects of the drug, therefore creating an overdose effect.

The user is never sure of the dosage level in his bloodstream.

Most of the deaths from these drugs are accidental as a result of lack of tolerance in the combination of the barbiturate and alcohol.

The most commonly used barbiturates are phenobarbitone (yellow jackets), quinalbarbitone (red devils), tuinal (tu-ies, rainbows) and sodium amylobarbitone.

These drugs can be bought illegally in containers with up to 100 capsules for up to $25.

According to Dr Robert Dymock, senior pathologist at the Queen Elizabeth Hospital, Adelaide, barbiturate drugs are now the major health problem among young Australians.

He said that in the course of a survey on the effects of the drugs he found they were usually obtained from chemists with fake prescriptions or genuine prescriptions from doctors who were conned by the user.

There is also some evidence to suggest that some doctors (called 'easy' among the users) deal out the drugs for profit.

Michael, 18, a heavy user of barbiturates, told me one of the most common methods of getting large quantities of barbiturates was to steal doctors' script sheets either by breaking into surgeries or stealing them from the doctor's desk while his back was turned during consultation.

He said he used barbiturates because there was 'nothing else to do.'

This item is typical in terms of the data derived from the content analysis: it is about drugs generally, it reports research statistics, nominates youth as 'victims' and generally focuses on medical-criminal consequences of drug use.

Television genres (such as social-problem documentaries and current affairs reports) realize similar discourse, often extending the analogy between sexual behaviour and drug use by the confessional ('exposure-of-the-intimate') mode of the medium. The following example quotes the final sequence of A.B.C.'s *Open File* (23/3/1983). Here the discourse of investigative journalism again locates the 'truth' about 'drugs' in the intimate self-confessed psychology of the young.

Although heroin is freely accessible, the televisual revelation still has something to talk about: viz. the behaviour, the suffering, of the socially sick. We might extend Foucault's point by claiming that the media's power is to *'invest life* through and through' because they *investigate behaviour* again and again.

'Open File', A.B.C., 23/3/83

LS of group of staff and residents (?) siting in circle in room. Cut to young woman (Angie) reading out loud.	Angie (On Camera)	Looking back over my life I consider that the environment that I grew up in was unhealthy and disruptive. Both my individuality and capabilities were squashed. I couldn't possibly live up to the expectations that were placed on me as a woman.
	Reporter (Voice-Over):	But total success at Odyssey does remain elusive. Long term resident Angie has decided to apply to leave Odyssey House. She now has to retell her story to staff and former residents...They'll then vote on her suitability to leave the program.
	Angie (On Camera)	Then I realized what was happening.
Wipe to psychiatrist (Dr Judi-Anne Densen-Gerber) in staff meeting.	D-G:	Again...a long term resident finally moving. I'd like to hear ah the reason that you felt it was an appropriate thing on her salary to buy a dress for three hundred and ninety dollars for her to read in front of me.
Cut to Angie	Welfare Worker	We have, we have gone around and around and

	(Voice-Over) (On Camera):	round with this one. We looked at it from the standpoint of the tremendous significance and sense of pride and accomplishment that she has in this particular endeavor. I mean it's amazing, her — her proposal, the way it's laid out, the whole thing just speaks of a tremendous amount of pride and given —
	D-G:	Very good from a woman who came in, who from a culture uh in which the female was the lowest of the low.
	Welfare Worker (On Camera):	And because of the amount of pride that she had and how special she feels about it we decided basically not to rain on her for....
	D-G:	So .... it's her birthday.
Wipe to Angie still reading but she is now weeping quietly as she does.	Angie (On Camera):	I asked myself how can you tell someone how to cope with the real world if you don't know how to yourself. I felt that my need to enjoy life is so great that our relation ship would have been disastrous. At twenty nine years of age I am only just beginning to enjoy life. At times I feel I am ready to take on the world, even though I see myself. . . (Voice fades down.)
Cut to Steve	Reporter (Voice-Over)	Steve left Odyssey after three days. He's never returned
Cut to CS Libbie.		Libbie's still undergoing treatment. Angie was

Cut to Angie, still reading and weeping.		not considered ready to leave and was recommended to stay at Odyssey. She did.
Cut to members of staff and residents (in room) one of whom is wiping away tears.	Angie (On Camera):	I feel I've come a long way from the first day I set foot in the doors of Odyssey House. I have disowned my own family (cough) but I have a new family that I will always be part of. I know...
Cut to D-G:	Reporter (Voice-Over):	Dr. Densen-Gerber, after her annual visit, went back to America.
Cut to Angie:	Angie (On Camera):	I have found my individuality and I know what my capabilities are. I have the strength to stand up for my rights as a person, and as a woman. These days I can walk down the street, holding my head up. I feel good about myself. All this Odyssey has given me and I will be forever grateful. (Voice fades down.)
Titles appear as Angie goes on talking.		

Foucalt emphasises not a conspiracy to subject citizens to State control but a location of subjects within discourses which incorporate power relations:

> *The exercise of power over the population and the accumulation of knowledge about it are two sides of a single process: not power and knowledge but knowledge-power* (Sheridan, 1980: 162).

In press constructions of what are termed 'social issues' such as drug-related problems, a consensual paradigm is not merely constructed through assumptions made about 'us', the 'normal reader'. Rather, a particular conceptualization of an administered social world is taken-for-granted. In this the agents of surveillance, control, rectification and support — both social and individual — are conspicuous. Experts pronounce, authorities judge, helpers warn, scientists debate, bureaucrats plan. Scientistic, technicistic information, recommendations, and solutions abound. Delinquency or deviance is not merely an anti-consensual threat. It is an 'effect' of these forms of knowledge-power. To quote Foucault again:

> *Delinquency, with the secret agents that it procures, but also with the generalized policing that it authorizes, constitutes a means of perpetual surveillance of the population: an apparatus that makes it possible to supervise, through the delinquents themselves, the whole social field. Delinquency functions as a political observatory. In their turn, the statisticians and the sociologists have made use of it, long after the police* (1979 (a): 281).

So drug-related news can be seen as representations founded on the very discourses which Foucalt identifies in relation to sexuality (or sensuality) and to 'delinquency'. By analogy with sexuality, news focusses on (1) the body of the consumer: her/his individual behaviour, health, pleasure: (2) the pedagogical: warnings to, information about, children, youth and other innocents; the family as socializing agent: (3) the need for and normality of surveillance and control of individual pleasure by means of elaborate corrective technologies of the State (medical, psychological, educational, penal).

By analogy with Foucault's history of the institutionalism of discipline and punitive institutions, drug news arguably embodies 'power-knowledge' relations appropriate to the 'universal reign of the normative' (1979 (a): 304).

I would therefore assert the need to move beyond the Consensual Paradigm by arguing two points. One is that what is significant in press reports of drug-related issues is *not* the construction of deviance per se, but the positive representation of the interventionist State: neither the Consensual Paradigm nor the media see the State as problematic. Both accept its roles as 'normal' ahistorical and natural.

The press generally assumes a reader who accepts the monitoring and interventionist roles of the State on behalf of individual victims and against individual villains. Much 'drug-news' is therefore 'good news' in the sense that it represents the data, the practices and the values of the helping and controlling apparatuses of the State in relation to social and personal *behaviour* as the focus of the State's various agencies.

A second criticism of the Consensual Paradigm concerns the notion of the actual 'consensus' which the press supposedly assumes. If one contrasts drug stories with some other social welfare stories then the very notion of a consistent consensual assumption can be questioned.

For example, Golding and Middleton (1982) have studied the way the British press represents social welfare issues, including unemployment benefits and other forms of economic support to 'the public'. But 'the public' is a problematic category in such reporting: 'the public' ('us') is frequently contrasted with the bureaucracy ('them') which spends 'our' (the public's — i.e. the taxpayers') money on victims (another class of 'them'). So in cases where social issues are seen as principally *economic,* Golding and Middleton did find a predictable consensus-supporting assumption:

> *A populist-pluralist mix of strong commitments to self-help, individualism, and anti-bureaucracy and the work ethic filtered the more liberal and compassionate perceptions of the welfare state that are common among journalists in the field* (1982: 152-3).

But anti-bureaucratic individualism and the normality of the work ethic are not unequivocally reflected in drug-related news. By defining the individual subject as biological-social, not as economic, drug-related news represents the subject's relation to the bureaucratic State in quite different terms. In particular, it does not see the Welfare State simply as a necessary interventionist evil.

* * * * * *

To summarize, the Consensual Paradigm sees the consensus assumed by the press as one aspect of ideology, and therefore as illusory and functional in the maintenance of class relations which are rendered natural and unproblematic within mainstream Western media. Young (1981) qualifies this view, emphasizing the penetration of these ideological forms by audience needs and by the struggle of media which are relatively autonomous of the State. But my criticisms of the model are different.

I have argued that the Consensual Paradigm is limited because it implies too monolithic an 'inferential structure' in the media. 'Social issues' such as drug-use and abuse are historically specific and ideologically complex: they incorporate deeply ingrained discourses concerning the relation between the individual and the Welfare State, deviance and the normative society, which may conflict with the consensual assumptions made in other areas. There is a specific contradiction in the press between representations of the relationship between the State and *economic* subjects on the one hand, and between the State and *bio-social* subjects on the other.

The Social Welfare State may be represented as friend or as foe, depending on which general social discourses an area of news is anchored to. 'Drugs' are represented as problems *for* the State because they are problems for, and of, individuals — i.e. they are *social*-administrative problems.

In drug items a structured set of interacting agents play out a limited set of stories, repetitively making sense of drugs in terms of how the professional agents of social knowledge and control (helpers and heroes) fight for, help, and save a society which is itself represented by analogy with the passive and ignorant (potential) victims of the intrinsic power of drugs or of the villainy of powerful exploiters. So 'society' is defended by, and defined by, the administrative arm of the State.

News stories are always about 'someone else' yet they imply a concerned (even personally threatened) reader who shares their values concerning the normality of passivity in a society where heroes and helpers are always on hand to control and monitor the ubiquitous threat that ignorance encourages. They see drug problems as social: almost exclusively concerned with *consumption by individuals* and the *behaviour* that this involves. They posit heroes and helpers acting on behalf of the administrative arm of society in just the right proportion to allay any excessive threat that the villainy of racketeers and the weakness of victims might arouse.

But they do more than this. They mark out the domain of the social as that in which the State is actively present, but positively so. It is an agent of knowledge and of control and rectification; necessary and benign. It is because the press constitutes its readers as *social* subjects that its 'knowledge' is a form of power.

Macquarie University

References

Bell, P. (1982) *Headlining Drugs,* Sydney: N.S.W., C.E.I.D.A.

Foucault, M. (1979) *Discipline and Punish: the Birth of the Prison,* transl. by A. Sheridan, New York: Vintage Books.

Foucault, M. (1979 (a)) 'On Governmentality,' *Ideology and Consciousness,* No. 6, pp. 5-22.

Foucault, M. (1981) *The History of Sexuality,* London: Penguin.

Gandy, O.H. (1980) 'Information on Health: Subsidised News,' *Media, Culture and Society,* 2, pp. 103-115.

Golding, P. and Middleton, S. (1982) *Images of Welfare,* London: Blackwell.

Hall, S., et al. (1978) *Policing the Crisis,* London: Macmillan.

Hartley, J. (1982) *Understanding News,* London: Methuen.

Kevelson, R. (1977) *The Inverted Pyramid: An Introduction to the Semiotics of Media Language,* Bloomington: Indiana University Press.

Kress, G., and Hodge, R. (1979) *Language as Ideology,* London: R.K.P.

Sheridan, A. (1980) *Michael Foucault: The Will to Truth,* London: Tavistock.

Young, J. (1974) 'Drugs and Deviance,' in Rock, P., and MacIntosh, M. (eds.), *Deviance and Social Control.*

Young, J. (1981) 'Beyond the Consensual Paradigm,' in Cohen. S., and Young, J. (eds.), *The Manufacture of News* (revised edition), London: Constable.

17

THE NEW JOURNALISM AND THE IMAGE-WORLD
Two Modes of Organizing Experience

David L. Eason

☐—*This essay provides a cultural analysis of the New Journalism. Two modes of New Journalism are distinguished based on their ways of constructing the relationship of image to reality, observing to living, and storytelling to experience. The two modes, designated* ethnographic realism *and* cultural phenomenology, *reflect alternative ways of responding to cultural change and organizing the experience of reporting. These approaches to understanding social reality are related to the problem of creating meaning in contemporary society.*

By THE END of the 1960s the doctrine of representation had crumpled in linguistics, philosophy, and even literary criticism. The center which separated image and reality was not holding, and the impact of this development was reflected in the popular arts and journalism as well.

Cultural criticism focused on how the self might find its bearings in a society characterized by a breakdown in consensus about manners and morals, and by the permeation of everyday life by a mass-produced image-world. Laing (1967) suggested that the true self might be regained only through a paradoxical journey outward through the edges of socially constructed unreality. McLuhan (1964) countered that the very idea of a journeying self searching for its center was an outdated metaphor of a dying print culture. Electronic people, he argued, live in a world the center of which is everywhere and nowhere. To Marxist critics such as Guy Debord (1970), McLuhan's electronic humans were socially abstracted individuals whose images had been appropriated by the corporate class. The alienated spectator confronted a double bind: ". . . the more he contemplates the less he lives; the more he accepts recognizing himself in the concomitant images of need, the less he understands his own existence and his own desires" (p. 30). Although more cautious in their assessment, Berger and Luckmann (1967) acknowledged that the marketing of worlds of experience transformed conceptions of reality and identity. "A society in which discrepant worlds are generally available on a market basis entails specific constellations of subjective reality and identity. There will be an increasingly general consciousness of the relativity of *all* worlds, including one's own, which is now subjectively apprehended as '*a* world,' rather than '*the* world' " (pp. 172–173).

Reflections on the relationships of self,

Mr. Eason is Associate Professor of Communication, University of Utah.

From David L. Eason, "The New Journalism and the Image-World: Two Modes of Organizing Experience," *Critical Studies in Mass Communication*, Vol. 1, No. 1 (March 1984), pp. 51-65.

image, and reality found expression in a variety of forms. One form was the New Journalism which revitalized reporting as a form of storytelling while giving shape to many of the cultural changes occurring. The New Journalism took its energy from the shifting relationship between the individual and the society, which located the process of creating meaning in diverse subcultures, and chronicled the symbolic quest for significance in a fragmenting society. New Journalists found their stories in trends and events already transformed into spectacles by the mass media. They used this image-world as a background for investigations into the cultural significance of the counterculture, political campaigns and conventions, prison rebellions, murders, executions and other spectacular events of the period.

Criticism of the New Journalism (Dennis & Rivers, 1974; Johnson, 1971; Hellman, 1981; Hersey, 1980; Hollowell, 1977; Murphy, 1974; and Weber, 1980) most often focuses on literary style, the resemblance between the reports and the novel, and ignores the relationship of the reports to other dimensions of culture.[1] Diverse texts that share stylistic commonalities are transformed into a model of New Journalism based, to a large extent, on the views of Tom Wolfe, one of the most prolific New Journalists. The effect of these strategies is to abstract the reports from their cultural contexts, to obscure significant differences among diverse texts, and to give only passing attention to the experiential contradictions represented in many of the reports.

The texts that have come to be characterized as New Journalism do share some important characteristics. The reporters usually focus on events as symbolic of some deeper cultural ideology or mythology, emphasize the world view of the individual or group under study, and show an absorption in the aesthetics of the reporting process in creating texts that read like novels or short stories (Eason, 1982). Despite these similarities, the reports reveal two approaches to organizing the experience of reporting. These two approaches reflect different ways of responding to cultural fragmentation and of locating the reporter in regard to the traditions of journalism and the broader history of American culture. One approach, most clearly reflected in the reports of Wolfe, Talese, Capote, and Sheehy, is best characterized as *ethnographic realism*. The other approach, most clearly reflected in the reports of Didion, Mailer, Thompson, Herr, and Dunne, is best characterized as *cultural phenomenology*.

Ethnographic realism responds to cultural fragmentation by giving accounts of "what it is that's going on here" that suggest "This is reality." The realism of the text constitutes the subculture as an object of display, and the reporter and reader, whose values are assumed and not explored, are cojoined in the act of observing. The effect of this strategy is to reinvent textually the consensus which cultural fragmentation had called into question. Cultural phenomenology describes what it feels like to live in a world in which there is no consensus about a frame of reference to explain "what it all means." Instead of arguing that "This is reality," the reports focus on the experiential contradictions that call consensual versions of reality into question. The phenomenological impetus is revealed in the multi-layered interrogation of communication, including that between writer and reader, as a way of constructing reality, and by the hesitancy to foreclose the question, "Is this real?" by invoking conventional ways of understanding.

The difference between the two modes of organizing social reality is revealed in three dimensions: (a) Ethnographic realism organizes experience in terms of the traditional duality between image and reality. The reporter penetrates the public facade or image in order to reveal the underlying reality. Cultural phenomenology describes a world in which image and reality are ecologically intertwined. The pervasiveness of this image-world calls into question commonsensical views of reality. (b) Ethnographic realism suggests the priority of cultural categories such as observed and lived experience. The reports are grounded in the assumption that observing is a passive act entailing no existential responsibility. In cultural phenomenology such assumptions are examined as ways of legitimizing ethical decisions. (c) Ethnographic realism reflects faith in the capability of traditional models of interpretation and expression, particularly the story form, to reveal the real. Although the reports acknowledge cultural relativism in their attention to the various symbolic worlds of their subjects, this awareness is not extended to the process of reporting which is treated as a natural process. Cultural phenomenology calls attention to reporting as a way of joining together writer and reader in the creation of reality. Narrative techniques call attention to storytelling as a cultural practice for making a common world.

IMAGES AND REALITIES

The impulse which guides the ethnographic mode is realism, in Wolfe's words (1973), "to show the reader *real life*—'Come here! This is the way people live these days! These are the things they do!' " (p. 33). To discover the reality of the other, the reporter must penetrate the image to reveal "the real" individual or group. Appearances may suggest that a situation is ambiguous or incomprehensible but the reporter reveals the continuity of an underlying cultural order by linking the visual realm to the experience of social actors. In *The Electric Kool-Aid Acid Test,* Wolfe (1968a) describes the process of interpretation. When he meets Ken Kesey and his Merry Pranksters, Wolfe cannot understand the relationship of their symbols to their shared reality. "Figuring out parables, I look around at the faces and they are all watching Kesey and I have not the slightest doubt, thinking: and that's what the cops-and-robbers game does to you. Despite the skepticism I brought here, I am suddenly experiencing their feeling. I am sure of it. I feel like I am in on something the outside world, the world I came from, could not possibly comprehend. . . ." (p. 25).

Making the phenomenon comprehensible for "the outside world" involves more than merely describing the scene and the actors' experiences. The scene must be explained by relating it to a social, cultural, or historical framework. Talese (1966, 1972, 1980) explains the interaction between his subjects and a changing social context by placing them in an historical framework. Sheehy (1973) places the culture of prostitutes within the larger class structure of the society. Capote (1965) infuses his account of the murder of a Kansas farm family with psychological and cultural explanations.

Wolfe, the most ambitious of the ethnographic journalists, furnishes the most elaborate explanations. Wolfe's reports establish a discontinuity between his subjects and previous cultural expressions. The reports then show how the subjects reflect traditional forms of culture. Although discontinuity serves as the motivation for the report, it is naturalized by linking the contemporary to a well-ordered, non-threatening past that promises to extend into the future. Underlying the ambiguous surfaces of contemporary reality is a cultural logic working itself out. The drug culture, symbolized by Ken Kesey and his Pranksters (Wolfe, 1968a), may appear to be a multitude of styles and symbols with no apparent meaning. Actually it is only a new manifestation of an ancient religious impulse and the group an elementary form of religious life. The "radical chic" of New York socialites (Wolfe, 1970) may appear to be a contradictory social rite for the elite to finance its own destruction. Actually it is only a particularly humorous manifestation of upper class status consumption traceable to the nineteenth century. The diversity of California lifestyles (Wolfe, 1965, 1968b) may suggest the loss of common culture. Actually they are only divergent expressions of a culture transformed by economic expansion that spread the idiosyncratic lifestyles of the upper class throughout society.[2]

Ethnographic realism takes its energy from an image-world which obscures the subjective realities of diverse subcultures. Exploring these alternative realities, however, poses no threat to the reporters' faith that they can discover, comprehend and communicate the real. Likewise these discrepant realities pose no threat to the society's identity. The ethnographic mode is organized around naturalizing discrepant views of reality within its own narrative conventions. Social reality may indeed be bizarre but it poses no threat to established ways of knowing and communicating. The disorder of society is only apparent and the reporter still able to state, "That's the way it is."

While ethnographic realism assures its readers that traditional ways of making sense still apply in society, cultural phenomenology describes the inability of traditional cultural distinctions to order contemporary reality. Didion (1968) introduces her first collection of reportage as a confrontation with the "evidence of atomization, the proof that things fall apart," (p. xi). She began working on the title piece of *Slouching Towards Bethlehem* after a time when she "had been paralyzed by the conviction that writing was an irrelevant act, that the world as I had known it no longer existed." The report, as well as many of the others in the volume, is an attempt "to come to terms with disorder" (p. xii).

Cultural phenomenology reveals that "coming to terms with disorder" is not synonymous with making events comprehensible for "the outside world." The phenomenological mode describes the image-world as a realm that blurs traditional distinctions between fantasy and reality. Didion (1968) describes a land where people have drifted away from the security of tradition in order "to find a new life style . . . in the only places they know to look: the movies and the newspapers" (p. 4). Everyday life which previously bound people together through time is invaded by media technology that cuts them loose in space. Technology, in the words of Mailer (1968), drives "insanity out of the wind and out of the attic, and out of all the lost primitive places" to "wherever fever, force and machines" come together (p. 174).

Mass media objectify dreams, transforming the fantastic into models for everyday life. Mailer (1968, p. 109), for instance, sees the counterculturists of the 1960s as "assembled from all the intersections between history and the comic books, between legend and television, the Biblical archetypes and the movies." Herr (1978, p. 7) describes the Vietnam War as one where a commander would risk lives solely for "a little ink." Didion (1968) suggests that the true significance of the California murder trial of Lucille Miller was that it made public the ways in which image and reality had become fatalistically intertwined in private lives. "What was most startling about the case of Lucille Miller was something that had nothing to do with the law at all, something that never appeared in the eight-column afternoon headlines but was always there between them: the revelation that the dream was teaching the dreamers how to live" (p. 17).

The dream-like nature of American reality in the 1960s and early 1970s is the major theme of Thompson's reportage (1971, 1973, 1979). Whether focusing on leisure, sports, or politics, Thompson describes a culture where the real has become so permeated by the fantastic that knowledge and ethics have become problematic in new ways. *Fear and Loathing in Las Vegas* (1971) is an account of "a savage journey to the heart of the American Dream." Las Vegas represents the metaphorical center of the image-world, a place where "everydayness" is created from surreal transformations of movies and television shows. Against this backdrop, Raoul Duke, who is a "monster reincarnation of Horatio Alger," and Dr. Gonzo search for "the main story of our generation." That story is the transformation of the American Dream, an ideal that previously had sustained and bound together people through time, into a neon nightmare organized around the hedonistic pursuit of "the now." Cut loose from community and tradition and filled with media-made paradigms of winning and losing, Thompson's Americans are transformed into pre-historic monsters who consume each other as they consume the culture itself.

In *The Image* (1961) Boorstin suggests nostalgically that Americans should return to previous distinctions between image and reality, recognizing extravagant expectations make reality more remote. In the phenomenological mode of New Journalism, such a return is impossible. The disorder of contemporary society is rooted in the interaction of "images of reality" and "the reality of images" that creates a realm where there is no exit.

OBSERVING AND LIVING

Human interest reporting traditionally requires a peculiar form of psychic distance that allows the reporter to find the "facts" in the "inner experiences" of the subject (Hughes, 1940). The practice requires that the reporter maintain a distinction between lived experiences and those experiences of the other observed in the reporting process. Ortega y Gasset (1948) gives an example of the kind of psychic distance the human interest reporter must maintain. A famous man is dying. Around his bed are a number of people including his wife, a doctor, and a reporter, each of whom participates in the scene differently. The wife is totally involved in the situation. She does not behold the scene, Ortega y Gasset argues, she lives it. The doctor is involved in the scene but only partially, responding to the man's needs through his professional self. The reporter likewise participates in the scene through his professional self. The doctor's professional code, however, demands he be involved, while the reporter's demands that he be aloof. "He does not live the scene, he observes it" (p. 17). Still, because within a matter of hours he must construct a compelling narrative that will move his readers by placing them in the scene, he observes in a peculiar way.

The reporter must be simultaneously

near and far from his subjects. He must vicariously penetrate their experiences while holding an aesthetic distance that allows the transformation of the experience within a set of narrative conventions into a story. Although the distinction between lived and observed experience may be difficult to justify on epistemological grounds, it is a commonplace cultural distinction that does point to different ways of being engaged in social reality. Moreover, it is a fundamental distinction for human interest reporting which sometimes requires the reporter to become involved in the existential realities of the subject. Since a reporter who treats each reporting assignment as an occasion for self-analysis likely will have difficulty legitimizing the practice of reporting over time, the distinction between lived and observed experience is a routine assumption that makes possible the daily construction of stories about the lives of other people.

Ethnographic realism maintains the traditional distance of human interest reporting, affirming the distinction between lived and observed experience. The distinction is, in fact, crucial to the mode's principle of realism which constitutes the reality to be reported as that of the other. "The subjectivity that I value in the good examples of New Journalism," Wolfe says in an interview (Bellamy, 1974, p. 85), "is the use of techniques to enable the writer to get inside the subjective reality—not his own—but the character he's writing about." Talese (Weber, 1974) makes a similar point, using the metaphor of the "movie director" to describe the process. "I'm like a director, and I shift my own particular focus, my own cameras, from one to the other. . . . I find that I can then get into the people that I am writing about and I just shift" (p. 97). Paradoxically, the distance of the "director" allows a more intimate portrait. In preparing a profile on Frank Sinatra, Talese did not interview him. Defending his style of research, Talese says, "I don't think I could have asked him—nor do I think he could have answered—those questions in any way that would have been as revealing of himself as I was able to gather by staying a bit of a distance away, observing him and overhearing him and watching those around him react to him" (p. 94).

In order to keep the subjects within the domain of the story type, the ethnographic realist must maintain the reality of the other as a discrete province of meaning, similar to that experienced in a film, play, or other cultural production. Wolfe (1973), for instance, cautions about the hazards of confronting the subject as more than a story type. "If a reporter stays with a person or group long enough they . . . will develop a personal relationship of some sort. For many reporters this presents a more formidable problem than penetrating the scene in the first place. They become stricken with a sense of guilt, responsibility, obligation. . . . People who become overly sensitive on this score should never take up the new style of journalism" (p. 51). Although ethnographic realism is criticized by some journalists for its investigations of subjectivity, the essential practices of the mode are consistent with the traditions of human interest reporting. Thompson (1979) is sensitive to this dimension of ethnographic realism when he writes of Wolfe, "The only thing new and unusual about Wolfe's journalism is that he's an abnormally good reporter . . . good in the classical—rather than the contemporary—sense" (pp. 122–123).

The "contemporary sense" to which Thompson alludes involves calling into question many of the traditional assumptions of the reporting process. Whereas ethnographic realism, like other forms of journalism, reveals the act of observing to be a means to get the story, cultural phenomenology reveals observing to be a vital part of the story. Observing is not merely a means to understand the world but an object of analysis. The well-ordered social dramas described in ethnographic realism become in cultural phenomenology disrupted spectacles in which the roles of actor and spectator are no longer clearly defined.

The phenomenological mode focuses on observing as a form of lived experience grounded in an epistemology and an ethics.[3] The spectators not only see reality, they organize it; they constitute reality as "out there" and themselves as neutral "camera eyes." The phenomenological mode explores the reality that actor and spectator create in their interaction, the dynamics through which each is created in the reporting process. It seeks to reveal that the presumed passivity of the act of observing is not grounded in nature but in culture and supports what Wicker (1975, p. 37) calls "the ethic of the press box." To become an observer is to see social reality as composed of active participants, who must take responsibility for their acts, and passive spectators, who bear no responsibility for what they watch.

Although Mailer, Didion, Herr, and Thompson focus on the relationship of observed and lived experience, the most extended treatment of the relationship is John Gregory Dunne's *Vegas* (1974). Dunne explores in *Vegas* the psychological motivation for his reporting and considers the ethical dilemmas implicit in creating worlds for anonymous readers. Dunne goes to Las Vegas because he is depressed and believes that reporting will be therapeutic. He plans to write a book in the ethnographic realist mode, an account of the "low life" of Las Vegas. He meets three people whom he believes will be great characters for his book: a young woman who works as a prostitute at night and attends beauty school during the day, a retired police officer from the Midwest who runs a private detective agency, and a small-time lounge comic who dreams of being a star. Although he desires to see the three as windows to the underlying cultural reality of Las Vegas, the characters function instead as mirrors for examining his own motivation for reporting.

Dunne concludes that he is a voyeur who lives his life through others in order to avoid dealing with his own problems. Previously he legitimized being an observer in life on moral grounds. "I was good at it, and imagined I had empathy for those I observed. I liked to think, I told myself then, and was still telling myself that summer in Vegas, that I could learn something about myself from the people whose lives I intruded upon, indeed that this was the reason I had taken up residence in an apartment behind the Strip" (p. 174). In Las Vegas Dunne comes to believe that the reporting project is less a search for stories containing morals about how to live than a search for an objectification of his own fantasy life. "It is always the other who populates our fantasies" (p. 87), Dunne writes. His fascination with the young prostitute, for instance, is less a quest for an understanding of the cruelties visited upon her than a socially legitimate way of having a prostitute without having to take responsibility for the act.

Dunne describes reporting not as an activity which prompts self-analysis about the socially responsible thing to do but as a flight from the existential responsibility for one's own acts through a socially approved role. "Reporting anesthetizes one's own problems. There is always someone in deeper emotional drift, or even grift, than you, someone to whom you can ladle out understanding as if it were a charitable contribution, one free meal from the psychic soup kitchen, just that one, no more, any more would entail responsibility, and responsibility is what one is trying to avoid in the first place" (p. 19).

Dunne describes the reporter as one who quests for a variety of experiences, believing that all knowledge can make one more morally aware. The reporter sustains the belief by focusing on the content of the observations, while ignoring the structure introduced by the act of observing. Observers believe they have no responsibility for what they are observing, since the action would occur even if they were absent. This passivity, however, is an illusion. Observing is a form of action which implicitly encourages events to continue. Dunne finds the paradigm for the active nature of observing in a situation that occurred shortly after he graduated from college. While living in an apartment building in New York, he became interested in the activities of a young woman whose apartment fronted on his own. The young woman, unaware that her private life was being invaded daily, rarely closed her windows. Dunne watched her for more than two years, gradually becoming aware of the most intimate details of her life. "Her life was a book whose pages I felt free to turn." One day, he became aware the lights in her apartment had been on for a couple of days. Although he worried she might be dead or injured, he feared his observing would be discovered and did not report the situation for more than two weeks.

Abstracted from a socially approved context, Dunne confronts observing as an existential experience that entails responsibility. Michael Herr makes this point explicit when he writes of the Vietnam War, "I went there behind the crude but serious belief that you had to be able to look at anything . . . it took the war to teach it, that you were as responsible for everything you saw as you were for everything you did" (p. 20). As a reporter, Dunne is able to rationalize his own psychological motivation as a requisite of the psychic distance necessary for satisfactory performance of the social role, thereby minimizing confrontation with implicit ethical dilemmas. *Vegas,* like the other phenomenological reports, makes problematic the epistemological and ethical dimensions of observing. Reporting is less a realm of certified activities than an activity in need of new intellectual and moral justifications.

STORIES AND EXPERIENCES

Although the New Journalism is largely understood as a stylistic phenomenon, remarkably little attention is paid to the relationship of literary style to the experience it embodies. Both modes of New Journalism reflect an absorption in aesthetic concerns. The emphases of the two modes, however, are distinctive.

A story is both a way of communicating and a way of comprehending (Eason, 1981). We not only tell stories, we also make sense in the process. Although it is commonplace to divide narratives into form and content, the two are actually bound together. Darnton (1975) exemplifies the interrelationship in an anecdote from his days as a reporter. After writing a straight-forward story about a boy whose bike had been stolen, Darnton was told by another reporter that such a format was inappropriate. The reporter showed Darnton what was needed by making up details and composing a fictional story. Using the fictional story as a model, Darnton returned to the reporting process, collecting facts appropriate to the new story type. The new story revealed the emotional dimensions of the event and contained a moral. It was well received at the newspaper and was prominently displayed on the front page. In learning how to tell the story, Darnton also learned to make sense of events in a particular way in the social world. The fictional story not only functioned as a model for communicating but also as a model for constructing social reality.

The distinctive aesthetic emphases of the two modes of New Journalism are derived from the different ways in which the two modes relate telling stories to making sense. Ethnographic realism represents style as a communicational technique whose function is to reveal a story that exists "out there" in real life. Cultural phenomenology represents style as an epistemological strategy that constructs as well as reveals reality. In ethnographic realism the dominant function of the narrative is to reveal an interpretation, in cultural phenomenology to show how an interpretation is constructed. Ethnographic realism is grounded in a perception of an underlying historical continuity between contemporary reality and American culture. The reporter, operating within a traditional role definition, penetrates the image to find the story. Since social reality can be understood and communicated within traditional cultural vehicles, questions of style are entertained as technical issues.

The ethnographic realist confronts narrative construction as a problem of mediating between the experience of the subject and the reader. All relationships necessary to complete the reporting process are subsumed in the creation of a symbolically unified set of scenes. What gives the report its novelistic quality is the invisible camera eye of the narrator which can record all of the objective details of the scene, then move in and out of the characters' experiences. The reporter's own experiences, the inevitable "jump cuts" of the reporting process, are either deleted or used as "cutaways" to unify the narrative.

Although the problem of mediating between the experience of the subject and the reader poses epistemological dilemmas, these problems are transformed into technical issues of communication. Wolfe (1973), for instance, justifies dealing with communication as a technical matter through what he terms "the physiology of realism." Print is an indirect medium that does not image what it represents. It operates by association, calling forth from the reader's experience typifications that provide a context of meaning for the story. "The most gifted writers are those who manipulate the memory sets of the reader in such a rich fashion that they create within the mind of the reader an entire world that resonates with the reader's own emotions" (p. 48). Although Wolfe's model of the reader making sense of a story is potentially that of the reporter "reading" signs to make sense of events, ethnographic realists rarely deal with their own acts of interpretation. Instead, they fall back on naturalistic arguments about the report as a valid, realistic statement. The ethnographic reporter's ability to keep the reportorial experience within his or her own typifications blunts analysis of the act of interpretation. As long as experience fits cultural categories, it exists as a taken-for-granted objectivity, "the way things are."

The aesthetic of cultural phenomenology arises out of an inability to state "the way things are." It is an aesthetic grounded in the inability of cultural typifications to order the reportorial experience. Unable, in Didion's words (1979, p. 11), "to impose the narrative line on disparate images," the phenomenological mode chronicles the interaction between consciousness and events. The story that is told is not one discovered out there in the world but the story of the writer's efforts to impose order on those events.

Although stories are told and not lived, "thinking as usual" transforms a way of communicating into a taken-for-granted reality. The narrative line is believed to exist in the events, not in the story. When experience fails to fit the typification, making conscious the relativity of the narrative line, a crisis occurs. As Schutz (1964, p 96) states, "The cultural pattern no longer functions as a system of tested recipes at hand, it reveals that its applicability is restricted to a specific historical situation." Didion (1979, p. 13) makes explicit the crisis that provides the ground for the phenomenological form in *The White Album*. "I was meant to know the plot but all I knew was what I saw: flash pictures in variable sequence, images with no 'meaning' beyond their temporary arrangement, not a movie but a cutting room experience. In what would probably be the middle of my life I wanted still to believe in the narrative's intelligibility, but to know that one could change the sense with every cut was to begin to perceive the experience as rather more electrical than ethical."

The most complex treatment of "coming to terms with disorder" and "the imposition of the narrative line on disparate images" is Mailer's *TheArmies of the Night* (1968). The report focuses on an anti-war march on the Pentagon in 1967, but its more abstract subject is communication and meaning in a mass-mediated society. Mailer discusses the relationship of images to realities, living to observing, and stories to experience in terms of the dual functions of any symbolic act. Mailer suggests that any symbolic structure is constituted in a dialectic of two functions. It is designed to fulfill a communicative function, to say something about something to someone, and an expressive function, to locate the speaker in the object world.[4] The conditions of modern society create a disjunction between the communicative and the expressive functions. The technology of mass media disengages subjects from their own expressions, separating messages from the intentions and values which motivate them. Transformed by technology, individuals become observers of their own acts, unable to find their own existential commitment in their mediated likeness while confronting an audience that treats symbolic packages as reality. As actions come to be negotiated in terms of a media aesthetic, both actor and spectator live a reality arbitrated by the assumptions of media technicians.[5]

The Armies of the Night was created against a background of mass media reports that established a conceptual framework for understanding the event.[6] The book removes the march from this taken-for-granted context and describes it as a mysterious, ambiguous event whose meaning is not readily apparent. Mailer argues that the event as reported in the mass media is paradigmatic of the routines and assumptions of the news media and instead focuses on the event in a larger cultural context as "a paradigm of the twentieth century" that occurs " in the crazy house of history." The absurdity of the event is bound up in the conditions for political action in a technological society that drives a wedge between the "symbolic" and "real" dimensions of events. Although the march is a real event that results from the commitment of individuals to stop the war in Vietnam, it is organized in terms of the way it will be seen in society. The expressive dimension of the event, reflected in the willingness of individuals to face personal injury and jail, is overwhelmed by its communicative dimension. "A protest which does not grow loses power every day, since protest movements depend upon the interest they arouse in mass media. But the mass media are interested only in processes which are expanding dramatically or collapsing" (p. 259). The need to appear to be a growing force demands a "revolutionary aesthetic," an absorption in the techniques of media production that threatens to transform protesters into actors.

Mailer is in the front ranks of the protesters because he is a celebrity, guaranteed to bring media coverage. His relationship to his own image exemplifies the transforming powers of mass media and the disjunction between the symbolic and the real that pervades modern culture. "Mailer's habit of living—no matter how unsuccessfully—with his image, was so engrained by now, that like a dutiful spouse he was forever consulting his better half" (p. 183).

The aesthetic of *The Armies of the Night* makes problematic the realm of appearances created by the mass media. Mailer substitutes for the predictable pattern of news reports a narrative strategy designed to reveal the disjunction between reported and experienced reality. The report is self-consciously punctuated with comments about narrative construction that reveal the transforming powers of all narratives. Essential to this strategy is the two-part organization of the book, "History as the Novel; The Novel as History," which emphasizes not events but the interaction of narrative forms and events. History, Mailer argues, deals with the realm of behavior. As a symbolic structure it places in the foreground the communicative function. The novel deals with the realm of the "emotional, spiritual, psychical, moral, existential, or supernatural" (p. 284), placing in the foreground the expressive dimension of the symbolic act.

Part one, "History as the Novel," deals with Mailer's experience of the march. Through an explication of his own experience Mailer removes the march from its symbolic packaging so that the reader might experience the event not as a repetition of the news formula but as an ambiguous event in need of interpretation. The strategy is novelistic because Mailer details his own experience "in the guise or dress of the novel" to show the variables which influence an interpretation of the event. Part two, "The Novel as History," which supplies the interpretation at least partially in the style of history, is "a real or true novel" (p. 184).

The two-part strategy of *The Armies of the Night* emphasizes that both social life and the report are constructions. The disjunction between the symbolic and the real in modern society, however, creates conditions where meaning cannot be deduced from behavior and appearances. The historian attempting to penetrate the realm of appearances surrounding the march can only weigh the various official versions that the event produced. These public versions, however, do not mirror the private existential realities of the march. In the face of such contradictions, the historian must become a novelist who invents the meaning of the event. Unlike the ethnographic realist who penetrates the image to find the reality of the other, Mailer argues that the image is impenetrable, that significance is privatized in the "novelistic" lives that make up the map of contemporary reality. Confronting such a dilemma, the individual cannot find the facts, but must invent an interpretation in an act of self-definition.

The mythology of a technological society, Mailer argues, is that disembodied facts communicate. *The Armies of the Night* takes as its object the demystification of this mythology. Its goal is less to convince the reader of an interpretation than to reveal the assumptions that ground interpretations. It seeks to create for the reader the disorder that interpretations transform, the experiential contradictions that usually remain outside the text. The book is an account of experience that is, in Didion's words, more electrical than ethical but from which an ethical stance must be created.

CONCLUSION

Although the two modes of New Journalism reflect different ways of responding to cultural change and of inventing the reporting project, the tendency to focus on the reports as purely formal structures has served to isolate the texts from broader considerations of modern culture. The reports, of course, can be read technically as a set of instructions on how to do in-depth reporting or how to write nonfiction. To do so without examining the problems that the texts investigate is to segregate journalism from its cultural context. The journalistic report, however, is a creature of modernization. It had its origins in the experience of modernity and it continues to reflect, in its various forms, transformations of that experience.

The two modes of New Journalism, considered most broadly, reflect two ways of responding to the experience of modernity in the late twentieth century. In "The Man on the Train" Percy (1975) captures the essence of the two positions in a comparison of the responses of two commuters to their placement on the train as being in the world they are traveling through and not in it in the sense of being there. "I mean that whereas one commuter may sit on the train and feel himself quite at home, seeing the passing scene as a series of meaningful projects full of signs he reads without difficulty, another commuter . . . is horrified at his surroundings—he might as well be passing through a lunar landscape and the signs he sees are absurd or at least ambiguous" (pp. 83–84). Percy concludes that "What causes anxiety in the one is the refuge from anxiety in the other" (p. 84).

For the ethnographic realist, the diversity of contemporary society is interesting but not threatening, "projects full of signs he reads without difficulty." Underlying the disparate images of culture are the same patterns which appear again and again in history. Social actors may wear a variety of masks but the spectators, the reporter and the reader, can still distinguish the artificial from the real. The relativity of human actions which motivates the reports poses no threats to traditional ways of comprehending and expressing reality. For the cultural phenomenologist contemporary reality is a "lunar landscape" where all that was fixed has become flux. The reporter has no privileged position, in Mailer's words, no tower to look down upon human actions. The changes that the reports chronicle are not merely changes occurring out there in the world and in the consciousness of the other, they are pervasive in society. The experience of these changes, however, is dulled by stories that transform the ambiguity of the new into a traditional narrative order. Cultural phenomenology seeks to transform what is taken for granted in writing and reading a report into an object of analysis. Reporter and reader are themselves implicated in the social changes. The transformation of the symbolic packaging creates for the reader an ambiguous situation as the relations among events, conventions and consciousness are pushed to the foreground. Meaning, the texts argue, is not something that exists out there independent of human consciousness, but something that is created and recreated in acts of interpretation and expression.

The New Journalism appears during a time when media scholars, utilizing the theoretical paradigms of ethnomethodology and phenomenology, are reflecting a heightened awareness of the relationship of reports to the construction of reality.[7] The phenomenological mode reflects an absorption in many of the same problems raised in this research focus. Moreover, the phenomenological mode confronts, in its most sophisticated forms, the central problem that troubles some of the media researchers, namely, the relativity of all frames of reference for understanding events in the social world.

To reduce the explicit treatment of these epistemological and ethical dilemmas to a matter of literary style is to blunt the mode's most essential theme: in a society organized around the production and consumption of images and reports which attempt to negate the distance between information and its referent, the individual must choose an interpretation, as Kierkegaard said in another context, "in fear and trembling." Barthes (1972) argues in *Mythologies* that, "The fact that we cannot manage to achieve more than an unstable grasp of reality doubtless gives the measure of our present alienation: we constantly drift between the object and its demystification, powerless to render its wholeness. For if we penetrate the object, we liberate it but we destroy it; and if we achnowledge its full weight, we respect it, but we restore it to a state which is still mystified. It would seem that we are condemned for some time yet always to speak *excessively* about reality" (p. 159). The phenomenological form of New Journalism is a mode of excessive speech that finds its home in the space between realism and relativism. It is a form of expression for a culture organized around the proliferation of realistic reports that simultaneously experiences the loss of standards for realism. That such a feeling is not pervasive is indicated by the ethnographic mode. The phenomenological mode, however, attests to just how fragile notions of realism are in a self-conscious culture, and to the impossibility, for many, of ceasing to speak excessively about reality. □

NOTES

[1]Notable exceptions are Lanigan (1983), Webb (1974), and Zavarzadeh (1976).

[2]See also Wolfe (1979) which distinguishes sharply between the image and reality of the astronauts.

[3]See Sontag (1978) on the epistemology and ethics of observing.

[4]For a discussion of the communicative and expressive dimensions of symbolic acts, see Gusdorf (1965).

[5]See Gitlin (1980) for another approach to this situation.

[6]See also Mailer (1968b, 1970). *The Executioner's Song* (1979) raises ethical dilemmas common to the ethnographic realist mode.

[7]The literature is extensive but see especially Tuchman (1978) and Schudson (1978).

REFERENCES

Barthes, R. (1972). *Mythologies* (A. Lavers, Trans.). New York: Hill and Wang.

Bellamy, J. D. (1974). *The new fiction: Interviews with innovative American writers.* Urbana: University of Illinois Press.

Berger, P. & Luckmann, T. (1967). *The social construction of reality.* Garden City: Anchor.

Boorstin, D. J. (1961). *The image.* New York: Harper & Row.

Capote, T. (1965). *In cold blood.* New York: Random House.

Darnton, R. (1975). Writing news and telling stories. *Daedalus 104,* 175–194.

Debord, G. (1970). *Society of the spectacle.* Detroit: Black and Red.

Dennis, E. & Rivers, W. (1974). *Other voices: The new journalism in America.* San Francisco: Canfield.

Didion, J. (1968). *Slouching towards Bethlehem.* New York: Delta.

Didion, J. (1979). *The white album.* New York: Simon and Schuster.

Dunne, J. G. (1974). *Vegas: A memoir of a dark season.* New York: Warner.

Eason, D. L. (1981). Telling stories and making sense. *Journal of Popular Culture, 15* (1), 125–130.

Eason, D. L. (1982). New journalism, metaphor and culture. *Journal of Popular Culture, 15* (4), 142–148.

Gitlin. T. (1980). *The whole world is watching.* Berkeley: University of California Press.

Gusdorf, G. (1965). *Speaking* (P. Brockelman, Trans.). Evanston: Northwestern University Press.

Hellman, J. (1981). *Fables of fact: The new journalism as new fiction.* Urbana: University of Illinois Press.

Hersey, J. (1980). The legend of license. *Yale Review, 70* (1), 1–25.

Herr, M. (1978). *Dispatches.* New York: Alfred A. Knopf.

Hollowell, J. (1977). *Fact and fiction: The new journalism and the nonfiction novel.* Chapel Hill: University of North Carolina.

Hughes, H. M. (1940). *News and the human interest story.* Chicago: University of Chicago Press.

Johnson, M. (1971). *The new journalism.* Lawrence: University of Kansas Press.

Laing, R. D. (1967). *The politics of experience.* New York: Ballantine.

Lanigan, R. L. (1983). Merleau-ponty on metajournalism: Signs, emblems and appeals in the poetry of truth. *Communication, 7* (2), 241–261.

Mailer, N. (1968a). *The armies of the night: The novel as history; history as the novel.* New York: New American Library.

Mailer, N. (1968b). *Miami and the siege of Chicago.* New York: New American Library.

Mailer, N. (1970). *Of a fire on the moon.* Boston: Little, Brown.

Mailer, N. (1979). *The executioner's song.* Boston: Little, Brown.

McLuhan, M. (1964). *Understanding media.* New York: McGraw-Hill.

Murphy, J. E. (1974). The new journalism: A critical perspective. *Journalism Monographs, 34.*

Ortega y Gasset, J. (1948). *The dehumanization of art.* Princeton: Princeton University Press.

Percy, W. (1975). The man on the train. In *The message in the bottle* (pp. 83–100). New York: Farrar, Straus & Giroux.

Schudson, M. (1978). *Discovering the news.* New York: Basic.

Schutz, A. (1964). The stranger. In M. Natanson (Ed.), *Collected Papers, Vol. 2* (pp. 91–105). The Hague: Martinus Nijhoff.

Sheehy, G. (1973). *Hustling*. New York: Dell.

Sontag, S. (1978). *On photography*. New York: Delta.

Talese, G. (1966). *The kingdom and the power*. New York: World.

Talese, G. (1972). *Honor thy father*. New York: Fawcett-World.

Talese, G. (1980). *Thy neighbor's wife*. New York: Doubleday.

Thompson, H. S. (1971). *Fear and loathing in Las Vegas: A savage jouney to the heart of the American dream*. New York: Popular Library.

Thompson, H. S. (1973). *Fear and loathing on the campaign trail*. San Francisco: Straight Arrow.

Thompson, H. S. (1979). *The great shark hunt*. New York: Fawcett.

Tuchman, G. (1978). *Making news*. New York: Free Press.

Webb, J. M. (1974). Historical perspective on the new journalism. *Journalism History*, 1 (1), 38–42.

Weber, R. (Ed.). (1974). *The reporter as artist: A look at the new journalism controversy*. New York: Hastings House.

Weber, R. (1980). *The literature of fact*. Athens: Ohio University.

Widker, T. (1975). *A time to die*. New York: Quadrangle.

Wolfe, T. (1965). *The kandy-kolored tangerine-flake streamline baby*. New York: Farrar, Straus & Giroux.

Wolfe, T. (1968a). *The electric kool-aid acid test*. New York: Bantam.

Wolfe, T. (1968b). *The pump house gang*. New York: Farrar, Straus & Giroux.

Wolfe, T. (1970). *Radical chic and mau-mauing the flak catchers*. New York: Farrar, Straus & Giroux.

Wolfe, T. (1973). *The new journalism*. New York: Harper & Row.

Wolfe, T. (1979). *The right stuff*. New York: Farrar, Straus & Giroux.

Zavarzadeh, M. (1976). *The mythopoetic reality: The postwar American nonfiction novel*. Urbana: University of Illinois.

18

INTERPRETIVE COMMUNITIES AND VARIABLE LITERACIES
The Functions of Romance Reading

Janice Radway

ONE OF THE MOST ENGAGING VOLUMES yet published on the subject of reading is the marvelous collection of photographs by André Kertész titled simply, *On Reading.*[1] Presented without commentary, this series of images of readers absorbed in apparently diverse materials, in both expected and unexpected contexts, is eloquent in its insistence that books and reading serve myriad purposes and functions for a wide variety of individuals. For that reason alone, this simple photographic essay provides an implicit but nonetheless profound commentary on some entrenched and familiar assumptions about literacy.

By grouping together readers as different as the well-dressed man perched on a library ladder in a book-lined study and the ragged young boy sprawled across a pile of discarded newspapers in the street, Kertész is able to suggest that whatever the differences and merits of the materials they peruse, all are engaged in some form of the engrossing behavior through which print is transformed into a world.[2] The very inclusiveness of the series equalizes readers and reading processes that would, in other contexts, be ranked hierarchically on an imaginary literacy scale. On that scale, the grade of

Writing of this paper was supported by a commission from the Annenberg Scholars Program, Annenberg School of Communications, University of Southern California, and delivered at the Scholars Conference, "Creating Meaning: Literacies of Our Time," February 1984.

Reprinted by permission of *Daedalus*, Journal of the American Academy of Arts and Sciences, "Anticipations," Vol. 113, No. 3 (Summer 1984), Cambridge, MA.

"truly literate" would be reserved for those educated individuals who were not only capable of reading texts that the culture deems "literature," but who also regularly choose to read such texts for utilitarian purposes, however broadly conceived. As Raymond Williams has observed, literature and literacy within this sort of system would be inextricably linked with the bourgeois ideology of taste and its concomitant construction of the "literary tradition."[3]

Kertész's book is useful, therefore, precisely because its resolutely democratic presentation of reading refuses to make the usual distinctions through which the truly literate are distinguished from the merely functionally literate or illiterate, and "literature" is segregated from all that is subliterature, paraliterature, or simple entertainment. Although his photographs are all in some sense "about" reading, what they demonstrate is the astonishing variety of circumstances within which reading occurs. Because they function at least partially as signifiers of "context" and difference, the photographs direct our attention to the question of whether such contexts are mere "settings" within which a single unitary process is carried on, or whether they are more significant situations that actively affect the character of that process and thus differentially transform the valence of the act. Kertész's photographs seem to suggest that we must give up our search for the essence and effects of literacy as a single process and look instead at the varied kinds of literate behaviors that people really engage in. The photographs, I would argue, pose the question of *how* each of these unique readers is literate in a particular time and place.

In effect, I am suggesting that Kertész's book echoes John Szwed's call for ethnographic studies of different kinds of literate behavior.[4] Like Kertész, Szwed foregrounds context and argues that in place of the usual theoretical accounts of the unavoidable psychological consequences of acquiring print literacy, we must have more specific studies of what people do with printed texts. I would repeat Szwed's call and suggest, additionally, that such ethnographies can be made more effective investigative tools for the study of literacy if they are grounded upon some recent theoretical arguments in reader-response criticism. Although reader criticism has been developed to explain the interpretation of literary texts, it has implications for the way we think about how people operate upon and use all sorts of printed matter.[5]

The reader and the reading process have come to occupy a central place in literary criticism in recent years, but investigators of these phenomena share no unified theoretical position. Indeed, reception theory or reader-response criticism includes approaches as diverse as the *rezeptionästhetik* of the Constance school, the structuralism of Roland Barthes, the semiotics of Umberto Eco and Jonathan Culler, the "interactionist" work of Louise Rosenblatt and Stanley Fish, and the subjectivist arguments of David Bleich and Norman Holland. Most of these reader theories were developed in response to the textual formalism associated with New Criticism and its caveat against the "affective fallacy." As participants in a widespread conceptual shift in the intellectual community from positivist positions to contextual or interpretive schemas, the various reader theorists sought to challenge the New Critical insistence on the absolute autonomy of the text. Troubled by the complete exclusion of the reader from accounts of the interpretive process, these theorists sought ways to reassert the essential dependency of meaning upon the interaction between the reader and the text.[6]

Yet, despite their preoccupation with the activities of readers, the theorists show a lingering tendency to grant primacy and ultimate power to the text itself. Although willing to acknowledge the reader's contribution to the process of producing a reading of a text, theorists like Roman Ingarden and Wolfgang Iser eventually claim priority for the text because they believe it inevitably directs, governs, controls, indeed, determines the reader's response to it.[7] To name their theories "reception theories" and their method "reader-response criticism" is entirely accurate, since they continue to posit a confrontation between two distinct and quite different entities, the reader and the text. The reader receives the text and responds to it in such a manner that the meaning—what its author desired to communicate and embodied within its textual structures—is, in Iser's words, "concretized" by the reader. Theories like Iser's are variations of the simple transmission-reception model of communication, whereby a sender's message is transmitted to a receiver via the medium of the printed text.

In continuing to accord primacy to texts, the theories remain compatible with the determinism inherent in many traditional conceptions of literacy and, accordingly, in the understanding of reading they imply. Previous theories of literacy have assumed that the character of print itself determines what can be done with it, and thus what it means to be literate. These more recent reading theories also argue implicitly that reading is a singular, skilled process, which many readers only partially master and some texts do not fully require. Thus their adherents can continue to accept the division of texts into the complex, or "great," and the simple, or subliterary, as well as the distinction between readers who are fully literate and those who are not. Despite their apparent interest in readers and reading activities, such theories continue to support the notion that all readers are alike and all reading really one, simply because they assume that the technology of print and the character of individual texts together determine the activities they initiate.

There are other reading theories, however, that call for a rethinking of the concept of literacy, precisely because they maintain it is the reader who controls the reading process, not the text. Although these theories are often lumped together with other reader-oriented criticisms as "reception theory" or "response criticism," they should not be so labeled. In fact, such versions of reader theory conceive of reading as "production" or "construction," as opposed to reception or even simple consumption. The individuals who have elaborated these theories do not belong to a single school, nor do they adhere to the same theoretical approach. Yet all hold that reading is a productive activity in which a reader actively *makes* sense of the verbal inscriptions on the page. The most important theorists in this branch of reader theory are Umberto Eco, Stanley Fish, Louise Rosenblatt, and Jonathan Culler.[8] The four vary in the degree to which they employ the jargon now associated with semiotic theory, but each has nonetheless elaborated a model of the text-reader interaction that can be called semiotic.

All, that is, conceive of textual meaning as the product of a complex transaction between an inert textual structure, composed of verbal signifiers, and an actively productive reader, who constructs those signifiers as meaningful signs on the basis of previously learned interpretive procedures and cultural codes. Although the reader often attempts to construe the text by referring to the codes and strategies she believes the author intended her to use, nothing in the text constrains her to do so, nor, if she does, is she necessarily successful. As Eco has observed, "The multiplicity of codes, contexts, and circumstances shows us that the same message can be decoded from different points of view and by reference to diverse systems of conventions."[9] Interpretation and textual meaning, then, are as dependent on who the reader is, on how she understands the process of reading, and on the cultural context within which she operates, as they are on the text's verbal structure itself.

Print is not determinant in such a view, nor is reading a simple mechanical matter of processing what is on the page. Rather, print functions as a kind of material with which and upon which readers operate in order to produce meaning. Reading, then, is a complicated semiotic and fundamentally social process that varies both in place and in time. That is to say, different readers read differently because they belong to what are known as various interpretive communities, each of which acts upon print differently and for different purposes.

The concept of the interpretive community, of course, has been discussed most recently by Stanley Fish.[10] Fish defines the notion rather narrowly, however, because he is interested only in different forms of academic literary criticism. For him, an interpretive community is a loosely connected group of literary scholars who share basic assumptions about the nature of literature, about the goals of literary criticism, and about the nature of the interpretive process. Different interpretive communities, therefore, at least as Fish discusses them, are composed of readers who may disagree about how to construct a literary interpretation, but who are nonetheless equally and similarly literate because all can produce coherent readings of difficult texts.

In spite of Fish's own lack of interest in other than professional readers, his concept of the interpretive community can be fruitfully rethought to apply more generally to readers outside the literary academy to help us understand why some readers prefer Westerns to the classics, detective stories to poetry, or the *Enquirer* to Shakespeare. Interpretive communities may not simply differ over what to do with metaphors and tropes; they may disagree even more fundamentally over the nature and purpose of reading itself. Different interpretive communities may actually be differently literate. We need to know, therefore, what exactly divides the vast community of individuals who buy and read books—in short, how book or print-related behaviors vary according to place and over time.

To call for such a project, however, is to confront obvious methodological problems almost at once. Because we do not know what an interpretive community actually is, we cannot identify one in order to study the ways in which its members are literate. Are such communities formally constituted groups to which individual members *know* they belong? Or are they much larger collections of people who, by virtue of a common social position and demographic character, unconsciously share certain assumptions about reading as well as preferences for reading material? Assuming that the latter is true, it is not at all obvious how we could ferret out the existence of such a group without first sharpening our understanding of how more formalized interpretive communities operate. If we can detect exactly what it is the readers in a formally recognized group share, and how this common fund of knowledge affects what they "do" with printed texts, we may be able to ask certain questions of apparently unconnected individuals that will also reveal the particular ways in which they behave with printed texts and, therefore, how they are literate.

A logical way to start such a project would be to make use of the publishing industry's own understanding of the book-buying public. The industry recognizes that certain readers are particularly interested in a specific "category" of books, and it therefore identifies mass-produced texts as belonging to one or another, usually by cover iconography. This has proved to be a reliable technique because there is indeed a portion of the book-buying community that reads only one kind of text. Time after time, such "category" readers, as they are known in the trade, will choose books from only this category. Many students of mass-produced literature, furthermore, assume that such readers choose their category because essential features of their social life create needs and demands that are somehow addressed and fulfilled by these books.[11] If this is true, an investigation of their preferences for, and interaction with, books of a particular category may in fact amount to an investigation of the place and function of literacy in their lives.

In this paper, I shall detail my attempt at just such a study, but must point out first that the group I investigated was even more formalized than the loose conglomerate who read a particular category—in this case, the romance.[12] It was necessary to begin with a small group of romance readers, one clustered about a bookstore clerk in "Smithton," because not enough information about this audience is available from publishers to construct a representative sample of romance readers as a whole. Thus my findings about the nature of romance reading are based on a self-selected group of women united by their reliance on a single individual who advises them about "good" and "bad" romances. Since all of the women in the group have been consulting Dorothy Evans, the bookstore clerk, for several years, I was not surprised to learn that as readers they are united by common purposes, preferences, and interpretive procedures. I also found that these aspects of their reading behavior seem to be a function of certain common social factors of their lives, a point I shall return to.

I must add, however, that my interpretive community of romance readers may not extend beyond the area served by this particular bookstore. These women, in fact, may not be part of a larger, genre-based interpretive community. We will know that only when we can test my findings against those of a much larger study, one that attempts to survey the behavior of *all* women who think of themselves as romance readers. While all may read romances, they may do so differently or for different purposes. They may indeed be category readers, but they may not constitute an interpretive community in the sense that they all select, use, and operate on printed texts in certain socially specific ways.

In turning now to the Smithton women and to their characteristic reading behavior, it seems important to describe first exactly how information was elicited about what they "did" with texts. Because I was interested in the women's own self-perceptions and understanding of romances and romance reading, I relied on ethnographic interviewing techniques to map the "world" of the romance reader. I interviewed sixteen women in two groups about all aspects of their leisure activity, and then talked more extensively with five, including Evans. Because I was well aware of the romance reader's wariness about the general public's scorn for her activity, I hoped the group situation would reassure each enough to answer my questions honestly. I was also aware, however, that the group situation might lead to a greater uniformity in response than actually existed, because of the influence of a single reader. I therefore also administered an anonymous questionnaire to the sixteen women as well as to twenty-six others. Since I found little discrepancy between my informants' oral and written responses and between the responses of the sixteen and others of Evans's customers, I concluded that the material elicited in the oral interviews was a reasonably accurate account of what the women thought they were up to.

My first task was to determine exactly how the members of the group made the necessary discriminations in order to select the texts they wanted. Because they are category readers, what was at issue was their definition of the category or genre and how they identified individual texts as examples of it. I sought such a definition through a variety of related questions to see whether their conscious understanding of the genre coincided with the definition they actually relied on in selecting reading matter.

What I found was that a definition of the genre was implicit in the way they used cover blurbs and illustrations, in their reliance on previous readings of certain authors, and in their use of Evans's recommendations to select their texts. Indeed, all of these activities seemed to be governed by their sense that "romance" had something to do with the manner and tone of presentation of a love relationship. Once I had determined the rudimentary content of the genre, I asked them to provide a "definition" of it to see whether their genre theory actually coincided with how they used individual instances of the category. What they told me was interesting, both because it tended to confirm their implicitly reported requirements and proved to be at once formalist and functional.

Their definition—"a man and a woman meeting, the problems they encounter, whether the relationship will gel or not"—not only identified the fundamental characters and events in the story, but also specified the evolution of the action and, implicitly, the nature of the response (tension or anxiety) it ought to evoke in the reader. By beginning with the definition, I was led to mark off two areas for further study. First, I pursued the issue of the plot structure itself by attempting to determine exactly how the women processed textual inscriptions to arrive at that particular abstract structure. I was trying, essentially, to describe their manner of textual production, to discover what they did with the text to produce their characteristic interpretation. At the same time, I attempted to explore the nature of their reaction to the plot structure, and thus got involved with questions of how the text made them feel and how it functioned in their daily lives. Here, I was investigating the readers' use of the activity of reading, asking what they accomplished *by* or *in* the process of reading these books. Before I pursue this aspect of their reading behavior, I would like to return briefly to the interpretive process itself and explore some of the problems encountered in trying to determine how people in real life arrive at a given reading of a particular book, and some of the possibilities as well.

It is somewhat difficult to shed light on the interpretive process simply because so much of it occurs automatically and unconsciously. While most readers can easily summarize a book or recount its plot, we have no sure way of knowing exactly what interpretive operations come into play in the redaction of a 200- or 300-page text. After hearing a plot summary, the investigator might read the text, noting both what the reader has designated as significant in her account and what she has ignored. These observations can then be used to infer the selection criteria that prompted the reader to identify the relevant textual features from which she constructed her final reading.[13] Those selection criteria themselves then point to what the romantic story is "about," at least for the individual summarizing the plot.

In the case of the romance readers, every plot summary ignored the fact that the hero and heroine were contrasted with foil figures with whom they were sometimes entangled. Their refusal to acknowledge these contrasts as essential to the plot suggested that the women's interest in the romance came not from any interest in sexual competition, same sex friendships, or contrasts, but from a deep-seated need to see an ideal relationship worked out between a man and a woman. Their responses to questions about the qualities of good and bad romances seemed to validate this inference. An ideal romance focused on "one woman-one man," while a poor example of the genre often involved the hero and heroine with too many other secondary characters. Their sense that the romance should be "about" a single relationship governed their selective perception of the significant features and events in each tale. This fundamental desire was ultimately responsible for the particular story they constructed.

With the women's essential evaluative criteria thus established, I then questioned them about their understanding or interpretation of the story they had constructed from each text's myriad details and events. Although this led to further observations about how the women treated language, particularly declarative statements, it went beyond simple textual operations and their conscious understanding of the story to the covert consequences of those operations and the tacit significance of that understanding. It was surprising to discover that the women saw these tales of "a man and a woman meeting" as stories about a woman's triumph, surprising, because so many feminist literary critics of the genre have argued that romances are about helpless, passive, weak women who relinquish their sense of self in the arms of the more important man.[14] I was tempted to attribute the interpretive difference to varying standards of judgment about female behavior, but certain of the women's statements about the authors' attitudes toward their heroines caused me to think twice about formulating such a conclusion.

Several of the women had observed repeatedly that their favorite writers always wrote about intelligent and independent heroines, so I decided to check this against the texts. If one focused only on verbal assertion, this was indeed the case. The authors always declared at the outset that their heroines were unusual, special, bright, and self-reliant, but later portrayed them as victims of circumstance. Apparently, the Smithton readers do not see this as contradictory because they do not use subsequent narrative action to revise a character portrait established by description at the beginning. Feminist literary critics, of course, applying what Jonathan Culler has described as a rule of unity, *do* try to produce a unified characterization that takes all of these details into account.[15] In their literary universe, character behavior is meant to comment on and alter preliminary portraiture[16]—hence, their final and quite different account of the romantic heroine as only a superficially independent woman, who is, in reality, deeply dependent and incapable of action herself. The argument for the accuracy of their interpretation is that as feminist critics, they are formally trained and thus fully literate. Romance readers, on the other hand, are neither well-educated nor fully conscious of what they do, and therefore simply don't know what the story *really* means. And because these women are somehow incompletely literate, they don't know how to interpret characters correctly. Nonetheless, the romantic text manages to exert its conservative power over them and thus functions to reinforce the patriarchal status quo.

I would like to suggest, however, that there is another equally plausible explanation of this difference in interpretations. The romance reader's failure to unify action and description may, in fact, be a function of a particular "philosophy" of language that effectively precludes such an operation. Their portrait of the heroine, in such a view, is not a result of their ignorance or lack of self-awareness, but a product of a particular attitude toward language. The women believe that words have meanings that are fixed and definite. Because those meanings are essentially contained *in* words, the women also believe that people choose words to say what they mean. Words are always already meaningful and can be selected for what they accurately say about a character or event. The Smithton readers assume that romance authors choose their words very carefully because they intend those words to describe correctly the characters in question. As a result, they do not judge verbal assertion by comparing it with the character's actions. If the writer says that her heroine is intelligent and independent, nothing she does or does not do later can alter her basic character. Consequently, the women believe that they are reading a story about an extraordinary woman who is overcome by unforeseen circumstances, but who nevertheless manages to teach the hero how to care for her and to appreciate her as she wishes to be appreciated. Because he always learns the lesson she has to teach and proposes a permanent commitment, the women can interpret this as the triumph of her values. Their interpretation follows logically from their textual operations, which are themselves dictated by a prior understanding of words and language. It seems to me that what we have here is not a form of partial literacy, but a different form of literacy altogether, founded on its own conception of the word and what can be done with it.

Another consequence of this attitude toward language surfaced again in a discussion about the women's reasons for reading romantic fiction. Although they agreed overwhelmingly that they read principally for enjoyment and to escape their daily problems, the Smithton women also maintained that they read romances to learn—not, as one might expect, about how to conduct a relationship but, rather, because they acquired factual information about geography, culture, and history from these books. This is so because they operate under two assumptions.

To begin with, they firmly believe that all romance authors research the historical and physical backgrounds of their stories. In fact, this is true. One has only to read the prefaces to romantic fiction to detect how important it is to the author to portray accurately both the physical setting of the story and the period in which it takes place. Indeed, romance writers constantly thank librarians and archivists for their assistance, and for those authors who travel to the foreign locales that form the backgrounds to their stories, there is gratitude to their guides as well.[17] Second, romance readers assume that when an author makes a factual statement about the background, she does so because it is "true." They therefore mark that statement as "information" and commit it to memory as "knowledge." Their *attitude* toward language, then, rather than the text alone, is responsible for one of their most important claims about the worth and function of romance reading. Although the books are works of fiction, the women use them as primers about the world. The romance for them is a kind of encyclopedia, and reading, a process of education.[18]

Romance readers are perhaps not alone in treating novels as compendia about the world. A good deal of popular fiction places important emphasis on setting and background. The readers of Irving Wallace and Arthur Hailey, for instance, believe they authentically experience the worlds of Hollywood, big city hotels, Hawaiian history, and Israeli culture because of the extensive research these authors conduct for their books. Louis L'Amour, perhaps the most popular writer of Westerns, is also well known as a careful student of the history of the American West. If his readers, as well as those of Wallace and Hailey, treat their texts as seriously as do the Smithton romance readers, it may well be that a large portion of the American public has learned its history and geography from the popular book. They must be considered literate despite the fact that they are uninterested in that large body of material sanctioned by the culture as "literature."

But for romance readers, we need to go beyond this level of analysis. Although romances clearly both provide an education and reassure their readers about the triumphant superiority of women and their values, it is likely that when the texts provide the opportunity for the women to realize these benefits through particular kinds of interpretive operations, those operations carry other tacit consequences and effects that the women are not aware of. This is the most difficult interpretive move in any reader study, since it is not at all clear either what constitutes evidence for an effect or how one validates an intuition that a reader benefits in ways other than those she can attest to explicitly. However, because reading and comprehension are surely not entirely conscious activities, it seems advisable to attempt to infer possible meanings to the reader and the effects of interpretive operations that she carries out but which she may not fully apprehend.

As an example, let me cite something I inferred from my observations about how the Smithton women treated the language of romantic texts. In exploring their methods for formulating character portraits and for processing "factual" material, I noticed that one of the reasons they operate on the texts as they do is a function of the fact that the authors had selected a vocabulary and syntax readily familiar to a middle-class housewife and mother with a year or two of college education. I inferred that this simple and resolutely familiar language use actually permits the women to rely heavily on their memory of previously learned cultural codes. When they encounter such a linguistic structure, they simply supply the most common referents for the words and phrases in question and thus actually construct a fictional duplicate of the world they are familiar with. Although the process of construction appears to the women as automatic and natural comprehension—as learning, in fact—it is actually a form of production that has the ultimate effect of naturalizing and therefore ratifying the world in which the women ordinarily live. Reading is a highly reassurring process, because it prompts them to use their most familiar methods for apprehending the world, and rewards them by enabling them to "find" only what they would have expected. Romance reading, it appears, allows a woman to believe she is learning and changing herself at the very same time it is reassuring her that she already knows how to make sense of an existence which always is as she expects, even in fiction.

Assessing the ultimate impact of these contradictory effects of the romance reader's interpretive activity is as difficult a task as trying to validate the fact that the covert consequences one detects or infers are actually experienced by the reader. One might argue that in learning more and more about her world, the romance reader comes to value herself and her abilities more, and thus feels powerful enough to seek change. Yet it is equally possible that the conservative nature of the interpretive process actually reassures her that nothing need be changed at all, precisely because the world *is* readable and hence fully meaningful. Corroboration of either effect can be sought in the reader's daily activities, but even then it would be virtually impossible to state positively that the interpretive activities performed in reading romantic novels resulted in changed behavior.

This is the point at which the analyst of reading becomes aware of the limits of the ethnographic method, an awareness that is quite like the anthropologist's recognition of how difficult it is to pierce the veil of cultural behavior to fathom its meaning and its fundamental roots in ideology. Even though reading can be investigated empirically, and the readers' own interpretations of texts taken into account, analytic interpretation cannot be done away with entirely. As Clifford Geertz reminded ethnographic anthropologists, "What we call our data are really our own constructions of other people's constructions of what they and their compatriots are up to. Cultural analysis," he concludes, "is . . . guessing at meanings, assessing the guesses, and drawing explanatory conclusions from the better guesses."[19] My account of what romance readers do to a text in the process of constructing an interpretation is just such a guess; but I think it is a better guess than it would have been if I had merely inferred the existence of such behavior on the basis of my own reading of the texts, a reading that none of the Smithton readers would have recognized as an interpretation of the books she knows so well.

Not only, however, do the Smithton women have an elaborate theory about the meaning and the significance of the romance as a literary form, but they can articulate to themselves a coherent explanation of the meaning of the act of reading itself as well. It is true, of course, that all acts of reading involve particular texts, and thus the overall significance of each complex act is intimately bound up with the meaning of the text and its implication in the reader's social and ideological life. Still, because the act of picking up a book is a form of social behavior that permits the reader to suspend momentarily all connections with the outside world, I think it is essential to make a distinction between book reading itself and the text constructed as a consequence of it.[20] Beyond knowing what the romantic story means to the Smithton reader, one wants to know also how she uses the activity of burying herself in the pages of a book. To ask this question is, in effect, to ask what she understands herself to be doing in reading, as well as to ask what she believes she conveys to others by reading.

The importance of these questions was made clear to me by the women themselves. Early in my initial interview with Evans, for example, I asked her what romantic novels "do" better than other novels available today. In posing the question, I expected her to concern herself with plots and ideas, that is, with the meaning and value of the romantic story. But she misconstrued my use of "do" and thought I had asked about the effects the reading of such novels has upon the reader. She talked at great length about the benefits these books provide the traditional wife and mother. The typical woman, she said, has many, many caretaking duties that are part of those intertwined roles, but her labors are inadequately appreciated by her family. Because individual family members do not sufficiently recognize her efforts nor compensate her for them by "taking care" of her, Evans believes such a woman must find a legitimate way of releasing her from her duties temporarily and of replenishing the energy that is constantly being drained in performing them. Romance reading, she explained, is the perfect solution. I think it would be worthwhile to quote Evans herself here, precisely because her remarks indicate so tellingly how conscious she is of reading as an activity that is an integral part of the readers' daily existence.

As a mother, I have run 'em to the orthodontist. I have run 'em to the swimming pool. I have run 'em to baton twirling lessons. I have run up to school because they forgot their lunch. You know, I mean, really! And you do it. And it isn't that you begrudge it. That isn't it. Then my husband would walk in the door and he'd say, "Well, what did you do today?" You know, it was like, "Well, tell me how you spent the last eight hours, because I've been out working." And I finally got to the point where I would say, "Well, I read four books, and I did all the wash and got the meal on the table and the beds are all made, and the house is tidy." And I would get defensive like, "So what do you call all this? Why should I have to tell you because I certainly don't ask you what you did for eight hours, step by step."—But their husbands *do* do that. We've compared notes. They hit the house and it's like "Well all right, I've been out earning a living. Now what have you been doin' with your time?" And you begin to be feeling, "Now really, why is he questioning me?"

Evans maintains, in effect, that romance reading is a "declaration of independence" for her and her customers. She believes that in picking up a book, each is effectively erecting a barrier between herself and the arena of her regular family ministrations. Because husband and children are told, "This is my time, my space, now leave me alone," they are expected to respect the signal of the book and to avoid interrupting her. Book reading allows the woman to free herself from her duties and responsibilities and provides a "space" or "time" within which she can attend to her own interests and needs.

It is here that the demographic character of this particular group of readers is relevant. For the most part, the Smithton women are married, middle-class mothers of children other than infants. More than 60 percent were between twenty-five and forty-four at the time of the study, and 70 percent had children younger than eighteen. Although 42 percent work outside the home, they nevertheless felt that family care was primarily their responsibility. In discussion after discussion, they referred to the unrelenting family demands made upon them and to the "tensions" these produced. Then, with a combination of defensiveness and belligerence, the women asserted repeatedly that the very difficulty of their double work burden earned them the right to do something pleasurable for themselves alone.

In assessing the correlation between the social character of the lives of these women and their understanding of the value of romance reading, it seems clear that what the women are doing is allowing themselves to abandon temporarily the self-abnegation that had been engrained in them all their lives as the proper attitude for a wife and mother. Within the context of their lives, romance reading appeared to be both an assertion of a deeply felt psychological need and a means for satisfying that need. Although the women themselves accept their need for respite and replenishment and for self-involvement as part of a role they willingly adopt, that they feel their romance reading is not simply pleasurable but necessary testifies to the enduring force of that need. Several of the women equated their reading to a form of addiction, and most were quite comfortable with a view of themselves as dependent on romances. Something specific and integral to their situation as wives and mothers apparently is the ultimate source of the romance's significance to them and, consequently, of their preference for the category.

It was at this point that I moved beyond the women's own construction of their behavior to look for a structural explanation of the social facts of their existence that led not only to the behavior itself but to their construction of it as well. Here, I was helped by recent work on the nature of patriarchy and middle-class marriage.[21] Within the context of such work, it seemed clear that the Smithton readers' need for respite and replenishment was a function of the fact that within traditional patriarchal marriage, no one is charged with the affective and emotional reconstitution of women.[22] Indeed, as one of Evans's customers put it, "You always have to be a Mary Poppins. You can't be sad, you can't be mad, you have to keep everything bottled up inside." Even if a woman is depleted by her efforts to care for others, she is nonetheless expected to restore and sustain herself within such a family structure, precisely because other family members do not conceive of their role as being one of nurturance. The women turn to romance reading because the activity itself temporarily permits them to identify with a heroine who receives all the attention and care of an extraordinary man. In effect, when they buy a romance, they are purchasing personal space and vicarious attention.

Before exploring exactly how the stories supply the longed-for reassurance and nurturance, we might take note of the fact that the Smithton readers feel a bit guilty about the time and money spent on indulging themselves in this way. Given their willing acceptance of the traditional female role with its implicit self-denial and self-abnegation, this is quite understandable. Although the women defiantly assert that they, too, have a right to some time for themselves (they often point to the amount of time their husbands spend watching televised sports), they worry about their families' disapproval of their book expenses and their self-preoccupation. Indeed, many of the women asked somewhat rhetorically whether I agreed that they had a right to do something for themselves alone, even though as a wife and mother they were supposed to be concerned with the interests of others. Their defensiveness and uncertainty suggests that their chronic reading causes them to experience a certain amount of role conflict. They feel a need to replenish the self and to attend to emotional needs created by the role they have willingly accepted, yet are not sure that this should be done at the expense of family responsibilities or through an activity that is so obviously pleasurable.

It is here that the other "use" of romance reading becomes important, because it acts to justify the time and money spent on books and reading. The Smithton women read primarily "to escape"—literally, to deny their presence in the family context. But they also read to learn. They enjoy the travelog and documentary aspects of the romance immensely, and even categorize books on the basis of their historical and geographic settings. More important, however, they actively use the factual materials they learn through reading to demonstrate to their skeptical families that they have indeed acquired something valuable in exchange for their expenditure of time and money. This strategy cannily defines the *act* of romance reading as goal-directed work, and therefore assigns to it a higher value in the male world, which is preoccupied with labor, self-improvement, and achievement.

Although the women are well aware of the fact that they use this aspect of romance reading to convince their husbands of the activity's validity, they are unaware of the benefits they derive by construing the activity in this way. Again, I am making an interpretive leap here, but it seems to be justified, given all the women have said about the confining aspects of domestic work and our culture's propensity to disparage women. By storing factual material as "information," and by displaying it to others as their own "knowledge," the women convince themselves that they have not languished as "mere housewives" but have continued to better themselves and to demonstrate their fundamental abilities. Thus, at the same time that romance reading gives them much needed personal time and space, it also enables them to believe that they are capable individuals and that they are changing for the better. Both "uses" of romance reading, therefore, act to deny the immediate present and to propel the women elsewhere. The act of romance reading first walls off pressing demands and then demonstrates to the participants that they are making themselves better or "other" than they were.

I think it can be seen from this example why it is so helpful to distinguish between the book read by an individual and the act of reading itself carried on within a specific social context. Although it is true that the two are not actually distinct components of the individual's behavior—simply because the act of reading must involve a text, which cannot help but contribute to the meaning of the larger activity—by separating them analytically, one can then isolate the social and material situation surrounding the actual event of reading. Books are always read within a set of specific circumstances, and their final meaning and impact may well be a function of the way those circumstances constitute the reader as a social being. In thus developing an account of how the act of book reading fits within the complex set of relations and behaviors that characterize the reader's social world, we can understand better why she might select such specific reading material in the first place. An important correlation may exist, in fact, between the needs that prompt the decision to read and the character of the books that are chosen for that activity. By taking account of that possibility, one is better prepared, finally, to return to the issue of textual interpretation in an effort to understand how the reader's particular construction of a text provides certain forms of intellectual and emotional gratification. Having sketched out how a reader actually uses her literacy, one is then prepared to investigate why she does so on these particular texts.

I can best demonstrate how intricate the connections can be between the social context surrounding a reader's activity and the texts that an individual chooses to read by referring one last time to Dorothy Evans and the Smithton women. Although I cannot detail all the ways in which the texts they selected addressed the specific needs and concerns that originated with their social role and their situation in the family context, I can at least show that by reading romances, their reading activity was made even more meaningful and beneficial to them. I discovered the special significance of the romance to them when I asked whether all romances were the same. Of course they weren't, the women replied, and then showed me that they could clearly distinguish the good romances from the bad. I then began to probe more deeply into their evaluative procedures and to examine more carefully the differences between the books they actually read and those they rejected.

Their favorite books were indeed characterized by the "one woman/one man" plot they claimed to prefer, stories in which the romantic hero focused all of his attention on a heroine with whom they identified. Although the initial interaction between the pair was characterized by the usual misunderstandings and emotional distance, the hero's treatment of the heroine was decidedly less cruel and violent than it was in what they considered to be poorer versions of the genre. In fact, his mistreatment of the heroine was always mitigated by temporary softenings of his demeanor, and his ultimate attitude toward her was transformed much earlier in the tale. Ideal heroes, it seemed, were also a good deal more androgynous than their less satisfying counterparts in that they combined masculine strength and power with a more feminine sensitivity and tenderness.

In indulging themselves in a few hundred pages of the hero's response to the heroine, the Smithton women allowed themselves to exist vicariously as the center of a spectacular man's attention. Not only did their reading activity permit them to give up their actively nurturant or servicing role in the family, but it also, because of the nature of the text, enabled them to become the passive recipient of another's total and tender care. What they achieved through romance reading was twofold: a temporary release from the demands of the social role that defined them, and psychological gratification for the needs they experienced because they had adopted that role. It might be said that romance reading functioned for the women as a kind of tacit, minimal protest against the patriarchal constitution of women: it enabled them to mark off a space where they could temporarily deny the selflessness usually demanded of them, to acknowledge the validity of the desires and needs created by the demeanor they otherwise accepted as part of that constitution, and to meet those needs by acquiring vicariously the nurturance and care that was lacking in their daily lives.

Before characterizing romance reading as incipiently subversive or oppositional behavior, however, we would do well to look carefully at the second way in which the reading of romances specifically addressed the Smithton readers' social situation as women. This aspect of romance reading was revealed to me through my exploration of their assertion that the stories were those of a woman's triumph. In looking at their favorite books very carefully, in fact, I could see a way in which their assertion was true. The typical ideal romance establishes at the outset that there is a clear opposition between the male and female worlds, the former dominated by competition, the desire for wealth, and the quest for social position, the latter characterized by the value placed on love and intimate human interactions. The romantic heroine, of course, as an inhabitant of the female world, understands the value of love, while the hero does not. Preoccupied with the goals of the typical male quest, he has no time in the beginning for sensitivity and tender gestures. In the course of the story, however, he learns the value of such things because he almost loses the heroine. In a sense, he is converted by the heroine into an occupant and proponent of the female world of love and emotional commitment—hence, the Smithton readers' understanding of these stories as tales of a woman's victory.

Romance reading, then, also demonstrates to these women that the domestic world they occupy is eminently valuable. They are told, in fact, that it is the way to true happiness, just as they are shown that it has the evangelical power to convert doubters to its purpose. The romance thus assures its readers that the world they have chosen already, or will likely choose in the future, is the world they ought to occupy. We might logically conclude, therefore, that one consequence of romance reading might be a reinforcement of the patriarchal constitution of women. Despite the fact that it enables women to resist some of that constitution's most difficult demands, romance reading might ultimately conserve patriarchy, because it reassures women that the sphere they occupy is right and fulfilling, and that all of their needs can be met within it. If so, this aspect of romance reading would contradict its existence as incipient opposition, and might override any positive force it could exert upon women to develop more effective ways of coping with their needs for nurturance and attentive care.

Unfortunately, assessment of the relative power of these two aspects of this highly complex form of behavior is nearly impossible without long-range, extensive observation of the women's actual behavior in the family. And should such a study be undertaken, it would still be extremely difficult to isolate and identify the causes of specific behavioral changes. Greater assertiveness on the part of the women might have nothing to do with the positive effects of romance reading, but might be the result of changes in the culture at large. In addition, continued acceptance of the traditional female role might in fact be the result of persistent economic dependence rather than the conservative impact of romance reading. Here again, we run up against the limitations of the ethnographic method. Although we can ask our informants what they believe they are accomplishing in reading—just as we can ask them to explain how they affect others *by* reading—we must get beyond their conscious comprehension and self-understanding if we are to make some sort of judgment about the cumulative impact of that activity both on them and on others. To ask about such an effect is, in fact, to pose a question about the relationship between the imaginary realm and the realm of material behavior in the world of actual social relations. The answer to this question can only be found through careful observation of just those behavioral changes over time. However, even when ethnographic observation leads to conclusions about significant alterations in women's behavior, attribution of those changes to specific causes will remain an inherently interpretive procedure, because the link between imagination and action will always be an inferred one.

Because I could not observe the behavior of the Smithton women over a long period of time, my account of their reading activity ends with an explanation of the multiple meanings that the activity has within the context of their daily lives. That explanation locates the ultimate source of the group's existence as an interpretive community in their roles as wives and mothers. Their preference for the romance genre, in my view, is a function of their particular social situation. The nature of their literacy, therefore—which is to say, the way they choose, understand, and use their books—is deeply affected by the circumstances of their lives. These, in fact, are both the very source of their desire to read and the set of conditions that determine and give meaning to the particular way in which they do.

The ultimate test of such an argument, of course, would be a series of related studies of romance readers that would begin by defining differently the interpretive communities to be investigated. One such study would have to begin with a group of unrelated romance readers who were demographically similar to the Smithton women. If these readers also read romances to escape and to learn, and chose only those books that supplied vicarious nurturance, then I think we might reasonably conclude that at least one form of romance reading is a function of the social and psychological consequences of patriarchal marriage. If a more extensive study of a demographically varied group of romance readers demonstrated that young, unmarried women, say, read different romances for different reasons, this would not necessarily upset that initial correlation. It is entirely possible, I think, that the interpretive community of romance readers, defined only by its members' preference for the romance category, may be subdivided into more specialized groups, whose reading behaviors vary with the particular circumstances of their daily lives. Although the interest of romance readers in the genre may be a function of the fact that all are women in a patriarchal society, and thus all fantasize about achieving self-definition through attachment to a spectacular man, the character of the man, the nature of the attachment, and the process of self-realization that are longed for may be determined by the particular situation of these women in patriarchal culture. All components of literate behavior, in short, including the desire to read, the decision to read a certain kind of material, the interpretation of that material, and the uses to which both the interpretation and the act of constructing it are put, may well be a consequence of the diverse material and social features that characterize the lives of real individuals. There may be, in fact, as many different forms of literate behavior as there are interpretive communities who buy and use books.

ENDNOTES

I would like to thank Horace Newcomb for his very helpful comments and suggestions on an earlier version of this paper.

[1]André Kertész, *On Reading* (New York: Penguin Books, 1982).

[2]Ibid., pp. 37, 10.

[3]Raymond Williams, *Marxism and Literature* (Oxford: Oxford University Press, 1977), pp. 45-54.

[4]John Szwed, "The Ethnography of Literacy," in *Writing: The Nature, Development, and Teaching of Written Communication,* vol. 1. *Variation in Writing: Functional and Linguistic Cultural Differences,* edited by Marcia Farr Whiteman (Hillsdale, N.J.: Lawrence Erlbaum Associates, 1981). I am grateful to Judy Levin for bringing this article to my attention in one of our many helpful conversations about literacy and romance reading.

[5]For a good introduction to reader-response criticism, see Jane P. Tompkins, *Reader-Response Criticism: From Formalism to Post-Structuralism* (Baltimore: Johns Hopkins University Press, 1980), and Susan B. Suleiman and Inge Crosman, *The Reader in the Text: Essays on Audience and Interpretation* (Princeton: Princeton University Press, 1980).

[6]For historical and critical discussion of reader theory, see Jonathan Culler, *The Pursuit of Signs: Semiotics, Literature, Deconstruction* (Ithaca, N.Y.: Cornell University Press, 1981), pp. 47-131, and *On Deconstruction: Theory and Criti-*

cism after Structuralism (Ithaca, N.Y.: Cornell University Press, 1982), pp. 31-83. See also Terry Eagleton, *Literary Theory: An Introduction* (Minneapolis: University of Minnesota Press, 1983), pp. 54-90.

[7]See Roman Ingarden, *The Literary Work of Art: An Investigation on the Borderlines of Ontology, Logic, and Theory of Literature,* translated by George Grabowicz (Evanston, Ill.: Northwestern University Press, 1973), and Wolfgang Iser, *The Act of Reading: A Theory of Aesthetic Response* (Baltimore: Johns Hopkins University Press, 1978).

[8]See, especially, Umberto Eco, *The Role of the Reader: Explorations in the Semiotics of Texts* (Bloomington: Indiana University Press, 1979) and *A Theory of Semiotics* (Bloomington: Indiana University Press, 1976); Jonathan Culler, *Structuralist Poetics: Structuralism, Linguistics, and the Study of Literature* (Ithaca, N.Y.: Cornell University Press, 1975); Stanley Fish, *Is There a Text in This Class?: The Authority of Interpretive Communities* (Cambridge: Harvard University Press, 1980); Louise Rosenblatt, *The Reader, the Text, the Poem: The Transactional Theory of the Literary Work* (Carbondale: Southern Illinois University Press, 1978).

[9]Eco, *A Theory of Semiotics,* p. 139.

[10]See especially part 2 of *Is There a Text in This Class?,* pp. 303-71.

[11]See, for example, John Cawelti, *Adventure, Mystery, and Romance: Formula Stories as Art and Popular Culture* (Chicago: University of Chicago Press, 1976).

[12]The present discussion of romance reading is based on my full-length study, *Reading the Romance: Women, Patriarchy, and Popular Literature* (Chapel Hill: University of North Carolina Press, forthcoming.) For another summary of my findings, see "Women Read the Romance: The Interaction of Text and Context," *Feminist Studies* 9 (Spring 1983): 53-78. The names Dorothy Evans and the Smithton women are pseudonyms designed to protect the privacy of my informants.

[13]As Stanley Fish has argued, "Linguistic and textual facts, rather than being the objects of interpretation, are its products" (*Is There a Text in This Class?* p. 9). Accordingly, the literary features used by the Smithton readers as the internal skeleton of their readings are actually isolated and deemed significant by them precisely because they come to the texts with a prior conception of what the stories should and usually do mean.

[14]See Ann Douglas, "Soft Porn Culture," *The New Republic,* August 30, 1980, pp. 25-29; Tania Modleski, "The Disappearing Act: A Study of Harlequin Romances," *Signs* 5 (Spring 1980): 435-48; Ann Barr Snitow, "Mass Market Romance: Pornography for Women Is Different," *Radical History Review* 20 (Spring/Summer 1979): 141-61.

[15]Culler, *Structuralist Poetics,* pp. 230-38, See also his *Ferdinand de Saussure* (New York: Penguin Books, 1976), pp. 117-18.

[16]For a demonstration of how such a reading strategy works, see William Veeder's discussion of *Portrait of a Lady,* in *Henry James—The Lessons of the Master: Popular Fiction and Personal Style in the Nineteenth Century* (Chicago: University of Chicago Press, 1975), pp. 106-83.

[17]In her acknowledgments to *The Proud Breed* (New York: Fawcett Crest Books, 1978), p. 7, for instance, Celeste De Blasis thanks the San Bernardino County library system as well as the Bancroft Library at Berkeley. She continues, "The Roman Catholic pastors of St. Joan of Arc, Victorville, St. David's, Apple Valley, Christ the Good Shepherd, Adelanto, and San Juan Capistrano Mission, and

a noted historian of the Archdiocese of Los Angeles were generous with their knowledge of early California's church ritual."

[18]In an essay on Ian Fleming's thrillers ("Narrative Structures in Fleming," in *The Role of the Reader,* pp. 144-72), Umberto Eco has argued that Fleming also indulges in minute description of familiar objects that appear in the background to the melodramatic action. Eco calls this strategy "the technique of the aimless glance" and maintains that it functions to seduce the reader into identifying with a character who thus appears to be "real" even though his activities are otherwise preposterous. Because Fleming rarely describes the unusual, Eco concludes, those descriptions do not occur as "encyclopedic information." Although the description in romances appears somewhat similar to that found in Fleming, it differs precisely because it focuses on the historically and spatially distant and thus can function encyclopedically.

[19]Clifford Geertz, "Thick Description: Toward an Interpretive Theory of Culture," in *The Interpretation of Cultures* (New York: Basic Books, 1973), pp. 9, 20.

[20]See Robert Escarpit's discussion of reading in *The Sociology of Literature,* translated by Ernest Pick (Painesville, Ohio: Lake Erie College Press, 1965), p. 88.

[21]See, for example, Kate Millett, *Sexual Politics* (Garden City, N.Y.: Doubleday, 1970), pp. 23-58; Heidi Hartmann, "The Unhappy Marriage of Marxism and Feminism: Towards a More Progressive Union," *Capital and Class* 8 (Summer 1979), pp. 1-33 and "The Family as Locus of Gender, Class, and Political Struggle: The Example of Housework," *Signs* 6 (Spring, 1981), pp. 366-94; Annette Kuhn, "Structures of Patriarchy and Capitalism in the Family," in *Feminism and Materialism: Women and Modes of Production,* edited by Annette Kuhn and AnnMarie Wolpe, (London: Routledge & Kegan Paul, 1978), pp. 42-67; and Roisin McDonough and Rachel Harrison, "Patriarchy and Relations of Production," in *Feminism and Materialism,* pp. 11-41.

[22]See Nancy Chodorow, *The Reproduction of Mothering: Psychoanalysis and the Sociology of Gender* (Berkeley: University of California Press, 1978).

19

THE BUSINESS VALUES OF AMERICAN NEWSPAPERS
The 19th Century Watershed in Chicago

David Paul Nord

Three major Chicago newspapers demonstrate the modern press role of mass mediators.

► The business history of American newspapers has been rather simply told by journalism historians. There are two versions of the story: the Great Forces version and the Great Man version. The Great Forces version is almost pure functionalism. Newspapers are portrayed as products of the mass media marketplace, pulled into existence by the tug of demand. As business enterprises, newspapers naturally shared the social values of other businesses of their time. The Great Man version, at the other extreme, is almost pure biography. Newspapers are portrayed as the tools, for good or ill, of powerful press lords. They are forced into existence by eccentric geniuses. In this version of the story, newspapers embody the personal values of their proprietors, which may or may not reflect the values of the business community at large.

This study argues for a view of newspaper business history that falls between the Great Forces and Great Man views. It seeks to discover the uniqueness of the newspaper as a business and to explain how that uniqueness helped shape the editorial values of editors and proprietors. It suggests that newspapers are peculiar sorts of businesses; they are neither shaped by Great Forces in precisely the same ways as other businesses nor are they the mere playthings of Great Men. As a group, newspapers have often been different from other businesses yet interestingly similar to each other in their social values, regardless of the men at the editorial or managerial helms.

Method and Background

Specifically, this article discusses the editorial values of Chicago newspapers during the formative years of the modern urban press, the late 19th century. The paper explores the reactions of three leading Chicago newspapers to three great business-labor crises: the 1877 railroad strikes, the 1886 eight-hour-day movement and Haymarket affair, and the 1894 Pullman strike. My thesis is that despite genuine ideological and idiosyncratic differences the newspapers were curiously similar in certain basic values, that this similarity was related in part to the special nature of the newspaper business, and that these values were "proto-progressive." Here proto-progressive means that newspapers seem to have been early proponents of progressive-era views on business and labor, notably a commitment to public interest consumerism, an obsession with commercial order and social harmony, and a growing faith in organizational modes of conflict resolution.

The 19th century was the age of laissez-faire in American business—or at least in American business values. Daniel Webster had set the stage in 1824. "Our age is wholly of a different character," he wrote. "Society is full of excitement; competition

► **The author is assistant professor of journalism at Indiana University.**

From David Paul Nord, "The Business Values of American Newspapers: The 19th Century Watershed in Chicago," *Journalism Quarterly*, Vol. 61, No. 2 (Summer 1984), pp. 265-273.

comes in place of monopoly; and intelligence and industry ask only for fair play and an open field."[1] The foundation of laissez-faire was private property, and the growth of laissez-faire in the 19th century was essentially an elaboration of traditional American notions of the rights and prerogatives of property. Classical economic theory had turned these personal rights into social virtues. Private ownership of property and its management by independent, self-interested proprietors would produce the most socially beneficial use of property through the magic of the marketplace. The role of government in the laissez-faire system was mainly to affirm and make legitimate emerging property relations—that is, those property relations generated by private power and by the marketplace.[2]

Conventional business views on labor in the age of laissez-faire were also linked to conceptions of private property. On the one hand, the right to work was viewed as a property right and the selling of one's labor as a property transaction. This made labor—a job—an individual-level contract between the employer and a single employee. Labor unions, especially if they used any sort of forced compliance, were widely denounced as infringements upon the individual worker's fundamental right to control his own labor, his own property. Furthermore, businessmen frequently argued that strikes or other concerted job actions infringed upon *their* property rights.[3]

On the eve of the great business-labor upheavals of 1877-1894, the Chicago newspapers generally shared the business and labor values of the age of laissez-faire—but not entirely or uniformly. The city's two dominant morning dailies, the *Times* and the *Tribune,* were quite conventional in their devotion to private property, free enterprise, limited government and the sanctity of the marketplace. On the other hand, the leading afternoon daily, the upstart *Daily News,* was much less committed to laissez-faire. In the maelstrom of the modern city, the *Daily News* saw serious social problems born of free markets, and the paper early argued for social action that moved beyond rigidly defined rights of private property.[4]

The 1877 Railroad Strikes

When the great railroad strikes of 1877 began to spread west toward Chicago, it was clear which side the Chicago *Times* would be on. The *Times* was the personal organ of Wilbur F. Storey, a self-made millionaire who believed steadfastly in the virtues of independence and hard work, in the absolute sanctity of private property, and in the morality and the efficiency of private enterprise.[5] Storey loved the great national railroads, and he blasted the "thugs and lawless mobs" that began to shut them down in July of 1877.[6] Even before the labor troubles turned violent, the *Times* denounced the whole idea of trade unionism and strikes as lunatic assaults upon private property. "The notion upon which all strikers act," the paper declared, "is that they have a right of employment upon other men's property.... Nothing could be more unreasonable." For the *Times,* men would be paid what they were worth, according to the laws of God and economics. "No human contrivance can ever alter the principle that underlies the relation of labor to capital, even as no statute can modify the motions

[1] Quoted in William Appleman Williams, *The Contours of American History* (Chicago: Quadrangle Books, 1966), p. 225. See also Sidney Fine, *Laissez Faire and the General Welfare State* (Ann Arbor: University of Michigan Press, 1956).

[2] William B. Scott, *In Pursuit of Happiness: American Conceptions of Property from the Seventeenth to the Twentieth Century* (Bloomington: Indiana University Press, 1977), Chapter 8. See also Morton Keller, *Affairs of State: Public Life in Late Nineteenth Century America* (Cambridge: Harvard University Press, 1977), Chapters 9-11.

[3] Gerald G. Eggert, *Railroad Labor Disputes: The Beginnings of Federal Strike Policy* (Ann Arbor: University of Michigan Press, 1967), Chapter 9; Sidney Lens, *The Labor Wars* (New York: Doubleday, 1973), Chapter 1.

[4] I discuss the philosophies of these papers in the 1870s in more detail in David Paul Nord, "The Public Community: The Urbanization of Journalism in Chicago," *Journal of Urban History* (in press).

[5] The best account of Storey's sensational career is Justin E. Walsh, *To Print the News and Raise Hell! A Biography of Wilbur F. Storey* (Chapel Hill: University of North Carolina Press, 1968). Storey's strident views on "the laws of political economy" can be found in dozens of editorials in 1876-77. See, for example, Chicago *Times,* Jan. 18, 1876, p. 4; Jan. 20, 1876, p. 4; Feb. 19, 1876, p 4; March 7, 1876, p. 4; Aug. 2, 1877, p. 4.

[6] The *Times* devoted most of a special July 4th issue in 1877 to praising the railroads of America. On the railroad strikes of 1877, see Philip S. Foner, *The Great Labor Uprising of 1877* (New York: Monad Press, 1977); and Robert V. Bruce, *1877: Year of Violence* (Indianapolis: Bobbs-Merrill, 1959).

of the planets or control the ocean tides."[7] Once the strikers become unruly and property was damaged, the *Times* called for complete suppression by armed force.[8]

Even more than the *Times,* the Chicago *Tribune* styled itself "the businessmen's newspaper." The *Tribune* was the organ of Joseph Medill, a prominent member of the Republican political and business elite of Chicago.[9] The *Tribune* believed, as ardently as did the *Times,* in private property and free enterprise. As a former mayor, Medill admitted more of a role for government than Storey did, but that role must be strictly limited to the protection of property and the preservation of individualism.[10] The *Tribune* opposed labor unionism in general and the 1877 railroad strikes in particular. In its first editorial on the strikes, the *Tribune,* in its usual pedantic fashion, lectured the strikers on labor economics. Wages were not set by the employers but by the market, the paper said. "If these men think they can't take the wages offered them, they can step out and let others take their places who feel that they can live upon the wages."[11] Like the *Times,* the *Tribune* became highly agitated when violence broke out. The news columns were now filled with sensational accounts of "Bloodshed" and "Red War." The *Tribune* urged the authorities to "shoot to kill"—for "a bullet in time saves nine."[12]

The Chicago *Daily News* was a different sort of paper from its morning contemporaries. The *Daily News* was a newcomer to Chicago, founded in 1875 as a small "penny paper" designed for the middle and lower classes. It was already a remarkable success by the summer of 1877.[13] The *Daily News* was founded by Melville E. Stone, a self-made businessman not unlike Storey and Medill. Despite a basic commitment to conventional business and social values, however, Stone guided his newspaper down a somewhat different ideological path. From the beginning, the *Daily News* was much more attuned to the idea of interdependence than to the notion of competitive individualism in the great cities of the late 19th century.[14] Unlike the *Times* and the *Tribune,* the *Daily News* promoted public works jobs for the unemployed, economic regulation, and other government intervention and enterprise, including the nationalization of railroads.[15] In short, the *Daily News* embraced the rudiments of a social understanding of property that was at odds with the prevailing business doctrine of laissez-faire.

In the 1877 railroad strikes, the *Daily News* sympathized with the striking workers. Far from preaching at the workers about the immutable law of wages,the *Daily News* denounced the railroads for their "infamous treatment" of their employees and excused the men for replying with the only weapon they had: a strike. The *Daily News* blamed the railroads for the strike and declared that the labor problem could not be settled "until the rights of workmen are properly acknowledged."[16] As violence spread to Chicago, the *Daily News* lost some of its sympathy. Like the other Chicago newspapers it condemned rioting in strong language, though after the strike had ended, the *Daily News* denounced the *Times* and

[7] *Times,* July 22, 1977, p. 6; July 30, 1877, p. 4. See also July 20, 1877, p. 4; Aug. 1, 1877, p. 4.

[8] *Ibid.,* July 25-31, 1877, *passim.*

[9] Chicago *Tribune,* May 1, 1876, p. 7. The best accounts of Medill's career are Lloyd Wendt, *Chicago Tribune: The Rise of a Great American Newspaper* (Chicago: Rand McNally, 1979); and John Tebbel, *An American Dynasty* (Garden City, N.Y.: Doubleday, 1947).

[10] *Tribune,* Jan. 24, 1876, p. 4; March 16, 1876, p. 4; May 20, 1876, p. 4; July 7, 1876, p. 4.

[11] *Ibid.,* July 20, 1877 p. 4. See also Feb. 4, 1876, p. 4; May 11, 1876, p. 4.

[12] *Ibid.,* July 23-27, 1877, *passim.* The outrage of the *Tribune* and the *Times* was fairly typical of other Chicago papers and papers around the nation in 1877. See Bruce, *1877,* Chapter 12; and Foner, *Great Labor Uprising,* Chapter 8.

[13] On the early years of the Chicago *Daily News,* see Donald J. Abramoske, "The Founding of the Chicago *Daily News,*" *Journal of the Illinois Historical Society,* 59:341-53 (Winter, 1966). See also Melville E. Stone, *Fifty Years a Journalist* (Garden City, N.Y.: Doubleday, 1921); and Charles H. Dennis, *Victor Lawson: His time and His Work* (Chicago: University of Chicago Press, 1935). Lawson was Stone's partner almost from the beginning.

[14] Chicago *Daily News,* April 1, 1876, p. 2; April 17, 1876 p. 2; May 10, 1876, p. 2; Oct. 9, 1876, p. 2; Dec. 18, 1876, p. 2.

[15] *Ibid.,* Jan. 18, 1876, p. 2; Jan. 25, 1876, p. 2; Feb. 26, 1876, p. 2; March 15, 1876, p. 2; March 30, 1876, p. 2; May 5, 1876, p. 2; May 8, 1876, p. 2; May 12, 1876, p.2; July 5, 1876, p. 2

[16] *Ibid.,* July 20, 1877, p. 2; July 25, 1877, p. 2; July 26, 1877, p. 2; July 28, 1877, p. 2. See also Dennis, *Victor Lawson,* pp. 41-44.

the *Tribune* for their bloodthirsty calls to arms.[17]

In some ways, then, these three papers were quite different in their ideologies and sympathies during the 1877 strikes. The *Times* and the *Tribune* were fairly similar in their anti-union stance and their commitment to laissez-faire; the *Daily News* was pro-striker and had begun to move, though hesitantly, toward a philosophy of activist government and social welfare. In spite of these differences, however, the editorials in these three newspapers during the 1877 strikes suggest some basic shared values.

Values Shared by Papers

The most obvious shared value was the obsession of all three newspapers with the public's role in the strikes. The "public interest" was central to the controversy. Notwithstanding their devotion to private property, all three newspapers insisted, as the *Daily News* put it, that "the whole question of railroads is a great public one." Even the *Times,* the most doctrinaire laissez-faire enthusiast of the three, declared that "railroad managers must be made to understand distinctly that they as well as other men owe duties to the public.[18] All three papers defined the public interest in the 1877 strikes as a kind of consumers' right. They professed to speak for the whole community of consumers of railroad services, whose interests superseded those of the direct participants in the conflict.[19]

A second basic value shared by the *Times,* the *Tribune* and the *Daily News* in 1877 was a rigid commitment to commercial order and social harmony. Each paper admitted at some point that there were two sides to the question of wages, but the question was irrelevant in the face of the violence. As the *Tribune* declared, "The first and most important duty is to quell mob rule."[20] The *Times* put it most bluntly: "The killing of some of the insurgents is not a matter which concerns society at all. If they stand in the way of society's peaceful order, the sooner they are killed the better." Even the *Daily News,* the strikers' best newspaper friend in Chicago, praised the heavy-handed force of the police and militia.[21] All agreed on the primacy of law and order.

A corollary to the papers' commitment to social order was their belief that most segments of society—including even the strikers,—*were* orderly. All the papers believed in consensus and in a broad community of interest between labor and capital, with stress on the idea of community.[22] For this reason, the papers portrayed the rioters as outsiders—not railroad workers at all. The papers blamed the violence on roughs and rowdies, communist loafers and vagrants, blackguard boys and guttersnipes. The *Daily News* was appalled by the "thugs, thieves, and hoodlums that the slums are now vomiting into our steets."[23] These were outsiders, aliens, violators of the natural, peaceful equilibrium of the consensus community.

This insistence upon social harmony was related to a third basic value that emerged in the newspapers' editorial reaction to the 1877 strikes: a pragmatic commitment to an organizational approach to conflict resolution. The *Times,* the *Tribune* and the *Daily News* all recognized that the railroad workers had legitimate grievances. They tended to view the strike as an unfortunate and unnecessary result of bad management —by both corporations and union leadership. They hoped that the turmoil of the strike would have the good result of rationalizing the organization of the industry, to the advantage of both capital and labor—and the public.[24]

Though the *Times* was hazy on how it

[17] *Daily News,* July 23, 1877, p. 2; July 27 1877, p. 2; July 31, 1877, p. 2; Aug. 7, 1877, p. 2.

[18] *Daily News,* July 25, 1877, p. 2; *Tribune,* Aug. 4, 1877, p. 4; *Times,* July 31, 1877, p. 4.

[19] *Times,* Aug. 3, 1877, p. 4; *Tribune,* July 21, 1877, p. 4; July 26, 1877, p. 4; July 27, 1877, p. 4; *Daily News,* July 27, 1877, p. 2.

[20] *Tribune,* July 23, 1877, p. 4; July 25, 1877, p. 4: *Times,* July 25, 1877, p. 6; July 29, 1877, p. 6; *Daily News,* July 23, 1877, p. 2; July 25, 1877, p. 2.

[21] *Times,* July 24, 1877, p. 6; *Daily News,* July 27, 1877, p. 2; *Tribune,* July 27, 1877, p. 4; July 29, 1877, p. 4.

[22] *Tribune.* Aug. 1, 1877, p. 4; July 28, 1877, p. 4; *Times,* July 29, 1877, p. 6; Aug. 2, 1877, p. 4; *Daily News,* July 27, 1877, p. 2.

[23] *Tribune,* July 26, 1877, p. 4; July 29, 1877, p. 4; *Times,* July 29, 1877, p. 6; *Daily News,* July 25, 1877, p. 2; Aug. 9, 1877, p. 2.

[24] *Times,* July 24, 1877, p. 6; *Daily News,* July 20, 1877, p. 2; July 26, 1877, p. 2; July 28, 1877, p. 2; *Tribune,* Aug. 3, 1877, p. 4; Aug. 4, 1877, p. 4.

expected the good to result, both the *Daily News* and the *Tribune* saw the need for some government intervention. In urging the workers to end the strike, the *Daily News* assured them that their "demonstration has taught the country a lesson it cannot forget.... The most important study of American statesmen for the next five years will be the proper adjustment of the relations between capital and labor." The *Tribune* urged again and again that the proper adjustment should be a national system of arbitration. Both papers believed in formalized negotiation; they believed in the power of facts and information in the rational settlement of conflict. The *Tribune* also advocated pensions and disability programs funded jointly by employees and employers. Such organizational arrangements would stabilize the industry and would be good for capital, labor and the public at large.[25] In short, these papers believed in the natural community of capital and labor, and they sought to strengthen that community through organizational means—assisted, modestly, by government.

The Eight-Hour Movement

The Chicago *Times,* Chicago *Tribune* and Chicago *Daily News* were still circulation leaders in their city in 1886, another critical year in labor and business history in America. In 1884-86, a series of strikes and boycotts and union organizing efforts came together in the movement for an eight-hour day, a movement which in turn culminated in nationwide work stoppages on May 1, 1886. In Chicago, the eight-hour movement became mixed up with other issues, including radical political agitation. For Chicagoans and for much of the rest of the country, the eight-hour movement was lost in the smoke of the Haymarket bomb, which exploded, with far-reaching repercussions, the night of May 4, 1886.[26]

The *Times,* the *Tribune* and the *Daily News* interpreted the eight-hour movement and the Haymarket affair much the same as they had the 1877 railroad strikes. As in 1877, the *Times* was the most thoroughly laissez-faire and the most stridently anti-labor. During the strikes for an eight-hour day, the paper denounced the eight-hour idea and damned all labor organzations, especially the Knights of Labor. The *Tribune* was as anti-strike as the *Times,* but it was not stridently anti-union. Though generally opposed on economic principle to the eight-hour idea, the *Tribune* was not completely hostile to it in practice if it could be worked out through negotiation. Once again, as in 1877, the *Daily News* was most sympathetic to labor's cause. Though it, too, opposed coercive strikes and secondary boycotts, the *Daily News* gave favorable coverage to the eight-hour movement, including the eight-hour strikes.[27]

In spite of fundamental ideological disagreements over the "labor question," the three newspapers again, as in 1877, shared basic values in their handling of the crisis of 1886. Once again, they all agreed that the labor-business confrontation was a great public question of vital interest to the community at large. The *Daily News* declared that public opinion would finally settle the question. "Out of all these varying views will come, in time, the fair, unprejudiced, controlling sentiment of general opinion which will set its seal of approval on these perplexing questions. To that decision all interests must in the end yield." All three papers declared that all parties to the dispute had great public duties that they must not ignore.[28]

The newspapers' commitment to commercial peace and social order was perhaps even more ardent in 1886 than it had been in 1877. After a mob smashed windows at the McCormick Reaper Works and espe-

[25] *Daily News,* July 25, 1877, p. 2; July 27, 1877, p. 2; Aug. 7, 1877, p. 2; *Tribune,* Aug. 3, 1877, p. 4; Aug. 4, 1877, p. 4; Aug. 8, 1877, p. 4.

[26] Henry David, *The History of the Haymarket Affair* (New York: Farrar & Rinehart, 1936); Bessie Louise Pierce, *A History of Chicago,* Vol. III: *The Rise of a Modern City, 1871-1893* (New York, Knopf, 1957), Chapters 7-8.

[27] *Times,* April 30, 1886, p. 4; May 1, 1886, p. 4; May 2, 1886, p. 4; *Tribune,* April 21, 1886, p. 4; April 24, 1886, p. 4; May 3, 1886, p. 4; May 10, 1886, p. 4; *Daily News,* May 1, 1886, pp. 1-2; May 3, 1886, pp. 1-2. For a study of the pro-business bias of New York papers on labor issues during this era, see Barbara C. Crosby, "Big Business Looks at Labor: How Major New York City Dailies Viewed Labor Unrest in the 1880s and 1890s," unpublished M.A. thesis, University of Wisconsin, 1980.

[28] *Daily News,* May 1, 1886, p. 2; *Tribune,* April 24, 1886, p. 4; May 2, 1886, p. 4; May 9, 1886, p. 4; May 12, 1886, p. 4; *Times,* May 1, 1886, pp. 2-3, 4.

cially after a bomb exploded near the Haymarket, all the newspapers called for retribution—swift and sure. "The community is menaced by a peril the magnitude of which it were folly to underestimate," the *Times* exclaimed. Even the *Daily News,* which was sympathetic to the working class, denounced this assault on law and order.[29] Again, as in 1877, the attack on the public peace was seen as coming from outside the legitimate community. For days after Haymarket, the newspapers produced streams of viciously anti-ethnic editorials. All agreed that it was the Poles, the Russians and other un-Americanized eastern Europeans who caused the trouble, who cause all the trouble in large American cities. All agreed with the *Tribune* that "Chicago has become the rendezvous for the worst elements of the Socialistic, atheistic, alcoholic European classes." The natural social relations between capital and labor in America were complementary and cordial. As in 1877, the dissidents were portrayed as illegitimate alien outsiders.[30]

All three papers approved of increased social force against industrial violence, including the use of police, militia and court injunctions. Though the *Times* did not go much beyond law enforcement as a means for conflict resolution, the *Tribune* and the *Daily News,* again promoted, though sometimes vaguely and indirectly, an organizational approach to economic conflict resolution. Both newspapers urged that the eight-hour-day issue be worked out in the "spirit of mutual concession." They argued for careful deliberation on the basis of facts and hard information. The idea of arbitration still seemed an especially attractive method for settling industrial disputes.[31]

The Pullman Strike

Less than a decade after the Haymarket affair, Chicago found itself the storm center of another major nationwide railroad strike. The so-called Pullman strike, in its full-blown form in early July, 1894, was actually a secondary boycott against railroads that used sleeping cars manufactured by the Pullman Palace Car Company of suburban Chicago. The boycott was mounted in support of striking Pullman workers by the year-old American Railway Union (ARU) under the leadership of Eugene V. Debs. The boycott quickly developed into a general railroad strike, tying up traffic nationwide. Throughout the turmoil, George M. Pullman absolutely refused to deal with the ARU or to negotiate with Pullman employees.[32]

Most Chicago newspapers opposed the secondary boycott, though they were not sympathetic to the imperious George M. Pullman.[33] The *Tribune* and the *Daily News* interpreted this new crisis on the basis of now familiar values. The *Times,* on the other hand, was an altogether different newspaper from what it had been during the earlier frays. With its flamboyant proprietor, Wilbur Storey, dead, the *Times* had fallen on hard times in the late 1880s. The popular Democrat Carter Harrison rescued it in 1891 and turned it into a political organ to boost his campaign for mayor in 1893. Under the editorship of his son, Carter Harrison II, the *Times* became an insurgent Democratic organ—the only paper in Chicago to support wholeheartedly the Pullman strikers.[34]

As in the earlier crises, the *Tribune,* the *Daily News* and the *Times* in 1894 held sharply different views of the "labor question." With the *Times* now practically converted to populism, the *Tribune* remained the most attuned to the philosophy of laissez-faire. The *Tribune* still hotly

[29] See the three papers' editorials for May 5, 1886, the day after the bombing. See also David, *Haymarket Affair,* Chapters 9-10.

[30] See editorials for May 6 and 7, 1886, in all three papers.

[31] *Times,* May 8, 1886, p. 4; May 12, 1886, p. 4; *Tribune,* April 21, 1886, p. 4; May 3, 1886, p. 4; May 10, 1886, p. 4; May 11, 1886, p. 4; *Daily News,* May 1, 1886, p. 2; May 3, 1886, p. 2.

[32] Almont Lindsey, *The Pullman Strike* (Chicago: University of Chicago Press, 1942). See also Eggert, *Railroad Labor Disputes,* Chapter 7; and Stanley Buder, *Pullman: An Experiment in Industrial Order and Community Planning, 1880-1930* (New York: Oxford University Press, 1967), Chapters 12-15.

[33] The Chicago (and national) press treatment of the strike is discussed in Lindsey, *Pullman Strike,* Chapter 13. See also Crosby, "Big Business"; and John R. Finnegan, Sr., "The Press and the Pullman Strike: An Analysis of the Coverage of the Railroad Boycott of 1894 by Four Metropolitan Daily Newspapers," unpublished M.A. thesis, University of Minnesota, 1965.

[34] Leroy F. Armstrong, "The Daily Papers of Chicago," *The Chautauquan,* 27: 541-42 (August, 1898). See also Carter H. Harrison II, *Stormy Years: The Autobiography of Carter H. Harrison, Five Times Mayor of Chicago* (Indianapolis: Bobbs-Merrill, 1935). Both father and son were multi-term mayors.

opposed strikes of any sort, and it denounced the secondary boycott tactic of the ARU. After July 1, almost every news story and editorial referred to Debs as "Dictator Debs." The *Daily News* generally supported the Pullman strike itself, though it too criticized the ARU's secondary railroad boycott. The *Times*, now shorn of all traces of Storey-style conservatism, thoroughly supported the original Pullman strike, the secondary boycott, and the union leadership of Eugene V. Debs.[35]

Despite these philosophical differences, all three newspapers again displayed basic shared values. As in 1877 and 1886, the papers in 1894 agreed that the Pullman strike/boycott was a great public issue. This was a central editorial theme of all three. The *Tribune* insisted that "the interest of the country are paramount to those involved in any merely personal dispute between the transportation companies and their employees."[36] Both the *Daily News* and the *Times* agreed with the *Tribune* on the deeply public nature of the strike, and they, like the *Tribune*, defined the public's interest as a consumers' right.[37]

A firm commitment to commercial order, social harmony and social control also ran through the newspapers in 1894. Not surprisingly, the *Tribune* immediately demanded the forceful suppression of the strikers the moment violence broke out. In the *Tribune's* view, all strikes were violent by nature. The *Daily News* also supported the federal government's show of force. "The workingman's best ally is the law," the paper said. Even the *Times*, which desperately desired that the strike and boycott succeed, supported almost all official efforts to enforce law and order. In an editorial titled "Suppress All Riots," the *Times* urged that all disorders be ended promptly, with "powder and ball and cold steel if necessary."[38]

As in earlier eras, the papers again attributed the violence and disorder to outsiders. The *Tribune* made Debs the scapegoat. It was Debs and the anarchistic leaders of the ARU that were bringing the sober, hard-working wage-earners of Chicago to ruin. The *Daily News* blamed "an excited minority" for the rioting—mainly the usual array of un-Americanized immigrants. The *Times* declared proudly "that no member of the American Railway Union took part in this lawless foray." The outbreaks instead were the work of "sinister influences."[39]

In 1894, all three papers had fully committed themselves to organizational schemes for the resolution of business-labor conflict. Despite their opposing sympathies in the strike, all three urged on-going negotiation and mutual compromise. George Pullman, the ever-faithful son of laissez-faire, was condemned by all three papers, because he stubbornly insisted upon his own selfish private rights in a great public controversy. All three pronounced Pullman a symbol of a dying age of labor relations.[40]

"Arbitration" was the watchword for all three papers. "This struggle is one for the principle of arbitration," the *Times* declared, and the *Daily News* and the *Tribune* agreed. When Pullman refused to arbitrate, he lost the sympathy of the newspapers. The strikers' desire to arbitrate proved to the *Daily News* that "they are for law and order and against anarchy and violence." The *Tribune* had favored arbitration for decades and pressed for the process again in the Pullman strike.[41] Despite their vastly different sympathies, even the *Tribune* and *Times* in 1894 shared a basic understanding of industrial government. The *Tribune* advocated company pensions and disability programs that

[35] *Tribune*, July 1, 1894, p. 1; July 2, 1894, p. 6; July 15, 1894, p. 12; *Daily News*, July 11, 1894, p. 4; July 13, 1894, p. 4; *Times*, July 3, 1894, p. 4; July 4, 1894, p. 9; July 5, 1894, p. 4; July 9, 1894, p. 1; July 15, 1894, p. 9.

[36] *Tribune*, July 6, 1894, p. 6; July 15, 1894, p. 6.

[37] *Tribune*, June 30, 1894, p. 2; July 2, 1894, p. 6; July 8, 1894, p. 12; *Daily News*, July 11, 1894, p. 4; *Times*, July 3, 1894, p. 4; July 5, 1894, p. 4; July 14, 1894, p. 1.

[38] *Tribune*, June 30, 1894, pp. 1, 12; July 1, 1894, pp. 1, 28; July 4, 1894, p. 6; July 8, 1894, p. 12; *Daily News*, July 7, 1894, p. 4; July 10, 1894, p. 4; *Times*, July 4, 1894, p. 4; July 5, 1894, p. 4; July 6, 1894, p. 4; July 7, 1894, p. 4.

[39] *Tribune*, July 2, 1894, p. 6; July 8, 1984, p. 12; July 11, 1894, p. 6; *Daily News*, July 10, 1894, p. 4; *Times*, July 6, 1894, p. 4; July 7, 1894, p. 4.

[40] *Times*, July 4, 1894, p. 9; July 15, 1894, p. 20; *Tribune*, July 10, 1894, p. 6; July 11, 1894, p. 6; *Daily News*, July 16, 1894, p. 4; July 21, 1894, p. 4.

[41] *Times*, July 8, 1894, p. 1; July 10, 1894, p. 4; *Daily News*, July 11, 1894, p. 4; July 13, 1894, p. 4; July 14, 1894, p. 4; *Tribune*, July 8, 1894, p. 12; July 17, 1894, p. 6.

would give employees more of a stake in the good fortunes of their companies. The *Times* urged that companies be forced to give labor "a broader field for the exertion of its power."[42] Yet, different as these proposals were, both papers expected the results to be largely the same, for both papers believed in the common interests of labor and capital. And both expected the results to come through negotiation and compromise, through a more rational organization of industry.

Shared Values

Thus, it happened that in late 19th century Chicago, newspapers with sharply opposing views on business-labor questions tended to share certain fundamental values: a commitment to public interest consumerism; an obsession with commercial order and social harmony; and a growing faith in organizational modes of conflict resolution. Neither the general business culture's philosophy of laissez-faire at the macro-level (Great Forces) nor the idiosyncracies of individual publishers and editors at the micro-level (Great Men) explain this tendency very well. The special nature of the newspaper business explains it better.

The newspapers' commitment to public interest consumerism seems to be an obvious reflection of the papers' own thoroughly public nature. Though editors such as Wilbur Storey and Joseph Medill were devoted to private property, private enterprise and privatism in general, their product was inherently public. The whole business of a newspaper is "publication"—making information and issues public. As urban newspapers began to expand their definition of news and to expand their circulations in the mid-19th century, the realm of public life expanded for them as well.[43] Through the act of publication itself, newspapers asserted that particular issues were no longer private matters. And this structural imperative of news came to dominate editorial values as well, and carried with it a subtle assault on the very private world of laissez-faire.

The modern newspaper, as it evolved in the 19th century, was a consumer product designed for broad circulation. Even a self-proclaimed businessman's paper such as the Chicago *Tribune* served an enormously diverse audience. To sell the product, newspapers sought to understand and to broaden shared public interests. Frequently, the citizens of the new giant metropolises of America shared more as consumers of the output of both private business and public government than they did as producers or wage-workers.[44] Thus, the consumer orientation was a natural one for newspapers, given the nature of their business.

As self-proclaimed custodians of the whole public's interest, newspapers not surprisingly abhorred conflict in the community. At one level, newspapers did choose sides in social conflict and sometimes secretly blessed the circulation-boosting side-effects of strikes and other upheavals. At a deeper level, however, conflict subverted the newspapers' social world, and they opposed it. In their efforts to do business with the *whole* public, or large segments of it, newpapers sought broad consensus. Though they often promoted political factions, modern urban newspapers almost always looked also to the broader public. They were becoming mass mediators—mass media.

As communication media, newspapers believed naturally in the efficacy of communication, and they had tremendous faith in the power and righteousness of "public opinion." But to be "informed," public opinion must be calm, rational, and deliberate. Violent conflict was alien to the newspapers' vision of communication, consensus, and community. If conflict was alien, it is not surprising that aliens were blamed for conflict. They stood outside the rational system of discourse—especially so

[42] *Tribune*, July 15, 1894, p. .2, *Times*, July 18, 1894, p. 4.

[43] On the gowth of the metro press, see Michael Schudson, *Discovering the News* (New York: Basic Books, 1978), Chapters 1-3; Gunther Barth, *City People: The Rise of Modern City Culture in 19th Century America* (New York: Oxford University Press, 1980), Chapter 3.

[44] On the unifying function of consumerism in the late 19th century, see David P. Thelen, *The New Citizenship* (Columbia University of Missouri Press, 1972). On the newspapers' role in this process, see David Paul Nord, *Newspapers and New Politics: Midwestern Municipal Reform, 1890-1900* (Ann Arbor: UMI Research Press, 1981).

if they could not even read English, the sine qua non of community membership for English-language metropolitan newspapers.

Devoted to what they conceived to be the general public interest, committed to public consensus and social harmony, newspapers quite naturally held the rational resolution of conflict to be a fundamental goal. Laissez-faire individualism on the one hand and organized labor strikes on the other hand were ideologies of conflict, and they ultimately fell before this goal—despite the nominal ideological sympathies of the newspapers. Newspapers, in a sense, urged the participants in controversy to follow what was essentially a newspaper model of conflict resolution: organize a formal communication system for the exchange of information, and compromise and consensus will follow.

Notwithstanding their widely varying editorial sympathies, Chicago newspapers by the 1890s were great proponents of *arbitration* in business-labor relations. Perhaps more than anything else, this faith in arbitration reflects the nature of the newspaper enterprise, for newspapers are themselves arbitrators in social relations—or so they conceived themselves. To champion arbitration as something more than a stopgap last resort, one has to believe that business-labor problems are questions that can be resolved rationally through the gathering, analysis, and application of information. Though it may be a will-o'-the-wisp, this faith in facts and information is the bedrock of journalism. For these Chicago papers, then, industrial arbitration became merely the continuation of newspaper work by other means.

For newspapers such as the Chicago *Daily News,* government could be trusted to participate more fully in the building of social welfare. For other papers, such as the Chicago *Tribune,* the lingering tug of laissez-faire was strong. But by 1900, the editorial policies of these two newspapers had gradually converged, in business-labor relations and in other areas as well, including government regulation of the public consequences of urban business and the municipal ownership of public utilities.[45] This convergence of editorial policy was highly pragmatic, forced by the circumstances of modern urban life in the 1890s. But its roots lay deep in the past. The underlying values that the newspapers shared by 1900 had grown up with the modern newspaper business itself.

The implications of this version of newspaper business history extend beyond journalism history, for the values that these Chicago newspapers shared in the 19th century became the values of progressive-era reform. Though the so-called progressive era of the early 20th century was a time much too variegated to characterize by a handful of social values, it is surely not too reckless to suggest that the values of public interest consumerism, commercial and social harmony, and organizational conflict resolution were central to the tenor of those times. Certainly, this was the case in business-labor relations,where the essence of progressivism was the working out of organizational structures and relationships for the rational resolution (or suppression) of conflict between organized labor and organized captial. But these values also infused the whole spirit of the progressive era, as laissez-faire in America gradually gave way to the organizational society and the regulatory state.[46]

The thesis of this article has been simply that urban newspapers were early participants in this great transformation and that their participation grew in part from the special nature of the newspaper business itself.

[45] Nord, *Newspapers and New Politics,* Chapters 6-7.

[46] Robert H. Wiebe, *The Search for Order, 1877-1920* (New York: Hill and Wang, 1967), Chapters 6-7. See also Paul Boyer, *Urban Masses and Moral Order in America, 1820-1920* (Cambridge: Harvard University Press, 1978), part four; and Richard L. McCormick, "The Discovery that Businesss Corrupts Politics: A Reappraisal of the Origins of Progressivism," *American Historical Review,* 86: 247-74 (April, 1981).

PART III

MASS MEDIA AND THE INDIVIDUAL

INTRODUCTION

Edward L. Fink

Ever since Babel, humans have realized that the means of cultural transmission are important for achieving cultural goals. In our time, this has resulted in the development of research on these means, which we now label "media." This section of *MCRY 5* examines the way the media affect individual members of the society. The selections advance our understanding of this process, and, at the same time, point out the theoretical quagmire that serves as the basis for this research. We thus have the paradox of concrete developments in the field built upon a shaky foundation: excellent examples of current social science research on media effects with a weak theoretical base. We turn now to these selections; we will return to discussing the foundations of this research at the end of this introduction.

The first two articles in Part III deal with the interdependency of the emotional states of the individual and exposure to and use of the media. Bryant and Zillman discuss the role that television plays in dealing with high levels of emotional arousal (stress) and low levels of arousal (boredom). In a carefully designed experimental study, they show that stressed subjects watch relaxing programs more than bored subjects, and that bored subjects watch exciting programs more than stressed subjects. Furthermore, watching the programs selected affects the excitatory state of the individual: excited subjects become more relaxed regardless of which programs they watch, and relaxed subjects become more excited if they choose exciting fare. Finally, only a few subjects express a reason for watching the programs they selected in terms consistent with the underlying mechanism that Bryant and Zillman provide.

Larson and Kubey look at the role that two media (television and music) play in the lives of adolescents. Using a novel technique that allows the sampling of experiences at relatively random times, they relate the subjective states of these youths to their social situation. They find that for these youths television watching is correlated with boredom and is less involving than listening to music. While the reported relationships are weak, it is found that television watching is associated with family interaction while listening to music is associated with peer interaction. In this study, the medium becomes the message: Media use is associated with different interpersonal and emotional contexts; the contents of the media are not themselves analyzed.

Violence, as a possible effect of imitation of media contents, has long been a concern of communication researchers. The next two selections represent a new controversy on this issue. The article by Phillips and Hensley is the latest in a series of investigations by Phillips and his associates that employ demographic data to test hypotheses about media influence on individual violent behavior. The authors posit a simple learning mechanism in which behavior displayed in the media is expected to be imitated if associated with appropriate sanctions. According to this study the homicide rate is predicted to increase as a result of publicized prizefights (rewarded violence) while publicized murder trials and executions (punished violence) should decrease the homicide rate. The authors test the relationship between homicides and publicized judicial actions using a seven-year time series of daily homicide data. The analysis requires controlling for trends and periodicities in the data, and incorporating lagged effects. With data on homicides of white victims, the authors conclude that "publicized punishments have a short-term deterrent effect" on these homicides. Considering that most publicized punishments involve white murderers and white victims, the imitation effect on black homicide victims was expected to be insignificant, and it was.

The work by Phillips and his collaborators is not without its criticism: the next article, by Kessler and Stipp, is an example. In this selection, the authors conduct a reanalysis of data in which Phillips attempted to show a modeling effect similar to the one discussed above—a previous study in which he claimed that television fictional suicides cause an increase in real suicides and single-vehicle motor fatalities. After correcting for errors in the original study and disaggregating the data to a daily time series, Kessler and Stipp find no support for Phillips's claim. Note that the two selections here merely hint at the extent of the controversy generated by Phillips: There are now many articles that discuss the statistical and theoretical adequacy of these "imitation of mass media" studies.

In addition to affecting emotions and behavior, media are presumed to affect human cognition. This idea has noble roots: Socrates indicated suspicion of writing because of the belief that human memory, and consequently human knowledge, would suffer as a result of it. Today this suspicion of media is translated into research questions; the next two articles are examples. The first, by Fetler, presents a study of the effects of television viewing on the school achievement of a sample of 10,000 Californian sixth-graders. Amount of daily television viewing explains only about 3 percent of the variance in achievement scores, and explains only about 1 percent of the variance of these scores after controlling for parental occupation and other variables. More viewing is generally associated with poorer achievement scores, but it also seems that moderate viewing has a slight positive effect on these scores. When controls for parental occupation are introduced, television seems to homogenize the achievement scores of the youngsters: The variability of achievement scores diminishes across the social groups as the amount of viewing increases.

A notion similar to the one above is provided by Gaziano in her review of studies of the "knowledge gap." Do the media serve to equalize knowledge across social classes, or, on the contrary, do they serve to increase the knowledge discrepancy between the haves and the have-nots? The review of the research on this topic provided in this article finds inconsistent results, with somewhat more support for the idea that media reduce knowledge gaps. This conclusion is not firmly established because the studies examined have different samples, measures, topics, media, extent of media coverage, and number of points in time, and these factors also seem to affect the outcome of these knowledge gap investigations. The article concludes with an agenda for knowledge gap research.

The media provide knowledge, including, presumably, knowledge of what is desirable or acceptable knowledge. Thus we often speculate about the media's power to bring about conformity—either because of the homogenizing effect discussed in the reference to the articles by Fetler and Graziano or, more sinisterly, because of social desirability effects that the media promote, intentionally or otherwise. In the next selection, Davison presents the intriguing idea that people "tend to overestimate the influence that mass communications have on the attitudes and behavior of others." Davison offers some evidence for this "third-person effect," and relates it to other communication phenomena (e.g., the idea that censors "know" that they are uncorrupted by the horrors that they must scrutinize, and also "know" that these same horrors will do grave harm to the general public). It would be interesting to attempt to integrate the third-person effect with other models of interdependency, such as the prisoner's dilemma game, the self-fulfilling prophecy, and the problem of the commons.

Fejes, in the last article in this section, contrasts the research perspective of "critical" mass communication scholars with those called "behaviorists." For critical scholars, the issues are writ large: They concern power, social class, culture, and ideology. The author discusses research approaches and sociologically based models of media that, he argues, are of relevance to critical scholars, and relates these to the fundamental issues that guide the critical perspective. One of these models, the spiral of silence, is relevant to Davison's article; another, the knowledge gap, is discussed by Gaziano; a third, the media dependency model, is relevant to several of the articles in this section. The author argues that the audience, however poorly represented in traditional behaviorist research, is "missing" for the critical researcher; as the audience is the nexus between power, class, culture, and ideology, Fejes advocates "bring[ing] the audience back into critical communications research."

In the research presented in this section, we see people employing media to affect their emotional states, to provide models of interpersonal relations, to gain knowledge, and to gain knowledge about knowledge. The subjects covered in the articles selected for inclusion in this part are quite varied, but certainly do not exhaust the phenomena that mass communication researchers study. In seeing the variety in these articles, we also see, in a negative sense, their unity: It is all too clear that there is no common set of variables, questions, or processes that underlies research on mass media and the individual. Had different topics, measures, or effects been selected for this section of the volume, the section might have reflected the same general level of quality. But it also would have generated the feeling that we lack the cumulation of findings into theories, as well as the sense that the research included is theoretically based only in a trivial sense.

The concern implicit in the above paragraph is not with the intelligence, diligence, or ingenuity of the scholars represented here; rather, it is with our conception of the research enterprise. Tannenbaum (this volume) describes research choices to be personal choices: While colleagues provide referees and advice, individual investigators select topics, methods, and models. However, the study of the sociology of science should teach us that this "individualism" is part of the rhetoric of science, but not a significant part of its practice. After all, scholars are socialized in cohorts that are differentiated by the schools that do the training; further, generations of students are trained in the methods and approaches in which, for the most part, their mentors were also trained. There are schools of thought and invisible colleges that are formed by networks of scholars.

Once this is noted, we cannot explain the lack of significant theoretical developments in mass communication by "individualism." Furthermore, while all sciences may be individualistic, not all are characterized by the incommensurability of their research that characterizes most research in mass communication. The obvious question is how to structure our work so that theoretical achievements are more likely. In briefest outline, I offer my suggestions.

First, the foundation of our research requires theories broader than those of mass media influence. These would be theories capturing the relations of social behavior, social cognition, social structure, and culture in which the influence of the mass media may be embedded. The theories should be stated ahistorically, but should be historically applicable and testable. They should employ models created by analogy to other domains. This ensures that a sense of closure can be established, as the processes to be investigated and variables for the investigation will be developed with these models and other, extra-model variables can be excluded or translated into the variables that the model provides. Such models, at least initially, should be simple enough to be precise and general. Finally, the measurement rules associated with the model that is employed should be integrated with it, so that calibration of the measures is equivalent to the establishment of functional relations among the variables.

The ideas articulated above are elaborated elsewhere; if adopted, they would represent a radical departure for mass communication research. Should we consider the web of interrelationships that we study to be complex, and should our theories be constructed to reflect this complexity, or should our conceptions and theories be simple, perhaps even naively so? This question suggests its own answer to each of us as we read the selections in Part III, and I have outlined mine. Consider these good selections, and consider next how we jointly create the structure for research and theory in communication.

20

USING TELEVISION TO ALLEVIATE BOREDOM AND STRESS
Selective Exposure as a Function of Induced Excitational States

Jennings Bryant and Dolf Zillmann

Bored versus stressed subjects were provided with opportunities to watch television. Bored subjects more frequently selected exciting than relaxing programs, while stressed subjects selected similar quantities of each program type.

An apparent paradox consistently emerges from surveys probing viewers' motives for watching television.[1] On the one hand, viewers say that they watch television in order to relax, and they attribute critical stress-reducing and revitalization powers to the balm of the set's cool glow. On the other hand, viewers report that they watch television in order to receive chills, thrills and excitement, and that television provides much-needed stimulation to compensate for the dull routine of daily life. The two positions were recently reviewed, conceptualized and labeled as "television the unwinder" and "television the exciter."[2]

There is, of course, no real paradox in the claim that television provides relaxation *and* excitement. It may be that some viewers consistently use television to unwind while other viewers rely more heavily on exciting fare in the hope of becoming more aroused. Or it may be that the same viewers use television for "R and R" at one time and excitement at another. Regardless of the "trait" versus "state" position, and regardless of the particular alteration in excitational state (i.e., down for relaxation vs. up for excitement), it is frequently asserted by viewers and media analysts alike that television consumption can greatly alter viewers' levels of arousal and, hence, influence their affective and emotional behavior.

It is obvious that in order for television to serve both as a readily available

---

Manuscript accepted for publication, October 1983.

See, for example, Robert T. Bower, *Television and the Public* (New York: Holt, Rinehart & Winston, 1973).

[2]Dolf Zillmann, "Television Viewing and Arousal," in *Television and Behavior: Ten Years of Scientific Progress and Implications for the Eighties*, eds. David Pearl, Lorraine Bouthilet and Joyce Lazar (Washington, DC: US Government Printing Office, 1982).

From Jennings Bryant and Dolf Zillmann, "Using Television to Alleviate Boredom and Stress: Selective Exposure as a Function of Induced Excitational States," *Journal of Broadcasting*, Vol. 28, No. 1 (Winter 1984), pp. 1-20. Copyright 1984 by The Broadcast Education Association. Reprinted by permission.

"upper" or "downer," a wide variety of types of programming must be available to viewers at any one time. Recent developments in the medium have certainly strengthened its potential in that regard. In little more than a decade, television has advanced from the stage in which the typical viewer had very few choices — programming from two or three networks and perhaps from an independent or public station — to a stage in which a combination of broadcast television with the new media technologies offers a rich choice of information and entertainment in the form of programming from numerous cable networks, specialty channels, prerecorded videocassettes and discs featuring fare ranging from family movies to pornography, interactive instruction, viewer-recorded or produced programs of an infinite variety, video games, video jukeboxes and other options just emerging with the explosion in television technology. In short, we have emerged from a time of signal scarcity to a time of programming plenty. Contemporary television should have no trouble delivering fare suitable for relaxation or for excitation.

As the ready availability of diverse programming becomes a cultural universal, and as the television consumer is faced with numerous choices, a number of important questions emerge regarding viewers' mastery of their new information-rich video environment. For example, how much purposeful control do viewers exert over the vast number of program selections currently available? If televised messages can serve to mediate excitational states, does the consumer use the medium in such a (psycho)logically valid way so as to take advantage of its power and potential? Research is just beginning to address these questions experimentally, primarily from the perspective of *selective exposure.*

Although the notion of selective exposure has played a role in mass communication research since the 1940s,[3] it has only recently been applied to entertainment programming. Atkin, Greenberg, Korzenny and McDermott[4] employed a time-order design with questionnaire administration to examine children's selective exposure to television violence. They concluded that children's predispositions toward aggression influenced their selections of a heavier diet of television violence. Employing an experimental procedure, Zillmann, Hezel and Medoff[5] examined the effect of affective states on selective exposure to televised entertainment fare. They found that subjects who were in negative affective states avoided comedy and action

[3]See, for example, Paul F. Lazarsfeld, Bernard Berelson and Hazel Gaudet, *The People's Choice* (New York: Columbia University Press, 1948).

[4]Charles Atkin, Bradley Greenberg, Felipe Korzenny and Steven McDermott, "Selective Exposure to Televised Violence," *Journal of Broadcasting* 23:5–13 (Winter 1979).

[5]Dolf Zillmann, Richard T. Hezel and Norman J. Medoff, "The Effect of Affective States on Selective Exposure to Televised Entertainment Fare," *Journal of Applied Social Psychology* 10:323–339 (July–August 1980).

drama, while subjects in conditions of positive affect watched more action drama and avoided the game show format. A subsequent investigation, reported in the same study, indicated that type of negative affect was a critical determinant of program selection: Provoked subjects avoided hostile comedy, which contained contents which apparently reminded them of their provocation, while frustrated subjects actively sought out such fare. These investigators concluded that persons selectively expose themselves to television programming that holds the greatest promise of providing prompt relief from their negative affective experiences.

Perhaps the two most frequently suffered general types of negative affect in contemporary American life are boredom and stress, two conditions which can be construed as defining opposing ends on a continuum of excitational states. If television is to offer relief from these divergent vexing states, very different types of programming may be required. The present investigation examines how bored versus stressed persons select television fare which holds "the greatest promise of providing prompt relief from negative affective experiences."[6] It also attempts to determine *how effective* the selected programming is in alleviating these presumably vexing excitational states. It examines how the relative degree of success of the programs in helping the person out of antecedent states affects viewers' *enjoyment* of the program, and it assesses the degree to which viewers can articulate their implicit "theories" or rationales which govern selectivity.

There can be no doubt that *boredom* is a prevalent characteristic of contemporary society. Millions of workers perform dull and routine tasks in factories, fields and offices. Millions of homemakers scrub floors, wash windows, shop for groceries and change diapers far more frequently than they desire. These bored, relatively unaroused persons should be ripe for and appreciative of increments in autonomic arousal.

The view that moderate increases in arousal are pleasurable has been espoused by numerous scholars. Early scholars taking this position were Bain[7] and Wundt.[8] Modern advocates include Berlyne[9] and McClelland.[10] Recent revisions of this position have been proposed by Schachter[11] and Zillmann.[12]

---

[6]*Ibid.*, p. 323.

[7]Alexander Bain, *The Emotions and the Will,* 3d ed. (London: Longmans, Green, 1975; originally published 1859).

[8]Wilhelm M. Wundt, *Grundzuge der Physiologischen Psychologie* (Leipzig: Englemann, 1893).

[9]Daniel E. Berlyne, *Aesthetics and Psychobiology* (Englewood Cliffs, NJ: Prentice-Hall, 1971).

[10]See, for example, David C. McClelland, John W. Atkinson, Russell A. Clark and Edgar L. Lowell, *The Achievement Motive* (New York: Holt, Rinehart & Winston, 1960).

[11]Stanley Schachter, "The Interaction of Cognitive and Physiological Determinants of Emotional State" in *Advances in Experimental Social Psychology,* vol. 1, ed. Leonard Berkowitz (New York: Academic Press, 1964).

[12]Dolf Zillmann, "Excitation Transfer in Communication-Mediated Aggressive Behavior," *Journal of Experimental Social Psychology* 7:419–434 (July 1971); Dolf Zillmann, "Attribution and

In a recent examination of the role of arousal in emotional behavior, the issue of how people suffering from boredom should come to select television's more arousing fare has been specifically addressed:

1. Persons who experience low levels of arousal — because of monotonous environmental conditions, repetitive nonstrenuous tasks or similarly unstimulating circumstances — are likely to respond more intensely than others to affect-inducing stimuli. To the extent that exposure to television fare fosters enjoyment and the magnitude of any evoked arousal fuels this enjoyment, persons who are initially rather unaroused can be expected to obtain comparatively great pleasure from watching television.
2. As the experience of comparatively great pleasure is repeated, a tendency to seek out this excitement should manifest itself through operant learning. Ultimately, initially rather unaroused persons should be drawn to watching television "for the excitement of it."[13]

Thus, people who are bored may be expected to choose television's more stimulating fare to take advantage of "television the exciter."

It is conceivable, however, that people who to outside observers appear to be bored, are actually comfortable with low levels of arousal, and that they are inclined to perpetuate their experiential states. These viewers may therefore choose less stimulating television fare over more exciting alternatives. It has been argued that individuals have very different optimal levels of activation.[14] This emphasis of individual differences has resulted in the typecasting of individuals as sensation seekers and, more importantly here, sensation avoiders.[15] Persons classified as sensation avoiders should make efforts to prevent exposure to exciting television fare, choosing nonstimulating programming whenever possible.

Stress is also a fixture of modern postindustrial existence, especially in the highly competitive job situations which characterize much of the management sector of our work force.[16] The demanding boss, the unmet quota, the imposing stack of unanswered mail, the annoying computer breakdown, the endless commute — all these are experiences that have produced the

---

Misattribution of Excitatory Reactions," in *New Directions in Attribution Research,* vol. 2, eds. John H. Harvey, William J. Ickes and Robert F. Kidd (Hillsdale, NJ: Erlbaum, 1970); Dolf Zillmann, "Anatomy of Suspense," in *The Entertainment Function of Television,* ed. Percy H. Tannenbaum (Hillsdale, NJ: Erlbaum, 1980).

[13]Zillmann, "Television Viewing and Arousal," *op. cit.,* p. 58.

[14]See, for example, R. Lewis Donohew, Philip Palmgreen and Jack Duncan, "An Activation Model of Information Exposure," *Communication Monographs* 47:295–303 (November 1980).

[15]See, for example, Marvin Zuckerman, "The Sensation Seeking Motive," *Progress in Experimental Personality Research* 7:79–148 (1974).

[16]See, for example, Hans Selye, *The Stress of Life* (New York: McGraw-Hill, 1956); and Lennart Levi, *Stress: Sources, Management, and Prevention* (New York: Liverright, 1967).

so-called "ulcer class." As these stressed persons return to their homes, the need for diversionary television programming to bring relief should be acute. What type of television programming should these persons select in order to provide relief from stress? Two competing rationales have been offered to answer this question.

On the one hand, it has been argued that cognitively involving, stimulating fare will best serve to relieve stress. This rationale runs as follows: A person who is stressed is in an inappropriately high state of arousal. Arousal is maintained by a continued cognitive preoccupation with the events responsible for the experience of stress. Disrupting this rumination[17] or this rehearsal process[18] should have the beneficial effect of reducing arousal, thereby providing relief. Television programs have the potential to disrupt this rehearsal or rumination process, with more highly cognitively involving programming,[19] which is unrelated to the state of stress,[20] being the most effective type of program for breaking into the rehearsal process and thereby reducing stress. The proposal has been summarized as follows:

1. Exposure to communication, especially to entertainment fare, is likely to disrupt rehearsal processes that would perpetuate states of elevated arousal associated with negative affective experiences. Exposure is thus likely to produce feelings of relief.
2. A communication's capacity to effect a diminution of arousal associated with negative affect and to bring on the experience of relief is proportional to its capacity to involve and absorb the individual, as long as the affinity between the individual's affective state and the events featured is minimal.
3. Contents likely to reinstate a negative affective experience tend to prevent the dissipation of arousal, thus perpetuating an aversive experience.[21]

On the other hand, the case can be made that the most effective type of programming in reducing stress is low-key, comparatively noninvolving fare. Exposure to stimulating programming, after all, may be somewhat arousing, and it might add to the stress dilemma. What these viewers may really need

---

[17]Cf. Albert Bandura, "Vicarious Processes: A Case of No-Trial Learning," in *Advances in Experimental Social Psychology,* vol. 2, ed. Leonard Berkowitz (New York: Academic Press, 1965).

[18]Cf. Dolf Zillmann, *Hostility and Aggression* (Hillsdale, NJ: Erlbaum, 1979).

[19]Dolf Zillmann and Rolland C. Johnson, "Motivated Aggressiveness Perpetuated by Exposure to Aggressive Films and Reduced by Exposure to Nonaggressive Films," *Journal of Research in Personality* 7:261-276 (November 1973).

[20]Jennings Bryant and Dolf Zillmann, "The Mediating Effect of the Intervention Potential of Communications on Displaced Aggressiveness and Retaliatory Behavior," in *Communication Yearbook I,* ed. Brent D. Ruben (New Brunswick, NJ: ICA-Transaction Press, 1977).

[21]Zillmann, "Television Viewing and Arousal," *op. cit.,* p. 56.

are programs that are emotionally incompatible with stress.[22] A recent newswire story described an emerging genre of specialized television shows featuring soaring birds, rippling waterfalls, logs burning in a fireplace, gently crashing ocean waves, slow-moving clouds or tranquil country scenes complemented by Muzak, all designed as a "visual and brain holiday" and advertised as "a relaxing way to unwind."[23] Television viewers in a state of stress may well elect to view such relaxing programs rather than cognitively more involving fare. There is some research evidence, in fact, that suggests that this type of programming — nature scenes, that is — has strong stress-relieving effects.[24]

Selective-exposure theorizing obviously presupposes viewers who are active in the sense of making deliberate choices that are based on having learned, though probably without awareness, what type of fare holds the greatest promise for generating excitement and for providing relief. The present study is designed to explore these proposed mechanisms and to determine the validity of the predicitive and explanatory rationales that have been posited. Essentially, subjects were placed in a state of boredom or stress and then provided with a choice between relaxing and exicitng programs under conditions simulating actual television watching.

Method

Subjects

One hundred and twenty undergraduates at the University of Massachusetts, 63 males and 57 females, served as subjects in the main experiment. A total of 80 additional subjects, 40 males and 40 females, served in various pretests and posttests. All were enrolled in an introductory communications course and received class credit for participating in the study.

Experimental Materials

Six 15-minute segments of television programs were selected as stimulus materials via a pretest. Three of the program segments were uniformly low-key and relaxing: a nature program on the locomotion of fish and other underwater creatures, an orchestra concert of classical lullabies and a travelogue of restful vacations for the harried executive. The remaining three programs were uniformly stimulating and exciting: a suspenseful segment

---

[22]Cf. Robert A. Baron, *Human Aggression* (New York: Plenum, 1977).

[23]Associated Press Newswire, 8 January 1983.

[24]See, for example, Lennart Levi, "The Urinary Output of Adrenalin and Noradrenalin During Pleasant and Unpleasant Emotional States: A Preliminary Report," *Psychosomatic Medicine* 27:80–85 (January–February 1965).

from an action-adventure pilot, an action-packed segment from a professional football game and a "play-off" quiz-show segment. Each segment was presented in color on a Sony 21" television monitor via video-cassette played on Sony U-matic recorder/playback units. Seven recorders fed the same monitor. Ten seconds of additional representative material from each of the programs from which the segments were taken was employed as preview or promotional material for each segment and was edited onto a separate cassette.

Pretest for the selection of experimental materials. Fifteen male and 15 female undergraduates enrolled in the same class as the subjects in the main experiment, none of whom participated in the remainder of the study, viewed 36 15-minute segments selected from broadcast television programs. These segments had been chosen from numerous broadcast programs which had been taped for research purposes; they were judged to represent a widespread differentiation in degree of excitedness, with 18 of the segments judged to be exciting and 18 judged to be relaxing.

The raters viewed each segment and rated each immediately after it was viewed. Five sessions were required to evaluate all 36 segments without undue fatigue. Evaluation involved eight scales. Each scale ranged from "0" to "10," was marked and numbered at each integer and was labeled "not at all _____" at "0" and "extremely _____" at "10," with the eight descriptors being: relaxing, stimulating, arousing, unwinding, peaceful, exciting, emotionally involving and restful.

Two composite indices were created by summing the responses to the four descriptors associated with *relaxation* (relaxing, unwinding, peaceful, restful) and the responses to the descriptors associated with *excitement* (stimulating, arousing, exciting, emotionally involving). The six segments chosen for the main experiment were ideally differentiated on each index. Composite means on the relaxing index for each segment were: nature = 38.4, lullabies = 37.2, travelogue = 37.6 versus action-adventure = 6.4, quiz-show = 5.7 and sport = 6.1. In contrast, on the excitement index, composite means were: nature = 5.1, lullabies = 5.6, travelogue = 4.7 versus action-adventure = 35.7, quiz show = 35.3 and sport = 35.1. Statistical tests confirmed the obvious, robust differentiation between relaxing versus exciting programs ($p < .001$) and substantiated the apparent high degree of concordance within categories (for all comparisons within category, $p > .50$).

Induction of Stress or Boredom

Conditions of stress versus boredom were experimentally induced by having subjects perform different tasks for one hour; each condition employed three tasks, each being performed for 20 minutes. Subjects in the *stress* condition solved intellectual puzzles, played solitary "Boggle" and took GRE/SAT-type tests which required reading difficult passages and completing comprehension questions immediately afterward. The number of puzzles to solve, games to play and questions to answer exceeded the subjects' abilities, no matter how hard they tried or how fast they worked. Moreover, each of these tasks was performed under time pressure and with the constant prodding of the experimenter who urged better and better performance on the part of the subject. In spite of his constant cajoling, the experimenter was neither hostile nor demeaning; rather he acted as a concerned and ambitious supervisor spurring his employee on to optimal productivity. Subjects in the *boredom* condition threaded metal washers on a shoe lace, drew very simple pictures using a dot-to-dot procedure, and repeatedly tightened and loosened a nut on a bolt. No time nor performance pressure was involved, and the experimenter did nothing to motivate improved performance.

Pretest for effectiveness in inducing stress or boredom. The effectiveness of these procedures in producing stress versus boredom was pretested. Subjects were 10 male and 10 female students recruited from the same population employed in the main experiment, yet none of whom served in the experimental or other pretest samples. Subjects were randomly assigned to conditions with an equal number of males and females in each condition. Excitatory state prior to and after task performance was assessed in measures of heart rate and systolic and diastolic blood pressures. Questionnaire ratings assessed experiential stress and boredom; additional questions assessed affective state. The questionnaire was administered immediately after the hour-long manipulation treatment.

Blood pressures were measured by the cuff method and heart rate was measured photoelectrically from the distal pad of the index finger. The measures were recorded on Whittaker apparati.

Changes in sympathetic activity expected to be produced by the stress-boredom treatment were analysed in changes from the basal (t_1) to the posttreatment measures (t_2) of the various indices employed. The treatment was found to produce significant activity changes on all indices. Employing delta scores ($t_2 - t_1$) throughout, systolic blood pressure increased in the stress condition (8.2 mm Hg) and decreased in the boredom condition (−3.6 mm Hg), the difference being associated with $t(18) = 21.83$, $p < .001$. Diastolic blood pressure changed similarly, though not so markedly: up 2.8 mm Hg for stress; down 1.6 mm Hg for boredom, $t(18) = 7.9$, $p < .001$. The pattern was also similar for heart rate. In the stress condition, heart rate increased substantially (7.3 bpm), while in the boredom condition, it decreased somewhat (3.5 bpm), with the differences associated with $t(18) = 12.3$, $p < .001$. Clearly, the treatment differentiated excitatory state.

Subjects' feelings of experiential stress were assessed in response to the direct question, "How much stress are you feeling right now?" Responses were made on a unipolar scale ranging from "0" to "10," marked and numbered at each integer, and labeled "no stress at all" at "0" and "extreme stress" at "10." Subjects in the boredom condition reported minimal stress (1.1), while subjects in the stress condition experienced considerable stress (8.4). The difference was associated with $t(18) = 36.4$, $p < .001$. The question assessing boredom was also direct: "How bored are you right now?" Responses were made on a similar scale, labeled "not bored at all" at "0" and "extremely bored" at "10." Subjects in the boredom condition reported being quite bored (7.7), while subjects in the stress condition were significantly less bored (2.2), the difference being associated with $t(18) = 19.4$, $p < .001$.

Previous research has demonstrated that affective state influences selective exposure to televised entertainment fare.[25] Therefore, two questions were included to determine subjects' affective state following task performance. One question asked, "How upset or angry are you right now?" The previously described scale was employed with labels of "not at all upset or angry" at "0" and "extremely upset or angry" at "10." Although subjects in the stress condition were somewhat more upset or angry (4.2) than their counterparts in the boredom condition (3.4), the difference, although close to significant, was not statistically reliable [$t(18) = 2.03$, $p > .05$]. A second question asked, "How frustrated are you right now?" The same scale skeleton was employed, with labels of "not frustrated at all" at "0" and "extremely frustrated" at "10." Subjects in the stress condition were significantly more frustrated than subjects in the boredom condition (6.1 and 3.9, respectively; [$t(18) = 2.43$, $p < .05$]. Frustration, then, covaried with stress and might be considered a salient element of it.

Procedure

Subjects were tested in individual sessions. At the time they were recruited, subjects were told that they would be participating in a two-part study which would take approximately two hours. Upon arriving at the laboratory, the subject was escorted into a testing/viewing room by a male experimenter who seated the subject in a comfortable, padded desk chair and instructed the subject to sit at the desk while prerecorded instructions were played.

The instructions reiterated the two-part nature of the experiment and informed the subject that the second part of the study would require physiological measures for which basal measures would be taken during a brief waiting period prior to beginning the second session. The first study was then introduced, with no further instructions given for the second portion of the study. In actuality, the second phase of the study was irrelevant to the

[25] Zillmann, Hezel and Medoff, *op. cit.*

present investigation and merely served as a pretext for the waiting period and for physiological measurement. The selective exposure assessment took place during the waiting period.

The first portion of the study was described as an assessment of key aspects of students' performance on certain types of tasks, the determination of which would purportedly be used as a factor in the second portion of the study. The subject was told that three tasks would be performed during the next hour, each lasting 20 minutes.

The experimenter then introduced and demonstrated the three tasks, informing subjects in the boredom condition that after any questions had been answered, his interactions with them would be minimal; that he was primarily to serve as timekeeper and indicate when the subject was to begin the second and third tasks. After questions were answered, the tasks were begun. The experimenter stayed in the room with the subject during this hour. In the boredom condition, he remained seated unobtrusively behind the subject except when it was time to provide the subject with materials for the next task. In the stress condition, the experimenter interacted frequently with the subject, purportedly to serve as a motivator to superior performance.

At the end of the hour, the experimenter told the subject that heart rate would be measured. The subject's index finger was inserted into a finger clip, and heart rate was assessed. Then, after the experimenter removed the clip, the subject was told that such a measure would be taken again in a few minutes, in order to determine a stable base measure for the second portion of the study in which an entire battery of physiological measures would be taken.

The experimenter informed the subject that it was permissible to watch television during the waiting period, and he oriented the subject toward a television set which was on the desk. In a casual manner, the experimenter told the subject that the programs available on the set were provided courtesy of Advent Cable Communication, which was making a bid to take over the local franchise operation and had wired the Communication Department with a closed-circuit system to attempt to win an endorsement of their programming and service. The subject was shown a page from a professionally printed program guide which indicated the program available on each channel at that time. The descriptions of each available program featured an adjective associated with either "excitement" or "relaxation." For example, the quiz program was described as "The exciting playoff contest. . . ."

The experimenter then turned on the set and quickly ran through the program selections by purportedly pushing each of six push buttons on a specially-created control panel built into the television set. Each button commanded access to one of the six experimental program segments, with the order of the program arrangement having previously been determined by a random procedure: Button A operated the action-adventure segment, Button B the lullabies segment, and so on. The button identification corresponded with that on the program guide. In actuality, the 10-second preview of each program was controlled by a separate, hidden button, and its operation locked out operation of the other buttons. Thus, while it appeared that the experimenter was punching the six buttons sequentially, a seventh tape was actually playing. This tape presented the preview/promo segments. After running through the program choices, the experimenter pushed the button of a vacant channel, told the subject to enjoy himself/herself for about 15 minutes, and then left the room, leaving the subject in control of the set.

After 15 minutes, the experimenter reentered the room, took a second measure of heart rate and turned off the set. Then the subject completed a four-item questionnaire "to provide feedback to Advent Cable Communication which provided us with the set and the programs," and the subject was ushered into the laboratory where another experimenter conducted a second, unrelated study.

At the completion of the testing, each subject was interviewed and was offered bonus points to reveal the "real" purpose of the study. No subject could. All subjects were fully debriefed in a later class meeting.

Dependent Measures

Measures of exposure. During the 15-minute waiting period, and after the experimenter had assessed heart rate and explained the operation of the television set, each subject's television exposure was recorded by an Esterline-Angus event recorder connected to the push-button channel selector. The recorder was located in an adjacent room with the seven cassette playback units. The room was soundproof, permitting unobstrusive monitoring of the time spent with each signal-carrying channel. Time spent with the *exciting* programs was one dependent measure of exposure. Time spent with the *relaxing* programs was a separate measure.

Measure of excitatory state. Heart rate as a measure of arousal was assessed to provide an index of relative relaxation or stimulation. Heart rate was assessed immediately after task performance (t_1) to determine if performing the stimulating versus relaxing tasks produced different levels of sympathetic activation. It was also assessed immediately after the 15-minute television exposure period (t_2) to determine whether and how watching either exciting or relaxing television programs affected the sympathetic activation of previously stressful versus bored subjects.

Subjects' self-reports of television viewing and program enjoyment and their rationales on selective exposure. To serve as a check on viewing and to determine whether subjects had any tacit understanding of their selective exposure behavior, four questions relating to their program selection and television viewing during the waiting period were included in the questionnaire. The first question was "How much television did you watch during this waiting period?" The subject answered the question by checking one of five response options: "I didn't watch any," "I watched less than half the time," "I watched somewhat more than half of the time," "I watched most of the time" and "I watched all of the time." The second question asked "What was the content of the television program that you watched the most?" A blank was provided for the response. A third question asked "How much did you enjoy the program you watched the most?" Responses were indicated on a scale skeleton identical to those previously described, with labels of "did not enjoy at all" at "0" and "enjoyed tremendously" at "100." The fourth question asked "Why did you choose to watch the program you watched the most?" Again, a blank was provided for the response.

Results

Manipulation of Boredom and Stress

The analysis of heart rate immediately subsequent to task performance indicated that, as in the more comprehensive pretest, the manipulation of excitatory state was effective. Heart rate was more than nine beats per minute faster in the stress condition (83.2) than in the boredom condition (74.0). As in the pretest, the difference was highly significant ($t(118) = 28.0$, $p < .001$).

Time of Exposure

The accumulated time of selective exposure to the two types of programs (relaxing, exciting) was analyzed in three time blocks of five minutes, covering the experimental period of 15 minutes. Preliminary analyses failed to show appreciable gender differences, and the gender variation was consequently collapsed. For the measure of selective exposure to the *relaxing* programs, the mixed-measures analysis of variance, with prior excitational state as the independent-measures factor and time blocks as the repeated-measures factor, produced a significant main effect for prior excitational state [$F(1,118) = 47.23$, $p < .001$]. Neither the main effect for time nor the interaction between these variables approached significance ($F < 1$ for both). The statistical decisions from the analysis of variance for selective exposure to the *exciting* programs were identical, the significant main effect for prior excitational state being associated with $F(1,118) = 36.02$, $p < .001$.

Table I displays the means associated with the significant main effects. As can be seen, stressed subjects watched nearly six times as much relaxing television (7 minutes 7 seconds) as did bored subjects (1 minute 14 seconds). In stark contrast, bored subjects watched nearly twice as much exciting fare (13 minutes 13 seconds) as did stressed subjects (7 minutes 21 seconds).

Table I
Selective Exposure to Relaxing and Exciting Programs as a Function of Boredom and Stress

Program Type	Experiential Condition	
	Boredom	Stress
Exciting	793[b]	441[a]
Relaxing	74[a]	427[b]
Combined	867	868

Note: Exposure time is in seconds. Maximally possible time was 900 seconds or 15 minutes. Statistical comparisons are within program type only (horizontal). Means with different letter superscripts differ significantly by F test at $p < .001$.

Looked at another way, whereas subjects under stress selected approximately the same amount of exciting and relaxing television, bored subjects exposed themselves to exciting programming about 10 times longer than to relaxing fare.

Two other facts of interest are revealed by detailed inspection of the exposure data. Subjects rarely changed channels. To present the normative exposure data: Initially, at the beginning of the exposure period, 12 bored subjects chose relaxing fare, 45 chose exciting programs and three opted not to watch television. In contrast, for stressed subjects, 32 chose relaxing programs while 26 opted for exciting offerings, and two had turned off the television set. Fifteen minutes later, at the end of the exposure period, the profile was similar: For bored subjects, 10 were watching relaxing fare, three were not watching at all, while 47 had by then opted for exciting television. For stressed subjects, 27 remained with relaxing fare, 30 with exciting material and three were not watching television. More than 75 percent of the channel changing came within the first minute of viewing. This apparent satisfaction with initial program selection and the resultant stable pattern of viewing over time, which is also indicated by the lack of statistical significance for the time-block factor, differ from earlier findings.[26] The difference may result from the more explicit program preview of the present study, together with the examination of the program-guide descriptions. Both procedures may have produced superior conditions for an informed initial program selection.

Effects of Exposure on Excitational State

Preliminary tests for gender differences failed to reveal appreciable differences for this and all of the remaining measures. Gender was consequently collapsed in all further analyses.

---

[26] *Ibid.*

At the time of initial program selection, heart rate — as an index of sympathetic activation — was clearly a function of the stress/boredom treatment. In order to determine what effect exposure to selected programs had on the preexposure excitational state, heart rate changes resulting from exposure were examined. The observed, stable pattern of exposure over time makes this procedure applicable. As will be recalled, most subjects stayed with the same program throughout the exposure session.

An analysis of variance was performed on the heart-rate scores, with prior excitational state (boredom, stress) and selective exposure to predominantly-viewed program type (relaxing, exciting) as independent-measures factors, and with time of assessment (before exposure, after exposure) as a repeated-measures factor. Program type was treated as a random factor. None of the main effects and two-factor interactions reached significance ($F^1 \simeq 1$ for all). However, the three-way interaction was highly significant [$F^1(1,116) = 18.41$, $p < .001$].

Table II
Excitatory Changes as a Result of Selective Exposure

	Experiential Condition			
	Boredom		Stress	
	Measurement Relative to Exposure			
Program Type	Before	After	Before	After
Exciting	74.3^{a}	81.3^{b}	82.8^{b}	76.3^{ab}
Relaxing	73.7^{a}	73.6^{a}	83.6^{b}	76.7^{ab}

Note: Mean scores report heart rate in bpm. Scores having no letter in their superscripts in common differ by Newman-Keuls' test at $p < .05$.

Table II presents this interaction. In the boredom/relaxing programs condition, heart rate was 73.7 bpm. It was significantly higher, 83.6 bpm, in the corresponding stress condition. Similarly, heart rate was 74.3 bpm in the boredom/exciting programs condition; and it was significantly higher, 82.8 bpm, in the corresponding stress condition. Those bored subjects who chose relaxing television evidenced almost no change in heart rate, their heart rate at the end of exposure having slowed .1 bpm. In contrast, bored subjects who selected exciting fare had the fastest heart rate at the end of the viewing period, their heart rate having increased 7.0 bpm from its initial level. Subjects under stress showed similar changes in heart rate whether they selected exciting or relaxing programs. In both instances, heart rate declined notably. In stressed subjects who selected relaxing programs, heart rate declined 6.9 bpm. In stressed subjects who watched exciting material, it declined 6.5 bpm. Subsequent tests show that after exposure only the two extreme mean scores were significantly different. Those two mean scores come from the initially bored subject who selected different types of viewing material. Heart rate at the end of viewing was 7.7 bpm different, indicating markedly different excitational states as a function of selective exposure to television.

Self-Perceptions

Watching the Programs. The selective exposure measures are analagous to the best known of the Nielsen ratings in that they record whether the set was on and to which of the available channels it was tuned while it was on. But they do not indicate whether the "viewers" were actually watching. Subjects' responses to the question "How much television did you watch during the waiting period?" were employed as a check on viewing. Overall, 39 of the 120 subjects reported viewing "all of the time" (32 percent); and 73 subjects reported viewing "most of the time" (61 percent). This 93 percent heavy viewing would seem to correspond rather well with the event-recorder data on the use of signal-carrying channels: 96 percent of the time.

To derive a more accurate index of viewing, subjects' individual event-recorder data were compared to their self-reports. This was done as follows: Self-report "all of the time" was determined to be equivalent to 100 percent exposure on the event-recorder record; "most of the time" was judged equivalent to 75–99 percent exposure as measured by the event recorder; "somewhat more than half the time" equaled 50–74 percent exposure, "less than half the time" equaled 1–49 percent exposure; and "didn't watch" equaled 0 percent exposure. Two judges independently determined the correspondence between record and self-report for each subject, with greater than 95 percent agreement between judges. Self-report was determined to correspond perfectly with measured exposure in 92.5 percent of the cases (111 of 120). The two measures were therefore considered highly related. A similar assessment made on the self-report item of "the television program you watched the most" compared with the event-recorder data yielded 90 percent agreement (108 of 120 subjects).

Enjoyment of the Programs. The question assessing program enjoyment was included to determine whether alteration in excitational state, particularly movement toward presumably more pleasant moderate levels of arousal from the more extreme levels associated with the noxious states of boredom and stress, would facilitate enjoyment. To make this determination, a one-factor analysis of variance was performed on the enjoyment ratings for subjects in the four experimental state/type-of-program conditions at the time television exposure was terminated. The analysis yielded significant findings ($F(3,116) = 3.01$, $p < .05$). The mean scores for enjoyment were: boredom/relaxing = 3.13, boredom/exciting = 6.4, stress/relaxing = 5.4 and stress/exciting = 5.9. Only the two extreme scores proved reliably different at $p < .05$ by Newman-Keuls' test.

Rationales for Selecting Programs. A content analysis was performed on subjects' answers to the question "Why did you choose to watch the program you watched the most?" A model statement of theoretical positions predicting each selective-exposure alternative was developed. For example, the rationale for why a stressful subject should choose exciting programs was, "I chose an exciting program because watching an involving message should take my mind off of the conditions that produced my stress." The two male experimenters served as coders. They collaborated on all judgments, examining each subject's response to see if it could be rephrased and then interpreted as fitting one of the model statements. If the judges could not agree after deliberation and argument (three instances), the response was omitted from analysis. Most of the responses (e.g., "I liked what I saw of it in the preview") were judged not to fit any of the model statements. Also, 27 questionnaires provided no response whatsoever to this question. In all, 21 of the responses were judged to be rephrasable into one of the exposure rationales posited. Of these responses, the subjects' perception of their selective exposure motives matched the exposure rationales expressed earlier in 17 of 21 cases (81 percent). This suggests that selective exposure can be thoughtful and deliberate — or alternatively, that some people are skillful rationalizers of their behavior. The type of selective exposure that was accurately explained most frequently was the condition in which bored subjects chose exciting television programs. Eight of the 17 theory-fitting explanations belonged to this condition, suggesting that the notion of "television as exciter" is widely accepted among college students. A typical sample of this kind of explanation is "I about went to sleep doing those stupid tasks the professor made us do, and I thought the quiz show would wake me up the best." Four explanatory attempts were made in each stress category. One of the subjects in the stress/exciting condition relied heavily on vernacular: "I was pretty strung out and thought the ball game would shake up my mind and let me get back down." A counterpart in the stress/relaxation condition was likewise informal: "Those tests got me excited and I thought the music would help me veg out." The only subject who explained in any acceptable fashion the preference for relaxing fare after being bored stated: "My roommate and I studied all last night and those tasks got me pretty num(b) [*sic*]. I thought the lullabys [*sic*] would finish setting me up for a good nights sleep."

Posttest

The present results are certainly consistent with the initially advanced rationales. However, an alternative account can readily be furnished for the findings that subjects experiencing stress underwent relaxation and that those experiencing boredom were stimulated by exposure. It may be argued that in the stress condition the selection of relaxing programs had no relaxing effect, did not disrupt rehearsal processes, etc., and that in the boredom condition the choice of exciting programs failed to arouse. Heart rate, it could be conjectured, simply increased in the boredom/exciting program condition or decreased in the stress conditions until it returned to normal, basal levels by homeostasis alone. Television viewing, then, may have had no effect. The fact that most of the mean scores for heart rate are located around a point of normalcy at the termination of exposure could be interpreted as supporting such an argument. Therefore, a posttest was conducted to examine and potentially rule out this possibility.

Method. Thirty subjects, 15 males and 15 females, none of whom had participated in other parts of the study, were recruited from the population employed in the main study. All of the subjects repeated the stress-inducing treatment. Twenty subjects were then randomly selected to repeat the selective-exposure procedures and the heart-rate assessment exactly as it had been done in the main experiment. The other 10 subjects, after receiving the identical stress treatment and heart-rate assessment, were left in the testing room without the potential for television exposure for the 15-minute waiting period. The latter group served as a control to determine the effect of selective exposure and television viewing on excitatory state.

Results. Selective exposure was similar to that in the main experiment; that is, the selection of relaxing versus exciting programming was rather evenly divided (407 seconds for relaxing; 423 seconds for exciting), failing to differ by t-test ($p > .50$).

Changes in heart rate from the conclusion of the stress treatment (t_1) to the end of the exposure or waiting period (t_2) served as the dependent measure of excitatory state. An analysis of variance performed on the difference scores ($t_2 - t_1$) for the three experimental conditions yielded significance [$F(2,27) = 10.47$, $p < .05$], with mean scores of -1.7 for the control, -6.3 for relaxing and -6.9 for exciting. The mean scores for the two selective-exposure conditions differed from the control, but not from each other, at $p < .05$ by Newman-Keuls' test.

The argument that exposure to the programs was without effect on excitatory state is thus unfounded, and the proposal that arousal levels homeostatically normalized does not constitute an acceptable explanation of the findings.

Discussion

Selective Exposure as a Function of Induced Boredom or Stress

The findings of the present study clearly support the tenet that acutely aversive states foster selective exposure to television programs capable of providing relief. Stressed subjects watched a far greater proportion of tranquil programming than did bored subjects; bored subjects selected a greater amount of exciting fare than did stressed subjects. Boredom and stress evidently motivated selective exposure. Subjects exhibited clear preferences for particular types of programming under the specific experimental conditions.

Rationales offered to explain why persons experiencing boredom or stress would select certain kinds of programs receive limited support from the exposure data taken alone. The notion that bored persons chose stimulating fare is perfectly concordant with the notion of "television the exciter." On the other hand, subjects suffering from stress selected relaxing versus exciting fare in almost equal proportions. On the basis of the exposure data, it might be argued that stressed people do not differentiate in their selection process. Or it could be argued that both rationales describe equally valid mechanisms for using television to provide relief from stress, and that some persons take advantage of cognitive intervention while others exploit emotional incompatibility — their prior learning history guiding their choice of programs according to what works most effectively for them. The data on subjects' self-interpretation of their own selective-exposure behavior lend some support to the latter rationale.

Effectiveness of Selections in Alleviating Boredom or Stress

Exciting television seems to be an effective prescription for alleviating feelings of aversion that characterize boredom. Viewers who selected exciting programs exhibited prompt elevation in levels of excitation. On the other hand, bored viewers who selected relaxing programs retained the low levels of arousal associated with their aversive experience. If it is assumed that the bored subjects who selected less stimulating fare sought to elevate their levels of arousal in order to return to normalcy,[27] their selection was obviously inadequate and ineffective. If, on the other hand, it is assumed that these subjects were sensation avoiders who may have had lower optimal arousal levels to begin with, then their selections can be deemed appropriate. The data on program enjoyment, to be discussed shortly, indicate that the former rationale may be superior. Further support is added by the fact that

---

[27]Cf. Harry H. Helson, *Adaptation-Level Theory: An Experimental and Systematic Approach to Behavior* (New York: Harper & Row, 1964).

during the last five-minute viewing block, only 10 initially bored subjects remained with relaxing fare.

As far as stressed subjects are concerned, either type of programming, relaxing or exciting, seemed to work equally well in returning arousal to normal levels. There was no indication whatsoever that viewing exciting programs under conditions of acute stress further elevates the high levels of arousal associated with that experimental state. It seems plausible that subjects who choose this type of fare under stress conditions have learned that for them it has utility in providing for relaxation. In other words, under the right conditions, and presumably for the right sorts of subjects, exciting television can be just as relaxing as so-called "relaxing" fare. Presumably, this is so because the excitatory potential of entertaining fare tends to be below that of acutely aversive experiences, and even arousing fare disrupts the rehearsal of information that would perpetuate the aversive state.

The enjoyment ratings seem to indicate that programming that is effective in alleviating noxious excitational states is enjoyed, whereas programming that fails to do so is not. The bored subjects who chose relaxing programming for the bulk of their viewing time and whose excitation remained at low levels rated the programs they watched as significantly less enjoyable than stressed subjects who watched the same type of fare.

These findings pertain to the earlier discussion of whether bored subjects who chose and stuck with relaxing material "made a mistake" or whether they were stress avoiders who were pleased with the results of their choice. The fact that they enjoyed the programs less suggests that they exercised poor judgment. The finding that stressed subjects who chose relaxing fare enjoyed it as much as their counterparts who chose exciting fare is also revealing. This similar degree of enjoyment might be taken as suggesting that different viewing strategies work for different people. It could also be interpreted as showing that "whatever works for people, they like."

Accuracy of Subjects' Rationales for Selective Exposure

Teleological theories of human behavior depict the person as an active processor of information who is constantly seeking to interpret events in light of the theories, plans and patterns available.[28] Although it is probably inadvisable to determine how much a plan or a "theory" guided behavior by asking a person after the fact why something was done, it is possible to at least determine the accuracy of persons' rationales — or perhaps more correctly, rationalizations — in light of the formal propositions and hypotheses.

In this instance, only a small proportion of the subjects (14 percent) were able to articulate a notion which might be considered an informal, personal

---

[28]See, for example, George A. Miller, Eugene Galanter and Karl H. Pribrum, *Plans and the Structures of Behavior* (New York: Holt, Rinehart & Winston, 1960).

theory. However, of those who did provide a theory-like answer the "why-they-did-it" fit their behavior (or vice versa) in excess of 95 percent of the time. This suggests that at least some persons are cognizant of the processes that govern their viewing decisions. Other subjects may have made "rational" selections also, but were unable to articulate their rationales.

All in all, the findings lend strong support to the utility of the selective-exposure propositions. In particular, they are supportive of the notion that subjects make intelligent program choices — mostly intuitively, but sometimes following comprehension of the circumstances — when using television exposure as a means for alleviating boredom and stress.

21

TELEVISION AND MUSIC
Contrasting Media in Adolescent Life

Reed Larson and Robert Kubey

In a recent article in *Daedelus*, humanist Wayne Booth (1982) proposes that various electronic and artistic media represent different modes of being in the world. Television watching, movie viewing, music listening, and reading each structure experience, shaping not only what a person encounters while directly engaged, but also the existence a person leads in other domains of life. Each medium or art form constitutes an expressive system of symbolic and explicit meanings that evoke feelings, values, and attitudes in its participants.

For adolescents, an important distinction can be made between watching TV and listening to music. Both are electronic media made available on a daily basis by innovations of the last 100 years. Both provide one-way reception of sequenced content. Television, however, is structured and packaged largely by middle-aged adults in the mainstream of society. Its narrative content is based on traditional American values and

---

For reprints or information, contact Robert Kubey, Department of Communication, Rutgers University, 4 Huntington Street, New Brunswick, NJ 08903.

From Reed Larson and Robert Kubey, "Television and Music: Contrasting Media in Adolescent Life," *Youth and Society*, Vol. 15, No. 1 (September 1983), pp. 13-31. Copyright 1983 by Sage Publications, Inc.

the Puritan Ethic (Goethals, 1981; Hirsch, 1980; Newcomb, 1974). Much of the music youth listen to, on the other hand, is created by individuals close to their own age who stand apart and may be at odds with adult society (Hebdige, 1979; Hirsch, 1971). The origins of rock music may be traced back to the music of American slaves and other downtrodden groups (Frith, 1981; Hebdige, 1979). The structure and content of these two forms of entertainment have different sources within the social system. Time spent with either medium, therefore, is time spent in contact with different loci in the society, loci that represent different goals and expectations, and hence different channels of socialization.

Much attention has been given to the symbolic content of these two media. What has been neglected is how young people respond subjectively, how each medium engages them psychologically. The influence of each as a socializing agent depends on its ability to draw teenagers in as participants, to mobilize their attention, their emotions, and their motivation into active communion with the medium's content. It is important, therefore, to consider what adolescents experience while attending to each, and how each relates to their experience in other life domains.

To investigate the subjective impact of television and music on youth, data used were obtained via the experience sampling method (ESM). For one week a sample of 75 adolescents carried radio-controlled pagers (the kind doctors carry). In response to transmitted signals they provided self-reports at random moments in their lives. This pool of over 2700 reports on daily emotion—involvement, excitement, loneliness, and boredom—serves as a base for analyzing the influence of TV and music on the subjective experience of adolescents.

TELEVISION AND MUSIC IN ADOLESCENT LIFE

Past research has demonstrated differences in how these two media are used and experienced by young people. First, rate of

TV watching is lower in adolescence than in any other period of life (Comstock et al., 1978) and it declines with age as the teenage years progress (Chaffee et al., 1971; Glick and Levy, 1962; Johnstone and Katz, 1957). Television is a medium in which teenage characters appear only one-third as often as their numbers in the population (Gerbner et al., 1980; Simmons et al., 1977) and the television image of adolescents is often negative (Peck, 1982). Hence the world of TV becomes increasingly alien to the growing teenager who has come to identify with the values of the peer group. Television is aimed at the broadest possible audience and many adolescents grow increasingly distant from the mainstream focus of this appeal.

With the decline in television viewing, there is an increase in rates of music listening during adolescence (Avery, 1979). Produced specifically for youth, much popular music speaks to salient adolescent concerns, from heterosexual relations to rebellion and autonomy. The lyrics, rhythms, and harmonies provide raw materials that youth may draw upon in learning sex roles and composing their sexual identities (Smothers, 1961). Hence music becomes an essential ingredient to the romantic rites of dances, parties, and dating so intrinsic to this transitional period of development. The lyrics also may provide support for dealing with ambivalent feelings about growing up and joining adult society. Youth music frequently presents the story of individuals who exist separate from the adult world and who wonder whether they will ever adjust to or join adult society (Carey, 1969; Cooper, 1978). Music may also serve as a focus for movements of collective rebellion, as illustrated by the teddy boys, skinheads, and punks of Great Britain (Hebdige, 1979).

The declining pertinence of TV to adolescents and the growing appeal of music should be manifest not only in rates of usage, but in the types of experiences adolescents have with each medium. Because the sound and message of popular music are created for youth and reflect their concerns, it is hypothesized that the experiential states accompanying music listening will reflect greater involvement and emotional participation than those accompanying television viewing. One would expect differences in the mood, motives, and level of activity occurring in conjunction with each.

The broader issue is how use of the two media is related to adolescents' overall experience: what they do and how they feel in other areas of their lives. Previous research suggests that heavy involvement with popular music conflicts with adherence to "adult" norms of academic achievement (Burke and Grinder, 1966; Coleman, 1961) and to other "middle-class" values, such as delay of gratification (Brown and O'Leary, 1971). Heavy use of television, on the other hand, has been found to be related to conventionality and conformity to adult norms (Rushton, 1979; Weigel and Jessor, 1973).

At no other period in life does the interplay between media and peer relations seem as crucial as in adolescence. Strong statistical relationships have been demonstrated between an adolescent's level of familiarity with and use of popular music and the same adolescent's popularity (Adoni, 1978; Brown and O'Leary, 1971; Johnstone and Katz, 1957). Clarke (1973) has shown that a substantial proportion of teenagers consider others' musical tastes in the impressions they form of their peers. Liking and being able to talk about music is crucial to an adolescent's participation in the world of other youth.

Television, in contrast, has been linked more closely to the family. Rates of adolescents' TV use are correlated with their parents' rates of use (Chaffee et al., 1971). Television, after all, is the medium most likely to be used at home and with other family members. With regard to peers, Hendry and Patrick (1977) found that heavy TV viewers have fewer friends, and Johnstone (1974) found that such adolescents were more likely to be individuals encountering "status frustrations." Heavy TV viewers may use television and family involvement as a substitute for relationships with friends.

Therefore, it is hypothesized that TV and music participation will exhibit different relationships to an adolescent's lifestyle, specifically to involvement in adult-structured domains of daily life, such as the family and the classroom, versus the adolescent-structured domain of the peer group. Involvement will be evaluated in terms of amount of time spent and mood in each domain. Hence, heavier television use is expected to correlate with more time with the family and less time with friends. Similarly, heavy TV use is expected to correlate with higher affective states with the family and lower affective states with friends. This overall pattern of relationship should be reversed for heavier music listening.

METHOD

The research was carried out in 1977, employing the experience sampling method (Csikszentmihalyi et al., 1977; Larson and Csikszentmihalyi, 1983). Adolescents in the study carried electronic pagers during a normal week in their lives and filled out self-reports in response to signals. Each pager could be set to receive the signals either by vibrating or by emitting a tone. The schedule specified signals at random times between 7:30 a.m. and 10:30 p.m. (8:00 a.m. to 1:30 a.m. on weekends), with one signal occurring within every two-hour block of time.

The research sample was composed of 75 students from a large and diverse suburban Chicago high school. It was selected by a random stratification procedure, structured to obtain approximately equal numbers of boys and girls, lower-middle-class and upper-middle-class students, and ninth, tenth, eleventh, and twelfth graders. More extensive details on sample composition are available in Csikszentmihalyi and Larson (forthcoming).

Participants' instructions were to fill out self-reports for as many of the signals as possible while they were awake, with a stipulation that they retained the right not to respond if they felt they "really needed privacy." The pool of completed self-reports represents 69% of the signals sent. Reports were missed due to going to bed, mechanical failure of the pager, as well as a range of other reasons, from misplacing the pager to traveling outside the 50-mile radio transmission radius. The total sample includes reports on 2734 moments in the participants' lives.

For each report, students responded to items asking about their objective situation and their subjective state at the time of the signal. The first included a multiple-choice question asking about their social context ("Were you with: parents(s), friend(s), alone, etc."), and open-ended questions regarding their physical context ("Where were you?") and their primary activity ("What was the MAIN thing you were doing?"). The open-ended responses have been coded into mutually exclusive categories, with a reliability of 82% and 80%, respectively. A major focus of this article is the self-reports for which the students' activity was coded as either watching TV or listening to music.

The subjective state items asked for scaled ratings in four areas reflecting subjective involvement: affective state, psychological activation, motivation, and cognitive state. The first two include four 7-point semantic differential scales, which were intercorrelated. The latter two include 7- and 10-point scales, grouped here only on theoretical grounds—items in these two areas are not highly intercorrelated (see Csikszentmihalyi and Larson, forthcoming). Responses to all items have been standardized to control for individual differences in response patterns; the means have been standardized to zero and the standard deviations to 1.0.

RESULTS

RATES AND CONTEXT OF MEDIA USE

The adolescents in the study indicated watching TV more often than listening to music (Table 1). Television watching was reported as a primary activity on 194 occasions, or 7.1% of the total set of self-reports. Music listening was reported as a primary activity 39 times, or 1.4% of the self-reports. Thus music was the main focus of attention one-fifth as often as television. But when reports of media use as secondary are added, the TV percentage rises slightly to 10.2%; the music percentage is more than quadrupled, to 6.4%. Music is more frequently used as background.[1]

Consistent with expectations, younger students reported more total TV watching ($t = 2.18, p < .05$); however, there were no significant age differences in extent of music listening (Table 1). Rates of TV and music use were unrelated to sex and socioeconomic status. These rates were also not significantly correlated with academic ability, as measured by the School and College Ability Test (SCAT), or creativity, as measured by the unusual uses test (Guilford, 1967). On the whole, extent of TV and music use was similar across different groups of adolescents.

Significant social context patterns were evident in the use of these two media (Table 2). When watching TV, respondents most often reported themselves to be with family members or alone and rarely to be with friends. When listening to music, they most often reported themselves to be alone, one-quarter of the time they were with their friends, and virtually never were they with their families.

The reported physical context of media use paralleled these differences in social context (Table 2). Television watching was most often reported in the living room, family room, or other common rooms of the home. It took place most frequently with other family members, in shared family space. Listening to music was reported most often in the adolescent's bedroom. It was typically a solitary activity carried out in the privacy of a person's personal space.

ADOLESCENTS' EXPERIENCE WITH TELEVISION AND MUSIC

For each of the self-reports the adolescents in the study rated their psychological state. These data allow consideration of what was experienced subjectively in conjunction with each medium. Table 3 shows the average self-ratings for all occa-

TABLE 1
Descriptive Information on TV and Music Self-Reports

	TV Watching		Music Listening	
	As Primary Activity	All TV Watching	As Primary Activity	All Music Listening
Number of Self-Reports	194	280	39	177
Average Rate of Self-Reports (%)	7.1	10.2	1.4	6.4
Average Rate (%) for :				
Boys	6.2	9.9	1.5	7.2
Girls	8.0	10.9	1.2	5.4
9th & 10th Graders	7.9	11.7	1.7	5.3
11th & 12th Graders	6.4	9.1	1.0	7.2
Lower-Middle Class	7.1	10.2	1.7	6.4
Upper-Middle Class	7.1	10.3	1.0	6.4

sions when TV and music were reported as a person's primary activity.

Consistent with the hypothesis, the data indicate that listening to music is typically more involving than watching TV. The largest differences are in the motivation items: The students reported a significantly greater wish to be in their current activity when listening to music, and they reported feeling significantly more "open" and "free." For all of these items, the z scores associated with music are well above the students' baseline daily responses (z = 0.0). Listening to music, then, is among the most highly motivating of daily adolescent experiences.

The affect and activation items also show music experience to be more favorable than watching TV, although only one of these items is statistically significant: The students reported feeling greater excitement (and less boredom) when listening to music. In sum, all domains except the cognitive items show a

TABLE 2
Contexts of TV Watching and Music Listening

	Percentage of all Self-Reports in Each Context	TV Watching	Music Listening
	(N= 2,734)	(N= 194)	(N= 39)
Social Context:[1]	%	%	%
Family	18	47	8
Friends	28	12	23
Alone	25	41	69
	71	100	100
TV vs Music Chi Square = 20.7, $p < .001$			
Physical Context:			
In bedroom	10	10	45
Elsewhere in Home	26	79	37
Outside Home	64	11	18
	100	100	100
TV vs Music Chi Square = 35.6, $p < .001$			

NOTE: Table shows the contexts in which media use was reported as a primary activity. Secondary usage follows closely similar percentages.
1. Times in class and times with people at work, accounting for 29% of all self-reports, are not included among the social contexts.

trend toward more favorable involvement with music than TV.[2]

In exploratory analyses, we considered how the states associated with each medium were related, first, to situational and, second, to subjective factors. The situational factor with the most probable impact was social context. Being alone is typically a negative experience for adolescents (Larson and Csikszentmihalyi, 1978, 1980), thus it was important to examine how this situation might interact with the experience of television and music.

Table 4 reveals that the differences between the two media were stronger when adolescents were alone. Watching TV alone was a more negative experience than is shown in Table 3

TABLE 3
The Experience of Watching TV and Listening to Music

	Watching TV (N=193)	Listening to Music (N=39)	TV vs Music t-value
	Z-score	Z-score	
Affect			
Happy-Sad	.02	.21	- .96
Cheerful-Irritable	.04	.22	-1.11
Friendly-Angry	-.13	.14	-1.40
Sociable-Lonely	-.24	-.08	- .82
Activation			
Strong-Weak	-.10	.14	-1.34
Alert-Drowsy	-.29	-.03	-1.55
Active-Passive	-.50	-.20	-1.69
Excited-Bored	-.10	.35	-2.80***
Motivation			
Wish to be Doing Activity	.08	.54	-3.24***
Control of Actions	-.04	.24	-1.70*
Free-Constrained	.13	.51	-2.62***
Open-Closed	-.05	.33	-2.21**
Cognitive State			
Concentration	-.19	-.09	- .53
Ease of Concentration	.17	.19	.13
Unselfconscious	.37	.34	.25
Clear-Confused	.05	-.10	.86

NOTE: Table shows average reported states for occasions when media use was the primary activity. Higher values correspond to a more positive state.
*$p < .10$; **$p < .05$; ***$p < .01$; ****$p < .001$; two-tailed.

in both affective and activation items. Watching TV in the presence of others is related to more favorable experiences, a finding parallel to what has been found with adults (Csikszentmihalyi and Kubey, 1981). However, music elicits virtually the same state whether it is listened to alone or with others.

It is notable that greater loneliness was reported when subjects were watching TV alone than when listening to music. Lyle and Hoffman (1972) found that teenagers reported choos-

TABLE 4
Watching TV and Listening to Music While Alone

	Watching TV (N=74) Z-score	Listening to Music (N=27) Z-score	TV vs Music t-value
Affect			
Happy-Sad	-.20	.28	-1.86*
Cheerful-Irritable	-.10	.22	-1.54
Friendly-Angry	-.22	.08	-1.29
Sociable-Lonely	-.65	-.22	-1.85*
Activation			
Strong-Weak	-.26	.07	-1.43
Alert-Drowsy	-.54	-.04	-2.44**
Active-Passive	-.66	-.26	-1.79*
Exicted-Bored	-.25	.35	-3.02***
Motivation			
Wish to be Doing Activity	-.05	.62	-4.36****
Control of Actions	-.16	.30	-2.09**
Free-Constrained	.08	.43	-1.84*
Open-Closed	-.06	.12	- .86
Cognitive State			
Concentration	-.17	.07	-1.00
Ease of Concentration	.10	.22	- .63
Unselfconscious	.33	.33	- .02
Clear-Confused	.06	-.24	1.31

*$p < .10$; **$p < .05$; ***$p < .01$; ****$p < .001$; two-tailed.

ing to listen to music as one of their most preferred methods of coping with anger or hurt feelings. It may be that teenagers feel in touch with their peers while listening to music, thereby escaping the more intense loneliness that accompanies time spent alone with television—a medium in which content is more alien to adolescent concerns and, thus, is less effective as a substitute for peer contact. The power of music is suggested by this capacity to raise moods and engage adolescents even in the normally dysphoric context of solitude.

In the second set of exploratory analyses interesting differences emerged in the subjective conditions associated with positive involvement in each medium. During TV viewing, being "in control of actions" was positively correlated with overall effect ($r = .19$, $p < .01$), but during music learning it was negatively correlated $r = -.29$, $p < .05$). In other words, when watching TV, feeling in control appeared to be favorable, but with music it was unfavorable. When listening to music the greatest involvement occurs when an adolescent feels out of control.

RELATIONSHIP TO THE REST OF LIFE

How does the amount of time spent with either of these media relate to experience in the other realms of an adolescent's life? Estimates of TV and music use were created by calculating the total percentage of self-reports each student reported being with each medium, either as a primary or secondary activity. For TV these estimates ranged from 0 to 33%; for music from 0 to 30%. The two measures were only slightly and negatively correlated ($r = -.13$, n.s.).

The central question was how use of each medium was related to a young person's participation in adult-structured segments of daily life (time with family and in the classroom) and in adolescent-structured segments (time with friends). Two indices of participation in these contexts were considered. The first was how much time a person spent in each social context, as estimated from his or her set of self-reports. The second was a person's relative affect in each context, measured by a person's average z score for the four affect items in that context. Occasions of primary and secondary media use were excluded from the computation of these two indices so as not to confound the analysis.

The relationship of media involvement to use of time is shown in Table 5. Rate of TV watching is positively correlated with amount of time spent with family, and negatively correlated with amount of time spent with friends. Consistent with expectation, TV watching shows greater compatibility with a lifestyle of family involvement and less compatibility with a lifestyle of involvement with friends. For rate of music listening the pattern is opposite, although the correlations are not quite significant.

A nearly parallel pattern is evident for affect with family and friends (Table 6). Rate of TV watching is correlated with feeling relatively worse with friends. In contrast, rate of music listening is correlated with feeling relatively worse with family. The findings confirm that TV and music have opposite association with an adolescent's involvement in the adult-structured domain of family and the adolescent-structured domain of friends.[3] These findings are robust with controls for age.

Several other significant correlations emerged that reflect the relationship of the two media to adolescents' adjustment to adult-structured domains. Amount of time spent watching TV is correlated with amount of time spent in the classroom ($r = .27, p < .05$). It also correlated with school performance (grade point average, controlled by aptitude; $r = .21, p < .05$).[4] Both school performance ($r = -.36, p < .001$) and time in class ($r = .26, p < .05$) were negatively related to music learning.

DISCUSSION

Television and music bring adolescents into contact with differing worlds of information, values, and emotion. The findings of this investigation demonstrate that music is much more successful in engaging youth in its world. When listening to music, adolescents reported greater emotional involvement. They reported higher motivation, greater excitement, and more openness. Watching television, in contrast, was associated with lower involvement. The adolescents reported feeling less motivated, more bored, and less free with this medium.

Music is more involving, it would seem, because it speaks to adolescent concerns, from heterosexual relationships to autonomy and individuation. Rock in particular may be embraced

TABLE 5
Rates of Media Use Correlated with Allocation of Time to Family, Friends, Solitude, and Class (N = 75)

Dependent Variables	Amount of Time Watching TV (r)	Amount of Time Listening to Music (r)
Amount of Time:		
With Family	.21*	-.13
In Class	.28**	-.26**
With Friends	-.26**	.15
Alone	-.03	.09

*p < .10; **p < .05; two-tailed.

by the young, because its very sounds and words mirror the intensity and turbulence of adolescent experience. The sound of adolescent music may be frenzied and hard driving, euphoric, melancholy, or seductive. The lyrics speak of loneliness, misunderstandings, adoration, desire, rejection, independence, bliss, remorse, and confusion. The music reflects the extreme emotional experiences adolescents encounter from moment to moment as part of their daily realities (Larson et al., 1980). Thus it is no wonder that this medium has such power to engage the young.

Adolescents do attend to television and their reported concentration is as high as with music. But their emotional involvement—their excitement, motivation, and openness—is lower, suggesting that, hour for hour, this medium may have less impact than music. The question, then, is why adolescents spend more time watching TV than listening to music. Why do adolescents choose a medium often associated with boredom and low mood states? One possibility is that television provides a means of relaxation (Csikszentmihalyi and Kubey, 1981) that permits teenagers a reprieve from the strong and changing emotions of this age period. In an earlier ESM study with adolescents, it was demonstrated that the dominant state during TV watching was one of nonfeeling or emotionlessness (Csikszentmihalyi et al., 1977). Television may provide adoles-

TABLE 6
Rates of Media Use Correlated with Average Affect with Family, with Friends, Alone, and in Class

	Amount of Time Watching TV (r)	Amount of Time Listening to Music (r)
Mean Affect:		
With Family	.04	-.20*
In Class	-.19	-.08
With Friends	-.16	.28**
Alone	.27**	-.07

NOTE: Table shows correlations between the percentage of self-reports in which individuals indicated TV and music to be a primary or secondary activity and the dependent variables. Occasions of media use have been excluded from computation of the dependent variables. The significance level of all correlations remains constant with controls for age, except for the correlation between music listening and amount of time spent in class, which drops to $r = -.20$, $p < .10$.
*$p < .10$; **$p < .05$; two-tailed.

cents an important chance to turn off strong emotions and regain a measure of control over their inner lives. Another explanation may lie in TV's relation to family life. Viewing occurs most frequently with the family, and a considerable body of research indicates that TV viewing stimulates family interaction and reinforces family solidarity (Faber et al., 1979; Glick and Levy, 1962; Lull, 1980). The opportunity to sit with family members and share a common experience may be personally valuable, particularly for younger adolescents.

These differences in the immediate experience of the two media appear to be translated into differences in the lifestyles associated with each. The data support expectations about the relationship of TV and music use to harmony with adult-structured and adolescent-structured domains. Television is watched more often by adolescents who spend more time with their families and who earn better grades. One might infer that the world of TV reinforces, or at least harmonizes with, the pursuit of adult goals and life in an adult-structured world.

Listening to music, in comparison, appears more compatible with life in the adolescent-structured peer group. Individuals who listen more to music report higher moods with their friends and lower moods with their families. The experience of charged participation in music appears to enrich particularly the part of their lives they share with friends. Music listening, then, may well represent a medium of conformity to the world of peers, just as TV appears to represent a medium of conformity to the world of adults.

The experiential alternatives presented by television and music have broader implications in a social-historical frame. Which medium a cohort of youth chooses to attend to may shape the path it will take into adulthood. If it has been socialized by the electronic medium of adult culture—television—we might expect greater social continuity in the transition between generations. But if it has been socialized by its own medium—youth music—the possibility of generational disjunctions is greater.

Television viewing may indeed be a common activity for adolescents, but it is music that stands ready to provide a model of expression, release, and autonomy from the adult world. Music has greater potential to catch the attention of a generation, to engage its members emotionally, and to galvanize them around a new set of symbols, impulses, and values.[5] The great popularity of rock music in the 1960s was certainly an element in uniting that generation's rebellion against adult values and norms. For the better part of a decade, the Beatles and other rock groups offered a worldwide network of young people their views on love, drugs, sex, religion, and politics. Punk rock has played a similar role for a smaller, though more alienated, group of youth in the seventies (Hebdige, 1979).

Perhaps Chuck Berry's classic lyric, "Roll over Beethoven/ Tell Tchaikovsky the news," best communicates rock music's subversive message that youth music is both superior to and separate from the adult world. And although smaller in number than previous cohorts of alienated youth, the very existence of today's punk rockers and "new wavers"—named for their music of preference—demonstrates music's power to arouse the collective experience of young people

NOTES

1. In a similar data base consisting of 107 adults, the amount of TV viewing was nearly identical, but adults reported music as a primary activity seven times less frequently than adolescents (Csikszentmihalyi and Kubey, 1981).

2. Instances of music listening as a primary activity were so rare in the sample of 107 adult workers (only 12 reports) that comparison is nearly impossible. Nonetheless, it is interesting to note that, in contrast to adolescents, adults reported feeling happier with TV than with music and reported wishing to be listening to music significantly less often ($p = .04$). Moreover, there was virtually no difference in the adults' reported levels of "excitement" experienced with the two media.

3. The positive correlation between amount of TV viewing and affect while alone extends findings by Hendry and Patrick (1977) and Johnstone (1974) that heavier adolescent viewers have fewer friends. Heavier viewers may have adjusted to being alone out of necessity in comparison to the more socially involved heavy music listeners, who appear to have more difficulty tolerating solitude (unless music is present).

4. This finding is inconsistent with Hendry and Patrick (1977) and others who have found that heavier TV viewers tend to do less well in school.

5. The ongoing decentralization of TV broadcasting, made possible by new cable and satellite technologies, may lead to the emergence of video channels run by and for youth. Our findings suggest that this might be a particularly powerful medium. Warner Amex's MTV (Music Television) is the first in a line of new video-rock outlets.

REFERENCES

ADONI, H. (1978) "The functions of mass media in the political socialization of adolescents." Communication Research 6: 84-106.

AVERY, R. (1979) "Adolescents' use of the mass media." Amer. Behavioral Scientist 23: 53-70.

BOOTH, W. (1982) "The company we keep: self-making in imaginative art, old and new." Daedelus 111: 33-59.

BROWN, R. and M. O'LEARY (1971) "Pop music in an English secondary school system." Amer. Behavioral Scientist 14: 401-413.

BURKE, R. and R. GRINDER (1966) "Personality-oriented themes and listening patterns in teen-age music and their relation to certain academic and peer variables." School Rev. 74: 196-211.

CAREY, J. (1969) "The ideology of autonomy in popular lyrics: a content analysis." Psychology 32: 150-164.

CHAFFEE, S., J. McLEOD, and C. ATKIN (1971) "Parental influences on adolescent media use." Amer. Behavioral Scientist 14: 323-340.

CLARKE, P. (1973) "Teenagers' coorientation and information-seeking about pop music." Amer. Behavioral Scientist 16: 551-566.

COLEMAN, J. S. (1961) The Adolescent Society: The Social Life of the Teenager and Its Impact on Education. New York: Macmillan.

COMSTOCK, G., S. CHAFFEE, N. KATZMAN, M. McCOMBS, and D. ROBERTS (1978) Television and Human Behavior. New York: Columbia Univ. Press.

COOPER, B. (1978) "The image of the outsider in contemporary lyrics." J. of Popular Culture 12: 168-178.

CSIKSZENTMIHALYI, M. and R. KUBEY (1981) "Television and the rest of life: a systematic comparison of subjective experience." Public Opinion Q. 45: 317-328.

CSIKSZENTMIHALYI, M. and R. LARSON (forthcoming) Being Adolescent: A Systematic Phenomenology of Daily Experience. New York: Basic Books.

——— and S. PRESCOTT (1977) "The ecology of adolescent experience." J. of Youth and Adolescence 6: 281-294.

FABER. R., J. BROWN, and J. McLEOD (1979) "Coming of age in the global village: television and adolescence," in E. Wartella (ed.) Children Communicating. Beverly Hills, CA: Sage.

FRITH, S. (1981) Sound Effects. New York: Pantheon.

GERBNER, G., L. GROSS, M. MORGAN, and N. SIGNORIELLI (1980) "The mainstreaming of America: violence profile no. 11." J. of Communication 28: 10-29.

GLICK, I. and S. LEVY (1962) Living with Television. Chicago: Aldine.

GOETHALS, G. (1981) The TV Ritual: Worship at the Video Altar. Boston: Beacon.

GUILFORD, J. (1967) "Creativity: yesterday, today, and tomorrow." J. of Creative Behavior 1: 3-14.

HEBDIGE, D. (1979) Subculture: The Meaning of Style. London: Methuen.

HENDRY, L. and H. PATRICK (1977) "Adolescents and television." J. of Youth and Adolescence 6: 325-336.

HIRSCH, P. (1980) "An organizational perspective on television (aided and abetted by models from economics, marketing, and the humanities)," in S. Withey and R. Abeles (eds.) Television and Social Behavior: Beyond Violence and Children. Hillsdale, NJ: Erlbaum.

——— (1971) "Sociological approaches to the pop music phenomenon." Amer. Behavioral Scientist 14: 371-388.

JOHNSTONE, J. (1974) "Social interaction and mass media use among adolescents: a case study," in J. Blumler and E. Katz (eds.) The Uses of Mass Communications: Current Perspectives on Gratifications Research. Beverly Hills, CA: Sage.

——— and E. KATZ (1957) "Youth and popular music: a study in the sociology of taste." Amer. J. of Sociology 17: 569-578.

LARSON, R. and M. CSIKSZENTMIHALYI (1983) "The experience sampling method," in H. Reis (ed.) New Directions for Naturalistic Methods in the Behavioral Sciences. San Francisco: Jossey-Bass.

——— (1980) "The significance of time alone in adolescent development." J. of Current Adolescent Medicine 2: 33-40.

——— (1978) "Experiential correlates of solitude in adolescence." J. of Personality 46: 677-693.

——— and R. GRAEF (1980) "Mood variability and the psycho-social adjustment of adolescents." J. of Youth and Adolescence 9: 469-490.

LULL, J. (1980) "Family communication patterns and the social uses of television." Communication Research 7: 319-334.

LYLE, J. and H. HOFFMAN (1972) "Children's use of television and other media," in E. Rubenstein et al. (eds.) Television and Social Behavior, Vol. 4: Television in Day-to-Day Life. Washington, DC: Government Printing Office.

NEWCOMB, H. (1974) TV: The Most Popular Art. Garden City, NY: Doubleday.

PECK, R. (1982) "Teenage stereotypes," in M. Schwartz (ed.) TV and Teens: Experts Look at the Issues. Reading, MA: Addison-Wesley.

RUSHTON, J. (1979) "The effects of prosocial television and film material on the behavior of viewers," in L. Berkowitz (ed.) Advances in Experimental Social Psychology, Vol. 12. New York: Academic.

SIMMONS, K., B. GREENBERG, and C. ATKIN (1977) The Demography of Fictional Characters in 1975-76. Project CASTLE, Report 2. East Lansing: Department of Communication, Michigan State University.

SMOTHERS, J. (1961) "The public and private meanings and uses of popular music for American adolescents." Ph.D. dissertation, University of Chicago.

WEIGEL, R. and R. JESSOR (1973) "Television and adolescent conventionality: an exploratory study." Public Opinion Q. 37: 76-90.

22

WHEN VIOLENCE IS REWARDED OR PUNISHED
The Impact of Mass Media Stories on Homicide

David P. Phillips and John E. Hensley

The number of homicides in the United States increases significantly after stories about prizefights, in which violence is rewarded, and decreases significantly after stories about murder trials and executions, in which violence is punished.

In the long history of scientific research, one major tradition has been concerned with the impact of the environment on health. Early epidemiological studies tended to focus on physical and biological features of the environment, such as Lind's study on the effects of diet on scurvy in 1751 and Pasteur's studies on the effects of micro-organisms in the late 1800s. Recent studies, such as those on the effects of smoking on cancer, have added a concern with the social and psychological features of the environment, including the mass media. This aspect of the environment is very pervasive, with the average American spending more time watching television than in any other activity, except for sleep and work (17). True to the epidemiological tradition, investigators have tended to focus on the negative aspects of this environment and thus have devoted many studies to the effects of mass media violence on aggression. After 2,500 investigations, researchers have reached a consensus on the effects of mass media violence *in the laboratory:* under certain circumstances, subjects exposed to portrayals of violence typically display more aggressive behavior than is true for matched control groups (1, 27, 28, 40, 42, 43).

David P. Phillips is Professor of Sociology and John E. Hensley is a Ph.D. candidate in sociology, both at the University of California at San Diego.

Reprinted from "When Violence Is Rewarded or Punished: The Impact of Mass Media Stories on Homicide," by David P. Phillips and John E. Hensley in *Journal of Communication*, Vol. 34, No. 3.

But defenders of the mass media have often argued that one cannot necessarily generalize from the artificial circumstances in the laboratory to the real-life effects of mass media violence. In particular, these critics have argued, there is no evidence that mass media stories about violence trigger serious antisocial behavior like rape or murder in the real world. This argument must be called into question, as there is now some evidence which indicates that some media stories do indeed trigger increases in fatal, antisocial behavior among the general population. After reviewing this evidence, we will also present new evidence indicating that another type of mass media story elicits *decreases* in such behavior. In sum, this article will present systematic evidence relating mass media stories about violence to real-life antisocial behavior.

A number of studies by Phillips and his colleagues examined the relationship between mass media coverage and those types of death that display a strong social and psychological component, i.e., suicide, accidents, and homicide. The first study (33) showed that suicides in the United States between 1947 and 1968 increased significantly just after a heavily publicized suicide story, e.g., that of Marilyn Monroe. Further, the more publicity devoted to a suicide story (measured by days of coverage), the greater the increase in suicides thereafter. This increase occurred primarily in the geographic area where the suicide story was most heavily publicized. The poststory peak in suicides has been replicated in a later study for the period 1972–1976 (12). All of these findings persist after correction for the effects of trends, seasons, and random fluctuations. At present, the best available explanation for the findings is that suicide stories elicit some imitative suicides.

Many researchers have suspected that some auto accidents have a suicidal component. If so, then auto accident deaths should also rise after publicized suicide stories. Research has shown this to be the case: auto accidents in California (34, 36) and Detroit (11) increased by more than 30 percent just after publicized suicide stories. Again, the more publicity given to the story, the greater the increase in auto deaths, with the increase occurring primarily in the geographical area where the story was most heavily publicized. Several pieces of evidence suggest that some of these auto deaths may have had a suicidal component. The number of single-car accident deaths rose more than the number of multiple-car accident deaths. Drivers (but not passengers) in single-car crashes occurring just after the story were significantly similar in age to the person described in the story, while drivers involved in crashes just before the story were not similar to the person described in the story. These results persist after correction for the effects of trends, seasons, and random fluctuations. At present, the only explanation that fits the data is that suicide stories trigger some imitative suicides, some of which are disguised as auto accidents.

The studies just reviewed have also found evidence that the car may sometimes be used as an instrument of murder-suicide. Publicized murder-suicide stories were followed by an increase in multiple-car passenger deaths but not by an increase in single-car driver deaths. In contrast, after "pure" suicide stories, there was an increase in single-car driver deaths but no increase in multiple-car passenger deaths. These findings are consistent with the hypothesis that some murder-suicide stories trigger imitative murder-suicides, which are disguised as auto crashes.

Two further studies (35, 37) examined the impact of murder-suicide stories and found that the number of crashes of private planes in the United States rose significantly just after heavily publicized murder-suicide stories. As before, the more publicity given to the story, the greater the rise in the number of plane crashes. The rise occurred mainly in the geographical area where the story was publicized.

The previous studies have been concerned with suicides and accidents. It would also be desirable to examine the impact of mass media stories on homicides. A direct approach to this problem would seek to determine whether the number of daily homicides in the United States rises just after publicized homicide stories. Unfortunately, this direct approach is not effective, because there are so many homicide stories in the mass media that it is very difficult to separate the effect of one from another. So one must choose a more indirect strategy for assessing the effects of mass media violence. Comstock (16) has noted that a violent story is most likely to be imitated in the laboratory if the violence in the story is presented as real, exciting, rewarded, and justified, and if the perpetrator of the violence is portrayed as intending to injure his victim. In view of these observations, one might want to examine the effects of real-life events that mirror these qualities.

One type of violent story that meets all of the above criteria is the heavyweight championship prizefight. In addition, these fights are heavily publicized and occur sufficiently seldom so that the separate effects of each story can be detected.

Using daily U.S. homicide statistics for the period 1973–1978, Phillips (41) showed that, after heavyweight championship prizefights, the number of U.S. homicides increases by 12.46 percent. Much-publicized fights tend to be followed by unusually large increases in homicides. The person beaten in the fight and the persons who are killed just afterward are unusually likely to be of the same race. Thus, after a young, white male is beaten in a fight, homicides of young, white males increase significantly, but the homicides of young, black males do not. Conversely, after a young, black male is beaten in a fight, homicides of young, black males increase significantly, but the homicides of young, white males do not. These findings are consistent with laboratory studies (6, 7, 8, 9) showing that prizefight scenes trigger aggressive behavior and that an individual is more likely to display aggression against a victim if that victim is similar to the losing boxer. The findings persist after correction for the effect of seasons, trends, and random fluctuations. Of the various explanations tested for the findings, the best available is that publicized prizefights trigger an increase in aggressive behavior, some of which results in homicide.

We have now reviewed eight studies indicating that some mass media stories are followed by increases in suicides, auto accidents, plane accidents, and murders. In all these studies, the more publicity given to the mass media story, the greater the increase in mortality thereafter. In a number of the studies, the person dying just after the story is similar to the person described in the story. Taken together, the evidence of these studies strongly suggests that some mass media stories trigger imitative increases in fatal violence.

The prizefight heavily* rewards *one person for inflicting violence on another and is at the opposite end of a continuum from a successfully prosecuted murder trial, which heavily* punishes *one person for inflicting physical violence on another.

Laboratory studies (2, 3, 4, 44) have shown that when a model is rewarded for aggressive behavior, the audience behaves more aggressively. Conversely, when a model is punished for aggression, the audience behaves less aggressively. When a model is neither rewarded nor punished for aggression, the audience response falls between these two extremes. If the population in real life behaves like the audience in these laboratory experiments, we would expect to find a rise in the number of homicides after a person is rewarded for violence (as in a prizefight) and a drop in the number of homicides after a person is punished for violence (as in a guilty-verdict murder trial).

Some intermediate fluctuation in homicides may be expected after a person is neither clearly rewarded nor punished (as in a not-guilty-verdict murder trial). Witnesses to the trial and its attendant publicity may impose different interpretations on the verdict of innocence. Some witnesses may believe that the accused is truly guilty and is in effect being rewarded by being allowed to "get away with murder." Others may believe that the accused is truly innocent and has been unfairly punished by having to endure a lengthy and nervewracking trial. Still a third segment of the audience may regard the not-guilty verdict as neither a reward nor a punishment.

Before presenting our findings, we should first consider a troubling question: why is it that the laboratory literature on punishment reveals a deterrent effect, while the nonlaboratory literature on capital punishment (5, 10, 13, 14, 15, 21, 23, 25, 26, 29, 46) reveals no such effect?[1] Failure to find a deterrent effect may occur for one of two reasons: either there is no such effect, or the methods used to seek evidence of deterrence are not sufficiently sensitive to reveal it.

The literature on capital punishment displays several characteristic methodological features. First, most research on deterrence examines the effect of changes in capital punishment legislation, rather than the effect of punishments which are carried out and publicized. It is possible that the potential murderer is more affected by a concrete example of punishment than by an abstract change in legislation. Second, nearly all research on deterrence examines yearly rather than daily homicide statistics. If the deterrent effect of a punishment is very short-lived, then this effect will not show up in yearly data but may nonetheless appear when daily figures are examined. We know of only three studies of deterrence using daily homicide data (18, 22, 45), and these studies examined only a small fraction of all U.S. homicides. In sum, past studies may have failed to uncover evidence of deterrence because deterrence effects may be too small or short-lived to be detectable by conventional research techniques.

In contrast, the current study employs techniques that have been specifically developed to detect short-lived fluctuations in mortality.

This is the first analysis to use *daily* homicides for a *large* population to compare the effects of stories in which violence is *rewarded, punished*, or *treated neutrally*. We will examine the patterns of more than 140,000 U.S. daily homicides before and after prizefights, innocent verdicts, and life sentences, death sentences, and executions. The term "homicide" was defined as a death coded E960–E969 in the 8th

[1] Two exceptions to this rule are a much criticized (10, 14, 26, 29, 32) study by Ehrlich (20) and a historical study by Phillips (38) of British weekly homicides before and after executions for the period 1858–1921.

Revision of the International Classification of Diseases. Homicide data for the years 1973–1979 were obtained from computerized death certificates distributed by the Inter-University Consortium for Political Science Research and generated by the National Center for Health Statistics.

A publicized acquittal, life sentence, death sentence, or execution was defined as one which was indexed in both *Facts on File*,[2] a comprehensive index of newspaper news, and the *Vanderbilt Television News Index*, which summarizes the network television evening news broadcasts. The complete list of heavyweight championship prizefights is taken from an earlier study by Phillips (41).

The effect of judicial actions on U.S. homicides can be assessed with a standard time series regression analysis (24, 31) that corrects for the impact of day of the week, month of the year, holidays, year, and prizefights. A separate dummy variable was coded for each day of the week (with Sunday being the omitted variable), for each month of the year (with December being the omitted variable), and for each year (with 1979 being the omitted variable). A dummy variable was coded to indicate the presence or absence of each public holiday (New Year's Day, Memorial Day, Independence Day, Labor Day, Thanksgiving, and Christmas).[3]

Earlier research (41) has shown that the effect of a prizefight "spikes" within four days of the fight. Consequently, we defined a series of dummy variables for detecting the effect of the fight 0 to 4 days after the fight. Since we are conceptualizing the prizefight as an event in which violence is rewarded, we have named the dummy variables associated with the prizefight as REWARD(0), REWARD(1),. . .,REWARD(4). Here, REWARD(0) measures the effect of the prizefight on the day of the fight, REWARD(1) measures the effect one day later, and so on.

All previous studies have found that a publicized event exerts its greatest impact on daily mortality within four days of the event (11, 34, 35, 36, 37, 41). In the light of this consistent finding, we will look for the impact of publicized judicial actions in the period from 0 to 4 days after the events occur (later we also examine a longer time period). Initially, we have used a single variable, PUNISH(0), PUNISH(1),. . .,PUNISH(4), to detect the effect of life sentences, death sentences, and

[2] These stories were sought under the index heading "Crime—Murder" in *Facts on File*. A case was included if (a) the description indicated clearly that the defendant was charged with "murder" or "homicide" (rather than, e.g., hiring someone else to commit murder), and (b) the judicial action taken was explicitly described as a death sentence, life sentence (or more than 100 years of penal servitude), acquittal, or execution. This article did not examine the effect of guilty verdicts that result in relatively mild sentences. Future studies should investigate this topic.

[3] Many of these holidays actually extend over several days, typically, a "holiday weekend." A holiday period was thus defined as beginning with the first day of the holiday and ending with the last day of that holiday. Any day falling in the holiday period was coded "1"; all other days were coded "0." A separate dummy variable was constructed for each of the six holidays in accordance with the above procedures.

executions. Later we will compare the effects of life sentences with those of death sentences and executions.

Nearly all the publicized punishments under study involve white murderers and white victims. If modeling plays an important role in deterrence, then these punishments are more likely to deter whites than blacks from murder. Since white murderers typically kill white victims (47), this implies that just after the publicized punishments the homicides of white victims should decrease more than the homicides of black victims.

Table 1: U.S. homicides of white victims regressed on publicized judicial actions, controlling for daily, monthly, yearly, and holiday effects, 1973–1979

R^2 = .438, $\bar{R}^2$ = .428, df = 2509, n = 2556

Regressor	Regression coefficient	t	Regressor	Regression coefficient	t
Intercept	39.06	37.14*			
HOMICIDE(1)	0.03	1.52			
Day of the week			Holiday		
Monday	−7.23	−15.82*	New Year's Day	12.96	6.97*
Tuesday	−7.52	−14.94*	Memorial Day	−0.45	−0.33
Wednesday	−8.38	−16.56*	Independence Day	2.91	1.68
Thursday	−7.04	−13.68*	Labor Day	2.68	1.94
Friday	−4.35	−8.63*	Thanksgiving	−1.05	−0.86
Saturday	4.12	8.55*	Christmas	5.32	3.06*
Month			Prizefights		
January	−3.40	−5.75*	REWARD(0)	1.08	0.83
February	−2.80	−4.64*	REWARD(1)	0.91	0.70
March	−4.11	−6.92*	REWARD(2)	0.59	0.45
April	−4.08	−6.83*	REWARD(3)	3.54	2.72*
May	−4.31	−7.05*	REWARD(4)	0.71	0.55
June	−3.12	−5.24*			
July	−0.80	−1.35	Acquittals		
August	−1.20	−2.02	NEUTRAL(0)	−3.45	−1.71
September	−1.78	−2.93*	NEUTRAL(1)	0.79	0.39
October	−1.95	−3.30*	NEUTRAL(2)	1.88	0.93
November	−0.94	−1.52	NEUTRAL(3)	0.30	0.15
			NEUTRAL(4)	−0.34	−0.17
Year					
1973	−6.55	−14.05*	Punishments		
1974	−4.55	−9.96*	PUNISH(0)	0.24	0.17
1975	−3.75	−8.28*	PUNISH(1)	0.85	0.62
1976	−6.03	−13.04*	PUNISH(2)	−0.58	−0.42
1977	−4.34	−9.53*	PUNISH(3)	−1.54	−1.12
1978	−3.08	−6.83*	PUNISH(4)	−3.32	−2.43**

Note: The variable HOMICIDE(1) indicates homicides lagged one day. Two-tailed t-tests are used for all seasonal variables; one-tailed t-tests for REWARD and PUNISH variables (because the direction of the effect can be predicted); and two-tailed tests for NEUTRAL variables (where the direction of the effect cannot be predicted).

* $p < .01$
** $p = .0076$

The results of the analysis of the impact of publicized punishments on the murders of white victims are shown in Table 1. The regression analysis allows us to determine whether the impact of any given variable is statistically significant, provided that there is no multicollinearity or serial correlation between the residuals in the regression equation. No such evidence was found.[4]

We can see from Table 1 that the day of the week is significantly associated with the fluctuation of U.S. homicides, with Saturday displaying the greatest number of homicides. In general, the number of homicides declines smoothly to a low in the middle of the week and rises to a peak on the weekend.

Next, the number of homicides varies significantly but not markedly by month, with no pronounced seasonal pattern. The number does rise very markedly in certain holiday periods, however, most notably during New Year's, Independence Day, Christmas, and, to a lesser extent, Thanksgiving. Finally, yearly effects are small and yield no pronounced pattern.

Turning to the influence of prizefights, coded as REWARD(0),. . .,REWARD(4), we can see that, on the third day after a heavyweight prizefight, the number of homicides rises significantly, by an average of 3.54. A very different effect is observed when we examine the influence of publicized punishments, coded as PUNISH (0),. . .,PUNISH(4). Four days after a person is sentenced to life imprisonment or to death or is executed for committing murder, there is a significant *decrease* of 3.32 homicides of white victims.[5] Turning finally to the effect of acquittals, coded as NEUTRAL(0),. . .,NEUTRAL(4), we can see that the number of homicides does not fluctuate significantly in either direction on the day of or just after an acquittal.

Up to now, we have been considering all harsh punishments in one category, without comparing the separate effects of life sentences, death sentences, and executions. This comparison is important, however, in

[4] The conventional test for serial correlation (the Durbin-Watson) is inappropriate when a lagged endogenous variable like HOMICIDE(1) is included in the regression equation (30). Of the two other tests of serial correlation suggested by Durbin (19) for use with lagged endogenous variables, the first is inappropriate for the present analysis (see 12, footnote 7). Durbin's second test for serial correlation revealed no evidence of first-order autocorrelation in any of the analyses reported in this article. For all tables examined, e(t) was not significantly related to e(t − 1). Autocorrelation of higher orders was sought by the methods described in Bollen and Phillips (12), with no evidence of serial correlation being uncovered.

[5] Under the null hypothesis, none of the five coefficients examined in Table 1, PUNISH(0), PUNISH(1),. . .,PUNISH(4), is likely to be a large, negative number. On the other hand, under the alternative hypothesis that harsh punishments deter homicides, one or more of these five coefficients is likely to be large and negative. If one or more of the PUNISH(X) coefficients is sufficiently large, we can reject the null hypothesis in favor of the alternative. One way to discover whether the null hypothesis can be rejected is as follows. Because the covariance matrix indicates that the estimates of the coefficients for PUNISH(X) are uncorrelated, and because of the asymptotic normality of the coefficient

light of the controversy surrounding capital punishment. If one finds that fewer homicides occur after a life sentence than after a death sentence or execution, this would support proponents of capital punishment. On the other hand, if one finds that just as many homicides occur after a life sentence as after a death sentence or execution, then this finding would undercut some arguments in favor of capital punishment.

Table 2 displays the observed number of homicides after each life sentence, death sentence, and execution and the expected number of homicides, given the null hypothesis that judicial actions have no effect on mortality. We notice first that the number of homicides declines after almost all judicial actions, no matter what their nature. The total of 559 homicides observed after the punishment stories, subtracted from the 623.18 homicides expected under the null hypothesis, yields a drop of 64.18 homicides, or a percentage decrease of 10.30.

Next we notice that homicides decline by an average of 2.73 after each life sentence and by 3.39 after each death sentence and execution.[6] The difference between these two figures, however, is not statistically significant, given that there were only four death sentences and three executions during the period under study. At present, we have no evidence that life sentences have a significantly weaker deterrent effect than death sentences or executions. This tends to weaken one argument in favor of capital punishment.

Are there different responses to judicial actions in which a murderer is punished for killing a white victim vs. those in which the victim was black?

If a murderer has been punished for killing a white victim, one would expect the murders of white victims but not necessarily black victims to decline substantially. If this argument is correct, then the percentage of

(cont'd from p. 108)

estimates, it follows that these coefficient estimates are in fact independent. This, in turn, implies that the t-statistics for each of these coefficients are independent. One can therefore use the binomial test to evaluate the probability of finding that *r* or more of the PUNISH(X) coefficients are statistically significant at a given level. Table 1 indicates that PUNISH(4) is statistically significant at .0076. For $n = 5$, $p = .0076$, $r \geq 1$, the binomial test indicates that the probability of finding one or more significance levels of .0076 in 5 independent trials is .0374. Hence, the drop in homicides after harsh punishments is significant, and we can reject the null hypothesis on the joint evidence provided by the five PUNISH(X) coefficients. See also Phillips (42) for another example of this conservative procedure for testing statistical significance.

[6] In making this comparison we must necessarily omit the two stories, Bianchi's life sentence and Bishop's execution, that occurred on the same day. It might be argued that having both stories publicized on the same day might distort our estimate of the average deterrent effect of a single publicized story. A straightforward way to correct for this problem is to compare the average drop in homicides (a) after all stories in Table 2, which yields 64.18/20 = 3.21, and (b) after all stories except for the Bianchi/Bishop story, which yields 55.89/19 = 2.94. Of course, the difference between these two figures (3.21 vs. 2.94) is not statistically significant, because only one "double punishment" is involved in the comparison.

Table 2: Fluctuation of U.S. homicides of white victims four days after publicized punishments, 1973–1979

Name of defendant	Publicized punishment: Date	Publicized punishment: Type	Race of victim	Observed no. of homicides	Expected no. of homicides	Observed minus expected
J. Corona	2-5-73	Life sentence	Mostly white	21	25.74	−4.74
"St. Croix Five"	8-13-73	Life sentence	Mostly white	23	27.94	−4.94
A. Martin	9-19-73	Death sentence	White	22	31.44	−9.44
E. Kemper	11-8-73	Life sentence	White	17	24.81	−7.81
E. Henley	7-16-74	Life sentence	White	36	38.64	−2.64
M. Chenault	9-12-74	Death sentence	Black	23	26.45	−3.45
R. Little and J. Remiro	6-27-75	Life sentence	Black	32	28.75	3.25
P. Gilly and C. Vealey	9-3-76	Life sentence	White	23	24.67	−1.67
J. Kallinger	10-14-76	Life sentence	White	34	24.80	9.20
G. Gilmore	1-17-77	Execution	White	26	27.43	−1.43
R. Zamora	11-7-77	Life sentence	White	25	30.22	−5.22
R. Chambliss	11-18-77	Life sentence	Black	31	26.93	4.07
P. Kearney	12-21-77	Life sentence	White	26	41.08	−15.08
M. Dunlap and J. Robison	1-10-78	Death sentence	White	32	37.30	−5.30
A. Provenzano and H. Konigsberg	6-21-78	Life sentence	White	34	34.12	−0.12
L. Van Houten	8-11-78	Life sentence	White	24	27.97	−3.97
J. Spenkelink	5-25-79	Execution	White	28	27.80	0.20
T. Bundy	7-31-79	Death sentence	White	42	42.93	−0.93
Dr. J. MacDonald	8-29-79	Life sentence	White	35	40.87	−5.87
K. Bianchi	10-22-79[a]	Life sentence	Mostly white	25	33.29	−8.29
J. Bishop	10-22-79[a]	Execution	White			

Note: Under the null hypothesis, judicial variables have no impact on the number of homicides. Thus, for Table 2, the expected number of homicides under the null hypothesis is calculated by omitting judicial variables from the regression variables listed in Table 1 and rerunning the regression equation. The dates given indicate when the sentence was publicized on the network evening news broadcasts. In almost all cases this date coincides with the actual date of sentencing. The one exception is E. Kemper, whose date of sentencing was 11-7-73, one day prior to the network coverage.

[a] The punishments for K. Bianchi and J. Bishop occurred on the same day; hence these two punishments have been treated as one story in computing the observed and expected number of homicides.

murder victims who are white should be unusually low just after a story in which a person is punished for killing a white victim—i.e., just after what we will call a "white victim" story.

This prediction can be checked by focusing on the fourth day after the publicized punishment, when the deterrent effect is strongest. Four days after a story in which a person is punished for killing a white victim, 49.37 percent (473 out of 958) of the murder victims are white. By contrast, this percentage is 52.22 percent (74,478 out of 142,630) for all the remaining days in our study period (1973–1979). These two percentages are significantly (though not markedly) different (p = .04, hypergeometric test, one-tailed; for another example of this use of the hypergeometric, see 35, 37). In sum, the murders of whites decline more than the murders of blacks just after a murderer is punished for killing a white victim.

Does the converse situation also hold? After a murderer is punished for killing a black victim, is the percentage of black murder victims unusually low? Four days after "black victim" punishment stories, 41.45 percent of murder victims are black (63 out of 152). A noticeably higher percentage is observed for all the remaining days in our study period—46.10 percent (66,127 out of 143,436). However, the difference between these two percentages (41.45 vs. 46.10) is not statistically significant, perhaps because there were only three "black victim" punishment stories in the period under study.[7]

Up to now, we have been concentrating on the effect of publicized punishments, defined as stories that appear both in the newspapers and on the network evening news. It is important to determine whether less publicized punishment stories also have a significant deterrent effect. Here, we will define a less publicized punishment story as one that appears in the newspapers (as indicated in *Facts on File*) but does *not* appear in the network evening news broadcasts.

To assess the effect of these stories, we have constructed the dummy variables, LESSPUB(0), LESSPUB(1),. . .,LESSPUB(10). We have extended the analysis to the tenth day, rather than the fourth day as before, to reduce the possibility of overlooking delayed effects. Adding these dummy variables to the regression variables specified in Table 1, and rerunning the regression analysis, yields the values displayed in Table 3. It is evident that relatively unpublicized punishments have no significant deterrent effect on homicides. This is to be expected if publicity is an important variable in the processes under study.

We have focused on the period from 0 to 4 days after the publicized punishments because previous research on daily mortality has shown that the effects of publicized stories appear within four days. In Table 4 we extend the analysis to the three-week period beginning with the day of the publicized punishment. Consulting this table, we can see that the great majority of the regression coefficients, PUNISH(0),. . .,PUNISH(20), are negative. This indicates that, on the whole, homicides continue to fall below the number expected in the period beyond the fourth day.

However, despite the fact that the coefficients on day 12 and day 16 have t-statistics with absolute values larger than 2.00, none of the sixteen

[7] We were not able to analyze what would clearly be an important relationship between the race of the murderer in the punishment story and the race of the people who murder just afterwards, because death certificates do not list the characteristics of the murderer, only of his victim.

Table 3: Impact of relatively *un*publicized punishments on U.S. daily homicides of white victims controlling for the effect of publicized judicial actions and daily, monthly, yearly, and holiday effects, 1973–1979

Regressor	Regression coefficient	t
LESSPUB(0)	1.38	0.96
LESSPUB(1)	0.14	0.10
LESSPUB(2)	−1.95	−1.36
LESSPUB(3)	2.72	1.89
LESSPUB(4)	−0.51	−0.35
LESSPUB(5)	1.85	1.29
LESSPUB(6)	−0.32	−0.22
LESSPUB(7)	−0.90	−0.62
LESSPUB(8)	1.68	1.17
LESSPUB(9)	−0.48	−0.33
LESSPUB(10)	1.85	1.28

Note: The term "relatively unpublicized" is as defined in the text. The stories in this category, with sentencing dates, are as follows: Steelman and Gretzler, 7-8-74; Clark, Moody, and Christian, 7-9-74; Brown and Brown, 11-2-74; Harvey, 1-6-75; Brooks, 3-5-75; Simon, Green, Moore, and Cooks, 3-29-76; Carter and Artis, 2-9-77; Chesimard, 3-25-77; Peltier, 6-2-77; Hayes, 2-18-78; Egenberger, 5-24-78; Martin, 6-15-79; and Acquin, 11-30-79. These stories all concern life sentences. The next set of stories concerns death sentences: Cuevas, 4-5-75; Simants, 1-29-76; Gilmore, 10-7-76; Cuevas, 1-26-79; and Harper, 11-7-79. (Cuevas is listed twice, because he had two separate trials.) The effect of these stories was calculated after controlling for the effect of all other regressor variables listed in Table 1. For reasons of clarity, the coefficients for these variables are not displayed in Table 3.

individual coefficients, PUNISH(5),. . .,PUNISH(20), is statistically significant (in the sense defined in footnote 5), because chance alone might produce two coefficients out of sixteen that appear to be significant at .05. In fact, one would find two or more "significant" coefficients .1892 of the time if chance alone were operating ($p = .1892$, binomial test, $n = 16$, $r \geq 2$). Thus, until new evidence is available, the most reasonable interpretation of the data is that the number of homicides significantly decreases for no more than four days after the punishment story.[8]

[8] It is evident from Table 4 that there are fewer homicides than expected on 15 of the 21 days under study. To examine the impact of a punishment on the entire 21-day period rather than on each of the 21 days separately, one could create a dummy variable labeled PUNISH(0–20) and code it "1" for a day that fell within the 21-day period and "0" for all other days. If we rerun the regression equation that produced Table 4 but substitute PUNISH(0–20) for PUNISH (0),. . .,PUNISH (20), we find that white homicides appear to drop significantly in the 21-day period following the punishment: the coefficient for PUNISH(0–20) is −.881, with an associated t-value of −2.53. However, the significance of this finding must be regarded as illusory, because the decision to create the variable PUNISH(0–20) and rerun the regression equation came after examination of the data in Table 4. Standard significance tests cannot be used with *ex post facto* analyses of this sort. Of course, the argument just made applies not only to the specific variable PUNISH(0–20) but to the general variable PUNISH(0–X) as well.

Table 4: Impact of publicized punishments on U.S. daily homicides of white victims for a 21-day period, starting with the day of punishment

Regressor	Regression coefficient	t
PUNISH(0)	0.17	0.13
PUNISH(1)	0.83	0.61
PUNISH(2)	−0.65	−0.47
PUNISH(3)	−1.64	−1.19
PUNISH(4)	−3.44	−2.52
PUNISH(5)	−1.79	−1.31
PUNISH(6)	1.45	1.06
PUNISH(7)	−0.86	−0.63
PUNISH(8)	−1.19	−0.87
PUNISH(9)	−1.59	−1.16
PUNISH(10)	0.04	0.03
PUNISH(11)	0.51	0.38
PUNISH(12)	−2.81	−2.06
PUNISH(13)	−1.31	−0.96
PUNISH(14)	−1.11	−0.81
PUNISH(15)	−0.56	−0.41
PUNISH(16)	2.95	2.17
PUNISH(17)	−0.88	−0.64
PUNISH(18)	−0.11	−0.08
PUNISH(19)	−2.58	−1.89
PUNISH(20)	−1.75	−1.28

Note: The effect of publicized punishments is calculated after controlling for all the variables listed in Table 1: HOMICIDE(1), day of week, month of year, holidays, year, REWARD(X), and NEUTRAL(X). For reasons of clarity, the coefficients of these variables are not displayed in Table 4, because the prime purpose of this table is to study the impact of publicized punishments for a three-week period.

We have been focusing only on white homicide victims because almost all the publicized punishments involve white murderers and white victims. If modeling plays an important role in the deterrence process, then whites are more likely than blacks to be deterred by the punishment stories.

In short, deterrent effects on blacks can be expected to be small. This expectation is supported by the data. When the regression analysis in Table 1 is rerun for black homicide victims, we find no significant drops in homicides just after the publicized punishments. The following are the values for the regression coefficients (RCs) and their associated t-statistics: PUNISH(0), RC = −1.73, t = −1.29; PUNISH(1), RC = .42, t = .32; PUNISH(2), RC = .16, t = .12; PUNISH(3), RC = .90, t = .67; PUNISH(4), RC = −1.61, t = −1.20.

In this article, we have provided what seems to be the first clear evidence that publicized punishments have a short-term deterrent effect on the homicides of white victims. Because this effect seems to be so short-lived, it is not surprising that it was not detected by earlier studies using yearly homicide data. Nor is it surprising that studies of small populations failed to uncover this effect. Even when the entire country is examined, one finds a drop of only 3.32 white homicide victims per punishment story. This implies that the drop would be much smaller, and probably undetectable, if smaller geographic units were studied. Future research on this topic, then, should examine the fluctuation of (a) daily homicide statistics (b) for a large population (c) after heavily publicized punishment stories.

REFERENCES

1. Andison, F. S. "Television Violence and Viewer Aggression: A Cumulation of Study Results 1956–1976." In G. C. Wilhoit and H. de Bock (Eds.) *Mass Communication Review Yearbook* 1. Beverly Hills, Cal.: Sage, 1980.
2. Bandura, A. "Influences of Models' Reinforcement Contingencies on the Acquisition of Imitative Responses." *Journal of Personality and Social Psychology* 1, 1965, pp. 589–595.
3. Bandura, A. "Psychological Mechanisms of Aggression." In M. von Cranach, K. Foppa, W. Lepenies, and D. Ploog (Eds.) *Human Ethnology: Claims and Limits of a New Discipline*. Cambridge: Cambridge University Press, 1979.
4. Bandura, A., D. Ross, and S. A. Ross. "Vicarious Reinforcement and Imitative Learning." *Journal of Abnormal and Social Psychology* 67, 1963, pp. 601–607.
5. Bedau, H. A. (Ed.). *The Death Penalty in America*. Lexington, Mass.: Heath, 1967.
6. Berkowitz, L. and J. T. Alioto. "The Meaning of an Observed Event as a Determinant of its Aggressive Consequences." *Journal of Personality and Social Psychology* 28, 1973, pp. 206–217.
7. Berkowitz, L. and R. Geen. "Film Violence and the Cue Properties of Available Targets." *Journal of Personality and Social Psychology* 3, 1966, pp. 525–530.
8. Berkowitz, L. and R. Geen. "Stimulus Qualities of the Target of Aggression: A Further Study." *Journal of Personality and Social Psychology* 5, 1967, pp. 364–368.
9. Berkowitz, L. and E. Rawlings. "Effects of Film Violence on Inhibitions Against Subsequent Aggression." *Journal of Abnormal and Social Psychology* 66, 1963, pp. 405–412.
10. Beyleveld, D. "Ehrlich's Analysis of Deterrence: Methodological Strategy and Ethics in Isaac Ehrlich's Research and Writing on the Death Penalty as a Deterrent." *British Journal of Criminology* 22, 1982, pp. 101–123.
11. Bollen, K. A. and D. P. Phillips. "Suicidal Motor Vehicle Fatalities in Detroit: A Replication." *American Journal of Sociology* 87, 1981, pp. 404–412.
12. Bollen, K. A. and D. P. Phillips. "Imitative Suicides: A National Study of the Effects of Television News Stories." *American Sociological Review* 47, 1982, pp. 802–809.
13. Bowers, W. J. *Executions in America*. Lexington, Mass.: Heath, 1974.
14. Bowers, W. J. and G. L. Pierce. "The Illusion of Deterrence in Isaac Ehrlich's Research on Capital Punishment." *Yale Law Journal* 85, 1975, pp. 187–208.
15. Canadian Department of the Solicitor General. *A Study of the Deterrent Effects of Capital Punishment*. Ottawa: Queen's Printer, 1972.
16. Comstock, G. "Types of Portrayal and Aggressive Behavior." *Journal of Communication* 27(3), Summer 1977, pp. 189–198.
17. Comstock, G., S. Chaffee, N. Katzman, M. McCombs, and D. Roberts. *Television in America*. Beverly Hills, Cal.: Sage, 1978.
18. Dann, R. H. "The Deterrent Effect of Capital Punishment." *Friends Social Service Series*, Bulletin 29, 1935.

19. Durbin, J. "Testing for Serial Correlation in Least-Squares Regression When Some of the Regressors are Lagged Dependent Variables." *Econometrica* 38, 1970, pp. 410–421.
20. Ehrlich, I. "The Deterrent Effect of Capital Punishment: A Question of Life and Death." *American Economic Review* 65, 1975, pp. 397–417.
21. Gibbs, J. P. *Crime, Punishment, and Deterrence.* New York: Elsevier, 1975.
22. Graves, W. F. "A Doctor Looks at Capital Punishment." *Journal of the Loma Linda University School of Medicine* 10, 1956, pp. 137–142.
23. Great Britain Royal Commission on Capital Punishment. *Report.* London: Her Majesty's Stationery Office, 1953.
24. Johnston, J. *Econometric Methods.* New York: McGraw-Hill, 1972.
25. Junker, J. A. "Testing the Deterrent Effect of Capital Punishment: A Reduced Form Approach." *Criminology* 19, 1982, pp. 626–649.
26. Klein, L. R., B. Forst, and V. Filatov. "The Deterrent Effect of Capital Punishment: An Assessment of the Estimates." *National Research Council,* 1978, pp. 336–380.
27. Murray, J. and S. Kippax. "From the Early Window to the Late Night Show: International Trends in the Study of Television's Impact on Children and Adults." *Advances in Experimental Social Psychology* 12, 1979, pp. 253–320.
28. National Institute of Mental Health. *Television and Behavior: Ten Years of Scientific Progress and Implications for the Eighties,* Vol. 1: *Summary Report.* Washington, D.C.: U.S. Government Printing Office, 1982.
29. National Research Council. *Deterrence and Incapacitation.* Washington, D.C.: National Academy of Sciences, 1978.
30. Nerlove, M. and K. F. Wallis. "Use of the Durbin-Watson Statistic in Appropriate Situations." *Econometrica* 34, 1966, pp. 235–238.
31. Ostrom, C. W. *Time Series Analysis: Regression Techniques.* Beverly Hills, Cal.: Sage, 1978.
32. Passell, P. "The Deterrent Effect of the Death Penalty: A Statistical Test." *Stanford Law Review* 28, 1975, pp. 61–80.
33. Phillips, D. P. "The Influence of Suggestion on Suicide: Substantive and Theoretical Implications of the Werther Effect." *American Sociological Review* 39, 1974, pp. 340–354.
34. Phillips, D. P. "Motor Vehicle Fatalities Increase Just After Publicized Suicide Stories." *Science* 196, 1977, pp. 1464–1465.
35. Phillips, D. P. "Airplane Accident Fatalities Increase Just After Stories About Murder and Suicide." *Science* 201, 1978, pp. 148–150.
36. Phillips, D. P. "Suicide, Motor Vehicle Fatalities, and the Mass Media: Evidence Toward a Theory of Suggestion." *American Journal of Sociology* 84, 1979, pp. 1150–1174.
37. Phillips, D. P. "Airplane Accidents, Murder, and the Mass Media: Towards a Theory of Imitation and Suggestion." *Social Forces* 58, 1980, pp. 1001–1024.
38. Phillips, D. P. "The Deterrent Effect of Capital Punishment: New Evidence on an Old Controversy." *American Journal of Sociology* 86, 1980, pp. 139–148.
39. Phillips, D. P. "Strong and Weak Research Designs for Detecting the Impact of Capital Punishment on Homicide." *Rutgers Law Review* 33, 1981, pp. 790–798.
40. Phillips, D. P. "The Behavioral Impact of Violence in the Mass Media: A Review of the Evidence From Laboratory and Nonlaboratory Investigations." *Sociology and Social Research* 66, 1982, pp. 386–398.
41. Phillips, D. P. "The Impact of Mass Media Violence on U.S. Homicides." *American Sociological Review* 48, 1983, pp. 560–568.
42. Phillips, D. P. "The Found Experiment: A New Technique for Assessing the Impact of Mass Media Violence on Real World Aggressive Behavior." *Public Communication and Behavior* 1, 1984 (forthcoming).

43. Roberts, D. F. and C. M. Bachen. "Mass Communications Effects." In M. R. Rosenzweig and L. W. Parker (Eds.) *Annual Review of Psychology*. Palo Alto, Cal.: Annual Review, 1981.
44. Rosekrans, M. A. and W. W. Hartup. "Imitative Influences of Consistent and Inconsistent Response Consequences to a Model and Aggressive Behavior in Children." *Journal of Personality and Social Psychology* 7, 1967, pp. 429–434.
45. Savitz, L. "A Study in Capital Punishment." *Journal of Criminal Law, Criminology, and Police Science* 49, 1968, pp. 338–341.
46. U.N. Economic and Social Council. *Capital Punishment*. New York: United Nations, 1973.
47. Uniform Crime Reports. *Crime in the United States*. Washington, D.C.: U.S. Department of Justice, 1983.

23

THE IMPACT OF FICTIONAL TELEVISION SUICIDE STORIES ON U.S. FATALITIES
A Replication

Ronald C. Kessler and Horst Stipp

In a recent issue of this *Journal,* Phillips reported evidence from a time-series analysis of U.S. fatalities in 1977 that fictional suicide stories on daytime television serials, "soap operas," trigger subsequent real-life suicides and single-vehicle motor vehicle fatalities. This paper calls attention to a serious mistake in Phillips's data which invalidates his results. In addition, the paper describes a more precise approach which produces no evidence linking soap opera suicide stories to subsequent real-life fatalities. The error in Phillips's paper stems from the fact that he used newspaper summaries as sources for the soap opera suicide stories and, in eight out of 13 cases, misspecified the date of the event. This mistake invalidates his before-after analysis strategy. Analyses presented here correct this error and disaggregate the time series to daily information. Several stories that Phillips overlooked are included.

In a recent issue of this *Journal,* Phillips (1982) presented evidence that fictional suicide stories on daytime television serials, "soap operas," are associated with subsequent suicides and single-vehicle motor fatalities (SVMFs) in the U.S. population. The author proclaimed this demonstration "the first systematic, quantitative evidence" (p. 1342) that fictional television violence triggers serious real-life violence.

Phillips's statement reflects a conviction that his research demonstrates a significant causal relationship, not established in previous research,

[1] We would like to thank Kenneth Bollen, George Comstock, Barry Cook, David McDowell, Roberto Franzosi, Ronald Milavsky, and William Rubens for helpful comments on an earlier draft; Jon Michael Reed for his assistance in obtaining data on television suicide stories; and Roger Brown, Adam Dolgins, Dana Herko, Richard Hogan, Jane McLeod, Katherine Rice, and Margalit Tal for research assistance. The Inter-University Consortium for Political and Social Research supplied the mortality data. Requests for reprints should be sent to Ronald C. Kessler, Department of Sociology, University of Michigan, Ann Arbor, Michigan 48109.

From Ronald C. Kessler and Horst Stipp, "The Impact of Fictional Television Suicide Stories on U.S. Fatalities: A Replication," *American Journal of Sociology*, Vol. 90, No. 1 (July 1984), pp. 151-167.

between violent depictions in television entertainment programs and acts of serious violence in the real world. His review of this research is largely based on Comstock (1975, 1980), who points out that most research in this area is experimental with necessarily artificial settings and measures of exposure and aggression that often do not resemble television exposure or aggressive behavior in the real world. Furthermore, Phillips points out that most research is restricted to children and adolescents. We would add to this assessment that practically all research in this field deals with relatively mild forms of aggression (such as play aggression) and that Phillips's is one of the very few studies that have investigated a possible link between fictional portrayals of violence and serious aggression.[2]

If Phillips's results are accurate, they would be the most powerful evidence to date that fictional television violence can lead to serious real-life aggression. However, as we show in this paper, there is a mistake in Phillips's analysis that invalidates his results. A more precise analysis that avoids this error fails to provide evidence for a causal link between fictional suicides and real-life fatalities.

A CRITIQUE OF PHILLIPS'S ANALYSIS

The approach Phillips took is a variant on one he used in previous studies of imitative suicides (e.g., Phillips 1974, 1979). Beginning with a time series of suicide stories, drawn in this case from television soap operas and one spoof of that genre ("Mary Hartman, Mary Hartman"), he set out to compare the number of real-life suicides and SVMFs that occurred shortly before and shortly after each story. The significance of the average before-after difference was taken as a test of television's effect.

In his previous work on the impact of real-life suicides of celebrities, Phillips looked at *daily* time series and documented the finding that imitative suicides occur three days after the beginning of media coverage. In his analysis of fictional suicide stories in soap operas, however, he used *weekly* newspaper soap opera plot summaries as his source of information. He realized that this made his results less sensitive than they might otherwise be and thus called for further analysis with a more detailed measure of soap opera episodes. This was what we originally set out to do in our extension of his work.

The newspaper soap opera summary used by Phillips is "The Soaps," written by Jon Michael Reed and syndicated in over 100 major papers throughout the country. Phillips used the *Los Angeles Times* version of this summary as his source. In 1977, the *Los Angeles Times* usually

[2] Serious aggression is dealt with in a cross-sectional survey by Belson (1978) and in a longitudinal panel study by Milavsky et al. (1982).

published the column in the Saturday edition. Phillips found 13 separate "suicide stories" from this source during 1977.

Since Phillips had available to him only weekly summaries of each soap opera, he did not know the exact day on which the suicide story was aired on television. Despite that, he was able to devise a before-after analysis. He reasoned that since Monday is the first day the event could have occurred, a three-day lag effect of the sort found in his earlier work should show up as a rise in fatalities on Thursday, a Tuesday soap opera story should show up as a rise in fatalities on Friday, and so on. Consequently, he focused on real-life fatalities in the second part of each week, Thursday through Sunday, and he contrasted the Thursday-through-Sunday suicide and SVMF counts the week before the televised soap opera attempt ("control period") with the counts in the week of the attempt ("experimental period"). If a suicide story was presented on Monday, Tuesday, or Wednesday, the comparison of fatality counts was clearly a before-after design. If a story appeared on Thursday or Friday, the "control period" fell before the event and the "experimental period" at the time of the event or a few days after it.

This is a reasonable approach, given the limitations of the data. However, Phillips made one assumption that turns out to be incorrect and invalidates the entire analysis. He assumed that the Saturday newspaper columns summarize episodes aired the previous Monday through Friday. In reality, the summary generally covers the period from Friday of the previous week through Thursday. The reason for this is that lead time is needed to prepare the column for the Saturday edition.[3]

The erroneous assumption about the date of the suicide stories in "The Soaps" column has important consequences for Phillips's analysis. If a suicide attempt was shown on a Friday, it was reported one week later than Phillips assumed. As a result, his "control period" was the Thursday through Sunday of the telecast and the "experimental period" was the Thursday through Sunday one week later.[4] As it happens, eight of the 13

[3] For example, a newspaper column published on Saturday the 10th would not cover Monday the 5th through Friday the 9th, as assumed by Phillips, but, rather, Friday the 2d and Monday through Thursday the 5th through the 8th. Episodes shown on Friday the 9th would be summarized in the column published on the 17th.

[4] Let us stay with the example given above. An event presented on Friday the 9th would be summarized in the column published on Saturday the 17th. Phillips, however, assumed that this event took place on Friday the 16th. Thus, his "control period" would be the previous Thursday through Sunday, the 8th through the 11th, and his "experimental period" Thursday the 15th through Sunday the 18th. Therefore, Phillips compared suicide and SVMF rates at the time of the suicide story (the day before, the day of the event, and one and two days after it) with rates one week later. The exception to this is a story from "Mary Hartman," the only nonnetwork "syndicated" program in his analysis. The episode in question (with a story involving Merle Jeeter; see table 1) was aired in Los Angeles on Friday, February 18, but appeared in the *Los*

stories analyzed by Phillips culminated on a Friday[5] (see table 1). Thus, in only five instances did he compare before-after fatality rates—the instances in which the "control period" was Thursday through Sunday *before,* and the "experimental period" was Thursday through Sunday *after* the telecast. Nothing about television effects can be learned from this hybrid set of comparisons.

RESULTS OF A REANALYSIS

We set out to overcome the limitations and errors in Phillips's work by a detailed content analysis. To obtain information of this sort we used a two-step process. First, we reviewed "The Soaps" column as well as two other soap opera summaries: *Soap Opera Digest* and the *Daytime Serial Newsletter.*[6] From this review we found three additional suicide stories overlooked in Phillips's research. Second, we contacted Jon Michael Reed, author of "The Soaps." His detailed file on 1977 soap opera stories provided us with the exact date of each story and, in addition, a description of the nature and the context of the suicide attempts. Table 1 contains a complete list of the 15 soap opera suicide stories televised during 1977.[7] As shown in the table, the 15 stories produced 19 separate episodes during which the audience observed some kind of suicide attempt. In four

---

Angeles Times summary published on the 19th. This was possible because "Mary Hartman" was taped and available for prescreening some days before it appeared. There is another problem with the Jeeter case. Because it was syndicated, it was not aired at the same time in all U.S. markets and not aired at all in many smaller markets. It might have been televised in, e.g., Milwaukee two or three weeks after it was shown in Los Angeles. Also, in contrast to network daytime serials, "Mary Hartman" episodes were repeated during the summer. Therefore, this story may have been shown again. These problems are also present in the story with Tom Hartman on June 30.

[5] Aside from the Jeeter case, all seven other Friday attempts counted by Phillips were misdated. In addition, the attempt of Ann Martin on Wednesday, May 4, was misdated. Phillips counted it as occurring during the week of May 11–15. This mistake can be explained by the fact that the attempt was not mentioned in "The Soaps" until the week after its occurrence.

[6] In 1977, *Soap Opera Digest* was published by S.O.D. Publishing, New York. Despite great efforts, we were able to obtain only six of the 12 issues. The *Daytime Serial Newsletter* is no longer published. In 1977 it was published monthly by D.S.N. Publications, Mountain View, Calif. We obtained all issues. We reviewed "The Soaps" for all weeks in the year, not just those in which it was published in the *Los Angeles Times*.

[7] The 13 stories in Phillips's list, plus the three additional ones we uncovered, produce a total of 16 stories. As is explained below, though, we discarded one of those in Phillips's original list, leaving us with 15.

TABLE 1

SOAP OPERA SUICIDE STORIES USED IN THE ANALYSIS

Character	Soap Opera	Date of Occurrence (1977)	Counted by Phillips	Phillips's "Experimental" Period (1977)
Merle Jeeter	Mary Hartman	2/18 (Fri.)	Yes	2/17–20
Heather Grant	General Hospital	3/3 (Thurs.)	Yes	3/3–6
Delia Ryan	Ryan's Hope	3/4 (Fri.)	Yes	3/10–13*
Sharon Duval	Days of Our Lives	3/29, 30 (Tues., Wed.)	Yes	3/31–4/3
Pierre Namath	General Hospital	4/13 (Wed.)	Yes	4/14–17
Paul Summers	The Doctors	4/15 (Fri.)	Yes	4/21–24*
Ann Martin	All My Children	5/4 (Wed.)	Yes	5/12–15*
Sharon Duval	Days of Our Lives	5/20 (Fri.)	No	...
Mary Ellen Dante ...	General Hospital	5/20 (Fri.)	Yes	5/26–29*
Tom Hartman	Mary Hartman	6/30, 7/1 (Thurs., Fri.)	No	...
Naomi Vernon	One Life to Live	7/8 (Fri.)	Yes	7/14–17*
Eleanor Conrad	The Doctors	9/20, 21 (Tues., Wed.)	No	...
Ron Becker	Young and Restless	10/7 (Fri.)	Yes	10/13–16*
Eleanor Conrad	The Doctors	10/14, 17 (Fri., Mon.)	Yes	10/20–23*
Laurie Dallas	The Edge of Night	11/11 (Fri.)	Yes	11/17–20*

NOTE.—All "experimental" periods are from Thursday through Sunday.
* Instances in which Phillips incorrectly dated the week of occurrence.

cases the very same event was repeated in two consecutive episodes. (This type of repeat performance, first used in the Saturday afternoon theater movie serials produced in the 1930s and 1940s, is not uncommon in the soaps.)

It is noteworthy that only two of these stories resulted in fatalities (Namath and Vernon). Most others were unsuccessful attempts. Three of the stories not involving fatalities were apparent fakes (Grant, Ryan, and Dante). We make no distinction among these various types of stories in the analysis presented here, as our main purpose is to replicate Phillips's analysis. In further work with these data, though, we are investigating whether variations along these lines are related to the ability of episodes to provoke imitative suicides.

Of these 15 stories, 12 were included in Phillips's list. He apparently did not find two (Sharon Duval on May 20 and Eleanor Conrad on September 20–21), and he omitted one because it occurred during the week of a major holiday (Tom Hartman on June 30–July 1).[8] He included a thirteenth story that we have omitted from our list. This is the case of Meredith Hartford in "Search for Tomorrow." Phillips included her suicide story for the week of October 24–28. Our more detailed analysis of the story line shows that this episode involved only a discussion of a past, unsuccessful suicide attempt and that Meredith was not even seen by the audience.[9]

Some justification of this decision is in order. We discarded the Meredith Hartford case from our analysis because a great many other discussions of past or impending suicides were televised on the daytime serials in 1977.[10] If we included the discussion about Meredith, we would have to count these others. And in the absence of a detailed content analysis of every soap opera for every day of the year it would not be possible to obtain the data needed to create a time series of all such discussions.[11]

A REPLICATION OF PHILLIPS'S ANALYSIS

Since we have much more detailed data than Phillips used, we did not replicate his Thursday through Sunday comparison of fatalities before and after fictional suicide stories. Instead we compared the number of

[8] Phillips did not consider stories occurring on or near holidays that his previous research had found to be significantly related to suicide rates, since the effect of the suicide story and of the holiday would be confounded in his analysis scheme.

[9] Meredith was away from home at a boarding school in Europe and so was never introduced as a character (although her name was mentioned occasionally). In October, her father (a regular character in the soap opera) went to Europe for a visit and stopped to see Meredith. On October 21 he was informed by a member of the school staff that Meredith had suffered a "most serious tragedy." On October 24 he learned that the "tragedy" was an unsuccessful suicide attempt precipitated by Meredith's learning that her lover was a married man. The audience was not told when the attempt occurred, nor was Meredith ever seen as a character.

[10] To give some idea of how frequently suicides were discussed on soap operas in 1977, we can report that there were 90 days in the weeks shortly before or after one of the suicide attempts in table 1 during which there was some discussion either of the possibility of the character committing suicide (prior to the actual attempt) or of the fact that he or she had done so (after the attempt). This is over a third of all weekdays in the year. And even this is a conservative estimate, because we did not systematically examine the topics of discussion on soaps during the periods of time other than those near one of the attempts we were studying.

[11] One could also argue that the mere discussion of a suicide in a program is unlikely to have the same impact on actual suicides as the dramatic portrayal of a suicide attempt. If this view is correct, eliminating mere discussions of suicide from the analysis would increase the likelihood of finding that the stories analyzed have an effect. However, we know very little about the mechanisms by which fictional suicide stories may trigger real-life suicides; therefore we do not know what kind of fictional suicide story may or may not have an effect.

fatalities over the four days beginning the day of the soap opera story with the number expected on the basis of control models.

Like Phillips, we combined stories that were so close to each other that their independent influences could not be discriminated. This yielded a set of 11 before-after comparisons, as shown in table 2. (One story included in table 1, concerning Tom Hartman, has been excluded here because the four-day lag interval overlaps with the Independence Day weekend. Phillips excluded Hartman for the same reason.) For each of these, the number of U.S. suicides and SVMFs completed from the day of the telecast through the third day after the telecast was calculated.[12] These totals are presented in columns 4a and 5a of table 2. In the case of multiple stories, as in the Grant/Ryan stories on March 3 and 4, this experimental period was modified to include the time period from the day of the first story through the third day after the second story. The totals reported in table 2 for these multiple-story cases have been adjusted to approximate the four-day total found in the other rows. For example, in the Grant/Ryan case there were 381 suicides in the five-day interval March 3–7. This means that the average four-day count was 80% of 381, or 304.8. The entry in table 2 has been rounded off to the nearest whole number.

The control period is defined as the closest time interval preceding the suicide story that contains the same days of the week as the experimental period and does not contain any holidays, real-life celebrity suicides, or other soap opera suicide stories. By defining the control period in this way we correct for the effects of public holidays, day-of-the-week fluctuations, and seasonal variations. The number of suicides and SVMFs that occurred in the control periods for each story are presented, respectively, in columns 4b and 5b.[13]

[12] We followed Phillips in counting as suicides all deaths coded in categories E950–E959 and as SVMFs all deaths coded in categories E815–E818 of the National Center for Health Statistics' Mortality Detail File for 1977. This person-specific file was aggregated to daily totals. We also followed Phillips in limiting our analysis to people described on their death certificates as "white." His reason for limiting the sample in this way was that most soap opera characters are white, so an imitation effect is probably more pronounced among whites. Phillips also limited his motor vehicle analysis to persons aged 15 or more, noting that suicides begin at approximately age 15. We followed him in this and also limited our suicide analysis in the same way. Although our decision to extend the age limitation to suicide makes no important difference to our results (suicides among children younger than 15 make up less than 1% of all suicides), we felt that it might marginally strengthen our chance of detecting a significant television effect, as most children younger than 15 are in school during the hours soap operas are televised.

[13] Phillips defined his control periods in the same way, though in one case he deviated from this procedure. The control period for the Jeeter episode would normally be February 10–13, but Phillips selected January 20–23 instead, on the grounds that the

TABLE 2

FOUR-DAY (Zero- to Three-Day Lags) BEFORE-AFTER COMPARISON OF U.S. SUICIDES AND SINGLE-VEHICLE MOTOR FATALITIES (SVMFs) AROUND THE TIME OF SOAP OPERA SUICIDE STORIES, 1977

CHARACTER	DATE OF STORY (1)	EXPERIMENTAL PERIOD (2)	CONTROL PERIOD (3)	SUICIDES (4)		SVMFs (5)	
				Experimental (a)	Control (b)	Experimental (a)	Control (b)
Jeeter	2/18	2/18–21	2/11–14	315	325	131	132
Grant/Ryan	3/3, 4	3/3–7	2/24–28	305	284	125	130
Duval	3/29, 30	3/29–4/2	3/22–26	314	303	125	133
Namath/Summers	4/13, 15	4/13–18	4/6–11	325	307	148	146
Martin	5/4	5/4–7	4/27–30	299	244	156	140
Duval/Dante	5/20	5/20–23	5/13–16	296	330	187	197
Vernon	7/8	7/8–11	6/24–27	299	299	174	194
Conrad	9/20, 21	9/20–24	9/13–17	282	286	142	157
Becker	10/7	10/7–10	9/30–10/3	303	289	169	182
Conrad	10/14, 17	10/14–20	9/30–10/6	289	279	143	159
Dallas	11/11	11/11–14	11/4–7	237	279	166	182
Total				3,264	3,225	1,666	1,752
Mean				296.73	293.18	151.45	159.27
SD				23.23	23.80	20.74	25.51
Mean difference				3.55		−7.82	
SD of mean difference				26.65		10.41	
t-test of mean difference				.4		−2.5	
df				10		10	

NOTE.—All figures are for U.S. white fatalities, aged 15 or older, 1977. Tom Hartman has been omitted because a zero- to three-day lag after his attempt overlaps with the Independence Day holiday. Phillips omitted Hartman for the same reason. Three pairs of stories (Grant/Ryan, Namath/Summers, and Duval/Dante) were combined because they occurred within three days of each other. Three stories overlap with holidays that were not considered by Phillips but which are nonetheless federal holidays: Jeeter overlaps with Washington's Birthday (2/21), Becker with Columbus Day (10/10), and Dallas with Veterans' Day (11/11). With these three removed, the *t*-tests of the mean differences are 0.93 (suicide) and −1.71 (SVMF).

Constructed in this way, the experimental and control periods are comparable to those created by Phillips. Our figures differ from his in only two important respects that have not been noted already (see nn. 12 and 13). Both of these constitute improvements over his calculations. First, we corrected his mistake in dating the telecast of eight stories. Second, we based our construction of the experimental and control periods on information about the precise day of the telecast rather than on the week of the telecast.[14]

A rigorous comparison of the experimental and control periods shows that there is no significant effect of soap opera suicides on real suicides. There are approximately 3.5 more suicides during an experimental period than during a control period, a difference that is well within the bounds of

---

suicide of comedian Freddie Prinze (on January 29) could have inflated the number of suicides committed in the period February 10–13. A careful inspection of Phillips's table 1 shows that his decision here had an important effect on his results. The experimental-control difference in the Jeeter case, using January 20–23 as the control period, is far larger than that in any other case he considers. (It accounts for a full 35% of the total experimental-control difference found in all nine contrasts taken together.) The reason: the number of suicides committed in January is lower than the number committed in any other month in the year. As shown in table 3, there is an average of 13 more suicides each day in February than in January. Indeed, of the 52 Thursday–Sunday periods in 1977, January 20–23 had the third lowest number of suicides (the two lower being April 28–May 1, which happened to be the control period for the Martin story, and December 22–25, during Christmas week). The suicide totals during the last three Thursday–Sunday periods in January and the first three in February were 241 (the control period Phillips selected), 251, 246 (the week of Prinze's death), 293, 298, and 294 (the week of the Jeeter story). It is clear from an inspection of this array that there is no evidence here for an effect of either the Prinze suicide or the Jeeter suicide story.

[14] There is an additional difference that should be mentioned. Phillips included a correction for linear trend based on a regression of weekly suicide counts on time. We did not include this in our replication because a simple linear trend model seriously distorts seasonal changes in suicides and SVMFs. January and December are very similar in fatality rates, not far apart as a linear model assumes. A polynomial model is consequently more appropriate. In analyses of these data with time-series models, described later, we include a more appropriate representation of trend, one that parallels closely the method used by Bollen and Phillips (1981, 1982) in collaborative work completed subsequent to Phillips's analysis of the television soap opera data. (We note, incidentally, that Bollen and Phillips, in their before-after analogue of our table 2, discovered that a correction for daily trend made no difference to their results, and therefore they excluded it from their final model. See table 1 in their 1982 paper.) The exclusion of Phillips's time trend is of no importance, as it amounts to no more than a weekly decrease of suicides by one-half. Applying this "detrending" to the data in our table 2 leaves the standard deviation of the suicide control period unchanged to the second decimal place and increases the mean experimental-control suicide difference by only 0.6. The t-test using detrended data is 0.91 (compared with 0.85 based on the data in table 2). The trend Phillips estimated for SVMFs is *positive*, which means that correcting for it would yield an even *lower* (more negative) television effect estimate than is reported in our table 2 already.

chance ($t = 0.4$, $df = 10$). There are about 7.8 fewer motor vehicle deaths during an experimental period than during a control period, a difference that is significant at the .02 level ($t = 2.5$, $df = 10$). These results refute Phillips's claim that fictional television suicide stories cause an increase in subsequent real-life fatalities in the four days after the telecast. Evidence for a positive television effect also failed to emerge when we repeated these calculations for a lag of one week.[15]

AN AGGREGATED ASSESSMENT OF TELEVISION EFFECTS

We carried out a parametric analogue of the before-after comparison just presented to see whether the greater precision of a regression-based approach would uncover evidence of a positive television effect. We did this by estimating a daily time-series model for 1977 containing four types of control variables: (1) six dummy variables for days of the week, (2) 11 dummy variables for months of the year, (3) 10 dummy variables for holidays,[16] and (4) dummy variables for two highly publicized celebrity

[15] Nor did we find any such evidence in an analysis of total motor vehicle fatalities rather than SVMFs. A one-week lag was used because Bollen and Phillips (1982) found this to be more appropriate than three days in their analysis of the relationship between publicized suicides and subsequent U.S. suicides. For the week-long (days 0–7) aggregations and before-after comparisons, *t*-tests were 0.7 (suicide) and −0.4 (SVMF), each with 10 *df*. Both of these tests are well within the bounds of chance.

[16] Phillips (1982), following Phillips and Liu (1980), included five public holidays in his analysis: Independence Day, Labor Day, Thanksgiving, Christmas, and New Year's Day. These are five of the seven federal holidays celebrated in all 50 states and the District of Columbia. (The other two are Washington's Birthday and Veterans' Day.) In subsequent work, Bollen (1983) and Bollen and Phillips (1981, 1982) included Memorial Day along with these five. Memorial Day is a federal holiday that is celebrated in 40 states and the District of Columbia on the last Monday in May. Several southern states celebrate Confederate Memorial Day instead (on the last Monday in April). Some states celebrate Memorial Day on May 30 or on the fourth Monday (rather than the last Monday) in May. Despite all this inconsistency, Bollen and Phillips found the suicide-holiday relationship quite strong during the federally defined Memorial Day weekend. They did not, however, investigate the relationship between suicide and other federal holidays celebrated in a large number of states. We have included all 10 of these holidays in our analysis, except that we have substituted New Year's Eve for New Year's Day. In addition to the eight mentioned above, those include Columbus Day (celebrated in 38 states and Washington, D.C.) and Election Day (celebrated in 27 states and Washington, D.C.). We followed the procedures adopted by Bollen (1983) for coding these holidays, with a single dummy variable used to define all the days in each holiday period (thus yielding 10 dummy variables in all). We also experimented with a more detailed holiday code. Phillips and Liu (1980) showed that suicides dip in the three days before a major holiday and rise during the three days after it. A single dummy variable used to characterize the entire holiday period, then, runs the risk of overpredicting the number of fatalities before the holiday and underpredicting the number after it. This is a particularly serious possibility as neither holidays nor soap opera suicide stories were well distributed over the days of

deaths that occurred in 1977—the January 29 suicide of Freddie Prinze and the August 16 death of Elvis Presley. Separate dummy variables were entered for the day of the death through the tenth day after the death in each of these two cases.

A time-series model containing all these controls gives us a much more precise way of evaluating the influence of television suicide stories than does Phillips's before-after method. Rather than choose a single control period for each soap opera story, we use the entire day-to-day series for 1977 to generate a no-effect baseline. By introducing dummy variables for the day of a suicide story, for the day after such a story, for two days after, and so on, we obtain a parametric estimate of the soap opera effect over different lag times.

We began the analysis by estimating a baseline equation containing only control variables. Here we found some results consistent with previous time-series investigations of fatality (Bollen 1983). The suicide rate is higher on Mondays than on other days of the week, while SVMFs peak on weekends. December and January bring fewer suicides than other months, while SVMFs are highest in the summer months and lowest in the winter months. There are fewer suicides on holidays than we would expect on the basis of chance, although this is significantly so only for the Memorial Day, Independence Day, and Thanksgiving holidays in this one-year series. For SVMFs, by comparison, the Memorial Day, Independence Day, and Labor Day holidays are associated with higher-than-average levels of fatality. Finally, we found no evidence that the number of suicides or SVMFs occurring in the days after the deaths of Freddie Prinze or Elvis Presley differed from baseline expectations. Consequently, we omitted controls for these celebrity deaths from our subsequent prediction equations.

Table 3 presents two time-series equations for the effects of soap opera suicide stories.[17] The first equation predicts daily variation in suicides,

---

the week. (Fully half of the holidays occurred on Mondays, and the great majority of soap opera suicide stories occurred on Fridays.) Consequently, we replaced the 10 holiday dummy variables with a series of before-holiday, day-of-holiday, and after-holiday dummies spanning the period from three days before to three days after each holiday. We recognize that this increases substantially the number of holiday control variables that one needs to include in the time-series equation and thus decreases the degrees of freedom in the equation. Therefore, all analyses were done three times: once with the 10 less detailed holiday dummies, again with the full set of detailed holiday dummies, and a third time with only those detailed holiday dummies that were found to be significant in the second set of analyses.

[17] In their most recent work on celebrity suicides, Bollen and Phillips (1981, 1982) estimated a model similar to this one in all important respects but one: it contained a lagged endogenous variable which is omitted from our model. We discovered that the lagged endogenous variable was not significant in this one-year series for either suicide

TABLE 3

DAILY TIME-SERIES REGRESSIONS OF U.S. SUICIDES AND SINGLE-VEHICLE MOTOR FATALITIES (SVMFs) ON SOAP OPERA SUICIDE STORIES AND CONTROLS, 1977

REGRESSORS	SUICIDES		SVMFs	
	b	SE	*b*	SE
Intercept	59.5**	2.4	32.7**	1.9
Story(0)	−.2	2.5	.2	1.9
Story(1)	−1.6	2.9	−3.6*	2.2
Story(2)	1.0	3.0	−3.0	2.3
Story(3)	.2	3.0	−.6	2.3
Story(4)	−2.0	2.9	−1.2	2.3
Story(5)	−1.6	2.9	−1.3	2.3
Story(6)	2.2	2.9	1.8	2.3
Story(7)	1.2	3.0	−4.1*	2.4
Story(8)	.6	3.0	4.8**	2.4
Story(9)	−3.7	3.0	−1.0	2.4
Story(10)	2.8	3.1	−2.1	2.4
Monday	11.3**	2.1	−19.5**	1.6
Tuesday	8.0**	2.0	−21.7**	1.5
Wednesday	3.8*	2.0	−20.8**	1.6
Thursday	2.4	2.0	−19.2**	1.6
Friday	2.1	2.0	−11.3**	1.5
Saturday	−.3	2.1	6.2**	1.6
February	12.8**	2.8	7.4**	2.2
March	13.0**	2.7	9.2**	2.1
April	12.2**	2.8	14.7**	2.1
May	12.5**	2.8	19.4**	2.2
June	8.9**	2.6	21.4**	2.0
July	12.9**	2.8	23.6**	2.2
August	10.2**	2.6	22.3**	2.0
September	10.8**	2.7	18.1**	2.1
October	10.8**	2.8	18.8**	2.2
November	6.7**	2.9	16.5**	2.2
December	.2	2.7	10.0**	2.1
Washington	3.3	5.2	.5	4.1
Memorial	−12.5**	5.1	6.9*	4.0
Independence	−8.4*	5.1	10.4**	4.0
Labor	−4.4	5.0	13.8**	3.9
Columbus	2.3	5.1	−1.3	3.9
Election	3.5	9.5	−.6	7.4
Veterans'	−5.1	5.9	1.3	4.6
Thanksgiving	−8.8*	4.6	3.2	3.6
Christmas	−4.0	5.6	4.9	4.4
New Year's Eve	−.4	9.4	−6.9	7.3
R^2	.360**		.781**	
D-W	1.95		1.96	

NOTE.—N = 355. See n. 16 for a discussion of the holiday codes. See n. 18 for a discussion of the story(i) codes.

* Significant at the .10 level.

** Significant at the .05 level.

whereas the second predicts daily variation in SVMFs. Television effects from the day of the story through the tenth day after the story are estimated, yielding a total of 22 television coefficients in the two equations together.[18] There is no meaningful evidence in these coefficients for a consistent television effect. In the suicide equation we see that none of the story(i) coefficients is statistically significant at the .10 level. Nor could we detect any evidence that any sets of these coefficients taken two or more at a time are significant when evaluated by an R^2 increment test. In the SVMF equation we find three significant coefficients, but two of these suggest that soap opera suicide stories lead to a drop in SVMFs. This is counterintuitive and in all likelihood due to chance. In fact, the story(1) coefficient is not associated with a significant R^2 increment. The opposite-sign story(7) and story(8) coefficients do pass the R^2 increment test individually but are nonetheless consistent with chance variation in a set of nine coefficients, as the R^2 increment test evaluating the overall significance of the set of coefficients for stories(0)–(8) is insignificant with 9 *df*.[19]

Like Phillips, we also studied subgroups. Separate time-series equations were estimated for subgroups defined by sex, urban-rural location, and the cross-classification of these two variables.[20] In none of these eight subgroups did we find more substantial evidence of television effects than in table 3. The television coefficients for these subgroup equations are presented in tables 4 (suicide) and 5 (SVMF). Only three of 88 coefficients are significant at the .10 level in the suicide series. Eight are significant in

---

or SVMF and so omitted it from the final model. The results presented do not change when the lagged endogenous variable is included as a predictor.

[18] We could not code story(i) for the first i = 10 days of 1977, as we did not know anything about the soap opera stories telecast during the last 10 days of 1976. These days were consequently dropped from the analysis, which explains why the sample size is 355 rather than 365. For the remaining days of the year a variable was coded for story(i) if one or more of the soap opera suicide stories listed in table 1 occurred 10 days or less prior to the day in question. When a day was part of the series for two stories (like October 14, the day of the second Conrad story and a week after the Becker story) or was part of a story that was televised on two or more days (like March 31, two days after Duval's first televised attempt but only one day after this attempt was retelevised), it was coded only in terms of the more recent story.

[19] These equations were replicated with the Hartman and Jeeter cases omitted to see whether the syndicated "Mary Hartman" episodes were responsible for the insignificant association. (See n. 4 above for a discussion of the problems in dating the telecast of "Mary Hartman" episodes.) Results did not change. None of the 11 story(i) coefficients shown in table 3 remained significant in the SVMF equation. As is reported in n. 16 above, we also investigated the possibility that more detailed holiday codes would change the results but found no evidence for this in replications.

[20] As in Phillips's analysis, an "urban" location is defined as a place with 100,000 or more inhabitants.

TABLE 4

DETAILS OF SUBGROUP DAILY TIME-SERIES REGRESSIONS OF U.S. SUICIDES ON SOAP OPERA SUICIDE STORIES AND CONTROLS, 1977 (N = 355)

Regressors	Subgroups			
	Male	Female	Urban	Rural
Story(0)	1.2	−1.4	−.2	1.0
Story(1)	−.5	−1.0	−1.3	.3
Story(2)	1.4	−.4	−.8	2.0
Story(3)	1.6	−1.4	−.3	−1.6
Story(4)	−1.7	−.3	−1.0	1.6
Story(5)	−2.1	.4	−1.2	−.5
Story(6)	2.5	−.3	−1.0	2.2
Story(7)	.3	.9	−.8	−.4
Story(8)	.9	−.3	2.0	−1.2
Story(9)	−2.3	−1.4	−.3	−.7
Story(10)	4.9*	−2.0	.9	−.0
D-W	1.90	2.20	2.06	2.08
	Urban Male	Urban Female	Rural Male	Rural Female
Story(0)	.2	−.4	.4	.6
Story(1)	−1.3	.0	.4	−.1
Story(2)	−.8	.0	1.3	.7
Story(3)	−.5	.2	−.7	−.9
Story(4)	−.2	−.8	.7	.9
Story(5)	−.6	−.6	−.4	−.1
Story(6)	−1.5	.4	1.5	.7
Story(7)	−1.5	.7	−.2	−.2
Story(8)	1.9*	.1	−1.5	.3
Story(9)	.1	−.3	.7	−1.4*
Story(10)	1.3	−.4	.7	−.7
D-W	1.93	2.25	2.07	1.97

NOTE.—The regression model in which these coefficients were estimated is identical to that presented in table 3, with the exception that subgroups rather than the total U.S. population are used in estimation. Coefficients for control variables are omitted here.
* Significant at the .10 level.

the SVMF series, but half of these are negative.[21] It is of particular interest to note that there is no hint of a sex difference in the magnitude of these coefficients for either outcome variable even though women make

[21] As with the equations presented in table 3, the subgroup results were subjected to a series of additional evaluations. An F-test for the R^2 increment of each story(i) coefficient was conducted as well as an evaluation of its t-test in the complete equation. As the 11 story(i) variables have only modest intercorrelations (the condition number of their correlation matrix is 1.6), these F-tests yielded evidence of significance very similar to that provided by the t-tests in tables 4 and 5. We also evaluated the

TABLE 5

DETAILS OF SUBGROUP DAILY TIME-SERIES REGRESSIONS OF U.S. SINGLE-VEHICLE MOTOR FATALITIES (SVMFs) AND CONTROLS, 1977 (N = 355)

Regressors	Subgroups			
	Male	Female	Urban	Rural
Story(0)	−.2	.4	1.6**	.3
Story(1)	−1.3	−2.3**	−.4	.7
Story(2)	−2.3	−.8	−.6	−1.1
Story(3)	−.3	−.4	.5	−.4
Story(4)	−1.3	.1	−.1	−1.0
Story(5)	−1.8	.5	.1	−1.2
Story(6)	2.0	−.3	.2	1.6
Story(7)	−2.8	−1.3	−.2	.0
Story(8)	4.4**	.4	.2	1.3
Story(9)	−.7	−.3	−.9	−.3
Story(10)	−.4	−1.7*	−.6	1.2
D-W	1.84	2.19	2.08	1.91
	Urban Male	Urban Female	Rural Male	Rural Female
Story(0)	1.0*	.6**	.7	−.4
Story(1)	−.1	−.3	.5	.2
Story(2)	−.1	−.5*	−.6	−.5
Story(3)	.7	−.1	−.1	−.3
Story(4)	−.2	.2	−.7	−.3
Story(5)	−.1	.2	−1.1	−.1
Story(6)	.4	−.2	1.2	.4
Story(7)	.5	−.6*	−.1	.1
Story(8)	.2	−.0	.9	.4
Story(9)	−.8	−.1	−.6	.3
Story(10)	−.2	−.4	1.2	−.0
D-W	2.09	2.16	1.94	1.94

NOTE.—The regression model in which these coefficients were estimated is identical to that presented in table 3, with the exception that subgroups rather than the total U.S. population are used in estimation. Coefficients for control variables are omitted here.

* Significant at the .10 level.

** Significant at the .05 level.

up the vast majority of soap opera viewers. (According to Nielsen [1977] ratings, in November 1977 the average "daytime drama" had a rating of 1.5 among men and 6.4 among women.) If television suicide stories trig-

significance of multiple story(i) coefficients; those in lags 0–3, 4–7, 8–10, 0–7, and 0–10. In 45 replications (each of these five multiple R^2 increment tests for the eight subgroups and the total sample), none was significant in the suicide equations, and only two for urban females were significant in the SVMF equations. These tests were replicated with equations that used the more detailed holiday codes described in n. 16 above. This refinement made very little difference in the results.

gered real-life imitations, we would almost certainly have observed a specification along these lines.

DISCUSSION

We have presented a replication and extension of Phillips's research on the effect of 1977 soap opera suicide stories on fatalities in the U.S. population. Our work improved on his by obtaining accurate dates for the telecasts, disaggregating to the day, and applying a powerful analytic technique to the data. Our analysis did not produce evidence supporting Phillips's claim of a substantial and statistically significant effect. Indeed, if we combine the effect coefficients in table 3 over the time period examined by Phillips (zero to three days after the story was telecast), we find an average decrease of one-half of a suicide and a decrease of seven SVMFs.

Although our results clearly contradict Phillips's claims about the effect of soap opera stories in 1977, they are mute on two questions: are there any kinds of fictional suicide stories that may affect real-life suicides, and, if so, under which conditions do effects occur? Since our analyses were based on data from only one year, the findings are restricted to the kind of stories presented during that year. A more thorough investigation should obtain a large and varied set of suicide stories and use a larger sample than is provided by a single year. If a particular story context could be found that links fictional television suicides to real suicides consistently across multiple years, we would have evidence of a meaningful television effect. Until such time, though, the weight of evidence argues against any influence of fictional televised suicide stories on real-life fatalities like that documented by Bollen and Phillips (1981, 1982) for celebrity suicides.

REFERENCES

Belson, William. 1978. *Television Violence and the Adolescent Boy*. London: Saxon.

Bollen, Kenneth A. 1983. "Temporal Variations in Mortality: A Comparison of U.S. Suicides and Motor Vehicle Fatalities." *Demography* 20:45–59.

Bollen, Kenneth A., and David P. Phillips. 1981. "Suicidal Motor Vehicle Fatalities in Detroit: A Replication." *American Journal of Sociology* 87:404–12.

———. 1982. "Imitative Suicides: A National Study of the Effects of Television News Stories." *American Sociological Review* 47:802–9.

Comstock, George. 1975. *Television and Human Behavior: The Key Studies*. Santa Monica, Calif.: Rand.

———. 1980. *Television in America*. Beverly Hills, Calif.: Sage.

Milavsky, J. Ronald, Ronald C. Kessler, Horst Stipp, and William S. Rubens. 1982. *Television and Aggression: A Panel Study*. New York: Academic Press.

Nielsen, A. C., Co. 1977. *National Audience Demographics Report, November 1977*. Northbrook, Ill.: Nielsen.

Phillips, David P. 1974. "The Influence of Suggestion on Suicide: Substantive and Theoretical Implications of the Werther Effect." *American Sociological Review* 39:340–54.

———. 1979. "Suicide, Motor Vehicle Fatalities, and the Mass Media: Evidence toward a Theory of Suggestion." *American Journal of Sociology* 84:1150–74.

———. 1982. "The Impact of Fictional Television Stories on U.S. Adult Fatalities: New Evidence on the Effect of the Mass Media on Violence." *American Journal of Sociology* 87:1340–59.

Phillips, David P., and Judith Liu. 1980. "The Frequency of Suicides around Major Public Holidays: Some Surprising Findings." *Suicide and Life-threatening Behavior* 10:41–50.

24

TELEVISION VIEWING AND SCHOOL ACHIEVEMENT

Mark Fetler

Using the results of the statewide California Assessment Program, this study of over 10,000 sixth-graders finds that heavy television viewing affects school achievement most significantly for students who are* more *socially advantaged.

The ubiquity of television in the United States is proverbial. Even so, only modest effects of television on student achievement have been documented, many of which diminish once intelligence is taken into account (8). The very pervasiveness that makes television an attractive research topic also makes it difficult to study. Experimental and statistical controls for program content, amount of viewing, and theoretically interesting background variables, such as social class and intelligence, are difficult to implement. Longitudinal studies that permit the monitoring of academic growth and viewing habits over a period of years (1, 9) are rare.

This article reports findings from a California Assessment Program survey of the television viewing habits of sixth-grade students, conducted in the spring of 1981. The California Assessment Program is a state testing program that annually assesses public schools in California and investigates factors that influence students' achievement. Here I examine the relationship of television viewing to student achievement, taking into account related variables such as study habits, characteristics of the home viewing environment, and social class.

Mark Fetler is a research and evaluation consultant for the California Department of Education. A preliminary version of this article was presented at the annual meeting of the American Education Research Association, New York, March 1982. Thanks are owed to Dr. Dale Carlson, Director of the California Assessment Program, and to two anonymous reviewers for their insightful comments. The views expressed here are not necessarily those of the California Department of Education.

Much recent writing on television has focused on its relationship to a variety of social issues (e.g., 4, 5, 10, 11, 17). Of special interest here is Gerbner et al.'s comprehensive theory of the social effects of television (6, 7) that uses the construct of "mainstreaming" to account for differences between groups of viewers. Mainstreaming refers to a tendency for television to cultivate a commonality of outlooks; heavier viewing diminishes differences related to social factors. Given that variables measuring aspects of socioeconomic status have been found to correlate with achievement, especially with aggregated units of analysis (15), the notion of mainstreaming was thought to be applicable to the relationship between television viewing and achievement. It seems plausible that heavier viewing of television diminishes differences in academic achievement in groups defined on the basis of variables that are associated with socioeconomic status.

The attraction of television for school-aged children has led to an increasing amount of research on the relationship between television and academic achievement (see, e.g., 12). Several recent and extensive reviews document current interest. Hornik's (8) review of studies and hypotheses relating home television use to schooling found that many studies showed a modest effect of viewing on reading achievement. Effects were greater for bright children but diminished after intelligence was statistically controlled.

Morgan and Gross's (9) examination of studies relating television use to schooling and education found a modest negative relationship between viewing and achievement. Heavier viewing was associated with lower intelligence and lower social class. For lower IQ students, especially girls, there was a positive association between viewing and achievement. Morgan and Gross cited two reasons for the modest correlations. One was the curvilinear relationship between amount of viewing and achievement, which was more pronounced for elementary school students than for high school students. Another reason for small correlations had to do with subgroup differences. For example, there were stronger negative effects of television on achievement for high IQ students than for low IQ students.

Williams et al. (16) synthesized the results of 23 different studies spanning the years 1954–1980. They found a median correlation of −.06 between amount of viewing and achievement. There was a significantly greater impact for high IQ students. Viewing up to ten hours per week had a positive effect on achievement, and viewing more than ten hours was associated with lower achievement.

This article examines the interaction of effects of amount of viewing, measures of social class, study habits, and the home environment on sixth-grade student achievement in reading, mathematics, and written expression.

For the purposes of this study, a strict home television environment was defined as one in which students were less likely to do homework in front of the set, less likely to watch before school or late at night, and less likely to be permitted to watch according to their own preferences. It was expected that television viewing would have fewer adverse effects on achievement in a strict home environment than in a less strict one. I also examined the proposed corollary of mainstreaming: that differences in academic achievement related to measures of social class are diminished with greater amounts of viewing. For example, heavy-viewing students from lower social classes should either benefit somewhat from their viewing or should not experience the same magnitude of decrease in achievement as students from higher social classes.

Data on student achievement were taken from the 1981 version of the California Assessment Program test, *Survey of Basic Skills: Grade Six,* administered annually to about 250,000 California public school children. The design of the test reflected instruction in California schools. The reading subtest contained items from four skill areas: word identification, vocabulary, comprehension, and study locational skills. The written expression subtest assessed standard English usage, language choices, sentence recognition, sentence manipulation, capitalization, and punctuation. The mathematics subtest covered arithmetic, geometry, measurement, probability, and statistics.

The test was constructed in a matrix format. There were a total of 128 reading items, 128 written expression items, and 160 mathematics items distributed among 16 unique forms of equal length. Each student took one form of the test, and roughly equal numbers of students in each school were given each form. The test was administered under standardized conditions by school personnel during the last two weeks of April each year. Individual tests were short enough so that they could be completed in 30–35 minutes, during a single class period, under unspeeded conditions. Test documents were mechanically scored and processed off-site; results were delivered on computer tape to the California Department of Education.

KR-20 reliability coefficients for the 16 forms range from .55 to .76 for the reading subtest, from .44 to .78 for the written expression subtest, and from .48 to .70 for the mathematics subtest (2). The median reliability was .68 for reading, .64 for written expression, and .60 for mathematics. When considering average scores of large groups of students, form-by-form reliabilities are less meaningful than aggregate scores, which reflect the content of all 16 forms. Using the Spearman-Brown formula, KR-20 reliabilities for the composite test can be estimated at .97 for reading, .96 for written expression, and .96 for mathematics. Given that the 16 forms are not exactly parallel in content or difficulty, these values are probably overestimates.

Results from a test that is designed and administered according to a matrix format must be interpreted differently than those from traditional, shorter, single-form tests. Matrix sampling permits economies of student time while assessing broad areas of content. Even though all important skills are represented on each form, each student sees only a small sample of the total item pool. Of necessity, specific content and average difficulty of forms differ. Average test scores for large groups are reliable and valid estimates of group achievement in the many skills assessed by the tests. The average percentage of correct scores represents the level of mastery of test content in the group tested.

Correlations of individual pupil level achievement scores with other variables are not as easily interpreted. Because the test forms differ slightly in specific content and difficulty, the correlations are attenuated from what they would be if everyone had received the same or exactly parallel tests. But there is evidence that this attenuation may not be substantial. White's (15) meta-analysis of 200 studies of the relation between social/economic status and achievement found a correlation of $r = .22$, using individuals as the unit of analysis. This compares with a correlation of $r = .35$ between parent occupation and total achievement in the study reported here (see Table 3). This higher correlation may be due to the large heterogeneous samples that take each form of the test and the general similarity of the forms.

A measure of parents' occupation was recorded for each student. On the back of each test booklet, the teacher identified the occupational category corresponding most closely to the occupation of the student's father, mother, or guardian. The five categories used were (a) unknown, (b) unskilled employees (and welfare), (c) skilled and semiskilled employees, (d) semiprofessionals, clerical and sales workers, and technicians, and (e) executives, professionals, and managers. The collection of information related to social class, such as parents' occupation, by the Department of Education is limited by laws regarding rights of privacy and by costs associated with its collection and processing. Parents' occupation is a limited proxy for a measure of social class; other desirable variables, such as income and education, unfortunately were not available. Teachers are, in general, quite familiar with their students and capable of making reliable judgments about them by the end of the school year, when the test is administered. Statewide, about 7.6 percent of the occupations of students' parents were classified as unknown. Possible reasons for this include the recent arrival of the student in the school, the suspected indigence of the parents, or the teacher's unwillingness to provide information. For this reason, if a parent's occupation was coded as unknown, it was treated as a missing value.

The schools included in the study were sampled systematically and ranked, based on 1980 sixth-grade test results, by the number of students tested (a proxy for school size) and an average index of parent occupation.

Every thirteenth school was selected from the ranked list, resulting in a set of 316 schools. The resulting sample did not differ significantly from the population in terms of achievement scores, parent occupation, or number of students tested. The three forms of the questionnaire were sequenced for distribution so that approximately equal numbers of each form were obtained by each school and class within a school. Initially, 15,385 questionnaires were returned by 292 schools. Student names were not collected in order to maintain confidentiality. Information on the questionnaires was used to match and merge student responses with their achievement scores. The merging procedure was done according to school, sex, and birthdate. Uniquely corresponding television survey and achievement records were combined. The result was 12,417 usable cases.

There were three circumstances under which students had to be eliminated from the study. First, non-English-speaking students (n = 673) were excluded because they were not required to take the achievement test. Second, students for whom socioeconomic data were missing (n = 1,012) were eliminated. Socioeconomic status was an important variable in several analyses, and to maintain cases with missing socioeconomic status data in some analyses and exclude them from others would have meant difficulty in comparing results. Finally, those students who indicated that they watched no television at all or did not respond to the question were eliminated (n = 245 and 77, respectively, for a total of 322). The number of students not watching television at all was too small, compared with the numbers in the other categories, to warrant analysis of their data. The final number of usable cases was 10,603.

Three separate forms of the survey were developed to minimize the time needed for administration and to maximize the amount of information collected. Each form began with a common set of questions regarding time spent watching television, doing homework, reading for pleasure, and ease of doing schoolwork.

Obtaining a reliable and valid measure of amount of viewing in a survey is difficult. Ideally, one would have a detailed account of shows watched and concomitant activities over a period of weeks or even longer. Measures of students' attitudes toward television, their cognitive abilities, and their viewing skills would be useful, as well. As this was unfortunately not practical, two measures were used here. The first was the student's response to the question: "On a typical weekday, about how many hours do you watch TV?" (0–½, ½–1, 1–2, 2–3, 3–4, 4–5, 5–6, 6 or more). Problems with this measure include the reliability of student judgment, the possibility of social response biases, and the fact that it does not supply an exact numerical estimate of amount of viewing.

Therefore, a second measure of viewing was also used, based on student estimates of how frequently they watched each of 27 television shows that were on the air before or after school or in the evening (regularly = 3, sometimes = 2, seldom or never = 1). The ratings were averaged for each student to obtain a measure of amount of viewing. Although different shows appeared on each form, care was taken to make the forms comparable in terms of content. This measure does not provide an actual estimate of time, although compensating for this fault is the likelihood that students can judge accurately how frequently they watch specific shows. This measure would seem to be less vulnerable to social response biases than the "typical weekday" measure; it also takes into account variations in viewing across time, and it provides a finer metric than the other measure. The estimates of amount of time were used in the breakdowns of achievement averages, and the average frequency of viewing programs was used in the correlational analyses.

Other questions asked whether students did homework in front of the set, watched the same programs as their parents, discussed what they viewed with their parents (all three questions scaled from 5 [every day] to 1 [not at all]), watched TV before school (from 5 [every day] to 1 [not at all]), watched late at night (from 9 [later than 2 A.M.] to 1 [7 P.M. or earlier]), were permitted to watch what they wanted (from 5 [all of the time] to 1 [never]), and how frequently they watched programs on public or educational television (from 5 [every day] to 1 [not at all]).

The use of survey data collected at one point in time places certain limitations on the interpretation of results. The limitations of control inherent in a large survey study severely restrict causal inferences regarding amount cf viewing and academic achievement. Furthermore, behavior in school is in reality affected by many individual psychological traits and by social relations in the family, neighborhood, and the school. Television viewing behavior is affected by a similar complex of

Table 1: Polynomial regression of achievement on amount of viewing

Parameter estimate	Reading	Writing	Mathematics
Intercept	44.1189	40.2315	34.1529
Viewing	2.3118	2.2569	2.4984
Viewing squared	−.0491	−.0447	−.0579
Viewing cubed	.0002	.0002	.0004
R-square	.0329	.0291	.0244

Note: All parameter estimates and R-square values are significant at $p < .0001$.

variables. With large aggregates of persons, associations between many of these variables can be documented, but the presence of such associations does not demonstrate causal relationships for individuals.

Achievement test scores in reading, written expression, and mathematics (expressed as the percent of correct answers) are plotted by amount of viewing in Figure 1. The percent of students in each viewing category is: 0–½ hour per day, 3 percent; ½–1 hour, 7 percent; 1–2 hours, 17 percent; 2–3 hours, 19 percent; 3–4 hours, 18 percent; 4–5 hours, 14 percent; 5–6 hours, 8 percent; 6 or more hours, 13 percent. The separation of the three achievement curves indicated that the mathematics test was the most difficult and the reading test the easiest. Polynomial

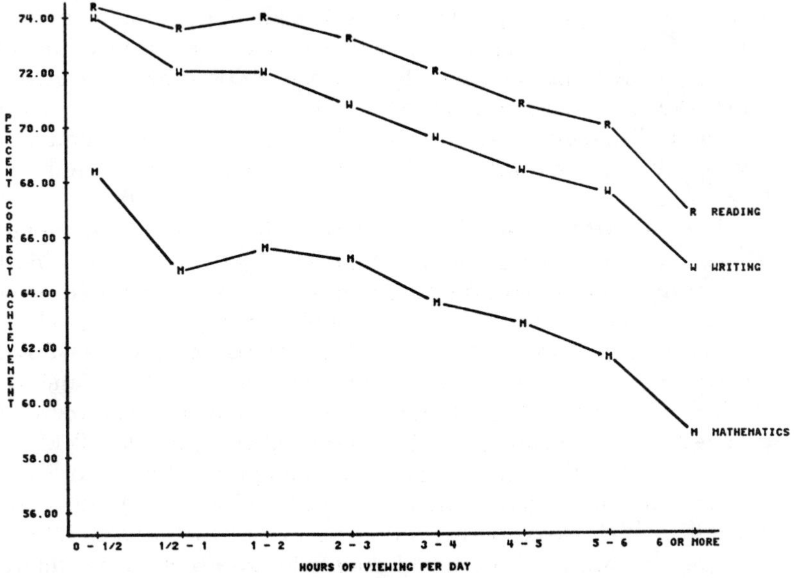

Figure 1: Plot of achievement in reading, written expression, and mathematics by amount of viewing

regression was used to measure curvilinearity by regressing achievement scores on powers of the amount of viewing (see Table 1). To the extent that squared or cubed terms contributed significantly to the regression, the results can be interpreted as a description of curvilinearity. The differences in the intercept terms in Figure 1 reflect the difference in the height of the three curves. When compared across regressions, the other parameter estimates were roughly equal, confirming the approximate parallelism of the three curves in Figure 1.

Students who viewed more than six hours of television per day had sharply lower achievement scores in all three content areas.

In reading and mathematics, scores were relatively higher for students watching one to two hours per day, compared to those who watched a little more or a little less. Correlations of achievement with amount of viewing were modest: for reading, $r = -.09$, $p < .0001$; for written expression, $r = -.10$, $p < .0001$; and for mathematics, $r = -.11$, $p < .0001$. The correlation of total achievement with amount of viewing was a little higher: $r = -.15$, $p < .0001$.

Prior research has tended to confirm an effect of achievement in reading but not in other content areas. The results here of an effect on written expression and mathematics as well as reading confirm the outcome of a previous California Assessment Program study (3), which found similar curves. The larger sample size may explain this finding, since a larger number of cases results in a greater likelihood of finding effects where they exist. Moreover, if there is a relationship between viewing and achievement, whether simple or complex, there is little a priori reason for it to apply to the area of reading alone. To the extent that homework, drill, or practice is necessary to improve achievement, and viewing interferes with these activities, the results should be general. Although this study was not designed to test specific hypotheses regarding competition for resources, the results are suggestive of Hornik's (8) theory of displacement.

Other researchers have found that the relationship between viewing and achievement is diminished once intelligence is taken into account. Although IQ scores were not available in this study, we do know that correlations between IQ and achievement scores typically range from .70 to .90 (13). This means that between one-half and three-fourths of the variance in achievement scores can be accounted for by intelligence. Considering that there would be a certain amount of "error" in the achievement residuals, it is likely that a control for IQ would diminish this relationship as well.

There was evidence of a curvilinear relationship between amount of viewing and achievement, in accordance with previous findings for elementary students. It is interesting that students watching relatively moderate amounts of television have higher achievement scores than those who report watching less. The data collected here provide little explanation for this finding. One can speculate, however, that television offers some information that is relevant to success in school. This information would most plausibly relate to vocabulary and English language usage and would therefore help to explain the relative change in reading and written expression, but not in mathematics. At any rate, the helpfulness of this type of learning to success in school is presumably limited. Formal instruction is typically guided by specific educational objectives, which are often reflected in the content of standardized tests of achievement; television rarely addresses such objectives. To the extent that more time is spent watching television, less is spent on mastery of educational objectives, and lower test scores may result. Of course, both viewing habits and school behavior are nested in a larger context of social relationships that should be taken into account.

The overall achievement scores are plotted by amount of viewing for different groups according to the parents' occupation (social class) in Figure 2. Sixteen percent of the students' parents were unskilled; 38 percent were skilled or semiskilled; 24 percent were semiprofessional; and 21 percent were professional. The curves showed the expected effects of social class: students from professional families scored better than those from skilled or semiskilled families, and so on. The correlation between total achievement and parent occupation was r = .33, $p < .0001$. A trend of consistently lower achievement was associated with

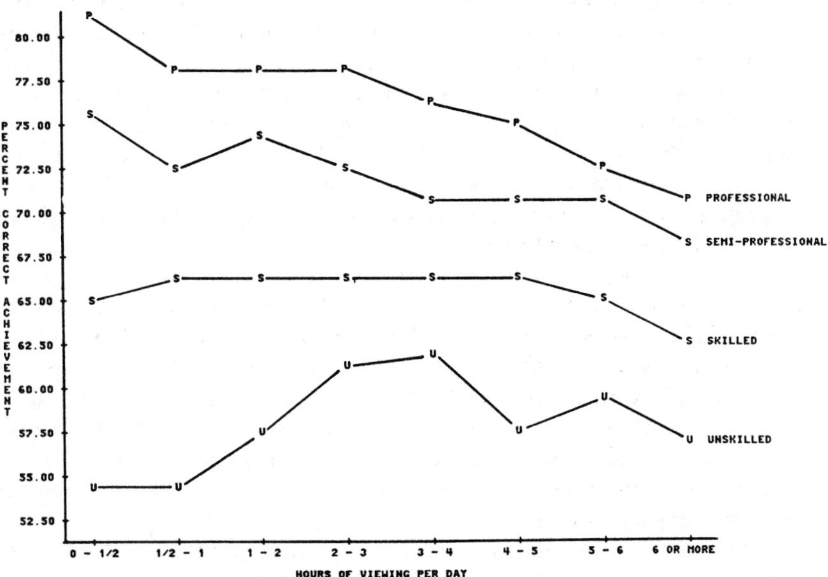

Figure 2: Plot of total achievement by amount of viewing for different levels of social class

heavier viewing for students from professional families. A relative increase in achievement, associated with moderate amounts of viewing, was evident for the students whose parents were semiprofessional or skilled workers and was most pronounced for students in the unskilled group.

The hypothesized corollary of mainstreaming pertaining to social class and achievement is supported by the findings of this study.

Differences in achievement for students of different social classes (as measured by parents' occupation) were large when viewing was light; they diminished as the amount of viewing increased (see Figure 2). The suggestion that students who would otherwise do well by virtue of aptitude or environment seem to be the most adversely affected by increased viewing is borne out here. This does not mean that advantaged students achieve less than very disadvantaged students under any circumstances, but that the downward trend in achievement for advantaged students was greater and more consistent than for disadvantaged students.

What could account for this? One possibility is that more affluent homes are more likely to contain books, magazines, stimulating games, and parents who encourage their children to read, do homework, and do well in school. The more time spent watching television in these homes, the less time could be spent in activities that sharpen skills relevant to success in school. Television would be a less academically stimulating activity than some of the other options available in such homes. Less affluent homes would be less likely to contain books, magazines, and other intellectually stimulating activities that would be displaced by television. Thus, compared to what is available, television would be relatively stimulating, providing new ideas, vicarious experiences, and new vocabulary, and might translate into academic improvement, at least when in moderation. It is worth noting, however, that although the students from less advantaged homes were most likely to be heavy viewers, the viewing of more than four hours of television per day was associated with lower achievement for all students, regardless of social class.

Overall achievement scores are plotted by amount of viewing for students giving different ratings of their ease of doing schoolwork in Figure 3. Nine percent of students rate homework as very easy, 28 percent rated it as easy, 48 percent rated it as neither easy nor hard, and 11 percent rated it as somewhat hard. Because only one percent of students rated schoolwork as very hard, no curve for them is shown. These ratings correlate with total sixth-grade achievement at $r = .24$ ($p < .0001$) and with parents' occupation at $r = .09$ ($p < .0001$). Lower achievement scores were associated with greater television viewing

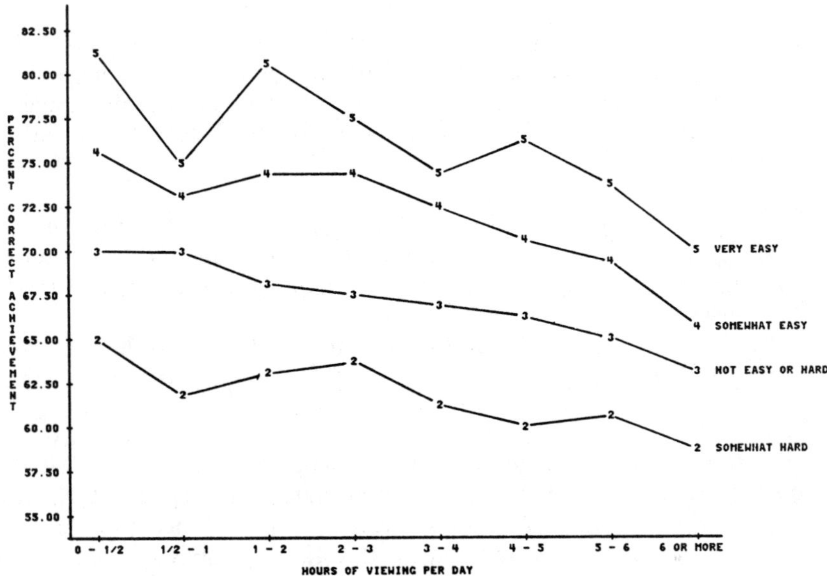

Figure 3: Plot of total achievement by amount of viewing for self-ratings of ease of schoolwork

among those students who consider homework "very easy" and "somewhat easy" and less so for those who consider it "neither easy nor hard" and "somewhat hard." For all groups, viewing in excess of six hours per day was associated with the lowest achievement scores.

Although these results support the mainstreaming corollary, they are not as strong as were those for parents' occupation and television viewing. The reason may be that ratings of ease of schoolwork were not as highly correlated with viewing or achievement as was the parents' occupation. The curves here were bunched more closely together for heavier than for lighter amounts of viewing, indicating a greater homogeneity with respect to achievement of heavier viewers. Students who found homework easy had higher achievement scores than others, and yet they were more prone to be affected by increased viewing. This appears to reaffirm the observation that those who would otherwise do well were most adversely affected by viewing.

Heavy and light viewers, each constituting about ten percent of the total sample, are compared in Table 2.[1] The objective of this analysis was to compare groups of students at either extreme on a continuum of amount of viewing. Those viewers in the upper and lower ten percent of

[1] To facilitate comparisons, I scaled all variables to have a mean of fifty and a standard deviation of ten, a method described by Wainer and Thissen (14). For convenience in making behavioral interpretations raw scores are included, as well.

Table 2: Scores of heavy and light viewers

	Heavy viewers		Light viewers	
	Scaled	Raw	Scaled	Raw
Amount of viewing	68.7	2.14	34.6	1.03
Overall achievement	44.2	58.30	53.4	74.14
Parent occupation	46.2	2.13	53.6	2.87
Homework while viewing	53.0	4.03	46.5	3.18
Viewing before school	53.9	1.77	45.7	1.18
How late do you watch TV?	54.3	4.10	44.9	3.00
Parents watch the same programs?	52.4	3.70	46.8	3.18
Discuss TV with parents?	53.9	2.99	47.8	2.31
Permitted to watch what you want?	51.3	3.79	47.6	3.48
How often do you watch the public station?	45.1	2.15	51.8	3.35

the sample met the criteria for extreme heavy or light viewing and constituted groups large enough for meaningful analysis. Heavy viewers scored below average in achievement and parent occupation; light viewers scored above average on these variables. Heavy viewers were more likely than light viewers to do homework in front of the set, to watch the same programs as their parents, to discuss programs with their parents, and to watch more often in the morning and later at night. Light viewers were less likely to be permitted to watch their preferences than heavy viewers. Heavy viewers watched markedly less public television than the average viewer; light viewers watched slightly more. Between-group comparisons were significant at $p < .001$ for all variables in the profile.

The profile of heavy viewers suggests that viewing habits are characteristic of the family unit and not just the individual.

Heavy viewers tend to watch the same programs as their parents and to discuss program content with their parents. Heavy viewers were permitted more often than light viewers to watch the shows they preferred. A further suggestion of a family viewing habit was the tendency of heavy viewers to do homework in front of the television set.

Heavy viewers watched all shows significantly more often than the average viewer, and light viewers watched all shows significantly less often. There was a marked difference between the types of shows most often watched by the heavy and light viewers. The ranked list of ten shows most frequently watched by heavy viewers was: "Midnight Special," "Vega$," "Dance Fever," "Flamingo Road," "Lou Grant," "Real Kids," "Quincy," "Soap," "Hart to Hart," and "Dynasty." Most of these shows can be classified as light entertainment. The ranked list of ten shows most frequently watched by light viewers was: "Bill Moyers' Journal," "Nova," "700 Club," "Sunrise Semester," "MacNeil-Lehrer

Report," "Washington Week in Review," "Masterpiece Theatre," "PTL Club," "Meet the Press," and "Firing Line." Most of these shows can be classified as public affairs, performing arts, or educational, with public television strongly represented. None of the programs most watched by light viewers was among those most watched by heavy viewers.

It is unlikely that these differences in viewer preferences could account for differences in achievement, since even educational programming does not necessarily present what children are expected to learn in school. Light viewing was correlated with a stricter home television environment, i.e., an environment in which parents more actively control the amount and type of programming. The shows most often watched by light viewers—public affairs and news programs—may be of little intrinsic interest to sixth-graders, as suggested by the fact that light viewers did not often discuss the shows they viewed with their parents. Possibly most of these shows were selected by the parents, and the student could either view them or not view at all.

Correlation coefficients for selected variables are contained in Table 3, and the results of a multiple regression using these variables are contained in Table 4.[2] Table 4 includes standardized b values to permit comparisons of the relative influence of variables on achievement. The weight for amount of viewing was about half that of ease of schoolwork and about a third that of parent occupation.

Table 3: Correlations of selected variables concerning TV habit and achievement scores

	Achievement	*Amount of viewing*	*Parent occupation*	*Amount of homework*	*Pleasure reading*	*Ease of schoolwork*	*Homework by the TV*
Achievement	—	−0.15	0.35	−0.07	0.08	0.25	−0.08
Amount of viewing	−0.15	—	−0.13	0.01	0.01	0.01	0.13
Parent occupation	0.35	−0.13	—	−0.00	0.03	0.11	−0.08
Amount of homework	−0.07	0.01	−0.00	—	0.21	−0.07	0.03
Reading for pleasure	0.08	0.01	0.03	0.21	—	0.10	−0.01
Ease of schoolwork	0.25	0.01	0.11	−0.07	0.10	—	0.01
Homework by the TV	−0.08	0.13	−0.08	0.03	−0.01	0.01	—
Mean	68.27	41.33	2.51	3.64	3.05	3.33	2.36
Standard deviation	17.18	8.82	1.00	1.31	1.53	0.84	1.20

Note: Correlations greater than .03 are significant at $p < .0001$.

[2] The 292 schools in the study do not constitute a simple random sample of pupils. Given the large cluster size, an average of 36 students per school, the design effect might be as low as 1.5 or as high as 9. Thus, true standard errors might be 1.2 to 3.0 times as large as those in Table 4. Probability levels are so low that substantive conclusions would be little affected even if the t-ratios were divided by 3, although "homework by the TV" might no longer be statistically significant.

Table 4: Multiple regression of TV habit and achievement scores

Variable	Parameter estimate	Standard error	t	Standardized b
Intercept	53.2622	1.1700	45.5236	
Amount of viewing	−0.2293	0.0179	−12.8458	−0.1176
Parent occupation	5.2272	0.1567	33.3630	0.3059
Amount of homework	−0.8496	0.1211	−7.0183	−0.0650
Reading for pleasure	0.7198	0.1039	6.9272	0.0643
Ease of schoolwork	4.0974	0.1872	21.8918	0.2004
Homework by the TV	−0.4935	0.1304	−3.7833	−0.0344

Overall $R^2 = .1863$

Note: Results of all t tests are significant at $p < .0001$, with the exception of that for homework by the TV, which is significant at $p < .0002$.

The correlations in Table 3 and the multiple regression analysis in Table 4 support the hypothesis of an association between viewing and achievement, even after parents' occupation and variables describing the home environment have been taken into account. The magnitude of the association for hours spent on homework, reading for pleasure, and doing homework in front of the set is relatively small. The weight for hours spent on homework was negative, indicating that those who reported spending more time on homework tended to have lower achievement scores. Apparently, sixth-graders who spent more time on homework had more difficulty in school; higher-achieving students did homework more quickly.

The relationship between amount of viewing and achievement is not simple, and this study does not purport to demonstrate a causal relationship between these two variables. Hornik (8) has noted that such a demonstration would require the development of an explicit theoretical model. Strict experimental tests, requiring random assignment of subjects to treatment groups, and statistical control requiring measurement of all relevant background variables are needed. Even then, experimental studies are criticized for artificially manipulating situations and the use of statistical control is criticized for overlooking some important but difficult to measure variable. Given these difficulties, the demonstration of a truly causal relationship must await more sophisticated social research methods.

Nonetheless, the results of this study are striking, especially when considered in the context of other studies. There appears to be a "threshold" amount of viewing beyond which television has a striking negative association with achievement which is not easily explained by other variables. There is a curvilinear relationship between amount of viewing and achievement, in which moderate amounts of viewing are associated with higher achievement. Finally, this curvilinear relationship, interacting with parents' occupation, shows a mainstreaming effect.

The strength of the relationship between amount of viewing and achievement, as measured by the polynomial regression taking curvilinearity into account, was quite modest. Had it been possible to measure intelligence, even this modest association might have disappeared. This finding suggests that further research should concentrate on identifying subgroups of students that may be particularly affected by television viewing, such as students who report watching either a great deal of television or very little.

REFERENCES

1. Bachen, C., D. Roberts, and M. Hornby. "Television Viewing Behavior and the Development of Reading Skills." Paper presented at the annual meeting of the American Educational Research Association, New York, 1982.
2. California Assessment Program. *Technical Report of the California Assessment Program*. Sacramento: California State Department of Education, 1977.
3. California Assessment Program. *Television and Student Achievement*. Sacramento: California State Department of Education, 1980.
4. Comstock, G. *Television in America*. Beverly Hills, Cal.: Sage, 1980.
5. Comstock, G., S. Chaffee, N. Katzman, M. McCombs, and D. Roberts. *Television and Human Behavior*. New York: Columbia University Press, 1978.
6. Gerbner, G., L. Gross, M. Morgan, and N. Signorielli. "The 'Mainstreaming' of America: Violence Profile No. 11." *Journal of Communication* 30(3), Summer 1980, pp. 10–29.
7. Gerbner, G., L. Gross, M. Morgan, and N. Signorielli. "Charting the Mainstream: Television's Contributions to Political Orientations." *Journal of Communication* 32(2), Spring 1982, pp. 100–127.
8. Hornik, R. "Out-of-School Television and Schooling: Hypotheses and Methods." *Review of Educational Research* 51, 1981, pp. 215–236.
9. Morgan, M. and L. Gross. "Television and Educational Achievement and Aspirations." In *Television and Behavior: Ten Years of Scientific Progress and Implications for the '80s*. Washington, D.C.: National Institutes of Mental Health, 1981.
10. Palmer, E. and A. Dorr (Eds.) *Children and the Faces of Television*. New York: Academic Press, 1980.
11. Roberts, D. and C. Bachen. "Mass Communication Effects." In M. Rosenzweig and L. Porter (Eds.) *Annual Review of Psychology*. Palo Alto, Cal.: Annual Reviews, 1981, pp. 307–356.
12. Salomon, G. *Interaction of Media, Cognition and Learning*. San Francisco: Jossey-Bass, 1979.
13. Stanley, J. and K. Hopkins. *Educational and Psychological Measurement and Evaluation*. Englewood Cliffs, N.J.: Prentice-Hall, 1972.
14. Wainer, H. and D. Thissen. "Graphical Data Analysis." In M. Rosenzweig and L. Porter (Eds.) *Annual Review of Psychology*. Palo Alto, Cal.: Annual Reviews, 1981, pp. 191–242.
15. White, K. "The Relation between Socioeconomic Status and Academic Achievement." *Psychological Bulletin* 91, 1982, pp. 461–481.
16. Williams, P., E. Haertel, G. Haertel, and H. Walberg. "The Impact of Leisure Time Television on School Learning." *American Educational Research Journal* 19, 1982, pp. 19–50.
17. Withey, S. and R. Abeles (Eds.) *Television and Social Behavior*. Hillsdale, N.J.: Lawrence Erlbaum, 1980.

25

THE KNOWLEDGE GAP
An Analytical Review of Media Effects

Cecile Gaziano

Two of the earliest findings in the mass communication literature are that some portions of the public tend to be chronically uninformed and that, in general, the greater the level of education, the greater the knowledge of various topics. Introduction of a formal knowledge gap hypothesis has stimulated much recent research and comment on the implications of support for this hypothesis.

The purpose of this article is to examine research evidence about knowledge gaps and to ask how strong the evidence is for knowledge gaps associated with education differences, particularly when amount of mass media publicity is taken into account.

AUTHOR'S NOTE: An earlier version of this article was presented to the Theory and Methodology Division of the Association for Education in Journalism at its July 1982 meeting in Athens, Ohio. The article has benefited from critiques by Phillip J. Tichenor, Professor of Journalism and

From Cecile Gaziano, "The Knowledge Gap: An Analytical Review of Media Effects," *Communication Research*, Vol. 10, No. 4 (October 1983), pp. 447-486.

The knowledge gap hypothesis states (Tichenor et al., 1970: 159-160),

> As the infusion of mass media information into a social system increases, segments of the population with higher socioeconomic status tend to acquire this information at a faster rate than the lower status segments, so that the gap in knowledge between these segments tends to increase rather than decrease.

Predictions are made for both one-time and multiple measurements:

1. *Over time*, acquisition of knowledge of a heavily publicized topic will proceed at a faster rate among better educated persons than among those with less education; and
2. *At a given point in time*, there should be a higher correlation between acquisition of knowledge and education for topics highly publicized in the media than for topics less highly publicized (Tichenor et al., 1970: 165).

Research concerning knowledge differentials based on levels of education has had two consequences in particular. One is that strong positive relationships between level of education and knowledge are accepted almost as axiomatic by social scientists.[1] The other is that the idea of knowledge gaps based on differences in formal schooling has become controversial. Some researchers believe that focusing on education as a variable implies that less educated persons are deficient in abilities or inferior to more educated persons, and these researchers have desired to shift emphasis to other variables.[2] Concomitant with this trend has been the abatement of interest of many social scientists in studying social problems of the disadvantaged. This abate-

---

Mass Communication, P. Jean Frazier, Associate Professor of Health Ecology and Ph.D. student in Mass Communication, both of the University of Minnesota, and an anonymous reviewer.

ment parallels the decline in government's interest in social programs.

The term "knowledge gap" appears in the literature with several different meanings. It is important to distinguish between (a) gaps found at one point in time, and (b) gaps which may occur over time and may change in magnitude. Another important distinction is between (c) knowledge gaps which refer only to the relationship between education and knowledge without reference to media, and (d) gaps which are an outcome dependent on media treatment or media exposure.

The knowledge gap hypothesis describes three variables: level of *mass media publicity* in a particular social setting, level of individuals' *education*, and level of individuals' *knowledge*. *Time* can be considered a fourth variable. A brief description of the evidence for relationships among these variables follows. It includes many news diffusion studies and public opinion poll data, because results of news diffusion research and polls often are cited as evidence of knowledge gaps or lack of gaps. A number of studies specifically designed to test hypotheses about knowledge gaps are described.

Many varying characteristics of 58 studies with relevant data are analyzed. Discussion of related work supplements this analysis. Theoretical and methodological differences among the studies are pointed out, and some conclusions are drawn about media effects on knowledge disparities and conditions under which knowledge gaps may occur or may not occur. Some reasons for conflicting results in the literature are explained and suggestions are made for future research on knowledge differentials.

BACKGROUND DESCRIPTION OF THE STUDIES

This section briefly describes the kinds of research which led to development of the knowledge gap hypothesis.

INFORMATION DIFFUSION: EARLY STUDIES

Results of a number of public opinion polls led Hyman and Sheatsley (1947) to discuss the nature of the problems that make it difficult to inform certain segments of the public; they called for research on these "chronic know-nothings."

For example, despite voluminous amounts of information disseminated in a 6-month-long information campaign about the United Nations in Cincinnati, the number of persons who knew anything about the U.N. was disappointingly low, and the more educated were far more likely to have been reached by the campaign than the less educated (Star and Hughes, 1950). Similar education and knowledge results were noted for candidates' stands on issues during the 1948 presidential election campaign in Elmira, New York (Berelson et al., 1954).

Several studies of news diffusion cited knowledge differentials related to education differences (Bogart, 1950-1951; Medalia and Larsen, 1958; Deutschmann and Danielson, 1960; Budd et al., 1966; Allen and Colfax, 1968; Adams et al., 1969; and McNelly et al., 1968).

In contrast, a couple of studies found "reverse gaps," in which the less educated were more likely to know of an event than the more educated (Larsen and Hill, 1954; Fathi, 1973). For example, at the time of the interview, more respondents among a laboring community in Seattle had heard the news of the death of Senator Robert A. Taft (93%) than respondents in a college faculty community (88%); however, methodological and other factors may have influenced this result.[3]

When news of the assassination of President John F. Kennedy was studied, no knowledge differentials emerged. Under the conditions of an event with astounding impact on the nation and unusual in the enormous, concentrated, and simultaneous focus of all media on the event, all respondents contacted were aware of the event (Greenberg, 1964).[4] This finding was confirmed by six other studies of the same event (Spitzer and Denzin, 1965). When, however, detailed or depth knowledge of the assassination was examined, respondents who were poorly informed were likely to have blue-collar occupations, to live in low-income residential areas, to be older, and to be male.[5] Spitzer and Denzin suggested a "know-nothing" hypothesis, which is somewhat like the knowledge gap hypothesis. They reviewed five other studies supporting their hypothesis.

PUBLIC OPINION POLL DATA

Public opinion poll data tend to exhibit a positive association between knowledge and education (Erskine, 1962, 1963a, 1963b, 1963c; Wade and Schramn, 1969; Gallup, 1977; Douglass and Stacey, 1972). There are a few exceptions (Erskine). Robinson's (1967: 24) inspection of some poll data led him to conclude that "expecting to raise public information levels through mass media efforts would be naive." Additional data and literature review reinforced this point (Robinson, 1972).

KNOWLEDGE GAP STUDIES

Tichenor et al. presented a formal knowledge gap hypothesis in 1970. Four pieces of evidence supported it: (1) the findings of the news diffusion study by Budd et al. (1966); (2) public opinion poll data on three science topics; (3) results of a study contrasting a community with a newspaper strike with a non-strike community (Samuelson, 1960); and (4) the authors' 1968 research in two Minnesota cities, measuring recall of medical, biological, and social science topics in the news, and comparing recall by previous amounts of newspaper publicity given to these subjects.

Later work by this research team has expanded on conditions under which the gap may widen or narrow with regard to a number of issues in Minnesota communities (Tichenor et al., 1973; Donohue et al., 1975; Tichenor et al.,

1980).[6] Their work has influenced at least fourteen other investigations of knowledge gap phenomena,[7] and it has stimulated several critical essays.

Not all of these studies of knowledge gaps hypothesis is stated, its test requires comparison of high and low levels of media attention to topics.

Investigations in addition to those of the Tichenor-Donohue-Olien team that do treat media publicity as a variable are those of Brown et al., (1981) and Gaziano (1982). Readers and nonreaders were contrasted by Abbott (1978) in an evaluation of an information campaign in a newspaper. Exposure to media forums is a variable in the work in India of Shingi and Mody (1976)[8] and Galloway (1977).

Genova and Greenberg (1979) varied duration of news event for two topics, and Fry (1979) contrasted dependence on newspapers with dependence on television. Nnaemeka (1976) compared urban respondents' exposure to newspaper articles relying on established news sources and rural respondents' exposure to newspaper articles using relatively more nonestablishment sources.

The impact of a high level of publicity for one issue was Bailey's (1971) focus. Neuman (1976) interviewed persons who watched evening television network newscasts (nonviewers were discarded from the survey). Gunaratne (1976) sampled residents of four Ceylon villages but did not measure media publicity for the five topics studied. Data on two topics were compared with earlier data which apparently also did not measure media publicity (Ryan, 1952).[9]

In addition to associations between education and knowledge, Brown et al. looked at links between motivation and knowledge, finding a gap based on motivation widening and a knowledge gap based on education closing under the influence of an information campaign. When interest in topics was compared with education as a predictor of knowledge, a measure of composite interest (self-interest and social interest combined) did about as well as education in predicting factual knowledge, but composite interest was a better predictor of structural knowledge than education was (Genova and Greenberg, 1979).[10] The relative influence of activity on issues by organized groups has been compared with the impact on knowledge gaps of neighborhood newspapers (Gaziano, 1983a).

OTHER SUPPORTING DATA

Additional studies with data on knowledge differentials related to education level in a variety of U.S. and foreign settings are described in the Analysis section.

Another related group of studies pertaining to disadvantaged children may be mentioned briefly. These studies are relevant to this analysis but are not included in the tables. They include the Coleman Report (1966) on school achievement differences and the reports on the effects of the educational television program *Sesame Street* (Ball and Bogatz, 1970; Bogatz and Ball, 1972). Cook et al. (1975) criticized the latter work because of errors of measurement and statistical inference and suggested that the show helped to widen the achievement gap between advantaged and disadvantaged children. Liebert (1976) has also taken issue with the Bogatz and Ball effort for not being designed to measure closure of any achievement gaps.[11]

CRITICAL COMMENT ON THE KNOWLEDGE GAP HYPOTHESIS

Since gaps do not always occur or increase, several scholars have discussed potential reasons for conflicting results (Ettema and Kline, 1977; Brown et al., 1981), and several have attempted to specify conditions under which gaps may develop or change (Katzman, 1974; Ettema and Kline, 1977; Tichenor et al., 1973, 1980; Donahue et al., 1975).

Genova and Greenberg (1979) suggested reformulating the original hypothesis as a proposition about gaps based on differences in interest, not education. Ettema and Kline (1977) proposed a reformulation based on differences in motivation. These might be treated as alternative hypotheses, however, because education, motivation, and interest all could explain knowledge disparities. Also, their influences might vary under certain conditions and education might sometimes be related to motivation and interest. Education was positively related to interest in at least two studies (Gaziano, 1983a, 1983b; Graber, 1978).

It is actually a "communication effects gap," as some have suggested (see Rogers, 1976). It is suggested that the gap is more than an information gap or a communication effects gap in the discussion section of this article. This evidence derives from study of social organization and stratification, including the structure of media and other information delivery systems.

Clarke and Kline (1974) have expressed concern about research that relates knowledge to education because resources and policy would be directed toward the school system rather than toward mass media in attempts to reduce knowledge differentials.

Dervin (1980) contends that the large body of support for the knowledge gap hypothesis buttresses the proposition only due to its underlying model of a source pitching messages to a receiver, who either catches the message or misses it and is to blame if the message is fumbled.[12] She argues that the knowledge gap is not a "real" phenomenon, however, because of difficulties with the traditional source-receiver model that measures the receiver of messages against irrelevant standards set up by academicians. She faults the logical positivist philosophy behind the traditional model and favors instead the relativist model in social science which underlies information-seeking and uses and gratifications perspectives. Researchers working within these orientations start with messages as seen from the standpoint of receivers' needs.

In contrast, some researchers working with the traditional source-receiver model place that model within a larger context of social, political, and economic organization of society. For example, one study found that gaps in knowledge of neighborhood public affairs issues were related to social stratification because the most important knowledge sources were more accessible to the most educated residents (Gaziano, 1983a, 1983b). Jencks et al. (1972) relate differentials in children's school achievement to many types of inequalities. Nowak (1977: 246) has helped to develop a "resource distribution approach" to communication research, and he suggests that knowledge gaps are related not only to SES differences but also to "variations in cultural conditions and culturally defined patterns of behavior." Other work has stressed the role of existing power structures in knowledge control and maintenance of unequal distribution of knowledge (Olien, et al., 1982; Tichenor et al., 1980).

ANALYSIS OF KNOWLEDGE GAP DATA

This analysis includes all of the studies that could be located, including both published and unpublished works, that contain any data on relationships of education and knowledge, regardless of the original investigators' interests. Indexes consulted included the *Readers' Guide*, the *International Index, Urban Affairs Abstracts, Communication Abstracts, Journalism Abstracts, Psychological Abstracts,* and the *Social Science Citation Index*. Other sources included Weaver (1978), Troldahl (1965), Gorelick (no date), and Frazier (1981). In addition, the footnotes and references of articles and chapters found were checked for further studies.[13]

The conclusions about knowledge gap evidence presented are not necessarily those of the primary researchers. The unit of analysis is "the finding"—that is, the finding of a knowledge gap or lack of one at one point in time or the finding of change or no change over time. Several studies reported more than one findings.

IDENTIFICATION OF KEY CHARACTERISTICS

As many pertinent qualities as possible were identified according to suggestions by Rogers (1981) and treated as variables in developing the analysis.[14] These characteristics include: date and location of research, sample size, completion rate, type of population sampled, research design (according to criteria outlined by Campbell and Stanley, (1963), number of measurements in time and method of data collection. Also included are type of topic studied, type of knowledge measured (awareness or depth), operational definitions of knowledge, type of media studied, operational definitions of education and of knowledge gap, an assessment of the amount of media publicity involved wherever possible, and knowledge gap findings (education-knowledge data).

Findings are discussed first according to these classifications and then according to evidence relevant to the knowledge gap hypothesis. The term "knowledge gap" in this discussion refers to positive education-knowledge relationships without reference to media impact. Wherever necessary, distinction is made between one-time and multiple measurement studies. The influence of media on gaps will be described later in the article.

RESEARCH DATE, LOCATION, AND POPULATION

The predominance of knowledge gap findings across varying settings (including several other countries), populations, and a period of about 35 years indicates that the frequent findings of knowledge gaps are fairly easily generalizable to present-day U.S. populations and some foreign ones. Date, location, and population do not seem to help to explain gaps.

SAMPLE SIZE, COMPLETION RATE, AND DESIGN

Knowledge gap findings persist in both methodologically weak and strong studies. Many studies have small sample sizes, although some are quite large; a number of surveys either have low completion rates or do not report them. Some studies report knowledge-education data for a small proportion of the sample due to low response rates or due to theoretical interest in a small part of the sample, such as only television news viewers. These studies are not easily compared with those reporting data for most of the sample.

Most of the 58 surveys are one-shot case studies, and many of these do not have even a comparison group. One-time measurements do not allow assessment of causal influences of media. Results favor existence of knowledge disparities relatively consistently.

In contrast, studies collecting data at more than one point in time tend to find that gaps decreased or did not change over time if they existed initially. This occurred regardless of design or size of time interval between measurements. These studies, however, tend to have certain other characteristics which may explain declines in gaps.

METHOD OF DATA COLLECTION

No conclusions can be drawn about method of data collection, although reports in which narrowing, unchanging, or no gaps occur tend to have used in-person interviewing techniques.

TYPE OF TOPIC

Examination of topic studied does suggest several conditions under which gaps develop or change.

First, gaps are likely to occur when topics appeal more to high SES persons than to low SES individuals (Bailey, 1971; Bogart, 1950-1951; Wade and Schramm, 1969). When the topic is of specific interest to the less educated, they may be as likely as the more advantaged to possess information (Erskine, 1962, 1963a; Neuman, 1976; Genova and Greenberg, 1979). Also, within an occupational group, communication variables related to employment or organization membership may affect knowledge more than education level Buss and Hofstetter, 1981; Scherer, 1977).

Second, every study on international or foreign topics included in this analysis reproted SES-related knowledge gaps (Budd et al., 1966; Erskine, 1962, 1963b; Gunaratne, 1976; McNelly and Molina, 1972; McNelly et al., 1968; Robinson, 1967, 1972; Star and Hughes, 1950).

Third, gaps frequently develop when national topics are studied (Allen and Colfax, 1968; Budd et al., 1966; Hofstetter et al., 1978; Deutschmann and Danielson, 1960; Edelstein, 1973; Kraus et al., 1963; Erskine, 1962, 1963a; Atkin et al., 1976; McNelly and Deutschmann, 1963; Kent and Rush, 1976; Gunaratne, 1976; Clarke and Kline, 1974; Robinson, 1972).

Fourth, whether or not topics are local may make a difference. Education was a strong predictor of knowledge of national issues in the work of Palmgreen (1979), but it was of little or no use in predicting local issue knowledge. The relationship between education and knowledge was stronger for national issues and weaker for local issues, according to Becker and Whitney (1980). And the Tichenor-Donohue-Olien team has noted that when a local issue is of basic concern to a community, the knowledge gap will decline (Donohue et al., 1975; Tichenor et al., 1980). Even though knowledge gaps were found for four local issues in a study emphasizing issues of potential importance to residents of an inner-city neighborhood, all the gaps were relatively modest in magnitude (Gaziano, 1982). The evidence to date, therefore, indicates that knowledge gaps are likely to be found when national or international issues are studied, but that gaps may not occur or are small when local issues are of interest.

Fifth, when knowledge is conceptualized as public affairs topics in civics class or textbook terms, knowledge differentials related to educational level are almost always found (Becker and Whitney, 1980; Rogers, 1965-1966; Fry, 1978; Gunaratne, 1976; Atkin et al., 1976; Kanervo, 1979; Wade and Schramm, 1969; Erskine, 1963c).

Sixth, although people of all educational backgrounds tend to be highly interested in health matters, they may still exhibit knowledge disparities (Erskine, 1963a; Tichenor et al., 1970, 1980; Gallup, 1977; Douglass and Stacey, 1972). Nevertheless, an extensive information campaign on good cardiovascular health did tend to close an initial knowledge gap over time (Brown et al., 1981).

OPERATIONAL DEFINITIONS OF KNOWLEDGE

Another explanation for inconsistent findings in the diffusion studies is the way in which these studies measure knowledge. Examples are Fathi (1973) and Larsen and Hill (1954) that report less educated respondents to be more likely to have information than more educated members of the sample. This conflicts with a number of other studies. The reason for the variation in results is likely to be that knowledge was measured as of the time of interview, or by the evening of the day news was announced. Had interviewing taken place later, results might have been different. In addition, the gap in time of interviewing of the two communities and the newspaper strike also probably affected the findings of Larsen and Hill. Diffusion studies in which interviewing took place some time after the event have found knowledge disparities among education groups (Bogart, 1950-1951; Levy, 1969; Medalia and Larsen, 1958). The major exceptions to this finding are the studies by Greenberg (1964) and others (cited by Spitzer and Denzin, 1965) on the assassination of President Kennedy which established that all respondents were aware of the event.

The unusual features of this event were simultaneous sustained media coverage and great national importance. SES-linked differentials, however, in-depth knowledge of this event did emerge in one study (Spitzer and Denzin, 1965).

A second consideration in measurement of knowledge is that using open-ended questions that allow respondents to define topics in their own terms does not necessarily lead to findings of no knowledge gaps (Edelstein, 1973; Benton and Frazier, 1976; Gaziano, 1982, 1983a, 1983b; Clarke and Kline, 1974; Palmgreen, 1979). The only study to use this technique and report little or no effect of formal schooling on knowledge is Palmgreen's, and this occurred only for local issues. Edelstein did state, however, that he believed this method reduced knowledge differentials in his study. Also, all correlations for education and knowledge noted in the other four investigations using open-ended questions are moderate.

A third consideration is that using the same measurement of knowledge over time affects findings. Studies in which knowledge questions were identical or the amount of knowledge measured was the same at each time have tended to find either no change in gaps (Abbott, 1978; Star and Hughes, 1950; Bogart, 1957-1958) or narrowing gaps (Galloway, 1977; Bailey, 1971; Brown et al., 1981; Douglas et al., 1970). One reported no gaps at either sampling period (Shingi and Mody, 1976). Responses to the same poll questions over time were, however, quite variable: responses to five questions showed increases (Tichenor et al., 1970; Erskine, 1963c), three demonstrated decreases (Erskine, 1963a, 1963b, 1963c), one gap remained unchanged (Erskine, 1963c), and one could not be evaluated because the breakdowns into education groups differed (Douglass and Stacey, 1972, compared with Gallup, 1977, on the same topic). In one case, two of six items remained the same (Genova and Greenberg, 1979).

Among studies with time-trend data, the tendency is to indicate unchanging or narrowing gaps; however, the reason for these findings may be ceiling effects as a result of limiting the amount of knowledge to be measured. The most knowledgeable could advance no further, and those who were less knowledgeable could then catch up. Three additional studies measured knowledge by different questions over time, or else measured any accurate statement as possession of knowledge; but whether or not gaps changed is not clear in two studies (Becker et al., 1978; Miller and MacKuen, 1979). In the third study, the ongoing one of Tichenor, Donohue, and Olien (Tichenor et al., 1973, 1980; Donohue et al., 1975), gaps tended to narrow over time, but the explanation is that certain conditions were operating: (a) high levels of conflict associated with issues; (b) high levels of newspaper coverage (1973); (c) high levels of personal discussion (1980); (d) homogeneous as opposed to heterogeneous social structure of community; (e) high level of basic concern of issue to a community; and (f) waning levels of public attention to issues over time (1975).

TYPES OF MEDIA STUDIED

Scrutiny of media measured also permits better understanding of conditions under which knowledge disparities may be reduced. It may be, for instance, that when a newspaper emphasizes a particular topic over a long time, its readers are more likely to know about that subject, regardless of education level—that is, that readers with grade school educations have more knowledge than nonreaders with grade-school level educations, and so on (Brinton and McKown, 1961; Abbott, 1978). The work of the Tichenor-Donohue-Olien team (Tichenor et al., 1973) also indicates that high levels of newspaper coverage of local issues served to narrow gaps. High levels of neighborhood newspaper coverage contributed somewhat to reduced gaps (Gaziano, 1982, 1983a). It is also possible that greater reliance by newspapers on established sources of news has some effect in widening knowledge gaps and greater reliance on nonestablished sources may reduce gaps, although urban-rural differences may be the explanatory variable (Nnaemeka, 1976).

Second, television may be a knowledge-leveler. Findings from two field surveys of network news support this assumption (Neuman, 1976, and Gantz, 1978, who report on a subset of respondents who view TV news), although a laboratory experiment with a network news show does not do so (Stauffer et al., 1978).[15] Further, although better educated people tend to watch televised presidential election debates, less educated persons who attend to the debates showed knowledge gains that may be comparable to the gains of the more highly educated who watch (Miller and MacKuen, 1979; Becker et al., 1978). Though a third survey of the 1976 debates turned up a moderate knowledge gap, this survey did not measure information gain per se (Bishop et al., 1978).[16] The introduction of television into rural Norwegian provinces may have increased levels of recognition of national political leaders' pictures (Torsvik, 1972). In a developing country, television forums may have reduced knowledge disparities (Galloway, 1977).

Less is known about the influence of interpersonal contacts. High levels of discussion about local issues may tend to lessen gaps (Tichenor et al., 1980), but greater reliance on interpersonal news sources which may be less accurate than media may depress knowledge levels (Spitzer and Denzin, 1965).

The withdrawal of media—such as in a newspaper strike—may contribute to gaps (Samuelson, cited by Tichenor et al., 1970). Waning public attention to issues over time may decrease disparities as overall levels of knowledge dissipate (Tichenor et al., 1980; Donohue et al., 1975).

In contrast, the concerted focus of several media on any event may raise knowledge levels of all educational groups. This was especially clear in the case of a president's assassination (Levy, 1969; Greenberg, 1964). It is possible that the three assassinations of public figures recalled by all of Levy's sample received far more media play than the three assassinations which were less remembered. One information campaign decreased knowledge disparities between more and less educated persons (Brown et al., 1981), although three other campaigns essentially had no effect on knowledge differentials (Star and Hughes, 1950; Abbott, 1978; Bogart, 1957-1958). Another campaign led to change of a community's attitudes in the intended direction, but did not affect knowledge levels (Douglas et al., 1970).[17]

MEASURE OF EDUCATION

The operational definitions of education levels are impossible to assess because only four studies give information about exact measurement.[18] One of these apparently treated education as a continuous variable, although it was coded as six categories (Genova and Greenberg, 1979). Two other surveys both coded and analyzed education data as categories (Kent and Rush, 1976; Nnaemeka, 1976). Only one study is known to have measured education as a true continuous variable (Kanervo, 1979).[19]

OPERATIONAL DEFINITION OF KNOWLEDGE GAP

The main ways of measuring knowledge gap were (1) differences in mean knowledge scores between the high-highest education group and the low-lowest education group, computed by subtraction or by analysis of variance; (2) differences in proportions of two or more education groups with any knowledge of the topics, computed by subtraction or by chi-square analysis; and (3) correlation coefficients for education and knowledge. Other indicators were path coefficients in path analysis, betas in regression analysis, and comparison of high SES communities with low SES communities.

ASSESSMENT OF KNOWLEDGE GAP EVIDENCE

The knowledge gap hypothesis states that as the amount of mass media publicity increases, high SES individuals will acquire knowledge at a greater rate than low SES persons, so that the gap in knowledge between social strata tends to increase rather than decrease. Evidence from data for a single point in time and from several points in time will be examined separately.

SUMMARY: MEDIA EFFECTS ON GAPS IN ONE-SHOT STUDIES

Because the studies vary greatly in media measurement characteristics and in information given about amount of publicity, division of the studies into categories according to relationship between amount of coverage and knowledge gaps can be only a rough assessment (see Table 1). Most of the topics studied appear to have been either moderately or highly publicized.

The overwhelming bulk of the evidence from one-time case studies is for knowledge gaps related to differences in formal education. High and moderate levels of mass media publicity in some cases may reduce knowledge gaps, but type of topic and geographic scope of topic may be more important factors in the development and maintenance of gaps, as well as in their reduction. The finding of gaps in one-time case studies does not necessarily mean that media publicity contributed to increased gaps between high and low SES strata in the population. Many of the education-knowledge correlations in the studies discussed above are moderate (for instance a Pearsonian correlation of .24). Such a moderate correlation may instead point to a narrowing of gaps, but one-shot case studies do not permit confident conclusions about either increased or reduced knowledge gaps under the influence of high levels of mass media publicity.

Several tentative generalizations may be made about media publicity in one-shot case studies. First, results are

TABLE 1
Knowledge Gap Findings for One-Time Measurement, for Each Topic Studied, by Amount of Media Publicity or Exposure*

Findings and Amount of Publicity	Researchers	Number of Topics	Total
I. Gap found			
A. High level of publicity	1. Allen and Colfax (1968)	1	8
	2. Berelson, et al (1954)	1	
	3. Brinton and McKown (1961)[a]	1	
	4. Hofstetter, et al (1978)[b]	1	
	5. Kraus, et al (1963)[c]	1	
	6. Medalia and Larsen (1958)	1	
	7. Robinson (1972)	1**	
	8. Spitzer and Denzin (1965)	1	
B. Moderate to high publicity	1. Adams, et al (1969)	1	10
	2. Atkin, et al (1976)	1**	
	3. Benton and Frazier (1976)	1	
	4. Bogart (1950-51)	1	
	5. Budd, et al (1966)	2	
	6. Edelstein (1973)	1	
	7. Kent and Rush (1976)	1	
	8. McNelly and Deutschmann (1963)[c]	1**	
	9. Bishop, et al (1978)[d]	1	
C. Moderate publicity	1. Levy (1969)	3	6
	2. McNelly, et al (1968)	3	
D. Low to moderate publicity	1. Becker and Whitney (1980)[e,f]	2	2
	2. Fry (1979)[e]	(1)	
E. Publicity varies	1. Gaziano (1982)[g]	4	11
	2. Nnaemeka (1976)[h]	3	
	3. Palmgreen (1979)[i]	1**	
	4. Tichenor, et al (1970)[j,k]	2**	
	5. Tichenor, et al (1973,'75,'80)[ℓ]	1	
F. Exposure to media varies	1. Stauffer, et al (1978)	1**	1
G. Amount of media publicity or exposure is not known	1. Clarke and Kline (1974)	1**	45
	2. Deutschmann and Danielson (1960)	3	
	3. Douglass and Stacey (1972)	1	
	4. Erskine (1962,1963a-c)	26	
	5. Gallup (1977)	1	
	6. Gunaratne (1976)	5	
	7. Kanervo (1979)	1**	
	8. Lounsbury, et al (1979)	1	
	9. McNelly and Molina (1972)[m]	1**	
	10. Robinson (1967)	2	
	11. Rogers (1965-66)	1**	
	12. Wade and Schramm (1969)	2**	
II. No gap or very slight gap			
A. High publicity	1. Levy (1969)	3	3
B. Publicity varies	1. Palmgreen (1979)[n]	1**	1
C. All respondents exposed	1. Gantz (1978)[p]	1**	2
	2. Neuman (1976)[p,r]	1**	
D. Amount of publicity or exposure is not known	1. Deutschmann (1963)[s]	1**	7
	2. Erskine (1962,1963a-c)	6	
III. "Reverse" gap found[t]			
A. Moderate to high publicity	1. Fathi (1973)	1	2
	2. Larsen and Hill (1954)[u]	1	
B. Low to moderate publicity	1. Buss and Hofstetter (1981)[v]	1	1
C. Publicity varies	1. Nnaemeka (1976)[h]	1	1
D. All respondents exposed	1. Neuman (1976)[w]	1	1

*Some studies report on more than one topic, and findings may have differed; therefore, some studies are listed more than once.

(continued)

TABLE 1 Notes continued

**Topic is defined relatively broadly.
a. Readers of newspapers have more knowledge than nonreaders within each education group.
b. Media use is highly associated with information holding, especially for low and medium education groups.
c. Gap occurs regardless of amount of media exposure.
d. Data reported for panel study but knowledge gain not measured? data are for one point in time.
e. Becker and Whitney (1980) and Fry (1979) report on different aspects of the same data.
f. Larger gap found for national issues than for local issues, regardless of dependency on either television or newspapers.
g. Larger gaps found for issues on which organications were highly active, compared with issues attracting little activity. Neighborhood newspapers contributed to narrowing of gaps in awareness knowledge when publicity was high.
h. When publicity is high or moderate, greater gaps occur for urban sample using newspapers that utilize established sources; gaps are smaller or are "reverse" gaps for rural sample using newspapers utilizing less establishment sources. Gaps are small or "reverse" among both urban and rural newspapers when publicity is relatively less.
i. Gaps occur for national issues, regardless of amount of publicity (see also note n).
j. Although Tichenor et al. (1970) include findings of Budd et al. (1966), this evidence is accounted for under a separate listing for Budd et al. in this table.
k. The greater the publicity, the greater the gap in recall of newspaper articles.
l. The greater the publicity, the greater the gap when several communities are compared.
m. Education predicts well for high SES strata; media use predicts knowledge better for low SES strata.
n. Gaps are not found for local issues, regardless of amount of media publicity (see also note i).
p. Results are based only on that portion of the sample which saw a TV newscast.
r. Only a slight gap occurred for unaided recall or aided recall with details (see also note w).
s. Comparison is of literate and elliterate groups, not education groups.
t. "Reverse" gap means that more of the less educated knew of a topic, compared with the better educated members of a sample.
u. However, see note 3 in text.
v. Variables related to employment predict knowledge better than education; however, mean score differences are not very large among four education groups drawn from steelworkers.
w. Reverse gap found for aided recall without details (also notes p and r).

mixed for high media coverage situations. Readers of a newspaper covering an issue heavily knew more about the issue than did nonreaders, regardless of educational level (Brinton and McKown, 1961). High newspaper coverage led to reduced gaps in local issue knowledge (Donohue et al., 1973). When media publicity is high, sustained, and concentrated, gaps in *awareness* knowledge may close or be nonexistent (Greenberg, 1964; Levy, 1969; Erskine, 1962, 1963a, 1963, 1963c). Yet, even if media attention is highly focused on an issue for some time, SES-related gaps may be observed in *depth* knowledge (Spitzer and Denzin, 1965).

Further, some surveys of highly covered issues and events report gaps, but these tend to be medical, biological, and social science topics (Tichenor et al., 1970), or national or international topics (Edelstein, 1973; Erskine, 1962, 1963a 1963b; Douglass and Stacey, 1972; Berelson et al., 1954). Other surveys of relatively well-publicized national subjects find modest gaps (Deutschmann and Danielson, 1960; Clarke and Kline, 1974; Bishop et al., 1978; Genova and Greenberg, 1979).

Second, results are also mixed for low publicity situations. Withdrawal of a daily newspaper because of a strike was linked to increased knowledge gaps (Samuelson, 1960). Decline in media attention to local issues over time was associated with reduced gaps (Donohue et al., 1975). When amount of media coverage and geographical scope of issue were varied, amount of media attention did not contribute to gaps, but scope did—gaps developed for national issues but not local ones (Palmgreen, 1979). In a study varying amount of neighborhood newspaper publicity for four local issues, higher coverage was associated with smaller knowledge gaps when compared with gaps for issues receiving less publicity (Gaziano, 1982). When dependence on a particular medium varied and media attention was low, the strength of the relationship between education and knowledge was weak or nonexistent for local topics and stronger for national ones (Becker and Whitney, 1980). In a field experiment, the more publicized the news stories on medical, biological, and social science topics, the larger the knowledge gap when compared with recall of less publicized articles on these subjects (Tichenor et al., 1970).

When media exposure and non-exposure are contrasted, some evidence suggests that media exposure leads to knowledge gap reductions. In Peru and Venezuela, degree of media exposure was a stronger predictor of foreign affairs or public affairs knowledge of low SES respondents than was level of education (McNelly and Molina, 1968;

Kanervo, 1979); and in Colombian peasant villages, media use or exposure contributed to public affairs knowledge (Rogers, 1965-1966; Deutschmann, 1963). Among a national U.S. sample, media use was highly associated with political information increases, especially for low and medium education respondents (Hofstetter et al., 1978). In contrast, a gap in knowledge of the radioactive nuclear fallout issue occurred regardless of amount of total media exposure (Kraus et al., 1963). Exposure to televised news may have led to narrowed gaps in two studies, although non-exposure was not studied (Neuman, 1976; Gantz, 1978), but gaps were found in an experimental study (Stauffer et al., 1978). The limitations of studies of television viewers for comparison with those discussed previously have already been noted.

When media are viewed in terms of media dependence, Fry (1979) examined the same data as Becker and Whitney (1980) and concluded that the higher the dependence on newspapers, the greater the knowledge gap for public affairs information (not a statistically significant finding). There was no knowledge difference among respondents who were dependent on television. The data of Brinton and McKown (1961) can also be compared in terms of readers versus nonreaders: the knowledge gap on a fluoridation issue among readers is smaller than the gap among nonreaders. On the other hand, other data on federal budget deficit and nuclear freeze issues revealed larger gaps among newspaper readers than nonreaders. (Results depended on topic for television viewers, who evidenced a greater gap on the national budget issue when contrasted with nonviewers; nonviewers showed a greater gap for the nuclear freeze issue.)[20] A survey of an occupational group—steelworkers—found that variables related to being employed versus unemployed were more related to knowledge than was education level (Buss and Hofstetter, 1981). Employment connected respondents to interpersonal communication networks.

SUMMARY: MEDIA EFFECTS ON GAPS OVER TIME

Among reports based on separate samples over time (listed in Table 2), four indicate reduction in knowledge differences between more and less educated persons in the United States under certain conditions (Tichenor et al., 1973, 1980; Donohue et al., 1975; Miller and MacKuen, 1979; Bailey, 1971; Becker et al., 1978). A portion of Gunaratne's (1976) data suggested increasing gaps when compared with the data of Ryan (1952), although the limitations of this comparison have been pointed out in note 9. Poll questions asked over time produced contradictory results—increased gaps for five topics (Tichenor et al., 1970; Erskine, 1963c), decreases for three topics (Erskine, 1963a, 1963b, 1963c), and one gap unchanged (Erskine, 1963c). Tichenor et al. (1970) contended that media coverage was increasing for topics they studied, but no media information is known for Erskine's data.

Among surveys with panels or combinations of panels with other designs that permit inferences about causality, four indicate a decrease in knowledge inequalities under certain conditions—in U.S. settings, unless otherwise noted (Brown et al., 1981; Douglas et al., 1970; Galloway, 1976, in a developing country; Genova and Greenberg, 1979). Three show no change in knowledge gaps over time (Star and Hughes, 1950; Bogart, 1957-1958, in Greece; Abbott, 1978). One report of no gap at either measurement focused on a teleclub for peasant farmers in a developing country (Shingi and Mody, 1976).

A very recent time-trend study not included in the preceding analysis provides evidence about gaps under the condition of dependence on newspapers and television (Miyo, 1983). This study involved a sample of randomly selected Wisconsin children and their parents, and panel data were reported for the parents' depth knowledge of the 1980 presidential election campaign during three waves of interviewing (9 months before the election, 1 month before

TABLE 2
Knowledge Gap Findings for Studies Over Time, for Each Topic Studied, by Amount of Media Publicity or Exposure

Findings and Amount of Publicity	Researchers	Number of Topics	Total
I. Gap found, which increases			
A. High level of publicity	1. Abbott (1978)[a]	1	1
B. Moderate to high publicity	1. Genova and Greenberg (1979)[b]	1	1
C. Publicity appears to have increased over time	1. Tichenor, et al (1970)	3	3
D. Amount of media publicity	1. Erskine (1963c) 2. Gunaratne (1976)[c]	2 2	4
II. Gap found, which decreases			
A. Moderate to high publicity	1. Bailey (1971)[d] 2. Genova and Greenberg (1979)[e]	1 2	3
B. Publicity varies	1. Brown, et al (1981)[f] 2. Douglas, et al (1970)[g] 3. Tichenor, et al (1973,'75,'80)[h]	1 1 8	10
C. Exposure varies	1. Galloway (1977)[i]	15	15
D. Amount of publicity or exposure is not known	1. Erskine (1962,1963a,1963b)	3	3
III. Gap found, which does not change			
A. High publicity	1. Abbott (1978)[j] 2. Star and Hughes (1950)	1 1	2
B. Moderate to high publicity	1. Genova and Greenberg (1979)[k]	1	1
C. Moderate publicity	1. Bogart (1957-58)[ℓ]	1**	1
D. Amount of publicity or exposure is not known	1. Erskine (1963c)	1	1
IV. No gap found at T_1 or T_2			
A. All subjects exposed to medium	1. Shingi and Mody (1976)[m]	2	2
V. Gap may narrow, but evidence is unclear			
A. Moderate to high publicity	1. Becker, et al (1978)[n] 2. Miller and MacKuen (1979)[p] 3. Bishop, et al (1978)[r]	1	1

*Some studies report on more than one topic, and findings may have differed; therefore, some studies are listed more than once.
**Topic is defined relatively broadly.
a. Gap increased if respondents did not see any newspaper articles during year-long information campaign in newspaper (see also note j).
b. Gap increased somewhat for "structural" knowledge of an event in the news for a relatively short duration during a ten-day period (see also notes e and k).
c. Two of Gunaratne's topics are comparable to Ryan's (1952) data for a subgroup in Gunaratne's sample with some limitations to the comparison. See note 9 in text.
d. The less educated showed slightly greater gains than more educated respondents in a 6- to 7-week period.
e. Gaps decreased in "factual" knowledge of two topics, differing in duration of event, during a period of ten days between T^1 and T^2. (See also notes b and k.)
f. Knowledge gap closed between T^1 and T^3 (after two 20-week information campaigns) in a community receiving information campaign. Gap did not close in comparison community not receiving an information campaign.
g. Gap narrowed because the low education group gained and higher education groups decreased in knowledge during an 8-month-long information campaign in a small community. Data are given for comparison community without a campaign, but response rate for this community was only 44%.

TABLE 2 Notes continued

h. Gaps in local issue knowledge decrease under conditions of high conflict, high newspaper coverage, high discussion, homogeneity of community, when issue is of basic concern to a community, and when public attention to issues wanes over time.
i. Although results were mixed, the tendency was for gaps to narrow over time in a village in India with radio and reading forums. Apparently, gaps did not narrow in a comparison village without the forums.
j. Gaps either did not increase or else showed a slight increase if respondents saw any articles during a year-long newspaper information campaign (see also note a).
k. A gap in "structural" knowledge of an event of relatively long duration did not change in magnitude during a 10-day measurement period (see also notes b and e).
l. Gaps did not change in a Greek community receiving an information campaign. Data for gaps in a comparison community without a campaign are not reported.
m. No knowledge gap based on SES differences found at either time of measurement in a small sample of farmers in India attending a teleclub. Non-teleclub farmers in another village tested only at T^1 but not at T^2.
n. Less educated people exposed to 1976 presidential election debates gained information, but amount of gain is unclear.
p. All respondents gained information during 1976 presidential election debates, but amount of gain for each education group is not clear.
r. These researchers also studied the 1976 presidential election debates and found a knowledge gap based on differences in education, but knowledge gain over time was not measured. Their data are shown in Table 1.

it, and 1 year later). A knowledge gap found at Time 1 decreased slightly by Time 2 (statistically nonsignificant), and it remained virtually unchanged by Time 3.[21] Newspaper-dependent respondents consistently were more knowledgeable than television-dependent respondents, and this finding held for both high and low education groups. For each education group, the gap between newspaper-dependent and television-dependent groups decreased between Time 1 and Time 2 when the level of media publicity about the campaign was high, and this gap widened by Time 3 when publicity had decreased.[22]

Incidentally, a reanalysis by Cook et al. (1975) of "Sesame Street" data suggested that learning gaps between advantaged and disadvantaged children increased. Cook et al. pointed out that the independent variable in the work of Bogatz and Ball (1970, 1972) was not exposure to the children's program but was rather encouragement to view. Another study of "Sesame Street" which did measure viewing found that learning gaps increased between advantaged and disadvantaged children (Minton, 1972).

Much of the time-trend evidence does not support a hypothesis of increasing gaps with higher levels of media publicity. Instead, the evidence favors decreases in gaps or no change when media publicity is high. *Several strong notes of caution, however, should be heeded.* First, ceiling effects may be confounding the findings of decreased gaps since the same questions were asked each time (Erskine, 1962, 1963a, 1963b, 1963c; Galloway, 1977; Bailey, 1971; Brown et al., 1981; Douglas et al., 1970). (Three surveys reporting no change in gaps used the same questions each time.) Second, type of topic and geographic scope of topic play an important role in narrowing knowledge differentials. Third, several special conditions seem to influence findings of reduced gaps, such as presence of conflict in issues, high level of organized group activity on issues, individuals' motivation or interest, and type of community social structure.

DISCUSSIONS AND CONCLUSIONS

The majority of the 58 reports examined support the proposition that *the higher the education, the greater the knowledge of various topics.* This is not the same phenomenon as described in the knowledge gap hypothesis, which requires a comparison of varying levels of mass media publicity for topics.

In one-time case studies, the frequent finding of moderately sized gaps may indicate that media publicity played a part in decreasing initially larger gaps. No firm conclusions, however, can be drawn about the effect of high versus low levels of media coverage in one-shot studies.

The time-trend studies, taken as a whole, suggest that increasing levels of media publicity may reduce gaps but several other factors may be equally or more influential in narrowing gaps.

The most frequent characteristics associated with knowledge inequalities in either one-time or time-trend surveys seem to be type of topic and geographic scope of topic studied. Content areas related to gaps include international and national issues, topics of greater interest to high SES persons than to low SES individuals, and knowledge conceptualized in civics class or textbook terms. Gaps occur less frequently or are small when topics are local and are likely to appeal to lower SES strata.

Inconsistent results in the diffusion studies—in which the less educated tend to be more aware of issues than the more educated—are most likely to be explained by the operational definition of knowledge as awareness of topic by time of interviewing or by evening of first news announcement. Results might have been different had interviewing taken place later.

In addition, utilizing open-ended questions which allow respondents to define knowledge in their own terms does not necessarily lead to findings of no differences, but it may lead to findings of smaller gaps than other methodologies.

Characteristics of research efforts which do not seem to influence results are populations studied, method of research, date and location of research, and operational definition of knowledge gap. Results may differ, however, for awareness knowledge as opposed to depth knowledge (Gaziano, 1983a).

Whenever studies are compared, one must account for a variety of measurement and conceptual differences and the particular set of conditions under which the findings hold.[23]

Comparability of research findings is a key issue. If results conflict, perhaps different phenomena were measured. Operational definitions of knowledge may be dissimilar (for instance, in depth versus awareness knowledge). Even if the type of knowledge is the same, question wording or measurement may differ (that is, one study may use a set of 16 knowledge items and another may use open-ended questions). Types of media studied may vary, as may measurement of media contact—use, frequency of exposure, ownership, message discrimination, and so on. An additional difficulty is that not only is measurement of education usually not explained but also there is no standard way to measure it.

Proportions of samples being contrasted may vary. Findings based on a small portion of a sample—such as the 14% who are television news viewers—are not comparable to results based on the majority of another sample. A further problem is that many authors do not give information on response rate at all.

Populations may vary. Random samples drawn from telephone listings, registered voters, and peasant farmers may yield differing data because populations were not equivalent. These, in turn, are unlike a purposive sample of adult nonreaders. Results based on a comparison of low SES and high SES communities are not entirely comparable to findings based on individuals who differ in level of education or other SES indicators.

Finally, complicating factors in comparisons of poll data (even though questions over time are identical) are the order in which questions were asked, the nature of preceding questions, and differences in sampling methods (such as early quota samples and later samples when methods were more sophisticated and representative).

A great deal of empirical evidence for knowledge gaps exists; therefore, we may believe that we know much about gaps under the influence of media publicity. In fact, we do not know much at all. Very little research with data on associations between knowledge and education has involved mass media coverage of issues and news topics as a *variable.* In particular, little is known about changes in the education-knowledge relationship over time as media coverage of topics varies.

FUTURE CONSIDERATIONS FOR RESEARCH

If scholars are interested in future knowledge gap investigations, they may wish to be guided by several considerations:

(1) Since little is known of the causal influence of media on knowledge gaps, not only should measurements be

taken at more than one point in time, but also panel designs (or panels in combinations with other designs such as the Solomon 4-group design) are desirable in order to demonstrate causal influence of media. Conclusions from an analysis of 56 studies of newspaper effects underscore this point (Weaver, 1978).

(2) Future knowledge gap research should systematically vary media publicity.[24]

(3) The amount of time which has elapsed between measurements is a variable. Bursts of publicity may reinforce learning from media but competing information and the forgetting process may intervene to alter knowledge gaps. The amount of media attention to various topics is in a constant process of change, and gaps may continually change over time as well.

(4) Measurement of knowledge, especially knowledge *gain,* is fraught with problems. A small pilot study of learning from the 1976 presidential debates points out a number of such difficulties (Graber, 1978). In addition, scholars may wish to know of the variety of operational definitions of knowledge in past research and to select those which will best answer their research questions. They may desire to avoid textbook types of knowledge definitions and they may prefer to use open-ended questions so that respondents can define knowledge in their own terms. Also, if statistical analyses assuming interval-level data are desired, researchers will want to measure knowledge and education as continuous variables (this does not preclude treating them as categorical variables as well). In the same vein, a 10-item test of knowledge at more than one point in time can aid assessment of knowledge gains; however, this limits the knowledge that can be studied. The facts of many issues are complex and, in theory, may have no limit, or be so complex that the limit is difficult to achieve.[25] Further, even if results demonstrate a reduction of a knowledge gap for a set of ten items, perhaps the gap increased for other aspects of knowledge of that particular issue. Limiting the

knowledge to be acquired to a set of ten specific items may be justified in terms of the goals of a particular information campaign, but in other situations, such as a complicated issue, setting knowledge limits may not be justified or realistic.

(5) It may be possible that measurement of knowledge as simple awareness of topics may produce different results than measurement of depth knowledge. The differences in findings of Greenberg (1964) — who measured awareness of President Kennedy's assassination—and of Spitzer and Denzin (1965)—who measured depth knowledge—suggests this, as does the work of Gaziano (1983a).

(6) Other variables besides education may affect knowledge gaps and therefore be of interest, but these variables may also be related to differences in education. Level of education has been found to be related to interest (Graber, 1978, interest in Presidential debates, to opinion holding (see Schreiber, 1978) and to behavior (Werner, 1975, buying of children's books advertised on television).

(7) Since level of education frequently is positively associated with knowledge, some scholars may want to explore this relationship from any of several vantage points. One is the explanation of the relationship (see Samuelson et al., 1963; Palmgreen, 1979; Childers with Post, 1975; Tichenor et al., 1970). Another is from the view that social-structural variables frequently predict behavior because social processes tend to be relatively stable. But certain situations and events can disrupt these social processes. It is in such cases that media may play a role that is not constrained by social structural variables (Davis, 1977).

Further, knowledge differentials depend on how information campaigns and information delivery systems are organized. Health and agricultural diffusion programs in developing nations tend to be set up not to benefit the poor but to serve the well-to-do farmers, landowners and the government in power (Roling et al., 1976; Rogers, 1976). Diffusion studies that find positive relationships among such variables as knowledge, adoption, income level, educational level, mass media exposure, and so forth "have failed to perceive these variables as parts of a broader and more crucial factor: society's power structure" (Beltran, 1975: 2, 190). American media also are structured to benefit the upper stratum.

Upper SES strata have access to more information and to more accurate information than do lower SES strata through print media—especially specialized print media, organization memberships, formal schooling, family norms fostering achievement, and high-status personal contacts. Groups are often parts of networks of larger organizations that further enhance opportunities to acquire knowledge. The result is a severely constricted flow of accurate information about public affairs to low SES groups, a flow that consigns low SES strata to a more closed information system than that of upper SES strata. Messages circulating in the lower SES subsystem tend to concern gossip, rumor, and folklore more often than public affairs topic (Childers with Post, 1975).

It is sometimes argued that low SES persons have a different kind of knowledge than do high SES persons; however, low SES knowledge is not necessarily useful for social mobility or advancement of low SES individuals vis-a-vis the center of power in society. Frequently, it is detrimental from the point of view of providing them with information that they can use to advance their interests. Public affairs knowledge is the kind of knowledge upon which social power is based. Researchers may elect to examine public affairs topics of potential interest to the disadvantaged. Scholars working within an information seeking framework may want to follow up on the observations of Suominen (1976) and Childers with Post (1975) that the disadvantaged may not be able to view their problems in terms of information needs and, when they do seek information, may not be very active in the search.

(8) Knowledge disparities may be exacerbated by the relatively recent change in the structure of the national economy, which increasingly is based on information allocation (Smith, 1975). In light of this, scholars also may wish to consider Katzman's (1974) hyptheses that new communication technologies may increase knowledge inequalities, not only because of unequal access but also because of unequal use, especially if access and use are linked to socioeconomic differences.

(9) Scholars may wish to review several policy implications of knowledge gap research in light of the evidence presented in this article and the suggestions for further research. In cases in which positive assocations between education and knowledge are weak, researchers may desire to specify more conditions under which the relationship is attenuated. Perhaps the mass media have greater influence on reduction of knowledge gaps than previously believed. In situations in which evidence for positive relationships between education and knowledge is substantial, some scholars may wish to consider how such social disparities should be addressed with regard to decisions about research topics, allocation of resources, and formulation of social policy. The shift in research emphasis from the traditional model to other perspectives which de-emphasize SES variables indirectly may be supportive of the Reagan administration's stance that the less advantaged do not require much support from social programs. To what extent is research presently concentrated on topics linked to social programs? Have social scientists stopped studying social inequalities because the orientation of government has changed?

Scholars interested in knowledge gap research may wish to investigate the complex sets of factors that bind social classes, impede social mobility, and lead to further unequal distribution of knowledge. Creating a more equitable knowledge distribution—assuming that this is a desirable goal in a democratic society—is not just a matter of redistributing information: The knowledge gap reflects disparities in information as one among many resources which are less available to lower SES groups in society.

NOTES

1. For example, Clarke and Kline (1974: 228) report, "Survey research commonly finds that correlations between use of mass media and levels of information pale by comparison with correlations between educational attainment and information." Robinson (1967: 24) states, "it is well known that correlations between educational level and printed mass media usage are almost as high as those found between educational and information level . . ." Dervin (1980: 78) notes, "When research is conducted using the traditional communication model, the results consistently show that those with less education and lower incomes are less likely to be information seekers, use expert information sources, be informed generally."

2. For example, Dervin (1980) asserts that research on knowledge gaps has resulted in a "blame-the-victim" syndrome. See also the discussion in this article under "Critical Comment on the Knowledge Gap Hypothesis."

3. One factor which may have affected this result is that a newspaper strike had idled the afternoon paper, a likely news vehicle for the faculty group. Another is that the faculty community was canvassed about a day after the event and the laboring community not interviewed until three and a half days had elapsed after the event.

4. Awareness of the Kennedy assassination was compared with awareness of five other assassinations of public figures (Levy, 1969). All respondents knew of three of the deaths, those of President Kennedy, Senator Robert Kennedy, and the Reverend Martin Luther King. In contrast, those with high education were considerably more likely to know of the violent deaths of Malcolm X, Medgar Evers, and George Lincoln Rockwell than were the less educated. A "reverse gap" appears for two events, however, when the sample is divided by race. Nonwhites tended on the whole to be less educated than the whites. Nonwhites had heard of the deaths of the two black public figures, Malcolm X and Evers, in greater proportions than whites. (More whites than nonwhites were aware of the death of Rockwell, a white American Nazi Party leader.)

5. Although some early diffusion studies, polls, and other research tended to find more men than women aware of a topic, this was not always the case, and gender differences seem to have been dependent partly on topic. In more recent research, sex differences in knowledge are not often found.

6. These three research reports deal with an ongoing study. The 1975 (Donohue et al.) and 1980 reports (Tichenor et al.) are updates on the 1973 article.

7. Three studies testing knowledge gap hypotheses are not reported in detail here because their content is not as relevant to this analysis as the other studies described. They are Tainter (1978), Egueke (1979), and Schere Tainter (1977).

8. The comparison group of farmers was tested at T_1 only but not at T_2.

9. Gunaratne's data collected in 1971 and Ryan's data from 1951 are not directly comparable because Ryan's respondents were male heads of households and Gunaratne's respondents were females, male heads of households, and male non-household heads. Further, Gunaratne excluded one of the three villages in Ryan's study and added two other to his investigation. Gunaratne's comparison over time was of Ryan's male household heads and the 1971 data on all males for only two villages and two types of knowledge.

10. "Structural" means knowledge of relationships, reasons, and so on. "Factual" means names, dates, places, and so on.

11. Liebert also cites the work of Minton (1972) which showed that the first year of viewing *Sesame Street* led to gains for advantaged children only in the sample. In addition, Salomon (1976: 14) discussed an Israeli study which also found SES differences; however, "low SES children . . . learned more in areas of perceptual analysis and discrimination, whereas middle-class children learned more in areas of abstraction and synthesis."

12. Beltran (1975) makes a distinction that others have also made between "system-blame" and "person-blame." He would not necessarily discard the traditional model but he would shift his analysis to characteristics of the social system rather than to characteristics of the individual. I would suggest that to place "blame" is not the point of scientific analysis; rather the goal is to determine causes of phenomena. These causes may not necessarily be "fault."

13. Other studies with relevant data may well exist but were not found.

14. Detailed tables showing more information for each study than is given here are available from the author.

15. Two reports of three Israeli surveys note gaps in recall of radio and television news items (Adoni and Cohen, 1978; Katz et al., 1977. It is not clear what proportion of the total sample these respondents represent nor whether or not the samples are random.

16. This survey (Bishop et al., 1978) states that the "knowledge-rich" got "richer"; however, this assumption is based on Graber's (1978) data on 21 individuals and on a mimeographed report of Abramowitz (1977). I have not examined the latter report. Graber's pilot study of learning in depth included two persons with a grade school education, six with high school educations, and thirteen with college educations.

17. There was a slim gain of .41 in the average score of the grade school educated group, but scores of groups with more education had *declined* by the end of the campaign.

18. Some scholars contend that categorical and ordinal data may be treated in statistical analysis as if they were equal interval data. Others argue that considerable error will result if this is done.

19. One study not included in the analysis apparently coded education as a continuous variable, but what was actually measured was educational level of the household head. This was compared with the respondent's knowledge of the issue, but the respondent was not necessarily the head of the household. The study is Bultena et al., 1978 (a knowledge gap for the issue was found).

20. This information is from a letter to the author from David W. Moore, Associate Professor of Political Science, University of New Hampshire, Durham,

N.H., on May 26, 1982. He cited data analyzed by his student, Carolyn Eisenhut, in her paper, "Does a Knowledge Gap Exist in New Hampshire????", May 10, 1982.

21. Miyo suggests that the measure of political knowledge may not have captured actual depth knowledge, thus imposing an artificial ceiling on the amount of knowledge to be acquired by more educated respondents.

22. When Miyo examined knowledge gaps among respondents low in dependence, she concluded that newspapers tended to widen knowledge gaps based on education and television appeared to narrow gaps over time. Among respondents high in dependence, newspapers appeared to decreased knowledge gaps and television appeared to increase them over time. When I looked at Miyo's data, however, by graphing average knowledge scores for each education group by high and low dependence on each medium, the following pattern appeared: the knowledge gap between more and less newspaper-dependent respondents tended to decrease for each education group between Time 1 and Time 2, and the gap increased between Time 2 and Time 3. This pattern occurred also for television-dependent respondents.

23. All of this discussion assumes that findings reported in the literature described are not due to measurement error.

24. An anonymous reviewer suggests that the hypothesis might be extended to predict SES-based knowledge gaps on specific topics when mass media coverage declines over time. (Some evidence on this point is provided by Donohue et al., 1975, and by Miyo, 1983).

25. Sometimes the argument is made that if researchers use simple measures of knowledge, an increasing gap based on education is untenable over the long term because eventually everyone with high education will know and those less well educated will catch up. There is reason to believe, however, that the less educated will not catch up if access to information and understanding depend on high socioeconomic status, even if interest is equally distributed within all SES groups.

REFERENCES

ABBOTT, E. A. (1978) "Effects of year-long newspaper energy series on reader knowledge and action." Presented to the Association for Education in Journalism, University of Washington, Seattle.

ABRAMOWITZ, A. (1977) "The first debate: a study of attitude change." Williamsburg, VA: College of William and Mary. (mimeo)

ADAMS, J. B., J. J. MULLEN, and H. M. WILSON (1969) "Diffusion of a 'minor' foreign affairs news event." Journalism Q. 46: 545-551.

ADONI, H. and A. A. COHEN (1978) "Television economic news and the social construction of economic reality." J. of Communication 28, 4: 61-70.

ALLEN, I. L. and J. D. COLFAX (1968) "The diffusion of news of LBJ's March 31 decision." Journalism Q. 45: 321-324.

ATKIN, C. K., J. GALLOWAY, and O. B. NAYMAN (1976) "News media exposure, political knowledge and campaign interest." Journalism Q. 53: 231-237.

BAILEY, G. A. (1971) "The Public, the Media, and the Knowledge Gap," J. of Environmental Education 2, 4: 3-8.

BALL, S. and G. A. BOGATZ (1970) The First Year of Sesame Street: An Evaluation. Princeton, NJ: Educational Testing Service.

BECKER, L. B., I. A. SOBOWALE, R. E. COBBEY, and C. H. EYAL (1978) "Debates' effects on voters' understanding of candidates and issues," in G. F. Bishop et al. (eds.) The Presidential Debates. New York: Praeger.

BECKER, L. B. and D. C. WHITNEY (1980) "Effects of media dependencies: audience assessment of government. " Communication Research 7: 95-120.

BELTRAN, L. R. (1975) "Research ideologies in conflict." J. of Communication 25, 2: 187-193.

BENTON, M. and P.J. FRAZIER (1976) "The agenda setting function of the mass media at three levels of 'information holding.'" Communication Research 3: 261-274.

BERELSON, B. R., P. F. LAZARSFELD, and W. N. McPHEE (1954) Voting: a Study of Opinion Formation in a Presidential Campaign. Chicago: Univ. of Chicago Press.

BISHOP, G. F., R. W. OLDENDICK, and A. J. TUCHFARBER (1978) "The Presiential debates as a device for increasing the 'rationality' of electoral behavior," in G. F. Bishop et al. (eds.) The Presidential Debates. New York: Praeger.

BOGART, L. (1957-1958) "Measuring the effectiveness of an overseas information campaign: a case history." Public Opinion Q. 21: 475-498.

———(1950-1951) "Spread of news on a local event: a case history." Public Opinion Q. 14: 769-772.

BOGATZ, G. A. and S. BALL (1972) The Second Year of Sesame Street: A Continuing Evaluation. Princeton, NJ: Educational Testing Service.

BRINTON, J. E. and L. N. McKOWN (1961) "Effects of newspaper reading on knowledge and attitude." Journalism Q. 38: 187-195.

BROWN, J. W., J. S. ETTEMA, and R. V. LUEPKER (1981) "Knowledge gap effects in a cardiovascular information campaign." Presented to the Association for Education in Journalism, East Lansing, MI.

BUDD, R. W., M. S. MacLEAN, Jr., and A. M. BARNES (1966) "Regularities in the diffusion of two major news events." Journalism Q. 43: 221-230.

BULTENA, G. L., D. L. ROGERS, and K. A. CONNER (1978) "Toward explaining citizens' knowledge about a proposed reservoir." J. of Environmental Education 9, 2: 24-36.

BUSS, T. F. and C. R. HOFSTETTER (1981) "Communication, information and participation during an emerging crisis." Social Sci. Journal 18: 81-91.

CAMPBELL, D. T. and J. C. STANLEY (1963) Experimental and Quasi-Experimental Designs for Research. Chicago: Rand McNally.

CHILDERS, T. with J. A. POST (1975) The Information-Poor in America. Metuchen, NJ: Scarecrow.

CLARKE, P. and F. G. KLINE (1974) "Media effects reconsidered: some new strategies for communication research." Communication Research 1: 224-240.

COLEMAN, J. S., et al. ["the Coleman report"] (1966) Equality of Educational Opportunity: Summary. Washington, D.C.: U.S. Government Printing Office.

COOK, T. D., H. APPLETON, R. F. CONNER, A. SHAFFER, G. A. TAMKIN, and S. J. WEBER (1975) Sesame Street Revisited. New York: Russell Sage.

DAVIS, D. K. (1977) "Assessing the role of mass communication in social processes: a comment on decline and fall at the White House.'" Communication Research 4: 23-34.

DERVIN, B. (1980) "Communication gaps and inequities: moving toward a reconceptualization," in B. Dervin and M. J. Voigt (eds.) Progress in Communication Sciences, Vol. II. Norwood, NJ: Ablex.

DEUTSCHMANN, P. J. (1963) "The mass media in an underdeveloped village." Journalism Q. 40: 27-35.

——— and W. A. DANIELSON (1960) "Diffusion of knowledge of the major news story." Journalism Q. 37: 345-355.

DONOHUE, G. A., P. J. TICHENOR, and C. N. OLIEN (1975) "Mass media and the knowledge gap: a hypothesis reconsidered." Communication Research 2: 3-23.

DOUGLAS, D. F., B. W. WESTLEY, and S. H. CHAFFEE (1970) "An information campaign that changed community attitudes." Journalism Q. 47: 479-487, 492.

DOUGLASS, C. W. and D. C. STACEY (eds.) (1972) "Demographical characteristics and social factors related to public opinion on fluoridation." J. of Public Health Dentistry 32, 2: 128-134.

EDELSTEIN, A. S. (1973) "Decision-making and mass communication: a conceptual and methodological approach to public opinion," in P. Clarke (ed.) New Model for Mass Communication Research. Beverly Hills, CA: Sage.

EGUEKE, C. G. (1979) "Involvement in news events and the knowledge gap hypothesis." Master's thesis, University of Wisconsin.

ERSKINE, H. G. (1963a) "The polls: exposure to domestic information." Public Opinion Q. 27: 491-500.

———(1963b) "The polls: exposure to international information." Public Opinion Q. 27: 658-662.

———(1963c) "The polls: textbook knowlege." Public Opinion Q. 27: 133-141.

———(1962) "The polls: the informed public." Public Opinion Q. 26: 669-677.

ETTEMA, J. S. and F. G. KLINE (1977) "Deficits, differences, and ceilings: contingent conditions for understanding the knowledge gap." Communication Research 4: 179-202.

FATHI, A. (1973) "Diffusion of a 'happy' news event." Journalism Q. 50: 271-277.

FRAZIER, P. J. (1981) "Trends in attitudes toward fluoridation." Paper presented to the American Association for Public Opinion Research. Buck Hill Falls, PA (May).

FRY, D. L. (1979) "The knowledge gap hypothesis and media dependence: an initial study." Paper presented to Association for Education in Journalism, University of Houston, TX.

GALLOWAY, J. J. (1977) "The analysis and significance of communication effects gaps." Communication Research 4: 363-386.

Gallup Omnibus, The (Gallup poll) (1977) "A Survey Concerning Water Fluoridation." (Appendix II.) Princeton, NJ: The Gallup Organization.

GANTZ, W. (1978) "How uses and gratifications affect recall of television news." Journalism Q. 55: 664-672, 681.

GAZIANO, C. (1983a) Neighborhood Newspapers, Citizen Groups, and Knowledge Gaps on Public Affairs Issues. Unpublished Ph.D. dissertation, Univ. of Minnesota.

——— (1983b) "Social stratification and the knowledge gap: some influences on knowledge disparities." Paper presented to the International Communication Association, Dallas (May 29).

——— (1982) "The influence of news media and citizen groups on the knowledge gap in an inner-city neighborhood." Paper presented to the American Association for Public Opinion Research, Hunt Valley, MD (May).

GENOVA, B.K.L. and B. S. GREENBERG (1979) "Interests in news and the knowledge gap." Public Opinion Q. 43: 79-91.

GORELICK, S. M. (No date) "Effects of the 1976 presidential debates: agenda-setting and issue learning." Unpublished paper, Teachers college, Columbia University, New York.

GRABER, D. A. (1978) "Problems in measuring audience effects of the 1976 debates," in G. f. Bishop et al. (eds.) The Presidential Debates: Media, Electoral, and Policy Perspectives. New York: Praeger.

GREENBERG, B. S. (1964) "Diffusion of news of the Kennedy assassination." Public Opinion Q. 28: 225-232.

GUNARATNE, S. A. (1976) "Modernisation and knowledge: a study of four Ceylonese villages." Communication Monographs. Singapore: Asian Mass Communication Research and Information Centre.

HOFSTETTER, C. R., C. ZUKIN, and T. F. BUSS (1978) "Political imagery and information in an age of television." Journalism Q. 55: 562-569.

HYMAN, H. H. and P. B. SHEATSLEY (1947) "Some reasons why information campaigns fail." Public Opinion Q. 11: 412-423.

JENCKS, C. et al. (1972) Inequality: A Reassessment of the Effect of Family and Schooling in America. New York: Basic Books.

KANERVO, E. W. (1979) "How people acquire information: a model of the public affairs information attainment process." Paper presented to the Association for Education in Journalism, University of Houston.

KATZ, E., H. ADONI, and P. PARNESS (1977) "Remembering the news: what the picture adds to recall." Journalism Q. 54: 231-239.

KATZMAN, N. (1974) "The impact of communication technology: promises and prospects." J. of Communication 24, 4: 47-58.

KENT, K. E. and R. R. RUSH (1976) "How communication behavior of older persons affects their public affairs knowledge." Journalism Q. 53: 40-46.

KRAUS, S., R. MEHLING, and E. EL-ASSAL (1963) "Mass media and the fallout controversy." Public Opinion Q. 27: 191-205.

LARSEN, O. N. and R. J. HILL (1954) "Mass media and interpersonal communication in the diffusion of a news event." Amer. Soc. Rev. 19: 426-433.

LEVY, S. G. (1969) "How population subgroups differed in knowledge of six assassinations." Journalism Q. 46: 685-698.

LIEBERT, R. M. (1976) "Evaluating the evaluators." J. of Communication 26, 2: 165-171.

LOUNSBURY, J. W., E. SUNDSTROM, and R. C. DeVAULT (1979) "Moderating effects of respondent knowledge in public opinion research." J. of Applied Psychology 64: 558-563.

McNELLY, J. T. and P. J. DEUTSCHMANN (1963) "Media use and socioeconomic status in a Latin American capital." Gazette 9, 1: 1-15.

McNELLY, J. T. and J. R. MOLINA (1972) "Communication, stratification and international affairs information in a developing urban society." Journalism Q. 49: 316-326, 339.

McNELLY, J. T., R. R. RUSH, and M. E. BISHOP (1968) "Cosmopolitan media usage in the diffusion of international affairs news." Journalism Q. 45: 329-332.

MEDALIA, N. Z. and O. N. LARSEN (1958) "Diffusion and belief in a collective delusion: the Seattle windshield pitting epidemic." Amer. Soc. Rev. 23: 180-186.

MILLER, A. H. and M. MacKUEN (1979) "Learning about the candidates: the 1976 presidential debates." Public Opinion Q. 43: 326-346.

MINTON, J. H. (1972) "The impact of Sesame Street on reading readiness of kindergarten children." Ph.D. dissertation, Fordham University.

MIYO, Y. (1983) "Knowledge-gap hypothesis and media dependency: is television a knowledge leveler?" Paper presented to the International Communication Association, Dallas (May).

NEUMAN, W. R. (1976) "Patterns of recall among television news viewers." Public Opinion Q. 40: 115-123.

NNAEMEKA, T.I.O. (1976) "Issue legitimation, mass media functions and public knowledge of social issues." Ph.D. dissertation, University of Minnesota.

NOWAK, K. (1977) "From information gaps to communication potential," in M. Berg et al. (eds.) Current Theories in Scandinavian Mass Communication Research. Grenaa, Denmark: GMT.

OLIEN, C. N., P. J. TICHENOR, and G. A. DONOHUE (1982) "Structure, communication, and social power: evolution of the knowledge gap hypothesis." Paper presented at "Sommatie '82" conference, Veldhoven, The Netherlands (March 26).

PALMGREEN, P. (1979) "Mass media use and political knowledge." Journalism Monographs, No. 61 (May).

ROBINSON, J. P. (1972) "Mass communication and information diffusion," in F. Gerald Kline et al. (eds.) Current Perspectives in Mass Communications Research. Beverly Hills, CA: Sage.

——— (1967) "World affairs information and mass media exposure." Journalism A. 44: 23-31.

ROGERS, E. M. (1981) "Methodology for meta-research." Presidential address paper presented to the International Communication Association, Minneapolis (May 21-25).

——— (1976) "Communication and development: the passing of the dominant paradigm." Communication Research 3: 213-240.

——— (1965-1966) "Mass media exposure and modernization among Colombian peasants." Public Opinion Q. 29: 614-625.

ROLING, N. G., J. ASCROFT, and F. WA CHEGE (1976) "The diffusion of innovations and the issue of equity in rural development." Communication Research 3: 155-170.

RYAN, B. (1952) "The ceylonese village and the new value system." Rural Sociology 17: 9-28.

SALOMON, G. (1976) "Cognitive skill learning across cultures." J. of Communication 26, 2: 138-144.

SAMUELSON, M. E. (1960) "Some news-seeking behavior in a newspaper strike." Ph.D. dissertation, Stanford University.

——— R. F. CARTER and L. RUGGELS (1963) "Education, available time, and use of mass media." Journalism Q. 40: 491-496, 617.

SCHERER, C. W. (1977) "Differential knowledge gain from a media campaign: a field experiment. Ph.D. dissertation, University of Wisconsin.

SCHREIBER, E. M. (1978) "Education and change in American opinions on a woman for President." Public Opinion Q. 42: 171-182.

SHINGI, P. M. and B. MODY (1976) "The communication effects gap: a field experiment on television and agricultural ignorance in India." Communication Research 3: 171-190.

SMITH, A. G. (1975) "The primary resource." J. of Communication 25, 2: 15-20.

SPITZER, S. P. and N. K. DENZIN (1965) "Levels of knowledge in an emergent crisis." Social Forces 44: 234-237.

STAR, S. A. and H. M. HUGHES (1950) "Report on an educational campaign: the Cincinnati plan for the United Nations." Amer. J. of Sociology 55: 389-400.

STAUFFER, J., R. FROST, and W. RYBOLT (1978) "Literacy, illiteracy, and learning from television news." Communication Research 5: 221-232.

SUOMINEN, E. (1976) "Who needs information and why." J. of Communication 26, 4: 115-119.

TAINTER, S. P. (1978) "Local media coverage of community issues: does it widen the knowledge gap?" Master's thesis, University of Wisconsin.

TICHENOR, P. J., G. A. DONOHUE, and C. N. OLIEN (1980) "Conflict and the knowledge gap." Community Conflict and the Press. Beverly Hills, CA: Sage.

——— (1970) "Mass media flow and differential growth in knowledge." Public Opinion Q. 34: 159-170.

TICHENOR, P. J., J. M. RODENKIRCHEN, C. N. OLIEN, and G. A. DONOHUE (1973) "Community issues, conflict, and public afairs knowledge," in Peter Clarke (ed.) New Models for Mass Communication Research. Beverly Hills, CA: Sage.

TORSVIK, P. (1972) "Television and information." Scandinavian Pol. Studies 7: 215-234.

TROLDAHL, V. C. (1965) "Studies of Consumption of Mass Media Content." Journalism Q. 42: 596-614.

WADE, S. and W. SCHRAMM (1969) "The mass media as sources of public affairs, science, and health knowledge." Public Opinion Q. 33: 197-209.

WEAVER, D. H. (1978) "A summary of newspaper social effects research." Paper presented to the Association for Education in Journalism, University of Washington, Seattle.

WERNER, A. (1975) "A case of sex and class socialization." J. of Communication 25, 4: 45-50.

26

THE THIRD-PERSON EFFECT IN COMMUNICATION

W. Phillips Davison

IN 1949 or 1950, while combing through cartons of U.S. Marine Corps documents from World War II, a young historian at Princeton University came across a series that piqued his curiosity. He stepped across the corridor and described his find to an even younger sociologist:

"You're supposed to know something about public opinion. What do you make of this? There was a service unit consisting of Negro troops with white officers on Iwo Jima Island in the Pacific. The Japanese learned about the location of this unit and sent planes over with propaganda leaflets. These leaflets stressed the theme that this was a white man's war and that the Japanese had no quarrel with colored peoples. They said, more or less, 'Don't risk your life for the white man. Give yourself up at the first opportunity, or just desert. Don't take chances.' The next day that unit was withdrawn."

"Why do you find this so interesting?" asked the sociologist.

"Because I can't find any evidence that the propaganda had an

---

Abstract A person exposed to a persuasive communication in the mass media sees this as having a greater effect on others than on himself or herself. Each individual reasons: "I will not be influenced, but they (the third persons) may well be persuaded." In some cases, a communication leads to action not because of its impact on those to whom it is ostensibly directed, but because others (third persons) think that it will have an impact on its audience. Four small experiments that tend to support this hypothesis are presented, and its complementary relationship to a number of concepts in the social sciences is noted. The third-person effect may help to explain various aspects of social behavior, including the fear of heretical propaganda by religious leaders and the fear of dissent by political rulers. It appears to be related to the phenomenon of censorship in general: the censor never admits to being influenced; it is others with "more impressionable minds" who will be affected.

W. Phillips Davison is Professor of Journalism and Sociology at Columbia University. The author wishes to thank Robert L. Cohen and two anonymous referees for reading an earlier version of this article and making helpful comments.

effect on the troops at all. But it sure had an effect on the white officers. The leaflets seem to have caused a substantial reshuffle of personnel."[1]

The sociologist mumbled something about probable guilt feelings on the part of the white officers and a tendency of the military to prefer solutions that involve physical action. But he couldn't escape the feeling that something else was involved.

A few years later, in the course of investigating the role of the West German press in the formation of Bonn's foreign policy, the sociologist had occasion to ask a series of journalists how much influence they thought newspaper editorials had on the thinking of their readers (Davison, 1957). One of the replies given frequently was along the following lines: "The editorials have little effect on people like you and me, but the ordinary reader is likely to be influenced quite a lot." Since evidence to support such a judgment could not be located, this line of inquiry was eventually abandoned, but the researcher remained impressed with the extent to which many journalists were convinced that editorials had an effect on other people's attitudes, while discounting the effect on people like themselves.

Some time after that, the sociologist became involved in the local phase of a national election, serving as a volunteer for his preferred candidate's organization. Two days before the election a leaflet supporting the rival candidate appeared in his mailbox. He was impressed with its quality. It would undoubtedly swing a lot of votes. Some counteraction would have to be taken. Without thinking further, he procured a pile of political literature from his own party's local office and spent the rest of the day distributing it door to door.

Informal postelection analyses (no systematic studies were conducted at the local level) suggested that neither set of propaganda materials had exerted much influence on the voters. It was as though a page had been taken out of *The People's Choice*.[2] The sociologist

[1] The historian in question, Jeter Isely, died tragically shortly thereafter. The book resulting, in part, from his research includes no direct reference to this incident; indeed, it makes no reference at all to Japanese leaflets, but it does contain the following passage: "About 200 of the enemy slipped through into the rear zones. There they were liquidated by the Fifth Pioneer Battalion and other service troops, many of them Negroes. The corps shore party commander was 'highly gratified with the performance of these colored troops. . . . While in direct action against the enemy for the first time . . . they conducted themselves with marked coolness and courage'" (Isely and Crowl, 1951:500). It would seem probable that the leaflets were dropped following this engagement.

[2] It is scarcely necessary to remind readers that this study of the 1940 election campaign found that very few voters were converted by political propaganda (Lazarsfeld et al., 1944).

(who is identical with the writer of this article) began to ask himself why he had assumed that the rival candidate's leaflet would be so effective.

These personal experiences, and probably others that have been forgotten, led to the formation of a proposition that, for want of a better label, may be called the "third-person effect hypothesis." In its broadest formulation, this hypothesis predicts that people will tend to overestimate the influence that mass communications have on the attitudes and behavior of others. More specifically, individuals who are members of an audience that is exposed to a persuasive communication (whether or not this communication is intended to be persuasive) will expect the communication to have a greater effect on others than on themselves. And whether or not these individuals are among the *ostensible* audience for the message, the impact that they expect this communication to have on others may lead them to take some action. Any effect that the communication achieves may thus be due not to the reaction of the ostensible audience but rather to the behavior of those who anticipate, or think they perceive, some reaction on the part of others.

The phenomenon under consideration has been called the "third-person effect" because third persons are involved from two different observational standpoints. In the view of those trying to evaluate the effects of a communication, its greatest impact will not be on "me" or "you," but on "them"—the third persons. From the standpoint of a propagandist or other persuasive communicator, on the other hand, the third persons are those who are in some way concerned with the attitudes and behavior of the ostensible audience. Indeed, the propagandist may try to manipulate the behavior of these third persons by apparently seeking to influence someone else.

This second definition of the "third person" may have been in the minds of the Japanese strategists who arranged to have leaflets dropped over the black service units on Iwo Jima. They may not have expected the leaflets to have an effect on the troops themselves, but were instead trying to goad the white military command into taking the action that it apparently did take in fact—namely, to withdraw the service units.

Imputation of such reasoning to Japanese military propagandists is supported by the fact that British and American psychological warfare in Europe made use of a very similar tactic. The History of the Psychological Warfare Division, Supreme Headquarters, Allied Expeditionary Force (Bad Homburg, Germany, 1945), tells us about Operation Huguenot—a project for undermining the efficiency of the German Air Force by suggesting that German flying personnel were deserting in their machines to the Allied side. Planting such suggestions was not difficult. It was known that Allied radio broadcasts were systematically monitored by the German government and that monitoring reports were distributed to all high political and military officials. Hints about desertions from the *Luftwaffe* could include, for example, a "slip" by an announcer indicating that a plane officially reported as being shot down had in fact landed safely in England. It could be assumed that at least some of these hints would be picked up by alert radio monitors in Berlin. The Psychological Warfare Division history tells us:

> The dividends from this operation were expected not so much in the actual number of desertions as in the effect of the countermeasures which the German authorities would be induced to take against flying personnel . . . sharpening up of anti-desertion measures and instructions to field police to keep a suspicious eye on everyone—a course which would have serious effects on morale. Also, the promotion of officers on account of reliability rather than efficiency (p. 53).[3]

It seems probable that practical persuaders throughout the centuries have been aware of this use of the third-person effect. Lovers, certainly, have frequently tried to influence the behavior of the loved one by seeming to direct their attentions to someone else.

Four Small Experiments

During the past several years, the writer has made a series of minor efforts to test one variant of the third-person effect hypothesis: that an individual who is exposed to a persuasive communication via the mass media will see this communication as having a greater effect on other people than on himself or herself. All these tests have been conducted with small groups under informal conditions. Elegant experiments they were not. Nevertheless, care was taken to insure that the groups did not contaminate each other and that their members did not supsect that a particular hypothesis was being tested. Even though no single experiment can be regarded as particularly impressive in itself, the results all tend to confirm the hypothesis. Taken together, they are reasonably convincing, at least to this writer.

The first trial was conducted with the help of a good-natured group of 33 graduate students taking a course on mass communication at

[3] According to an academic student of Allied psychological warfare in World War II, a number of desertions were claimed as a result of Operation Huguenot, even though the principal purpose of the undertaking had not been to encourage desertions (Lerner, 1949:268).

Columbia University in 1978. It was just after the New York State election of that year and also just after a strike that had shut down the three major New York City newspapers. A questionnaire included items about both the election and the strike, and was divided into two sections, one including "questions about New Yorkers in general," and the other "a few questions about your own experiences." One of the items in the first section read as follows:

> As you probably know, Governor Carey repeatedly called on Mr. Duryea [the Republican challenger] to make his income tax returns public, and used Mr. Duryea's failure to do so as a major campaign theme. About how much influence do you think this had on the way New Yorkers voted in the gubernatorial election? Please indicate this by making a mark at the appropriate point on the scale below.

The scale ran from 0 (No Influence at All) to 7 (Very Great Influence).

At the end of the second section of the questionnaire, there was the following item:

> And how about Governor Carey's emphasis on Mr. Duryea's failure to make his income tax returns public? If you had been a New York voter (or if you actually were a New York voter), how much influence do you think this would have had (or actually did have) on your vote in the gubernatorial election? Please indicate this by making a mark at the appropriate point on the scale below. [The same scale was used as in the first question.]

When the scores for New Yorkers in general were tabulated, it was found that they had an arithmetic mean of 3.4, falling close to the middle of the influence scale. The scores for personal influence had a mean of only 2.26, indicating that, as predicted, the respondents evaluated the persuasive communication as having a greater effect on others than on themselves. Since the standard deviations of both distributions were huge, however, the replies given by each respondent were scored so as to ascertain how many individuals did in fact see the communication as having more influence on New Yorkers in general than on themselves. The results showed that about half the respondents perceived the effect on others to be greater than on the self, and that very few evaluated the effect as being greater on self than on others:

More influence on New Yorkers in general	48%
More influence on self	6
Same influence on public and on self	36
No answer/no opinion	9

Another experiment designed to confirm or disconfirm the third-person effect hypothesis was embodied in a small poll on mass media and socialization that was administered to 25 graduate students in the spring of 1981. This time, the effect of communications on self was asked about before an evaluation of the effect on others was requested. Respondents were asked how often their parents had read to them when they were small children, about how old they had been when they learned to distinguish television commercials from program content, and a few other personal questions. Then they were asked:

And how about attitudes toward commercial products? Did exposure to TV influence you to ask your parents to buy things you otherwise wouldn't have wanted?

The questionnaire went on to request observations about "other people, especially other people's children." One item was:

Does exposure to TV cause kids to ask their parents to buy them things they otherwise wouldn't want?

Again, the hypothesis seemed to be confirmed, although the small number of respondents and the distribution of replies, as shown in Table 1, leave adequate room for those who prefer to remain skeptical.

In discussing the results, several respondents pointed out, quite correctly, that the two questions had different wordings and that their comparability was further diminished by the fact that they dealt with different time periods. One noted that perhaps advertising techniques had improved during the past 20 years to such an extent that today's children are indeed more influenced by television commercials than those of the 1960s.

The hypothesis was tested also during the primary campaigns prior to the 1980 presidential election. A group of 25 adults, about equally divided between those under 30 and over 30, who were attending a lecture series at the Museum of Broadcasting in New York, were asked a number of questions regarding the upcoming election and the role of media in it. Again, the questions about the effects of com-

Table 1. Television's Ability to Make Children Ask Parents to Buy Commercial Products

	Self Influenced by TV as Child	*Children of Others Influenced by TV*
Quite a lot	32%	68%
Some	24	28
Not very much	20	4
Not at all	16	0
Didn't watch as a child	8	0

munications on self and other were widely separated in the questionnaire, and subsequent discussion showed that no respondent had become aware that a particular hypothesis was being tested. The question on self read as follows:

Let's assume that you are planning to vote in the upcoming presidential election. Would you say that your voting intention has been influenced by the results of the New Hampshire primary?

Two pages later, there were two additional questions about the effects of the New Hampshire primary on voters in general, although the phraseology made it possible, perhaps mistakenly, to interpret the questions as applying to other factors in additon to voting:

How much effect do you think the results of the New Hampshire primary will have on the political fortunes of Ronald Reagan?
And how about Jimmy Carter? How much effect will the results of the New Hampshire primary have on his political fortunes?

The results obtained for these three questions are shown in Table 2. Again, some comfort is given to supporters of the third-person effect hypothesis.

In this case, of course, the persuasive communications were not necessarily of a propagandistic nature, and more likely consisted of news reports. And the questions were not strictly comparable.

A fourth trial, again at the Museum of Broadcasting, followed the same general format but asked a different group of respondents to evaluate the effect on their own votes and the votes of people in general of charges that Ronald Reagan would pursue a "hawkish" foreign policy. About twice as many respondents felt that other people would be influenced more than they would be themselves.

Two further experiments, conducted in the fall of 1981 and the spring of 1982, showed results very similar to the ones already described.

Table 2. Effects of New Hampshire Primary on Personal Voting Intentions and on Political Fortunes of Two Major Candidates

	Will Influence Own Intention	*Will Influence Reagan's Fortunes*	*Will Influence Carter's Fortunes*
Quite a lot	0%	52%	32%
A little	24	24	48
Not at all	72	20	20
Not sure	4	4	0

Third-Person Effect in the Literature

Numerous scholars seem to have noted what has here been called the third-person effect, but none so far as I know has paused to comment on it. For example, the hypothesis seems to be supported by several studies of the "Roots" television series. First aired in January 1977, this eight-part dramatization of Alex Haley's story about his forebears' painful progress from Africa, through slavery, into the post-civil war period in the United States attracted over 130 million Americans to one or more episodes—the largest television audience for any program up to that time. Even before all episodes in the series had been shown, research organizations had started efforts to gauge its effects on the public. Several of these research projects were able to compare expected effects with observed effects. Most respondents predicted that the series would have substantial impact on the attitudes of both blacks and whites. The white reaction was expected to be increased tolerance and sympathy; blacks were expected to be angry and to show bitterness and hostility (Howard et al., 1978). When asked for their *own* reactions, however, substantial pluralities of both blacks and whites reported that a feeling of sadness was the principal effect of watching "Roots." Two researchers commented that, in general, the program did not have the widespread effects on racial attitudes attributed to it by observers (Hur and Robinson, 1978). An analyst who reviewed five of the "Roots" studies concluded that they provided little evidence of change in actual racial attitudes, even though these had been widely expected (Surlin, 1978).

Somewhat similar observations were made in the course of an investigation of American attitudes toward Jews during the period following World War II. It was hypothesized that the brutal persecution of European Jews by the Nazis and the strong support of the Allied cause by Jews everywhere might have caused Americans generally to look with greater favor on their Jewish fellow citizens. Two separate surveys by the Opinion Research Corporation in 1945 showed that this was not the case. Nearly four out of five respondents in both surveys said that the mass killings of Jews in Europe had caused no change in their attitudes toward Jews in the United States. When asked in one of the surveys, however, over half of the respondents said that they expected other people's attitudes to change, in either a favorable or an unfavorable direction (Stember, et al., 1966:142–43). Many influences in addition to the mass media were involved here, of course, but newspaper and radio were certainly the principal channels through which most people learned about the persecution of European Jewry.

A number of scholars have speculated that "experts" are particularly likely to overemphasize the effects of the media. A journalist turned political scientist attributes this tendency especially to students of politics and to communication theorists, explaining that this may be because they are isolated from the actual operation of media organizations (Diamond, 1978).

Another reason for misevaluation of media effects on the part of experts is suggested by a study of the role of the press in community conflict. In connection with an interview with an expert on a locally controversial issue the authors note: "This expert's view is typical, in the sense that it includes the belief that media affect people in general but not the individual who has specialized expertise" (Tichenor et al., 1980:130).

A similar observation was made in the course of a study of perception of public opinion by decision makers in the field of nuclear power. Many of these experts expressed the belief that the public was being misled by biased coverage of nuclear power in the mass media, since most people did not have access to good sources of technical information (Cohen, 1982).

In a sense, we are all experts on those subjects that matter to us, in that we have information not available to other people. This information may not be of a factual or technical nature; it may have to do with our own experiences, likes, and dislikes. Other people, we reason, do not know what we know. Therefore, they are more likely to be influenced by the media.

The literature contains fewer instances of cases in which people's behavior has been influenced by their expectations that the media would persuade others. Nevertheless, examples can be found, especially in connection with voter behavior. The third-person effect seems to have been at work in the 1978 gubernatorial primary election in Maryland, where "a reform candidate breezed by the incumbent and his principal challenger while neither of them was looking" (Hollander, 1979:405). According to repeated polls by two different organizations, only about 5 percent of the electorate expressed the intention of voting for this reform candidate, although he had an excellent reputation. Then he received the editorial endorsement of the *Baltimore Sun* and *Evening Sun.* A poll in progress when the endorsement was made showed the reform candidate as being the choice of 4 percent before the "Sunpapers" editorial stand and 11 percent afterwards. His performance in subsequent polls continued to improve and he won a narrow victory in the election. As a public opinion researcher in Baltimore put it, "The newspaper endorsement made Hughes a plausible candidate and the voters did the rest" (Hollander, 1979:407).

To interpret these data as supporting the third-person effect hypothesis one has to assume that the newspaper endorsements did not change the attitudes of many people toward Hughes; they rather changed expectations about the support he would receive from others. Individuals may have reasoned: "I am going to vote for him because the newspapers have probably convinced other people of something I already know—namely, that he is the best candidate—and therefore he has a good chance of winning."

Such an interpretation was given by the campaign manager of former mayor Carl Stokes of Cleveland, who mentioned at a Columbia University seminar on public communication that the endorsement by the Cleveland *Plain Dealer* was one of the major reasons for Stokes' victory in the 1967 mayoralty race.

"Do you think the *Plain Dealer*'s support really changed many people's opinions," he was asked.

"I don't think it changed any," was the reply. "But it convinced some individuals and organizations that he had a chance; so they started sending in campaign contributions."

A similar observation about campaign contributions was made by the press secretary of Senator Fred Harris, who ran for the Democratic nomination in the primaries prior to the 1976 presidential election:

> But in order to raise that kind of money dispersed among twenty states, then you need national media exposure. You need it because people do judge by national media exposure as to whether the campaign is serious or not and, believe me, they hesitate before they give money. . . . They're going to wait until they see Fred's smiling face on national television (quoted in Arterton, 1978:9).

It is probable that advertisers and marketers are aware of the action-inducing potential of the third-person effect, although I have not noted references to this in the research literature. The frequently used appeal, "Buy yours while the supply lasts," certainly suggests that others will be persuaded by the advertising and that one had therefore better make a purchase promptly.

Relationships to Other Phenomena

Media bias is frequently perceived in situations where it is clearly absent or where it is present to a very limited extent. For example, in the 1972 presidential campaign, many of those who preferred McGovern thought their newspaper was giving more attention to Nixon; and many who were for Nixon thought McGovern was receiving more exposure in the same medium. The same judgments were made with regard to television news, although less frequently. Yet analysis of the media in question showed that they were giving fairly evenhanded treatment to the two major candidates (Mendelsohn and O'Keefe, 1976:148, 150).

A somewhat similar observation was made in the study of perceptions of public opinion by decision makers in the nuclear energy sector that was referred to above. The decision makers frequently complained that their field of operation received negative and sensational coverage by the mass media, and that this was a major reason why many people opposed nuclear power. At the same time, opponents of nuclear power showed themselves to be equally dissatisfied with news coverage in this area, and accused the media of an establishment bias (Cohen, 1982).

One possible explanation for the fact that people on both sides of an issue can see the media as biased against their own point of view is that each observer assumes a disproportionate effect will be achieved by arguments or facts supporting the "wrong" side of the issue. Others (the third persons), the observer reasons, will be unduly impressed by these facts or arguments; they do not have the information that enables me to form a correct opinion. It is probable that, from the point of view of partisans, balanced media presentation would require a sharp tilt toward the "correct" side of the issue. This would compensate for the intellectual frailty of third persons and would, according to a partisan, ensure that the media achieved a truly balanced presentation.

But, if the third-person effect hypothesis is correct, why are not the facts and arguments on the "correct" side as well as the "wrong" side seen as having a disproportionate effect on others? Perhaps the material on the "correct" side is not seen as persuasive at all; it is merely a statement of the obvious and therefore cannot be expected to have an impact on attitudes.

Pluralistic ignorance, and the misperception of others' attitudes in general, may also involve the third-person effect, at least in some cases. If individuals assume that they are virtually alone in holding particular attitudes and expectations, not knowing that many others privately share them (Merton, 1968:431), it may be because they assume others have been brainwashed by the mass media. Indeed, the tendency to perceive the media as being biased toward the "wrong" side of an issue, combined with the tendency to impute persuasiveness to the media insofar as others are concerned, creates a strong presumption that the attitudes of other people on any controversial issue that is in the focus of public attention will be widely misperceived.

Empirical studies of pluralistic ignorance of which I am aware do *not* offer much support for the above proposition. But neither do they disconfirm it with any vigor. These studies have not treated public communication as a major variable to be built into their research designs (for example, Schanck, 1932 and 1938; Colombotos et al., 1975; Fields and Schuman, 1976; O'Gorman and Garry, 1976). Schanck does, however, remark in connection with one controversy in Elm Hollow that "continuous advocacy of a position by a minority leads them (the majority) to a belief that this stand may be fairly universal in their group" (Schanck, 1938:93).

To test the notion that the third-person effect plays a part in the creation of pluralistic ignorance one could, for example, determine whether misperception of others' attitudes is more likely to occur on issues that have been extensively discussed in the mass media than on issues that are discussed mainly in primary groups. The data presented by Fields and Schuman suggest that this might well be the case, in that pluralistic ignorance appears to be greater in regard to issues such as race relations (discussed widely in the media) than in regard to issues involving ethics or morals (discussed more in primary groups).

It is also possible that public communication diminishes misperception of others' attitudes among people in part of the media audience while it increases misperception among some. In this connection, the concept of reference groups may prove useful in explaining the third-person effect. Are people "like me" or "different from me" seen as being more affected by persuasive messages? Or is the degree of similarity not a relevant factor? If perceived congruity of others' attitudes and values with one's own is a factor in the selection of normative reference groups (Singer, 1981:73), then one would expect there to be little exaggeration in the perceived impact of a communication on members of such groups. On the other hand, the importance of not overlooking a possible change in attitude on the part of a significant other might make one assume, conservatively, that some reference group members had indeed been affected. There is plenty of room for research and speculation.

The third-person effect is probably involved in the "spiral of silence" which, according to a recent theory about the formation of public opinion, leads those on one side of an issue to express their opinions with more and more volume and confidence, while those on the other side of the issue tend to fall silent (Noelle-Neumann, 1980). In particular, exaggerated perceptions of the effects of mass media election propaganda on others would help to explain the situations in which polls show that respondents think Party A will win an election even though a majority of the respondents retain their intention of voting for Party B. Each person may reason: I haven't been influenced by this widely publicized nonsense, but *they* probably have been.

Thus, in both the 1965 and 1972 election campaigns in West Germany, expectations as to which of the major parties would win the election changed by as much as 15 percentage points during the months prior to election day, while at the same time voting intentions remained fairly stable (Noelle-Neumann, 1980:15–17). At the last minute, again consistent with the third-person effect hypothesis, undecided voters opted disproportionately in favor of the party which seemed to be attracting the greater number of supporters. The reasoning of at least some of these late deciders was probably along the following lines: I don't find much difference between the parties, but the fact that others seem to be persuaded by the arguments or image of Party A probably means that this is the better party. A bandwagon effect was created.

As in the case of observed media bias, the question arises why the impact of Party B's propaganda is not exaggerated as much as that of Party A's propaganda. Perhaps there is simply more of the latter. This was the case with some of the West German elections that were studied. But it seems likely that other factors, presently unknown, interact with the third-person effect to produce the observed result.

The Third-Person Effect in Our Lives

Fluctuations in the stock market are not infrequently accounted for by reference to rumors or news reports—perhaps that a subcommittee of the House of Representatives is considering a tax on widgets or that the Ambassadors from Israel and an unnamed Arab state have been seen sharing a taxi from Kennedy Airport to the United Nations headquarters. The reasoning seems to be that these reports will cause others to sell (or buy) certain categories of shares; therefore I will sell (or buy) in order to anticipate their action.

In times when supplies of consumer goods are irregular, there are always some people who will rush to the stores the moment they hear reports of any possible shortage. If you ask them why, the answer is likely to be that they are concerned about the effects of these reports on other people. They want to stock up before the hoarders remove all goods from the shelves.

When news stories about the possibly dangerous effects of aerosol on the earth's atmosphere began to appear, according to an item in the *New York Times* (September 16, 1975), manufacturers of products sold in aerosol cans changed quickly to spray and squeeze containers. Of course, there could have been a number of explanations for such behavior (expectations of government regulations, the lower cost of squeeze containers, etc.), but one possibility is that manufacturers expected stories about the dangers of fluorocarbon propellants to turn the public against aerosol cans and were thus providing another example of the third-person effect at work.

The phenomenon of censorship offers what is perhaps the most interesting field for speculation about the role of the third-person effect. Insofar as faith and morals are concerned, at least, it is difficult to find a censor who will admit to having been adversely affected by the information whose dissemination is to be prohibited. Even the censor's friends are usually safe from pollution. It is the general public that must be protected. Or else, it is youthful members of the general public, or those with impressionable minds. When Maryland's State Board of Censors, which had been filtering smut from motion pictures since 1916, was finally allowed to die in June 1981, some of its members issued dire forecasts about the future morals of Maryland and the nation (*New York Times,* June 29, 1981). Yet the censors themselves had apparently emerged unscathed. One of them stated that over the course of 21 years she had "looked at more naked bodies than 50,000 doctors," but the effect of this experience was apparently more on her diet than on her morals. "I had to stop eating a lot of food because of what they do with it in these movies," she is quoted as having told the Maryland Legislature.

Throughout history, heretical doctrines and political dissidence have aroused concern, sometimes terror, among priests and potentates. How much of this apprehension and the resulting repression was due to the third-person effect? It certainly must have played a role, and probably has accounted for a grisly percentage of the world's suffering and horror. Exaggerated expectations about the effects of dissident communications have caused countless people to be incarcerated, tortured, and killed. Even today, prisons in authoritarian and totalitarian countries contain people whose crime is alleged to be "propaganda against the state," or "spreading destructive rumors."

Why are exaggerated expectations about the effects of communications on others so common? Do they occur in response to all categories of persuasive communications, or only certain categories? Or, is it possible that we do not overestimate effects on others so much as we underestimate effects on ourselves?

References

Arterton, F. Christopher
1978 "Campaign organizations confront the media-political environment." In James

David Barber (ed.), Race for the Presidency. Englewood Cliffs, N.J.: Prentice-Hall.
Cohen, Robert L.
1982 "The perception and evaluation of public opinion by decision makers: civilian nuclear power in the United States." Ph.D. dissertation, Columbia University.
Colombotos, John, Corrinne Kirchner, and Michael Millman
1975 "Physicians view national health insurance." Medical Care 13:369–96.
Davison, W. Phillips
1957 "The mass media in West German political life." In Hans Speier and W. P. Davison, eds., West German Leadership and Foreign Policy. Evanston, Ill.: Row Peterson.
Diamond, Edwin
1978 Good News, Bad News. Cambridge, Mass.: MIT Press.
Fields, James M., and Howard Schuman
1976 "Public beliefs about beliefs of the public." Public Opinion Quarterly 40:427–49.
Hollander, Sidney
1979 "On the strength of a newspaper endorsement." Public Opinion Quarterly 43:405–7.
Howard, John, George Rothbart, and Lee Sloan
1978 "The response to 'Roots': a national survey." Journal of Broadcasting 22:279–88.
Hur, Kenneth K., and John P. Robinson
1978 "The social impact of 'Roots'." Journalism Quarterly 55:19–24.
Isely, Jeter A., and Philip A. Crowl
1951 The U.S. Marines and Amphibious War: Its Theory and Its Practice in the Pacific. Princeton, N.J.: Princeton University Press.
Lazarsfeld, Paul F., Bernard Berelson, and Hazel Gaudet
1944 The People's Choice. New York: Duell, Sloan & Pearce.
Lerner, Daniel
1949 Sykewar: Psychological Warfare Against Germany, D-Day to VE-Day. New York: George W. Stewart.
Mendelsohn, Harold, and Garrett J. O'Keefe
1976 The People Choose a President. New York: Praeger.
Merton, Robert K.
1968 Social Theory and Social Structure. New York: Free Press.
Noelle-Neumann, Elisabeth
1980 Die Schweigespirale. München and Zürich: Piper Verlag.
O'Gorman, Hubert, and Stephen L. Garry
1976 "Pluralistic ignorance—a replication and extension." Public Opinion Quarterly 40:449–58.
Schanck, Richard L.
1932 "The community and its groups and institutions." Psychological Monographs 43, No. 2.
1938 "Test-tube for public opinion: a rural community." Public Opinion Quarterly 2:90–95.
Singer, Eleanor
1981 "Reference groups and social evaluations." In Morris Rosenberg and Ralph H. Turner (eds.), Social Psychology: Sociological Perspectives. New York: Basic Books.
Stember, Charles Herbert, et. al.
1966 Jews in the Mind of America. New York: Basic Books.
Surlin, Stuart U.
1978 "'Roots' research: a summary of findings." Journal of Broadcasting 22:309–20.
Tichenor, Phillip J., George A. Donohue, and Clarice N. Olien.
1980 Community Conflict and the Press. Beverly Hills, Calif.: Sage.

27

CRITICAL MASS COMMUNICATIONS RESEARCH AND MEDIA EFFECTS
The Problem of the Disappearing Audience

Fred Fejes

As is evident from even a quick glance at the major research approaches over the last thirty years, the major focus of traditional mainstream communication research has been on media effects. Fueled by popular concern and financed by private and public monies, effects research has almost become synonymous with mass communication research. In the minds of many, including some communication scholars, the major—if not only—significant question, that communication research should address is what effect do the media have on the audience. After all, it is the presumed power of the media to capture and sway the hearts, minds and behavior of the national public that account for both the fear and anxiety, and the hope and excitement, with which the media are regarded.

Within the community of American communication scholars, the issue of effects has been most often formulated in terms of behaviorist interpretations of human nature and society. Drawing upon the dominant behaviorist ideas in psychology, sociology, political science and their hybrids, communication researchers generally approach the study of effects utilizing some type of stimulus-response model of human behavior and media impact. Among individual researchers approaches differ greatly. Nonetheless the goal of such study is to produce some science-like knowledge about the rôle of the media in human affairs. And this science-like knowledge more likely than not is cast in a behaviorist mold.

While a behaviorist focus on media effects still dominates American research, there has emerged recently a new line of communications inquiry and work. This new approach, often termed the critical communications perspective, seeks to shift sharply the context of the discussion and research about the relations among the media, society and the individual. In contrast to the behaviorist orientation of mainstream communications research, critical research seeks to examine the relationship among media, communications and social power.[1] Also in contrast to traditional American research, much of the impetus for this new research perspective comes from researchers in Great Britain and on the Continent. Although it is difficult to generalize or define precisely the character of this new school of thought, it is evident that researchers with this perspective locate their work and debates within the broad tradition of a Marxist critique of industrialized capitalist societies. Drawing upon fields of scholarship and research as diverse as sociology, economics, semiotics, political philosophy, literary studies, psychology and history, critical researchers seek to examine the rôle the media play in maintaining the class

From Fred Fejes, "Critical Mass Communications Research and Media Effects: The Problem of the Disappearing Audience," *Media, Culture and Society*, Vol. 6, No. 3 (July 1984), pp. 219-232.

stratified societies of the Western capitalist world. Rejecting as forms of self-delusion the claims of value-neutrality of American behaviorist research, researchers in the critical school explicitly acknowledge the Marxist based assumptions about society and humankind built into their research. These scholars believe that the political and epistemological commitments that underlie their work are as much open to examination and debate as their research methods and conclusions.

While this new critical perspective encompasses a wide variety of theoretical and empirical concerns and approaches, following Curran, Gurevitch and Woollacott (1982), it is possible to define three major research approaches within it. The first, the structuralist approach to media analysis, draws upon ideas found in linguistics, anthropology, semiotics and psychoanalysis. The major goal has been the study of the system and processes of signification and representation in the media. Empirical structuralist research focuses on an analysis of media texts such as films, television programs, advertisements and so forth. With an Althusserian notion of ideology that sees ideology less as a simple, if somewhat distorted, reflection of the economic base and more as an optic through which one frames the world, structuralist research seeks to examine the implicit catagories of thought in media texts through which the individual experiences the world.

The second major critical approach, the political economy approach focuses upon the economic structure and processes of media production (Murdock and Golding, 1977). The major thrust of this research has been the study of the trend toward increasing monopolization and concentration of control within the media industries. Relying on a more classic notion of ideology utilizing a base and superstructure model, the political economy approach sees the media producing and disseminating a false consciousness which legitimates the class interests of those who own and control the media. While this is seen as the media's ultimate effect, most of the research taking this approach concentrates on an investigation of the structures of control within the media.

The third critical perspective, cultural studies, is similar to the structural approach in that it focuses on the media message. However, in contrast to the autonomy the structuralist approach ascribes to such messages, the cultural approach assumes that media content and impact are shaped by the societal environment in which media messages are produced and received (Hall, 1980).

The cultural approach also rejects the simple base-superstructure division by which political economy scholars explain cultural phenomena. This approach argues that culture is a far more complex dialectic between social being and social consciousness than the metaphor of base-superstructure would allow. In the media message one sees an important expression of this dialectic.

Taken together these critical perspectives constitute a radical departure from traditional American communications research. The major differences between the two streams of research extend from basic assumptions about the nature and purpose of the research enterprise to methods, and finally to the concepts imbedded in scholarly discourse. In the behaviorist tradition such concepts such as ideology, and hegemony are regarded as meaningless if not inherently polemical and anti-scientific while in the critical tradition they are central. Historically, the behaviorist research tradition has been mainly concerned with the effects of the media. The critical perspective, on the other hand, focuses either on the control and production of media messages or their content in the context of examining how the media develop a specific ideology that supports a class-dominated society.

One can go to great lengths in detailing and discussing the differences between the behaviorist and critical traditions. Nonetheless one is struck with the fact that the major element underlying traditional behaviorist research—a concern with effects—seems to play such a minor rôle in critical research. A number of explanations can be offered for this situation. Critical researchers can argue that by focusing on control, production and the content of media messages, they are examining aspects of the media process overlooked by behaviorist researchers. In slighting the issue of effects, they are only reciprocating the behaviorist's long-standing neglect of media structure. Moreover casting their research in a Marxist context of power and ideology, they are raising issues about the relations between media and society that are rarely present in more traditional research. According to this view, a concern with effects has a very low priority on the theoretical and research agenda.

Another possible reason for the lack of attention to effects is that critical research is still at an early stage of development. The conceptual and theoretical framework is still being articulated. For example, given the major differences in the notion of ideology among the structuralist, political economy and culturalist approaches, critical research is as yet unable to advance upon the terrain of effects. Only when there emerges a theoretical consensus about the nature of ideology, and thus the character of critical communications research, can the whole issue of effects be addressed.

Another set of explanations revolve around the fact that, given the theoretical assumptions and orientation of critical research, the notion of effects, as generally conceived, is not so much wrong-headed as irrelevant. In critical research, to the extent that effects are dealt with at all, they are subsumed under the more general heading of ideology and hegemony. The impact of the media on the audience is seen in terms of creating and maintaining a hegemonic order. The concepts of ideology and hegemony, much like the Marxist notion of alienation, are structural concepts that cannot be easily translated into analytical notions. They cannot be simply operationalized in terms of discrete variables open to ordinal or higher levels of measurement. Moreover, if somehow overcoming these difficulties, one attempts to study the ideological effects of the media on the audience, one is faced with a predicament. As Bennett notes, the operations of ideology are not inherently invisible.

> . . . (T)heir invisibility is a condition of their effectiveness. They have to be *made* visible (in order to be studied). It therefore follows that the proposition that the media are influential in proposing certain ideologically derived definitions of reality is one that cannot be dependent for its validation solely upon the subjective reports of those whose consciousness is said to be produced, without their being aware of it, by this process. It is a proposition that would automatically lose its theoretical power were it to be operationalized in this way. (1982b: 298)

Finally critical researchers can argue that the lack of attention to effects is more apparent than real. There are examples, although not very many, of researchers working within the critical perspective using audience response data in examining audience adaptation of media-relayed ideologies (Hartman, 1979; Morley, 1980). Moreover, it can be argued that the critical researchers do focus on effects, but different kinds of effects. Studies such as Cohen's *Folk Devils and Moral Panics: The Creation of the Mods and Rockers* (1973) and Hall *et al.*'s *Policing the Crisis* (1978), for example, examine the rôle the media play in an 'amplification spiral' or a 'signification spiral' in which a particular incident or phenomenon comes to be associated through the media with a larger problem of social crisis. As noted by Hall *et al.* in their analysis of the British media's presentation of mugging, other institutions such as the police and the courts are mobilized by the media and in turn act upon the media, expanding the scope of the original phenomenon and increasing the importance and the intensity of the meanings ascribed to it by the media. The end effect in general is a re-enforcement and expansion of the existing institutional means of social control and a clearer definition of deviant and acceptable behavior. In this case the effect is seen as being reciprocal between the media and the other institutions in society as they create a spiral of signification that in turn reinforces the existing social and political order (Bennett, 1982b).

Aside from having an effect on institutions, the media can be seen as having a major effect on social collectivities and social movements. Gitlin's (1980) study of the interaction between the media and the American New Left is a very good example of how the notion of effects can be conceptualized in a manner different from that of traditional behaviorist research.

All of these reasons may be advanced to explain why critical communication research does not focus on effects as traditionally conceived. And all of these reasons make a certain amount of sense. Yet one cannot help but wonder whether, in the long run, the tendency against looking at traditional audience-centered notions of effects will ultimately prove debilitating to the optimum development of a critical perspective.

There is an assumption in critical research that the impact of the media is powerful. In some ways, perhaps, the situation of critical research is analogous to research on propaganda conducted by Lasswell and others, before and during World War II. Both assume the media are powerful. Thus the focus is away from an analysis of the media effect and more toward an analysis of message content and, in the case of critical research, message production. Yet there is a danger that for critical communications research, as with propaganda research, the audience will be regarded as passive. As more and more research is focused towards message content and production, the audience will become more and more invisible in the theory and research of critical scholars. For critical communications research, there is a distinct danger of a disappearing audience.

For example in a discussion about the reality defining rôle of the media as conceived by critical researchers, Bennett (1982b) argues that there is often a duality present in such conceptions. There is a 'media' reality and the 'real' reality of the world which the media interprets. According to Bennett this leads to one seeing 'media' reality primarily as a distortion of 'real' reality. This view de-emphasizes the complex dialectic of signification that occurs in the process of the production of the media message. Whether one accepts Bennett's point or finds the notion of duality more compatible, one is struck by how another reality, the reality of the audience, is downplayed. The style, manner and rules by which the audience incorporate, accommodate, alter or reject media reality as part of their own everyday reality are overlooked. If one goal of critical communications research is to develop a politics of the media where popular struggle over the production and character of media presentations is developed, it is quite odd that so little attention is paid to the audience and their relation to the media.

Most critical researchers have rejected most if not all of the behavioral tradition of effects research as either inherently uninteresting and/or biased in terms of the liberal pluralist assumptions built into it. Very few can deny that much of such research is marked by a dearth of stimulating questions, ideas or prose; or that neo-Marxist critique of behaviorism in the social sciences applies with special vigor to behaviorism in communication research.

However, a total and blanket rejection by critical scholars of the behaviorist tradition of effects research is hasty and ill advised. If critical researchers admit the need to develop some conception of the audience and media impact on the audience, they will at some point have to confront the body of traditional effects research. Most likely such a confrontation will assume the form of a thorough-going critique of such research. Ideally critical researchers will learn from this what the failings of such research were and such mistakes will not be repeated again in critical research.

However, there is another reason critical researchers should investigate traditional behavioral effects research. The traditional field of effects research may not be totally devoid of ideas or insights helpful to critical communication scholars. Current mainstream research is beginning to concentrate more and more on the learning and informational effects of the media as opposed to individual persuasive effects. There is a growing realization that what has been regarded in the past as the effects of the media are more truthfully to be seen as the effects of the specific manner in which production and distribution of media messages are organized (Hirsch, 1978). Also current research is beginning to develop a view of the media as more powerful than a previous limited effects model would allow. Thus, it seems that mainstream research is becoming more relevant to some of the issues and concerns of critical communications research. If critical researchers want to develop a conception and analysis of the audience and its relation to the media, the field of traditional research should not be dismissed out of hand.

Not all types of mainstream research are of equal value or use to critical research. Theories and models of media effect developed in the context of psychological models tend to have little relevance at this point for critical scholars. Such models, because of their focus on individual psychological level phenomena, often tend to ignore the larger social and historical environment in which the individual exists and in which media messages are produced. Such models tend to be ahistorical, seeking to define universal traits about human behavior. Moreover, they generally neglect the dimension of power that is central to a critical approach.

Mainstream models that are based on sociological theory are of more relevance as they deal with media impact in a larger social context. Over the last ten years four sociological-based models of media impact in particular have been developed that are germane to the concerns of critical research. These are the agenda setting, the spiral of silence, the knowledge gap and the media dependency models. As McQuail and Windahl (1981, pp. 60-61) have noted, these models view effects as long-term and indirect. They differ from other behavioral models as they center on such issues as the informal learning of social rôles; the tendency of the media to convey implicit ideology, the formation of the climate of opinion; the differential of knowledge in society; and long term changes in culture, institutions and social structure. In the remainder of this paper these four models will be discussed both in order to present their basic and essential features and to outline their relevance to critical communications research. It is not argued that these models be accepted fully and at face value. As shall be evident in the discussion, they have many deficiencies. Nonetheless critical researchers will find some elements of these models helpful to their thinking about audiences and media impact.

Some critical researchers (cf. Gitlin, 1978) have noted that the agenda setting model presents a promising if still somewhat narrow approach to a consideration of media effects. The basic idea behind the model is that the media develop agendas for the audience (McCombs, 1981). The media select from a wide range of possible issues and topics and, by giving them differential attention and emphasis, generally measured in terms of volume and frequency of media space or time, define for the audience the relative importance of each. The model is tested by comparing the emphasis and attention the media give to certain issues with the emphasis and attention the audience give to the same issues. The impact of the media, then, is not what it tells people to think, but what it tells people to think about. Figure 1 summarizes the model.

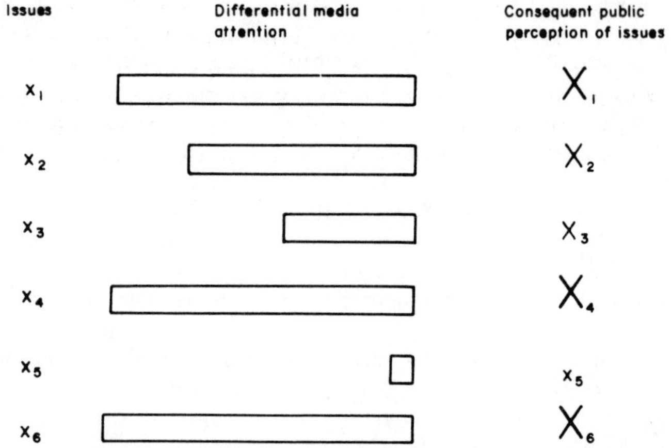

Issues | Differential media attention | Consequent public perception of issues

X_1 X_1
X_2 X_2
X_3 X_3
X_4 X_4
X_5 X_5
X_6 X_6

Figure 1. The agenda-setting model; matters given most attention in the media will be perceived as the most important (McQuail and Windahl, 1981)

While the agenda setting model has been influential within the mainstream American tradition, there has been an ongoing debate about the empirical validity of studies designed to test it. (Becker, 1982). Nonetheless, critical researchers should note that the agenda-setting model and research represent one attempt to examine the impact symbolic media realities have on the audience. The emphasis is on how the media shape the larger cultural environment of the audience, not only in terms of the issues they raise, but also, and equally important, in terms of the issues or topics they de-emphasize or ignore. Yet the agenda-setting model represents a crude attempt to explore media realities. The model says little about the actual symbolic realities portrayed by the media. It is very insensitive to the specific content and the nuances of the cultural meanings created. Yet the ability to demonstrate, if only in a small and crude way, the manner in which the audience accepts the symbolic universe created by the media should not be dismissed by critical researchers. In this sense the agenda-setting model touches some of the central concerns of critical research.

The spiral of silence model developed by the West German media sociologist Elizabeth Noelle-Neumann (1974, 1980) is in some ways the negative mirror image of the agenda setting model in that it centers on the ability of the media to remove from public view and discussion certain issues and topics. This model is based on the assumption that individuals strive to avoid isolation by avoiding holding attitudes, beliefs or opinions not held by the majority in the society. Individuals scan the environment to see what views are held by the majority or are gaining strength and what views are in the minority or are declining. One is more likely to express one's views if they are perceived to be consistent with the majority. On the other hand, if they are perceived to be in the minority, one is more likely to suppress them. The perception of the dominance of one set of views often has little relation to whether or not a majority of people actually have such views. Perceived majority opinions are many times only held by a minority. Nonetheless the perception that one set of views are in the majority sets off a spiraling process by which people who hold opposing views begin to become silent and the perceived majority view is established as the actual prevailing one. The spiral of silence develops as people look to the media for prevailing definitions of reality. Because of the monopoly nature of the media and the inherent routines of media production, there is a high degree of agreement or consonance among the media as to which views of reality to present. While interpersonal communication also provides information, the media tend to be the major factor. Figure 2 summarizes the model.

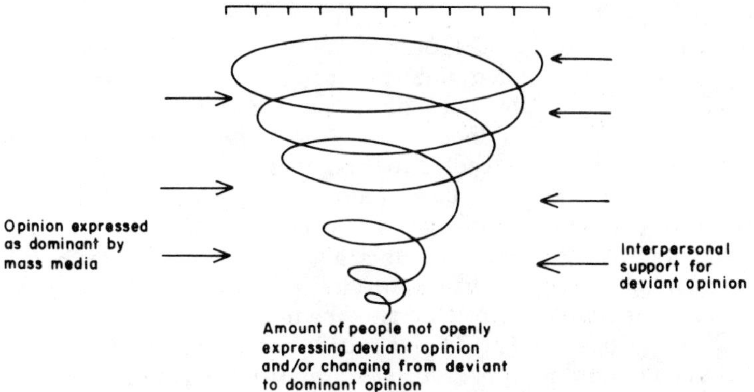

Figure 2. An example of a spiral of silence; mass media expressing dominant opinion together with an increasing lack of interpersonal support for deviant views bring about a spiral of silence, with an increasing number of individuals either expressing the dominant opinion or failing to express deviant ones (after Noelle-Neumann, 1974) (McQuail and Windahl, 1981)

While some have noted the difficulties inherent in operationalizing and testing this model fully (McQuail and Windahl, 1981), some of its key elements have received empirical support (Taylor, 1982). This model is particularly provocative in the way it shows how the media operate to legitimate or de-legitimate certain symbolic realities. Moreover, it can be useful in talking about past phenomena that have emerged as central to an understanding of the rôle of media in culture and society. For example, a major concern of the Frankfurt School theorists, an influential source of ideas for critical research, was to understand how the Nazis were able to take control of German society and cultural life with so little opposition. Their explanation was based on notions of mass society (Bennett, 1982a). This model offers an alternative understanding of how the media could operate to assist in the acquiescence by an entire society of a political and cultural order seemingly at odds with its history and tradition. The example of Nazi Germany was the ultimate case. There was total control of the media and so the spiral of silence operated effectively. Neumann's explanation is far more interesting and useful for a wide range of cases than that provided by the Frankfurt School. The spiral of silence does not imply a mass society view of the relations between the human individual, society and the media. Room is left not only for the rôle of interpersonal structure and communication, but also for the possibility of individuals and groups to contest the power of the media. Not expressing one's view because it is not perceived to be in the majority does not necessarily mean one's view is changed. Minority or oppositional views may be kept alive in interpersonal settings where social support exists for a view.

Dramatic changes in public opinion are due less to the persuasive or conversion effects of the media and more to the fact that the spiral of silence has been broken. Opinions held by the majority but perceived to be in the minority are suddenly recognized to be in the majority. Suddenly they emerge and are expressed (Katz, 1981). This suggests that aside from the world of expressed public opinion there exists a subterranean universe of attitudes, views and opinions that are held in check by the power of the media and that stand in opposition to the perceived majority position. A breakdown in the power of the media to present and enforce only one set of views would presumably bring to fore attitudes, views and opinions long suppressed.

As with the agenda-setting model, the spiral of silence model is insensitive to the complexities involved in an understanding of media content. It treats the issues of media signification and representation in a crude way. In this sense it is incomplete. Nonetheless, this model, along with the agenda-setting model provides a useful way for critical scholars to think about media impact. While being aware of the vast differences in language and concepts between the behavioral and critical traditions, one perhaps can suggest that both the agenda-setting and the spiral of silence models can be one way, albeit a rough way, of studying empirically the ideological impact of the media on the audience.

The knowledge-gap model focuses on another area of media impact (Tichenor, Donohue, Olien, 1970; Tichenor, 1982). Utilizing a social systems perspective, this model examines the relationships between media impact and social power in terms of the distribution of media information among various social classes. The basic idea behind the model is that 'as the infusion of mass media information into a social system increases, segments of the population with higher socio-economic status tend to acquire this information at a faster rate than the lower socio-economic segments, so that the gap in knowledge between the segments tend to increase rather than decrease (Tichenor, 1982, p. 81)'. The media act not only to maintain inequalities in the class structure, but to increase and amplify them. Lower classes remain information poor or even become poorer in a relative sense, while higher social class segments become information richer. This model is summarized in Figure 3.

In studies on this model, educational level is generally used as the index of class status. Empirical research conducted both in industrialized and Third World societies tend to support the basic 'tenets of this model' (Dervin, 1980). What has occupied much recent research is a search for the conditions under which the knowledge gap does not exist or is closed. One major condition that seems to inhibit the knowledge gap dynamic is the interest and motivation on the part of lower social classes to learn about a specific issue that is of concern to them or the entire community (Ettema and Kline, 1977; Genova and Greenberg, 1979).

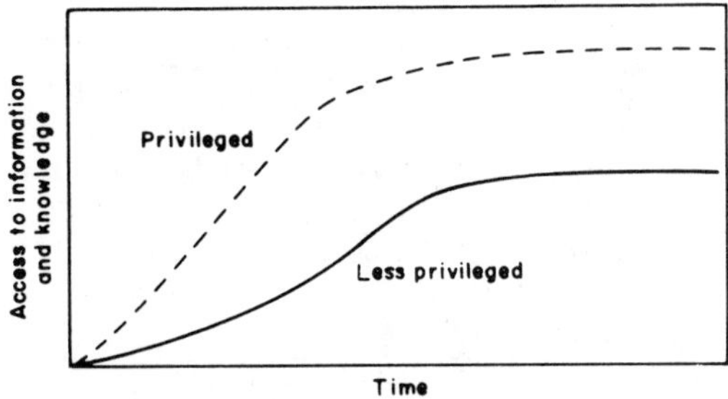

Figure 3. Non-closing information gap (after Thunberg *et al.*, 1979) (McQuail and Windahl, 1981)

Another condition that is in some ways related to interest is social conflict. The greater the conflict surrounding a certain issue, the smaller the knowledge gap (Donahue, Olien and Tichenor, 1974).

The knowledge-gap model presents some insights into the manner the media can act to strengthen the political and economic structure of class-stratified capitalist societies. In terms of a simple base-superstructure model, the knowledge gap demonstrates that the inequalities inherent in the realm of the economic base are reproduced in the sphere of culture. Marx's notion of the increasing immiseration of the working class under capitalism can be extended to the area of the media. In this sense this model provides a powerful critique of the argument that increasing the power and scope of the media provides benefits to all segments of society (McQuail and Windahl, 1981). More importantly the idea that the gap can be lessened by conflict surrounding an issue suggests that conflict plays a constructive rôle in the process of social change. The knowledge-gap model can present a starting point for critical researchers to consider some of the larger social consequences of the media in a class-stratified society.

The final model to be considered, the dependency model of media effects, is an example of an extremely promising approach whose possibilities so far have not been realized, or even appreciated by traditional mainstream research. Formulated by Ball-Rokeach and DeFleur (1976, 1982) the dependency model views audience effects in the context of the larger social structure in which the media and the audience exist. It attempts to explain the interaction between audience, media systems and the larger societal system. As societies become more complex, individuals become more dependent on the media for information about, and orientation to the larger social world. The type and degree of dependency vary, depending in large part on the structural conditions of society and the degree to which society is in a condition of change, conflict or instability. Audience dependency on media information, and thus the type and intensity of effect (cognitive, affective and behavioral) increases as the level of structural conflict and change increases. Likewise the rôle of the mass media will vary in quantity, diversity, reliability and authority according to societal conditions. The model is summarized in Figure 4.

In its basic outline, the dependency model seeks to explain variance in media effects in terms of variances in the historical conditions of a society and its media. This relationship leads to a number of interesting consequences. First, the effects of the media are not strictly comparable across time or across societies because the

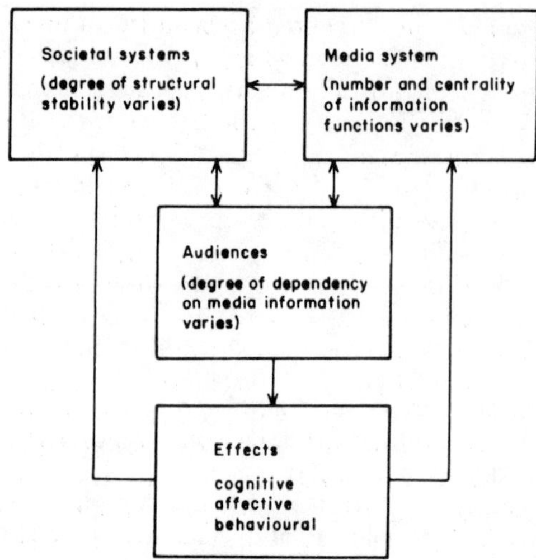

Figure 4. Ball-Rokeach and DeFleur's dependency model, showing the interdependence between society, mass media, audience and effects (after Ball-Rokeach and DeFleur, 1976) (McQuail and Windahl, 1981)

structural conditions necessarily vary. This allows for a consideration of a number of different effects. Ball-Rokeach and DeFleur, drawing upon mainstream communications research, list a number of different cognitive, affective and behavioral effects that the media can produce under different conditions. Second, the model suggests that audience effects may lead in turn to effects on the social system and institutions. A continual series of war combat footage on the nightly news, such as occurred during the Vietnam War, could lead to opposition to the fighting that then changes the structure of foreign policy making in the government. Third, the model emphasizes the factor of social stability and instability as major conditions of the type and strength of media effect. Ball-Rokeach and DeFleur are suggesting here that the important issue is not one of powerful media effects versus limited effects. Rather it is the societal conditions that determine the power and type of media effects. Finally, this model strongly posits the need for analysis of societal condition in relation to the media and the audience. If the emphasis is on the inter-relationship among social structure, the media and the audience, there is thus the need to map out these inter-relationships. This requires that an understanding of the media be integrated with an understanding of political theory, political sociology and history. The dependency model suggests an analysis of the media and the audience that requires placing both in a larger societal context.

As is evident, the dependency model comes close to the orientation and some of the concerns of critical communication research. Unfortunately, research based on the dependency model has yet to realize any of its interesting possibilities for understanding the relations among media, society and audience. While the model paints large the picture of media-society relations, the related research has focused primarily on the dependency relations between audience and media. Empirical research based on this model uses it more as an 'audience centered' model of effects (Becker and Whitney, 1980; Nigg 1982). Its larger societal and historical implications have generally been ignored by mainstream researchers. Nonetheless it remains a suggestive set of ideas on which critical researchers could follow up.

The four models of media impact on audiences suggest that critical researchers need not necessarily reject all aspects of the behaviorist tradition. On the other hand one should not overestimate the value of these models or suggest that they can replace the many other avenues of research found in critical communications studies. While these models offer some insight and ideas about audience effects and the power of the media, one can easily find major deficiencies in each. As a whole the models offer little about the social and historical context of the control and production of media messages. If agenda setting is one demonstrable effect of the media, then the next logical question should be what is the process by which the media's agenda is formulated in the first place. This raises issues of the organizational structure of the media, the rôle of professionalism, the larger structure of control of the media such as ownership, and the media's relationship to other social and political institutions, all of which mainstream research on agenda setting ignores. If the media play a central rôle in a spiral of silence, by what process and under what conditions is the uniformity or consonance of the media's messages created and maintained? This again raises the question of media production and control. The knowledge gap and dependency models are likewise mute about media production and its relation to a larger societal environment.

Another major deficiency of these models are their assumptions and treatment of the media messages. As noted earlier these models conceive of media messages in a simple way, as discrete measurable units of information transmitted to receivers. To a critical researcher whose aim is an analysis of media messages as a system of representation and signification, this view of media content would be regarded as crude. These models are not alive to the notion of media messages as cultural and ideological phenomenon whose specific meanings have to be carefully examined and interpreted.

One should not argue, as some have (Blumler and Gurevitch, 1982), that the existence of mainstream models such as these strongly suggest the possibility of a easy convergence between Marxist and behavioral approaches to communication issues. To utilize Gouldner's terms, the 'world hypotheses' and 'background assumptions' inherent in each of these two approaches are too radically different and opposed to allow an easy merging of these two traditions (Gouldner, 1970: 20-60). Critical research is organized around an examination of the rôle that the media play in maintaining and changing the structures of power in society. The researcher is not a neutral observer but a member of society and a committed participant in the larger social processes. Research is thus a political act and the nature of research is open to examination and debate. Finally, traditional behavioral communications research is based on an analytical mode of argument in which a phenomenon is broken down into its components and each part studied as a separate entity. In contrast critical research is based on the holistic mode or argument which attempts to deal with a phenomenon such as the social rôle of the media as a complex integrated system of power relations. The goal is to understand the parts in relation to the whole.

The models outlined are at best, preliminary ideas, sketches or frameworks, for critical researchers; these must be extensively reformulated in the context of critical concerns and orientations. The fact that they reintroduce the notion of a powerful media and suggest that the societal context of the media is a factor to be considered should cause critical researchers to examine them for possible ideas about media impact on audiences.

Of course one is not limited to these models in a formulation of media impact. Ethnographic studies of media effect can provide a new approach to an understanding of impact. A reconceptualization of the audience from individuals to collectivities, interpretive communities or social movements can prove equally fruitful. In general, in seeking to address the question of media impact, critical researchers must rethink the entire issue of the nature and definition of the media, audience and effect and the relation among them. In doing so, they should draw upon a wide range of bodies of thought and work for their ideas. Behaviorist models should not automatically be excluded.

Indeed it needs to be pointed out that these traditional models raise some significant issues for critical researchers. While critical researchers may stress the analysis of the type and range of meaning in media content, they have not demonstrated what difference it all makes. Behavioral researchers may treat the media message in a comparatively naive way. Yet they have successfully demonstrated that differences in media content have different consequences. At a more fundamental level lies the issue of where meaning is located. At the theoretical level, critical researchers are aware of the complex interaction between messages, meaning and receiver. Yet at the empirical level, their work suggests that meaning is located in the message. This conclusion is due more to the lack of attention to the relation between the message and the audience than to a clearly worked out theoretical stance. Behavioral researchers, on the other hand, assume that the meanings are in people—that in themselves messages have no meaning. They only act as stimuli and people create meanings in response to these stimuli. One could argue that the burden of proof is on critical researchers to show that all the meanings uncovered in media content make a difference.

For critical researchers, a theory of the media is incomplete without a 'theory of reception'. The ideal of course is to develop an understanding of the mass communication process that is able to examine and explain media production, messages and effects in the framework of a specific and clearly articulated theory of society, history, culture and power. The need now, though, is to bring the audience back into critical communications research.

Acknowledgements

I wish to thank Sam Becker and Eileen Meehan of the University of Iowa for their extremely helpful comments on an earlier draft of this paper. The author, of course, is solely responsible for the content.

Notes

1. One can argue that a concern with power is not absent from mainstream American research. While critical researchers ask about the rôle of the media in the maintenance of a class society, mainstream scholars focus more on the rôle of the media in creating and maintaining the power of a particular politician, party or interest group. In this sense the concern with power is shared by both groups of scholars. The main difference, of course, is the theory of society and the resulting conceptions of power that underlie their questions about power and the media.

References

BALL-ROKEACH, S. J. and DEFLEUR, M. L. (1976). A dependency model of mass media effects, *Communication Research*, vol. 3, no. 1

BALL-ROKEACH, S. J. and DEFLEUR, M. L. (1982). *Theories of Mass Communication* (4th edn). New York: Longman

BECKER, L. B. (1982). The mass media and citizen assessment of issue importance: a reflection on agenda setting, in Whitney, D. C., Wartella, E. and Windahl, S. (eds), *Mass Communication Review Yearbook*, vol. 3. Beverly Hills: Sage

BECKER, L. and WHITNEY, D. C. (1980). Effects of media dependencies: audience assessment of government, *Communication Research*, vol. 7, no. 1

BENNETT, T. (1982). Media, 'reality,' signification, in Gurevitch, M., Bennett, T., Curran, J. and Woollacott, J. (eds), *Culture, Society and the Media*. London: Methuen.

BLUMLER, J. G. and GUREVITCH, M. (1982). The political effects of mass communication, in Gurevitch, M., Bennett, T., Curran, J. and Woollacott, J. (eds), *Culture, Society and the Media*. London: Methuen

COHEN, S. (1973). *Folk Devils and Moral Panics*. St Albans: Paladin

CURRAN, J., GUREVITCH, M. and WOOLLACOTT, J. (1982). The study of the media: theoretical approaches, in Gurevitch, M., Bennett, T., Curran, J. and Woollacott, J. (eds), *Culture, Society and the Media*. London: Methuen

DERVIN, B. (1980). Communication gaps and inequities: moving towards a reconceptualization, in Dervin, B. and Voigt, M. J. (eds), *Progress in Communication Sciences*, vol. II. Norwood, New Jersey: Ablex

DONOHUE, G. A., OLIEN, C. N. and TICHENOR, P. J. (1974). Communities, pollution and the fight for survival, *Journal of Environmental Education*, vol. 1., no. 1

ETTEMA, J. S. and KLINE, F. G. (1977). Deficits, differences and ceilings: contingent conditions for understanding the knowledge gap, *Communication Research*, vol. 4, no. 2

GENOVA, B. K. L. and GREENBERG, B. S. (1979). Interest in the news and the knowledge gap, *Public Opinion Quarterly*, vol. 43, no. 1

GITLIN, T. (1978). Media sociology: the dominant paradigm, *Theory and Society*, vol. 6, no. 1

GITLIN, T. (1980). *The Whole World is Watching*. Berkeley: University of California Press

GOULDNER, A. W. (1970). *The Coming Crisis of Western Sociology*. New York: Avon

HALL, S. (1980). Cultural studies: two paradigms, *Media, Culture and Society*, vol. 2, no. 1

HALL, S., CRITCHER, C., JEFFERSON, T., CLARKE, J. and ROBERTS, B. (1978). *Policing the Crisis: the State and Law and Order*. London: Macmillan

HARTMANN, P. (1979). News and public perception of industrial relations, *Media, Culture and Society*, vol. 1, no. 3

HIRSCH, P. M. (1978). Television as a national medium, in Street, D. (ed.) *Handbook of Contemporary Urban Life*. San Francisco: Jossey Boss

KATZ, E. (1981). Publicity and pluralistic ignorance: notes on the spiral of silence, in Baier, H., Kepplinger, H. M. and Reuman, K. (eds), *Public Opinion and Social Change*, Wiesbaden: Westdeutscher Verlag

McCOMBS, M. E. (1981). The agenda setting approach, in Nimmo, D. D. and Sanders, K. R. (eds), *Handbook of Political Communication*. Beverly Hills: Sage

McQUAIL, D. and WINDAHL, S. (1981). *Communication Models*. London: Longman

MORLEY, D. (1980). *The 'Nationwide' Audience: Structure and Decoding*. London: British Film Institute

MURDOCK, G. and GOLDING, P. (1977). Capitalism, communication and class relations, in Curran, J., Gurevitch, M. and Woollacott, J. (eds), *Mass Communication and Society*. London: Edward Arnold

NOELLE-NEUMANN, E. (1974). The spiral of silence: a theory of public opinion, *Journal of Communication*, vol. 24, no. 2

NOELLE-NEUMANN, E. (1980). Mass media and social change in developed societies, in Wilhoit, G. C. and de Bock, H. (eds), *Mass Communication Review Yearbook*, vol. 1, Beverly Hills: Sage

NIGG, J. M. (1982). Communication under conditions of uncertainty: understanding earthquake forecasting, *Journal of Communication*, vol. 32, no. 4

TAYLOR, D. G. (1982). Pluralistic ignorance and the spiral of silence, *Public Opinion* Quarterly, vol. 46, no. 2

THUNBERG, A. M., NOWAK, K. and ROSENGREN, K. E. (1979). *Samverkansspiralen*. Stockholm: Liber Förlag

TICHENOR, P. J. (1982). Status, communication and social evolution: evolution of the knowledge gap hypothesis, *Masscommunicatie*, vol. 10, no. 3

TICHENOR, P. J., DONOHUE, G. A. and OLIEN, C. N. (1970), Mass media flow and differential growth in knowledge, *Public Opinion Quarterly*, vol. 34, no. 2

PART IV

MASS COMMUNICATION TECHNOLOGY AND POLICY

INTRODUCTION

James G. Webster

Designing and implementing media policies that will have desirable social outcomes has never been an easy task. We must decide what is or is not desirable, and understand enough about the processes and effects of media to identify the means by which those outcomes can be realized. The rapid emergence of new communication technologies has done little to make matters easier. Technological innovations can alter the character and definition of media systems, and so challenge many of our assumptions about media use and influence. They can open new avenues for achieving social change, and so force us to consider the hazards and benefits of change. Included in this section are articles that deal in various ways with these issues of mass communication technology and policy.

Babe raises fundamental questions about the ability of traditional microeconomic theory to deal with information as either the input or output of an economic system. Babe argues that conventional economic analyses have an inadequate conception of information, and are further unable to quantify or value information in a meaningful way. He suggests that policy research and policymaking might profit by considering information's more qualitative aspects and its anticipated effects on recipients.

Should government act affirmatively to ensure that a representative mix of programming is made available to the public, or rely upon the marketplace to provide appropriate offerings? Glasser focuses on the legal controversy surrounding radio format regulation to explore the merits of competition as a means for achieving diversity in electronic media. He argues that the marketplace solution, popular among U.S. policymakers, "typically mitigates against the ideal of pluralistic programming." In a response, Krasnow and Kennard chide the author for failing to identify a realistic alternative to the marketplace.

The medium of television has long been characterized by the transient nature of its broadcasts, a quality that has undoubtedly circumscribed both the uses and effects of television. With the widespread adoption of home video recorders, however, this feature of the medium and its messages can be changed. Levy and Fink provide a theoretical framework for understanding message transience and develop a mathematical model that predicts the "half-life" of different program types. The authors then go on to suggest the elements of a more general theory of mass media transience.

Perhaps no single technological innovation is thought to have more far-reaching social implications than the computer. As computer technology has become more commonplace, so too has the wisdom of advocating educational programs designed to promote "computer literacy." Is such training necessary for people to function effectively in a modern society? Will those who are not computer literate be left behind? Noble examines the alleged benefits of computer literacy and argues that its advocates' practical claims are "both hollow and full of danger, both ludicrous and grave."

For some years now, the demand for a "new information order" has been at the center of debate on international communications policy. No element of that debate has been more hotly contested that the extent to which Western news agencies dominate and distort the flows of international news. Sreberny-Mohammadi reports on the "World of the News" study that examined news coverage in 29 countries. In a reaction to the study, Stevenson argues that the findings do not substantiate the assertion that Third World media are maintained in a state of dependence by Western news organizations. In a second reaction, Nordenstreng argues that the results should not be taken at face value because "vulgar" content categories lent themselves to "a false interpretation in support of the cause of those who are opposed to the New International Information Order." The debate, it would seem, goes on.

McCormack compares Canada's 1981 Kent commission report and the MacBride (UNESCO) report to explicate different criteria for judging press performance. As she notes, "the former assumes that competition is the major safeguard of diversity; the latter written from the perspective of the Third World countries, regards social inequality as the primary obstacle to the free flow of information." McCormack offers an alternative model of the media and political culture that places special emphasis on the concept of access.

These selections, like many others in this volume, serve to remind us of the vitality and dynamism of this field of study. They might also serve to remind us that no single theoretical perspective or well-defined body of literature serves as a point of departure for the study of communications policy. If there is no all-encompassing framework that binds these works together, there are at least recurrent themes and concerns that can be identified. Often times, these themes manifest themselves as responses to one of two questions. Where do we want to go, and how are we going to get there?

The answer to the first question occurs with a surprising degree of regularity. Diversity, at least in Western societies, is frequently identified as the objective of communications policy. There are, of course, debates about what diversity really means. Glasser, for example, cautions that we not mistake variety for diversity.

Generally, however, we are agreed that our policies should create media systems where people are free to choose from a broad and varied range of news and information, opinion and criticism, art and entertainment. Within the U.S. context, such an objective seems entirely in keeping with the goals of a "free marketplace of ideas." Even among those less wedded to First Amendment ideals, increasing the free flow of information is often a goal of communications policy.

If there has been some consensus about where we ought to be going, there has been anything but consensus about how we are to get there. Many policy-makers extoll the virtues of unfettered competition and advocate a course of deregulation. To others, this route appears to serve corporate interests far more than the public interest. As alternatives, they have variously proposed that we limit or control patterns of ownership, encourage greater professionalism in the media, guarantee citizens some means of access (to send and/or receive messages), mandate that different kinds of material be made available regardless of demand, or otherwise affirmatively regulate the content of the media. All these mechanisms for achieving the goal of diversity have been proposed before. All are evident here in Part IV.

What is less evident is a careful consideration of the goal itself. The technologies of satellite, cable, computer and recorder, mean, if nothing else, that the hardware for delivering, storing, and retrieving a wealth of messages is at hand. Suppose we succeed, by whatever means, at filling those systems with the diverse media offerings we so desire. What will become of people who live with such media at their disposal? Will they use their freedom of choice to exploit the full range of opportunities before them, or retreat, as never before , into private worlds of familiar images and comfortable ideas? Will mass publics that had previously shared the common ground of mass media gradually regroup into more isolated communities of interest? Will diversity breed a more vital and rewarding society in which to live, or facilitate social polarization, manipulation, and alienation?

Our ability to answer these questions, and so inform the process of policymaking, depends in large part on understanding how people will use the options and opportunities presented by the new media. It is primarily for this reason that Nicholas Garnham has urged effects researchers to shift their attention to the consumption of information, and Denis McQuail sees the need to develop some theory of how choices are made.

The articles that follow, then, offer a variety of insights into a rather broad area we have labeled "Mass Communication Technology and Policy." The reader may find this a curious collection. At their worst, these works can seem like pieces of a puzzle that defies solution. They do not lock neatly into place, yet somehow they belong together. At their best, they challenge us to develop a broader framework for understanding media policies by forcing us to address some very fundamental questions. What will be the social impact of technological change? Do our current theories and models provide an adequate basis for understanding these changes? Where do we want to go, and how are we going to get there?

28

INFORMATION INDUSTRIES AND ECONOMIC ANALYSIS
Policy-Makers Beware

Robert E. Babe

We look not to things that are seen but to things that are unseen; for things that are seen are transient, but the things that are unseen are eternal.

St. Paul (2 Corinthians 4:18)

I. THE INFORMATION AGE AND ECONOMIC ANALYSIS

Studies indicate that both the stock and the flow of information are increasing exponentially each year (Bell, 1977, pp. 54–57); that information workers now account for just slightly under 50 percent of the U.S. labor force, up from 25 percent in 1940 (Porat, 1976, p. 189). Technological change in industries associated with the creation and movement of information has been extensive and rapid over the past several decades.

Consequently, many believe that western societies are entering a new era, variously termed Post-Industrial Society (Bell, 1973), The Information Age or The Information Economy (Porat, 1976), The Global Village (McLuhan, 1964), The Age of Discontinuity (Drucker, 1968), The Third Wave (Toffler, 1980). Characterizing this new era is unprecedented activity in the production and distribution of information.

Accompanying the growing economic significance of information has been an increasing attention paid thereto by economists. Patents, copyright, trademarks, newspapers, book and periodical publishing, broadcasting, cable television, the economics of knowledge production and education are among the industries, practices and activities receiving growing attention from economists.

This article addresses some of the major assumptions and modes of analysis of traditional microeconomic theory, concluding that this theory is of limited usefulness for analyzing or prescribing policies respecting the production or creation of information.

The term "information industries" is correctly applied to all industries engaged in the creation or production, distribution and/or storage of infor-

From Robert E. Babe, "Information Industries and Economic Analysis: Policy-Makers Beware," in Oscar H. Gandy Jr., Paul Espinosa, and Janusz A. Ordover, eds., *Proceedings from the Tenth Annual Telecommunications Policy Research Conference* (Norwood: Ablex, 1983), pp. 123-135. Reprinted by permission of Ablex Publishing Corporation.

mation. The analysis and critique put forth in this paper, however, is applied only to the creation or production of information, and to industries whose activities in storage and/or distribution are ancillary to creation or production. Therefore, telephones, telegraphs, and other common carriers are not considered.

Foremost among the deficiencies of microeconomics, as applied to information creation, is an inadequate conception of what information is. Information, as we shall see, is one universal concept binding together many diverse phenomena. A second such universal concept is money; money happens to be the one employed by economists for purposes of analysing and comparing otherwise diverse economic situations.[1] Money is a medium of exchange, a measure of value, and a store of value. Therefore, it can be viewed also as a carrier of information. In this sense, it both measures situations (markets) and carries or transmits these measurements to those concerned through its circulation.

The question addressed by this paper may be put as follows: Can money, as the measuring rod of value and as the carrier of information concerning value, itself measure the value of information or carry information concerning the value of information?

There are two conceivable situations in which money could either measure information and/or carry information concerning the value of information; neither situation, however, generally holds. First, conceivably, money could *be* itself information and information could *be* money, in the way that mass and energy (two other universal measures) are but different states of the same concept; if this were true, money would "map" information, or be precisely convertible into information, and *vice versa*. If not, any attempt at direct conversion would be an error analogous to measuring length by units of mass or to measuring mass (for all objects) by money. (see Leshan and Margenau, 1982, pp. 55–60).

Alternatively, money conceivably could measure the value of information as it purportedly measures the value of other items exchanged in markets. For this situation to exist, however, it is required that information can be measured. If units of information cannot be specified, then how can one know the value of a unit of information? In addressing information industries, it is essential that economists know that which they are analysing, namely the production of information.

This paper addresses the realism of each of the foregoing hypothetical situations. To repeat, for microeconomic analysis of the information industries to be valid, one of these situations must exist.

II. INFORMATION

Information has been defined as an increment to knowledge (Malchup, 1980, p. 8; von Weizsäcker, 1980, p. 279). This definition raises questions of the definition of knowledge, a topic I need not pursue here apart from noting that knowledge is variable from one person to another, and hence that which constitutes an increment to knowledge is also variable from one person to another.

Information has also been defined as disconnected and apparently random events, data, impressions, stimuli and so forth which, if and when connected systematically by means of theory, story, history, model or otherwise, come to constitute knowledge or meaning (Malchup, 1980, p. 8). Information in this sense is the raw, unprocessed data from which knowledge is constructed and by which it is subsequently tested. In the absence of such connections, information is either invisible (unperceived) or constitutes noise (uncomprehended).[2]

Information has also been defined as that which provokes a response in, or in some manner affects or transforms, the recipient (Thayer, 1970; Weiner, 1950, p. 27). In this view, if a receiver remains untouched by the stimuli confronting him, he has not been "in-formed".

Finally, but not necessarily exhaustively, information is viewed as a limitation of or selection from possibilities, a "closing of entropy" (Klapp, 1978, p. 10). As such, information is the *formation* of, or ordering from, conceivable chaos. For example, a word is a selection of a specific sound (or arrangement of written symbols) from an infinite variety of conceivable sounds (or scribbles). Accordingly, in this view, information is a measure of the improbable, and indeed the "less probable an event is, the more information it furnishes" (von Weizsäcker, 1980, p. 278; see also Darnell, 1972, pp. 156–161). Information provides the recipient with an awareness of the unexpected, the unusual, the improbable; on the other hand, events with complete certainty of occurrence provide no information; they are not news.

These various conceptions of information however diverse they may appear to be do entail some common features. First, information does not inhere objectively in the originator or source alone, although information emanates or proceeds from its source; rather, information entails an interaction between source and recipient, whereby the emanations from the former are processed, comprehended or otherwise assimilated by the latter (Wood, 1978). Information entails *the formation within* the recipient of characteristics of the originator; it may entail more than this of course (as in the case of an "objective" scientific dissertation on some esoteric topic) but information always entails an in-forming of the source for the receiver since information proceeds from its source and is assimilated by its receiver.

Second, information comprises symbols or signs which represent or point to something else (Porat, 1976, p. 3). Information does not stand alone but is inevitably in reference to something else. Light waves reflected from an object and perceived by a viewer transmit the surface characteristics of the object but the light waves do not constitute the object. Likewise, the word "chair" signifies an object or a class of objects but is not itself that object or class of objects.

Inasmuch as information represents or signifies something other than itself, and always entails an interaction between its source and its recipient, we arrive at a third characteristic of information: its immateriality. Information is immaterial in destination, often in origin, and always in transmission. The following paragraphs justify this statement.

Signs point to something else, but their meanings (or significations) are products of custom, learning, sensory perception and interpretation. For example, the words "house" and "la maison", while quite dissimilar in sound and written appearance, signify the same thing, albeit to different language groups (custom, learning). Similarly, a very high profit rate will signify one meaning to a businessman (excellent performance) and a completely different meaning to an antitrust economist (monopoly). Information is inevitably processed by the mind, by which its meaning or signification is constructed. And, as far as we can conceive, there is an immaterial (or nonphysical) realm to the mind.[3]

Much, if not most, information originates in one mind and is transmitted to other minds and therefore much, if not most, information is immaterial in origin as well as in destination.

Not only is information often immaterial in source, and always in destination, it is also immaterial in transmission. To say this is not to deny that information must be transmitted through physical or material means (otherwise, we would be entering the realm of parapsychology); it is simply to point out that the means whereby information is encoded is not the information itself. Light waves, paper, air and so forth are media which can be encoded (formed, shaped, impressed) so as to be capable of imparting significations to the recipient. If the medium used for encoding were itself the information, there would be no extractable meaning carried by the medium (and hence McLuhan's aphorism that "the medium is the message").

Two illustrations may help clarify the point. Microelectronics can make possible the storage in a relatively tiny space (the size of a paperback book) of information previously requiring libraries (Evans, 1979, p. 106); obviously, the information stored is something other than the physical means of storage. Likewise, a three letter equation ($E = mc^2$), or a well-turned sentence ("In the beginning was the Word, and the Word was with God, and the Word was God") can speak worlds of meaning more than the collected works of a pulp novelist or even a learned dissertation on the properties of linear, homogenous production functions; quantification of the symbols used imparts no knowledge respecting the information content of the symbols when conjoined.[4]

There is then no definite, fixed relationship between the means of transmitting or storing information and the "amount" of information so transmitted or stored. Consequently, information is quite immaterial.

III. INFORMATION AND ECONOMIC ANALYSIS

A. General Economic Modelling

Modern (neoclassical) economics is a rather complex system of thought, with deep-seated origins in eighteenth and nineteenth century libertarian and utilitarian philosophies,[5] purporting to describe and explain economic phenomena (namely, the production and exchange of goods and services). Of chief concern to us is the adequacy of the economic modelling process when applied to information.

The economic process is viewed as one of exchange whereby goods and services possessed by one are traded for goods and services held by another; the exchange will occur when it benefits both parties due to differences in valuations of the articles in question. Money mediates the exchange process by valuating goods and services. The valuation process is a result of the interaction of demand (the valuation placed on the good or service by those without) and supply (the valuation by those who possess the good or service prior to exchange). Underlying demand is the "utility" or the usefulness of the item in satisfying wants or needs; underlying supply is the cost (or foregone utility) in losing the item through sale. Money is the measure of both anticipated utility from purchase and foregone utility from sale.

Production is frequently undertaken for purpose of sale. In such cases, the firm must purchase factor inputs (land, labour, capital, energy) and such purchases represent the decline in utility to the firm (costs). Production will be undertaken only if costs can be recouped through sale (exchange) of outputs over the long term.

Economic analysis is frequently employed to reach policy recommendations as to how the production and distribution processes can be improved. In this regard, the criteria most frequently employed are those of "economic efficiency".

There are several dimensions to the economic conception of efficiency. First, the good or service should be produced at the lowest attainable cost (i.e., it should utilize the least cost combination of factor inputs), given the level of output; technically, the firm or industry should be producing at the lowest attainable point on the "short run average cost curve";[6] this condition entails the equality of average cost and short run marginal (or incremental) cost. Second, the "optimal" volume of output should be produced; technically, the quantity supplied should be such that price equals the marginal cost of production and, since marginal cost equals average cost, no excess profits are earned. Third, in recognition that over time firms may expand or contract production in response to secular demand shifts, output levels should create equality between price and long run marginal (or incremental) costs.[7]

Fundamental to the foregoing are the notions that costs of production should be as low as possible and greater than benefits created for the level of output chosen, and that at the margin (the last unit produced and purchased) costs should equal benefits.

Economists take the demand "curve"[8] (a temporally fixed relation between quantities demanded and prices, all other relevant factors constant) as the measure of marginal benefits to the user (purchaser). Price paid is viewed as the monetary expression of the benefits received (or anticipated) from the last unit purchased. Consequently, the demand curve, depicting the unique relationship between possible prices and varying quantities, also depicts incremental benefits inhering in the various quantities.

Within the foregoing conceptual framework economists analyse information industries and make recommendations that would improve economic efficiency. In this regard, depending upon the particular situation being analysed, information can be viewed either as a factor of production or as a final commodity.

As a factor of production information is an input in the process of producing outputs, and in this case economists compare the costs of attaining information with the reduction in costs attributable to its use. At the margin, the cost saving from applying information should equal its acquisition cost.

As a final commodity, the quantity of information produced or made available for sale should be such that, at the margin, the price paid equals its cost of production and distribution. (Stigler, 1961; Demsetz, 1969).

B. Limitations to Economic Analysis of Information

We noted in the foregoing section that the traditional economic model distinguishes information as an *input* in the process of production, and as a final commodity or *output* purchased by consumers for its own utility. In this former instance, information is seen as substituting for, and conserving, other productive factors (traditionally land, labor, capital and energy). In the latter instance, information is itself a commodity, subject to substitution for other goods and services comprising the consumers' "utility function"; and its purpose is to satisfy consumer demand.

1. Information as Economic Input

Information is not merely an input interchangeable with other inputs. It defines, permeates and transforms the production process. Technically, information changes the production function and the resulting cost curves. In this respect, it is totally unlike other inputs.

Information, then, can be another name for technological change. As soon as information is admitted into economic analysis as a productive input, static analysis on the cost side (given cost curves, a given production function) becomes dynamic (changing cost curves, changing production functions).

But efficiency is an ambiguous and dubious concept in the world of economic dynamics, for efficiency implies that output levels should be chosen such that "the" marginal cost of production equals "the" benefits derived from use. Information, as a factor of production, however, inherently means that production processes are continually changing with the result that the marginal cost is evanescent.

Moreover, information is embodied within the other factors of production, making them inseparable from the information they embody. Labor contains knowledge; capital items encapsulate knowledge; management combines capital and labor, and this combining process utilizes knowledge contained in management.

2. *Information as Economic Output or Commodity*

For purposes of economic analysis, information, when viewed as output, is treated as a commodity not dissimilar from other commodities. Its function is to satisfy consumer wants or preferences, and consumers are assumed to procure information in such quantities that price equals marginal utility.

Treating information as a commodity implies that there is a unit of output that can be specified and measured; otherwise, no conclusions can be reached respecting optimal outputs and prices per unit of output. Treating information as a commodity also implies that information is a final output in the sense that it satisfies pre-existing tastes and preferences. Otherwise, if information transforms that which it purportedly satisfies (namely, consumer demand), dynamic analysis must replace static analysis on the demand side (shifting demand curves); but, as we have seen, all notions of efficiency become quite ambiguous and dubious in the face of economic dynamics.

a. *Limitations to Information as Commodity.* Information possesses characteristics which weaken its status as commodity. For one thing, it is intangible. While information can be, and often is, materially encapsulated (print, film, videotape), it need not be the case. The first methods developed by civilized society for exchanging information entailed no material encapsulation at all: gesture, music, speech.

The disembodied or incorporeal character of information presents difficulties for economic analysis. One of these is the quantification of information. Economic analysis is concerned with prices of outputs and costs of inputs; consequently, in treating information as an economic commodity, there is an essential need to reduce information to some standardized and quantifiable indicator: number of pages, words, bits, hours of television program transmission, feet of film and so forth. In each case, quantification is applied to the material or physical means of encapsulating information, rather than to the information itself.

A second factor weakening the status of information as a commodity is the absence of any final consumption; there is no final consumption, only dissipation and transformation. Any piece of information created by one and imparted to another transforms ("in-forms") the second person, affecting his or her thinking processes and actions (i.e., his or her output). Information continues to spiral down through the ages in dissipated forms, being altered to varying degrees through each transmission process.[9] This total continuity through time weakens the capacity of economists to analyze information industries, since economists try to isolate an interval of time within which all final effects are resolved, an impossibility for information. From these remarks, it can also be seen that information exemplifies the economist's notion of externalities (i.e., spillover or third party effects) which have always been troublesome for empirical work in any event. (Chase, 1968).

A third characteristic of information detracting from its status as commodity is its public good nature. Public goods comprise those outputs (1) for which it is difficult or costly to exclude from benefiting those who choose not to pay, and/or (2) for which the use or consumption by one does not substract from, and may even add to, the use or consumption by others (Musgrave, 1959, and Ferguson, 1972, p. 498). Information bears both of these characteristics insofar as (1) the disembodied qualities of information can be trapped and encapsulated on material form at low cost through reprography or otherwise, or even intercepted in transmission in the absence of any material encapsulation at all;[10] and (2) use of information by one does not detract from use or possession by another; indeed, information tends still to reside with the producer after sale. Economic theory, virtually all economists admit, offers no guidelines as to efficient pricing or production in such circumstances. (Besen et al, 1978; Samuelson, 1964).

b. *Information as Essence.*[11] Information is never a final output, consumed and thereby annihilated. Rather, it is ingested by the receiver and the receiver is thereby altered.

Nor is information mere input to the production process. We have seen that it permeates and transforms production processes.

Moreover, information permeates and transforms societies (Berger and Luckman, 1966). For example, the process of modernization of economies and cultures is viewed by some as being highly dependent upon and interrelated with the flow, in high volume, of communications which extol and facilitate market transactions. (Lerner, 1958). Moreover, information patterns can unify a nation, fragment a nation, or lead to cultural dependency. It is the position of many Third World nations that restrictions on the flow of information from outside their borders must be imposed in order to permit national sovereignty and induce economic development; this is the call for the New World Information Order. (Righter, 1978; Smith, 1980).

By approaching information from the standpoint of power or energy or essence as opposed to commodity or input, one is evaluating information by its intrinsic qualitative aspects and its anticipated effects upon recipients, rather than upon the basis of price alone. *Commodity* gives orientation toward the quantitative, while *essence* gives orientation toward the qualitative. *Commodity* gives orientation toward the static (satisfying existing demands) while *essence* emphasizes the dynamic, transformative effect of information as regards whatever it comes in contact with. Information as *commodity* is precise and objective, as least if and when quantitative measures have been agreed to. As reality transformer or *essence,* information is qualitative and hence subjective; when viewed as essence, emphasis is on the interaction of the receiver with the information and consequently judgements depend upon how the information is processed, in addition to the intrinsic qualitative characteristics of the information itself. This means that information as essence is more ambiguous, less amenable to objective, "scientific" analysis. Nonetheless, this conclusion in no way minimizes the extreme importance of the notion of information as essence.

For the information industries, qualitative factors are most significant. Virtually every manifestation of man's presence on the planet has had its origins in the immaterial realm of the mind and in the exchanges of that ethereal essence known as information, from one mind to another. These impalpable foundations of society have led both to man's most glorious achievements and to his most ignoble atrocities. Witness John Milton:

> The mind is its own place, and in itself can make a heav'n of hell, a hell of heav'n. (Milton, 1674).

To ignore, or assume away as unimportant, the qualitative aspects of information, to "commoditize" information and value it only in accordance with price, is at best simplistic and partial.

IV. CONCLUSIONS

Economic analysis is highly complex, both theoretically, and in application, and this complexity may cause one to mistake as rigor all of the underlying confusions, ambiguities, inconsistencies and reductionist assumptions. Policy makers are advised, therefore, to be quite circumspect in reviewing analyses of information industries prepared by economists who view information only, or primarily, as a commodity or input and who take "economic efficiency" as the criterion for analysis.

The notion of information as commodity or input has an added danger. It means that the suppliers and procurers of information need value the same only in terms of market price, outside of any ethical or moral framework; the "eyes of the heart" become blinded by price. This tendency threatens freedom.

Walter Lippmann (1955, pp. 88–108) noted that freedom of speech does not encompass freedom to lie, cheat, incite to violence. Each freedom must be responsibly exercised or it will be jeopardized in the name of protecting the common weal. The increased commoditization of information, in the absence of renewed social responsibility, will threaten the very freedoms the hucksters of information value so highly. (Lasch, 1978; Bell, 1976).

Continued research into the information industries is of vital importance in our era, which has been termed the "Information Age". But, in the course of these investigations, we would do well to bear in mind the caution sounded by Theodore Roszak (1973):

> What science can measure is only a portion of what man can know. Our knowing reaches out to embrace the sacred; what bars its way, though it promise us dominion, condemns us to be prisoners of the empirical lie. (p. 67)

V. FOOTNOTES

[1] Alfred Marshall, father of modern (neoclassical) microeconomic theory, wrote:

> Economists deal with facts which can be observed, and quantities which can be measured.... The problems which can be grouped as economic, because they relate specially to man's conduct under the influence of motives that are measurable by a money price, are found to make a fairly homogeneous group. ("Principles of Economics", p. 27, quoted in Mitchell [1969], p. 141.)

[2] One can argue, however, that paradigms or theories develop first, and that information (facts, data) is inevitably perceived and selected in a manner so as to support or justify the model (Kuhn, 1970). In reality, there is undoubtedly an interactive process between information and knowledge whereby information supports or refutes models while, at the same time, the model tends to limit or suppress perceptions of information hostile to it.

[3] A materialist theory of the mind must answer the question how we can know anything; such theories are always falsified in self-reference. Behaviorism, for example, in taking the position that all human actions and "thoughts" are the determined outcome of physical stimuli, negates its own validity in self-reference; the writings of behavioral psychologists, while claiming to be universally true, must be the outcome of their own unique conditioning, quite destroying the general applicability of the theory. Similar remarks apply to sociobiology, whereby all actions and thoughts are held to be chemically (genetically) determined.

It is the unique characteristic and capability of humans to stand apart both from phenomena and from self, to possess conscious self-awareness and to see oneself from the "outside". No totally materialist theory of the mind can account for this capability.

[4] While any given medium may possess a theoretical maximum to its capacity to transmit or store "bits" (quantity of symbols), this bandwidth or memory capacity provides no indication as to the amount of information (which depends *inter alia* upon the synergy conjoining bits) so transmitted or stored.

[5] The intellectual presence of Adam Smith, Jeremy Bentham, John Stuart Mill and lesser of the classical economists is still strongly felt in virtually every standard microeconomics textbook. For discussions on the evolution of economic thought from these classical precursors see, *inter alia,* Mitchell (1967), Blaug (1968), Robinson (1962) and Oser (1963).

[6] The "short run" is the current period when firms have in place fixed productive factors, and hence output can be expanded (beyond capacity) only with difficulty. Marginal cost is the increment in cost attributable to production of the last unit.

[7] The "long run" comprises the time period over which all costs become variable and the firm can adapt to new demand levels.

The firm always operates in the short run, while looking at the long run. Economists have never been able to adequately deal with the question of which marginal cost schedule should pertain for efficient operations—short run marginal costs or long run marginal costs, or one of the infinite number of marginal cost schedules between the two extremes. Economic analysis, it can be seen, is much less rigorous than is often presumed.

[8] Quotation marks about the word "curve" signify the general logical inconsistency in the notion of a demand curve. Demand curves are held to depict various prices and quantities, other relevant factors constant. But movement from one price to another *on* the curve will inevitably have repercussions on the exogenous variables. For example, the prices and quantities of substitutes will change in response to the movement down the demand curve; but this change in the price and quantity of substitutes annihilates the demand curve, since it was drawn under the assumption that all such related factors are constant.

Economic analysis, it can be seen, is much less logical than is often presumed.

[9] Note the insights of Northrop Frye (1957):

> Just as a new scientific discovery manifests something that was already in the order of nature, and at the same time is logically related to the total structure of the existing science, so the new poem manifests something that was already latent in the order of words.... Poetry can only be made out of other poems; novels out of other novels. (p. 97)

[10] And hence the problematic nature of copyright in the age of electronic diffusion. See, *inter alia,* Hamilton and Ploman (1980).

[11] Essence: "That which makes something what it is; an existent being, especially an immaterial being or spirit". *Standard College Dictionary,* Canadian Edition.

VI. REFERENCES

Bell, D. (1973). "The Coming of Post-Industrial Society." New York: Basic Books.

Bell, D. (1976). "The Cultural Contradictions of Capitalism." New York: Basic Books.

Bell, D. (1977). Teletext and technology. *In* "The Winding Passage: Essays and Sociological Journeys 1960–1980", pp. 34–65, New York: Basic Books, 1980.

Bell, D. (1978). The Social Framework of the Information Society. *In* M. Dertouzos and J. Moses (Eds.), "The Computer Age: A Twenty-Year View", pp. 34–65, Cambridge, MA: MIT Press.

Berger, P., and Luckman, T. (1966). "The Social Construction of Reality." Harmondsworth, England: Penguin.

Besen, S., Manning, W., and Mitchell, B. (1978). Copyright liability for cable television. *Journal of Law and Economics 21* (No. 1), 67–95.

Blaug, M. (1968). "Economic Theory in Retrospect." Homewood, IL: Irwin.

Chase, S. (Ed.) (1968). "Problems in Public Expenditure Analysis." Washington, DC: Brookings.

Darnell, D. (1972). Information theory: An approach to human communication, *In* R. Budd and B. Ruben (Eds.), "Approaches to Human Communication," pp. 156–169, Rochelle Park, NJ: Hayden.

Demsetz, H. (1969). Information and efficiency: Another viewpoint. *Journal of Law and Economics 12* (No. 1), 1–22.

Drucker, P. (1968). "The Age of Discontinuity." New York: Harper and Row.
Evans, C. (1979). "The Mighty Micro: The Impact of the Computer Revolution." London: Victor Gollancz.
Ferguson, C. (1972). "Microeconomic Theory." 3rd ed. Homewood, IL: Irwin.
Friedman, M. (1962). "Price Theory: A Provisional Text." Chicago, IL: Aldine.
Frye, N. (1957). "Anatomy of Criticism." Princeton, NJ: Princeton University Press.
Hamilton, C. and Ploman, E. (1980). "Copyright: Intellectual Property in the Information Age." London: Routledge and Kegan Paul.
Kahn, A. (1970). "The Economics of Regulation: Principles and Institutions," Vol. 1. New York: John Wiley and Sons.
Klapp, O. (1978). "Opening and Closing: Strategies of Information Adaptation in Society." Cambridge, England: Cambridge University Press.
Kuhn, T. (1970). "The Structure of Scientific Revolutions." 2nd ed. Chicago, IL: University of Chicago Press.
Lasch, C. (1978). "The Culture of Narcissism: American Life in An Age of Diminishing Expectations." New York: Norton.
Lerner, D. (1958). "The Passing of Traditional Society: Modernizing the Middle East." New York: Free Press.
Leshan, L. and Margenau, H. (1982). "Einstein's Space and Van Gogh's Sky: Physical Realty and Beyond." New York: Macmillan.
Lippmann, W. (1955). "The Public Philosophy." New York: Mentor.
Machlup, F. (1980). "Knowledge: Its Creation, Distribution and Economic Significance." Volume I: Knowledge and Knowledge Production. Princeton, NJ: Princeton University Press.
McLuhan, M. (1964). "Understanding Media: The Extensions of Man." New York: Mentor.
Milton, J. (1674/1969). Paradise Lost. *In* Douglas Bush (Ed.), "Milton: Poetical Works." Oxford, England: Oxford University Press.
Mitchell, W. (1967/1969). "Types of Economic Theory." 2 vols. New York: Kelly.
Musgrave, R. (1959). "The Theory of Public Finance: A Study in Political Economy." New York: McGraw-Hill.
Oser, J. (1963). "The Evolution of Economic Thought." New York: Harcourt, Brace and World.
Porat, M. (1976). "The Information Economy." Stanford, CA: Centre for Interdisciplinary Research.
Righter, R. (1978). "Whose News? Politics, The Press and the Third World." New York: Times Books.
Robinson, J. (1962). "Economic Philosophy." Chicago, IL: Aldine.
Roszak, T. (1973). "Where The Wasteland Ends." Garden City, NY: Anchor Books.
Samuelson, P. (1964). Public goods and subscription TV; correction of the record. *Journal of Law and Economics 7,* 81–83.
Smith, A. (1980). "The Geopolitics of Information." London: Faber and Faber.
Stigler, G. (1961). The economics of information. *Journal of Political Economy 69* (No. 3).
Stigler, G. (1966). "The Theory of Price." 3rd ed. New York: Macmillan.
Thayer, L. (1970). "On Human Communication and Social Development." (Paper presented at the first World Conference on Social Communication for Development, Mexico City).
Toffler, A. (1980). "The Third Wave." New York: Bantam.
von Weizsäcker, F. (1980). "The Unity of Nature." New York: Farrar, Straus and Giroux.
Weiner, N. (1950). "The Human Use of Human Beings: Cybernetics and Society." New York: Avon Books.
Wood, N. (1978). "The Trinity in the Universe." Grand Rapids, MI: Kregel Publications.

29

COMPETITION AND DIVERSITY AMONG RADIO FORMATS
Legal and Structural Issues

Theodore L. Glasser

The FCC's laissez-faire approach to format allocation underscores the Commission's aversion to diversity as a goal of the First Amendment. The FCC's format policy confuses variety with diversity and thus fails to recognize that competition in the marketplace typically mitigates against the ideal of pluralistic programming.

It has never been clear what Congress and the courts intended as the proper relationship between broadcasting and the realities of free enterprise. The legislative history of the Communications Act of 1934 suggests that Congress did not want broadcasters to be constrained by federally imposed programming priorities.[1] As the Supreme Court recognized in 1940, broadcasters are not common carriers: "Congress intended to leave competition in the business of broadcasting where it found it, to permit a licensee . . . to survive or succumb according to his ability to make his programs attractive to the public."[2] At the same time, however, Congress expects licensees to be responsive to the "public interest, convenience, and necessity,"[3] and the judiciary has cautioned broadcasters about their "enforceable public obligations."[4] In its effort to "secure the maximum benefits of radio to all the people,"[5] the Federal Communications Commission must thus acknowledge that, at times, the consumer's right to hear outweighs the broadcaster's right to be heard.[6]

To reconcile these contrasting and often conflicting views of the role of broadcasting, the FCC has established a "double standard" approach to broadcast regulation, a policy intended to strike a balance between, as the

---

Manuscript accepted for publication, November 1983.

[1]*For a review of the history of the Communications Act, see the FCC's Notice of Inquiry and Notice of Proposed Rulemaking: Deregulation of Radio,* 44 Fed. Reg. 57636, 57637–57639 (October 5, 1979).

[2]*FCC* v. *Sanders Brothers Radio Station,* 309 US 470, 475, (1940).

[3]Communications Act of 1934, 47 USC, Sections 303, 307, 309, 310(d) (1976).

[4]*Office of Communication of United Church of Christ* v. *FCC,* 359, F.2d 994, 1003 (DC Cir., 1966).

[5]*National Broadcasting Co.* v. *U.S.,* 319 US 190, 217 (1943).

[6]*Red Lion Broadcasting Co.* v. *FCC,* 395 US 367, 390 (1969).

From Theodore L. Glasser, "Competition and Diversity Among Radio Formats: Legal and Structural Issues," *Journal of Broadcasting*, Vol. 28, No. 2 (Spring 1984), pp. 127-142.

Supreme Court puts it, "the preservation of a free competitive broadcast system, on the one hand, and the reasonable restriction of that freedom inherent in the public interest standard provided in the Communications Act, on the other."[7] Accordingly, the FCC requires a certain degree of equity, balance and accountability insofar as public affairs programming is concerned,[8] but generally leaves entertainment programming to the demands of the marketplace.

The viability of a laissez-faire approach to entertainment programming, however, remains a major policy issue. That the marketplace for broadcasting may not yield a sufficiently heterogeneous mix of programming has long been the subject of debate among policymakers, and nowhere has this debate been more acrimonious than in its application to the diversification of radio formats. While the judiciary ordinarily upholds the Commission's disparate treatment of public affairs and entertainment programming, for nearly a decade the DC Circuit Court of Appeals had been encouraging the FCC to temper its marketplace approach to format allocation by providing a "safety valve" procedure that would accommodate exceptions to — and thus exemptions from — its policy of nonintervention.

In *FCC* v. *WNCN Listeners Guild,* the Supreme Court recently rebuked the Court of Appeals and — at least tacitly — endorsed the Commission's desire to rely on "market forces to promote diversity in radio entertainment formats and to satisfy the entertainment preferences of radio listeners."[9] Ultimately, though, the Court's decision rested not on the wisdom of the FCC's policy but on the fact that the Commission offered a "rational" and "reasonable" preference for its policy.[10] In contrast, this paper focuses on the wisdom of the FCC's policy, especially in the context of the broader legal and structural issues it raises.

In an effort to identify and assess the legal and structural issues endemic to the FCC's marketplace model, this paper: (1) reviews the proposition that the marketplace for radio is structurally deficient; (2) offers a brief chronology of the conflict between the Court of Appeals and the FCC, including the

---

[7]*Sanders Brother,* 390 US at 474.

[8]Through the FCC's recent efforts to deregulate radio, nonentertainment programming guidelines have lost much of their specificity. See generally *Report and Order,* FCC 81-17, 46 Fed. Reg. 13888 (February 24, 1981). "Rather than specify precise actions," the Commission explained, "we have sought to define broad obligations, leaving the fulfillment of those obligations to the operation of a broadcaster's good faith discretion. See *Memorandum Opinion and Order,* In the Matter of Deregulation of Radio, DC Docket 79–219 (FCC 81–366), paragraph 40, released August 28, 1981.

[9]*FCC* v. *WNCN Listeners Guild,* 101 S. Ct. 1266, 1279 (1981).

[10]"Our opinions have repeatedly emphasized that the Commission's judgment regarding how the public interest is best served is entitled to substantial judicial deference." *WNCN,* 101 S. Ct. at 1275. See also *FCC* v. *National Citizens Committee for Broadcasting,* 436 US 775, 793 (1978) and *FCC* v. *WOKO, Inc.,* 392 US 223, 229 (1946).

Court's rather conservative attempt to impose limits on the FCC's policy; (3) explicates the Supreme Court's decision in *WNCN*; and (4) appraises the broader public policy question of format diversity, particularly as this question comes to bear on industry structure and First Amendment jurisprudence. Notwithstanding the FCC's recent efforts to deregulate broadcasting, particularly entertainment programming, the issue of format diversity remains an important policy question because the relationship between the marketplace and media content is likely to continue to inform the larger discussions on the proper structure of the communications industries.

Structural Deficiencies in the Marketplace

Occasionally, someone may naively suggest that broadcasters will simply select whatever format is unrepresented or underrepresented in their market,[11] but generally it is an accepted truism that broadcasters will select whatever format will maximize profits — regardless of how many competing stations may be using the same format. Moreover, it is no longer always true that the largest number of listeners will necessarily maximize profits, a proposition advanced by Steiner in one of the earliest — and still one of the most insightful — analyses of competition in radio broadcasting.[12] Broadcasters today are very much aware of audience *quality,* not just quantity; a smaller but demographically attractive audience may indeed be more profitable than a larger but demographically unattractive audience. Assumptions about format duplication, therefore, must rest not on audience maximization, as Steiner proposed, but on profit maximization: *a station will duplicate an existing format rather than produce a unique format if its share of the audience for a duplicated format yields higher profits than the profits generated by the entire audience for a unique format.*

Since the market share commanded by a duplicated format often exceeds a new or different format's share of the market, format duplication is the rule, not the exception. As Table I illustrates, format duplication among the most profitable radio stations in the larger markets is often as high as 40 percent. To be sure, in some markets there are more duplicated formats than there are

[11]For example, a recent study of commercial radio formats, written by a broadcast consultant and two broadcast educators, offers this advice to professionals and students: "Each format should be designed to provide, if not a unique service, at least one that is markedly different from those already in use. This is easy if there is no All-News, no Classical, no Contemporary, no MOR. One simply fills the void." Edd Routt, James B. McGrath and Fredric Weiss, *The Radio Format Conundrum* (New York: Hastings House, 1978), p. 33.

[12]Peter O. Steiner, "Program Patterns and Preferences, and the Workability of Competition in Radio Broadcasting," *Quarterly Journal of Economics* 66:194–223 (May 1952).

Table I
Format Duplication Among Top 10 Stations in Four Selected Markets

	Houston	Cleveland	Columbus	Oklahoma City
Country	3	1	2	2
Beautiful Music	2	2	2	1
Top 40	0	1	1	1
News/Talk	1	1	0	0
Middle of the Road	0	0	1	1
Adult Contemporary	0	3	3	3
Album Oriented Rock	1	1	1	2
Contemporary	2	1	0	0
Urban Contemporary	1	0	0	0
Percent of Duplication	40	30	40	40

Source: *Broadcasting,* 17 August 1981, pp. 78–86.

distinctive formats.[13] Format diversity exists, it follows, but only to the extent that consumer preferences cluster into large and profitable audiences.

Format duplication, however, is not in itself *prima facie* evidence of a structurally deficient marketplace. While it can be readily demonstrated that the range of formats does not fully accommodate listener's divergent tastes and interests,[14] consumer dissatisfaction is only a necessary — not a sufficient — condition of a structurally deficient marketplace.[15] Only if it could be demonstrated — theoretically if not empirically — that the marketplace for radio offers less variety and choice than a truly "free" marketplace, would there be sufficient reason to conclude that the marketplace for radio is structurally deficient.

Theoretically, the marketplace for radio is structurally imperfect — and deficient from a listener's perspective — in three ways. First, since commercial radio is supported entirely through advertising, broadcasters tend to be more responsive to advertisers than to listeners. Inevitably, broadcasters are concerned more with advertiser welfare than listener welfare because the advertiser, not the listener, is the consumer. Since a broadcaster's goal is to provide the most attractive product (audience) for the consumer (advertiser),

---

[13]According to figures released by the FCC in 1976, for example, there are more stations in Chicago using the same format (16 using a "middle-of-the-road" format) than there are distinctive formats (13). Figures reported in Bruce M. Owen, "Regulating Diversity: The Case of Radio Formats," *Journal of Broadcasting* 21:305–319 (Summer 1977).

[14]The fact that the FCC receives complaints from citizens groups is ample evidence that the range of formats does not entirely satisfy consumer preferences.

[15]Consumer dissatisfaction is only a necessary — not a sufficient — condition of a structurally deficient marketplace because even in an ideal marketplace not every consumer is likely to be fully satisfied.

radio programming is more likely to reflect advertisers' interest in a particular kind of audience than listeners' interest in a particular kind of programming. Although advertiser and listener interests may at times converge and perhaps even overlap considerably, to the extent that advertiser satisfaction and listener satisfaction do not actually *coincide,* the marketplace for radio can be said to be structurally deficient.

Second, since broadcasters are engaged in the production of audiences, not programs, there is no real index of what listeners would be willing to pay for the programs of their choice; consequently, there is no reasonable measure of the *intensity* of listener preferences, which ordinarily would be interpreted as the economic value of a program. Under the existing structure of broadcasting, therefore, minority preferences "are probably systematically discriminated against," at least insofar as minority preferences are defined as "preferences for material that are held by relatively small groups, each member of which might be willing to pay quite a lot for them."[16]

Third, instead of using marketplace forces for purposes of spectrum allocation, Congress has chosen to have frequencies assigned — and licenses granted — at no cost to the broadcaster. As a result, there are no incentives for broadcasters to use their share of the spectrum efficiently and thus economically. Specifically, without a pricing mechanism whereby frequencies are defined in terms of their economic worth, it is virtually impossible to assess the relative benefit and cost of a radio format; not only are taxpayers deprived of payment for a presumably public resource, but broadcasters are afforded an extraordinary — and an econoically distorted — return on their investment. Moreover, since broadcasters neither buy nor lease the use of an obviously valuable resource — the electromagnetic spectrum — there is no opportunity for individuals or firms to prevent over-consumption of frequencies. "A private-enterprise system cannot function properly," concluded economist Ronald Coase in his now frequently-cited critique of the regulation of broadcasting, "unless property rights are created in resources, and, when this is done, someone wishing to use a resource has to pay the owner to obtain it."[17]

Although Coase does not include "that administrative allocation of resources is inevitably worse than an allocation by means of the price mechanism,"[18] and while economist Bruce Owen agrees that even with direct listener payment and an abundance of frequencies there may still be discrimination against minority preferences, it would be reasonably prudent

---

[16]Bruce M. Owen, *Economics and Freedom of Expression* (Cambridge: Ballinger, 1975), p. 114.

[17]Ronald H. Coase, "The Federal Communications Commission," *Journal of Law and Economics* 2:1–40 (October 1959); Excerpted in Douglas H. Ginsburg, *Regulation of Broadcasting* (St. Paul: West, 1979), pp. 47–48.

[18]*Ibid.,* p. 50.

to posit that under a truly free system of competition, as Owen puts it, "things probably would not be as bad."[19]

The FCC and the Marketplace for Entertainment Programming

While the FCC has long acknowledged the imperfections of its marketplace model, it has nonetheless maintained that format allocation — and thus format diversity — should not be subject to regulatory scrutiny. In a *Memorandum Opinion and Order* in 1976, the Commission reaffirmed its commitment to the marketplace as "the best way to allocate entertainment formats in radio, whether the hoped for result is expressed in First Amendment terms (i.e., promoting the greatest diversity of listening choices for the public) or in economic terms (i.e., maximizing the welfare of consumers of radio programs)."[20] Whether an administrative allocation of formats might yield a greater diversity of programming was not germane because, in the Commission's view, there was no requirement "to measure any system of allocation against the standard of perfection;" the marketplace model was both convenient and "the best available means of producing the diversity *to which the public is entitled.*"[21]

Significantly, the 1976 *Opinion and Order* made clear the Commission's "long and continuing reluctance to define and enforce" a public interest standard as it might be applied to radio entertainment programming. As a review and restatement of policy, it served to fortify the FCC's conviction that the "regulation of entertainment formats as an aspect of the public interest would produce an unnecessary and menacing entaglement in matters that Congress meant to leave to private discretion."[22] But the FCC's *Opinion* was much more than a policy statement, for its was a considered repudiation of a format diversity philosophy promulgated by the District of Columbia Court of Appeals. The FCC's *Opinion* not only identified its "fundamental disagreement" with the Court's philosophy but in effect rejected what had become "a vexing series of reversals."[23]

What the Commission sought to reject, specifically, was an emerging "format doctrine," an effort by the Court of Appeals to apply a public interest

---

[19]Owen, *Economics and Freedom of Expression, ibid.*, p. 114.

[20]*Memorandum Opinion and Order,* 41 Fed. Reg. 32950, 32952 (August 6, 1976).

[21]*Ibid.* (emphasis added).

[22]*Ibid.* at 32953.

[23]For a review of the conflict betwen the FCC and the DC Court of Appeals, see John H. Pennybacker, "The Format Change Issue: FCC vs. US Court of Appeals," *Journal of Broadcasting* 22:411–424 (Fall 1978). See also Frank J. Kahn, "Regulating Format Diversity," *Journal of Communication* 32:181–191 (Winter 1982).

standard to entertainment programming: if broadcasting is to be regulated in the public interest, the Court had maintained, it follows that the "FCC would seek to assure that, within technical and economic constraints, as many as possible of the various formats preferred by segments of the public would be provided;" and if indeed the Commission "is to pursue the public interest, it may not be able at the same time to pursue a policy of free competition."[24] In short, the Commission's *Opinion* stood in opposition to the Court's requirement that, should circumstances dictate, the FCC would be obliged to consider whether the "disappearance of a distinctive format may deprive a significant segment of the public of the benefits of radio."[25]

The Format Doctrine

Between 1970 and 1974, in a series of four cases,[26] the District of Columbia Court of Appeals established its format doctrine, essentially a "set of criteria for determining when the 'public interest' standard requires the Commission to hold a hearing to review proposed changes in entertainment formats."[27] While the Court did not expect the Commission to "restrain the broadcasting of any program, dictate adoption of a new format, force retention of an existing format, or command provision of access to non-licensees,"[28] it did want the FCC to at least hold a hearing when a proposed format change raised "substantial and material questions of fact."[29] The FCC's role in reviewing format changes would thus be limited to those special circumstances when: (1) notice of a format change brought about "significant public grumbling;" (2) the "grumbling public" was large enough to be accommodated by available frequencies; (3) the proposed format change would leave the service area without a "unique" format — i.e., there was no adequate substitute for the format being abandoned; and (4) the format being abandoned was economically feasible.[30] The Court viewed these critieria as defining those unusual circumstances when the FCC's policy of nonintervention constituted an evasion of its statutory responsibility to hold evidentiary

---

[24]*Citizens Committe to Save WEFM* v. *FCC,* 506 F.2d 246 (DC Cir. 1974). Excerpted in Ginsburg, pp. 300, 305.

[25]*Ibid.* at p. 301.

[26]In addition to *WEFM,* see *Citizens Committe to Keep Progressive Rock* v. *FCC,* 478 F.2d 926 (1973); *Lakewood Broadcasting Service, Inc.* v. *FCC,* 478 F.2d 919 (1973); and *Citizens Committee to Preserve the Voice of the Arts in Atlanta* v. *FCC,* 436 F2d 263 (1970).

[27]*WNCN,* 101 S. Ct. at 1270.

[28]*WNCN Listeners Guild* v. *FCC,* 610 F.2d 838, 851 (DC Cir. 1979).

[29]610 F.2d at 843.

[30]These criteria logically apply to renewal as well as transfer applications. *WNCN,* 101 S. Ct. at 1270, n.6. For a worthwhile review of these criteria, see Pennybacker, pp. 414–421.

hearings.[31] As a matter of policy and procedure, however, the format doctrine was not intended to contravene the FCC's preference for a marketplace approach to format allocation. Indeed, the format doctrine was devised as an exception to — not a substitute for — the imperfect system of free competition.

The Commision, nonetheless, viewed the format doctrine as

> flatly inconsistent with our understanding of congressional policy as manifested in the Communications Act, contraproductive in terms of maximizing the welfare of the radio-listening public, administratively a fearful and comprehensive nightmare, and unconstitutional as impermissibly chilling innovation and experiementation in radio programming.[32]

The FCC's 1976 *Opinion and Order* interpreted the format doctrine in general — and in particular the Court's decision in *WEFM* — as having "far-reaching ramifications to our entire scheme of radio broadcast licensing;" if the Court intended for the format doctrine a limited and well-defined role, the FCC saw it as imposing "comprehensive, discriminating, and continuing state surveillance."[33] Although the Commission acknowledged its responsibility to comply with the Court's mandate in *WEFM,* its 1976 *Opinion* described the format doctrine as an "extremely unwise policy" and, in the end, rejected it as neither administratively tenable nor necessary in the public interest."[34]

Three citizens groups[35] petitioned the Court of Appeals for review of the FCC's *Opinion and Order,* and in June of 1979 the Court, sitting *en banc,* held the FCC's policy "to be unavailing and of no force and effect."[36] Taking the Commission to task for comparing its "policy" to the "policy" of the Court, Judge McGowan reminded the FCC that the judiciary interprets the *law* — it does not make "policy;" the format doctrine was "an interpretation of a statute" and, as such, qualified as a decision "in which the judicial word is final."[37] Notwithstanding the "deference owed the Commission's construction of the Communications Act," any contrary construction by the judiciary clearly takes precedence: it is the "Commission's obligation," the Court

---

[31]Section 309(a) of the Communications Act of 1934 provides that citizens may petition the FCC to deny a broadcast license if granting the license would be inconsistent with the Act's public interest standard. 47 USC Section 309(a) (1976).

[32]Quoted in *WNCN,* 610 F.2d at 845.

[33]*Memorandum Opinion and Order,* 41 Fed. Reg. at 32953.

[34]*Ibid.,* n.8.

[35]WNCN Listeners Guild, Classical Radio for Connecticut, and The Office of Communication of the United Church of Christ.

[36]*WNCN,* 610 F.2d at 858.

[37]*Ibid.* at 855.

ruled, "to accept and carry out in good faith its legal duties as interpreted by the court."[38]

WNCN and the Demise of the Format Doctrine

In response to writs of certiorari filed by the FCC, the National Association of Broadcasters and two broadcasting companies, the Supreme Court ruled in favor of the Commission's marketplace approach to format allocation. Justice White, writing for the Court, identified the controversy in its most narrow terms: "The issue before us is whether there are circumstances in which the Commission must review past or anticipated changes in a station's entertainment programming when it rules on an application for renewal or transfer of a radio broadcast license."[39] The Court's ruling was similarly narrow: since the FCC's policy on format diversity neither conflicted with the Communications Act of 1934 nor violated the First Amendment, the Court of Appeals had no basis for invalidating it. Without assessing the merits of either the format doctrine or the FCC's 1976 *Opinion and Order,* the Court found the latter to be "a reasonable accommodation of the policy of promoting diversity in programming and the policy of avoiding unnecessary restrictions on licensee discretion."[40]

While it could be difficult to read *WNCN* as an enthusiastic endorsement of the FCC's marketplace model, it would be just as difficult to ignore the significance of the Court's desire to empower the Commission with broad discretion in determining how much weight should be given to the goal of promoting diversity in radio programming and what policies should be pursued in realizing that goal.[41] Decidedly, *WNCN* focused not on the larger question of radio diversity and the role that government might properly play in achieving it but on the institutional competence of the Federal Communications Commission. In the Court's view, since "the construction of a statute by those charged with its execution should be followed unless there are compelling indications that is wrong,"[42] and since the Communications Act does not specifically require format regulation by the Commission, it follows that the Court of Appeals' format doctrine violated the FCC's "broad rulemaking powers."[43] Whether the format doctrine was itself a rational and reasonable approach to the diversification of radio programming was irrele-

---

[38]*Ibid.*
[39]*WNCN,* 101 S. Ct. at 1269.
[40]*Ibid.* at 1275.
[41]*Ibid.* at 1277.
[42]*Ibid.* at 1276.
[43]*Ibid* at 1281, n.11.

vant because the FCC's policies are entitled to "substantial judicial deference."

Apparently, the FCC's "broad rulemaking powers" are to be protected even when the Commission decides *not* to make rules. Whereas the FCC expressly declined to regulate radio formats "as an aspect of the public interest,"[44] the Supreme Court took this to be a "constitutionally permissible means of *implementing* the public interest standard."[45] Citing its 1940 ruling in *FCC* v. *Pottsville Broadcasting,* the Court described the public interest standard as a "supple instrument for the exercise of discretion by the expert body which Congress has charged to carry out its legislation;"[46] and it was certainly within the FCC's competence, the Court reasoned, for it to conclude "that its statutory duties are best fulfilled by not attempting to oversee format changes."[47]

Of course, that the FCC had chosen to remove itself *entirely* from the process through which formats would be allocated was the principal justification for the Courst of Appeal's format doctrine. If the lower court was willing to accept the logic of the Commission's marketplace model, it wanted to be sure that the FCC had at least provided a "waiver provision" or a "safety valve" procedure whereby citizens could petition for a hearing.[48] In at least two earlier decisions — *NBC* v. *U.S.* (1943) and *U.S.* v. *Storer Broadcasting* (1956) — the Supreme Court had considered the validity of the FCC's rules "in light of the flexibility provided by the procedures;"[49] and so the Court of Appeals was confident that its format doctrine was firmly rooted in administrative law, if not Constitutional law. In *WNCN,* however, the Supreme Court inexplicably retreated from its earlier rulings. The Court "did not hold," Justice White explained in a footnote, "that the Commission may never adopt a rule that lacks a waiver provision."[50]

Consumer Welfare, Pluralistic Programming and First Amendment Values

The FCC's commitment to the marketplace as the most desirable — or least objectionable — means of achieving format diversity not only underscores the ambiguity of diversity as a First Amendment ideal but illustrates the Commission's indifference toward the relationship between economic

[44] *Memorandum Opinion and Order,* 41 Fed. Reg. at 32953.
[45] *WNCN,* 101 S. Ct. at 1279.
[46] *Ibid.* at 1274.
[47] *Ibid.* at 1275.
[48] *WNCN,* 610 F.2d at 847–849.
[49] *NBC* v. *U.S.,* 319 US 190 (1943); *U.S.* v. *Storer Broadcasting,* 351 US 192 (1956).
[50] *WNCN,* 101 S. Ct. at 1278, n. 44.

incentives, industry structure and democratic values. From a policy perspective, the Commission's abiding faith in the principles of free enterprise is manifestly inimical to the needs of a culturally plural society because it effectively precludes consideration of the importance of pluralistic programming.

Cultural Pluralism and the First Amendment

While freedom of speech may be "essential as a means of assuring individual self-fulfillment,"[51] the self-fulfillment function of speech "finds little counterpart in relation to the press."[52] Arguably, the free press clause — in contrast to the free speech clause — denotes an essentially instrumental value, an effort to safeguard those conditions necessary for the survival of a wise and sophisticated electorate. Accordingly, freedom of the press is an important constitutional guarantee not because a free press is inherently valuable but because a free press can best meet the public communication needs of a democratic society: First Amendment protection for the print and electronic press is desirable because it fosters a robust and uninhibited press; a robust and uninhibited press is desirable because it is a press able and presumably willing to accommodate divergent points of view; divergent points of view are desirable because they sustain public debate; public debate is desirable because it nurtures an informed citizenry; and an informed citizenry is desirable because it brings about a more perfect polity and, in the end, legitimates the very idea of self-government. The goal of the free press clause of the First Amendment, it follows, is to protect and enhance the *public's* ability to govern itself; an *individual's* opportunity to be heard publicly warrants First Amendment protection only because it contributes to what Alexander Meiklejohn calls the "public understanding" essential to self-government.

From a Meiklejohnian interpretation of the free press clause, the First Amendment is not intended to promote "unregulated talkativeness;" what is crucial, Meiklejohn argues, is "not that everyone shall speak" but that "everything worth saying shall be said."[53] Meiklejohn's theory of the First Amendment is fundamentally political; appropriately, it appears in a work entitled *Political Freedom.* There is, however, an important corollary to Meiklejohn's theory, a *cultural* interpretation of the goals and objectives of the First Amendment.

---

[51]Thomas I. Emerson, *The System of Freedom of Expression* (New York: Random House, 1970), p. 6.

[52]Melville B. Nimmer, "Is Freedom of the Press a Redundancy?" *Hastings Law Journal* 26:639–658 (1975). Excerpted in *Free but Regulated: Conflicting Traditions in Media Law,* eds. D. L. Brenner and W. L. Rivers (Ames: Iowa State University Press, 1982), p. 28.

[53]Alexander Meiklejohn, *Political Freedom* (New York: Oxford University Press, 1965), p. 26.

From a cultural perspective, a Meiklejohnian interpretation of the free press clause would call for a robust and uninhibited press not for purposes of accommodating an enlightened electorate but for purposes of accommodating a plurality of cultural associations. If the political goal of the free press clause is an informed citizenry, its cultural goal is a citizenry firmly rooted in what John Dewey described as the "principles of associated life;" for as Dewey reminds us, democracy is more than a type of government: democracy is primarily a form of association, a kind of "conjoint communicated experience."[54]

By "conjoint communicated experience" Dewey meant to emphasize that "a clear consciousness of a communal life, in all its implications, constitutes the idea of democracy."[55] Only a culturally plural society, in Dewey's view, can embody the spirit of democracy; and only the spirit of democracy can nourish a sense of community and an appreciation for the integrity of diverse cultures. Dewey's understanding of the connection between democracy and community is founded on the premise that "community is inherently democratic, and democracy is inherently communal."[56]

In the context of broadcasting, a commitment to cultural pluralism translates into First Amendment protection for truly pluralistic programming. In contrast to the kind of cultural oligarchy resulting from an advertiser-dominated system of broadcasting, pluralistic programming is programming designed to reflect and thus enhance cultural diversity; pluralistic programming, to borrow sociologist Robert Nisbet's distinction, responds to individual listeners as "indistinguishable from a culture" rather than as "simply a numerical aggregate" regarded for "administrative puposes as discrete and socially separated."[57]

Although the Supreme Court appeared to have recognized the importance of pluralistic programming when in *Red Lion* in 1969 it made reference to the listener's First Amendment right "to receive suitable access to social, political, esthetic, moral, and other ideas and experiences."[58] Justice White in *WNCN* made it clear that the *Red Lion* court "did not imply that the First Amendment grants individual listeners the right to have the Commission review the abandonment of their favorite entertainment programs."[59] Thus

---

[54]John Dewey, *The Public and Its Problems* (Chicago: Swallow Press, 1927), pp. 145–154. For a more general discussion of the values of a culturally plural society, see *Pluralism in a Democratic Society,* eds. M.M. Tumin and W. Plotch (New York: Praeger, 1977).

[55]Dewey, *ibid.,* p. 149.

[56]Lary Belman, "John Dewey's Concept of Communication," *Journal of Communication* 27:29–37 (Winter 1977).

[57]Robert A. Nisbet, *The Quest for Community* (New York: Oxford University Press, 1953), p. 249.

[58]*Red Lion Broadcasting Co.* v. *FCC,* 395 US 367, 390 (1969).

[59]*WNCN,* 101 S. Ct. at 1279.

the failure of *WNCN* — at least from a cultural point of view — is the failure of the Court to see any connection between *Red Lion* and the FCC's format policy; and the failure of the FCC's policy is the failure of the Commission to look beyond the marketplace for the standards with which to assess program diversity.

The FCC's format policy is inherently flawed if only because it views diversity in strictly economic terms, what the Court of Appeals describes as a "mechanistic deference" to free enterprise.[60] Since the Commission's format policy safeguards the broadcaster's right to compete, not the listener's right to "receive suitable access" to a sufficiently diverse range of programming, the FCC appears to be willing to settle for whatever diversity competition might yield. In practice, the FCC thus accepts the competition — not diversity — as the goal of the First Amendment. In fact, the only standard used by the Commission to define and measure diversity is the ideal of "free" competition.

When measured against the standard of "free' competition, the FCC readily admits that the marketplace for radio is structurally deficient (for the reasons outlined earlier) — but not deficient to the point where government intervention would be required. Remarkedly, the FCC's understanding of the deficiencies of the marketplace is limited to the marketplace's *economic* imperfections; at no time has the Commission extended its inquiry into the marketplace's *cultural* imperfections. If the Commission is reluctant to decide whether competition brings about "insufficient" diversity because "insufficient" raises a cultural and thus normative issue, it is administratively and politically comfortable with its laissez-faire approach to format allocation because its marketplace model is portrayed as an entirely empirical, apolitical and value-free resolution of the diversity issue.

Competition, Diversity and Pluralistic Programming

That the FCC's conception of diversity is inextricably wedded to competition in the marketplace is, however, striking evidence of the Commission's bias, not its impartiality. Principally, it is a bias in favor of the broadcaster, not the listener; and a bias in favor of competition, not diversity. To no avail, former FCC Commissioner Nicholas Johnson tried to call attention to the Commission's bias when he argued that the "conclusion of the marketplace advocates that the pricing mechanism produces the most equitable and efficient allocation of resources is itself a normative, not an empirical, judgment;" furthermore, Johnson wrote:

> To assume that market allocation of a good is a normal situation, to be departed from only in exceptional situations, is to determine an industry's

[60] *WEFM*, 506 F.2d at 268.

goals and principles by considering only economic factors and ignoring the social impact of the industry.

The market allocation proposal ignores public policy considerations in its failure to encourage "good" use of the spectrum.[61]

It is ironic that the FCC's expressed interest in diversity turns out to be a commitment to competition; for as Owen goes to great lengths to explain, competition has very little to do with diversity. Actually, Owen — who the Commission cites with approval — sees diversity as "at best irrelevant and at worst seriously debilitating to the consumer interest."[62]

Inevitably, when consumer welfare is defined economically instead of culturally, *variety* will be mistaken for *diversity*. And this is precisely what has happened in radio broadcasting: the marketplace for formats has failed to distinguish between intra-format diversity, which is mere variety, and inter-format diversity, which comes closer to the goal of pluralistic programming. As the FCC puts it, there "exists no *economically* rational basis"[63] for deciding whether intra-format or inter-format diversity best serves the public interest. In other words, when diversity is defined solely in terms of competition, there would appear to be no meaningful distinction between, say, a market with 12 unique formats and a market with one format duplicated by 12 stations. In many markets, therefore, pluralistic programming may give way to a great variety of essentially similar programs — and in Owne's and the Commission's view, consumer welfare would be the better for it.

To fully appreciate the folly of the FCC's conception of diversity — and to better illustrate the importance of the distinction between variety and diversity — consider the marketplace for automobiles. Should automobile manufacturers limit their production to only subcompacts but design an impressive *variety* of subcompacts (analogous to only intra-format diversity), would consumer welfare be as well served as when automobile manufacturers produce a *diversity* of models — from subcompacts to full-size cars — but offer only one design for each size model category (analogous to only inter-format diversity)? Given limited resources, if automobile manufacturers had to limit *either* variety *or* diversity, which would be the higher priority? In its most stark terms, is it more important to allow consumers to choose between a yellow, a blue or a green subcompact or between a subcompact and, say, a nine-passenger station wagon?

The difference between variety and diversity is, essentially, the difference

[61]In Ginsburg, *ibid.*, pp. 69, 70.

[62]Bruce M. Owen, "Diversity in Broadcasting: The Economic View of Programming," *Journal of Communication* 28:43–47 (Spring 1978).

[63]*Memorandum Opinion and Order,* 41 Fed. Reg. at 32957. Intraformat diversity refers to diversity *within* a particular format category; interformat diversity refers to diversity among distinctive formats.

between wants and needs. *Wants* are typically private and idiosyncratic; they focus on personal perference and individual gratification. *Needs,* however, are typically public and shared; they transcend individual preference and focus instead on purposes and interests common to a class of people. Whereas wants emerge from a fundamentally hedonistic calculation of pleasure and pain, needs emerge in response to a desire to achieve or maintain a reasonably comfortable quality of life.[64] There is indeed an important difference between the need of low-income families for a small, fuel-efficient car and one family's preference for a particular package of options.

Just as automobile diversity is essential if automobile manufacturers expect to meet the needs of a society increasingly dependent on private transportation, format diversity is essential if broadcasters expect to meet the needs of a society committed to the ideal of cultural pluralism. And if there is a lesson to be learned from the automobile industry, it is that economic incentives alone often mitigate against diversity: without government intervention, variety tends to displace diversity and the consumer is left with the illusion of choice. Be they automobiles or radio programs, it is a fundamental economic maxim that "wherever there is a demand for diversity of product, pure competition turns out to be not the ideal but a departure from it."[65]

In sum, to advocate greater diversity in radio programming is not to advocate diversity for the sake of diversity. Rather, pluralistic programming is programming intended to sustain the cultural diversity in a given market; it is what Jacklin calls "representative diversity," programming diverse enough to correspond to the diversity in the community.[66] As a practical matter, the goal of diversity in radio broadcasting is no more unworkable than the goal of fuel-efficiency in the automobile industry. It *will* require corrective measures but not the kind of insidious state control that would suppress expression. On the contrary, a restructuring of the marketplace for radio[67] could bring about a greater diversity of communication and thus extend to listeners the freedom of choice to which they are entitled under the First Amendment and the Communications Act of 1934. As the Court of Appeals recognized over a decade ago, "it is surely in the public interest, as that was conceived by a

---

[64]For an argument in favor of the "recognition of the limits of resources and the priority of needs" over wants, see Daniel Bell, *The Cultural Contraditions of Capitalism* (New York: Basic Books, 1976).

[65]E. H. Chamberlin, "Product Heterogeneity and Public Policy," *American Economic Review* 40:85–92 (May 1950, Papers and Proceedings).

[66]Phil Jacklin, "Representative Diversity," *Journal of Communication* 28:85–88 (Spring 1978).

[67]For a proposal to restructure the marketplace for radio for purposes of increasing program diversity, see Harvey C. Jassem, Roger J. Desmond and Theodore L. Glasser, "Pluralistic Programming and Radio Diversity: A Review and a Proposal," *Policy Sciences* 14:347–364 (August 1982).

Congress representative of all the people, for all major aspects of contemporary culture to be accommodated by the commonly-owned public resources whenever that is technically and economically feasible."[68] That goal is certainly technically feasible and would be economically feasible if legal and structural issues were not defined solely in terms of marketplace forces. The important point is not that the marketplace for radio is structurally deficient because it is a departure from the ideal of competition but that competition itself is a departure from the ideal of pluralistic programming.

30

COMPETITION AND DIVERSITY AMONG RADIO FORMATS
A 1984 Response

Erwin G. Krasnow and William E. Kennard

There is an old saw that a liberal looks at government and asks, "What wonderful things can we do with this splendid machine," while the conservative looks at the machine and says, "What terrible damage can this rough beast do."

"Competition and Diversity Among Radio Formats" is clearly written from a liberal perspective. The article is essentially a plea for government intervention in the selection of radio program formats. The reader has to wait until the last paragraph, however, to find out how the author would accomplish this task without, to use his words, "the kind of insidious state control that would suppress expression." The proposed solution—a restructuring of the marketplace for radio—is never explained in the article. There is a reference in the penultimate footnote to an article in the August, 1982, edition of *Policy Sciences* which calls for the formation of local radio boards; the local boards would be responsible for identifying and describing existing local communities of taste.

The creation of local programming councils is a novel approach—it is an old idea whose time has never come. The proposal would run 180 degrees counter to the direction taken by the FCC, the Supreme Court and most members of Congress. Such an approach would necessarily result in the entanglement of mini-FCCs in matters that Congress meant to leave to private discretion. Implementation of program format regulation—be it on a local or federal level—would raise constitutional questions because "a comprehensive, discriminating and continuing state surveillance will inevitably be required to ensure that these restrictions are obeyed." *FCC Policy Statement,* 60 FCC 2d 858, 865 (1976), *quoting Lemon* v. *Kurtzman,* 403 US 602, 619 (1971).

The article devotes scant attention to the legal and policy issues posed by establishing the FCC—or worse yet, local programming councils—as the arbiter of such a nebulous concept as pluralistic programming. Any interpretation of the Communications Act which would require the Commission to

From Erwin G. Krasnow and William E. Kennard, "Competition and Diversity Among Radio Formats: A 1984 Response," *Journal of Broadcasting*, Vol. 28, No. 2 (Spring 1984), pp. 143-145.

regulate the selection of radio program formats is directly contrary to decisions of the US Supreme Court which make clear that the Communications Act embodies a policy of leaving the selection of programming to broadcasters and is designed "to preserve editorial control of programming in the licensee." *FCC* v. *Midwest Video Corp.,* 440 US 689, 705 (1979); *see also CBS* v. *Democratic National Committee,* 412 US 94, 105 (1973). In this connection, Congress, during the consideration of the Radio Act of 1927 and the Communications Act of 1934, focused generally on the question of whether the agency should be authorized to set program priorities in assigning radio licenses, and specifically on the question of whether the agency should be empowered to regulate the types of music to be broadcast (for example, "high class music" as opposed to "jazz"). A proposal to permit the agency to establish programming priorities was eliminated from the bill because of fears of censorship, and these concerns led directly to Section 326 of the Communications Act, 47 USC § 326, which explicitly prohibits agency censorship. Thus, the only legislative history bearing on the Commission's authority to regulate program formats demonstrates that Congress desired to leave the choice of program formats to broadcasters.

The broad public interest standard embodied in the Act does not lend support to a proposal to regulate program formats, for the standard necessarily "invites reference to First Amendment principles." *CBS* v. *DNC,* 412 US at 122. Such principles strongly support the Commission's determination not to engage in format regulation. For example, the fairness doctrine has been sustained only because it "contemplates a wide range of licensee discretion" and does not dictate or control broadcasters' initial choices of programming. *Midwest Video,* 440 US at 705 n.14. In contrast, format regulation would require the Commission to dictate a licensee's entire program schedule by restraining the broadcast of a proposed format and by forcing the licensee to retain an existing format when the broadcaster has affirmatively exercised a contrary editorial judgment. In requiring a broadcaster to present a certain type of programming in place of another, the Commission would be imposing a prior restraint on speech and would be violating the fundamental principle that government regulatory action must be neutral and may not favor one side of an issue or one public taste over another. *See FCC* v. *Pacifica Foundation,* 438 US 726, 745–46 (1978).

In rejecting format regulation, the Commission found that it was not possible to devise adequate standards to regulate radio formats because the boundaries between format types are extremely elusive, because there is no method of objectively gauging public dissatisfaction with the format change, and because it is impossible to compare the relative "public interest" in the existing and proposed formats. The agency would therefore be compelled to make a wide variety of unguided and subjective judgments that would lead to the imposition of its own program preferences on broadcasters. Professor Glasser has failed to grapple with the unworkable nature of corrective measures designed to implement an elitist or "force them to eat cake" approach to "reforming" the marketplace for radio. To paraphrase Gilbert and Sullivan, a carping critic's lot is not a happy one—the author has presented ideas that are totally out of step with the regulatory philosophy of the FCC and court precedents, and has proposed a solution that is as elusive as the quest for the Holy Grail; however, we acknowledge that he is a pretty good speller.

31

COMPETITION AND DIVERSITY AMONG RADIO FORMATS
A Rejoinder

Theodore L. Glasser

That Messrs. Krasnow and Kennard find that my "ideas are totally out of step with the regulatory philosophy of the FCC and court precedents" brings to mind an Oliver Wendell Holmes adage: "It cannot be helped, it is as it should be, that the law is behind the times."

Curiously, the substance of the repsonse focuses on what is in my view the least important, the least interesting, and the least consequential aspect of my article. I am taken to task for not explaining how I would restructure the marketplace for radio, and I am criticized for not grappling with the "unworkable nature" of such corrective measures. Curious indeed, since my *only* mention of a proposal to restructure the marketplace was in my very last paragraph.

I do wish the Krasnow and Kennard comment had concentrated on—and responded to—my attempt to assess the Commission's assumptions about the relationship between competition and diversity. Instead, the authors strain valiantly to resuscitate the time-worn assumptions that underlie the FCC's decision to use marketplace forces as the sole basis for allocating radio formats. They worry about a government agency being compelled to make "unguided" and "subjective" judgments. And so we are left with the unhappy and entirely unsupported proposition that the marketplace will operate democratically—that an entrepreneur's judgments are somehow properly guided, less subjective, and presumptively consistent with the needs of the community.

Much is being written these days about a "new charter for telecommunications;" and much is being said about how the state might properly enhance the quality of telecommunications.[1] At a time when communications policy is going through fundamental changes, it is so important, as the Court of Appeals observed, that we "not equate what is habitual with what is right."[2]

---

[1]See for example Thomas I. Emerson, "The Affirmative Side of the First Amendment," *Georgia Law Review* 15:795–849 (Summer 1981) and David L. Bazelon, "The First Amendment and the 'New Media'—New Directions in Regulating Telecommunications," *Federal Communications Law Journal* 31:201–213 (1979).

[2]*Business Executives' Move* v. *FCC,* 450 F.2d 642, 665 (DC Cir. 1971).

From Theodore L. Glasser, "Competition and Diversity Among Radio Formats: A Rejoinder," *Journal of Broadcasting*, Vol. 28, No. 2 (Spring 1984), p. 147.

32

HOME VIDEO RECORDERS AND THE TRANSIENCE OF TELEVISION BROADCASTS

Mark R. Levy and Edward L. Fink

A model of the recording and replaying of television programs predicts the "half-life" of recorded fare and suggests the impact of seriality, frequency, and availability on home recording.

Historically, mass media have been characterized by a high degree of message transience. With few exceptions, mass media are "usually meant to be consumed immediately, not to be entered into permanent records" and the content is "regarded as expendable" (34, pp. 6–7). Compared to print, television programs have been distinguished by an especially high degree of transience. Once broadcast, a television program becomes unavailable for repeated viewing unless it is rebroadcast. Indeed, it has been said in an inelegant but nonetheless revealing phrase that television "goes in one eye and out the other" (12).

The transient quality of television broadcasts has a number of important consequences for the mass communication process. For audiences, for example, the catch-it-or-miss-it nature of television broadcasts affects both media consumption patterns and leisure time budgets more generally (31). Moreover, the fleetingness of TV messages may significantly constrain the ability of viewers to comprehend or otherwise be affected by content (see, e.g., 32). From the perspective of content creators, the speed with which television messages "disappear" may encourage an emphasis on timeliness, superficiality, or sensationalism

Mark R. Levy is Associate Professor in the College of Journalism and a Research Associate in the Center for Research in Public Communication, University of Maryland. Edward L. Fink is Associate Professor in the Department of Communication Arts and Theatre and a Research Associate in the Center for Research in Public Communication, University of Maryland. An earlier version of this article was presented at the 33rd Annual Conference of the International Communication Association, May 29, 1983, at Dallas. The authors contributed equally to this article.

Reprinted from "Home Video Recorders and the Transience of Television Broadcasts," by Mark R. Levy and Edward L. Fink in the *Journal of Communication*, Vol. 34, No. 2, Spring 1984.

in what is fundamentally a one-time chance to attract large audiences (13). Finally, the transitory character of television broadcasts may even partially explain the disdain expressed for that medium by many high culture critics (e.g., 10, 25): if one criterion of artistic merit is longevity of appeal, then television's fleeting fare cannot meet the test of time.

The introduction of home video recorders in the mid-1970s has raised the technological possibility that the transient quality of television broadcasts may be altered, however, for these new recorders have the potential to permanently preserve television programs on videotape *at home*. Such a change would be consistent with the great sweep of communication history, a history in which messages have simultaneously become less transient and more widespread (30).

In this article we provide a framework for understanding message transience and apply it to television programs. We will also test a mathematical model dealing with the technology that has the capability to alter the transient character of television broadcasts, the home video cassette recorder. At least six million U.S. households have video cassette recorders (VCRs), and conservative estimates project that, by 1990, VCRs will be found in one-quarter or more of all U.S. homes (5, 7). The rapid diffusion of home video recorder technology has important behavioral and theoretical implications for the transience of television broadcasts.

Behavioral issues in VCR use. At present, the principal use of VCRs is to record broadcasts directly from the home television set. The average VCR household records approximately four broadcasts per week and replays an average of three or four recordings weekly (1, 17). On the average, less than one prerecorded cassette that has been bought, borrowed, or rented is played per week by VCR households.

Most report using the VCR for time shifting, that is, to record broadcasts for relatively immediate replay at a more convenient time (2, 19). Several researchers have found, for example, that three-quarters or more of all tapes replayed were initially recorded within a week or less of their first playback. Moreover, more than half of all VCR recordings are made through use of a built-in timer that records programs while the TV set is turned off and potential viewers are engaged elsewhere (18).

A second use for video recorders is the taping of programs, especially motion pictures and "specials," in order to save them in a home videotape "library." A recorded movie or special concert may be replayed years later, giving it the aura of uniqueness and longevity that is typically associated with "classics" in other media. All that is required is the relatively small luxury of enough blank videotape and some storage space.[1] However, discussion of this so-called "library-building" use of VCRs has been largely speculative, with little evidence offered on the frequency of its occurrence or its behavioral and motivational correlates.

Thus, in both types of VCR use—time shifting and library building—users are actively responding to and altering the existing broadcast schedule, recording programs for future viewing. In doing so, they are also affecting, to a greater or lesser degree, the transience of television broadcasts.

Theoretical issues in VCR use. The transience of mass media messages in general and television programs in particular has two general determinants: first, the technical characteristics of the transmitted signal, and second, the public definitions of the media, their content, and their uses (21).

In the case of television, the technical aspects are fairly simple: home video recorders capture and retain that medium's electronic signal on half-inch videotape. Thus, the transience of television broadcasts can be more usefully examined as a function of how audiences perceive and use the resulting videotapes.

Such audience perceptions and uses might be fruitfully studied from a uses and gratifications perspective, which suggests that individuals select specific types of media content according to their expectations and experiences with a given medium (16). This general observation is

[1] The median number of "blank" cassettes owned by VCR households reportedly is less than a dozen (see 22). This suggests that the average VCR household has enough cassettes for both time shifting and some limited library building.

particularly germane to VCR users. While VCR households *watch* the same average number and types of television programs as do other households, previous studies (2, 18) report that most VCR users regularly record and play back only a relatively small number of program types (e.g., movies, soap operas, situation comedies) and that they tend to "specialize" in only two or three of these types. This specialization in recording and replay can be interpreted as an attempt by VCR users to maintain and perhaps increase those gratifications associated with certain types of television programs. As a result, the transience of certain programs may be reduced.

At least four factors affect the decision to record a television program for future replay, whether that recording will be replayed ("consumed"), and the degree to which the taped broadcast will be considered "expendable" by the viewer.

Seriality of program content. This refers to (a) the degree to which the plot and characters of a television program are perceived by viewers to have some continuity and (b) the degree to which audience members believe that exposure to one episode, installment, or broadcast is necessary to their understanding or enjoyment of previous or subsequent programs. For example, we would argue that soap operas and dramatic series (e.g., "Hill Street Blues," "Dallas"), with story lines that develop from episode to episode and with continuing character portrayals, exhibit a high degree of content seriality. Knowing what is happening from installment to installment may be an important element in viewer enjoyment.

Other programs and program types are probably characterized by lower degrees of content seriality. In situation comedies, for instance, the characters remain more or less constant, but each program installment offers a relatively self-contained plot. By contrast, motion pictures and "specials" are comparatively "free-standing."

In general, we would expect that the higher the seriality of a program's content, the more likely that a video recording of that program would be replayed.

Frequency of program transmission. Programs such as soap operas, talk shows, and newscasts are broadcast daily; network situation comedies, dramatic series, or police-detective programs air weekly; a given motion picture or "special" may be broadcast only once. If a new episode of an already recorded program is to be broadcast soon, then the VCR user may consider the already taped program to be relatively expendable and, instead of replaying the tape, simply wait for the fresh broadcast.

However, both program transmission frequency and program content seriality will also affect the "speed" (i.e., the elapsed time between recording and replay) of program playback. For example, recordings of programs that are comparatively high in content seriality *and* that are also broadcast frequently would be more rapidly replayed, if they are replayed at all, than low-seriality, infrequently broadcast programs. Indeed, in principle, it should be possible to map all television programs into the two dimensions of content seriality and transmission frequency to predict their likelihood of replay.

Availability of other broadcasts. If a viewer believes that similar gratifications will result from watching a fresh broadcast of a program perceived to be similar in type and/or use to an already taped broadcast, then that viewer may decide not to replay the recorded program or to replay it more "slowly." Whether such a substitution or delay actually occurs will be a function of such things as program seriality, frequency of program transmission, viewer loyalty to a given program, viewer perceptions of program genre, and the timely scheduling of functionally equivalent broadcasts.

Nontelevision competition for the viewer's time and attention. While mass media are relatively interchangeable in their ability to gratify many social and psychological needs (16), these same gratifications often may be found outside the media. VCR use allows television to be defined by audiences as resembling other stored, on-the-shelf media like magazines and books, or other daily sensory choices (e.g., food). Thus, a more complete understanding of VCR use also requires an assessment of how VCRs affect the comparative position of television as a source of these gratifications and under what circumstances the recording and replay of TV programs are replaced by utilizing other media or engaging in other behavior.

By examining the time elapsed between recording and replay, the model we will develop allows precise estimation of the impact of VCRs on the transience of television broadcasts.

Several investigators have attempted to create mathematical models of the mass media, dealing either with historical or economic trends (see, e.g., 26) or with viewing patterns or message survival (9, 14, 15, 20, 28). Following in that general tradition, we are proposing a model that focuses on the "speed" with which video recordings are played back.

The model focuses first on overall replay behavior and second on the relationship between playbacks and the frequency of program transmission, using data based on a sample of VCR households and on a sample of television programs. To assess the viewer's conception of the other three factors identified above as affecting broadcast transience (program seriality, frequency of program type transmission, and nontelevision competition) would require data that are not available to us. Indeed, we know of no data base that measures all four factors along with VCR use and replay behavior. Thus, we expect the analyses provided below to be only gross estimates of the effects we seek to evaluate.

Two types of VCR use have already been discussed. The time-shifting use suggests that TV programs are replayed rather quickly, while the library-building use suggests that programs are replayed long after their initial recording. Note, then, that the two uses of VCRs are associated with different levels of broadcast transience: time shifting implies quick replay and then tape reuse, which erases the previous program; library building implies extended program life, in the sense of both possible multiple replays and prolonged shelf storage.

Also note that a single program or program type may be associated with either type of use. One may record the news for time shifting, but save the newscast of, say, a royal wedding or a presidential address. We hypothesize that, in general, the time-shifting function should be most associated with programs that are scheduled daily, next most with programs broadcast on a weekly basis, and least with one-shot programs, that is, broadcasts whose general content is unlikely to be repeated.[2] However, we would also suggest that, in general, a program recorded for time shifting is unlikely to also have been recorded for library building.

How can we evaluate the extent to which specific programs or types of programs are being recorded for time-shifting purposes? To the extent that a program is recorded solely for time shifting, we should find that

—the cumulative proportion of recorded broadcasts replayed (which, of course, is zero initially) approaches some maximum finite value with the passage of time;

—the additional proportion of recordings replayed declines over time; and

—the impulse to replay a newly recorded program is greatest initially and diminishes over time.

The greater the extent to which a program or program type can be described as meeting these three criteria, the more we can assume that the time-shifting function is relevant to that program or program type.

A model that follows the above stipulations is the exponential decay model $Y_t = \alpha \exp(-\beta t)$, where α = the Y intercept, β = an empirically derived constant whose sign is positive, t = time, and Y_t = the

[2] In the test of the model presented below, we have classified programs solely by the criterion of scheduling. However, it would be preferable to obtain viewer perceptions of how programs should be classified, especially since ambiguous cases sometimes arise. For example, a news program (daily) may contain a report of a dramatic event (e.g., a royal wedding) and thus be considered by some viewers to be a one-shot program.

height of the curve at the instant t. The exponential decay curve has a number of properties. First, the cumulative area under the curve follows the equation $Y_{cum} = (\alpha/\beta)[1 - \exp(-\beta t)]$. Thus, Y_{cum} is 0 at $t = 0$ and approaches α/β as t approaches infinity. Second, the slope of the curve follows the equation $dY/dt = -\alpha\beta \exp(-\beta t)$. Therefore, with $\alpha > 0$, the slope is always negative. At $t = 0$, the slope is $-\alpha\beta$, and as t approaches infinity, the slope approaches 0. Third, the acceleration of the curve follows the equation $d^2Y/dt^2 = \alpha\beta^2 \exp(-\beta t)$. Acceleration is positive and greatest initially; it declines, as t approaches infinity, to 0. Finally, the slope and acceleration of the curve at any point are proportionate to the height of the curve at that point.

The exponential decay model has been used to describe forgetting (11), drug distribution in the body, radioactive decay, and the response of sales to advertising (see 8). When applied to communications, this model allows for the calculation of a summary measure of content transience that we call "message half-life." By message half-life, we mean that point in time at which 50 percent of a set of mass media messages will have been seen by the aggregate audience.[3] This does not mean that any particular person has a 0.5 probability of exposure, but rather that half of the messages have been read or viewed.

For example, studies of newspaper reading have shown that virtually all daily newspapers are read within one day of the paper's publication (6). By contrast, some sections of the Sunday newspaper are retained and read for four or more days. Thus, the content of daily newspapers can be said to have a message half-life of less than one day, while Sunday sections have a message half-life of a few days. Similar, but more precise, half-life calculations can be made for television programs that have been videotaped, yielding a comparative measure of message or content longevity.

If our exponential decay model is correct, the half-life of VCR-taped broadcasts may be computed in the following fashion. The model assumes: $50\% = Y_{cum} = (\alpha/\beta)[1 - \exp(-\beta t)]$. Since α and β are empirical parameters that may be estimated, the half-life—$t_{(Y_{cum} = .50)}$—may be estimated as: $(-\log[1 - .50(\beta/\alpha)])/\beta$. Note that the definition of half-life

[3] An alternative definition for the half-life of a set of messages is that point in time at which fifty percent of the set of messages that will ever be perceived will have been perceived by the aggregate audience. We call this the fifty percent of ultimate exposure half-life. For example, in the case of VCR use, if 80 percent of the recordings will ultimately be replayed, then under this alternative definition, the message half-life will be the point in time at which 40 percent of the recordings have been replayed. A third way to define message half-life has been used in the study of scientific citations (see, e.g., 9, 14, 27, and 29). In those studies, message half-life is the point in time at which half of a potential audience has been exposed to a given message.

assumes that at least 50 percent of recordings will be replayed. Also, the measure of half-life used here is not for any particular message, but for messages grouped in some fashion, such as by program type, frequency of transmission, etc.

The data used in this study were obtained from television viewing diaries placed in VCR households by Media Statistics, Inc.

An initial sample of VCR households was identified by telephone screening of some 40,000 households selected at random by systematic sampling in 15 metropolitan areas nationwide.[4] A random subsample was then drawn from that pool of VCR households, and 249 households completed usable diaries for a one-week period between September 10 and October 17, 1981.[5]

We find this subsample to be similar to other samples of VCR users. As previous studies (2, 18) have found, this sample was distinctly upscale. More than one-third, for example, reported family incomes in excess of $50,000 a year, and four-fifths of household heads had attended college (23). Some 36 percent of the VCR households sampled subscribed to cable and/or pay television—about twice the average cable/pay TV penetration in the 15 markets surveyed. However, despite the demographic skew of the sample, an inspection of programs recorded and replayed, as well as findings from other studies (2, 18), suggests that these VCR households view and record the same general types of programs that are watched and not recorded by the non-VCR-owning audience.

One diary was kept for each TV set in the home. Entries from each diary were compiled by Media Statistics, Inc., into a household composite in which was listed, among other things, the title of every program recorded and/or played back and the diary day of recording or replay. All programs replayed during the diary week were classified as "daily," "weekly," or "one-shot," depending on the frequency of program transmission. Programs classified as daily were soap operas and talk shows. Weekly programs were situation comedies, dramatic series, entertainment series, police-detective programs, weekly children's pro-

[4] The metropolitan areas surveyed were New York City, Los Angeles, Chicago, Cleveland, Denver, San Francisco, Philadelphia, Dallas–Fort Worth, Boston, St. Louis, Milwaukee, Minneapolis, Washington, D.C., Houston, and Seattle.

[5] While the type of program available to be recorded and replayed may, of course, vary somewhat with the season and broadcast schedules, previous studies (2, 3, 18) have found that program preferences in VCR households and patterns of VCR use are relatively stable and comparatively independent of seasonal and programming influences.

grams, and public affairs and science programs. Programs classified as "one-shot" were motion pictures, entertainment specials, and cultural specials.[6]

To avoid understating the proportion of recordings actually played back within a week of broadcast, we cross-tabulated diary day of recording with elapsed days to replay and calculated the mean percentage of recordings replayed on each day of the "extended" week. This procedure can be better understood through the example in Table 1, based on all programs played back.

Table 1: Diary day of recording, by elapsed days to replay, for all broadcasts recorded (in percent)

	Elapsed days to replay									
Day recorded	0 %	1 %	2 %	3 %	4 %	5 %	6 %	Not replayed %	%	n
1	24.1	14.6	7.6	5.1	1.9	1.3	0.6	44.9	100.0	158
2	24.0	20.7	8.0	2.7	2.7	1.3		40.7	100.0	150
3	23.4	20.7	9.0	2.1	2.1			42.8	100.0	145
4	25.2	17.5	4.9	2.9				49.5	100.0	103
5	25.7	25.7	7.6					41.0	100.0	105
6	22.1	18.9						58.9	100.0	95
7	22.2							77.8	100.0	126

To calculate the mean percentage of recordings replayed on Day 0 (that is, on the same day as recorded), we summed the percentages in the column headed with a 0 (e.g., 24.1, 24.0, 23.4, 25.2, etc.) and divided the total by seven. To determine the percentage of recordings replayed after one elapsed day, we summed the row percentages in the next column and divided by six. Similar calculations were then made for the remaining five days. The percentage of recordings played back in Days 0 to 6 was summed and that total was subtracted from 100 percent to give the estimate of recordings not replayed within an "extended" week. This procedure was also followed for daily, weekly, and one-shot programs.

It should be noted that, because the data were not available in a more precise form, the diary format "time" is not the same as the time parameter in the exponential decay model. For example, a program recorded at 11:59 P.M. and replayed at 12:01 A.M. (two minutes later) is treated in the diary as if it had been replayed *one day* later. In the exponential decay model, the replay would properly be treated as occurring on Day 0, with t being more precisely estimated as 0.0014 days

[6] Because of either the original coding scheme used to classify recordings or broadcast scheduling idiosyncracies, 173 programs recorded in the overall sample could not be satisfactorily assigned to the daily, weekly, or one-shot categories. These excluded programs were sports (n = 71) and miscellaneous (n = 102).

after recording. We assume that this difference in the use of time will not greatly affect the utility of the model. Further, since time was treated as having only seven levels (replay 0–6 days from recording), we will also assume that replays are evenly distributed within each day. Thus, to test our model, diary Day 0 will be treated as the interval 0 to 1 and estimated as Day 0.5 in the model.

The exponential decay curve was fitted to these data with the following assumptions:

1. A stochastic error term, u, is multiplicative, so that $Y_t = \alpha[\exp(-\beta t)]\, u$.

2. The exponential decay equation may be linearized by taking the logarithms of both sides: $\log(Y_t) = \log(\alpha) - \beta t + \log(u)$, where log (u) is assumed to be normal, homoscedastic, and non-autocorrelated.

3. Days on which no playbacks were reported were not utilized for estimating the parameters of the curve. This is because we expect that with a larger sample of VCR households and programs, this number might be expected to be other than zero, and a nonzero value is required for curve-fitting. Rather than arbitrarily add a nonzero value (see, e.g., 33), we excluded such points. If this procedure were incorrect, predicted values for cumulative replays would differ considerably from observed values. Thus, even with a small sample of time points, the validity of the procedure can be evaluated.

The largest proportion of initial replays occurred very shortly after the recordings were made.

For example, 43.5 percent of all recordings were played back either the day of broadcast or the next day, with 72.0 percent of daily programs receiving this speedy replay (see Table 2). Similarly, tapes of weekly and one-shot programs also received their largest proportion of playbacks soon after recording, although in absolute terms the proportions of those two program types replayed within a day or less of recording was substantially smaller than the 0–1 day totals for either all or daily programs.

Furthermore, as the exponential decay model predicts, the additional proportion of recordings played back declines precipitously with time. On the second day after broadcast, for example, only 7.4 percent of all recordings were given their first playback, and six days after recording, fewer than one percent of all programs received their initial taped viewing. This pattern held generally for all program types.

There was a substantial difference between program types in the cumulative proportion of recordings played back by the end of the extended diary week. While more than half (58.2 percent) of all broadcasts were replayed within six days of recording, more than three-

Table 2: Observed (from diaries) and expected (from exponential decay model) percentage of replays by elapsed time since recording and by program type

Elapsed time[a] (in days)	All (n = 882)[b] Obs. %	Exp. %	Daily (n = 194) Obs. %	Exp. %	Weekly (n = 206) Obs. %	Exp. %	One-shot (n = 309) Obs. %	Exp. %
0–1	23.8	27.7	54.8	56.8	15.3	28.5	8.2	12.7
1–2	19.7	14.7	17.2	18.1	26.4	15.0	17.8	8.9
2–3	7.4	7.8	5.1	5.7	9.2	7.9	7.6	6.2
3–4	3.2	4.2	1.8	1.8	4.6	4.2	3.0	4.3
4–5	2.2	2.2	0.0	0.6	2.1	2.2	2.2	3.0
5–6	1.3	1.2	0.0	0.2	0.9	1.2	2.0	2.1
6–7	0.6	0.6	0.0	0.1	0.0	0.6	1.9	1.5
0–7	58.2	58.3	78.9	83.3	58.5	59.6	42.7	38.7
0–15	—	59.0	—	83.3	—	60.3	—	42.0
0–∞ (α/β)	—	59.1	—	83.3	—	60.3	—	42.2
	$\chi^2 = 22.00$, df = 5, $p < .05$		$\chi^2 = 3.18$, df = 2, n.s.		$\chi^2 = 31.43$, df = 3, $p < .05$		$\chi^2 = 36.43$, df = 5, $p < .05$	

[a] The time interval "0–1" days means greater than 0 and less than 1 day.

[b] The Ns refer to the number of programs of the given type that were recorded. Included in the "all" category are 173 programs not classified as daily, weekly, or one-shot (see footnote 6).

Note: In computing χ^2 values, we combined cells so that the minimal expected cell frequency was about 5. For the weekly programs, we combined the cells representing the last three days. If we had combined the data for only the last two days, then $\chi^2 = 31.86$, df = 4.

quarters (78.9 percent) of daily broadcasts had been similarly replayed. On the other hand, far fewer than half (42.7 percent) of one-shot programs that had been taped were played back in the same time period. Taken together, these results suggest that it is appropriate to model VCR replay patterns with an exponential decay curve, since the assumption of initially high levels of use followed by rapidly declining proportions of playbacks appears to have been met. Again, note that the exponential decay equation is modeling the time-shifting rather than the library-building function.

The parameters of the curves estimated for these data are presented in Table 3, and the comparison of the observed replay results and those expected from the exponential decay model is found in Table 2.

As can be seen in Table 2, the exponential decay model does a good job in predicting the percentage of replays day by day. The expected cumulative proportion of replays for the observed period (the figure corresponding to 0–7 days in Table 2) is within 4.4 percent of observed replays in each column, and the average absolute error day by day for the category "all programs" is 1.5 percent. As shown in Table 3, each linearized exponential decay model has a higher R^2 than its comparable

Table 3: Exponential decay curve parameters by program type

Parameter estimate	All programs	Daily programs	Weekly programs	One-shot programs
α	.3731	.9550	.3867	.1506
β	.6318	1.1463	.6415	.3571
R^2	.9833	.9991	.8999	.7777
R^2 linear equation	.8199	.8261	.6769	.5502
$t(Y_{cum} = .50)$	2.9682	.7997	2.7572	(undefined)

Note: The R^2s are from the linearized equation $\log (Y_t) = \log (\alpha) - \beta t + \log (u)$. The sample size for each curve is the number of days with replay greater than zero. These are 7, 4, 6, and 7 respectively. The R^2 for the linear equation is from $Y = c + dt + v$, where v is the error term. These R^2s are based on the same sample size and are solely for comparison with R^2s from the linearized exponential decay model. $t(Y_{cum} = .50)$ is the half-life of the program type, expressed in days.

linear equation. A chi-square test of the goodness of fit of the exponential decay model indicates that the model is not rejected (at $p < .05$) only for daily programs. The order of the chi-square values indicates that the model is most adequate for daily programs, next best for weekly programs, and least adequate for one-shot programs.[7]

The α parameter indicates the initial impact of the program periodicity on the likelihood of replay, and the β parameter shows how quickly this initial impact declines over time. Daily programs have higher estimated initial impacts than weekly programs and, in turn, weekly programs have higher estimated initial impacts than one-shot broadcasts. Further, daily programs are estimated to decay (in their replay likelihood) more rapidly than weekly programs, while weekly broadcasts are estimated to decay more quickly than one-shot programs.

The estimated half-life of all programs is about three days, which means that 50 percent of all recordings will be replayed initially within that time. The half-life of daily programs is estimated at 0.80 days, and the half-life of weekly programs is estimated at 2.76 days. We cannot estimate a half-life for one-shot programs, since the model predicts that fewer than fifty percent of such programs will ever be replayed.

The prediction of the cumulative percentage of replays after infinite time has passed is estimated by the ratio α/β. These estimates are found

[7] One reason the exponential decay model fails by the chi-square test to fit weekly and one-shot programs is that the data for these programs (Table 2) exhibit a "bump" at Day 1. These bumps may be due both to the scheduling of weekly and one-shot programs later in the day and to their longer broadcast duration. This results in these programs being more likely to be played back one day later. If we collapse data from Day 0 and Day 1 and, as a conservative strategy, utilize the previously estimated parameters, the exponential decay model is not significantly rejected (weekly: $\chi^2(df = 2) = 1.15$; one-shot: $\chi^2(df = 4) = 6.77$). While the order of the chi-square statistics changes, the order of the αs, βs, and R^2s remains the same. Hence, the argument that follows is still valid even taking into account plausible reasons for a one-day lag in replay.

in Table 2. If we compare these estimates with the observed proportion of replays within one week, we see that, except for one-shot programs, the model predicts only a modest increment of additional playbacks after the first week. For example, while 58.2 percent of all tapes are replayed the first week, the model predicts that, at most, the proportion of replays will equal 59.1 percent. For one-shot programs, the predicted proportion of replays (42.2 percent) is *smaller* than the actual replays in the first week (42.7 percent). Finally, returning to Table 3, we see that, judging by R^2 values, the linearized exponential decay model works best for daily programs, next best for weekly programs, and least well (but still quite well) for one-shot broadcasts.[8]

Home video recorder use has the potential to affect program longevity, but that potential remains incompletely fulfilled.

There can be little doubt that home VCR use reduces the transience of some television broadcasts. However, that conclusion must be strictly qualified, since this study has also shown that about 42 percent of all recordings go unplayed the first week. A television broadcast that is recorded but not played back is no different in its effects from any other nonperceived message.

We have also proposed that video recording may have a time-shifting and/or library use and hypothesized that the time-shifting use is most associated with daily programs, next most with weekly programs, and least with one-shot programs. Moreover, one-shot programs were hypothesized to be most associated with library building. We have found that the exponential decay model, which is predicated on the time-shifting use, is adequate for all types of programs and most adequate for daily broadcasts. The model predicts that both the initial decision to replay programs and the "decay" of programs are ordered as we expected. Further, the proportion of variance explained by the model is similarly ordered by program type. The fact that the model is least adequate for one-shot programs, and the fact that it underestimates the replay potential of one-shot programs, are, we expect, because replay of these programs is most likely associated with library building. Hence, quick replay is neither desired nor necessary, and the observed curve of replay percentages for one-shot programs should be (and is) flatter than replay curves for daily and weekly broadcasts. Still, the exponential

[8] Of course, the R^2s are a function of sample size. Given the small number of time points, statistical tests of significance are not employed, nor is a correction for shrinkage. There is no statistical test to evaluate the extent to which the linearized exponential decay model is superior to the linear model, since neither is nested within the other.

decay model does an adequate job with one-shot programs within the time frame of one week (see footnote 7). This raises the possibility that there is some overlap between the library-building and time-shifting uses and their respective motivational and behavioral correlates.

Our study has several implications for understanding the transience of television broadcasts. First, to assess the impact of VCR use on ultimate audience size, one must be aware that (a) only about 58 percent of all programs are replayed within one week of their recording, (b) if daily and weekly programs are not played back the first week after recording, it is unlikely that they will *ever* be replayed, and (c) for one-shot broadcasts, replays may be quite extended in time.

Further, as one-shot programs are recorded and stored, they have the potential to compete with "on-shelf" (hence, "on-demand") print items such as magazines and books. This competition may significantly change both media use during leisure time and the kinds of one-shot programs that suppliers will provide. For example, "how-to-do-it" books now have little competition from "how-to-do-it" TV programs. However, if such broadcasts are presented, recorded, and shelved, they may directly compete and are likely to be especially successful in providing instructions for crafts and the like.

The old debate concerning television viewing and literacy (see, e.g., 24) may also become more salient as stored TV programs provide new competition to reading. Paradoxically, this competition may come not from what many decry as television's worst programs (the regularly scheduled broadcasts) but rather from that which potentially is television's best fare, the "special."

The ideas presented here also suggest a more general theory of mass media transience. One element of such a theory is "over-time fungibility," that is, the extent to which audiences perceive a message as being replaced by an equivalent one over time. Equivalence will be a function of content seriality, frequency of content transmission, and competition from similar types of content.

The second element of a more general theory is "over-media fungibility." It reflects the extent to which medium-specific content distinguishes itself and its medium by competing successfully with the content and situational experience of other media. Some television content, for example, may be sufficiently distinctive to command an audience even years after its initial broadcast. Its competitors are other "classics," regardless of media source, available in other "libraries." Of course, the media source may affect the apparent distinctiveness of the program.[9]

[9] For evidence concerning the distinctiveness of content due to the medium, see (4, 16).

Finally, the transience of mass communications can be seen as a function of competition from other environmental stimuli, constraints that affect attention, and the recording/storage capabilities of audiences. Additional data can clarify the role of these elements as general determinants of media transience and media use.

REFERENCES

1. Agostino, E., H. Terry, and R. Johnson. "Home Video Recorders: Rights and Ratings." *Journal of Communication* 30(4), Autumn 1980, pp. 28–35.
2. Arbitron Company. *Home Video Cassette Recorders: Ownership/Usage 1978.* New York: Arbitron, 1979.
3. Arbitron Company. *VCR Diary Pilot Test: Phase I (November/December, 1980), Phase II (February, 1981), Research Department Communication No. 162.* Laurel, Md.: Arbitron Research, June 11, 1983.
4. Barnett, G. "Bilingual Semantic Organization: A Muitidimensional Analysis." *Journal of Cross-Cultural Psychology* 8, 1977, pp. 315–330.
5. Benton & Bowles, Inc. *The New TV Technologies: The View from the Viewer,* II. New York: Benton & Bowles, 1983.
6. Bogart, L. *Press and Public: Who Reads What, When, Where, and Why in American Newspapers.* Hillsdale, N.J.: Lawrence Erlbaum, 1981.
7. *Broadcasting* magazine. "In brief." August 23, 1982, p. 81.
8. Burghes, D. and A. Wood. *Mathematical Models in the Social, Management, and Life Sciences.* Chichester, England: Ellis Horwood Ltd., 1980. Distributed by Halsted Press, New York.
9. Burton, R. and R. Kebler. "The 'Half-Life' of Some Scientific and Technical Literature." *American Documentation* 11, 1960, pp. 18–22.
10. Cater, D. "Television and Thinking People." In R. Adler (Ed.) *Television as a Social Force: New Approaches to TV Criticism.* New York: Praeger, 1975, pp. 11–18.
11. Ebbinghaus, E. *Memory: A Contribution to Experimental Psychology.* New York: Dover, 1964 [1885].
12. Gans, H. *Popular Culture and High Culture.* New York: Basic Books, 1974.
13. Gans, H. *Deciding What's News.* New York: Pantheon Books, 1979.
14. Garfield, E., M. Malin, and H. Small. "Citation Data as Science Indicators." In Y. Elkana et al. (Eds.) *Toward a Metric of Science: The Advent of Science Indicators.* New York: Wiley, 1978, pp. 179–208.
15. Goodhardt, G., A. Ehrenberg, and M. Collins. *The Television Audience: Patterns of Viewing.* Westmead, England: Saxon House, 1975.
16. Katz, E., M. Gurevitch, and H. Haas. "On the Uses of the Mass Media for Important Things." *American Sociological Review* 38, 1973, pp. 164–181.
17. Levy, M. "Home Video Recorders: A User Survey." *Journal of Communication* 30(4), Autumn 1980, pp. 23–27.
18. Levy, M. "Program Playback Preferences in VCR Households." *Journal of Broadcasting* 24, 1980, pp. 327–336.
19. Levy, M. "Home Video Recorders and Time-Shifting." *Journalism Quarterly* 58, 1981, pp. 401–405.
20. McPhee, W. *Formal Theories of Mass Behavior.* New York: Free Press, 1963.
21. McQuail, D. *Mass Communication Theory.* Beverly Hills, Cal.: Sage, 1983.
22. Media Statistics, Inc. *Results of Special Mediastat Survey Conducted in Video Recorder Homes.* Silver Spring, Md.: Media Statistics, Inc., 1979.

23. Media Statistics, Inc. *Summary 1981 VCR Report.* Silver Spring, Md.: Media Statistics, Inc., 1981.
24. Murray, J. *Television and Youth.* Boys Town, Neb.: Boys Town Center for the Study of Youth Development, 1980.
25. Novak, M. "Television Shapes the Soul." In R. Adler (Ed.) *Television as a Social Force: New Approaches to TV Criticism.* New York: Praeger, 1975, pp. 19–34.
26. Pool, Ithiel de Sola. "Tracking the Flow of Information." *Science* 221, 1983, pp. 609–613.
27. Price, D. de Solla. "Networks of Scientific Papers." *Science* 149, 1965, pp. 510–515.
28. Price, D. de Solla and D. Beaver. "Collaboration in an Invisible College." *American Psychologist* 24, 1966, pp. 1011–1018.
29. Reeves, B. and C. Borgman. "A Bibliometric Evaluation of Core Journals in Communication Research." *Human Communication Research* 10, 1983, pp. 119–136.
30. Resnikoff, H. "Information Systems Theory and Research: An Overview of the Societal Significance of Information Science." In D. Nimmo (Ed.) *Communication Yearbook* 4. New Brunswick, N.J.: Transaction Books, 1980, pp. 115–122.
31. Robinson, J. and L. Jeffres. "The Changing Role of Newspapers in the Age of Television." *Journalism Monographs* 63, 1979.
32. Sahin, H., D. Davis, and J. Robinson. "Improving Television News." *Irish Broadcasting Review* 11, Summer 1981, pp. 50–55.
33. Tukey, J. *Exploratory Data Analysis.* Reading, Mass.: Addison-Wesley, 1977.
34. Wright, C. *Mass Communication.* New York: Random House, 1975.

33

THE UNDERSIDE OF COMPUTER LITERACY

Douglas Noble

WE ARE WITNESSING the installation of an enormous computer education infrastructure in this country. Each day offers new assertions of the urgent need to bring "Computer Literacy" (CL) to the masses of students, teachers, grandmothers, and businessmen ready to participate in the new computerized society. The coffers, federal and corporate, are opening wide as an urgent need for high skill in a high-technology world assumes central importance. As the computer insinuates itself further and further into our jobs and our lives, the need for some form of Computer Literacy for everyone comes to be accepted as reasonable, even reassuring.

Not surprisingly, computer education has become very big business. Although its focus has recently shifted from the child to the adult, CL educators are in fact advancing on many fronts, from management and parent workshops to teacher's colleges to computer camps. The number of computers in American schools is growing at the rate of 56 percent per year, with 90,000 microcomputers already in place. Atari, Apple, IBM, and Radio Shack all are pouring money and free computers into teachers' colleges, school districts, and universities across the country. One observer notes that "securing shares of the education marketplace may be critical in determining which computer manufacturers will still be in business several years from now." And it has been predicted that by 1986 training directed at the neophyte will be a $3 billion market. CL, the attempt to introduce the masses to computers, has become one of the nation's fastest growing businesses.

CL is a *mass* movement in education. Computer clubs and workshops, technical and vocational programs, graduate courses in computer science and engineering, constitute an understandable response to the new technology. Computer Literacy education, however, is more difficult to understand. CL does not propose to make engineers, programmers, and technicians out of everyone. Indeed, the focus is precisely the opposite: to provide

From Douglas Noble, "The Underside of Computer Literacy," *Raritan*, Vol. III, No. 4 (Spring 1984), pp. 37-64.

the masses with some *minimal* introduction to computers so that we all may be "comfortable" with the new technology. There is considerable debate about what CL courses should contain: the history of computers? the social impact of computers? hardware basics? flowcharts and logic? programming and software evaluation? But the common goal of all CL advocates is to "give as many people as possible the sense of belonging in a computer-rich society."* This sense of belonging is the main attraction of CL.

This is the first time in this century, if not in history, that a mass educational movement has followed so closely on the heels of a technological innovation. Seventy-five years ago automobile schools (most of them short-lived and out for a quick buck) sprang up overnight to train mechanics and drivers for the new horseless carriage. Radio, television, and telephone all generated thousands of clubs and technical schools, but there was no thought of reaching *everyone*, as with CL. None of these inventions, despite their promise for transforming society, triggered any such mass educational campaign as we are seeing with the computer. Nor were these inventions compared to the invention of print; competence with automobiles or television, however interpreted, was never equated with functional literacy, as Computer Literacy so often is. Nor did it seem urgent that everyone feel comfortable overnight.

The public interest in CL is essentially defensive; the oil lubricating the movement seems to be the fear of the uninitiated that they will be left behind by the "Computer Revolution." CL advocates, designating themselves as pioneers in a wave of enlightenment akin to the spread of print in the fifteenth century, feed this anxiety with warnings that "the ability to use and understand computers will [soon] be equivalent to understanding the printed word," and that "those who are not computer literate will be at as much a disadvantage in society as someone who cannot read is to-

*The quotations in this paper represent a selection from the inexhaustible rhetoric generated by computer enthusiasts in the past few years, much of which has been preserved in a single volume edited by Robert J. Seidel, entitled *Computer Literacy: Issues and Directions for 1985*, Academic Press, 1982. Similar sentiments may be found in countless journal, magazine, and newspaper articles.

day." Failure to learn to use computers, we are told again and again, will leave one functionally illiterate, devoid of the skills needed to survive in a computerized world.

Such talk has caught on. "I'm an intelligent person," admits my mother, echoing the thoughts of millions, "but I feel dumb. I feel like an immigrant in my own country." Her solution? Take a computer course. This is the antidote, Jane Pauley of the "Today" show delights in telling us, for "computerphobia," a disease striking the vitals of (among others) uninitiated managers fearing replacement by others more "literate" than themselves. The computer is here to stay, everyone seems to be saying, so we have no choice about whether to get on board; our only choice is whether we will be eager or resigned as we do so.

Defensive self-preservation is the purpose of job-seeking kids, of their well-intentioned parents, of phobic executives, or grandmothers like my own mother, for whom learning about computers is as alarmingly demanding as going to the moon. It is also the motive of school administrators, who are heard saying that "nobody came to me to ask if a computer revolution should take place, but it's here and my students must be prepared for it."

It is taken as a given that everyone must be educated in computers, and, indeed, any suggestion that we allow segments of the population to be denied this knowledge sounds heretical in a democratic society. The powerful mythology of equality of opportunity, and the omnipresence of the computer itself, provide the most convincing justification for the necessity of CL.

The computer is here, everywhere, and we all must be helped to understand and use it. How can anyone argue with that? When a sense of urgency about our national priorities is added, the inappropriateness of debate seems clearer still:

> A computer literate work force is necessary to maintain our national defense and to improve our national productivity.
>
> A computer literate populace is as necessary to an information society as raw materials and energy are to an industrial society.
>
> Due to the decline in national productivity, the increase in foreign trade competition, and national defense and safety

> needs, computers have emerged as the major force ameliorating these conditions. Consequently, the shortage of computer specialists and knowledge-workers has raised the problem of computer literacy to the level of a national crisis.

But what particular decline in productivity? Which "knowledge-workers"? What shortage of computer specialists? What "problem" of computer literacy? Never mind. We are asked not to question even specious arguments when the Japanese are whipping us, and our own high technology (the answer to all our economic problems) is supposedly being stunted by American computer illiteracy. Although the authors of such statements systematically confuse minimal computer literacy with high technical skill, and although their appeals to productivity, national defense, and safety are characteristically vague, still they manage to make the crisis seem real enough to stifle debate.

Equally unexamined is the basic assumption about the importance of CL to the individual, namely, that computers are everywhere and so it is in everyone's interest to understand them. As well as indiscriminately confusing the future with the present (Are computers everywhere now? Is the Information Society here yet?), this assumption in its simplicity begs most of the important questions of fact and value. Where are computers used? What are they used to do? What do people need to know in order to use them? Does the computer enhance anyone's life? Whose? Does it hurt anyone's life? Whose? Who decides when and where computers will be used?

The alleged benefits of CL in meeting the needs of the American public can be grouped into four principal categories, each representing one role in the daily life of the individual—the individual as consumer, as student, as worker, and as citizen.

1. "The opportunities available to those who become educated consumers . . . will be . . . great" and therefore "federal emphasis should be on the production of a population able to cope rather than merely exist in an information society." CL will afford us the "survival" and "coping" skills we will need in the home-computer revolution, which promises totally to transform our domesticity, our leisure, our shopping, and banking.

2. "To function effectively as students, our nation's youth needs to know how to use and program computers," since "computers contribute to the intellectual growth of human beings," and "computer literacy maximizes our problem-solving abilities." One benefit of CL, then, is its enhancement of learning by showing students how to participate in the computer-induced "revolution in learning" now beginning in the nation's schools.

3. "To function effectively as scientists, engineers, managers and teachers, the professionals of today . . . need to learn how to use computers to enhance their specialized skills." Everyone will need to "emerge from school with the knowledge and skills that let them begin to work productively in the information sector" as more and more jobs are redefined as "hi-tech occupations that will require high-order skills." In a word, CL will help us get or keep a job, and may indeed determine whether we are employable at all.

4. "Some understanding of computer programming is necessary for the exercise of the rights and responsibilities of citizenship," for in order "to function effectively as citizens . . . we will need to know how the computer impinges on and enhances our everyday lives." CL will create an informed citizenry which will determine the shape of the new technology and prevent abuse. It will also ensure equality of opportunity by making the technology accessible to all. CL will empower us by putting ultimate control of computer technology in our hands.

These advantages, then, are what CL has to offer, according to its proponents. Leaving to others an examination of the questionable relevance of CL to national defense and international competition, let us examine in turn the home, the school, the job site, and the political arena, to see if the reality corresponds to the promise.

Time's "Man of the Year" for 1982 was a machine, the computer, which is supposedly transforming the home into an "electronic cottage" and our daily lives into a sequence of interactions with microcircuitry. Estimates for the number of personal computers in use in the U.S. by the end of the century range as high as 80 million. (By comparison, there are now 83 million American homes with TV sets.) Already we are being bombarded by computerized telephones, autos, washer/dryers, watches, games, and toys. Outside the home we see computers in supermarkets, banks, airports, and libraries. Tiny chips of silicon are helping people find mates, protect their houses, record their favorite music. Computer buffs are transforming their houses into "smart homes," even as the first personalized robots come waddling off the assembly lines.

Meanwhile we are continually told how much we ourselves need a home computer to manage the bills, store the recipes, and edit the correspondence (although four out of five home computers are used exclusively for games). The future of the home computer promises to be truly revolutionary, once TV, computer, and telephone are linked together and become "videotex," with which we'll be able to shop, bank, and read the newspaper without ever leaving the screen. With such powerful telecommunications, more and more office jobs will be done at home, computer networks will provide community, and home entertainment systems will fill our leisure hours. Such are the predictions, for better or worse.

A number of observers have begun to warn of the dangers of videotex to individual security; they warn as well of the total marketization of the home. "With personal computers and two-way TV we'll create a wealth of personal information and scarcely notice it leaving the house. The TV will know what X-rated movies we watch." Our banking, shopping, and viewing habits will all become part of some data bank. "There will be tremendous incentive to record this information for market research or sale."

Even today the threat posed by the computer to home and family has become a growing concern of psychiatrists and marriage counselors. They are witnessing the "social disease" of the "computer widow" whose spouse spends all his free time in front of the computer, and they worry about the impact of the computer on children for whom playing with electronic machines takes the place of playing, or even just being, with other kids. "Bit by bit

[sic] computers are changing the way people relate" and "hardly anybody is looking at the impact on family life." Specifically, CL educators are not looking. In fact, they are proceeding at an accelerated rate to "prepare" the public for the wondrous transformation of the home in a computer-rich world.

What is most evident, yet rarely noted, in all of this, aside from the fact that it's all happening without public knowledge or consent, is that one doesn't have to know very much in order to reap the benefits. Computerized telephones, watches, and dryers require no computer understanding by the user. However much the market, bank, garage, or airline relies on computers, still the consumer, even the wise consumer, needs to know nothing about computers in order to function or cope. Even where our direct interaction with a computer terminal is required, as in a library or using a bank "moneymatic" or home computers for budgets or games, what one needs to know about computers is minimal.

It might be argued that the consumer needs to know how to shop for computer products and how to fix or maintain all the computerized paraphernalia which one has become dependent upon. In fact, however, one doesn't need to understand the bewildering variety of competing computer products in order to make intelligent purchases. All one needs is a friend who is somewhat knowledgeable about computers, just as one may consult a mechanically inclined acquaintance when buying a used car. Even without such a friend, one can usually pick up enough information from the sales people at the computer store or take a look at *Consumer Reports* to make an intelligent decision.

The same may be said for fixing or maintaining one's computer or computerized gadgets once they are purchased. If they break, one need only bring them to the shop for servicing, just as most people now do with TVs and cars. Although it is unquestionably an advantage to be able to fix one's car, or washer, or typewriter, those who depend upon the mechanic or serviceman are not failing to cope or function in a world of cars and typewriters. So it is and will be in the world of computers. In fact, considering the relatively few parts in a personal computer, repair might very quickly become possible for many consumers. The high technology of the computer is the microprocessor itself, which is simply replaced if a problem arises. To repair the rest of the computer requires electrical or electronic know-how, not computer literacy.

Those of us who have grown up around cars, televisions, and telephones are sufficiently literate in their use. No one ever trained us, as children or adults, to manage everyday technologies. We simply learned about them as we grew up with them, just as children who are interested now learn a great deal about computers from hanging around computer stores or their friends' houses.

The analogy will be clearer as computers become more and more "user friendly." Just as the automobile became accessible to millions once the electric starter and (later) the automatic transmission were added, so the personal computer will enter 80 million homes when its use requires only pressing a few buttons. (The new "Lisa" computer, at the moment an expensive business-oriented device, ushers in the age of friendly computing with its remarkable simplicity, which reduces instructional time from forty hours to forty minutes.) As advanced user friendliness reaches the average computer consumer (and there is no doubt that it soon will), what will happen to the urgency of CL? Will we continue to be told that we need CL to cope, function, or survive in the world of computers? Even today, such a claim makes astonishingly little sense. One just does not have to know very much to be a consumer in a computerized world, and one will need to know still less in the future.

Uncritical acceptance is the order of the day in the nation's schools, too. School districts are buying up microcomputers and commercially available software as if these would solve all of their considerable difficulties. Thousands of these shiny new symbols of high technology are being put in place by administrators eager to impress their school boards, enhance their school's image, or ease the pressures from affluent parents who already own home computers. Some of these administrators are themselves reluctant boarders of the technology bandwagon; others are among its prime movers. Eager or resigned, however, no one wants his or her school left behind. So the computers pour in and the NEA calls for "a massive infusion of funds to help schools close the 'computer gap' between students' and teachers' need to gain literacy in the new technology" and the schools' dwindling financial resources.

Impoverishment is but one of the problems for school districts anxious to bring computer literacy to their students. Some of the more cautious CL advocates have begun to warn against rushing too quickly into high tech. Although none suggests that CL is unneccessary, they worry that many administrators are making unwise purchases because they have not sufficiently defined their "instructional objectives"; the result too often is a roomful of unused hardware and inappropriate software. Teachers, too, are often unprepared to work with the computers. Often a single teacher becomes the resident expert, and some math or science teachers are coaxed into offering computer classes, learning as they go. The shortage of qualified computer teachers is in fact a primary complaint of CL enthusiasts, which is why their focus has shifted more and more to teachers' colleges and in-service workshops.

Doubts about the quality of commercial software and the reliability of some of the hardware have also begun to be heard. Most packaged learning materials now available are considered educationally unsound ("90 percent garbage" is the phrase often used), and free trial periods are seldom offered to the teacher who wants to know exactly what he or she is buying. Hardware servicing is often said to be erratic as well. None of these obstacles, however, seems to be deterring school districts from buying, even though the steadily decreasing price of computers suggests that they might do well to go slowly.

What is all the rush? Behind it is a belief in the power of the computer to transform education: "Just as education was reshaped five centuries ago by the printing press, education is going to be reshaped by computers." Never mind how much CL educators really know about the influence of printing on education 500 years ago; the historical allusion, the unexamined assumption buried within the term computer *literacy* itself, serves CL proponents by suggesting the totality of the computer transformation of the school. This transformation envisions the use of computers both as powerful instructional aids and as instruments for creative problem-solving. The potential value of such uses seems limitless to enthusiasts; let us examine some of the grounds for their enthusiasm.

The oldest, and lowliest, form of computer-aided instruction is drill-and-practice, in which the computer simply takes the place of a workbook, adding video-induced motivation and sound or graphic reinforcement for correct answers. The computer really does very little "teaching" of concepts, apart from providing printed text which might just as well be in a book. The big draw of this unsophisticated use is its ability to attract the attention of otherwise unmotivated students. The staying power of such motivation is very doubtful, although the student gains some "keyboard familiarity" and "enhancement of self-image."

A newer form of computer-aided instruction uses computers to teach in ways otherwise impossible, as in the use of sophisticated simulations of the circulatory system, number patterns, election returns, or conflicting physical forces. An example in game format is "lunar landing," which asks the student to make decisions simultaneously affecting fuel consumption, velocity, thrust, and distance from the moon's surface. Advocates of this sort of use claim that it gives students radically new opportunities to learn about complex relationships in a variety of subject areas. But such use is extremely rare; what "courseware" exists has been developed in a few schools blessed with high levels of commitment, funding, and personnel. And it proposes an arena of experimentation and risk which is scarcely feasible for the typical school district. Existing courseware, therefore, has not found a wide market, and it is relatively untested. Yet the dream of teaching a variety of subjects in a totally new way is selling a lot of computers in school districts where the dream may never be realized.

Computer-aided instruction, then, is either too sophisticated to be more than a wish, or too simple to justify much excitement. There are some interesting things going on in computer-assisted instruction; but they are far from becoming a "revolution in education," and there seems little reason for CL educators to be alarming students or their parents about such remote eventualities. Computers are used in another way in the schools, however, as the locus for creative problem-solving and new ways of thinking. "Children-friendly" programming languages such as Logo have encouraged many educators to believe that computers can lead children to more expansive ways of thinking and solving problems. Many teachers, myself included, are thrilled to observe young children programming computers to draw sophisticated shapes or "converse" intelligently, and it becomes seductively easy to believe that the key to intelligent cognitive behavior, and even to the "problem" of motivation, lies buried in the act of programming a computer.

Unfortunately, such enthusiasm is premature. "There is little objective evaluation data confirming the contention that computer programming enhances intellectual functioning or problem-solving." Despite the fact that "computer programming is often used explicitly to teach problem-solving . . . current research has only begun to scratch the surface in exploring whether what students learn about problem-solving by programming computers has any carryover into non-computer situations." "The general picture from research on problem-solving and thinking is that the conditions under which transfer occurs from one domain to another are subtle and limited; . . . one is more impressed by the extent to which transfer doesn't occur."

It appears, despite our intuitions, that we really know very little about the cognitive processes involved in programming, and still less about the transfer of these processes to other areas of intellectual activity. What about the motivational possibilities? Don't computers turn kids on to sustained, self-directed, eager learning? All of the evidence available is anecdotal; my own experience is that the flashy computers attract all kids for a short time but that only the ten percent or so who are truly interested stay involved past a month or two. It seems that the only thing learned from a century of research on motivation, namely that it is linked to interest, holds true with computers too, despite all the current excitement, my own, as teacher and programmer, included. The Learning Revolution in this form is barely off the ground. What is more, the very act of programming computers might itself become obsolete in the wake of ever "friendlier" computers, and "writing computer code will . . . become redundant, [as] the ability to write programs [becomes] as relevant as the ability of an airline pilot to fly a kite." What is a curriculum planner to do?

A seldom addressed danger in this premature enthusiasm about the Learning Revolution is the widening of the gap between rich and poor school districts. While the NEA places "some hope for solution" in the $425 million American Defense Education Act recently passed by the House, and while Apple's Steven Jobs wants to put one free computer in each of the nation's 80,000 schools, these measures will not make computers as accessible to poor students as to wealthy ones. Some call for state intervention in computer distribution and funding to prevent a have/have-not society. Unequal access to computers has become a real concern to many CL enthusiasts, who argue that the solution is to provide more computers to poor schools and more training to their teachers. So long, however, as they also push for similar increments for affluent schools, there is no solution at all, since rich schools have access to alternative funding unavailable to poor ones.

No one seems ready to argue that rich districts be forced to wait while the have-nots catch up; waiting is not in the CL scenario. A better solution, unfortunately, is fast becoming untenable. If, as I am suggesting, CL is not very important (and if, as we shall see later, computer jobs—both in skill and in numbers—are greatly overrated), it could be argued that access to computers in schools is not very important, and that the exacerbation of inequality caused by computers is exaggerated. Reality supports this argument, but unfortunately we live in a world of appearances which function as reality. Consequently, we are seeing the invention ex nihilo, of a "need" for computer access, in the form of high school graduation requirements, college prerequisites, teaching qualification, and hiring practices. Overnight, the "need" for CL has begun to be manufactured, and survival, in education and employment, has become linked to computer access in school; the "inequality gap" and the "computer gap" have become one, and the answer to both is: more computers, more literacy. At this point the exaggerated claims about the revolution in education leave the realm of wishful thinking and start to become dangerous.

The hole card of the CL movement is jobs. Above all, CL educators invoke job preparation to explain the urgency of their enterprise. In fact, personal experience shows that some teachers are annoyed by any suggestion that they delay their students' preparation for the new jobs long enough to find out what these jobs will be. Most educators' knee-jerk acceptance of the mythology surrounding the "high technology workforce," and their astonishing ignorance of the real impact of computers on jobs in 1984, testify to the defensiveness underlying the computer education movement.

The basic supposition of the CL movement is that high-tech jobs require high-tech skills. Early in this century, the introduction of machinery into unskilled jobs automatically made these jobs "semiskilled"; just so, we are told, the introduction of computers will transform many jobs into "knowledge work" or "mind work." Somehow, mere interaction with a computer will transform the skills required and radically raise the level of intellect needed. Since computers are in fact being introduced into a vast number of jobs, it seems to follow that future employment will demand high levels of intellect and computer understanding. This is the prevailing view, and it sells CL to millions of people.

The currency of this view rests on a failure to examine how computers are used in various sorts of jobs. True, computers are being introduced into millions of jobs; but it hardly follows that the skills required for these jobs therefore become intellectually more demanding or stimulating. In fact, the contrary is more often the case: the jobs become deskilled, less creative, more highly controlled, and mindless.

It is important to realize, first, that many jobs are simply eliminated by the introduction of computers, and, second, that a large part of the service sector of the future will remain unaffected by computers. Examples of the former include craftspersons, machinists, textile cutters, compositors, auto workers, printers, telephone repairers, filing and billing clerks, and keypunchers. Regarding the latter, one observer notes that "the major demand for workers in the next decade will not be for computer scientists and engineers but for janitors, nurses' aides, sales clerks, cashiers, nurses, fast-food preparers, secretaries, truck drivers and kitchen helpers." Only seven percent of new jobs will be in high-tech areas, and the rest will not involve computers at all. And the computer assembly jobs themselves, upon which the entire industry depends, are rapidly being moved to places like Hong Kong and Taiwan, where labor is cheaper.

The surviving jobs that will be transformed by computers fall into four categories: 1) jobs that involve computers but require no interaction between the computer and the worker; 2) jobs that involve minimal interaction between computer and worker; 3) the "computer occupations" themselves, which require some level of computer knowledge; 4) the professions that require the use of computers as a tool.

The real estate agent reading a printout of listings, the supermarket checker using a scanner, the airline baggage handler using a computerized conveyor system, the retail clerk, the bank teller: these are some of the people whose jobs involve computers. In fact, the presence of the computer in such occupations is what leads to the idea that computers are everywhere. Yet what do these millions of workers need to understand about computers? The truth is that this sort of computer impact will be the most typical; yet in each case the degree of skill demanded by the job is reduced, not increased, by the presence of the computer (even though one supermarket manager suggested to me that passing groceries over a scanner requires more skill than running a cash register). Furthermore, any knowledge about the computer itself is quite irrelevant to the actual performance of the job.

Jobs which do require minimal interaction with a computer include those in computer-assisted manufacturing, drafting, machining, word processing, and data retrieval. Such jobs are significantly transformed, and some form of retraining is required.

However, the retraining is far less than often imagined, rarely lasting more than a few weeks, and it usually is restricted to learning to operate specific instruments, something seldom included in a computer literacy curriculum. Here, too, it is arguable that the new skills demand far less intellectual participation by the worker than those which they replace. One need only compare a word processor to a secretary who used to run the office, or an N/C machine operator to a skilled machinist. Such jobs will represent a very high proportion of the computer-related work of the future.

Some argue that the office worker and industrial worker of the future "will soon have access to managerial information – and, hence, the ability to engage in tough and interesting problem solving along with her [sic] supervisor" and that "the new technologies [will] blur the invidious distinctions between the secretary and the boss and between the blue- and white-collar worker, [thereby providing] tremendous opportunities to those office and factory workers who are prepared by . . . education to accept increased responsibilities." It is difficult to comprehend such observations, which represent a remarkable distortion of political realities. The evidence is uncontestable that computers give industrial and office management new and tighter forms of control and supervision, and that the push for greater efficiency and productivity reduces the worker's opportunity for skilled, knowledgeable participation in his or her own work. Nevertheless, the mythology that computers enhance all jobs they touch, transforming them into "mind jobs" filled with new responsibility, persists to feed the fears of those who hope for help from CL. For the vast majority of future workers, whether their jobs will be touched by computers or not, Computer Literacy education is a waste of time.

The last two categories are jobs in the "computer occupations" themselves, such as systems analysts, programmers, and operators, and the professionals involved in sophisticated computer use, such as scientists, business managers, and engineers. These categories constitute a relatively small fraction of the total employment picture of the next decade. The computer occupations, for example, are projected to increase in number by only one million in the next decade (totalling two million by 1990). This number is small when contrasted to the three million jobs predicted to be lost to computers by 1990, or when set against the millions of people who will be seeking employment in these valued occupations.

What about the businessmen, engineers, teachers, and scientists who will be using computer technology in sophisticated professional ways? To argue that teachers will need to be capable of sophisticated computer use would beg the very question we are discussing; if computer education is largely unnecessary, then teaching does not require sophisticated computer knowledge. Second, most independent businessmen and corporate managers who will be using computers will chiefly rely on prepackaged technical services or increasingly user-friendly computer systems (such as Lisa). The computer skills and knowledge they need will, like those of so many other workers, be far less awesome than computerphobics have been led to fear.

More importantly, those jobs that will continue to demand high levels of computer knowledge and understanding—in engineering, scientific research, statistics, finance, and specialized areas of medicine—constitute an extremely small part of the whole spectrum of jobs. These are the true mind workers of the future, but it seems certain that they will remain few in number despite fantasies of a workforce filled with engineers, scientists, and statisticians. There is virtually no room at the top of the labor market pyramid, given existing social relations of work in America, and high technology will almost certainly be used to preserve existing relations of power, status, and income rather than disturb them. The relative distribution of mind work, sophisticated, intellectually stimulating, and potent, will undoubtedly remain at or below present levels for the next few decades, if the masters of high technology continue to remake our world as they have begun to.

What does this brief survey of tomorrow's jobs tell us about the need for CL? First, many jobs will involve no computers at all. Second, the majority of jobs will involve only indirect use of computers or, at most, a level of computer use requiring a week or two of practical instruction. In all such jobs a prior introduction to computers such as CL is quite unnecessary, since no prior computer knowledge is required. Third, since, according to one CL educator, "for many years to come people will be able to acquire needed levels of computer-oriented skills on the job or in higher education programs," CL is even unnecessary in the training of those who will eventually become sophisticated computer workers. Fourth, the number and quality of jobs in the computer field itself is greatly overstated, and thus these jobs cannot be used to justify universal CL. Fifth, the number of knowledge workers, in any significant sense, will remain small despite the spread of CL. On all accounts, even from this admittedly cursory view of the future, CL makes no sense as job preparation. The hole card turns out to be the joker.

Nevertheless, the joke may be on us. We saw earlier how new educational requirements, however groundless, are rapidly making the need for CL a fact of life for today's students. Similarly, new hiring practices will most likely render CL necessary for employment. Just as good spelling is now required to fill out an application for a janitor's job and a high school diploma is needed to become a nurse's aide, and a college diploma is necessary for just about everything else, so tomorrow CL will be a requisite for many jobs that actually require no computer knowledge. With such credential barriers in place, CL will have created its own necessity, and employability will depend in part upon a parcel of useless knowledge about computers. Mythology will become the new reality. In the words of Atari's chief scientist, used originally in a different although not entirely unrelated context, "The best way to predict the future is to invent it." CL might turn up an ace whatever is in the deck.

Many teachers will argue that however few real knowledge-work jobs there may be, they want their students to have them. This competitive spirit (which parents share) feeds the momentum of CL: everyone wants his or her kid to become an engineer or a programmer, and an introduction to computers seems the best place to start. It is next to impossible to convince a particular parent or teacher that this does not make sense. A larger view, however, would unravel the twin mythology supporting this attitude. The idea that, no matter how few good jobs there are, there is still one out there for my child, depends upon a lingering hope that there will be enough for all; it assumes also that everyone gets an equal chance, and that success or failure depends solely on individual competence and preparation. There is nothing, even in the rhetoric of CL, to encourage a hope for equal opportunity in the world of high technology; all the evidence points in the opposite direction. Similarly, there is little reason to expect an abundance of decent jobs in the new workforce, despite the rhetoric. Some of us should begin to ask why.

Many will be squeezed out by the computer revolution. The disenfranchised segments of the population, those who are already out of the running for jobs because of discrimination and inequality, will undoubtedly be pushed still further from access to jobs in the world of high technology. In a society where perhaps 25 percent of the population is functionally illiterate, in the original sense of that term, such people will be doubly condemned for being computer illiterate as well. The invented necessity of CL, in the form of credential barriers to employment, will serve to blame the victim in a new, insidious way: those who don't know computers will be firmly locked out of a workforce barely open to them now. Considerable lip service is being paid to these people, just as there is considerable discussion these days about the millions of people being replaced by automation. In all the talk, however, the only solution ever discussed is education or retraining: Let these unfortunate people learn computers so they can become knowledge workers. As we have begun to see, this is really no solution at all. CL, as job preparation, is in fact an obstacle to possible futures which might include these people. Perhaps the fundamental attitude behind CL, and the high-technology movement in general, is best expressed in the words of one of its popularizers: "The real measure of a revolution is not its casualty count, but its effects on the survivors."

We have seen that CL has very little to do with whether we will survive—as consumers, students, or workers—in the new world of high technology. There remains, however, one last justification for CL which we have not yet examined. It is frequently argued that the public needs to become informed about the new technology if, as citizens in a democracy, we are to be able to determine how computers will shape our lives. Public empowerment is an oft-stated goal of CL advocates, and it certainly appears reasonable that some understanding of the new technology is needed for controlling it. So long as computers remain a mystery to the majority of citizens, it is argued, the public will be an easy prey to vested interests, large scale abuse, and runaway technology. Society will be shaped by the designs of the few, and the masses will suffer the consequences, unless they are educated into computer literacy.

The irony of this argument is that we are already surrounded by computers and high technology without ever having been asked if we wanted to be. There has been virtually no public debate about whether the American people want the computerized information society we are now being forced to enter. The truth is that our society is already shaped primarily by the designs of the few and the momentum of technology, and it makes no sense to suggest that a minimal understanding of computers will empower an already technologically impotent citizenry. Computer literacy does not provide the public with the tools for wresting control of these technologies from the hands of corporate decision-makers. In fact, it is much more likely that a focus on minimal technical competence, as in CL, will lead to a sort of pseudocontrol, a false sense that one has power simply because one can make a computer do a little something. Real control of the direction the new technology will take involves political understanding, not trivial technical understanding, and it must focus on decisions which affect the design and use of large systems, not on the ability to create catchy little BASIC programs.

A few CL advocates are at least aware of this larger picture, but the overwhelming tendency is to ignore it. The trend in CL curriculum development is to turn away from what is derisively referred to as "computer awareness" (that is, a general overview of the social impact of computers) and to encourage instead a more hands-on, technical understanding. Basic to this tendency is the assumption that the control of a technology requires technological expertise. Control of nuclear energy in the hands of experts, however, proved dangerous in the case of Three Mile Island. People learned there that the experts did not really know what they were doing, that they did not genuinely consider the safety of the public as their top priority, and that ordinary citizens could confront and change the direction of a technology without having any technological understanding whatsoever. In the same way, control of computer technology by a few has created unmanned factories, offices of the future, useless gadgetry and games, "smart homes" and "electronic battlefields," all of which, it could be argued, lead to deterioration of people's jobs, skills, social relations, power, dignity, and even their chances of survival. Public debate on all of these transformations has been virtually nonexistent, and we must examine the public empowerment aspirations of CL in this context. We must ask whether CL is a movement which might help us confront existing policy, or whether it is in fact an extension of this policy, a vehicle for its dissemination, even a tool being used, often unknowingly, to further its public acceptance.

The content of CL courses now available contradicts any claim that they could possibly enlighten or empower anyone (unless "empowerment" is reduced to the keyboard familarity required to vote via videotex). Even if technical understanding were important for democratic participation, the minimal technical information available in such courses is many orders of magnitude removed from any significant understanding which might serve to enhance public deliberation. And any token attention to "social impact," in those courses that address it at all, is typically one-sided and delimited. For example, the New York State Association of Math Teachers, in its state-wide curriculum proposal, defines social-impact objectives in this manner: "The student will be aware of some of the major uses of computers in modern society . . . and the student will be aware of career opportunities related to computers." The nontechnical components of CL courses generally are reduced to a cursory look at the history of computers (often ignoring the military contribution), a brief survey of benign computer uses, an unrealistic description of computer careers, and a gee-whiz glance at the marvels of the future. One popular CL course, now being introduced throughout the nation, is called Computeronics. Except for one or two comments about the frustrations of computer errors and a short parody of the dehumanized home of the future, the "Computers in Society" text of this course reads virtually as propaganda for the status quo. Job loss or social disenfranchisement are not mentioned, and the student is asked to "imagine that you are an executive," never an unemployed autoworker or assembler, when the effects of computerization are examined.

Even more disturbing was the attitude of teachers and trainers at a Computeronics teacher workshop I recently attended. Neither the teachers nor the trainers appeared very knowledgeable about computers or their impact, and there was a collective inclination to keep things light and uncomplicated. One trainer asked that we pretend not to know anything about computers so that he could practice his craft, and discussions about social questions were kept amusing and friendly, even as some real concerns were expressed. When one woman jokingly suggested we go down to the gym, get baseball bats, and destroy the micros surrounding us, the response was uncomfortable laughter. Teachers left that workshop with only the slightest knowledge of computer programming, with negligible understanding of the social impact of this technology, and with very little desire to find out more. Yet such people as these, all nice folks, will be the ones conferring Computer Literacy upon millions of students. Not one participant appeared to realize the part he or she might be playing in the dissemination of such diluted, uncritical, uninformed, and possibly harmful education. This is hardly what Thomas Jefferson had in mind.

One further word about pseudocontrol. The computer differs from the TV and telephone in that, although it appears alien and menacing to the uninitiated, it can be tamed, controlled by the user, once some simple programming is learned. The possibilities for learning to control one's computer appear limitless because of the variety of functions it can be made to perform. Thus the home computer hobbyist enjoys a tremendous sense of power over his or her small piece of the technology: "When you program a computer, you feel a great deal of control and mastery" because "to program a computer is to enjoy power." The danger is that this sense of control, or pseudocontrol, becomes a substitute for real control, deluding one into thinking that one has mastered a technology when in reality one is only playing God with a chip of silicon.

This false sense of empowerment blocks any real participation in the social control of the technology as a whole. The result is a nation of individual computer masters who can't see the forest for the trees. The intensity of the debate about the impact of computer technology seems to have diminished in recent years, and discussions of its effect on human values appear to be out of fashion. If CL is truly a campaign for public enlightenment, one would have expected just the reverse, and this might tell us something about the real nature of CL. Is it possible that the failure, not the success, of CL might bring us closer to a collective understanding of where we are heading and what we might do about it?

CL is, in its practical claims, a bunch of nonsense, both hollow and full of danger, both ludicrous and grave. An examination of its specious content may alarm some readers, but probably not many. This is because almost everyone, including most CL advocates themselves, has already swallowed its faults of logic and distortions of reality without so much as a second thought. There is no question that the majority of those who are pushing CL into every corner of this country honestly believe that CL makes sense. There are some advocates of CL, however, who, it seems reasonable to assume, are using CL as a means to furthering their objectives at the expense (literally and otherwise) of a defensive American public. It is time to look at the weavers of the emperor's new clothes.

Hans Christian Andersen's weavers claim to be making cloth

which is invisible to fools and incompetents. The swindlers' success requires a population which is sufficiently insecure about its intellectual competence to be willing to deny the obvious truth, a scenario not very different from the present state of affairs in America. Many Americans question their abilities and fear for their present or future jobs, to the point of being persuadable that what appears obvious to them (for example, that computers are troubling or dehumanizing) is false. The important thing is that oneself and one's children not be left behind.

As the country now agonizes over its presumed intellectual deficiencies, comparisons between our education and skills and those of the Japanese or Soviets proliferate in the press; one reads everywhere that we won't be able to "problem-solve" or "think critically" as well as our competitors or enemies unless we "create another Sputnik" and proceed full speed ahead. Add to this a climate of recession, loss of jobs to foreign industry, and high unemployment, and we are ready for the weavers: "The general context," writes one strong CL advocate, "that I think it is essential to assume, *even if we have to engage in a deliberate suspension of disbelief in order to assume it*, is an overarching national goal: to reverse the trend of decline of the U.S. relative to its main competition in productivity, prestige and leadership" (emphasis mine).

Enter High Tech. "America Rushes to High Technology For Growth," *Business Week* announces on a recent cover. Just as the promoters of the electrical and chemical technologies in the first decades of this century saw World War I as their great opportunity, so the promoters of computer technology are seizing this opportunity to establish their technology at the center of our economy. Only the acquiescence of the American people is needed: "It is clear that in the coming years we are going to retool our industry, and it should be made clear that we must, at the same time, retool ourselves." Enter computer literacy. But cui bono? Who might benefit most from such a massive "retooling" of the American people? Two obvious parties come to mind. First, there are the manufacturers and retailers of hardware and software, who envision an enormous educational demand for their wares.

"We're looking at an infinite market," says the chairman of one such manufacturing firm. Anyone who is at all skeptical about CL usually comes to this answer first: CL is just a way to sell computers. This, then, is one not-so-hidden agenda behind CL.

A second party which stands to benefit from the push for CL is the education profession, in schools, colleges, industry, and small, profitable computer schools. As new graduate programs in computer education start up, as thousands of laid-off workers look to be "retrained," as millions of students need computer courses in order to graduate, as twenty-six million managers look reluctantly at the computers in their futures, as millions of teachers line up for in-service training, the realm of the educator has suddenly acquired a large and rich new province. "School administrators are laying their bets on a sure ticket to a better life for schools—technology." This, then, is a second agenda behind CL.

The content of CL is largely irrelevant for both agendas so long as demand for the hardware, software, and instruction remains high. This helps to explain how CL has spread so quickly despite its dubious content and justification. Many educators sincerely believe in what CL promises, and many sincerely want to provide the best possible CL curricula for their students. Nevertheless, very few have examined the assumptions and context of their effort and, given what they stand to gain, it is altogether understandable that they have not bothered. This is even more true for the manufacturers and retailers of computers and software; their business is selling products, and if CL expands their markets, who are they to question it? Educators, manufacturers, and retailers all follow agendas which have expanded the perceived need for CL among the American people. These groups are primarily responsible for the CL movement in this country. They have intensified high-tech fever, and have responded with predictable enterprise to the "needs" of a defensive population. They are, however, merely spreading someone else's vision of a new world.

It seems reasonable to interpret CL as propaganda which parades as public enlightenment, and to conclude that it means to create a populace that can comfortably accept the prospect of a computerized world. The common thread running through the various definitions of Computer Literacy encourages a suspicion that something like this is the program:

> The goal of CL should be to give as many of [the masses] as possible the sense of belonging in a computer-rich society.
>
> Give all people, at least, a minimal amount of computer knowledge that would enable them to become "computer comfortable."
>
> [CL leads] to a favorable or well-informed affective orientation.
>
> [CL will enable people to] take reasonable positions on information-related issues.
>
> [CL will help people to] understand the concept of compromise . . . with respect to policy issues such as informational privacy and security.
>
> Many individuals today are apprehensive about privacy, misuse, attitudes and automation in general. [CL] is the way to eliminate these concerns.
>
> Training is a concrete basis for understanding the value of computers and . . . leads to greater acceptance of other societal applications as well.

It is difficult to ignore the implication here. The weavers of CL's dubious cloth are the prime movers behind the computerized society itself, the fabricators of "high tech," "telecommunications," "information society," and "computer revolution." Catchwords such as these have convinced the nation that it is entering a social transformation which is both total and inevitable. Those corporate leaders and their ideological allies who mean to transform the workplace, the home, the school, and the functions of government into an efficient, highly controlled, and easily monitored technological marketplace, are the real originators of CL, if not by that name, because they need something like it to make their social transformation a reality. (Whether the transformation is taken to be conspiratorially organized, or largely a matter of implicit common interests, scarcely matters.) Whereas educators and computer merchants have only enlarged upon an existing demand, the makers of the Information Society, those who would transform our world to suit their needs, have perpetrated CL in order to ensure public acquiescence in their grand design.

How does the propaganda of Computer Literacy ensure this acquiescence? First, it introduces people to computers, gives them some hands-on experience, and deludes them into thinking that all computers are friendly and easily controlled because their little micro is so. In this way, CL mystifies in the name of demystification. The very act of making computers accessible conceals the more socially significant, and far less accessible, purposes of the technology. The one-sided presentation of marvelous computer uses in CL courses furthers this deception in the name of "awareness."

Second, as manufacturers and designers work to produce computers which are ever more user-friendly, so CL is used to "produce" people who are ever more computer-friendly. A person who is familiar with a school computer, or even better, one who has a personal computer at home, is far less likely to be suspicious of a computerized society than one who is uninitiated and scared.

This brings us to a third way CL ensures public acquiescence in the information society. It is used to psychologize dissent. Anyone who might for whatever good reason be reluctant to get involved with computers is called "computerphobic," which means that he or she is really afraid of computers out of mere ignorance. Few people who have been labelled computerphobic don't somehow believe it themselves. It is powerful stuff; those accused of fearing something new become disoriented as old truths lose ground. CL exists not only to inform but also to give such people an easy way out, when a more difficult way might lead them to the truth.

A fourth use of CL propaganda is to stifle debate and to depoliticize discussion. The focus on the technical, and the establishment of a carefully delineated arena for discussions of "social impact," render any genuine criticism illegitimate, even irrational. And the portrayal of the computer society as a given discredits any discussions of human values and dignity as being wishful thinking or nostalgic reverie.

The fifth influence of CL propaganda is perhaps the most effective. The unequivocal message of CL is this: computers are important, very important, and knowing about them is equally important. There is hardly a way that a society bombarded with such exhortations to become computer literate, as we have been, can continue to believe that knowing about computers might not be very important. Some of the hysteria of parents, schoolmen, and management results from this bombardment. One certain way to ensure public cooperation and acquiescence is to make people feel that they have no choice, and the CL campaign is designed to do just that. When a fervent appeal to national pride and prestige is added, and a resolve to overcome our foreign competition in trade and international leadership, it becomes hard to find someone who will even admit the possibility that all this computer talk may be exaggerated. Many people breathe a noticeable sigh of relief at such a suggestion, and many have thanked me for mentioning the unmentionable. But the relative unimportance of computer knowledge must be stated plainly and often before people can learn to hope that the picture of the future woven into the CL tapestry is, as yet, essentially a fiction.

The weavers of the emperor's new clothes wanted to line their pockets with gold. Those who weave the far-reaching strands of Computer Literacy want to redesign our world. It is especially troubling, therefore, to find that several of the more visible proponents of CL have historical associations with an ideology whose focus is military and whose methods are decidedly scientistic and antidemocratic. Only a few pieces of the puzzle are yet in place, unfortunately. They include the author of "The Next Great Crisis in American Education – Computer Literacy," who is also a National Science Foundation convenor of national CL conferences. His work prior to the rise of CL included a study for the Army on "undergrounds in insurgent, revolutionary and resistance warfare," in which he states that "the most effective countermeasure is the use of immediate, overpowering force to repress the first signs of insurgency or resistance. Nations with a representative or constitutional form of government are often restrained from such action by moral, legal and social considerations." HumRRO,

Human Resources Research Organization, a major recipient of CL grants and also a convenor of national CL conferences, was founded by the Army in 1951 to "improve human performance through behavioral and social science research." It is unclear at this time what the connections may be between such backgrounds and CL, but the matter certainly warrants closer examination. Some agendas will remain hidden until then.

Hans Christian Andersen chose a child to break the spell of the weavers. Our story is different. We can hardly count on our children to point out the fraudulence of Computer Literacy. They are already too comfortable, for the most part, within the new world, and their fearlessness, often admired by a cautious older generation, could in fact be their greatest weakness. The naked truth must be declared by those who can still see it, so that we may still have a chance to choose our future.

It must be stated that computers are not the problem. A word processor would have facilitated the writing of this paper tremendously, and I would not reject a CAT scan at the appropriate time. Too often, however, when one intones the homily that "computers aren't harmful, people are," one is assuming that "people" are reasonable beings like us, or, if they are not, that they can be replaced. But things are not that simple, and the people who are forging the information society cannot readily be assumed to share our idea of what is reasonable. The distinction between computers and the people who control them once again becomes blurred, and Luddism takes on fresh appeal.

But the subject of this paper is not computers. It is Computer Literacy. Although the two are assuredly related, it is important that they be kept separate. One does not have to be "anticomputer" to choose to reject the Computer Revolution or to see through the transparent fraudulence of Computer Literacy. What is desperately needed at this time is the resurrection of critical debate, a renewal of public discourse about how computers might be understood and used in ways which enrich our lives. This would be the first step toward a truly computer-literate society.

34

THE "WORLD OF THE NEWS" STUDY
Results of International Cooperation

Annabelle Sreberny-Mohammadi

If ever it was clear that good evidence doesn't prove a case, that is true of the international research project that started under the title of the "Foreign Images" study, circulated as "The World of the News: The News of the World," and is being published as *Foreign News in the Media*. Emerging out of the international concern with the imbalance of news flows and news content, it was guaranteed a political life, to be used as ammunition in both social scientific debate about the nature of research and the role of evidence, and in the political debate that centers on UNESCO and the demand for a New International Information Order.

Perhaps no aspect of the NIIO debate has been more contentious and controversial than the question of international news. In the mid-1970s, argument about news flows and presentation, the imbalances of international communications structures, and the dominance of the Western news agencies agitated all concerned with the mass media: international organizations, national policy-makers, media researchers, and media practitioners. Bias in the flows of international news and distortion in its content, particularly regarding the image of the South, were the central themes. These were raised yet again at the General Conference of UNESCO in Nairobi in 1976, and a resolution was passed calling for study of this problem. This resulted in the joint study by UNESCO and the International Association for Mass Communication Research that is reported here (20).[1]

[1] Other discussions of the report appear in (18, 19).

Annabelle Sreberny-Mohammadi is Research Associate, Centre for Mass Communication Research, University of Leicester. The full report upon which this article is based is being published by UNESCO (20).

Reprinted from "The 'World of the News' Study: Results of International Cooperation," by Annabelle Sreberny-Mohammadi, "Pseudo Debate," by Robert L. Stevenson, and "Bitter Lessons," by Kaarle Nordenstreng in the *Journal of Communication*, Vol. 34, No. 1 (Winter 1984), pp. 121-142.

This project was planned as an inventory of international news reporting. Earlier studies have had similar aims, although their focus has often been far more limited, dealing with one particular region or one kind of media presentation only. Among the most famous pioneering efforts in the field are Kaiser's comparative study of 17 major daily newspapers (10) and the International Press Institute's study, *The Flow of the News* (9), both of which were published in 1953. More recently, Gerbner and Marvanyi (3) mapped out the various "worlds" presented in selected press systems, and Golding and Elliott (4) examined international news presentation within the context of a study on the production of broadcast news. Schramm (15) has devoted particular attention to news presentation in and about Asia. Indeed, there has been an increasing flow of materials relating to news flow in recent books and journal symposia; the studies range from limited empirical exercises to methodological issues and the need for extra-media indicators, to the theoretical questions underpinning the debate about news flow imbalance (7, 8, 13, 22, 24, 25).

The central merit of this study is its breadth.

It covers all "worlds of development," all the regions of the world, and includes data from both broadcasting channels and the press. There were 13 full participating teams and the U.S. team covered an additional 16 media systems, providing a very wide and significant data base of 29 media systems. The 13 participating teams were from Australia, Finland, the Federal Republic of Germany, India, Iran, Hungary, Lebanon, Malaysia, the Netherlands, Nigeria, Poland, the United States, and Yugoslavia. In addition, quantitative data were generated for Algeria, Argentina, Brazil, Egypt, Greece, Iceland, Indonesia, Ivory Coast, Kenya, Mexico, Thailand, Tunisia, Turkey, U.S.S.R., Zaire, and Zambia.

The idea for the project stemmed from a resolution passed at the 1976 General Conference of UNESCO in Nairobi; the responsibility for undertaking the research was transferred to the IAMCR in the summer of 1977, and by the summer of 1979 the above teams had volunteered as possessing the necessary resources.

All participants were to adhere to a core schedule for sampling, coding, and analysis. While some undertook additional historical and other kinds of analysis, only the results of the core schedule are reported here; the other materials are available in the respective national reports. The press sample included three or four of the largest daily papers in each country. For the radio and television broadcasting sample, only the "main news bulletin of the day" was selected and taped for subsequent analysis. Beyond such general instructions, each national team was free to select those press and broadcasting channels that best represented their particular national system. Some reflected political diversity, as in the Finnish selections, while others focused on the diverse presentations of ethnic/linguistic communities, as in the Malay choices. Some focused only on national newspapers, while countries without a national press selected regional papers. The variations in selection mean that the figure used for some countries represents only a single channel (Greece, Turkey); it rises to a maximum of twelve channels studied (Malaysia).

We grouped the 29 media systems into seven geo-political regions for reporting large patterns, so many differences were equalized in collapsing these data. For example, the data on North American television are derived from a single national media system, that of the United States, while the data for Africa included seven media systems.

The time sample was based on one chronological week, in April 1979, and a composite week, which spanned April through June. Our week was in fact six days, since Sunday editions were excluded; these tend to break with the normal pattern of weekly presentation and many countries publish no Sunday or equivalent paper. Only the "general news" pages of the press were included. All specialized sections of a paper, such as finance, travel, women, etc., were omitted, as were any special reports and supplements that appeared during our time period. This was intended to maximize the comparability of results, cut coding time, and help make the press results more comparable with those from broadcasting, where no special programming of a news-oriented kind could be included.

To some extent, this focus on the "general news" pages biased the outcome of our findings, orienting the sample toward a comparatively limited set of hard news topics. Clearly, too, our study does not pretend to reflect the complete universe of news and news-related information available within any of the participating nations. It focuses only on the main formal mass media channels and their particular modes of news presentation and through the formal coding instrument provides information on the rough volume and overall structure of international news presentation.

The news item was the unit of analysis. Each item was coded on the following variables: *location*—where the news item originated; *source*—from whom the news item originated; *position and nationality of actor*—who made the news; *topic*—what the news was about; and *theme*—what is the news context. The length of an item was also coded, but since the correlations between the two sets of figures for frequency and length were high, we report only the total number of items here.

Even the definition of international news became a key issue.

Not all items included were "foreign" or "external" news in terms of origin or strictly *international* in terms of dealing with events in more than a single country. The widely adopted story-type classification that

Table 1: Amount of international news on an average day by selected channels (press, radio, and TV)

	International news stories	
	x̄	% of all news*
NORTH AMERICA		
U.S. (N = 1,487)		
New York Times	33	39
Washington Post	26	42
Los Angeles Times	21	25
New York Daily News	14	19
Minneapolis Tribune	14	30
Charlotte Observer	11	
Television—CBS	4	19
LATIN AMERICA		
Argentina (N = 1,017)		
Clarín	20	43
La Opinion	27	53
Cronica	21	25
Radio—Rivadavia	11	n.a.
Television—11	3	n.a.
Television—Tele Noche	4	n.a.
Brazil (N = 630)		
O Estado de São Paulo	29	33
Jornal do Brasil	24	28
Mexico (N = 1,188)		
El Universal	40	33
Excelsior	39	43
AFRICA		
Algeria (N = 935)		
El Moudjahed	35	44
Television	13	68
Ivory Coast (N = 390)		
Fraternité Matin	22	51
Television	33	82
Kenya (N = 501)		
Nairobi Standard	13	45
Daily Nation	14	36
Radio	15	64
Nigeria (N = 205)		
Daily Times	9	5
New Nigerian	3	16
Punch	2	13
Radio	3	17
Television	1	3
Tunisia (N = 1,303)		
La Presse	36	76
L'Action	25	51
Television	14	77
Zaire (N = 419)		
Elima	9	29
Salonga	7	25
Radio	18	61
Zambia (N = 516)		
Zambia Times	13	43
Zambia Daily Mail	13	81
Radio	10	47
Television	7	80
MIDDLE EAST		
Egypt (N = 1,322)		
al-Ahram	30	25
al-Akhbar	38	17
al-Gomhuria	30	12
Radio	14	92
Iran (N = 453)		
Kayhan	15	16
Ettela'at	12	18
Ayandegan	11	17
Lebanon (N = 2,049)		
al-Nahar	48	35
as-Safir	57	41
al-Amal	31	30
Radio Lebanon	22	62
Tele-Liban	13	65
ASIA		
Australia (N = 1,032)		
Australian	23	29
Herald	30	28
Telegraph	16	46
Radio—ABC	7	52
Radio—2AD	2	18
Television—ABC	6	30
Television—9/8	2	16
India (N = 1,649)		
Hindu	24	24
Times of India	33	21
Indian Express	22	24
Hindustan Times	27	23

Table 1: Amount of international news on an average day by selected channels (press, radio, and TV), continued

	International news stories	
	x̄	% of all news*
Statesman	32	29
Radio	5	18
Television	6	34
Indonesia (N = 811)		
Kompas	11	18
Sinar Harapan	14	34
Merdeka	27	44
Radio	6	n.a.
Television	9	n.a.
Malaysia (N = 2,070)		
New Straits Times	39	39
Utusan Malaysia	18	16
Sin Chew Jut Poh	37	26
Tamil Nesan	18	23
Radio (E)	7	54
Radio (M)	13	35
Radio (C)	5	43
Radio (T)	5	38
Television (E)	10	54
Television (M)	10	39
Television (C)	9	45
Television (T)	7	30
Thailand (N = 500)		
Siam-Rath	9	17
Thai-Rath	18	20
Dao-Sham	4	11
Radio	2	19
Television 3TV	14	58
EASTERN EUROPE		
Hungary (N = 2,931)		
Népszabadság	55	32
Népszava	43	25
Magyar Nemzet	60	31
Magyar Hírlap	61	37
Esti Hírlap	25	30
Radio	16	33
Television	11	40
Poland (N = 713)		
Trybuna Ludu	42	73
Zycie Warszawy	26	58
Express Wieczorny	30	45
Radio 1	9	41
Radio 111	6	55
TV News	8	26
U.S.S.R. (N = 997)		
Pravda	35	55
Izvestiya	25	55
Komsomolskaya Pravda	15	46
Television	8	32
Yugoslavia (N = 1,144)		
Delo	50	60
Dnevnik	24	39
Večer	12	19
Radio	11	36
WESTERN EUROPE		
Federal Republic of Germany (N = 3,068)		
Bild-Zeitung	31	41
Die Welt	59	52
Frankfurter Allgemeine	50	48
Suddeutscher Zeitung	65	60
Frankfurter Rundschau	37	41
Television—ARD	14	17
Television—ZDF	15	24
Finland (N = 881)		
Helsingin Sanomat	26	39
Aamulehti	18	23
Kansan Uutiset	14	22
Savon Sanomat	11	10
Television	5	36
Greece (N = 205)		
Ta Nea	16	18
Iceland (N = 689)		
Morgundbladid	25	23
Thjódviljinn	11	24
Dagbladid	11	16
Radio	6	20
Television	4	18
Netherlands (N = 991)		
Telegraaf	16	26
NRC/Handelsblad	38	42
Tubantia	23	17
Television—Nos	6	53
Turkey (N = 327)		
Milliyet	27	33

* General news-hole, omitting special sections and supplements.

allows for "foreign news at home" and "home news abroad" eliminates any neat dividing line between what is purely domestic news and what is international. There was also a high level of what we call "natiocentric coverage," or international news items being included in media output when their domestic relevance is clear. Thus, as soon as we began to examine the disparities between the total amounts of international news carried by the various systems and to try to determine what could be considered an acceptable or desirable balance between domestic coverage and international reporting, analytic difficulties arose. Sometimes a strong international focus would appear to draw attention away from necessary domestic investigation, while a weak international focus seemed to result in an isolationist and introverted outlook.

Table 1 shows the selected channels for each participating team, the total data base, and the average amount of international news carried by each channel daily. The results of the study can be presented here only in the most general and schematic manner. Results are presented in a single composite figure for each national media system. This leaves out the interesting question of differences between press and broadcast news. Perhaps what was most notable about the findings of the limited quantitative analysis was that, although the participating nations reflected different levels of development and a variety of political perspectives, the overall pattern of attention paid to certain kinds of events was remarkably similar.

Despite the diversity of systems analyzed, the structure of international news coverage was quite similar across systems.

In terms of the topics covered by international news, we found that politics dominated international news reporting everywhere (for results by region, see Table 2). Our two categories of international politics and

Table 2: Coverage of selected topics in international news by region[a]

	North America %	Latin America %	Africa %	Middle East %	Asia %	Eastern Europe %	Western Europe %
International politics	18	20	32	42	16	26	18
Domestic politics	21	28	19	17	17	18	20
Military	16	9	11	14	12	10	10
Economic matters	9	11	8	6	13	12	10
Crime	12	10	8	4	9	4	9
Culture	2	2	2	2	2	8	2
Sports	2	3	2	3	1	4	3
Personalities	1	1	2	1	2	1	2
Natural disasters	4	4	2	1	3	2	3
Total	85	88	86	90	75	85	77

[a] The other topics were: international aid, social service, religion, science, entertainment, human interest, student matters, ecology, and other.

domestic politics accounted for between 32 percent and 66 percent of all international news coverage in all participating media systems but three (Nigeria and Australia had less; Iran even more). Indeed, "hard" news, represented by these two political categories and by items on military and defense and economics, accounted for the majority of all stories. This was even more the case in the news media of the South, where few "soft" stories are either generated or reported. Similarly, we found that political figures dominate, embracing 25 percent to 60 percent of all actors in international news; few other categories of actors received significant mention. Political news with political actors constitutes the bulk of international news coverage everywhere.

The other overall finding was the prominence of regionalism. Every national system devoted most attention to events happening within and to actors belonging to its immediate geographical region. This focus characterized between 23 percent and 63 percent of all international news in every system. Thus, Nigeria was most concerned about African affairs and African actors, Argentina featured Latin American news most prominently, and so on. Table 3 shows this phenomenon by grouping the countries into regions and ranking their focus of attention; the diagonal line of number-one-ranked regions is clear. Although there is little evidence of a "Third World perspective," a "continental orientation" is strong.

The only instances in which this regional focus did not hold true were in the Polish and Yugoslav systems, where as much attention was paid to news events in Western Europe as in the East. Indeed, the Eastern European region was the only one to be more fully represented in international news through its actors than through location of events within its territory (see Table 3). The separation of *actors* from *location* in the great mobility of international affairs again raises the question of how "balance" is to be achieved in international news production. Our data show that extra-regional concern for other developing areas is still weak, so that Galtung's assessment of a decade ago that "the peripheral nations do not read much about each other, especially not across bloc borders" still holds (2). Thus, again, balance can be achieved in the "reciprocity of indifference" whereby Latin America ranks last in the

Table 3: Rank ordering of regions in international news by location of event

	Participating media systems								
Regions	North America	Latin America	Africa	Middle East	Asia	Eastern Europe	Western Europe	Location	Actor
North America	1	3	5	3	3	6	2	3	2
Latin America	6	1	8	6	8	8	8	7	8
Africa	5	6.5	1	4	5	7	5.5	5	6
Middle East	2.5	4	2	1	4	4.5	3	2	1
Asia	4	5	5	5	1	3	5.5	4	5
Eastern Europe	7	6.5	7	7	6	1	4	6	4
Western Europe	2.5	2	3	2	2	2	1	1	3
General	8	8	5	8	7	4.5	7	8	7

attention of the African media, and Africa ranks low in the Latin American. Western Europe and North America manifest a "reciprocity of concern," as each accords the other the most attention after themselves. Balance achieved by the equalization of the flow of news "bits" may still leave more basic issues unsettled.

In regard to news content, news everywhere appears to be defined as the "exceptional event," with coups and catastrophes being newsworthy wherever they occur. That the South is so often portrayed in such a manner is a function of the limited amount of attention paid to developing areas outside their own regions. The media of the South both exhibit less interest in covering and are less a source for "soft" news items such as human interest stories, culture, entertainment; further, the fewer the number of international news items, the more those items are concentrated in a few subject areas and reflect very immediate events. Only in the Eastern European media is any significant amount of attention paid to what might be termed "positive" news about culture and science.

The most contentious area of current debate on international communication has been the role of the Western news agencies as the dominant creators and gatekeepers of news flows. Our methodology proved rather crude for distinguishing the source of a news item. Examining the press only, we found a very high rate of non-attribution of news sources, as shown in Table 4. Given that constraint, however, there was a high reported use of local sources, mainly national news agencies, and of national correspondents. While this may mask the exact origination of a news item, it does reveal a significant amount of possible *secondary* gatekeeping in the selection, interpretation, and processing of news that originally may have been culled from external sources. Yet it was indeed the "big four" Western agencies that figured as the second most

Table 4: Attributed sources of international news by region (for press only)

	North America %	Latin America %	Africa %	Middle East %	Asia %	Eastern Europe %	Western Europe %
Home country agency	4	—	11	3	16	36	15
Reuters	6	—	5	12	14	2	14
UPI	9	10	1	7	5	2	4
AP	22	7	1	9	14	1	14
AFP	—	12	5	20	10	2	6
TASS	—	—	—	—	—	16	1
Other agency		17		12	2	2	3
Own staff	36	9	9	8	26	22	27
Other medium—home	1	—	—	—	—	1	1
Other medium—foreign	1	2	3	5	3	3	4
Other source	6	12	5	10	6	5	7
Unidentifiable	11	39	65	28	18	27	21

Note: Multiple coding was permitted, so totals may exceed 100 percent.

important set of sources for international news, and our figures quite probably do not reflect all the news from these sources. It may be the case that the "big four" provide a limited news diet, but there was no evidence to suggest even a sampling of alternative news menus from the many other types of sources that now exist.

A qualitative analysis supplemented the quantitative findings of international news coverage.

From the beginning of this project, we intended to balance the formal exercise in quantification with a more delicate, nuanced, interpretative analysis of the deeper content of international news presentation. This would provide the context for interpretation of the statistical data and a real taste of the news coverage available within each national system. Devising such an interpretative schema proved a bigger task than anticipated, and this great aim was reduced to an analysis of selected "dominant" stories. Decisions as to how "dominance" was constructed within each media system (by length of story, presence on front page, repetition throughout the period, etc.) were left to each national team. Three or four items were to be selected and a summary made of the perspective and news angle adopted and the journalistic devices and language styles used to report the item. Some differences emerged between the findings from the quantitative study and those of this qualitative analysis, which suggest that analysis based on only one kind of evidence might be very misleading.

The categories used for quantification tended to reflect similarities in coverage, while the qualitative analysis revealed some differences in outlook. The qualitative analysis produced a different geographic focus from the quantitative findings. For example, Africa was repeatedly said to have furnished major news stories, relating to elections in what was then Rhodesia and to the routing of Idi Amin from Uganda. The statistical ranking of the region, however, was not high. Conversely, Western Europe and North America were not found to have produced many significant stories, yet both achieved a higher ranking for amount of news coverage than did Africa. These two regions seem to provide a second tier of attention after "own region" as "consistent newsmakers," even overtaking the global "hot spots." The implication of this divergence—whether a continual and low-key or a short-term and dramatic focus has the greater effect on audiences of media news—deserves attention.

Differences in focus, perspective, and value orientation became clearer in this qualitative analysis. Varying attitudes toward the Camp David agreements were revealed, as was the contrasting jubilation or cynicism with which Salt II talks were greeted. Yet, at the same time, many national studies showed considerable reverberations of the concepts and descriptive terminology used by the big agencies themselves, as Weaver and Wilhoit have discussed in their study of agency output (see, e.g., 23). The widespread adoption of news agency language suggests that there is less real secondary gatekeeping than many would wish for. It is clear, however, that tone, moral judgments, and political orientations form the wider ideological frame of each media system and are as, if not more, important in the construction of social consciousness than the total amount of news coverage. The differences and contradictions between the two—quantitative and qualitative—sets of data suggest that caution is needed in the evaluation of the project. Adequate understanding of international news presentation requires several levels of analysis; any one set of findings alone may be ambiguous and open to very different interpretations.

As our interest lay in a general mapping of international news presentation, we could not answer many intriguing questions.

Given the vast amount of data generated by even the simplest of 29-country surveys, we limited ourselves to the central questions.[2] We made no special analysis of the position of a news item, so a front-page leader counted the same as a news brief on a middle page. We gave no ranking to the relative "influence" of the paper being analyzed nor to any of the radio and television channels, although this issue is legitimately raised in the national reports. According to our sample comparisons, the analyses based on the number of items and those based on total amount of space proved to be remarkably similar. Although differences do appear when the data are divided into small subcategories, at the level of analysis by country—which is the level we use in the final report—the similarities are striking. It seems to make very little difference whether the number of stories is counted or whether total space covered is measured: the results for each country are nearly identical.

Some tests were also made on a sample of U.S. papers of the effect of including only the general news sections from six-day samples (the method used in the study) as compared with analysis of international news items culled from the entire newspaper and including the Sunday editions. As the results in Table 5 show, care is needed with the interpretation of the data. Sports news in particular, but also other materials usually found in special sections of a paper, are underrepresented in our study. So too is material not written to meet a daily deadline, so that "soft" news is underrepresented, while the fast-breaking, event-oriented news of politics, foreign affairs, and war tends to be overrepresented. The total amount of international news available in the American press is also underrepresented, by about 45 percent, and this may hold true for other national systems. On the other hand, any

[2] This section draws heavily on an unpublished paper by Robert L. Stevenson (21).

Table 5: Comparison of general news section, six-day analysis and total paper, seven-day analysis in U.S. media sample

	Full sample (n = 2,675) %	Limited sample (n = 1,487) %
Geographic origin of news		
North America	35	26
Latin America	6	7
Africa	7	10
Middle East	11	16
Asia	13	14
Western Europe	17	16
Eastern Europe	7	6
General	5	5
	r = .94	
Main topic		
International politics	13	18
Domestic politics	15	21
Military, defense	11	16
Economics	14	9
International aid	1	2
Social services	2	2
Crime, justice, legal	9	12
Culture	7	2
Religion	2	2
Science	1	2
Sports	10	2
Entertainment	1	1
Personalities	4	1
Human interest	3	3
Student affairs	0	0
Ecology	2	2
Accidents, natural disasters	3	4
Other	2	2
	r = .84	

kind of sampling procedure creates certain distortions and this study does not claim to have analyzed the total universe of international news available in any one country: that would be a quite formidable, albeit fascinating, task.

And yet, the validity of our quantitative findings is supported by and in turn reverberates the general findings of many other such studies conducted over the past decade. For example, a look at the geographic emphasis of international news from the data of 42 countries (culled from 10 separate empirical studies)[3] reveals a strong, consistent, and simple pattern. Regional news is emphasized in the media of all countries.

[3] The ten studies analyzed were by Dajani and Donohue (1), Gerbner and Marvanyi (3), Golding and Elliott (4), Harris (5), Hester (6), McQuail (11), Pinch (12), Rimmer (14), Schramm et al. (16), and Skurnik (17).

Behind the dominance of own region, in second place, is news from North America and Western Europe, while the "invisible" parts of the world are Eastern Europe and the rest of the developing world outside own immediate area. Likewise with topic, where the degree of slippage between categories is greater, all the studies examined found that news emphasizes a narrow range of hard news topics and actors: politics, or politics-by-other-means such as war and economics, mainly through the activities of decision-making elites. But again, in this study as in most of the others, exactly those parts of the mass media and also alternative media were omitted where a more analytic, contextualized, and perhaps more positive approach toward international news might be found.

We would suggest that it is time to move away from this kind of study, since the accumulated data are vast and the central findings reasonably validated. We could do with more studies that focus on and help to explain how and why this almost universal process of news selection has evolved: studies of the news "gatekeepers," especially in Third World contexts, and their professional training, organizational contexts, news orientations; studies on the production and distribution processes and content of non-Western news agencies, particularly those aiming to promote a development orientation; studies that examine existing alternative perspectives on the news, from a feminist outlook on British Channel Four to a Third World perspective in an African paper, to see how "difference" is created.

We might concentrate more on the news product itself, to provide a "deeper" reading of the content of international news and thus improve on our attempt at qualitative analysis. Also, the inherent presumption that the mass media are central and crucial carriers of information and imagery about foreign countries itself needs to be tested again, balanced by investigations of exactly what various audiences do "receive" from such international news presentation and what alternative sources they use.

Finally, if the demands for a New International Information Order are to have any bite, then the rhetorical teeth need to be sharpened. Central notions like balance and distortion need to be clarified. Balanced news in an unbalanced world would be an empty victory.

REFERENCES

1. Dajani, Nabil and John Donohue. "A Content Analysis of Six Arab Dailies." *Gazette* 19, 1973, pp. 155–170.
2. Galtung, Johan. "A Structural Theory of Imperialism." *Journal of Peace Research* 8(2), Spring 1971.
3. Gerbner, George and George Marvanyi. "The Many Worlds of the World's Press." *Journal of Communication* 27(1), Winter 1977, pp. 52–66.
4. Golding, Peter and Philip Elliott. *Making the News*. London: Longman, 1979.
5. Harris, Phil. "Final Report to UNESCO of a Study of the International News Media." Mimeo, University of Leicester, 1977.
6. Hester, Al. "Five Years of Foreign News on U.S. Television Evening Newscasts." *Gazette* 24, 1978, pp. 86–95.

7. Horton, Philip (Ed.) *The Third World and Press Freedom.* New York: Praeger, 1978.
8. "Humanising International News." Symposium in *Media Asia* 5(3), 1978.
9. International Press Institute. *The Flow of the News.* Zurich: IPI, 1953.
10. Kaiser, Jacques. *One Week's News.* Paris: UNESCO, 1953.
11. McQuail, Denis. *Analysis of Newspaper Content.* Research Series 4, Royal Commission on the Press. London: Her Majesty's Stationery Office, 1977.
12. Pinch, Edward T. "A Brief Study of News Patterns in Sixteen Third World Countries." Murrow Reports. Tufts University, Medford, Mass., 1978.
13. Richstad, J. and J. Anderson (Eds.) *Crisis in International News.* New York: Columbia University Press, 1981.
14. Rimmer, Tony. "Foreign News in UPI's 'A' Wire in the USA: A Descriptive Analysis of Content for February 13–18, 1977." Paper presented to the International Communication Association, Acapulco, 1980.
15. Schramm, Wilbur and Erwin Atwood. *Circulation of News in the Third World: A Study in Asia.* Hong Kong: Chinese University Press, 1981.
16. Schramm, Wilbur et al. "International News Wires and Third World News in Asia." Murrow Reports. Tufts University, Medford, Mass., 1978.
17. Skurnik, W. A. E. "Foreign News Coverage Compared: Six African Newspapers." Paper presented to the African Studies Association, Los Angeles, 1979.
18. Sreberny-Mohammadi, Annabelle. "More Bad News Than Good: International News Reporting." *Media Information Australia* 23, February 1982.
19. Sreberny-Mohammadi, Annabelle. "The World of the News: The News of the World." In *New Structures of International Communication? The Role of Research.* International Association for Mass Communication Research, 1982.
20. Sreberny-Mohammadi, Annabelle with Kaarle Nordenstreng, Robert L. Stevenson, and Frank Ugboajah. *Foreign News in the Media: International Reporting in Twenty-nine Countries.* Reports and Papers on Mass Communication No. 93. Paris: UNESCO, 1984.
21. Stevenson, Robert L. "Other Research and the World of the News." Unpublished paper, University of North Carolina at Chapel Hill, 1981.
22. "Third World News and Views." Symposium in *Journal of Communication* 29(2), Spring 1979.
23. Weaver, David H. and G. Cleveland Wilhoit. "Foreign News Coverage in Two U.S. Wire Services." *Journal of Communication* 31(2), Spring 1981, pp. 55–63.
24. "What's News?" Symposium in *Communications and Development Review* 2(2), 1978.
25. "A World Debate on Information—Flood-tide or Balanced Flow?" Symposium in *UNESCO Courier*, April 1977.

Pseudo Debate

Robert L. Stevenson

Let us begin by noting what this study does *not* show. It does not show that Western media and news agencies ignore the Third World. It does not show that they single out the Third World for unfair negative coverage. It does not show that they see the Third World through a filter of cultural bias. It does not show that Third World media are hostage to a Western news monopoly. It does not show that the socialist and Third World media systems that claim to represent an alternative model operate much differently than their Western counterparts.

One point that stands out in this and every other comparable study (10, 11) is the importance of geographic proximity in foreign news. The percentages of foreign news from the immediate geographic region (including the home country itself) range from 22 percent in the Yugoslav media and 26 percent in the U.S. media to 56 percent in the Ivory Coast and 63 percent in Malaysia. On the average, slightly more than half of foreign news in Third World media comes from the immediate geographic region.

Assertions that the Western media and news agencies ignore the Third World are not true. About one-third of foreign news in Northern media systems originates in the Third World; in Third World countries, two-thirds to three-quarters of all foreign news is from other Third World countries.

News from the Third World accounts for about 60 percent of foreign coverage on domestic regional wires in the United States (15). Regional files of the Associated Press, United Press International, Agence France-Presse, and Reuters serving Latin America, the Middle East, and Africa contain 40 percent to 50 percent of stories originating in the receiving nations. Comparable studies (1, 9) document a similar pattern in other parts of the world. The big gaps in world news are not the Third World in

Robert L. Stevenson is Associate Professor in the School of Journalism, University of North Carolina at Chapel Hill. The complete analysis by the American team is reported in Robert L. Stevenson and Donald Lewis Shaw (Eds.) *Foreign News and the New World Information Order* (Ames, Ia.: Iowa State University Press, 1984).

Western media but Eastern Europe in all other areas of the world and Third World regions in other Third World regions. Africa is mostly invisible in Latin American media; Latin America, in turn, is poorly represented in Asian media. Is this the result of a lack of information or a lack of interest? The evidence suggests the latter, although we do not know enough about how Third World gatekeepers choose their modest "diet" of foreign news from a large and varied "menu."

The question of whether the Third World is singled out for negative coverage—even held up to ridicule, according to Masmoudi (8)—is more complex. The distribution of topics in Third World coverage is similar to the distribution of topics in First World coverage in the media of all of the 17 countries my colleagues and I have studied (7, 10, 11). However, Weaver and Wilhoit (15, 16) found that news agencies did give greater attention to certain categories of political disruption in their Third World coverage than in their coverage of the North. In pursuing that question (12), we found similar patterns in the media of several countries but noted important caveats: political disruption is, in fact, more prevalent in the Third World than in the North, so that coverage may be *accurate* even if *unbalanced;* Third World gatekeepers themselves often overselect Third World "bad news" from the menu available to them; the attention given to disruptive news in the Third World is characteristic of all media systems, particularly those in the Third World itself.

"Cultural bias" is also difficult to define and measure, but the set of 33 themes and references that were designed to capture something of the cultural and ideological context of foreign news comes close. Coders were instructed to note the presence of a theme only if it was clearly present. It is instructive to note how little of the news contained any themes. In the U.S. sample, almost half (48 percent) of all stories contained none of the themes, a figure identical to that of the Soviet media (49 percent). Two-thirds of the stories in the international regional files of the Western agencies were without these explicit cultural values.

From a category we added that assessed overall direction or affect of each story, we found that few stories in any country were explicitly positive or negative. This was consistent with earlier research (13) in which we concluded that most of what people see as "bias" in the news is a function of the expectations they bring to it.

The question of cultural bias in foreign news can be addressed qualitatively as well. Harris (3) noted how adjectives were edited into copy of the Ghana News Agency to reflect the "African interest." In the Zambian media, we found frequent references to "the racist puppet Ian Smith" and the "sham, bogus election" for a prime minister in what was then Rhodesia. In the Algerian press were headlines such as "Demonstration at El-Menia Against the Treason of Sadat" and stories about "the treasonous accord signed by Sadat with the Zionist enemy" (2). Is this evidence of what Masmoudi calls the media's "reference to moral, cultural or political values peculiar to certain states, in defiance of the values and concerns of other nations"? It is, but the responsibility for it does not lie with the Western agencies.

What is, in fact, the influence of the Western news agencies on what is eventually selected as international news?

Tracing the origins of foreign news was one of the most difficult parts of the project, because there was so much variance in how sources were identified. In some cases, like Tunisia and Zaire, 90 percent of the published stories were not credited. In others, like Zambia, nearly 60 percent were credited to the national agency or newspaper staff, although many were clearly rewrites of agency material.

Throughout the Third World, the proportion of stories credited to domestic sources varied from about 10 percent in Nigeria and Zaire to 53 percent in Indonesia. In most cases, the proportion credited to the four Western news agencies was in the range of 25 percent, although in reality it is certainly higher. In considering the flow of foreign news to the Third World, two points are important to remember. The first is that alternatives to the Western news agencies are available, even if they are not often used or credited. Sources as diverse as UNESCO itself (14), the International Organization of Journalists (5), and case studies (3, 4) document the availability to national news agencies of six to twelve separate agencies as different as Xinhua, the Non-Aligned News Agencies Pool, and neighboring national agencies.

It also should be kept in mind that nearly all Third World national agencies—Latin America is the main exception—operate as monopolies for all information coming into the country and sometimes for information going out as well. In even the most undeveloped countries, these national agencies exert total control over what trickle of information will get into the country from the flood available internationally. We have found that Western agencies typically influence geographic and topic emphasis in national media but are less influential in transmitting cultural values (7). From this, we conclude that the influence of Western agencies derives from their ability to provide timely, straightforward accounts of major events of news value around the world.

We turn to the question of whether the results of this study support the contention that mass media in the Third World are maintained in a state of dependence through the transnational system.

The foreign news carried by Western media can be explained, however superficially and incompletely, by Marxist arguments of cultural imperialism. And, by extension, one would expect the media of Third

World countries oriented toward the West—Mexico, Nigeria, and Egypt, for example—to be similar. But how can one then account for the finding that media in very different countries—Zambia, Algeria, the Soviet Union, for example—show very similar (or "worse") patterns?

This study suggests that the ideological rhetoric is misplaced in three ways. First, many of the charges against the Western media and news services are without evidence to support them. Second, the lack of difference among media of very different political systems argues against the theory of cultural imperialism. And third, much of the rhetoric addresses outdated questions.

A number of studies enable us to look at changes in media content worldwide over the last ten years. Larson (6) has shown that there was a significant increase in the amount of foreign coverage on U.S. network television from the 1960s through the 1970s. An update of their study of U.S. domestic wire service files by Weaver and Wilhoit (16) showed an increase in foreign coverage since 1979. And this study shows far less reliance on the Western agencies around the world than similar studies published in the 1960s and early 1970s.

Too much of the New World Information Order debate has focused on assertions that were probably never true and are certainly no longer true. This study helps clear the air of the pseudo debate.

REFERENCES

1. Bishop, Robert L. "How Reuters and AFP Coverage of Independent Africa Compare." *Journalism Quarterly* 52(4), Winter 1975, pp. 654–662.
2. Cooper, Anne Messerly. "Affect of Arab News: Post-Treaty Portrayal of Egypt and Israel in the Mass Media of Three Arab Countries." Paper presented to the Association for Education in Journalism, East Lansing, Michigan, 1981.
3. Harris, Phil. "News Dependence: The Case for a New World Information Order." Mimeo, University of Leicester, 1977.
4. Golding, Peter and Philip Elliott. *Making the News*. London: Longman, 1979.
5. International Organization of Journalists. *Handbook of News Agencies*. Prague: IOJ, 1969.
6. Larson, James F. "International Affairs Coverage on US Evening Network News." In William C. Adams (Ed.) *Television Coverage in International Affairs*. Norwood, N.J.: Ablex, 1982.
7. Link, Jere M. "A Test of the Cultural Dependency Theory in Seven Latin American Newspapers." Paper presented to the Association for Education in Journalism, Athens, Ohio, 1982.
8. Masmoudi, Mustapha. "The New World Information Order." *Journal of Communication* 29(2), Spring 1979, pp. 172–185.
9. Schramm, Wilbur and Erwin Atwood. *Circulation of News in the Third World: A Study in Asia*. Hong Kong: Chinese University Press, 1981.
10. Stevenson, Robert L. and Richard R. Cole. "Foreign News Flow and the Unesco Debate." Paper presented to the International Studies Association, Los Angeles, 1980.
11. Stevenson, Robert L., Richard R. Cole, and Donald Lewis Shaw. "Patterns of World News Coverage: A Look at the UNESCO Debate on the 'New World Information Order.'" In Gertrude Joch Robinson (Ed.) *Assessing the New World Information*

Order Debate: Evidence and Proposals. International Communication Division, Association for Education in Journalism, 1982.

12. Stevenson, Robert L. and Gary D. Gaddy. " 'Bad News' and the Third World." Paper presented to the International Communication Association, Boston, 1982.
13. Stevenson, Robert L. and Mark T. Greene. "A Reconsideration of Bias in the News." *Journalism Quarterly* 57(1), Spring 1980, pp. 115–121.
14. UNESCO. *World Communications.* Paris: UNESCO Press, 1975.
15. Weaver, David H. and G. Cleveland Wilhoit. "Foreign News Coverage in Two U.S. Wire Services." *Journal of Communication* 31(2), Spring 1981, pp. 55–63.
16. Wilhoit, G. Cleveland and David H. Weaver. "Foreign News Coverage in Two Wire Services: Study No. 2—1981." Paper presented to the Association for Education in Journalism, Athens, Ohio, 1982.

Bitter Lessons

Kaarle Nordenstreng

In order to properly evaluate this study, we must recall its original aims and objectives. As prescribed by a resolution passed at UNESCO's General Conference in Nairobi in 1976 (4), it was supposed to be "a study on the image of foreign countries representing different social systems and developmental stages as portrayed by mass-circulated press in respective countries." The resolution went on to suggest that particular attention be paid "to the image given over the past twenty years by mass media in industrialized countries of the developing countries and of the changing economic and political relations in the international community."

The nature of the image in question was further illuminated by references made in the resolution to three vital documents of international politics: first, UNESCO's Constitution of 1946 ("contributing to peace and security *inter alia* by advancing the mutual knowledge and understanding of peoples through all means of mass communication"); second, the Helsinki Accords of 1975 ("the participating States recognize the need for an ever wider knowledge and understanding of the various aspects of life in other participating States"); and third, the Colombo Summit of the Non-Aligned Countries in 1976 ("all countries of the world should have the right to inform and be informed objectively and accurately").

Accordingly, the initiative was born out of an understanding that the mass media play a delicate role in international relations—that is, that the media are far from apolitical by nature—thus linking the media to

Kaarle Nordenstreng is Professor of Journalism and Mass Communication at the University of Tampere, Finland.

such areas of high politics as national and international security, détente, human rights, and a new international economic order. Moreover, the initiative carried with it a normative assumption that the media, instead of remaining neutral, should actively contribute to peace, international understanding, and other related universal values defined by the international community in forums such as UNESCO and the Conference on Security and Cooperation in Europe (for closer analysis, see 5, 6). In short, the project was inspired by what might be called a "U.N. ideology" that has since been manifested in landmarks such as UNESCO's Mass Media Declaration (2) and the MacBride Report (1).[1]

Within this context, the study was supposed to examine the performance of mass-circulated media in different countries, with a view toward indicating empirically how "biased" or "objective" the coverage of foreign countries actually is, identifying possible inadequacies, and thus helping to improve media performance. The idea called for the use of a delicate methodological instrument that would get at the qualitative sphere of image building, instead of just employing conventional categories of content analysis such as topics/types of news, countries/regions covered, etc.

The execution of the project turned out to be far from the original idea.

The final project was dominated by "vulgar" categories that capture *ad hoc* aspects of the media content, rather than a comprehensive image carried by the content. In other words, it became more of a quantitative than a qualitative exercise, whereas the original idea was to make it more "intensive" than "extensive." Accompanying this shift of emphasis is the reduction of any historical perspective; what remains is a simple contemporary measurement of media performance devoid of "the changing economic and political relations in the international community." All this revision took place in the process of operationalizing the study, under the pressures of limited resources and differing opinions among participants about what to do. The scientific and political point of departure was left without further elaboration and the project began to lead its own life, mainly determined by various pragmatic aspects—not the least of which was the need to get a minimum common core of hard quantitative evidence across various national media systems.

This is not a unique case in the history of social science research; there are good excuses and there is even room for some sympathy to

[1] I feel competent to testify about the true origin of the study since I initiated the idea and wrote the draft resolution in question (as chairman of the communication subcommittee in the Finnish National Commission for UNESCO; for details, see [4]).

those involved in a large international exercise. However, one may ask how this outcome can occur even in such "better families" as the leading quarters of the International Association for Mass Communication Research—especially after a pilot study had warned against using only instruments of a quasi-objective nature that would be unable to tackle the contents in a comprehensive and in-depth manner (4). At this stage, we must frankly admit to the methodological dilemmas that (mis)lead us quite far from the original idea, as well as point out that a proper "qualitative analysis" is by no means necessarily less scientific or exact than a "quantitative analysis."

A demonstration of this point is provided by a closer look at how Salt II was treated in the *New York Times* and *Pravda* (7). Although the profile of these papers across the "vulgar" categories of the quantitative analysis looks more or less the same, the images involved appear quite different when more specific aspects of the content are taken into consideration. For example, *Pravda* devoted 28 percent of its total centimeters on Salt II to current news and human interest stories about the summit, as compared to 6 percent of the total by the *New York Times*. The *New York Times*, on the other hand, devoted 20 percent of its space to emigration and Soviet dissidents' problems and only 7 percent to East-West foreign policy, while *Pravda* devoted 38 percent to Soviet-U.S. policy, détente, and the benefits of international cooperation. Thus,

(text continues on page 634)

a quantification that bypasses such crucial aspects of content is not only incomplete; it may well be misleading and thus unscientific.

In fact, Stevenson (9) has given us an instructive lesson about this in early reports on that part of the project carried out in North Carolina. Examining the quantitative analysis, Stevenson concludes that there is no evidence "that any part of the world is held up to an unusually unfavorable light or, more important, that the Third World is singled out for any special negative coverage" (9, p. 15). Such a conclusion can be based only on blind reliance on the data provided by the "vulgar" categories. Even the primitive qualitative analysis included in the main study makes us doubt Stevenson's conclusion and understand that "we need to be very cautious in our interpretations, and particularly in any generalizations we may be tempted to make" (8, p. 119). More careless were those political writers who wasted no time in "proving" with the data of this study (as reported by Stevenson) that the whole offensive for a New International Information Order lacked scientific foundation and thus was open to serious challenge (see, e.g., 10).

Such sidetracks make this study a textbook example of how social science can be misused for political purposes.

At the same time, the project serves as a serious reminder to the communication research community about the fundamental problems of content analysis. Too often, the concept of content is accepted without critical scrutiny, with quantitative results on *some aspects* of the messages being taken as the "real" and comprehensive content. An understanding of foreign countries as reflected in news coverage requires a much more delicate methodology than the simple counting of how much attention is devoted to such categories as politics, natural catastrophes, etc., and how frequent is the use of such words as "imperialism" and "terrorism." Here we are faced with the general dilemma of positivism: the fact that certain aspects of reality lend themselves to convenient measurement (and subsequent statistical elaboration) does not mean that these aspects are necessarily most essential to our understanding of reality.

The study was originally planned to contribute to our understanding of reality as conceived in the spirit of Helsinki and Colombo. However, practical imperatives limited the scope of the project so that, in the end, it adds little to our common-sense knowledge and to the evidence provided by earlier studies. Ironically, the project's results have been given a false interpretation in support of the cause of those who are opposed to the New International Information Order. Thus, perhaps the greatest contribution of this enterprise has been through a negative case—by demonstrating the scientific inadequacy and political risks involved in one-sided quantitative consideration of mass media content.[2]

Nevertheless, the study was worth undertaking. Even if it did not manage to provide waterproof testimony for or against the crucial arguments of the NIIO debate, it was important simply in drawing serious attention to issues of mass media content. Keeping content (in particular the qualitative aspects) firmly on the agenda of international communication policy debate is no small task at a time when the Western counteroffensive is doing its utmost to distract a critical consideration of media content by turning attention exclusively to media infrastructures and other less "normative" aspects. It is imperative to follow up the study by "going deeper" into the analysis of the content proper.

REFERENCES

1. International Commission for the Study of Communication Problems (MacBride Commission). *Many Voices, One World.* Paris: UNESCO, 1980.
2. Nordenstreng, K. *The Mass Media Declaration of UNESCO.* Norwood, N.J.: Ablex, 1984.
3. Nordenstreng, K. "Three Theses on the Imbalance Debate." In J. S. Yadava (Ed.) *Politics of News: Third World Perspectives.* New Delhi, forthcoming.
4. Nordenstreng, K. and M. Salomaa. "Studying the Image of Foreign Countries as Portrayed by the Mass Media: A Progress Report." Paper prepared for the Scientific Conference of the International Association for Mass Communication Research, Warsaw, September 4–9, 1978.
5. Nordenstreng, K. and H. I. Schiller. "Helsinki: The New Equation." *Journal of Communication* 26(1), Winter 1976, pp. 130–134.
6. Nordenstreng, K. and H. I. Schiller (Eds.). *National Sovereignty and International Communication.* Norwood, N.J.: Ablex, 1979.
7. Rand, M. "Qualitative Analysis of Selected Topics: Follow-up of the Foreign Images Study." Unpublished master's thesis, University of Tampere, forthcoming.
8. Sreberny-Mohammadi, A. et al. *Foreign News in the Media: International Reporting in Twenty-nine Countries.* Reports and Papers on Mass Communication No. 93. Paris: UNESCO, 1984.
9. Stevenson, R. L. "The Western News Agencies Do Not Ignore the Third World." *Editor & Publisher*, July 5, 1980.
10. Sussman, L. R. "Freedom of the Press: Problems in Restructuring the Flow of International News." In R. D. Gastil (Ed.) *Freedom in the World: Political Rights and Civil Liberties 1980.* New York: Freedom House, 1980.

[2] For a more comprehensive appraisal of the lesson from a non-aligned point of view, see (3).

35

THE POLITICAL CULTURE AND THE PRESS OF CANADA

Thelma McCormack

1

The Royal Commission on Newspapers, chaired by Mr. Tom Kent, published its final report in July 1981.[1] Like the Davey report[2] which preceded it, the Kent report documents a decline in competition and an increase in the concentration of ownership, trends that have been developing at a more rapid and, in the eyes of many, an alarming rate over recent years. Mergers have eliminated competition; chains have displaced local control by absentee ownership; and conglomerates have begun to purchase newspapers for tax or other extraneous benefits which have little to do with the public good. The result has been that more and more people have been getting their print news and interpretations from fewer and fewer sources; and the sources themselves may be appendages of businesses as unrelated to journalism (and to each other) as hog futures, football teams and pharmaceuticals.

The commission also lifts the curtain on some of the new communication technologies with their potential for private power and private profit accruing to the few in positions of control. But that discussion constitutes a relatively minor part of the report which, for the most part, focusses on the fate of newspapers and a conventional technology.

It is not clear from the report whether the current state is simply a period of reorganization in a long-term development, a phase from which the press will eventually emerge transformed and more independent as well as more economically viable; or whether it is an irreversible trend downward, and, if the latter, whether the outcome will be the disappearance of daily newspapers or their ownership by a few super-conglomerates. The commission chose a worst-case scenario: "Under existing law and policy, the process of concentration will continue to a bitterer end; company will take over company,

1 *Royal Commission on Newspapers* (Ottawa: Supply and Services, 1981); hereafter cited as Kent. The other commissioners were Laurent Picard and Borden Spears.

2 Report of the Special Senate Committee on Mass Media, *The Uncertain Mirror* (Ottawa: Queen's Printer, 1970).

From Thelma McCormack, "The Political Culture and the Press of Canada," *Canadian Journal of Political Science*, Vol. 26, No. 3 (September 1983), pp. 451-472.

agglomeration will proceed until all Canadian newspapers are divisions of one or two conglomerates."[3]

Various remedies were recommended by the commission. Most of them, like press councils and ombudsmen, are voluntary; some, however, would call for new legislation, a Canada Newspaper Act that would limit further acquisitions and require the largest chains to divest themselves of certain of their properties. Existing anti-combines legislation was felt to be inadequate, primarily because the Supreme Court's interpretations in recent years have favoured the combines; for example, the Crown lost what seemed to be an airtight case against the K. C. Irving empire in New Brunswick. But, in any event, the problem is to anticipate or prevent concentration rather than wait and dismantle it.

The proposed legislation is mild. Stronger measures might have been expected, especially in view of the unwillingness shown by the press in the past to reform itself. Nothing the commission heard gave it reason to believe that the media owners would conduct themselves differently in the future. Indeed, Lord Thomson told the members that he was planning to make an investment in Canada, but that if he was not allowed to engage in other forms of business activity he would take his capital elsewhere—that is, to the United States where no such constraints on entrepreneurial initiative exist and where, given the present environment of deregulation, none is likely to be enacted in the near future.

Nevertheless, and despite the provocation of Thomson, the commission was reluctant to interfere with the market mechanism. Subsidies such as low-interest loans which have been used in Sweden, Holland, Germany, Italy and Belgium to assist faltering newspapers or to help new ones get started were not seriously considered. Nor did the commission hold out any hope for a nonprofit "print CBC." Like an earlier British commission which rejected a print BBC, the Kent commission dismissed the idea.

Analytically, the Kent report is based on a modernization paradigm which emphasizes the processes of rationalization, the development of a professional ethos and the autonomy of institutions. In this respect, the report is typical of much contemporary thinking about the direction of our communication media and the appropriate criteria for judging their performance.

There has, however, been growing criticism of the modernization model from the political left and, more significantly, from many intellectuals and political leaders in the developing nations. Their dissatisfaction and the limitations of the modernization paradigm are best understood by contrasting the Kent report with another recent

3 Kent, 220.

Abstract. The 1981 Kent commission report on newspapers is discussed and contrasted with the MacBride (UNESCO) report. The former assumes that competition is the major safeguard of diversity; the latter, written from the perspective of Third World countries, regards social inequality as the primary obstacle to the free flow of information. Together they reflect contemporary controversies about modernization. Trends toward rationalization, professionalization and autonomy are examined. Neither approach, Kent or MacBride, provides a satisfactory interpretation of Quebec's francophone press. An alternative model based on access is, we suggest, closer to the realities of Canada's changing political culture and class structure.

Résumé. Dans cet article on compare le rapport de la Commission Kent sur les journaux avec le rapport MacBride (UNESCO). La point de départ du premier est que la concurrence est la meilleure garantie pour la diversité de l'information; le deuxième, écrit à travers la perspective des pays du Tiers monde, considère l'inégalité sociale comme l'obstacle plus important à la libre circulation de l'information. Les deux rapports reflètent de discussions actuelles concernant la modernisation; ils examinent les tendances vers la rationalisation, la professionnalisation et l'autonomie. Mais ni le rapport Kent, ni le rapport MacBride donnent une interprétation satisfaisante de la presse francophone au Québec. Un modèle alternatif fondé dans l'accès serait plus près de la réalité canadienne, en ce qui concerne aussi bien les transformations de la culture politique que la structure de classes.

media document, the UNESCO (MacBride) report which looks at the media from the perspective of developing nations.[4]

The focus of the MacBride report is on inequality, inequality within nations but chiefly between, on the one hand, the wealthy industrial nations of Europe and North America and, on the other, the poorer ones of Asia, Africa and Latin America. It examines media trends in terms of power relationships; more precisely, it asks whether such media variables as technology, patterns of ownership and structure of organizations widen or narrow the knowledge gap, shorten or lengthen the social distance among different subcultures, increase or decrease the economic disparities between the haves and have-nots.[5]

The two reports offer an opportunity to examine some of the issues in contemporary communications theory. In the comments that follow we will be contrasting the two reports with particular reference to their societal models and their assumptions about political culture. Section 2 will discuss three dimensions of modernization: rationalization, professionalization and autonomy. This section will conclude with a discussion of the Kent commission's analysis of the Quebec French-language press which we consider here as a test case for the models. Section 3 will look more closely at the media and political culture with particular reference to the concept of access.

4 Sean MacBride, *Many Voices, One World* (New York: UNESCO, 1980).

5 What prompted the MacBride commission was the concern many Third World countries felt about the new technology of satellites. Not only would this technology put the poorer countries at a greater disadvantage than they already were; it would also increase the ability of advanced nations to impose their ideologies and value systems on emerging nations whose traditional cultures were already subject to considerable strain.

2

Rationalization

Where have all the newspapers gone? The pattern of ownership which the Kent commission described is not confined to Canada. Canadians have been spared the embarrassment of Britons in having their prestige papers purchased by outsiders like Rupert Murdoch or by American corporations; otherwise, the same trends—mergers, chain formations, takeovers by conglomerates—have been occurring elsewhere in Britain, Western Europe and Japan.

The commission believes this widespread phenomenon is endemic in advanced industrial societies, the only differences among them being the degree of concentration and the steps governments were willing to take to slow down or redirect the processes. Canada, the commission noted, has been slower than other countries to take any measures although the concentration here is greater.[6]

Still, no one really knows why newspapers are disappearing. Market forces are often obscured in the case of conglomerates where complicated fiscal strategies may be involved; profitable papers may be terminated while the less fit are allowed to survive. Nevertheless, the commission saw no economic reason for any drastic decline. According to the report, newspapers are a good investment; according to their publishers, they are not.[7] Every newspaper which closes its doors produces books which show more red than black, impressive losses over an extended period. But the purchase prices for many of these papers suggest another set of books. Newspapers are bought and sold on a market that excludes most ordinary individual and institutional investors. (Recently, the Gannett chain in the United States bought a small Arizona chain for $347 million.) If both sides are to be believed, the newspaper business is both a sick industry and a healthy one; some papers are better able to ride out inflation, featherbedding, lockouts, strikes, obsolete machinery and poor managerial practices than others. Meanwhile, the gloss put on this by the industry is: "fewer papers but better ones."

By better is meant more efficient, and efficient usually translates into dollars and cents: that is, the competitive advantages to be gained through economies of scale or when, as in the case of mergers, one newspaper can do the advertising work of two. As Keith Davey put it, "more voices may be healthier, but fewer ones are cheaper."[8] Like Senator Davey, the Kent commission was sceptical about the motives of

6 Kent, 17.

7 According to the report, the average rate of return between 1974 and 1980 was 33.4 per cent and represents an improvement over earlier figures (Kent, *Royal Commission*, 164).

8 Keith Davey, "The Davey Report: In Retrospect," in Benjamin D. Singer (ed.), *Communications in Canadian Society* (Toronto: Copp Clark, 1975), 182-92.

the media entrepreneurs. Against their thinly disguised drive for unlimited profits, the Kent commission postulated a countervailing norm of social responsibility. The commission did not, as we shall discuss later, question whether rationalization contributes to greater organizational efficiency, and what efficiency means in the context of communication. Instead, it emphasized the special nature of newspapers and the responsibility which owners must accept. Any rationalization, then, and any profit-taking through rationalization may not be at the expense of the public good or in conflict with it.

For some observers the current state of affairs is less a response to media-specific economics than to the nature of the larger economy. Symthe, for example, has argued that the media serve monopoly capitalism by managing consumption through advertising.[9] The primary function of a modern newspaper, he claims, is not to deliver news to readers but to deliver audiences to advertisers. If this notion were correct, we would expect that the newspapers at risk would be those in the weaker or smaller market areas. Yet recent closures have been in large cities—London, New York, Washington, Buffalo, Toronto, Montreal, Winnipeg and Ottawa—dense urban areas which constitute strong if not excellent markets. These events, newsworthy in themselves, may be symptomatic of a deeper structural disorder being masked by the high return of some newspapers and some chains.

Too much attention may be given to advertising as the source of the newspapers' difficulty or as the prime mover in the rationalization processes. Many of the newspapers of Western Europe have never been as dependent on advertising as ours have been, and they, too, have suffered from attrition. It would seem, then, that *any* crisis in the economy will have negative consequences for the privately owned media. Those which are largely dependent on advertising (indirectly, on levels of consumption in the economy) will reflect the crisis earlier and more acutely, while the others, based on public ownership or subsidies can slow down the rate and spread the impact more equitably among all the papers.

Economic explanations, however, may not be sufficient to account for that decline in the number of papers or to enable us to identify the qualitative changes that have been taking place. (In Toronto, for example, the *Telegram*, a solid middlebrow family paper was replaced by a tabloid, the *Sun*.) Qualitative changes may, as we shall suggest, be more significant for our political culture than quantitative ones. An alternative approach would start by asking whether the newspapers were themselves at fault, whether they lost touch with changes in both social structure and the political culture. As a new middle class of salaried professionals, white-collar workers, accountants, engineers

9 Dallas W. Smythe, *Dependency Road: Communications, Capitalism, Consciousness and Canada* (Norwood, N.J.: Ablex, 1981).

and others brought a new ethos to social life, and as a politics of social movements (most notably the Parti québécois) became more salient, the press remained rooted in the past, the voice of an older middle class and the mirror of a political culture based on parliaments and parties.

If it is correct to say that the press has been slow to comprehend the new modes of political participation, the next question concerns the rigidity. Why and what kinds of organizational variables—size, complexity, decision-making, degree of hierarchy—might make the gatekeepers less aware of changes in the social structure and less responsive to them?

One line of inquiry would be to consider whether the rationalization processes which were intended to streamline and increase efficiency have, in fact, had the opposite effect of making newspapers less and less resilient, robbing them of their creative sensors, making them more efficient in their commercial dealings but less efficient as communicators.

The perspective just discussed is closer to the MacBride report which examines communication as a process within a larger framework of social change. Whether the communication institutions are competitive or not is less important than how well they express the aspirations and concerns of emerging social groups. And, as we shall indicate in the following section, professionalization of the media may be a deterrent to the communicative process.

Professionalization

Although the Kent commission deplored the lack of competition in Canadian newspapers, its research indicated that newspaper readers were not particularly disturbed by its absence, nor were a younger generation of journalists.[10] But the commission was not ready to abandon the idea that a market mechanism, imperfect as it is, remains the best way to insure a marketplace of ideas. There is little evidence to support this view and much to show the opposite, that competition produces wasteful imitation, redundancy and poorer quality in slicker packaging. Every royal commission in Britain on the press since the 1940s has made the point that competition does not produce either better papers or more diversity.[11] More recently, the same theme was reiterated in the MacBride report.[12]

But if competition is no longer a reliable mechanism to guarantee diversity, what are the alternatives? One choice is to upgrade the press,

10 Kent, 38, 112.

11 *Royal Commission on the Press, 1947-1949* (London: HMSO, 1949), Cmd. 7700; *Royal Commission on the Press 1961-1962* (London: HMSO, 1962), Cmd. 1811; *Royal Commission on the Press 1974* (London: HMSO, 1977), Cmd. 6810.

12 MacBride, *Many Voices*, 22. If there is any further doubt about the dubious value of competition one can look at the intense rivalry between the two American weeklies *Time* and *Newsweek* to see how negligible their differences are.

to develop what the British call a "quality" press, or at least to put a floor under the popular press through professionalization. According to this view, as journalists acquired more and better education, as they acquired a new status and a new professional ethic of commitment, they would have greater leverage. Newspaper proprietors might treat their newspapers like any other business but journalists would not; and without the journalists, no press.

The other option is to change the institution rather than the occupational morality of the journalist, to build into the institution itself mechanisms of accountability and norms of excellence. The editorial collective is one example; another is *Le Monde*, the distinguished French newspaper which is staff-owned.

The Kent commission rejected the second. It recommended a special contract for editors-in-chief that would define the boundaries between editor and proprietor, an arm's length relationship, but opposed any notion of organizational self-government that might be construed as worker control. "We have emphasized that professionalism that should be the spirit of journalism,"[13] the commission wrote, adding: "We do not mean that journalists should be members of associations backed by statutory power to control admission to members."[14]

Other professions have this self government; indeed, it is often regarded as the sine qua non of a profession. In any case, by opting for a solution which reforms the organization by reforming the individual, the commission was following an established tradition in North American thinking about journalism. The philosophy was most clearly expressed in the late 1940s by the Hutchins report.[15] The media, it was said there, have become increasingly powerful in shaping our lives, too powerful to be left in the hands of amateurs or old-style media barons. Second, despite all the lip service paid to the ideal of competition, competition in the media was no longer a reality, nor was it necessarily desirable. Further, the complexities of the modern interdependent world could no longer be understood through the simplistic formula of our village journalism or though the bizarre formula of jazz-age, big-city tabloid journalism.

The solution was professionalization which would start at the training level where the education of journalists would no longer be left to chance or the slow methods of apprenticeship. Schools of journalism would have a broader, less specialized curriculum than the vocationally-oriented journalism schools. In addition, every newspaper, regardless of circulation, would have a mandate to reflect

13 Kent, 225.

14 Ibid.

15 Commission on Freedom of the Press, *A Free and Responsible Press* (Chicago: University of Chicago, 1947).

the range of intelligent opinion on any controversial subject. Editorial pages would become a place for thoughtful in-depth discussions, a seminar rather than a soapbox. Journalism would eventually begin to resemble the social sciences: timely, objective, well-researched and, apart from the editorial pages, value-free. It would be an environment in which journalists and scholars would or could form closer networks.[16]

If it worked, it would give us the newspapers a modern democracy deserved. If it failed, it would still have a salutary effect on the bottom of the scale, on the lowest standards of the sensationalist, anti-intellectual tabloid press. And, as the newer high standards became the rule rather than the exception, it would matter less and less whether communities had one newspaper or several, whether the owners were bankers or moralists, since citizens would have a press they could both trust and respect.

Behind this vision of the future was a confidence that the hope was not a utopian dream but a reasonable, credible expectation based on a larger societal evolution taking place as we moved from simple to complex organization, from sacred to secular modes of thought, and from communal to associational (or contractual) normative and legal systems. Thus, professionalization of the press was part of, and in harmony with, a larger social evolution in which all forms of economic activity would be professionalized.

For purposes of discussion we can look at the various parts of this model separately: the evolutionary scenario; the social science model with reference to objectivity; and the professionalization of the journalist.

The Evolutionary Scenario

The Kent commission was basically in agreement with the evolutionary scenario. The history of the press, it says, is a gradual evolution from "partisan to professional." It refers to many Third World countries as still being at the earlier partisan stage where the press "has yet to undergo its libertarian revolution and cut itself off from political power."[17] The libertarian period is a prelude to a more mature social responsibility.

But the development of the press in Latin America, for example, is more turbulent and revolutionary than peaceful and evolutionary, and editors in exile like Jacobo Timerman are not likely to delude themselves into thinking that without some drastic political intervention in the political environment of Argentina the "libertarian revolution" which took place in our press history will or could take place there.[18] A better

16 Thelma McCormack, "Intellectuals and the Mass Media," *American Behavioral Scientist* 9 (1965-66), 31-36.

17 Kent, 24.

18 Cornelia Butler Flora, "Contradictions of Capitalism in Mass Media in Latin

source to consult might be the history of the press in Nazi Germany.[19] Yet, leaving aside the question whether there is a natural progression from partisan to professional, there is a further one of whether we can provide a role model to the media in less developed countries, whether, apart from patterns of ownership, our experience and our press are examples of what might be done as these countries move forward in their own way.

Recent developments provide a mixed picture. We have had, just as the Hutchins commission hoped and predicted, the growth of a small number of prestige papers, a journalism acceptable and attractive to the new educated elites who see themselves—their tastes, interests, lifestyles—reflected in it. At the same time, the "trickle-down" effect has failed to have any influence on the lowbrow tabloids whose standards remain what they have always been and whose economic future seems to be as secure as any a newspaper can hope for.

What now appears to be happening—admittedly more in the United States and Britain than in Canada—was an unanticipated polarization of the press into elite and mass. The loss has been to a middle-class public whose cultural tastes have been ridiculed by both ends of the taste continuum and whose information needs have been increasingly ignored by the gatekeepers of the media who have written off this particular segment of the population as a historical, cultural and economic force. The full political price for this judgment in terms of mail-order journalism and New Right politics is not yet known; however, our point is that the political repercussions of numbers and ownership of newspapers may be less important than those related to the pattern of qualitative changes in the press.

Objectivity

The Kent commission reflected some of the criticism that both journalists and social scientists have made of objectivity and positivism in general in recent years. Is objectivity possible and is it desirable? Not the latter, the commission said. Objectivity was too often "a pretext for not taking a position, for maintaining a hypocritical neutrality that camouflaged complicity with those in power."[20] The limits of objective reporting were revealed, according to the report, during the McCarthy period when journalists felt obliged to report the malicious charges the senator was making without labelling them as lies. Having learned from that experience, the press then swung over to advocacy journalism, but

America," in Thelma McCormack (ed.), *Studies in Communications* Vol. 1 (Greenwich, Conn.: JAI, 1980), 19-36; Jacobo Timerman, *Prisoner Without a Name, Cell Without a Number* (New York: Vintage, 1982).

19 Oron J. Hale, *The Captive Press in the Third Reich* (Princeton: Princeton University Press, 1964).

20 Kent, 24.

that, too, was unsatisfactory, according to the report. Eventually, and in the aftermath of Watergate, the media did find a mean between objectivity and advocacy: fairness. The new protocol is a "more balanced position by treating people and events as fairly as possible."[21]

"Balance" in this context does not means a compensatory principle in which corrections are made for under-reporting; it is not affirmative action, nor does it place items on an unbalanced agenda; it refers only to items which had already been defined as newsworthy, and to various ethical considerations about the way these items are presented. Dissident groups, then, who feel their views are being overlooked by the press must still resort to attention-getting histrionics in order to get exposure, or, at best, they are called upon to defend their right to access and show why they have a better claim than other petitioners.

In the MacBride report balance is also a criterion of responsible journalism but it means here the correction of inequities. The Western concept of "free flow" of information is criticized as being one-sided, a monologue rather than a dialogue. The alternative is a "free and balanced" model of communication in which all receivers are senders and all senders are receivers. Fair communication, then, would be manifestly unfair if it left the existing system of social inequality intact.

Nor would it be communication. The MacBride report raises a set of fundamental questions about the nature of communication as a social process, about whether there can be any genuine reciprocal communication between unequals, or whether such relationships, on a local or world scale, are inevitably coloured by distrust and lack of empathy. The implication of this is that newspapers may be judged as excellent by Kent standards, satisfying the most exacting professional norms, yet low on a scale that measured interactive communication.

Thus, as we speculated earlier, one reason newspapers may fail is that they distance themselves from their publics. Conversely, however, newspapers may succeed too well: they may become too intimate and sectarian or they may become so close that they can, as most tabloids do, manipulate our anxieties. Unless, then, equality is built into the paradigm structurally, the way is open for a variety of dysfunctional directions.

Professionalization of the Journalist

The emphasis throughout the Kent report is on the journalist, the belief that with a professional education and a professional ethic and with enough opportunity to develop, the journalist would alter the industry itself. The empirical evidence to support the Kent commission's thesis about up-grading is missing. Existing literature on the organization and processes of production in the media suggests that the opposite may be

21 Ibid.

true—that, despite the higher education requirements for journalists, their occupation has been downgraded.

The idea of work becoming increasingly devalued and less skilled has come to be known as the Braverman thesis.[22] Briefly, it is that the new educational requirements proposed by Kent and others have more to do with the expansionist trends and opportunism of universities than they have with the nature of the work which journalists, as journalists, carry out. Having a university degree may enhance prestige, and working toward it may be an intrinsically worthwhile experience for the student, but compared to what happened in an earlier period when newspaper offices were small and the work largely undifferentiated, when journalists performed a wide range of activities such as newsgathering, writing, editing and various managerial tasks, the contemporary young journalist has lost ground.

Production of news is closer to an assembly line creating a standardized product which may already be semi-processed. Moreover, the modern bureaucratic structures in news organizations (these tend to be the larger, better paying and more prestigious ones) deprive young journalists of opportunities to complete their professional socialization through close contact with senior and experienced people. Instead, the young recruits often find themselves under-employed, over-educated and in subordinate roles, a classic condition of status discrepancy with all that implies for self-esteem, organizational loyalty and commitment to the profession.

The investment in education, then, appears to have little connection with job satisfaction; ironically, it may have even less connection with income. Johnstone found in his study that the range of annual earnings between those with the most and those with the least schooling was \$1,831.[23]

In short, journalism, which began as a craft, has moved away from becoming a professional career except for a few, the "stars" who have high status, substantial earnings, and fulfilling careers. They often have the satisfaction of inventing history and then finding themselves at its most dramatic and powerful nodes. But these special privileged careers are possible because of a large number of non-celebrities who carry out the routine work of the organization in a work environment notoriously hierarchical and where the mobility ladder has lengthened considerably.[24]

22 Harry Braverman, *Labor and Monopoly Capital* (New York: Monthly Review Press, 1974).

23 John W. C. Johnstone, Edward J. Slawski and William W. Bowman, *The News People* (Urbana: University of Illinois, 1967).

24 Herbert J. Gans, *Deciding What's News* (New York: Vintage, 1980), 85; H. Bagdikian, "Professional Personnel and Organizational Structure in the Mass Media," in W. Phillips Davison and Frederick T. C. Yu (eds.), *Mass Communications Research* (New York: Praeger, 1974), 125.

It is one thing to say that the professional paradigm which the Kent commission drew on is flawed and that empirical evidence casts doubt on its future, but it is another to jettison it completely. Many who are critical of the professional model hesitate for fear of throwing out the baby with the bath. The MacBride report does not. It makes a case against professionalization on the grounds that it contributes to inequality and dependency in both the communication relationship and in the larger social structure.

Professionalization of journalists is, the report notes, a more sophisticated form of one-way flow from communicators to audiences. It is the legacy of a Western tradition of the French and American revolutions which granted the right to receive information to all citizens; that is, a one-way flow from a few communicators to many readers, listeners and viewers. But this legacy, the MacBride report maintains, is neither historically nor functionally appropriate to developing nations which start from different cultural traditions and confront different exigencies.[25] In addition to overcoming poverty, the new nations must also overcome the passivity of people who have lived for so many generations under colonial rule, people whose habits and modes of cognition are shaped by their poverty, their social dependency and political exclusion. The professionally-trained communicator whose model of the press is a prestige paper in the West and who wishes to bring this model to people in the Third World contributes unwittingly to the dependency of the receiver, tending to "eclipse the equally important objective of encouraging access and participation for the public."[26]

The two-way flow described by the MacBride report should not be confused with interactional technology which puts computer terminals in households and invites persons to register their votes or indicate preferences without leaving home. The MacBride concept assumes a very low level of technology as a pervasive fact of life and a pattern of investment that would put productive technology ahead of consumer technology. The interactional relationship it envisages is a social one, not a technological one, a relationship in which the parties together construct the options available instead of selecting from those presented by a survey organization; it is agenda-building rather than responding to an agenda set by the media or other professional groups.[27]

25 Several publications in recent years have made the point that a different concept of communication was more suited to emerging nations. Everett M. Rogers, "Communication and Development: The Passing of the Dominant Paradigm," in Everett M. Rogers (ed.), *Communication and Development* (Beverly Hills: Sage, 1976, 121-48; Jeremy Tunstall, *The Media Are American* (New York: Columbia University Press, 1977); Peter Golding, "Media Professionalism in the Third World: The Transfer of Ideology," in James Curran, Michael Gurevitch and Janet Woollacott (eds.), *Mass Communication and Society* (London: Edward Arnold, 1969).

26 MacBride, *Many Voices*, 419.

27 Roger W. Cobb and Charles E. Elder, "The Politics of Agenda-Building: An

Communication in Western societies has, in principle, been interactive, but for a variety of reasons, some of them relating to internal organization and some to external factors, it has become less so. As a result the media-established agendas do not always correspond to the priorities of their regular readers, much less those of a larger public.[28] In the extreme, the media and the public face opposite directions; to a lesser degree this has been the case of the poor, racial minorities and the women's movement.

But that estrangement begins early, for the media are part of the process of political socialization to inequality. Studies of media use by children and young adults indicate how early in life the divergent paths of different classes are taken.[29] The MacBride report puts the same phenomenon on a larger scale, between nations that are rich and poor. Inequality, then, is not only damaging to the processes of communication at the micro-level between individuals and between small groups; it is as counterproductive at the macro-level. Thus, professionalization, whether it is imported from abroad or developed within the country with the assistance of experts, contributes to a dependency syndrome that is not offset by rhetoric about freedom of the press and professional excellence.

Media Autonomy

In countries like Canada the autonomy of the press, one measure of modernization, is assumed. The scholarly literature is full of discussions about whether the media lead or follow public opinion, whether their function is divisive or integrative, and whether they should arbitrate conflict or remain apart from it. All of these debates implicitly assume that, despite financial dependency of the press on advertising or on circulation, the media have a choice that they do not have in countries where governments control the press and, through it, public opinion.[30]

The Kent report holds this view, too. The special responsibility of the press lies in its autonomy, an independence that has been carefully nurtured by law and precedent, by the vigilance of civil libertarians. It

Alternative Perspective for Modern Democratic Theory," *Journal of Politics* 33 (1971), 893-902.

28 Jeffrey C. Hubbard, Melvin L. DeFleur and Lois B. DeFleur, "Mass Media Influences on Public Conceptions of Social Problems," *Social Problems* 23 (1975), 22-34.

29 Robert D. Hess and Judith V. Torney, "The Development of Political Attitudes in Children," in Edward S. Greenberg (ed.), *Political Socialization* (New York: Atherton, 1970), 64-82; Herbert Hirsch, *Poverty and Politicization* (New York: Free Press, 1971). The early studies of political socialization of children did not examine the use of the media.

30 Thelma McCormack, "Revolution, Communication and the Sense of History," in Elihu Katz and Tamas Szecskö (eds.), *Mass Media and Social Change* (London: Sage, 1981), 167-85.

provides a foundation of credibility without which there could be no media influence on public opinion. Cherished as an ideal in free societies, it is also instrumental to the integrity of the journalist.

In recent years, however, there has been discussion among scholars about just how much influence the media have, and whether the influence is on specific issues (for example, wage control) or on an agenda made up of a number of items; whether it is on the issues included on the agenda or those which have been left out; or whether it is on the ordering of the issues. The commission was not concerned with these conceptual problems but did assert that the press, in contrast with other media, is the agenda-setter for the nation; it is "the principal external influence on the agenda of public affairs,"[31] the major resource of opinion leaders, and the primary source for the top decision-makers.[32]

No evidence is provided to support the latter two claims. If leaders and others in positions of power did, in fact, depend primarily on daily newspapers for their awareness of problems and their calculated guesses about probable outcomes of action, the consequences would be good for democracy but disastrous for the country: good because the same information would be open and available to all of us; bad because the information is fragmentary, incomplete and conceptually unrefined. The reality is a modern data-gathering and data-processing technology which has created powerful, private information services accessible only through private subscription to select clients in the private and public sectors. While ordinary citizens are reading a newspaper, the executives of large corporations are reading indicator reports based on 200 newspapers.[33]

Still there are large numbers of people outside of these exclusive circles who have an interest in public affairs, who want to be informed and to have some individual or collective influence on public policy. They are the backbone of the new social movements concerned with nuclear installations, the environment, women's rights, alternative energy sources, separatism and other matters; they move in and out of shifting political coalitions rather than in and out of political parties. Do the media set agendas for these groups? The evidence is inconclusive.[34] A case can be made for saying that the media are part of an agenda-negotiating or agenda-building process; they do not have the great influence often attributed to them, but they engage their audiences

31 Kent, 216.

32 Ibid., 137.

33 Morris Janowitz, "Content Analysis and the Study of Sociopolitical Change," *Journal of Communication* 26 (1976), 10-21.

34 The agenda-setting literature is extensive and based largely on studies of elections. Investigators have attempted to show a correspondence between the salience of issues in the media (based on content analyses) and those in the public mind (based on opinion surveys). While it is clear that the two are not wholly dissimilar, the degree of correspondence is unclear.

who in turn engage them. It does not diminish the importance of the press to say that it does not set agenda but only proposes them and participates in a process where these proposals and counterproposals are sorted out.

The notion of agenda-building or agenda-negotiating is closer to the MacBride notion of public opinion as a process rather than a fixed entity. The MacBride report assumes that complete institutional autonomy is not in itself desirable, that unless the media are part of a social process they are unable to have any influence on others. Thus, the press may be housed separately and have some rules or guidelines about fraternizing with government or other officials, but it cannot stand apart from the social process: "The success of measures to improve communication in both form and content is inextricably linked with steps to make society itself less oppressive and unequal, more just and more democratic."[35] Public opinion in this context is not a response to something, a reactive phenomenon, but a form of active consultation, a process as much as a condition, "a consciousness formed by knowledge of public affairs and the experience of social practices" which endows ordinary people with the qualifications to make informed judgments. On an international scale, it means that Third World nations know themselves best, better than anyone else can know them; they are, therefore, uniquely qualified to participate in decision-making that has consequences for their futures.

To summarize, the three dimensions of modernization—rationalization, professionalization and autonomy, which correspond operationally to the institution, the labour force and the public—are strained in the case of the advanced developed nations and possibly destructive for the less developed ones. Critics of the MacBride report may find its analysis unsatisfactory for countries in the Third World without, at the same time, adopting the liberal model of the Kent report.

Meanwhile, in Canada, there is the case of Quebec where the political culture has been more volatile than in other parts of the country and where the social structure has changed more quickly and more drastically than elsewhere. The French-language press offers an opportunity to look at the various models and assess their heuristic strengths.

The French-Language Quebec Press

The Kent commission viewed the special characteristics of the Quebec press as a cultural expression. The French-language press was not just another ethnic press; but it was also not the ideological European press. The key to the francophone media, according to the commission, is

35 MacBride, *Many Voices*, 18.

Quebec's culture: its language, its unique institutions, its history and its social relationships. The French press, for example, did not turn to advertising as a source of financing in the nineteenth century; it was founded "on the support of elites, lay and clerical."[36] Lacking the Protestant entrepreneurial tradition, the Quebec journalists never had the individualistic psychology or respect for hard facts that journalists elsewhere in Canada had and which they shared with other journalists in the English-speaking world. "Because of the particular character of their society and culture," the report says, "French-speaking journalists have always regarded North American liberalism with distrust."[37] Their own way of thinking has been more collectively oriented. "The French-speaking journalist, like the priest or politician, has always willy-nilly, been invested with a certain nationalist mission."[38] And this nationalist mission interfered with the empirical style of the anglophone press; "it prompted a certain disdain for mere 'hard fact', and a strong inclination toward analysis, patriotic dissertations, and preaching. . . ."[39]

The cultural interpretation of the Kent commission is strongly contested by the Quebec left which is more favourably disposed toward a class analysis than a cultural one.[40] But much of the commission's own research contradicts its interpretation of the Quebec press. For better or worse, journalists in Quebec seem to respect hard fact.[41] Furthermore, the results of a survey conducted by the commission do not project a picture of the Quebec journalist as ideologue; nor do Quebec journalists perceive their own press as lacking in objectivity.[42]

A convergence between the two presses, French-language and English, may be developing that obliterates differences of the past. But an alternative thesis would be that Quebec chose the other route to change, altering the institution rather than the motivation of the individual journalist. Instead of putting its faith in professionalization as the solution to the abuses of a market concept, it created some of the most militant unions of the North American press community. Even more disturbing to the anglophone tradition is the stronger support in

36 Lysiane Gagnon, "Journalism and Ideologies in Quebec," in *The Journalists* (Research Publications of the Royal Commission on Newspapers Vol. 2 [Ottawa: Supply and Services, 1981]), 22-23.

37 Ibid., 30-31.

38 Ibid., 31.

39 Ibid., 23.

40 Pierre Fournier, *The Quebec Establishment* (Montreal: Black Rose, 1976); Marcel Rioux, *Quebec In Question* (Toronto: Lorimer, 1978).

41 In a survey of journalists on Quebec dailies carried out by the commission, more than three quarters said that "accurate reporting of what is said by prominent people you meet" was very important. On another question, the highest priority was given to "analyzing and interpreting difficult issues" as the most important function a journalist fulfills by 22 per cent. See *The Journalists*, Appendix, 195.

42 Ibid.

Quebec for a form of worker control in management. Whereas the Kent report favoured a special editor-in-chief contract, the Quebec journalists want greater involvement in management. In a survey which asked journalists about the most desirable form of ownership, 60 per cent said "Editorial Association" similar to the pattern in France.[43]

There may be a historical or cultural predisposition in these attitudes, but according to Florian Sauvageau the fight to gain more power over news content has been most aggressively pursued within the last 20 years.[44] If that is the case, it reflects neither culture nor class as much as a process of politicization that is taking place within the media as well as through them. Quebec's case, then, is more than just an exception to the Kent model that "proves the rule." On the other hand, it does not fit the low-technology MacBride model either. Certain European countries where both the press and their readerships are more politicized may provide parallels. But, more than anything else, the Quebec press points to the necessity and theoretical advantages of developing a third model.

3

A third model could be constructed on the premise of access, for nothing illustrates better the changes that have been taking place in contemporary thinking about communication and social structure than the concept of access. It reflects a radical philosophical shift in our understanding of freedom of the press. Whereas in the past freedom of the press meant the protection given to publishers and editors from interference and retributive measures by the state, in current discussion it often refers to a social right, the right of readers and other serious audiences to encounter a broad spectrum of ideas. The enemies of freedom of expression may have been the state in the past, and in many parts of the world (for example, Poland) that situation obtains today, but in the democracies and in modern highly industrialized economies based on private enterprise, it is more often the economic elites who present a problem. Freedom of the press for whom? Barron asks. For the monopoly proprietors or for the whole community?[45]

The Davey report took a view similar to Barron's, and more recently Senator Davey repeated the dictum. "Too many publishers," he said, "harbor the absurd notion that freedom of the press is something they own; their freedom of the press. . . . Of course, the exact

43 Ibid., 197.

44 Florian Sauvageau, "French-speaking Journalists on Journalism," in *The Journalists*, 49.

45 James Barron, "Access to the Press—A New First Amendment Right," *Harvard Law Review* 80 (1967), 1641-78; and James Barron, *Freedom of the Press For Whom?* (Bloomington: Indiana University Press, 1973).

opposite is the case. Press freedom is the right of the people."[46] But the Kent commission reverted to the older, more conservative position that press freedom belonged to the proprietor who could "do what he likes with his newspaper" providing that the newspaper was his principal property.[47] Access was not discussed either in the final report or in the volume of research papers entitled *Newspapers and the Law*, an omission which is consistent with the way the commission defined the role of editors and the need to protect them legally so that they could mediate between the public interest and the private interest of stockholders.

Access, however, is not dependent on the way editors define their responsibilities or on their legal protection. It is both an institutional obligation and a principle of entitlement. Editors, it assumes, will always be confronted with conflicts of interest in which one side is more powerful than the other. Access is simply a directive about how these inevitable conflicts of interest are to be resolved.

Within the general framework of entitlement, access has two meanings, political and cultural. The political one is reformulation of the doctrine that a free society guarantees its citizens freedom of expression. For many reasons and for many years the conditions supporting freedom of expression have been eroded and, as a consequence, the quality of public debate has deteriorated. Access, then, is a response to the structural problem. It is an ethos and system of hospitality to ideas, in particular to new and dissenting ones. The conservative biases of large-scale bureaucratic organization put a premium on such openness and tend to distance the exponents of new or controversial ideas. The ideas are viewed with suspicion and the social movements that espouse them are defined as "they." Under these circumstances, access must be regarded as imperative and, if necessary, mandated. (It is on this latter point of mandating access that Barron's critics have mainly objected. Mandating access, they say, would reimpose the state and thus defeat the intention of guaranteeing freedom of expression.)[48]

But whether access is formally mandated or informally achieved, it must be a genuine and not a token gesture. In an age of satellite television, a soapbox in a city park is not access; neither is a small underground periodical that circulates erratically. "The test of a community's opportunities for free expression rests not so much in an abundance of alternative media but rather in an abundance of opportunities to secure expression in media with the largest impact."[49]

46 Keith Davey, "How Misreading Jolted the Press," *Globe and Mail*, September 16, 1981.

47 Kent, 246.

48 Benno C. Schmidt, Jr., *Freedom of the Press vs. Public Access* (New York: Praeger, 1976).

49 Barron, "Access to the Press," 1653.

Radical, off-beat, marginal media may help to create a climate of opinion, an intellectual environment in which the coercive element implicit in Barron's thesis is gratuitous, but the acid test of access is what is readily available through the meanstream and prestige press, not what is tolerated at the fringe. In short, when access is defined as a social right, it must take into consideration the public's media habits and the means of reaching significant populations. Whether the newspaper is the principal property of the proprietor is interesting but irrelevant.

The cultural meaning of access is spelled out in the MacBride report where the emphasis is on *who* rather than *what*, and on *how* rather than *where*. "Who" concerns whether the journalists are insiders or outsiders, people who have experienced the Third World as members of it and who therefore understand its nuances and cultural uniqueness. Preference, then, is given to the insiders, those with ascriptive credentials to speak to the world community rather than outsiders who may be experts but cannot empathize with the groups on whom they are reporting. Merit is secondary, and whether it is compromised or not it will almost certainly be perceived that way by the foreign journalists who find themselves excluded from important sources. Western journalists trained to define access only in political terms will regard this kind of policy as a form of censorship, a calculated decision by the new elites to control the media, to manage the news and to conceal from the world at large the Gulags and the gross planning errors. In the extreme, the cultural meaning of access is less concerned with truth (as it is understood in the Western democracies) than with authenticity.

Authenticity is also a process, the active involvement of social movements and social groups in the press which, in turn, reflects back an image against which participants can judge themselves and reflect on what they and their movement are doing. The assumption here is that it is not access but accessing that restores to people their cultural self-respect and personal self-esteem.

Within our own community the MacBride concept of access is applicable to social groups which have been culturally disenfranchised through poverty and racism. But for those dissident social movements that are partially mobilized—feminists, environmentalists, peace movement people—the problem of access is different. On the one hand, it is nonrecognition, and, on the other, it is a form of recognition that either discredits or trivializes the movements.

Failure of the press to acknowledge the existence of insurgent social movements and their respective ideologies is an abuse of the political meaning of access. But manipulation by the media—when, for example, the press encourages the social movement to engage in foolish behaviour in order to get coverage—is an abuse of the cultural meaning of access. A similar abuse occurs when these social movements are forced to line up as petitioners in a queue marked "equal time." The serious movements are thus equated with the faddists, and the longer the queue the less exposure for each. Once again, the dimension of these movements that is abused is their authenticity. Readers and serious students of public affairs are thus called upon to judge a distorted image.

Whether the distancing mechanisms which discredit and trivialize such movements are responsible for pushing them toward more extremist thinking and types of direct action is problematic, but they make such options appear more reasonable. In any event, it is this kind of scenario, realistic enough in Canada and elsewhere, that recommends the concept of access as a starting point for a third model.

Conclusion

It is, perhaps, a Freudian slip that the Kent report, in its one and only reference to the MacBride UNESCO report, misspelled the chairman's name. The two reports are, as we have indicated, poles apart. Our purpose in discussing them together was not to cast one or the other of them in a more or less favourable light, but to illustrate some of the issues in contemporary communication theory.

When communication is understood as a process and when communication institutions are seen as serving a political culture as well as expressing the cultural and economic aspirations of different status and class groups, very different criteria are used to judge media performance than if we were drawing on the classical liberal model of the press in democracy. The Kent commission report comes closest to the liberal model; indeed, in some respects, it is closer than the earlier Davey committee report. The cracks in it are perhaps more easily seen by students who are so familiar with it than those in the MacBride report. But other critics (Marxists, for example) might find the MacBride report wanting, for implicit in it are the assumptions of world social democracy, a concept more often associated with Myrdal than with contemporary Marxist dependency theory.[50] In any event, the MacBride model is not the only alternative to the liberal one.

Nevetheless, juxtaposition of the two enables us to make certain points. It was suggested, for example, that although profit and loss are important determinants of life of an individual newspaper, ultimately any system of communication has a deeper social history. Newspapers rise and fall with the fate of classes. If they remain static, if they are unable to disengage themselves and adapt to the newer social map, they lose the loyalty and close experiential bonds with their readers. Rationalizing processes, we suggested, may act as a factor in concealing the changes the media must make if they are to maintain a close connection with social groups. A great deal of research, however, needs

50 Gunnar Myrdal, *Asian Drama* (New York: Pantheon, 1968).

to be done on the non-economic reasons for the success or failure of the newspapers.

The preoccupation with the number of papers and with the loss of competition tends to obscure other kinds of changes which may have more far-reaching consequences for our political culture. One can match the Kent's worst-case scenario with another: two types of press, elite and mass, with a third underground press of embittered ultra-conservative groups who either prefer or are forced into this more covert method of communication while the orthodox press, serving its own constituents, does not serve ordinary citizens.

The liberal assumptions of the Kent report are more clearly indicated in its faith that professionalization would raise the standards of the press, but only if the proper conditions of competition are also present. It is to its credit and to the satisfaction of the new graduates of journalism programmes that it did not dismiss competition. Shrinking employment opportunities are discouraging to the young and do not build into the media culture a social richness that good journalism requires. But despite the focus on the market mechanism in the Kent report, the commission recognizes that only professionalization could produce a press that meets the needs of a complex society. It is suggested here, however, that there have been trends that have impeded the professionalization processes. Our journalists now have professional educations, the proper degrees and credentials which qualify them for professional positions. But what this has done is to rationalize the system of recruitment to the media; once inside, the young recruits find themselves with little chance of ever realizing their potential. The political potential of this kind of disenchantment by young journalists has yet to be calculated, but it is not surprising to observe them in the vanguard of insurgent social movements. They do not merely report on a political culture; they become part of it.

The MacBride report, we note, challenged the entire concept of professionalization by suggesting that it compounded the problems of communication; it distanced the parties from each other. The report also challenged the concept of balance, whether it was a sensible, fair presentation of issues which were already defined as salient or whether it was a correction of inequities. Thus, although the Kent commission moved from conventional notions of scientific objectivity, it did not propose ways of altering the process by which media agendas are constructed.

In different ways, then, the two models, Kent and MacBride, offer alternative perceptions of society and of social change. The Kent model proposes to make the industry more responsible; the MacBride report proposes to make the have-not nations more articulate and to give them the legitimation they need to present their own agendas both to their internal populations and to the larger world community. But neither report, we suggest, adequately accounts for the French-language press of Quebec. Over-emphasis on the concept of culture by the Kent report, over-emphasis on public apathy and lack of technology in the MacBride report—in both cases, the Quebec example falls through the net. A third model based on the concept of access is proposed chiefly because it draws attention to changes in the political environment brought about by the formation of social movements. And to the extent that the political culture outside of Quebec is similarly being transformed by extraparliamentary politics, the importance of explicating the third model cannot be stated often or emphatically enough.